16th International Conference Information Systems 2023

Lisbon, Portugal
11-13 March 2023

Editors:

Miguel Baptista Nunes
Pedro Isaías
Philip Powell

ISBN: 978-1-7138-8465-1

Printed from e-media with permission by:

Curran Associates, Inc.
57 Morehouse Lane
Red Hook, NY 12571

Some format issues inherent in the e-media version may also appear in this print version.

International Association for Development of the Information Society (IADIS)
Rua Sao Sebastiao Da Pedreira
No. 100, 30, 1050-209
Lisbon, Portugal

Phone: 351 21 3151373
Fax: 351 21 3151244

secretariat@iadis.org

Additional copies of this publication are available from:

Curran Associates, Inc.
57 Morehouse Lane
Red Hook, NY 12571 USA
Phone: 845-758-0400
Fax: 845-758-2633
Email: curran@proceedings.com
Web: www.proceedings.com

TABLE OF CONTENTS

FULL PAPERS

SHORT PAPERS

POSTER

FULL PAPERS

TEACHING COMPUTER LITERACY IN A HIGHER EDUCATION: DETERMINING NEED AND CONTENT

Kobus van Aswegen and Estelle Taylor
North-West University, Potchefstroom Campus, South Africa

ABSTRACT

The importance of computer literacy on tertiary level cannot be over emphasized, as computers have become an essential part of students' academic life, and crucial to their success. Yet, students report a lack of knowledge, skills and competencies to optimally make use of devices, the internet, and software. Computer literacy education has become a mandatory subject at many undergraduate programs, but there are numerous challenges, complicated by a wide variety of curriculums, methods of teaching, and differences in the knowledge levels of incoming students from various schools and backgrounds. There has been much debate surrounding what specific basic computer literacy students should be required to know. The aim of this paper was to determine if computer literacy should be included as a compulsory module at a higher education institution in South Africa, as well as to determine the possible content that should be included in a computer literacy module taught at tertiary level. Two surveys were used to determine the perceptions of lecturers and students at a tertiary institution in South Africa. The results of these surveys were statistically analysed. The findings confirmed that computer literacy should be taught at tertiary level. This should include basic word processing skills, electronic communication skills, Internet skills, knowledge of computer components, more advanced knowledge of word processing and an introduction to presentation software (i.e. PowerPoint). Basic spreadsheet processing skills may be considered as part of the general content. The teaching and learning approach should take into consideration the needs of the students as well as the needs of the faculties, and the institution should consider identifying groups of students with specific needs, rather than a one-size-fits-all approach. It is clear that lecturers as well as students would prefer to have at least some contact sessions. The findings of this study contributed to the decisions made at this specific institution in regards to the teaching and learning of computer literacy on tertiary level. It may also guide other institutions in decisions in this regard.

KEYWORDS

Computer Literacy, Module Design

1. INTRODUCTION

Different terms are used to describe overlapping literacies, for example digital literacy. Digital literacy can be defined as the ability to use ICT and the Internet (Tafazoli *et al.*, 2017), or as an ability to comfortably use technology to accomplish basic computing tasks (Barker & Harris, 2018). Other terms used include, eLiteracy (skills that are necessary to operate comfortably in ICT supported environments) and ICT literacy (using digital technology and networks to access, manage and create information) (Tafazoli *et al.*, 2017).

In this paper we will use the term computer literacy. Fraillon *et al.* (2018) defines computer and information literacy as an individual's ability to use computers to investigate, create, and communicate in order to participate effectively in society. Computer literacy can also be defined as the ability to use computers for creation, communication and collaboration, or, from educational perspective, the development of knowledge and skills for competent use of general computer applications, software programs, and Internet tools (Tafazoli *et al.*, 2017). Wong *et al.* (2017) wrote that computer literacy includes, for example, knowledge such as how to use word processing, spreadsheets, presentations and database software, as well as Internet and online activities. The definition of Wong *et al.* (2017) will be used in this paper.

Tertiary institutions in many countries require students to attend computer literacy courses to raise their basic skills. Israel (2018) wrote that computers have become an essential part of students' academic life, and crucial for their success, and because of this the importance of computer literacy cannot be over emphasized. In a study by Israel (2018), done in the Philippines, the results indicated that the majority of the students acquired computer literacy skills through assistance of colleagues and friends, as well as through self-teaching. Very little students acquired their computer literacy skills through courses offered by their university. Israel (2018) recommends that universities introduce a compulsory, practical computer related course into the curriculum to endure a level of computer literacy in all students. In a study done by Wong et al. (2017) in Macao, China, it was found that even though students had to attend a computer literacy course, lecturers still complained about the weak IT skills of many students, which suggested that all students were not benefiting sufficiently from these courses (Wong *et al.*, 2017). Yaun and Shunru (2020) wrote that "Practical Computer Literacy", also referred to as "Computer Fundamentals" has been a compulsory course for all undergraduate programs in China for several decades. They also refer to challenges in regards to standards, and taking into account students with different cultural and educational backgrounds, learning, and language abilities. In another study done in Turkey, Ümmühan & Orçun (2020) found that computer literacy skills have not yet reached the desired levels. Here a computer literacy course is also compulsory for first year students, and carried out with distance education.

Results of a survey done by the Department: Higher Education and Training (DHET) in South Africa in 2020, confirmed that many students still reported a lack of knowledge, skills and competencies to optimally make use of devices, the internet, and software. Students reported that they did not know how to use computers and email, and did not know how to open Microsoft Word and how to type a document (Department: Higher Education and Training, 2020). Students also reported that having to complete a first year computer literacy module, helped them with understanding the required concepts. The report concludes that while there has been recognition at national level to prioritise digital skills development, DHET might need to lead initiatives in this respect. "Too many students commented that they did not know how to type and/or are not able to use their devices effectively due to a lack of skills and understanding of software and operating systems" (Department: Higher Education and Training, 2020).

Computer literacy education has become a mandatory subject at most undergraduate programs, and with this numerous challenges arise for the educators (Vasilache, 2016), complicated by a wide variety of curriculums and methods of teaching. To add to this, the knowledge levels of incoming students are varied. Students come from various schools and backgrounds, and with different levels of literacy, as well as different personal experiences with computers and information technology (Vasilache, 2016). There may also be a need to determine computer literacy standards for different fields of study (Dincer, 2016).

In typical computer literacy courses or modules, sometimes found in the general education requirements of a university, students study basic computer hardware concepts and traditional office suite software such as Microsoft Office. According to Ümmühan and Orçun (2020) course content in a computer literacy module in Turkey was (for example) basic computer literacy subjects such as information security, protection against infection, web and internet based communication, information and communication technologies, use of computer and file management, word processors, spreadsheets, database applications and presentations. In recent years, there has been much debate surrounding what specific basic computer literacy college-level students should be required to know. There seem to be a lack of an agreed upon standard on specific skills set to incorporate into a general computer literacy course that should be required of all undergraduate students (Barker & Harris, 2018).

When considering a computer literacy module for teaching and learning at tertiary level, the following questions should be answered:

Do students still need to be taught computer literacy at tertiary level? To answer this question, the perceptions of students as well as lecturers are relevant.

If we do need to teach students computer literacy at tertiary level, what content should this include?

If we do need to teach students computer literacy at tertiary level, what is the best way of doing this (online vs contact mode)?

The aim of this paper is to determine if computer literacy should be included as a compulsory module at a higher education institution in South Africa, as well as the possible content that should be included a computer literacy module taught at tertiary level.

In section 2 the methodology is described, while results are presented in section 3. The conclusion is discussed in section 4.

2. METHODOLOGY

Two surveys, developed by using Google Forms, were used to determine the perceptions of lecturers and students at a tertiary institution in South Africa. This was part of a broader study investigating different aspects of academic literacy. This study will report only on responses to the questions in regards to computer literacy. Links to the online surveys were distributed electronically via e-mail. The first survey (send out to lecturers) had 404 responses and the second one (send out to students) had 11570 responses. After the data was validated, cleaned and coded there were 150 usable responses for the lecturers' questionnaire and 4427 for the students' questionnaire. The lecturers' survey included 3 Likert scale questions, as well as 1 open question and were answered by lecturers from all 8 faculties. The students' survey included 5 Likert scale questions, as well as 1 open question and were answered by students from all 8 faculties and across 7 different years of their study. The results of these surveys were statistically analysed, and in the next section the most important results are discussed.

In figure 1 and figure 2 the different faculties that participated in the survey can be seen, while figure 3 represents the different groups of students that participated.

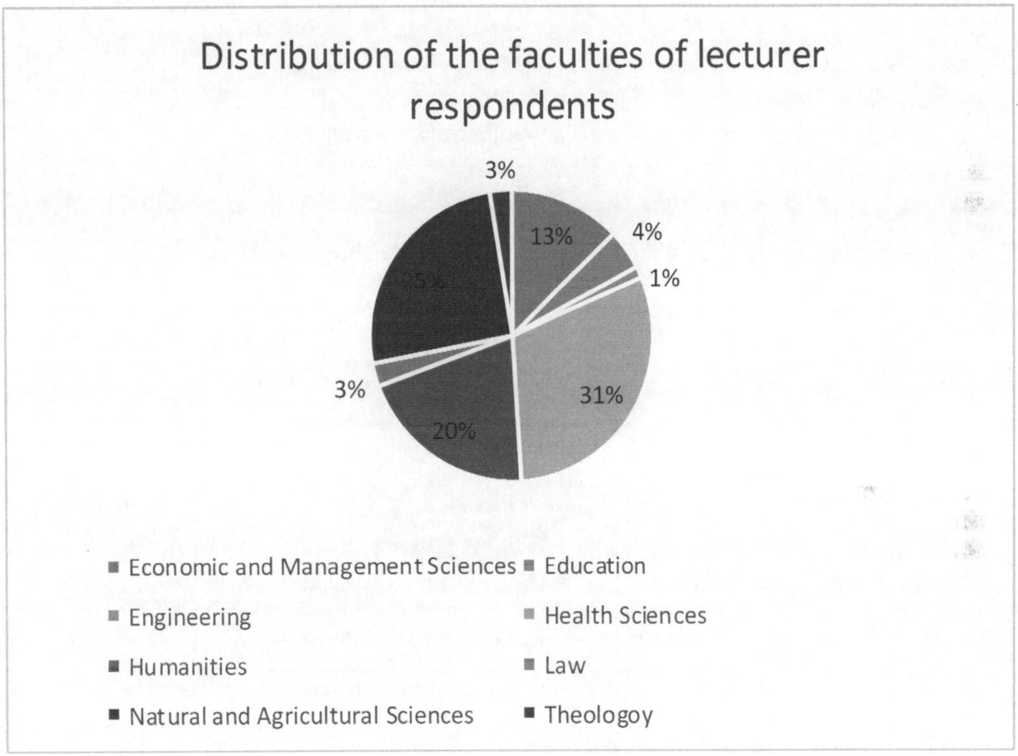

Figure 1. Participating faculties: lecturers

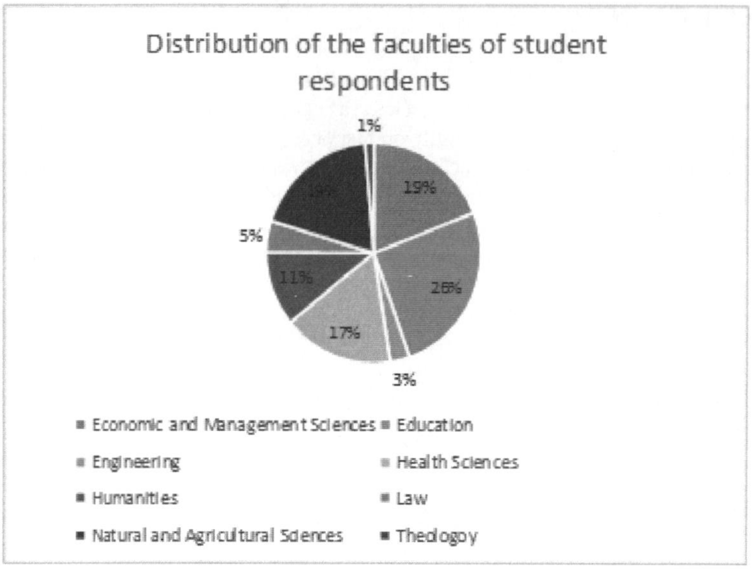

Figure 2. Participating faculties: students

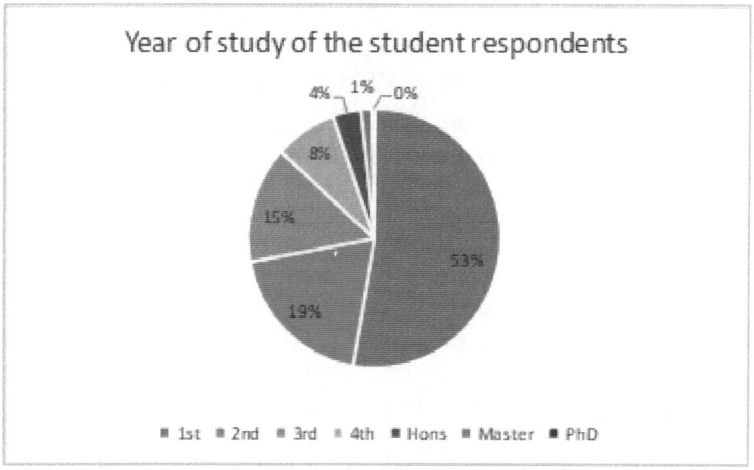

Figure 3. Year of study: students

3. RESULTS

In this section the results are discussed according to the questions stated in section 1. The question: "Should computer literacy be taught at tertiary level?" is addressed in section 3.1, teaching computer literacy at tertiary level. If we do need to teach students computer literacy at tertiary level, what content should be included in a computer literacy module? This is addressed in section 3.2, proposed content of a computer literacy module. If we do need to teach students computer literacy at tertiary level, what is the best way of doing this – online, with contact classes or blended learning. This is discussed in section 3.3.

3.1 Teaching Computer Literacy at Tertiary Level

When considering the responses to the open question 'Should students be taught computer literacy at tertiary level", the clearly prevalent answer was that it is necessary to teach university students computer literacy, with lecturers responding with 125 yes to 4 no responses. Looking at the different responses from lecturers to this open question, some respondents suggested using selection criteria for students, or grouping students according to specific training needs. This correlates with the findings of Vasilache (2016), as well as the recommendation of Dincer (2016) that there may be a need to determine computer literacy standards for different fields of study.

Most students also responded with a yes to the same question. An overwhelming number of students (n=3199) indicated that they believe a computer literacy course is needed at tertiary level with 791 of those stating that they believe this is necessary due *specifically to the lack of prior knowledge*.

The results in table 1 show that lecturers perceive the computer literacy of the average student not to be very good, as the highest mean is 2.89 (for basic word processing skills). For the different components listed, only 10% to 22% of lecturers rated the computer literacy of students as very good.

Table 1. Lecturer: Indicate your perception of the computer literacy of the average student in each of the following areas

Skill	Percentage				Mean
	Very Poor	Poor	Good	Very Good	
Knowledge of computer components and how a computer functions	7%	34%	36%	22%	2.73
Electronic communication skills	8%	35%	38%	19%	2.68
Basic word processing skills	5%	22%	53%	21%	2.89
More advanced knowledge of word processing	24%	40%	23%	13%	2.25
Basic spreadsheet processing skills	25%	35%	27%	12%	2.26
More advanced knowledge of spreadsheets	39%	33%	18%	10%	1.99
Introduction to presentation software	12%	33%	41%	14%	2.57
Internet skills	9%	31%	43%	17%	2.68

The results in table 2 and 3 show that most students felt that completing a component on computer literacy did actually improve their computer skills.

Table 2. Student: Before enrolling in the Computer Skills component at the university, how knowledgeable / competent were you in the following skills

Skill	Percentage				Mean
	Not at all competent	Somewhat competent	Competent	Very Competent	
Knowledge of computer components and how a computer functions	7%	19%	33%	41%	3.09
Electronic communication skills	5%	13%	37%	45%	3.22
Basic word processing skills	6%	12%	27%	54%	3.30
More advanced knowledge of word processing	10%	18%	30%	43%	3.06
Basic spreadsheet processing skills	19%	24%	26%	31%	2.69
More advanced knowledge of spreadsheets	23%	26%	25%	26%	2.54
Introduction to presentation software	14%	19%	28%	40%	2.94
Internet skills	8%	18%	35%	40%	3.07

Table 3. Student: After enrolling in the Computer Skills component at the university, how knowledgeable / competent were you in the following skills

Skill	Percentage				
	Not at all competent	Somewhat competent	Competent	Very Competent	Mean
Knowledge of computer components and how a computer functions	2%	4%	22%	73%	3.65
Electronic communication skills	1%	5%	27%	67%	3.59
Basic word processing skills	2%	4%	22%	72%	3.64
More advanced knowledge of word processing	2%	7%	27%	63%	3.51
Basic spreadsheet processing skills	5%	14%	32%	49%	3.25
More advanced knowledge of spreadsheets	6%	16%	33%	45%	3.16
Introduction to presentation software	3%	9%	25%	62%	3.47
Internet skills	3%	8%	29%	60%	3.47

A comparison is done in table 4, where it can be seen that the mean value improved for all the items in the list. This comparison is also shown graphically in figure 4. As can be seen there is a marked increase in the computer skills of students, especially in spreadsheet processing.

Table 4. Student: Mean values compared, before and after enrolling in the Computer Skills component at the university, how knowledgeable / competent students were in the following skills

Mean values before and after enrolling in the Computer Skills component			
Skill	Before	After	Difference
Knowledge of computer components and how a computer functions	3.09	3.65	0.56
Electronic communication skills	3.22	3.59	0.37
Basic word processing skills	3.30	3.64	0.34
More advanced knowledge of word processing	3.06	3.51	0.45
Basic spreadsheet processing skills	2.69	3.25	0.56
More advanced knowledge of spreadsheets	2.54	3.16	0.62
Introduction to presentation software	2.94	3.47	0.53
Internet skills	3.07	3.47	0.40

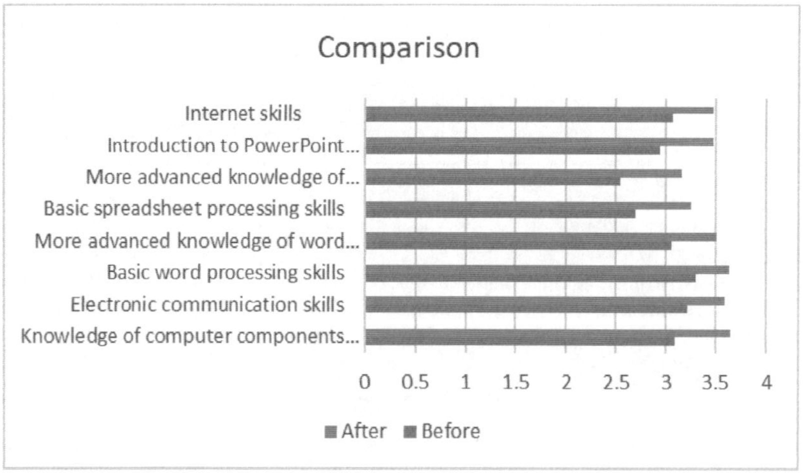

Figure 4. Comparison of mean values before and after

Lecturers were asked to indicate the importance of specific abilities in assisting students to succeed in their 1st and 2nd year courses. There results can be seen in table 5. A very large majority (96%) indicated that it is important or very important that students know how to effectively use the LMS. It is also important for the lecturers, that students know how to use academic search engines and the various journal databases (mean of 3.43), word and spreadsheet processing (mean of 3.70) and formulating formal emails (mean of 3.55).

Table 5. Lecturer: how important are the following abilities as addressed in the computer literacy course to assist students in succeeding in the 1st and 2nd year courses that you teach

Skill	Percentage				
	Not at all important	Somewhat important	Important	Very important	Mean
Know how to use and navigate the Sakai LMS students are using	3%	1%	9%	87%	3.81
Understand how to navigate Google Scholar or the various databases available on the university's library site	4%	11%	22%	63%	3.43
Understand how to use word- and spreadsheet processing packages	1%	5%	17%	77%	3.70
Formulating and sending of formal emails	1%	5%	30%	63%	3.55

This results in section 3.1 confirm the findings of Israel (2018), Wong et al. (2017) and the Department: Higher Education and Training (DHET) (2020), that computer literacy should be taught at tertiary level. This leads us to the next question – what content should this include?

3.2 Proposed Content of a Computer Literacy Module

From the results reported in table 6 it is clear that lecturers agree that students often need basic word processing skills (mean of 3.61), electronic communication skills (mean of 3.52), Internet skills (mean of 3.31), knowledge of computer components and the functioning of computers (mean of 3.21), more advanced knowledge of word processing (mean of 3.15). and presentation software skills (mean of 3). Only spreadsheet processing skills (2.75) and more advanced knowledge of spreadsheets (2.53) have a mean of lower than 3, but 57% of lecturers still indicated that students fairly often of often need basic spreadsheet processing skills to complete assignments.

Table 6. Lecturer: How frequently do students need the following computer skills to complete assignments in your module

Skill	Percentage				
	Never	Occasionall y	Fairly Often	Very Often	Mea n
Knowledge of computer components and how a computer functions	11%	11%	26%	53%	3.21
Electronic communication skills	5%	3%	29%	64%	3.52
Basic word processing skills	3%	6%	19%	73%	3.61
More advanced knowledge of word processing	7%	15%	34%	44%	3.15
Basic spreadsheet processing skills	13%	29%	27%	30%	2.75
More advanced knowledge of spreadsheets	23%	28%	21%	28%	2.53
Introduction to presentation software	11%	19%	31%	40%	3.00
Internet skills	4%	13%	30%	52%	3.31

The results in table 7 show that the responses from students mostly agree with those from the lecturers, with the same 3 items in the list of top 3, in the same order. Students responded that they often need basic word processing skills (mean of 3.61), followed by electronic communication skills (mean of 3.50) and Internet skills (mean of 3.47). Once again only spreadsheet processing skills (2.89) and more advanced knowledge of spreadsheets (2.833) have a mean of lower than 3, but 65% of students still indicated that students fairly often of often need basic spreadsheet processing skills to complete assignments.

Table 7. Student: How often do you use the following computer-related skills to complete assignments in various modules?

Skill	Not at all	Sometimes	Percentage Often	Very often	Mean
Knowledge of computer components and how a computer functions	5%	11%	26%	58%	3.38
Electronic communication skills	1%	8%	30%	61%	3.50
Basic word processing skills	2%	5%	23%	70%	3.61
More advanced knowledge of word processing	3%	12%	31%	54%	3.37
Basic spreadsheet processing skills	11%	23%	31%	34%	2.89
More advanced knowledge of spreadsheets	13%	24%	31%	32%	2.83
Introduction to presentation software	9%	18%	29%	45%	3.10
Internet skills	3%	9%	27%	62%	3.47

A comparison of the data in tables 6 and 7 are done in table 8 and the use of certain computer skills reported by the students, correlates to how often lecturers (according to them) require students to actually use those skills in their studies.

Table 8. Student: Mean values compared of how often lecturers require the use of certain computer skills against how often students actually use these skills

How often lecturers require certain skills vs. the students' actual use of these skills		
Skill	Lecturers require	Students' use
Knowledge of computer components and how a computer functions	3.21	3.38
Electronic communication skills	3.52	3.50
Basic word processing skills	3.61	3.61
More advanced knowledge of word processing	3.15	3.37
Basic spreadsheet processing skills	2.75	2.89
More advanced knowledge of spreadsheets	2.53	2.83
Introduction to presentation software	3.00	3.10
Internet skills	3.31	3.47

From the above results it seem that at least basic word processing skills, electronic communication skills, and Internet skills should be included. Knowledge of computer components, more advanced knowledge of word processing and introduction to presentation software also seem to be important, while at least basic spreadsheet processing skills may be considered as part of the general content.

3.3 Online vs Contact Mode

At the institution where the survey was done, computer literacy is currently presented fully online and self-paced, without any contact lectures. The results in table 9 show that most lecturers (77%) feel that this should change to include at least some contact sessions, combined with online learning (65%) or only contact sessions (12%). The results in table 9 show that most students (60%) agree that the presentation should include at least some contact sessions (combined with online learning (47%) or only contact sessions (13%)).

Table 9. Lecturer: How do you think the Computer Skills component should be presented

Procurement method	Percentage
Leave it as is, i.e. a self-paced online learning component	15%
Present it with contact sessions	12%
Have some lectures (contact sessions) and some self-paced online learning	65%
Other	9%

Table 10. Student: How do you think the Computer Skills component should be presented

Statement	Percentage
Leave it as is, i.e. a self-paced online learning component	37%
Present it with contact sessions	13%
Have some lectures (contact sessions) and some self-paced online learning	47%
Other	3%

These results are similar to the findings of a study done in Turkey, where half of the active students who participated in the study stated that face-to-face learning is more useful while the other half of active students suggested that distance education is more useful. The students having the opinion that face-to-face education is more useful specified the reasons as easy follow-up, interaction and participation and less impact of technical problems. Some of the participants in this study suggested that compulsory attendance is needed (Ümmühan & Orçun, 2020).

Other suggestions from lecturers showed very little overlap, but did indicate that there is need to change the presentation of this component. Lecturers feel that the approach should take into consideration the needs of the students as well as the needs of the faculties, and lecturers feel that more research may be necessary on this topic. The explanations from students who selected the 'Other" option mainly expressed that students wish to have contact sessions for the Computer Skills component. Students would like the institution to identify groups of students with specific needs, rather than a one-size-fits-all approach.

4. CONCLUSION

The aim of this paper was to determine if computer literacy should be included as a compulsory module at a higher education institution in South Africa, as well as to determine the possible content that should be included in a computer literacy module taught at tertiary level. The results of two surveys were used to determine the perceptions of lecturers and students at a tertiary institution in South Africa. The findings confirmed the findings of other studies reported on in section 1. Lecturers as well as students strongly felt that students should be taught computer literacy at tertiary level. Some suggestions were selection criteria for students, or grouping students according to specific training needs. Lecturers perceived the computer literacy of the average student to not be very good, and students did feel that completing a component on Computer Skills did improve their computer skills. This answered the first question asked in section 1, should students be taught computer literacy at tertiary level?

Looking at the computer skills, lecturers as well as students, feel is needed to complete assignments, it seems that at least basic word processing skills, electronic communication skills, and Internet skills should be included. Knowledge of computer components, more advanced knowledge of word processing and introduction to presentation software also seem to be important, while at least basic spreadsheet processing skills may be considered as part of the general content. This answers the second question in section 1, on the content that should be included in a computer literacy module.

On the issue of presentation of a computer literacy module (the third question in section 1), the approach should take into consideration the needs of the students as well as the needs of the faculties, and the institution should consider identifying groups of students with specific needs, rather than a one-size-fits-all approach. More research may be necessary on this topic. However, it is clear that lecturers as well as students would prefer to have at least some contact sessions.

A possible recommendation from these findings is that the institution should consider a separate, at least 8 credit module for Computer Skills (1 credit equals 10 hours), preferable in the first semester as the students need these skills as soon as possible. This can be divided as seen in table 11.

Table 11. From the results and from experience at least the following content and credits are needed

Component	Credit(s)
Introduction to computers	1
Basic word processing skills	2
More advanced word processing skills	2
Basic spreadsheet skills	2
Introduction to presentation software	1
Total	8

This should include at least some contact classes, while certain components can still be done online. A pre-test may be considered at the beginning of the year, where students who do have the necessary skills can be fast-tracked or exempted.

The need for further research was mentioned specifically in the surveys, and possibilities for further research include researching selection criteria for students, and looking into how students can be optimally grouped according to specific training needs. This should take into consideration the needs of the students as well as the needs of the faculties, rather than a one-size-fits-all approach. If the decision is made to use a pre-test at the beginning of the year to fast-track or exempt students from completing the module, research will be necessary to determine what should optimally be assessed in this test. Research should also be done to determine how computer literacy is taught at other institutions in South Africa, as well as in other countries.

The findings of this study contributed to the decisions made at this specific institution in regards to the teaching and learning of computer literacy on tertiary level. It may also guide other institutions in decisions in this regard.

REFERENCES

Barker, N., & Harris, L. 2018. Are Computer Science and Information Systems Students More Likely to Earn a Better Grade in Basic Computer Literacy Courses Than Their Peers: A Case Study. In 2018 International Conference on Computational Science and Computational Intelligence (CSCI) (pp. 580-583). IEEE.

Department: Higher Education and Training. 2020. Students' access to and use of learning materials. Survey report 2020. Available at:

Dincer, S. 2016. Assessing the computer literacy of university graduates. In Proceedings of the Third International Conference on Open and Flexible Education (pp. 294-303).

Fraillon, J., Ainley, J., Schulz, W., Duckworth, D., & Friedman, T. 2019. IEA international computer and information literacy study 2018 assessment framework. Springer Nature. 74p.

Israel, O. 2018. An Assessment of Computer Literacy among Undergraduate Students of Delta State University, Abraka. International Research: Journal of Library and Information Science, 8(2).

Tafazoli, D., Parra, M. E. G., & Abril, C. A. H. 2017. Computer literacy: Sine qua non for digital age of language learning & teaching. Theory and Practice in Language Studies, 7(9), 716.

Ümmühan, A. V. C. I., & Orçun, O. R. U. Ç. 2020. Computer Literacy Course with Distance Education: Students' Views on the Procedure, Content and Benefits. *Öğretim Teknolojisi ve Hayat Boyu Öğrenme Dergisi*, *1*(2), 138-156.

Vasilache, S. 2016. An adaptive model of teaching computer literacy in the context of multicultural instruction. In 2016 IEEE International Conference on Teaching, Assessment, and Learning for Engineering (TALE) (pp. 308-310).

Wong, K., Neves, A., & Negreiros, J. 2017. Computer Literacy Teaching Using Peer Learning and under the Confucian Heritage Cultural Settings of Macao, China. International Association for Development of the Information Society.

Yuan, R., & Shunru, J. 2020. An Exploration of Teaching International Students Practical Computer Literacy at Shanghai Dianji University. International Journal of Science Vol.7 No.4 2020.

THE INCREASING IMPORTANCE OF NATURAL LANGUAGE INTERACTION IN THE DESIGN OF INTELLIGENT TUTORING SYSTEMS

Kurt Englmeier
Schmalkalden University of Applied Science
Blechhammer, 98574 Schmalkalden, Germany

ABSTRACT

In the context of learning platforms for on-the-job training, we expect from an intelligent tutoring system (ITS) that it effectively brings learners to the learning program that suits their aspirations and ambitions and guides them through an individual course or even their entire course program. The better the ITS "understands" the learners' goals, behavior, misconceptions, and errors, the better it can guide the learners along their learning journey, and the more effectively learners acquire their desired knowledge. Guidance usually includes observation of learners, evaluation of their behavior, which leads to the analysis and evaluation of their input, and eventually provides helpful and useful feedback to the learners.
Digital learning platforms increasingly focus on self-paced or self-directed learning, which gives learners the freedom to learn whenever they want and at whatever learning pace that suits their personal learning preferences and attitudes. This trend fosters a shift away from predefined and rigidly wired sessions towards flexibly arranged learning nuggets and tests. There are different paradigms for the design of learner guidance or instructions in ITS. This paper draws attention to natural language (NL) as the prominent mean of communication between system and learners. The benefits of emphasizing natural language bring a number of benefits for guiding and instructing learners. The paper describes the architecture and design of an ITS in the context of a prototypical platform for self-paced learning and demonstrates the role and importance of natural language processing (NLP) as key technology for learner guidance and instruction.

KEYWORDS

Intelligent Tutoring Systems, Natural Language Processing, Digital Learning Environments, Learner Guidance and Instruction

1. INTRODUCTION

Intelligent tutoring system (ITS) have the capability to support new learning experiences by providing customized leaning paths through the learning material and individualized feedback (Guo et al., 2021; Mousavinasab et al., 2018; Paladines and Ramirez, 2020). They convey "domain knowledge in a two-way, *adaptive*, and *incremental* manner" (Yang, 2010). We can expect that ITS foster active learning, that is, the learners have much more impact on the behavior of the digital learning platform. The acquisition of sustainable knowledge, however, is a goal of outstanding importance in digital learning platforms. Their attractiveness raises if they support the learners' need for esteem and self-actualization as defined by Abraham Maslow (Maslow, 1943; Maslow 1962). This need may have many facets addressing many areas in the life of the learners, including advances in their professional life (Almotairi et al., 2019).

Consequently, the focus on ITS may comprise the formation of learners over a larger period of time covering more than just one course. Much like the adaptation of a course to the individual aspirations, requirements and capacities of the learner the curriculum (or training) planning needs to be put in the same focus. On-the-job training in the industry requires this focus on ITS in order to identify training opportunities for the continuous development of the skills of employees. The goal of curriculum planning is to determine which digital courses or further learning resources suit the actual employee's competence in combination with the skills and knowledge the learners aspire to achieve. Required skills and knowledge define the formation setting for the training. However, formation may vary among employees even if they have the same role in a company. The recommended training program, consequently, differs in the same way and evolves over time.

In the past, digital learning platforms provided their content through more or less predefined sequences of sessions and quizzes. From a modern ITS we can expect more flexibility and adaptability to the learners' individuality. Supporting self-paced learning as a leading paradigm provides well-known benefits to learning environments (Peterson, 1996). An ITS includes recommendation features (or a recommendation engine) pursuing the purpose to personalize the learner experience by suggesting learning items and steps that are most relevant and interesting to the individual learner journey. There are several types of recommendation features. In the context of learning platforms, we talk about suggestions of the next learning steps the learners should consider for their career and, later, their learning journeys.

The design of recommendation features for learning environments shall promote reliability, flexibility, and adaptability. However, these features need to be coordinated, too, along the instructional strategy of the course of the training and need to react on the learners' input.

There is no doubt, that symbols can support a very efficient interaction between learners and learning systems. However, it can be beneficial to consider the inclusion of natural language in the interaction design (Cohen, 1992; Ledgard et al., 1980). First, NL as means of communication between the ITS and learners can bring several benefits for guiding and instructing learners. These include:

- Immediate understandability: NL is an intuitive and natural form of communication for humans, making it easier for learners to understand the instructions and guidance provided by the ITS.
- Increased attractiveness: Using NL may enable that learners experience their learning environment more natural, personal, conversational, and, thus, more comfortable and convenient. This raises the system's attractiveness, which, in turn, increases learner motivation and engagement.
- Responsiveness: Natural language can be used to provide guidance that is more flexible and adaptable when allowing learners to express questions, preferences, or requirements in their language.
- Increased expressiveness: Metaphors and graphical interaction elements need to learned and not all interaction possibilities can be suitably expressed by graphical elements. Natural language steps in here to fill these communication gaps.
- Increased analytics: Tracking learners and representing their progress and performance by NL allows for more accurate and actionable insights into their learning experience.

This paper focuses also on the design of ITS that supports the individual layout of training programs for employees in the industry. Furthermore, it also fosters adaptive learner guidance and instruction in order to enable self-paced learning within a digital course. Completing a course does not compellingly and automatically lead to sustainable acquisition of knowledge, even when completed successfully. If newly acquired knowledge falls to oblivion too soon, the course failed to achieve its mission. The course shall encourage the learners to adopt the knowledge provided by the course and not just completing the course successfully. The goal shall be the self-contained learner's adoption of the knowledge domain. The ITS as described here is part of the research project eduplex that aims to develop a more adaptive learning environment for on-the-job training in the industry.

Based on these design principles, the second chapter outlines the architecture our ITS is acting upon and references to related work. Chapter 3 describes in more detail the recommendation features of our ITS. Chapter 4 shifts the focus towards natural language as key ingredient in the design and implementation of our ITS.

2. ARCHITECTURE AND RELATED WORK

Recommendation features of an ITS as discussed in this paper prominently focus on two areas:

1. The setting for coaching employees in the broader context of helping them to find and compose a suitable training program to satisfy their professional goals and aspirations in order to improve their skills and knowledge.
2. Guidance of trainees within a particular course that supports self-paced learning.

It is important to understand the layout of our digital courses in order to better understand the design and implementation of our ITS for self-paced learning. The architecture and design of the digital course is built upon a couple of key principles:

- The entire content of a course is split up into a small number of chapters.
- Each chapter comprises thematically related *learning nuggets*.
- *Learn controls* are provided adjacent to each subset of learning nuggets.

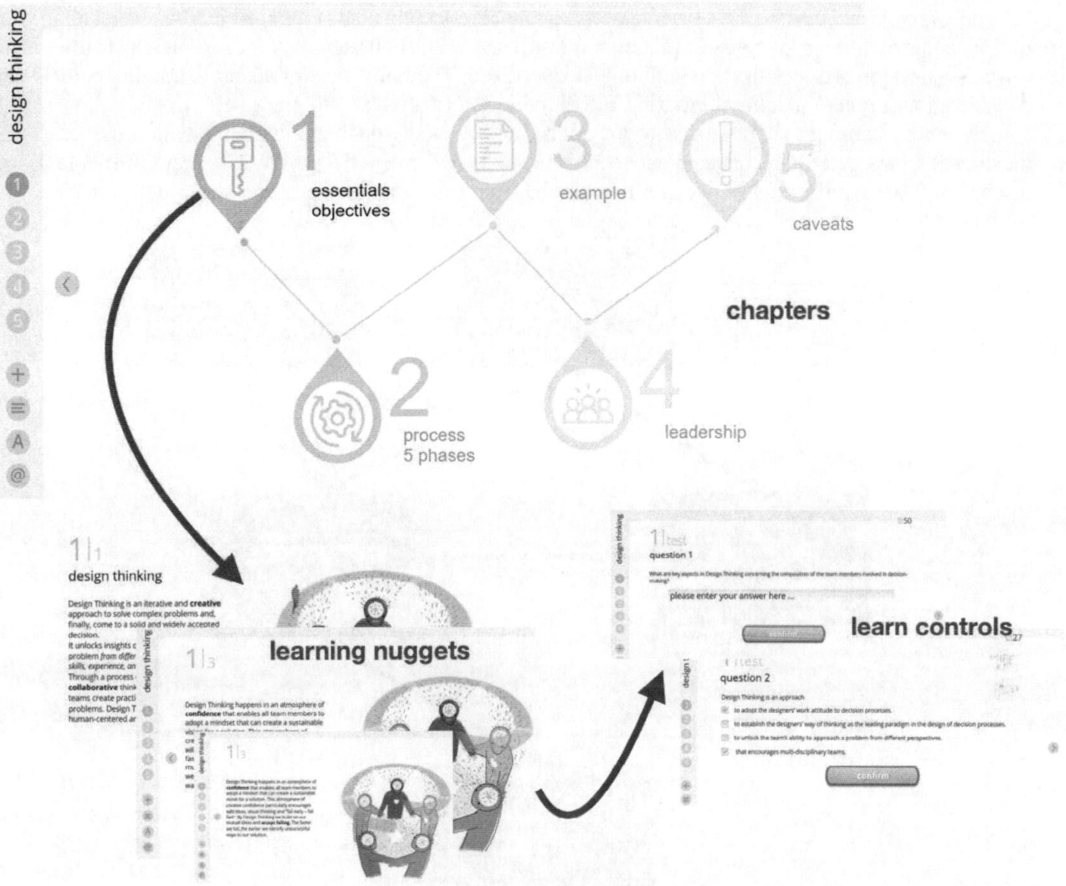

Figure 1. Example of the composition of a self-paced learning course (for Design Thinking) along chapters, learning nuggets, and learn controls

The *functionality of ITS* can be achieved through the collaboration of a number of system components addressing learners, instruction, adaptive training, the domain knowledge, and the interaction (inclined to Yang, 2010). The prominent role of NL suggests the consideration of an explicit language model.

The *domain knowledge* represents in a structured way knowledge and concepts within the *business* domain of the respective organization. It comprises all topics that are important in the training context of this organization. The annotation of the content related to this knowledge area is the first skeleton for the operationalization of NL for the purposes of learner guidance and instruction. The structure of annotation terms summarizes in an operational way the meaning of text in the knowledge base.

The *learner profile* is an operational summary of learner characteristics, preferences, and needs. It is essential when it comes to adapt the learners' journal according to their learning experience and progress. Adaptive instructions reflect the specific needs and abilities of the learners. A learner profile can include information such as:

- Prior knowledge and experience: what the learner already know and what they need or want to learn.
- Learning pace and results from the learn controls: what the learner has learned and in which time.
- Learning paths: the individual sequences of the course sections and quizzes visited along the learner journey.
- Statements reflecting further aspects of the individual learner journeys.

It is the learner profile that helps trainers and course designers to create more adaptive and engaging learning experiences by putting more emphasis on the unique characteristics and needs of each learner.

The *adaptive training model* is the overarching model reflecting the learners' formation over a larger period of time and over a range of courses. (Nkambou & Kabanza, 2001) It depicts, for example, the learner journey towards a new job or specialization within the existing job. The implement of adaptive training models can be considered as a meta model orchestrating the individual formation of an employee. It may reference digital courses, static learning material, class room events, or even individual appointments with a trainer. Usually, the model's parameters are updated in accordance with the learner's progress or new available learning resources. The adaptiveness of the training model emerges from the fact that the initial situation of the formation is not completely known at the beginning of the training.

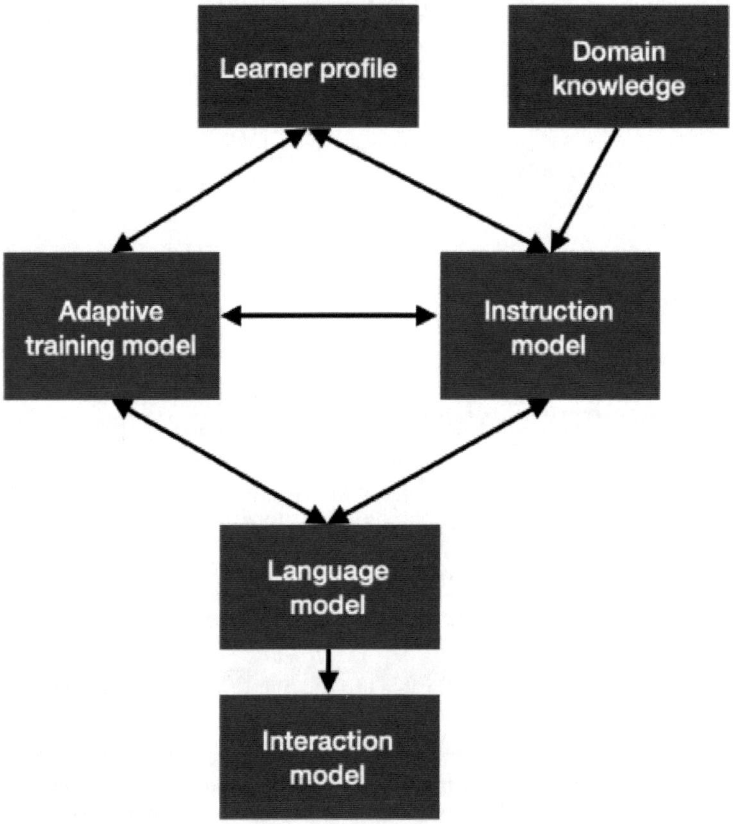

Figure 2. Architecture schema of an intelligent tutoring system (inclined to Yang, 2010)

The instruction model outlines patterns of learner guidance in order to successfully complete a course and to sustainably acquire knowledge. The instruction model describes the learning steps and the content of the learn controls including evaluation algorithms that express the learners' level of progress. Instruction models contain many references from learning nuggets to questions as part of the learning control. These references help, to provide proper feedback to the learners that help them understand their errors and misconceptions (Benbunan-Fich, 2002). In summary, the instruction model describes how learning nuggets are interconnected and how they are related to the learning controls. It also defines the reporting of the learner's achievements that are recorded in the learner's profile.

The interaction model defines the way in which the learning system with the learners. This includes the way it responds to inputs, actions, and the way it communicates. In the context of our ITS we apply a rule-based system that enables or disables navigation and interaction possibilities. They also include natural language processing and dialogue management for the interactions with the learners. Therefore, the language model is an integral part of the interaction model that supports the analysis of natural language instructions and learner statements in order to generate or trigger adequate actions of the learning system. The language model maintains the semantic context the recommendation features of the ITS are acting upon.

3. RECOMMENDATION IN THE CONTEXT OF ON-THE-JOB TRAINING

Recommendation for the professional or personal development on the job has a clear focus on the formation of employees in a certain work context. Recommendations shall answer the question "What to do next?". On the formation level, these recommendations emerge from the employee's goals and career aspirations. From this goal horizon, more specific goals can be derived that reflect development and improvement of skills, competences, and job-related knowledge. Usually with a person from the human resources department or functional management (or a training coach) the employee (or trainee) discusses her or his strengths and areas for improvement. Coaching an employee typically addresses specific areas of expertise, such as management, sales, production, technical skills, or soft skills like efficient and effective communication, emotional intelligence, leadership and the like. It may work in a variety of settings, including businesses, government agencies, and educational institutions.

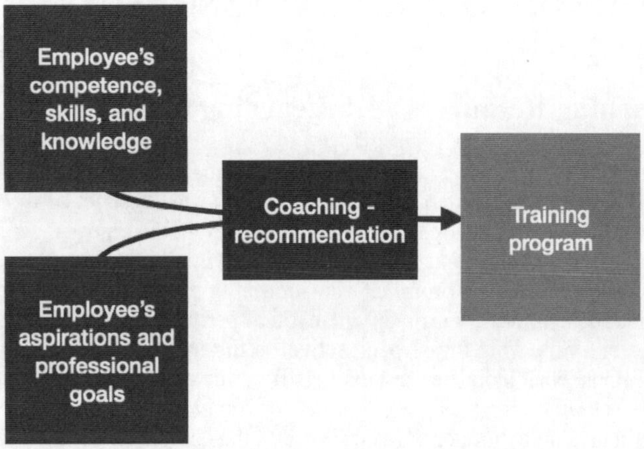

Figure 3. Schema for recommendation in the context of professional and personal formation

Formation-related recommendation comprise suggestions or endorsements considering the competences, skills and knowledge of the employees and the goals of their further development. Additionally, it would be beneficial if the recommendation also includes the expectations on the trainee's progress and how the acquired knowledge will form their job and career. An individual's career aspirations and goals greatly impact the types of training programs they need to choose to participate in. By understanding career aspirations and goals of their employees, organizations can tailor their training programs to better align with the needs and goals of their workforce. This ensures that the *recommended* training program are meeting the needs of the employees and are helping them to progress towards their career aspirations and professional goals. Recommendation on the formation level addresses the selection of the training resources (or courses) that help the employee to achieve personal and professional goals and career aspirations. It is important that the goals of the individual parts of the training program sum up to the overall goals as defined on the meta level. With this selection of training resources, the overall formation goal is broken down into more detailed goals reflecting the expectations connected with the training program.

Recommendations on the course level address the trainee's performance during the training period. They are used to assess the trainees' progress at the individual stages of each course and their readiness for further stages within the same course or advancement to the next consecutive course.

In a self-paced learning course, the automatic recommendations provided by the ITS are based on the following data:

- Points achieved as result from the learn control
- Time spent on studying a single learning nugget, subset of nuggets, or chapter
- Learning nuggets as marked by the trainees, because they are of special interest for them
- Notes left on the page of a learning nugget

From this information the ITS generates recommendations for the next step of the trainee, such as

- repeat one or more learn controls
- repeat one or more learning nuggets
- repeat an entire chapter and re-taking the associate learn controls
- proceed to the next chapter/learning nugget

It is important to note that the recommendation also consider the time elapsed between studying the different chapters of a course in order to take into account the fact, the humans can forget what they have learned. There are, thus, reminders that automatically appear after a certain number of weeks or months has been passed. The time span depends also on the results the trainee has achieved in the respective learn control of the chapter or learning nugget.

4. THE SPECIFIC ROLE OF NATURAL LANGUAGE

4.1 Matching Learning Resources with Learning Goals

There are some very prominent application areas for Natural language processing (NLP) in the context of the ITS as described in this paper. When coaching employees to find the best set of training program for their professional goals and aspirations, NLP helps to analyze and highlight the trainees' actual skills, competences, and knowledge and the ones they want to achieve through the training program. Learner profiles result from this NLP-based analytic step. NLP has a prominent position in this process, because required information is mostly contained in job descriptions, curricula vitae, and personal statements that sketch the aspired competence, knowledge or skills. This future perspective on the individual formation can also be achieved from job or skill descriptions. NLP identifies and extracts from the descriptions the *essential information* that *summarizes the actual and future stage in the formation of the employee*. This information constitutes the profile of the employee in the context of her or his training. In the end, it reflects the objectives of the training.

Courses, course chapters, and learning nuggets are part of the *knowledge base* among other learning resources. We can assume that each learning resource comes with a brief description summarizing its content and learning objectives. Applying NLP on these items extracts the essential information here, too. By matching the essential information on the learner's side and on the course's side NLP can identify all courses that are useful concerning the training goals for the employee.

4.2 Supporting the Interaction for Self-Paced Learning

It is important to note that many systems supporting self-paced learning do not really support NL input, in particular, when it comes to the design of learn control features. Because of their limited text analysis features, they support mostly single choice questions, multiple choice questions or similarly schematic question types that bypass types that enable free-text answers in natural language. For a more ambitious design of a learn control environment the eduplex project considered it important to provide learn control questions that require free text input. In this setting, NLP helps to identify the meaning of the correct answer and of the trainee's answer. The comparison of the two respective statements and, thus, the correct evaluation of the trainee's answer can only be achieved through a series of NL processes such as automatic correction of misspellings and estimating to what extend the learner's statement lies within the meaning of the correct answer.

In the same way, NLP identifies and extracts essential information from learning nuggets and learn controls as well as statements the learners left with a nugget or learn control. These statements can have the form of reminders ("Check this section again in a week"), questions ("How shall I compute the entries in the risk matrix?") or the like.

NLP helps to annotate all learning nuggets, learn control, and trainee statements with standardized terms. In the next step, NLP can relate these annotations forming a semantic net over these learning components and comments. This, in turn, is the source for the automatic and dynamic identification of navigation paths or to recommend the trainee what to do next.

4.3 Standardized Annotation

We use a variety of natural language processing (NLP) techniques to analyze all kind of textual information in the context of our ITS. This includes machine-learning based text analysis with a particular emphasis on named entity recognition. In our approach, we develop annotation features using domain-specific BERT transformers (Devlin et al., 2019) modelled on the European Skills, Competences and Occupations classification (ESCO) system. The models help to produce standardized semantic networks for each profile type (learner, knowledge, learning resource). Recursive text summarization produces hierarchically structured annotation sets from the descriptions that we link with the semantic networks. It is important to note that named-entity recognition (NER) is applied in this process to improve the expressiveness of the semantic profiles (Fort et al., 2009). They complete the definition of the ontologies that represent the different profiles (Hernandez, 2005). NER is useful when it comes to identifying time-related or quantity-related characteristics in job descriptions, such as the number of years a person practices in a particular field, for instance. The same holds for trainee statements like "I want to come back in one week". Beside NER, we also apply n-gram identification in order to increase the precision of our NLP features. The larger the value of n, the more context is taken into account, but also the sparser the data becomes. For our analysis features we restrict to 2-, 3- and 4-grams. By using all of these techniques together, we improve the accuracy and efficiency of our annotation tasks.

The use of a standardized vocabulary increases the correctness of the matching processes, in particular when it comes to compare the meaning in the annotations to be matched. For this purpose, we first expand all terms in both annotations by their synonyms. Before expansion, however, we restrict the set synonym terms to those terms that are part of the respective knowledge domain. If the course addresses Agile Computing, for instance, we take the vocabulary of the entire learning material of this course as controlled vocabulary where the synonyms for the text analysis are recruited from.

These techniques mentioned here can be used to extract insights from learner data and to describe the learners' movements along their journey. Once the data has been analyzed, results are going to be interpreted and draw conclusions about the learner's journey. This can include things such as identifying areas where learners struggled, determining which stages of the journey were successful, and understanding the overall their performance throughout the journey. The semantic network enables the learning platform to perform or propose actions suitable for the learners' journey.

In summary, in our ITS, the learner journey (including all the related profiles) is predominantly expressed in NL. The semantics of each stage of the journey, that is, of the learning nuggets and learn controls are mainly expressed in NL. They show:

1. Key stages and milestones that the learner will go through. These stages include studying learning nuggets, progress tracking, and learn control results.
2. Representations on the learner's interactions and statements.
3. The learner's competence and knowledge and the objectives the learner aspires to achieve.

5. CONCLUSION

The paper prominently describes the role of NLP in the design of analytical features for ITS. First, NLP first supports the adequate matching of employees with learning opportunities that meet their aspirations and career goals. NLP is probably the only instrument to produce digital profiles of the competences, skills, and knowledge of employees on a broad scale. Almost all information on these qualities is available in texts only. The same holds for all kind of learning resources that are usually described in texts, too. With the presentation of the employees' professionals in textual form, all three types of key sources of information for our ITS are candidates for NLP. Machine-learning tools like BERT are powerful instruments for the annotation of texts. However, our research shows, that for the proper annotation of text related to occupations and training the integration of features handling named entities and n-grams are indispensable. The use of nomenclatures like ESCO are also useful. However, their items cannot cover the details of the texts. Too many information is not addressed by ESCO. That, in turn, requires the application of automatic summarization techniques on the texts and the proper linking of the hierarchical structure of the summaries with ESCO.

The support of NL also significantly enriches the interaction in our prototypical course system for self-paced learning. Even though we haven't conducted yet a comprehensive evaluation of our platform for self-paced learning, from the feedback of our first users we can assume that our approach and, in particular, the natural language interaction will be appreciated.

Beside a profound evaluation of our approach, we will also extend the automatic production of references between learning nuggets. NLP can construct a coherent semantic network across learning nuggets and related learn controls. The expansion of this network towards learning entities that are part of other courses, for instance, appears appealing. It gives the learners the possibility to easily explore into knowledge areas akin to the one of the courses at hand but reaching beyond its content limits.

ACKNOWLEDGEMENT

Research as outlined here is part of the eduplex project under the research framework INVITE of the Federal Institute for Vocational Education and Training (BIBB) funded by the German Federal Ministry of Education and Research.

REFERENCES

Almotairi, M. et al., 2019. Enhance employees' competences through customized learning. *Proceedings of the 10th International Conference on E-Education, E-Business, E-Management and E-Learnings.* Tokyo, Japan, pp. 42-47.

Benbunan-Fich, R., 2002. Improving education and training with IT. *Communications of the ACM.* Vol. 45, No. 6, pp. 94-99.

Devlin, J. et al., 2019. BERT: Pre-training of deep bidirectional transformers for language understanding. *Proceedings of the 2019 Conference of the North American Chapter of the Association for Computational Linguistics: Human Language Technologies.* Minneapolis, USA, pp. 4171-4186.

Fort, K. et al., 2009. Towards a methodology for named entities annotation. *Proceedings of the Third Linguistic Annotation Workshop.* Suntec, Singapore, pp. 142-149.

Guo, L., Wang, D., Gu, F., Li, Y., Wang, Y., & Zhou, R., 2021. Evolution and trends in intelligent tutoring systems research: a multidisciplinary and scientometric view. *Asia Pacific Education Review*, Vol. 22, 441-461.

Hernandez, N., 2005. Ontologies pour l'aide à l'exploration d'une collection de documents. *Ingénierie des systèmes d'information, RSTI série ISI, Recherche, extraction et exploration d'information*, Vol. 10, No. 1, pp. 11-31.

Ledgard, H. et al., 1980. The natural language of interactive systems. *Communications of the ACM.* Vol. 23, No. 10, pp. 556-563.

Maslow, A. H., 1943. A theory of human motivation. *Psychological Review*, Vol. 4, No. 50, pp. 370-396.

Maslow, A. H., 1962. *Toward a psychology of being*. D. Van Nostrand Company, Princeton, USA.

Mousavinasab, E., Zarifsanaiey, N., Kalhori, S.R., Rakhshan, M., Keikha, L., & Saeedi, M.G., 2018. Intelligent tutoring systems: a systematic review of characteristics, applications, and evaluation methods. *Interactive Learning Environments*, Vol. 29, pp. 142-163.

Nkambou, R. and Kabanza, F., 2001. Designing Intelligent Tutoring Systems: A Multiagent Planning Approach. *ACM SIGCUE Outlook*, Vol. 27, No. 2, pp. 46-60.

Paladines, J. and Ramirez, J., 2020. A Systematic Literature Review of Intelligent Tutoring Systems With Dialogue in Natural Language. *IEEE Access,* Vol. 8, pp. 164246-164267,

Peterson, P. L., 1996. Self-paced training expanding educational opportunities. *Proceedings of the 24th annual ACM SIGUCCS conference on User services.* Chigago, USA, pp. 127-131.

Yang, F.J., 2010. The Ideology of Intelligent Tutoring Systems. *In acm Inroads*, Vol. 1, No. 4, pp. 63-65.

LESSONS LEARNT FROM AN ONLINE PILOT STUDY ABOUT STRATEGIC ALIGNMENT AT A HIGHER EDUCATION INSTITUTION

Thokozani Kachale, Wegene Demeke, Christos Chrysoulas and Imed Romdhani
School of Computing, Engineering, and the Built Environment
Edinburgh Napier University, 10 Colinton Road, Edinburgh, EH10 5DT, United Kingdom

ABSTRACT

This article is a report on the lessons learned when conducting an interpretive case study in a developing country. From the literature review, it was apparent that there are few reported lessons from pilot studies about strategic alignment in higher education institutions from a middle management perspective in the developing countries. The aim of this article is to fill that gap. The pilot study was conducted to assess the feasibility of collecting data from Malawi, one of the countries with low internet access in the world. The case study organisation was a university that had been identified during the time that governments across the world had imposed travel restrictions during the COVID-19 pandemic. The pilot study involved evaluating the feasibility of collecting data online using the Luftman questionnaire for assessing maturity level for organisations and the use of Microsoft Teams for conducting online interviews within the context of a country where the majority of the population do not have internet access, and English is the de facto lingua franca. Among the lessons learned were the need for researchers to be careful to match case study organisations to research topic, the need to support participants understanding questionnaires in qualitative case studies to minimise risk of drop out and ensure participants understand any technical language being used, the effect that external factors such as weather might have on a study, and the limitations of automatic voice recognition for interview transcription.

KEYWORDS

Strategic Alignment, On-Line Data Collection, Lessons Learned, Middle Management, Pilot Study

1. INTRODUCTION

The pilot study was conducted against a background of a dearth of research in the developing world in the areas of business strategy and information system strategy formulation and their strategic alignment, and middle managers' participation in these areas. The pilot study was based on an interpretive case study at a public university in Malawi. The inclusion criteria were that the participants should be middle managers who participate in the formulation of business strategy, information technology strategy and their strategic alignment.

According to Ismail et al. (2017) a Pilot Study (PS) is a small-scale research project that is carried out prior to the final full-scale study (Kim, 2010). It assists researchers in testing the feasibility of the research. It allows researchers, particularly novices, gain interviewing experience and refine the final road map for the main study (Aziz and Khan, 2021). A researcher can pilot a study to identify or refine a research question, determine which methods are best for pursuing it, and estimate how much time and resources will be required to complete the larger final version of the study. When conducting a qualitative study, it is critical to use a PS to test and identify how methods and ideas would work in practice (Aziz and Khan, 2021). According to (Ismail et al., 2017), PSs are commonly associated with quantitative studies but can still yield important feedback to inform the main study and reinforce methodological rigor.

As a principal investigator, the PS was not done from an entirely novice point of view. In previous line of work, the principal investigator had conducted many interviews during requirements elicitation for software development projects. The major concern for the principal investigator was that he had never undertaken any previous academic research work of this nature that placed him with the need for more self-awareness while using less familiar qualitative methods, instruments, and techniques with a view to knowledge generation required from PhD study.

This is a reflexive report regarding the PS that was conducted prior to the final extensive study in Malawi. The aim was to test the methodological feasibility of carrying out a remote study in a location that is known for its poor internet connectivity while the principal investigator was based in the United Kingdom. This paper compiles the lessons learned with respect to access to potential host organisations, recruitment of potential participants, data collection methods, and the researcher's personal development.

The rest of the paper is organised as follows: Section 2 addresses some of the literature that was reviewed, followed by a discussion in Section 3 of lessons learned starting with the issue of access to the case study. This is followed by participant recruitment strategy, the use of English language for data collection and the impact of technology on transcription before the article is concluded in Section 4.

2. LITERATURE REVIEW

According to Janghorban et al. (2013), a pilot study is "small scale of a complete survey or a pretest of a particular research instrument such as questionnaire or interview guide" which is concerned with the following areas: a) identification of issues that might arise with participants' recruitment, b) providing real-world qualitative research experience for the researcher, c) assessing the suitability of the interview protocol, and determination of the research methodology. Another area that might benefit from conducting a pilot study is the project management aspect of the final study in terms of refining the estimates about the time and cost required (Ismail et al., 2017). Aziz and Khan (2021) found that there is a lot of literature about pilot studies in quantitative studies, there appeared to be a challenge in allocating adequate literature on pilot studies in qualitative studies. This study also had challenges locating reported pilot studies using online data collection from the developing world in areas of strategic alignment from the middle management perspective.

Following these aspects of pilot study as good practice, the study proceeded to test the feasibility of on-line data collection method. One of the aspects of this method to be considered was the availability and access of reliable internet among potential participants. The Malawi National Statistics Office puts the latest population figure at 17.2 million (Malanga and Chigona, 2022). According to (Worldometer, 2022), the latest population figure is 20.3 million, 18.5% of which is urban-based and the median age is 18.1 years. Malanga and Chigona (2022) quotes the rural population at 87% implying that only 13% live in urban areas. Only 13.9% of the population have internet access (Kainja, 2022) attributed to lack of state investment in ICT infrastructure, high corporate tax, and value-added tax rates. These result in high internet prices making the internet inaccessible to the majority, especially those who live in the rural areas (Malanga and Chigona, 2022).

While there is low internet access across the general population, there is a reliable quality internet access in urban areas especially among institutions. The participants to the semi-structured interviews were all members of staff at public university with fiber optic broadband. In addition to the semi-structured interviews which were conducted using Microsoft Teams, they were also asked to complete an online assessment of strategic alignment maturity using Microsoft Forms.

A universally accepted definition of who are middle managers is elusive. The shifting collegial nature of leadership in universities makes the identification of middle managers particularly hard. Defined very succinctly, " middle managers have managers reporting to them and are also required to report to managers at a more senior level", (van Niekerk and Jansen van Rensburg, 2022) p.277. In a single case study that they conducted at a university in South Africa, they identified exclusion and inclusion criteria based on job title. The following titles were excluded because they were considered senior managers: executive director, vice principal, chancellor, and vice chancellor. The inclusion into the middle management for the study, the middle managers were those that had been employed in non-academic positions with the following job titles: director, deputy director, and assistant director. (ibid.). Floyd (2015) carried out a case study of middle managers from two "culturally different English universities" who had different ways of identifying middle managers. In one university, middle managers were externally recruited, while in another they were seconded from among the academic staff. As a result of changes in stakeholder expectations from universities, heads of department are increasingly viewed as managers. This has resulted in these academic managers and administrative managers sharing responsibility for budgets and resource allocation (Floyd, 2015).

These middle managers, regardless of career path, are strategically important owing to their situation as a bridge between top management and the lower levels of the organisation (Tarakci et al., 2018). Their activities may lead to realisation of divergent strategies due to imperfect communication, or understanding (Baker and Singh, 2019, Balogun, 2006), or self-interest (Ates, 2014, Gibson and Groom, 2021, Tarakci et al., 2018, Wooldridge et al., 2008). Although the latter might appear politically incorrect, sometimes the divergent actions of middle managers may lead to an overall improvement in the competitive position of an organisation (Baker and Singh, 2019). From the viewpoint of formulation and implementation of business and information system strategies, and their strategic alignment it is important to note these will usually be agreed by top management. Once they have been approved it is the middle managers who have the responsibility to oversee that these are implemented in their business units (Netland et al., 2020). Through sensemaking and issue selling, middle managers exert strategic influence on, and from the bottom layers (Balogun, 2006) in a feedback loop. Sensemaking is concerned with interpretation of top-down intended corporate strategies into relevant business strategies for their business units. Where there is self-interest, misunderstanding, or misinterpretation, top management strategic goals may not be implemented as intended within business units. Sometimes when business units may note that intended corporate strategies are not coordinated with customer expectations, or not yielding intended results, they may have to improvise or raise issues for consideration of top managers which are routed through middle managers in what is called issue selling. Top management may consider some of these issues and subsequently amend corporate strategies to reflect the recommendations from the bottom.

One area in which middle managers at a university may exert their influence in the foregoing ways is the area of strategic alignment. This has been an issue of concern for top managers for over three decades based on the assumption that there is a positive relationship between strategic alignment between business strategy and information technology strategy (Luftman et al., 2017). Strategic alignment has been defined using various terms such as “fit”, “harmony”, “fusion”, “linkage” to describe managerial behaviours between the information technology and non-information technology business units of an organisation that aim to provide new services, improve business processes, and decision making resulting in increasing business value for the organisation (Luftman et al., 2017). In the case of a university the way in which this value might be increased could take many forms such as providing support for learners using on-line learning management systems, publishing prospectuses on websites, and enrolling students into open and distance learning programs.

The section has reviewed the relevant literature for this study. This has covered the importance of pilot studies in qualitative studies, the level of internet access in Malawi, the challenges of identifying middle managers, and how they may influence the formulation of business strategy and information systems strategy, and their strategic alignment. The next section is a discussion of lessons that were learned from conducting the pilot study.

3. DISCUSSION

The participants for the pilot study were all drawn from a public university in Malawi after obtaining the necessary ethics approval and authorization. There were four participants in total who were requested to complete an assessment for the level of maturity for strategic alignment and to participate in semi-structured interviews. Each interview, which lasted about one hour, was conducted online using Microsoft Teams. A strategic alignment maturity assessment was completed using Microsoft Forms.

The study design was an interpretive single case study with two aims. The first aim sought to establish the level of maturity for strategic alignment of business strategy and information technology strategy. The second aim was to explore the lived experience of middle managers in the formulation of business strategy, information systems strategy and such strategic alignment. In order to answer the research questions, the principal investigator set out to approach managers of organisations with the following characteristics. The case study organisation should be capable of being characterized as having a middle management layer. As well as being involved in implementation of strategic directives set out by top managers, the middle managers should also be involved in contributing towards formulation of business strategy, information strategy and their strategic alignment. The following sections are a discussion of the lessons learned that were identified during the study starting with approaching case study organisations, participant access and recruitment.

3.1 Lessons from Obtaining Access to Case Study Organisation

To move the study forward, several organisations in Scotland and Malawi were contacted. For this purpose, the principal investigator contacted current and former work colleagues and former classmates during undergraduate study in Malawi and Scotland. This was at the beginning of the second year of studies. In total eight organisations were contacted as in table 1 below. Two of these organisations were based in Scotland. However, one was not as keen when it finally came down to start the data collection. The willing charity in Malawi was too small as it did not have a clearly distinguishable middle management layer with strategic responsibilities because they had only one person functioning as the information systems department. The willing charity in Scotland had a much flatter structure and was deemed unsuitable as well.

Table 1. List of potential case study organisations (source: authors)

	Location	Organisation type	Relationship between Contact Person and Principal Investigator	Observations
Charity 1	Scotland	Local Charity	Colleague. Works in same department	Showed signs of unwillingness to proceed
Charity 2	Scotland	International Charity	Social contact	Willingness but deemed not suitable for exploring research questions due to organisation form
Bank 1	Malawi	Subsidiary of international banking group.	Social contact. Works for former employer	Willingness but adversely impacted by adverse weather conditions
Bank 2	Malawi	Large local bank	Social contact of PI. . Studied at the same university	Became unresponsive at some point
Government Agency 1	Malawi	Compliance of fiscal laws	Social contact. Studied at the same university	Became unresponsive at some point
Government Agency 2	Malawi	Participation in democratic participation	Social contact. Studied at the same university	Willingness but PI decided to proceed elsewhere because they were recruiting new Executive Director
HEI	Malawi	Public university	Social contact. Studied at the same university	Successfully hosted study with other issues in participant recruitment
Charity 3	Malawi	Local charity	Social contact. Studied at the same university	Willingness but PI decided the organisation form not suitable for exploring research questions

Before moving on to the next section, it is interesting to point out that one of the banks that had been approached had indicated a strong interest to host the study. The negotiations had gone on well between December 2021 and January 2022. However, this is the rainy season in Malawi. During this season, the country was hit by severe weather systems resulting in unusually heavy rains that significantly affected public infrastructure including the power grid. As a result, many organisations, including the banks with metropolitan and wide area networks were required to work on their disaster recovery capabilities. The lesson learnt was that sometimes a planned study might be affected by events outside of the control of the researcher and the potential host organisation. This did not deter the study as negotiations went on with other organisations and until the principal investigator was able to identify alternative case studies through persistence. This highlights the reality that even with the best of intentions, organisations may not be able to host similar studies and there is a need for researchers to develop negotiation skills and be willing to be flexible as the situation requires. Sometimes the researcher must accept that willing organisations might prove not to be as useful due to their unsuitability for exploring research questions as was the case with some organisations in this study. That is a very important aspect of experience as a researcher.

3.2 Lessons from Potential Participant Recruitment

One of the areas that was tested during the pilot study was participant recruitment. This is important because a PhD study requires empirical data. This requires a substantial amount of time and effort (Wray et al., 2017).

Participants were recruited via a gatekeeper after Lilongwe University of Agriculture and Natural Resources had authorised the study. This was done after the Ethics Committee at Edinburgh Napier University had indicated that the study posed low to medium level of risk to participants. An email with a participant information sheet introducing the study was sent to the participants through a key informant. From the literature review that was conducted, it had been established that globally there was a small number of studies from middle management perspective in strategic alignment studies at higher education institutions in developing countries. Up to the time of the pilot study, it had not been possible to access such studies from Malawi and the study proceeded from that perspective.

Having gained access to a public university, four middle managers were introduced to the principal investigator. This snow-balled to six through referrals during the interviews. One participant dropped out of the interviews because she had indicated that she found the Luftman maturity level assessment questionnaire too technical in its wording. She did not indicate the exact items that were problematic for her, and she was no longer available to clarify. A second participant dropped out because there were urgent work-related issues, and he would not be available on the date that he had indicated that he would be available.

The principal investigator learnt that the personal networks that one cultivates are helpful not only for social purposes. Sharing personal goals with friends and being open with social contacts about how the principal investigator felt they could assist were some of the things that helped gain access to potential participants for the study. The participants were individuals that could not have otherwise been accessible to if not for the people who introduced them. Although this method might not appear to be very scientific and formal, the lesson learnt was that a student researcher can use this method successfully to find not only willing case study organisations, but also volunteers willing to participate in such studies.

3.3 Lessons from Data Collection

The data collection method has two aspects worthy of the readers' attention.

3.3.1 Conducting Online Research

The first aspect is that of conducting online interviews based in what is considered a developed nation where the principal investigator is currently based (United Kingdom) and a least developed country (Malawi) where the case study organisation is situated in with all participants. Malawi has low internet access among the general population, especially in rural areas. However, there appears to be a decent level of internet access in urban areas and institutions (Malemia, 2021). Only one session had a slightly poor quality compared to three interviews. However, the recorded file was still usable. For two interviews, it was possible to use video capabilities without problems.

Gruber et al. (2008) conducted an online study which enabled them to proceed in ways that would not have been possible otherwise. The respondents found it convenient to participate in the study without leaving the convenience of their homes. The main study with which this pilot study was associated had been conceived in the middle of lockdowns that were in place in many countries as a public health response to the Covid-19 pandemic.

The important lesson learnt was that online studies between the United Kingdom and Malawi are possible and this is an avenue that other researchers may wish to consider. This data collection method offers a cost-effective option (Gruber et al., 2008, Hewson, 2017) for those who wish to conduct research in remote places such as Malawi. The participants in the study were employees of a university who used their own equipment. However, where researchers who might wish to collaborate with participants, who cannot afford their own internet-connected equipment need to seriously consider what implications that might have on the overall data collection method and the financial cost implications and quality of their proposed study.

3.3.2 Data Collection Instruments

The next aspect to the data collection method is one regarding the instruments that were used for conducting semi-structured interviews. After conducting the literature review, the principal investigator produced research questions and decided to proceed with the study as an interpretive single case study using semi-structured interviews, Luftman Strategic alignment assessment model, and document analysis (Hewson, 2017, Yin, 2014, Torres-Moreno and Aponte-Melo, 2021).

- Semi-Structured Interviews

An important consideration during interviews is the establishment of rapport between interviewer and interviewee. Gruber et al. (2008) recognises that this is easy to do during one-to-one interviews and experience confirms this. Setting up the environment to make sure the participants were at ease was not a challenge as it might have otherwise been had the interviews been conducted face to face. As part of establishing rapport with the study participants, at the beginning of the interviews, participants were asked to talk about themselves, their education, length of employment, or if they had worked elsewhere before joining the university. Listening to participants talking about themselves helped the principal investigator to establish how the probes to the key interview questions would be framed.

Each interview session began by reiterating the introduction to the study and further notification that participation was voluntary. The principal investigator was under the impression that there was parity between himself as the interviewer and study participants. The interviews were conducted in English and there were no language barriers to be overcome. This is because not only is English the official business language in Malawi, but it is also the medium of business communication and lesson delivery at the public university. At the end of each interview participants were asked how they found the sessions. They indicated the language used during interviews and manner of presentation had put them at ease.

- Luftman's Strategic Alignment Maturity Alignment Assessment Tool

The first page of the assessment tool provided participants with details emphasising that participation to the study was voluntary. Should a participant decide not to continue with the study they could opt out at this point or simply close the tool at any point as they completed it. Once they completed and submitted the tool the information was saved anonymously on an Edinburgh Napier University server. The assessment tool was administered online using Microsoft Forms. The data was downloaded and analysed in Microsoft Excel.

Except for one out of six participants, all of them were able to complete all the thirty-nine questions within the model. Prior to the pilot study, the principal investigator had tested the instrument with colleagues at the School of Computing. One had stated that it could have been helpful to truncate the instrument because it might be considered too long in the field. However, none of the participants during the PS who completed the assessment had raised similar issues or any other issues with the tool.

The principal investigator's observations were that the layout for the tool was better rendered when using mobile devices (mobile phone or tablet) than it was on laptop computers. However, the PS participants did not raise these issues. So, the assessment tool will be used for the final study as it is. This position has been arrived after considering the findings of the PS which seem to indicate that the assessment tool may not fully explore the level of maturity for strategic alignment. However, the validation of the tool was carried out after it had been used in assessing maturity in 3000 participating companies(Luftman et al., 2017). So, any suggestions to amend the tool will invariably require more studies of similar institutions in Malawi to justify such amendment.

However, because a case study of this nature has a small number of participants compared to surveys, all care must be taken to encourage participants as much as possible to avoid dropping out of studies. To mitigate against loss of participants after going to great lengths to recruit them, it is recommended that the researcher must be careful to emphasise the availability of support for participants to explain any terms that might cause problems. To minimize the risk of dropping out, all potential participants who are willing to be interviewed for the main study using the Luftman questionnaire should be interviewed first and be encouraged to complete the assessment questionnaire with guidance from the research team.

3.4 Language

The data collection was conducted in English according to design. Participants were comfortable conducting interviews without the requirement to translate in any vernacular language. Although the principal investigator could not locate strategic alignment research articles in English conducted in Malawi, the use of English as the official lingua franca dates back to colonial times (Chilora, 2000). The language enjoys a predominance over vernacular languages in delivery of lessons in education (Reilly et al., 2022, Matiki, 2001). As a result, it has attained a de facto official language status and did not pose any challenge during semi-structured interviews.

However, a challenge rose due to the speech recognition software for automatic transcription that is offered in MS Teams. The overall quality of transcripts was poor but provided a better starting point than would have been had the whole exercise been done from scratch. This was due to the voice recognition system not being able to recognise some English words pronounced by Malawians as speakers of several languages. The principal investigator is familiar with several Malawian accents, and this assisted with the transcription. While this lack of automatic transcription might be deemed as drawback on the one hand, on the other hand it enabled us to get more acquainted with the semi-structured interview data which helped with coding and analysis. Someone who might not be familiar with how Malawians speak might require assistance with transcription but so far, the study shows that anyone familiar with English should be able to transcribe the interview data.

Once the transcription was done for each interview recording, copies were sent out to each participant to validate whether what had been transcribed represents an accurate record of what had transpired during interviews. All four PS participants affirmed that what had been transcribed was accurate. The transcripts were compiled in Microsoft Word which is one the popular word processors across the world. Participants did not indicate any problems using Word.

3.5 MS Teams

During interviews, two participants were willing to conduct interviews with their videos left on. Two participants switched off their videos. However, it was not possible to assess participants' body language even for the ones who had not turned off their video. Video interviews had a very slight edge over the audio interviews because it was possible to maintain some level of eye contact with participants. These did not appear to affect the quality of the interview process and the resultant data as there was a good flow of dialogue. The principal investigator was aware of the need to be respectful to the participants to enable them to speak and respond freely to the questions that were asked (Guillemin and Heggen, 2009). On average the interviews lasted around one hour.

4. CONCLUSION

The purpose of the PS was twofold. Firstly, to verify the feasibility of conducting such a study online at a time when there were worldwide travel restrictions. The pilot study participants were all based in Malawi which is known for low internet access. However, the PS has shown that it is feasible to conduct a study of this nature remotely suggesting that the quality of internet is acceptable for purposes of data collection using software such as Microsoft Teams.

A pilot study may also be useful to gain research experience and develop personal skills and abilities that can make a significant contribution to the main study. From the time the principal investigator started approaching organisations to host the study to the time the pilot study was conducted, invaluable lessons were learnt. The first issue that arose was the realisation that even though some organisations may be willing to host a study, they may be unsuitable for any number of reasons. For example, two of the organisations that had indicated a willingness were rejected by the principal investigator because they had been considered unsuitable due to their operational forms. Even though another organisation had also been willing to host the study, it was overtaken by the recruitment of an executive director which might have raised internal political issues and resulted in the new leadership not being supportive of hosting the study. Yet another organisation could not proceed with the study because of extreme weather conditions that had caused the target potential participants to focus their attention on the disaster recovery planning. The lessons learnt include that as a researcher, one must be flexible and tenacious while anticipating that issues might arise due to the researcher's preference or circumstances beyond the researcher's control.

Retaining participants in a qualitative study can be a challenge if sufficient care is not taken to support participants respond to some of the technical issues that are being explored in a study. Another issue that might arise is the researcher becoming too dependent on technology. This is particularly true of automatic voice recognition facilities in the software applications that are prolific on the market these days. At present, the automatic voice recognition for non-native speakers of English does not provide levels of acceptable accuracy. This means that any researcher planning to conduct interviews in places where English might be spoken need to provide sufficient time for transcription, or to enlist the services of speakers of English from that region to mitigate against the poor transcription quality provided by the automatic voice recognition systems available on the market.

REFERENCES

Ates, N. Y. (2014). *The Strategy Process: A Middle Management Perspective.* Doctor of Philosophy, Erasmus Research Institute of Management.

Aziz, A. & Khan, N. (2021). The Potential Uses of Pilot Studies in Qualitative Research. *Journal of Research and Reviews in Social Sciences Pakistan,* 3, 750-767.

Baker, J. & Singh, H. (2019). The roots of misalignment: Insights on strategy implementation from a system dynamics perspective. *The Journal of Strategic Information Systems,* Volume 28.

Balogun, J. (2006). Managing Change: Steering a Course between Intended Strategies and Unanticipated Outcomes. *Long Range Planning,* 39, 29-49.

Chilora, H. Language policy research and practice in Malawi. Comparative and International Education Society (CIES) 2000 Conference. San Francisco, USA, 2000.

Floyd, A. (2015). Supporting Academic Middle Managers in Higher Education: Do We Care? *Higher Education Policy,* 29.

Gibson, L. & Groom, R. (2021). Understanding 'Vulnerability' and 'Political Skill' in Academy Middle Management During Organisational Change in Professional Youth Football. *Journal of Change Management,* 21, 358-382.

Gruber, T., Szmigin, I., Reppel, A. E. & Voss, R. (2008). Designing and conducting online interviews to investigate interesting consumer phenomena. *Qualitative Market Research: An International Journal.*

Guillemin, M. & Heggen, K. (2009). Rapport and respect: negotiating ethical relations between researcher and participant. *Medicine, Health Care and Philosophy,* 12, 291-299.

Hewson, C. (2017). Research design and tools for internet research. In:eds. *In:* Fielding, N. G., Lee, R. M. & Blank, G. (eds.) *The Sage Handbook of Online Research Methods (2nd Ed.).* Sage London.

Ismail, N., Kinchin, G. & Edwards, J.-A. (2017). Pilot Study, Does It Really Matter? Learning Lessons from Conducting a Pilot Study for a Qualitative PhD Thesis. *International Journal of Social Science Research,* 6.

Janghorban, R., Latifnejad Roudsari, R. & Taghipour, A. (2013). Pilot Study in Qualitative Research: The Roles and Values. *Hayat,* 19, 1-5.

Kainja, J. (2022). The Media and Freedom of Expression in Democratic Malawi: A Formality or Reality? *In:* Adeola, A. & Mutua, M. W. (eds.) *The Palgrave Handbook of Democracy, Governance and Justice in Africa.* Cham: Springer International Publishing.

Kim, Y. (2010). The Pilot Study in Qualitative Inquiry. *Qualitative Social Work,* 9.

Luftman, J. N., Lyytinen, K. & Zvi, T. B. (2017). Enhancing the measurement of information technology (IT) business alignment and its influence on company performance. *Journal of Information Technology,* 32, 26-46.

Malanga, D. F. & Chigona, W. (2022). Users Expectations as Determinants of Continuance Intention towards mHealth amongst health workers: Case of Cstock in Malawi. *African Conference on Information Systems and Technology.* Malawi University of Science and Technology: Kennesaw State University.

Malemia, L. (2021). Bringing the gap between the information rich and the information poor in malawi. Inclusive Libraries and Information Services towards achieving Prosperity for Sustainable Development in Africa. *Mzuzu University Digital Repository,* XXXIV SCECSA, 120-127.

Matiki, A. J. (2001). The social significance of English in Malawi. *World Englishes,* 20, 201-218.

Netland, T. H., Powell, D. J. & Hines, P. (2020). Demystifying lean leadership. *International Journal of Lean Six Sigma,* 11, 543-554.

Reilly, C., Rescue, E. & Chavula, J. J. (2022). Language policy in Ghana and Malawi: differing approaches to multilingualism in education. *Journal of the British Academy,* 10, 69-95.

Tarakci, M., Ates, N., Floyd, S., Ahn, Y. & Woolidge, B. (2018). Performance Feedback and Middle Managers' Divergent Strategic Behavior: The Roles of Social Comparisons and Organizational Identification. *Strategic management journal,* 39, 1139-1162.

Torres-Moreno, M. E. & Aponte-Melo, J. H. (2021). Assessing Business-IT Alignment Maturity at a Colombian University. *Journal of Cases on Information Technology,* 23.

Van Niekerk, K. & Jansen Van Rensburg, M. (2022). Middle Managers' Strategising Practices to Effect Strategic Change. *Journal of Change Management,* 22, 273-291.

Wooldridge, B., Schmid, T. & Floyd, S. W. (2008). The Middle Management Perspective on Strategy Process: Contributions, Synthesis, and Future Research. *Journal of Management,* 34, 1190-1221.

Worldometer. 2022. *Malawi Population (LIVE)* [Online]. Available: https://www.worldometers.info/world-population/malawi-population/#:~:text=The%20current%20population%20of%20Malawi,the%20latest%20United%20Nations%20data [Accessed 11th December 2022].

Wray, J., Archibong, U. & Walton, S. (2017). Why undertake a pilot in a qualitative PhD study? Lessons learned to promote success. *Nurse Res,* 24, 31-35.

Yin, R. K. (2014). *Case Study Research: Design and Methods,* United Kingdom, SAGE Publications Inc.

STAKEHOLDERS FEEDBACK ON THE INDUSTRY-ACADEMIA GAP

Sebongile Mazibuko and Estelle Taylor
North-West University
South Africa

ABSTRACT

This study aims to research the industry-academia gap by obtaining feedback from stakeholders (industry and academia). Results may be used to support Higher Education Institutions (HEI) in addressing the industry-academia gap. This is an interpretive study, as the aim is to gain understanding by analysing feedback from industry and academia participants. Quantitative and open questions were used to gather this feedback. Data was collected using online questionnaires, completed by 22 industry contacts, as well as 20 IT-lecturers at a HEI in South Africa. Results from this study confirmed results from previous studies, proofing that the industry-academia gap is still an issue, and emphasizing specific issues and skills that HEIs can try to address in teaching and learning, e.g. addressing the problem of poor-quality student intake, improving academic collaboration, students volunteering or working in industry during their studies to acquire the needed skills, including work-integrated learning in the curriculum and focusing on the development of soft skills of students.

KEYWORDS

Industry-Academia Collaboration, Industry-Academia Gap, Higher Education, Information Technology

1. INTRODUCTION

This study aims to research the industry-academia gap by obtaining feedback from stakeholders (industry and academia). The research aims to determine whether participants from industry as well as HEIs agree with aspects mentioned in existing literature, and to determine guidelines that can be used to address this gap. This research also investigates the importance and development of soft skills. Results may be used to support Higher Education Institutions (HEI) in addressing the industry-academia gap. The paper starts with the background and problem statement (section 2), followed by a brief description of the methodology (section 3), the results (section 4) and conclusion (section 5).

2. BACKGROUND AND PROBLEM STATEMENT

According to Abbas and Sagsan (2020) a considerable amount of literature is available on the quality of service of HEIs, but not enough attention has been given to employability of graduates. They define employability as "*the ability of a person, not only to find the job but to retain it by consistently complying with its changing requirements*". Horváth-Csikós et al. (2022) defined employability as "*the attainment of work-related skills and competencies useful in employment*".). HEIs are increasingly concerned with improving the employability of students (Andreas, 2018; Horváth-Csikós et al., 2022).

In a study in South Africa, by Taylor (2016), one response from the industry was: "*…we find well-qualified individuals battling with these basic skills on an ongoing basis. Graduates are immature when they arrive at the workplace and a lot more can be done at university to address this.*" It is important to determine if what individuals are taught in higher education institutions will be beneficial for them when they enter the industry and to ensure that they will not struggle to adapt to the skills required (Benamati *et al.*, 2010; Foll *et al.*, 2018; Sahin & Celikkan, 2017). Academics must be guided in developing dynamic curricula that can be easily adapted to today's industry trends, with information that applies to students' careers (Sahin & Celikkan, 2020).

Studies suggest a gap between the needs of industry and the academic preparation or abilities of recently graduated students, affecting the employability of students. This is sometimes called a skills gap, an expectations gap or the industry – academia gap. In this paper the term industry-academia gap will be used. The industry-academia gap is the gap between the Information Technology education system and the industries' expectations from entry-level professionals (Bekkers & Bodas Freitas, 2008; Siegel *et al.*, 2003). When the COVID-19 pandemic commenced, most researchers and practitioners were sent to work from home, relying on online collaboration with their peers, which might have given rise to an even wider industry-academia collaboration gap (Marijan & Gotlieb, 2021).

According to Kashupi (2021), reports show that some graduates struggle to get jobs in industry due to limited skills. Andreas (2018) writes in his study that both industry and graduates attribute the lack of soft skills to the inability of universities to prepare students. Vrat (2009) wrote that, if steps are not taken to bridge the industry-academia gap, industries will continue to get graduates that do not have the acquired skills to do the job. Beckman *et al.* (1997) wrote "*An approach to closing this gap could be that the two parties, namely the industry, and higher education institutions, work together on the education goals*". This will increase the proficiency of the higher education institutions to meet the industry's expected training goals. Collaboration between industry and academia may help in addressing this gap. The relationship between any part of the higher educational system and industry, focusing on encouraging knowledge and technology exchange, is referred to as university-industry collaboration (Bekkers & Bodas Freitas, 2008; Siegel *et al.*, 2003).

Employers who participated in a study done by Hart Research Associates (2015) indicated that they are more likely to consider a job candidate who has participated in an internship, a senior project, a collaborative research project, a field-based project, or a community-based project (Hart research Associates (2015). The same recommendation was made in 2021 by the participants in a study by the Association of American Colleges and Universities, where representatives from companies indicated that completion of active and applied learning experiences gives job applicants an advantage, and internships lead the list of what makes employers more likely to consider hiring a candidate. Other advantages included experience that involved working in community settings with people from diverse backgrounds or cultures; work-study program or other form of employment during college; as well as a portfolio of work highlighting skills and experiences (AACU, 2021). In another study by Taylor (2019) recommendations were that students should work in the industry during holidays (exposure to work situations), collaboration with students from other programs or faculties, work on real-world projects, and include more teamwork in programs.

According to Pandi et al. (2012) the major factors that impact the quality of technical education negatively are outdated teaching-learning processes and curriculum, lack of management commitment, substandard computational resources, low level of research and development, inferior quality student intake, lack of academic collaborations, and poor alumni interactions.

HEI's need to know what skills are required to adjust the curriculum. According to Love *et al.* (2001), important personal attributes about graduates that employers pay the most attention to include flexibility, intelligence, adaptiveness, and the ability to deal with instantaneous transformation and uncertainty. They also argue that graduates need to have skills that allow them to work effectively with others to produce efficient results on time. The skills identified by Love *et al.* (2001) include communication, the ability to deliver what is required on time, academic achievement, acceptance of responsibility, adaptability to changing environments, problem-solving, time management, leadership, teamwork, and integrity.

Taylor (2016) argued that these personal attributes or soft skills (another term that is often used) are difficult to teach. This study also showed a difference of opinion on whether the development of these skills is the responsibility of the students, lecturers, or industry. Important soft skills that should be developed at Higher Education Institutions were identified as Communication skills, Interpersonal relations and teamwork, Leadership and Emotional intelligence, Professionalism and work ethic, Self-management, Conflict management, Critical thinking, and Multidisciplinary thinking (Taylor, 2019).

The following guidelines to address the industry-academia gap can be derived from this literature review:

- Collaborate with industry (Kashupi, 2021; Beckman et al., 1997).
- Update teaching and learning processes (Pandi et al., 2012).
- Frequently update the curriculum (Pandi et al., 2012).
- Use projects from the industry (Pandi et al., 2012).
- Work-integrated learning (Karim & Hasan, 2019).
- Develop personal attributes / soft skills of students (Love et al. 2001; Taylor, 2016).

3. METHODOLOGY

This is an interpretive study, as the aim is to gain understanding by analysing feedback from industry and academia participants. The study was done at a HEI in South Africa. Quantitative as well as open questions were used to gather this feedback. Data was collected using online questionnaires, completed by 22 industry contacts, as well as 20 IT-lecturers at a HEI in South Africa. The questions in the questionnaires were chosen after a literature study was done on the topic. The questionnaires and links to sources are available from the authors. An example is shown below:

Table 1

In your opinion what percentage of graduates is ready to enter the workforce immediately after graduation?	0-20% 21-40% 41-60% 61-80% 81-100%	Derived from comments by Mehra (2007), Mishra, 2016), Reddy (2012), and Vrat (2009).
The following aspects have been mentioned as possible reasons for the industry-academia gap. Indicate your agreement with each of these statements: a. The readiness of graduates to enter the workforce is impacted negatively by gaps or incompatibilities in the curriculum. b. The readiness of graduates to enter the workforce is impacted negatively by a lack of computational resources. c. The readiness of graduates to enter the workforce is impacted negatively by poor-quality student intake. d. The readiness of graduates to enter the workforce is impacted negatively by a lack of academic collaborations.	Strongly disagree / Disagree / Not sure / Agree / Strongly agree	Derived from comments by Pandi et al. (2012), and Kashupi (2021).
Please indicate your level of agreement with the following statements: a. Teaching and learning at Higher Education Institutions should focus more on theoretical content and less on practical content. b. Teaching and learning at Higher Education Institutions should focus more on practical content and less on theoretical content. c. Collaboration between Higher Education institutions and industry partners is essential to improve the readiness of graduates to enter the workforce. d. Students should work on projects from industry. e. Students should volunteer or work in industry during their studies to acquire the needed skills. f. Work-integrated learning is essential to improve the readiness of graduates to enter the workforce. g. Curricula in the fields of CS / IT should be changed frequently to keep up with the changing field. h. Technology education should be offered pre-tertiary as a compulsory subject. i. Students should create a portfolio of work during tertiary education that can be shown to prospective employers. j. Completing industry certifications would make students more employable.	Strongly disagree / Disagree / Not sure / Agree / Strongly agree	Derived from Beckman *et al.* (1997); Taylor (2016); Karim & Hasan (2019); Ankiewickz, 1995.

4. RESULTS

More information is provided on the participants in section 4.1, followed by description of the feedback received on specific issues in sections 4.2 to 4.7.

4.1 Participants

Responses were received from 22 participants from industry and 20 participants from academia. Participants from industry included one Business Intelligence Architect, one Business Consultant, two CEOs, one CIO, one Data Management Lead, three Directors, one General Manager, one Group IT Manager, one Head of Cloud, one Head of Applications, one head of CX, one MES Manager, one SAP Cloud Services Manager, one operations manager, one Principal Project Manager, two Senior BI Developers, one Senior Business Analyst, one Sessional Lecturer, and one VP Engineer. One respondent from the industry has 6-10 years of work experience, four have 11-15 years of work experience, five have 16-20 years of work experience, and fourteen have more than 20 years of work experience. The job titles as well as the years of experience show that the participants are mostly senior people in the industry with many years of experience. Results from the different questions will be discussed next.

Responses were received from 22 industry representatives, these consisted of one Business Intelligence Architect, one Business Consultant, two CEOs, one CIO, one Data Management Lead, three Directors, one General Manager, one Group IT Manager, one Head of Cloud, one Head of Applications, one head of CX, one MES Manager, one SAP Cloud Services Manager, one operations manager, one Principal Project Manager, two Senior BI Developers, one Senior Business Analyst, one Sessional Lecturer, and one VP Engineer. Based on the statistics, only one respondent from the industry has 6-10 years of work experience, four have 11-15 years of work experience, five have 16-20 years of work experience, and fourteen have more than 20 years of work experience. The job titles as well as the years of experience show that the participants are mostly senior people in the industry with many years of experience. Responses were also received from 20 lecturers, teaching at a Higher Education Institution (HEI) in South Africa. Results are reported in sections 4.1 to 4.5.

4.2 Percentage of Graduates Ready to Enter the Workforce Immediately After Graduation

Previous studies mention that low percentages of recent graduates are ready to enter the workforce (Mehra (2007), Mishra, 2016), Reddy (2012) and Vrat (2009). Participants in this study were asked to indicate their perception on the readiness of recent graduates in South Africa.

4.2.1 Industry

Based on the results in figure 1, a third (33.3%) of the industry participants think that very few graduates (0-20%) are ready to enter the workforce. A total of 62.5% (33.3% + 29.2%) think that less than 40% of graduates are ready to enter the workforce immediately after graduation. Only 12.5% of participants think that more than 80% of graduates are ready to enter the workforce immediately after graduation.

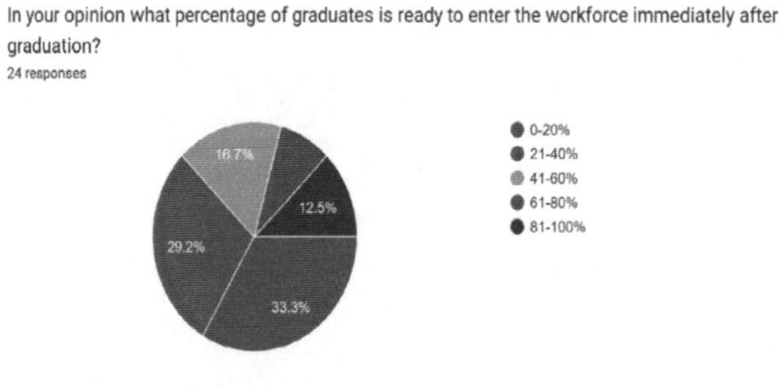

Figure 1. The percentage of graduates ready to enter the workforce (according to industry)

4.2.2 Lecturers

Based on the results in figure 2, a third (33.3%) of lecturers think that very few graduates (21-40%) are ready to enter the workforce. A total of 42.8% (33.3% + 9.5%) think that less than 40% of graduates are ready to enter the workforce immediately after graduation. None of the lecturers thinks that more than 80% of the graduates are ready to enter the workforce immediately after graduation.

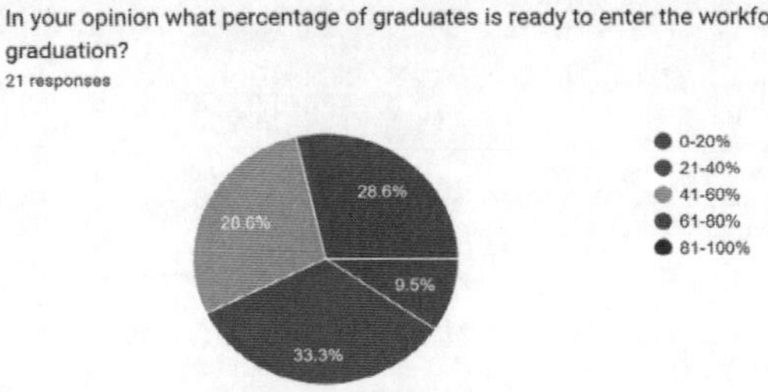

Figure 2. The percentage of graduates ready to enter the workforce (according to academia/lecturers)

4.2.3 Summary

These results show that most participants from industry and academia agree that many graduates are not ready to enter the workplace immediately after graduation. This is proof that the industry-academia gap exists.

4.3 Factors Impacting the Readiness of Graduates to Enter the Workforce

Four factors were identified during a literature review that may impact the readiness of graduates to enter the workforce (Pandi et al., 2012; Kashupi, 2021). The relevance of these factors was evaluated by asking participants to indicate their agreement with each statement. Participants from industry as well as lecturers mostly agreed with all four statements (mean of 3 to 3.85 on a scale of 0-4). Participants from industries strongly agreed that the readiness of graduates to enter the workforce is impacted negatively by a lack of academic collaborations (3.66), followed by gaps or incompatibilities in the curriculum (3.52). Lecturers agreed most strongly with the statement that the readiness of graduates to enter the workforce is impacted negatively by poor-quality student intake (3.85). These results can be seen in table 2.

Table 2. Factors impacting the readiness of graduates to enter the workforce (according to industry and academia/lecturers)

Statement	**Industry**	**Lecturers**
The readiness of graduates to enter the workforce is impacted negatively by gaps or incompatibilities in the curriculum.	3.52	3.2
The readiness of graduates to enter the workforce is impacted negatively by a lack of computational resources.	2.76	3.05
The readiness of graduates to enter the workforce is impacted negatively by poor-quality student intake.	3	3.85
The readiness of graduates to enter the workforce is impacted negatively by a lack of academic collaboration.	3.66	3.2

These results are also depicted in graphical format in figure 3.

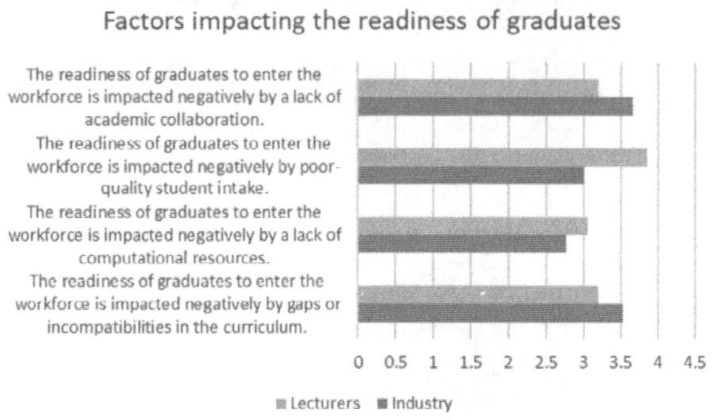

Figure 3. Factors impacting the readness of graduares to enter the workforce

Participants were also given the opportunity to list other aspects that have a negative impact on the readiness of graduates to enter the workforce. Feedback from industry will be described first, followed by feedback from lecturers and a summary.

4.3.1 Industry

As can be seen in table 3, practical / technical experience and understanding of how organizations operate were each mentioned by several participants from industry. Three participants from industries mentioned graduates' willingness to learn (or lack thereof), and 2 participants felt that lecturers are removed from the reality of the working world. One participant felt that specialization happens too late.

Table 3. Reasons that have a negative impact on the readiness of graduates to enter the workforce (according to industry)

Aspect	Number
Practical Experience	6
Understanding how organizations operate	5
Willingness to learn	3
Lecturers are removed from the reality of the working world	2
Specialization happens too late	1

4.3.2 Lecturers

Five lecturers pointed out that one of the aspects that negatively impact the readiness of graduates to enter the workforce is the willingness of students to take responsibility for their own studies. The second dominant aspect mentioned was the failure to incorporate various industry certifications into University curriculums, which was pointed out by four lecturers. Two lecturers also mentioned lack of practical experience. These results can be seen in table 4.

Table 4. Reasons that have a negative impact on the readiness of graduates to enter the workforce (according to academia/lecturers)

Aspect	Number
Most students do not take responsibility for their studies	5
Failure to incorporate various industry certifications into University curriculums	4
Not enough practical experience and problem-solving applications	2
Primary and Secondary schooling directly influence Tertiary education student quality	1
The speed at which technology changes	1
Covid-19	1
Work-ready skills, also known as employability skills, soft skills, and work-readiness skills	1

4.3.3 Summary

The aspects mentioned by both industry and lecturers were the unwillingness of students to learn and take responsibility for their own studies, as well as lack of practical experience. However, lecturers strongly felt that an important aspect is that more students should take responsibility for their own studies. More can be done at HEI to ensure that lecturers stay up to date with what is happening in industry,

4.4 Reasons for the Industry-Academia Gap

Possible reasons for the industry-academia gap were identified during a literature review (Beckman et al., 1997; Taylor, 2016; Karim & Hasan, 2019; Ankiewickz, 1995). Participants were asked to indicate their agreement with each of these statements. From the information in table 5, the participants from industries as well as lecturers mostly do not agree with the statement that teaching and learning at Higher Education Institutions should focus more on theoretical content and less on practical content. They both mostly agree with all the other statements (mean of 3 to 4.52 on a scale of 0-5). Participants from industries feel most strongly about the statement that collaboration between Higher education institutions and industry partners is essential to improve the readiness of graduates to enter the workforce (4.52) and that students should volunteer or work in industry during their studies to acquire the needed skills (4.42). Lecturers also feel most strongly about the same 2 statements, that collaboration between Higher Education institutions and industry partners is essential to improve the readiness of graduates to enter the workforce (4.3) and that students should volunteer or work in industry during their studies to acquire the needed skills (4.25), as well as the statement that work-integrated learning is essential to improve the readiness of graduates to enter the workforce (4.25).

Table 5. Level of agreement with specific statements (according to industry and academia/lecturers)

Statement	**Industry**	**Lecturers**
Teaching and learning at Higher Education Institutions should focus more on theoretical content and less on practical content.	2.14	2.75
Teaching and learning at Higher Education Institutions should focus more on practical content and less on theoretical content.	3.57	3
Collaboration between Higher Education institutions and industry partners is essential to improve the readiness of graduates to enter the workforce.	4.52	4.3
Students should work on projects from industry.	4.23	4.05
Students should volunteer or work in industry during their studies to acquire the needed skills.	4.42	4.25
Work-integrated learning is essential to improve the readiness of graduates to enter the workforce.	4.47	4.25
Curricula in the fields of CS / IT should be changed frequently to keep up with the changing field.	4.09	3.75
Technology education should be offered pre-tertiary as a compulsory subject.	3.66	4.1
Students should create a portfolio of work during tertiary education that can be shown to prospective employers.	4	4.1
Completing industry certifications would make students more employable.	3.80	4.05

Nine participants from industries agreed that Covid-19 and its challenges had a negative impact on the readiness of graduates to enter the workforce. All lecturers who participated in the study agreed that Covid-19 had a negative impact on the readiness of graduates to enter the workforce. Lecturers feel more strongly about the negative effect of Covid-19 and its challenges on the readiness of graduates. Since this study was done while many of the students effected by Covid-19 are still busy with their studies, it is possible that the effect will still be seen by those in industry. However, half of the participants from industry already agree with the negative effect. Academia as well as industry will need to put steps in place to address this.

4.5 Specific Areas/Topics Where Recent Graduates Lack Important Knowledge

Several topics were mentioned by participants as specific areas that recent graduates lack important knowledge in. Feedback from industry will be described first, followed by feedback from lecturers and a summary.

4.5.1 Industry

The areas or topics mentioned by participants from industry can be seen in table 6.

Table 6. Specific areas/topics where recent graduates lack important knowledge (according to industry)

Area	Number
Basics of computer programming	3
ERP and Cloud Integration platforms	2
Interpersonal skills, other soft skills	2
Lack of theoretical approach to systems design, development and problem-solving	2
Basic computer networking knowledge	2
Source control, architecture, advanced programming, communication, and client relations	2
Business skills	1
Real-life examples or situations / practical experience	1
How businesses work and their internal processes	1
DevOps	1

Participants from industry mentioned several topics that should be included in the curriculum. These topics can be seen in table 7.

Table 7. Important topics that should be included in the IT/CS/IS curriculum at the tertiary level (according to industry)

Topic	Number
Logic	1
Planning and estimating	1
Digital transformation	1
How a solution can meet business needs	1
DevOps	1
Work-integrated learning module	1
Ethical hacking	1
Conflict management, critical thinking, troubleshooting-when to ask for help	2
Cloud computing and presenting	2
Business Process Management	3
Data management and data warehousing	3

4.5.2 Lecturers

Five lecturers responded that graduates lack problem-solving, critical thinking, communication skills, and application of knowledge, and three that graduates lack practical understanding and applied knowledge. Other areas mentioned by lecturers can be seen in table 8.

Table 8. Specific areas/topics where recent graduates lack important knowledge (according to academia/lecturers)

Area	Number
Soft skills (e.g., Problem-solving, critical thinking, communication skills, time management, teamwork)	10
Lack of practical understanding and applied knowledge / A balance between learning and experience / Applying knowledge and skills to previously unknown scenarios	4
Programming Skills	2
The 4th Industrial Revolution	2
Cloud, cyber security, SAFE practices, portfolio generation, networking	1

Feedback from industry is mostly business specific, while lecturers mostly mention soft skills. Topics that can be added according to the curriculum according to lecturers are listed in table 9.

Table 9. Important topics that should be included in the IT/CS/IS curriculum at the tertiary level (according to academia/lecturers)

Topic	Number
Data structures and algorithms (Object-oriented programming)	1
A solid foundation in programming, architecture knowledge that is applicable to cloud and not just desktop applications, cyber security especially as it relates to making applications safe, artificial intelligence and automation, git culture and the creation of your portfolio of work, marketing of yourself as a knowledge worker	1
Human behaviour - including psychology may be good, legal issues and IT, governance, and IS /IT management	1
AI, IoT & Blockchain	1
Integrated learning and workplace environment. Transforming the developed skills for real-world practical application. Integrated learning curriculum for the workplace environment	1
Collaborative working tools, source code management, more practical application of database, and problem-solving skills	2
Being open to adaptability and being able to solve problems	2
Communication and Interpersonal skills	2

4.5.3 Summary

Participants from industry as well as lecturers mentioned that additional certifications are highly dependent on the industries graduates are interested in. Industry participants mentioned RPA, SAP, BPM, Java, DMBOK, Data Analysis, DevOps, SQL, C#, Angular, Microsoft, Google, and AWS Cloud, Python and Cloud certifications. Specific certifications mentioned by lecturers were Data Engineering, Advanced programming courses, UiPath developer certification, Microsoft developer certifications, Certified Ethical Hacker, Java certifications, Micro-credentials and other certificates issued by trusted organizations (i.e., LinkedIn), Scrum/Agile chat, Project Management, Security certification of some sort.

4.6 Other Comments/Suggestions

Participants were given the opportunity to add any other comments or suggestions. Comments from industry included:

Computer Science Graduates who understand the business context, are strong code developers, are familiar with systems integration, and can work independently researching topics they need to do their work are most valuable.

General IT skills will give a great head-start. Nevertheless, graduates must expect to continue their learning from day one in a career.

There should be a compulsory basket of about twenty-five common patterns that students master before they leave university.

We need more General Training in the first 2 years of the Degree and then choosing a specialization field where the Students need some real-world intern experience based on their selection.

Let companies participate in the success of our students- grad programs do not do much, what they need is a mentor- let people in companies volunteer to mentor 1 or 2 students once a week on soft workforce.

Comments from lecturers included:

We should not only give students qualifications, but we should also make sure we have projects with companies to enhance their learning in preparation for the workplace, business, etc. Is not only about learning but how can we perform the implementation.

Introduce the students to multiple different technology stacks.

4.7 Important Personal Attributes of Graduates

During the literature review, possible important personal attributes or soft skills were identified. These were Interpersonal relations and teamwork, Leadership and emotional intelligence, Professionalism and work ethic, Self-management, Conflict management, Critical thinking and Multi-disciplinary thinking (Love et al., 2001; Taylor, 2019). In this research, the participants from industries as well as lecturers agreed that all these skills are important (3 = of average importance, 4 = very important, 5= absolutely essential).

Table 10. Importance of different soft skills (according to industry and academia/lecturers, scale1-5)

Soft skill	Industry	Lecturers
Interpersonal relations and teamwork	4.28	4.4
Leadership and emotional intelligence	3.61	4.1
Professionalism and work ethic	4,57	4.65
Self-management	4.28	4.35
Conflict management	3.47	3.65
Critical thinking	4.19	4.75
Multi-disciplinary thinking	3.85	4.25

The results can be seen in table 10. According to the participants from industries, professionalism and work ethic is most important, followed by interpersonal relations and teamwork, as well as self-management, and critical thinking. According to lecturers, critical thinking is most important, followed by professionalism and work ethic, and interpersonal relations and teamwork. This means that both groups rated the same 4 soft skills as most important.

According to a literature review, the important soft skills of graduates are not develop as expected (Love et al., 2001; Taylor, 2019). Participants in this study were asked to indicate their perception on the level of the development of these skills in recent graduates. As can be seen in table 11, both groups rated the soft skills of graduates low (3 = Average, 2 = Below average). Participants from industries rated leadership and emotional intelligence as the lowest, followed by conflict management. They also rated all the skills below 3 except Communication and Interpersonal relations and teamwork. The lecturers also rated Leadership and emotional intelligence as the lowest, followed by self-management, conflict management, and critical thinking. The lecturers rated all the soft skills below 3.

Table 11. Rating of different soft skills of graduates (according to industry and academia/lecturers, scale1-5)

Soft skill	Industry	Lecturers
Communication	3.19	2.65
Interpersonal relations and teamwork	3.09	2.85
Leadership and emotional intelligence	2.57	2.45
Professionalism and work ethic	2.76	2.75
Self-management	2.80	2.5
Conflict management	2.71	2.5
Critical thinking	2.90	2.5
Multi-disciplinary thinking	2.76	2.65

Participants were asked to mention other skills (not included in the above list) that they deemed as important. Participants from industry mentioned the following additional soft skills as also important: Commitment, Maturity, Loyalty, Problem-solving, Willingness to succeed, Creativity, Self-empowerment, Self-development, Confidence, Respect, Curiosity (mentioned by 3 participants). Participants from academia also mentioned problem solving, self-development and creativity, as well as the following additional soft skills: Marketing and self-promotion, Self-awareness, Eagerness to learn.

5. CONCLUSION

Results show that most participants from industry and academia agree that many graduates are not ready to enter the workplace immediately after graduation. This is proof that the industry-academia gap exists. Aspects impacting the readiness of graduates to enter the workforce mentioned by both industry and lecturers were the unwillingness of students to learn and take responsibility for their own studies, as well as lack of practical experience. The participants from industries agreed most strongly with the statement that the readiness of graduates to enter the workforce is impacted negatively by a lack of academic collaborations, followed by gaps or incompatibilities in the curriculum. Lecturers agreed most strongly with the statement that the readiness of graduates to enter the workforce is impacted negatively by poor-quality student intake. The difference in opinion shows where the main concern of the industry is versus the issues academia faces.

Participants from industries as well as lecturers did not agree that teaching and learning at higher education institutions should focus more on theoretical content and less on practical content. Participants from industries felt most strongly about the statement that the collaboration between higher education institutions and industry partners is essential to improve the readiness of graduates to enter the workforce and that students should volunteer or work in industry during their studies to acquire the needed skills. Lecturers also felt most strongly about the same two statements, that collaboration between Higher Education institutions and industry partners is essential to improve the readiness of graduates to enter the workforce and that students should volunteer or work in industry during their studies to acquire the needed skills, as well as the statement that work-integrated learning is essential to improve the readiness of graduates to enter the workforce.

Nearly half of the participants from industry and all the participants from academia agreed that Covid-19 had a negative effect on the readiness of graduates. All stakeholders (academia as well as industry) will need to put steps in place to address this.

Participants from industry as well as academia felt that various certifications can be used to address the industry-academia gap. The lists of topics that should be included in the curriculum, as well as certifications deemed valuable for students to obtain, and additional comments reported on in this study can be used by academic institutions to address the industry-academia gap.

In section 2 of this paper, guidelines for addressing the industry-academia gap were derived from the literature review. These were:

- Collaborate with industry.
- Update teaching and learning processes.
- Frequently update the curriculum.
- Use projects from the industry.
- Work-integrated learning.
- Develop personal attributes / soft skills of students.

These guidelines were confirmed by the feedback received during this study. Guidelines that can be added to these from the results of this study include:

- Add more practical experience and understanding of how organizations operate to the curriculum.
- Consider incorporating industry certifications into curriculums.
- Add more emphasis on knowledge in the basics of computer programming.
- Ensure that lecturers stay up to date with what is happening in industry.
- Students should be motivated to take responsibility for their own studies and to realize the importance of life-long learning in the IT-environment.
- Academia as well as industry need to put steps in place to address the negative effect of Covid-19 on the readiness of graduates.

These guidelines, together with the lists of certifications and topics, can be used when evaluating or updating the curriculum, to address the industry-academia gap and deliver students ready to enter the workplace.

Participants from industries as well as lecturers indicated that all the mentioned soft skills are important. According to the participants from industries, professionalism and work ethic is most important, followed by interpersonal relations and teamwork, as well as self-management, and critical thinking. According to lecturers, critical thinking is most important, followed by professionalism and work ethic, and interpersonal relations and teamwork. This means that both groups rated the same 4 soft skills as most important.

Both groups rated the soft skills of graduates low. Participants from industries rated leadership and emotional intelligence as the lowest, followed by conflict management. Lecturers also rated Leadership and emotional intelligence as the lowest, followed by self-management, conflict management, and critical thinking.

Results from this study mostly confirmed results from previous studies, proofing that the industry-academia gap is still an issue. Results emphasized specific issues and skills that HEIs can try to address in teaching and learning, e.g., addressing the problem of poor-quality student intake, improving academic collaboration, students volunteering or working in industry during their studies to acquire the needed skills, including work-integrated learning in the curriculum, and focusing on the development of soft skills of students.

REFERENCES

AACU (Association of American Colleges and Universities). 2021. How College Contributes to Workforce Success. Available online: https://dgmg81phhvh63.cloudfront.net/content/user-photos/Research/PDFs/AACUEmployerReport2021.pdf

Abbas, J., & Sagsan, M. 2020. Identification of key employability attributes and evaluation of university graduates' performance: Instrument development and validation. Higher Education, Skills and Work-Based Learning.

Andreas, S. 2018. Effects of the decline in social capital on college graduates' soft skills. *Industry and Higher Education*, *32*(1), 47–56. https://doi.org/10.1177/0950422217749277

Ankiewickz, P. 1995. The planning of technology education for South African schools. *International Journal of Technology and Design Education*, *5*(1):245-254.

Beckman, K., Neal, C., Khajenoori, S. & Mead, N.R. (1997). Collaborations: Closing the industry academia gap. *IEEE software,* 14(6):49-57.

Bekkers, R., & Bodas Freitas, I. (2008). Analysing knowledge transfer channels between universities and industry: To what degree do sectors also matter? *Research Policy*, *37*:1837-1853.

Benamati, J. H., Ozdemir, Z. D., & Smith, H. J. (2010). Aligning undergraduate IS

Föll, P., Hauser, M., & Thiesse, F. (2018). Identifying the skills expected of IS graduates by industry: A text mining approach. In *Proceedings of 39th International Conference on Information Systems (ICIS 2018)*, San Francisco, California (USA). Vol 4. 2730-2747.

Hart Research Associates. (2015). *Falling Short? College Learning and Career Success*. Available online: http://www.aacu.org/leap/public-opinion-research/2015-survey-results.

Horváth-Csikós, G., Juhász, T., & Gáspár, T. (2022). Employers' perception of young workers' soft skills. *Prosperitas*, (in press) https://doi.org/10.31570/prosp_2022_0021

Karim, A., Campbell, M. & Hasan, M. (2019). A new method of integrating project-based and work-integrated learning in postgraduate engineering study. *Curric. J*, 0(0):1-17.

Kashupi, T.N. (2021). *Department of Informatics, Namibia University of Science and Technology*. Windhoek, Namibia.

Love, P.E.D., Haynes, N.S. & Irani, Z. (2001). Construction managers' expectations and observations of graduates. *Journal of Managerial Psychology*, *16*(8):579-593.

Marijan, D., & Gotlieb, A. (2021). Industry-Academia research collaboration in software engineering: The Certus model. *Information and software technology*, *132*, 106473.

Mishra, A. (2016). *Growing mismatch between graduates' skills, market needs-University World News.* http://www.universityworldnews.com/article.php?story=20140204171742828 Date of access: 2 Nov. 2016.

Pandi, A., Sethipathi, P. & Rajesh, R. (2012). A conceptual model for achieving global quality in engineering educational institutions in India. *Procedia Engineering*, *38*(1):3628-3634.

Sahin, Y. G., & Celikkan, U. (2020). Information technology asymmetry and gaps between higher education institutions and industry. *Journal of Information Technology Education: Research*, 19:339-365.

Siegel, D. S., Waldman, D., & Link, A. (2003). Assessing the impact of organizational practises on the relative productivity of university technology transfer offices: An exploratory study. *Research Policy*, 32:27-48.

Taylor, E. (2016). Investigating the perception of stakeholders on soft skills development of students: Evidence from South Africa. *Interdisciplinary journal of e-skills and lifelong learning*, *12*(1), 1-18.

Taylor, E. (2019, November). Investigating Soft Skills Development at a Higher Education Institution in South Africa. In *Proceedings of the 2019 3rd International Conference on Education and E-Learning* (pp. 140-146).

Vahid, G., Gorkem, G., Eray, T., Cagatay, C. & Michael, F. (2020). Closing the gap between software engineering education and industrial needs. *IEEE software*: 68-77.

Wallin, J., Isaksson, O., Larsson, E. & Elfstrom, O. (2014). Bridging the gap between university and industry. Three mechanisms for innovation efficiency: 1-15.

Wigdorowitz, M., Rajab, P., Hassem, T. & Titi, N. (2021). The impact of Covid-19 on psychometric assessment across industry and academia in South Africa. *African Journal of psychological assessment,* 3(21) Date of access: 31 Mar. 2021.

Vrat, P. 2009. Role of technical education in emerging Indian society. *Opportunities and challenges*, *11*(2):9.1-9.10.

DIGITAL SHADOW SUPPORTED BY AUGMENTED REALITY AND CLOUD FOR THE MONITORING OF AN INDUSTRIAL PROCESS

Erick Criollo, Gustavo Caiza and William Oñate
Universidad Politécnica Salesiana, Ecuador

ABSTRACT

The development of the new technological tools of the coming industrial revolution enables incorporating intelligent functions to traditional industrial systems; even though this demand increases discretely, it is important to promote the transition to this new industrial era. Therefore, this document describes an experimental study conducted for monitoring the distribution station of a MPS 500 modular production system, which for the project is set as physical twin, and the outcome of modeling it as digital shadow, synchronizing them by sending and receiving data to and from the cloud. For this purpose, once the station has been configured and programmed, a Raspberry Pi single-board computer was implemented to acquire the digital signals from the station sensors, and further process and send them to the cloud. For modeling the digital environment, it was replicated in the Blender software according to the area, length and diameter of the elements that constitute the station. At last, the synchronization between the environments and the visualization using augmented reality was obtained programming in Unity and Vuforia, respectively. The results obtained verified that the system matched to the supervision level of the automation pyramid, achieving a latency of 151.23 ms and fulfilling the general purpose of monitoring the station in real-time.

KEYWORDS

Digital Shadow, MPS 500, Augmented Reality, Unidirectional Communication

1. INTRODUCTION

Recently, a significant technological development, known as industry 4.0 (Ciffolilli and Muscio, 2018), has taken place in the industrial area, specifically in the fields of electronics and industrial systems; in industry 4.0, classical production techniques may share operations with new digital tools (Cortés et al., 2019). Due to industrialization in the production circuit, different processes that involve a set of sensors, actuators and controllers, are implemented to enable the plant to fulfill its purpose (Davis and King, 2019); the common denominator of these processes is that they perform automated and sequential tasks (Requena, 2018). The Modular Production System (MPS) is one of these systems since it executes more than one task in real-time to achieve its objective (Villacreses, 2021; Castillo and Guerrero, 2020). Analogously, the distribution station used in this project is an educational laboratory equipment that puts together the principles used in industry industry (Hermann et al., 2016), providing students with knowledge, expertise, and skills to prepare them for a future work environment.

The easiest way to monitor a plant is in person (Jiang et al., 2019), the design of a digital shadow or Digital Shadow allows to obtain a dynamic virtual replica in a unidirectional way (Bergs et al., 2021), when there is a variation in the physical model, the digital shadow automatically recreates these new parameters (Sepasgozar, 2021), that is, the digital environment updates its behavior in the face of any change in the physical environment, but not the other way around, providing any classic process with new virtual, digital and technological resources (Guo, 2019). Data storage in the cloud enables immediate processing and acquisition of the information stored on internet servers, such that it is available for the user independently of the moment or time interval in which he/she requires it; its scalability of reduced costs and accessibility (Alam, 2020) enable that this technology consolidates as a research and development area for the current decade, and both the data storage and data download subscriber functions are mainly used in this project. Augmented reality is another tool that promotes user´s understanding of a specific application but transferring this technology to the industrial field would be considered unnecessary if it is not established the base for its use (Diegmann et al., 2015). For this reason, working on augmented reality over a digital shadow improves the performance being sought, and it even contributes with variables that may guide the operator in a detailed manner (Zhao et al., 2020).

As a consequence of what has been previously pointed out, this paper delves on the procedure to monitor the MPS 500 distribution station using augmented reality, grouping the aforementioned concepts and principles, such that a unidirectional communication system is employed based on the data platform stored in the cloud. In order to accomplish the development of the digital shadow system, it is necessary to model the laboratory station at a real or natural scale. For this purpose, it is initially used a system which is part of the Blender software, that will be further automated using Vuforia and Unity (Hamid et al.,2020) once the virtual environment has been created. A circuit or PCB is made to condition the input signals or the signals from the 24V station sensors connected to the GPIO pins of the Raspberry Pi board (Caiza and García, 2017), such that the data are received, processed, and sent to the Firebase Database platform, to which the station model application is subscribed. This model receives, interprets, and controls the augmented reality application, while observing the performance of the physical and digital stations synchronized in real-time. The paper is structured as follows: section II describes the main concepts and the methodology employed, section III explains the design and implementation, section IV presents the results obtained and section V finalizes with the conclusions.

2. MATERIALS AND METHODS

2.1 MPS 500 Distribution Station

In industry, the modular production system (MPS) is the result of an automated electronic process (Cortés et al., 2019) that consists of sensors and actuators controlled by a PLC S7-300, with a 313C CPU. The distribution station performs three tasks, namely storage, classification, and distribution of a set of pieces or bodies of cylinders, which are classified and distributed according to the color and the material composition. These operation principles are constantly employed in the manufacturing industry (Davis and King, 2019).

2.2 Blender Platform and Vuforia

Blender is a software that can be used for modeling, animation, creation and rendering of 3D graphics (Requena, 2018). It is open source and generally used for graphical design, enabling to model scenarios at real scale with a great level of detail.

Vuforia Unity is a virtual kit that enables the development of software in augmented reality (Villacreses, 2021). It employs planar images as a base for presenting the augmented reality; such images are further converted into a 3D environment to generate the mixed reality effect which, for the case of the project, places the elements of the station and interprets the signals that enable synchronizing the digital shadow with the physical twin.

2.3 Google Firebase Platform

The Google Firebase cloud platform is a cloud-based cross-device digital system (Castillo and Guerrero, 2020), for developing mobile applications and web sites. Its function covers four fundamental pillars such as data analysis, development, growth, and monetization (Hermann et al., 2016). The development group includes the Realtime Database tool, which enabled storing and downloading the data for the system employed. As it was mentioned above, this is one of the tools of the Firebase development group. Its role is to synchronize in real-time the data stored in its independent database; these data are stored in the cloud and are arranged in JSON format, enabling that the data remain updated even when there is no connection, momentarily providing the alternative of publishing or discarding changes stored in the cache until the connection is restored and they are updated automatically (Jiang et al., 2019).

2.4 Realtime Database Firebase SDK for Unity

Broadly, a software development kit (SDK) enables the assistance in the concept, development and results processes, besides solving possible errors (Bergs et al., 2021); for Unity versions 2019.x and above, the connection to the Firebase database is managed from the Realtime native SDK, as opposed to previous versions where it was required to install Google LLC packages from Package Manager to be able to connect to Firebase; this enables the functions for publishing and/or subscribing to the database, and the subscriber function was used in this case.

2.5 Publisher, Subscriber and Data Structure

The syntax that enables the subscriber to obtain the data and the publisher to share them is the JSON structured data format (Alam, 2020). Data are set as objects within the Firebase Realtime Database, and for this reason the database may be defined as a JSON tree, i.e., each node has an associated key, and the set of nodes has an associated ID, such that for the publisher to issue a change in the same database that is received by the subscriber, they should necessarily share the JSON file to enable the communication to be established.

3. DESIGN AND IMPLEMENTATION

The objective of this study is to design a digital environment of the MPS 500 distribution station. Therefore, a digital modeling was made based on the physical station to reproduce its behavior, establishing a unidirectional communication through the publisher and the subscriber, as it is visualized in Figure 1; every subprocess is described in the subsequent sections.

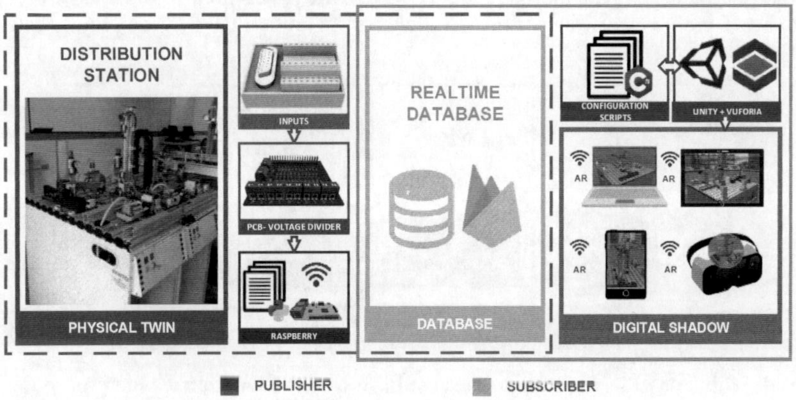

Figure 1. General diagram for the project design

3.1 General Performance of the Station

To implement the operation, the station was automated using ladder programming logic in the Tia Portal software, where each subprocess corresponds to the programmed behavior of the actuators according to the animation mentioned in section 3.8.

3.2 PCB to Adapt the Signals to the Raspberry and Configuration

The Raspberry Pi General Purpose Input/Output (GPIO) pins are adaptable as digital inputs and outputs only at 3.3 V. On the other hand, the station sensors operate with values of 0 V corresponding to logical 0, and 24 V corresponding to logical 1. For this reason, a PCB was built for connecting the input signals; this PCB scales the values of 0 V as logical 0 and 2.9 V as logical 1, since these values can be interpreted by the board.

Once the Debian Buster operating system was installed, the VNC and SSH protocols were enabled to remotely control the Raspberry, as shown in Figure 2. The PIP and PIP3 packet management systems, the GPIO library, Python and Pyrebase were installed through the console of the operating system.

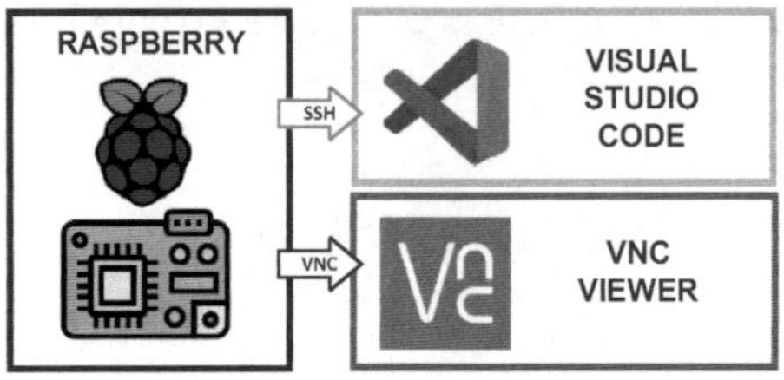

Figure 2. SSH and VNC protocols for Raspberry

3.3 Raspberry as Publishing Element

From the Google Firebase platform, the account was validated with the Realtime Database tool, with the location us-central1 corresponding to Iowa, United States. Subsequently, the JSON file folder and the main file were created in a directory in the Raspberry Pi, in which the Firebase, Pyrebase and GPIO libraries were imported by means of Visual Studio Code with Python as the programming language. The signal of each station sensor was assigned to a GPIO pin and also to a unique node in the database that captured the sensor state at that instant; then, the program was executed, and the first Boolean data were sent. It was also verified at each node that the logical state of the sensors is the correct one. The JSON file provided by Firebase, which is responsible for publishing in the database created, was saved in the same directory as the main file; similarly, to avoid problems, it was verified from the configuration tab that the project data matched the data of the JSON file.

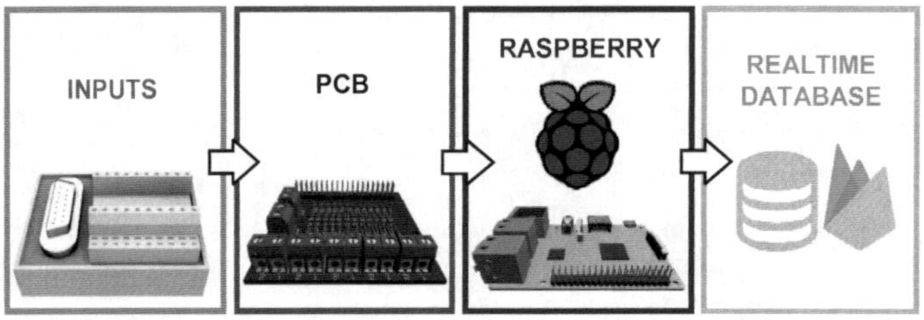

Figure 3. Process that uses the Raspberry Pi as a publisher

As a result of this process, the design presented in Figure. 3 summarizes the procedure, where the sensor signals were published in the platform, each one with its corresponding logical state; then, the data of the sensors that enable the operation of the station or physical twin are published; these data also enable that the digital station or digital shadow emulate its behavior. Subsequently, the digital environment is modeled.

3.4 Evaluation of the Features of the Physical Twin

Prior to modeling the station, it is measured the dimensions of all the elements that constitute it, and it determined their position, arrangement, materials, and all physical features that can be visually captured from every object, including the base of the station.

Once each element has been measured and evaluated, the station is modeled; the entire virtual environment was created in Blender at a natural scale from the real dimensions obtained. The process initiated modeling the sensors, then the actuators; subsequently, textures are imported to the structures of the elements, and finally animation is added to replicate the movements of the cylinders or pieces, exchanger module, elevator module and stacking module; the remaining elements are static, and thus do not need movement, Figure 4 shows the procedure implemented.

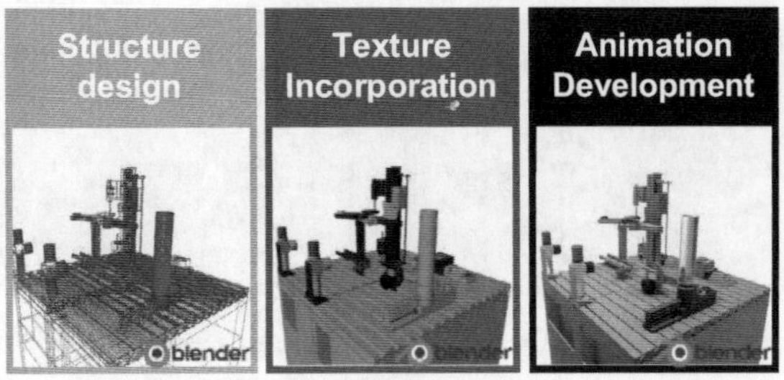

Figure 4. Modeling of the Physical Twin to Digital Shadow

3.5 Integration of Vuforia and Unity for Rendering with Blender

Once the final virtual environment was consolidated, it was imported to Unity as shown in Figure 5; on the other side the input enters as a variable, a QR input in the case of this project, to be further interpreted by Vuforia, which also imports the data from the results obtained from the QR and from the plugins with updated information about the position, amount of light, amount of shadow, among others. After this process was finalized, the file was exported as an executable file for the Android platform.

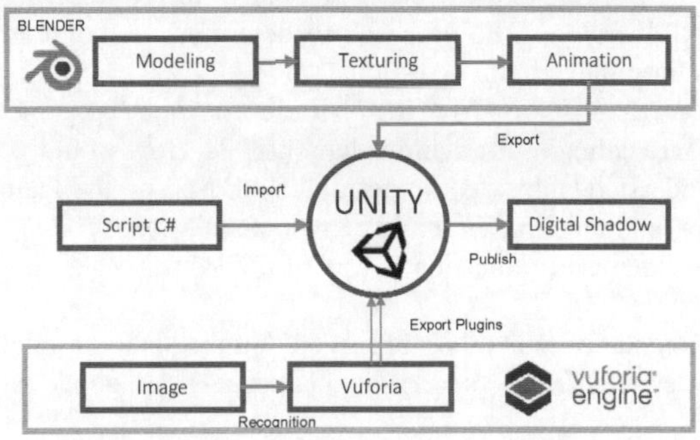

Figure 5. Process for creating the digital shadow with augmented reality

3.6 Collection of Data from the Subscriber

Conditions for developing the animation were established from the model imported by Unity from Blender; these conditions validate that the process of the digital environment is executed at the same time than the process of the physical twin. These variables are stored in the Realtime Database (Martinez et al., 2021), i.e., the ones updated by the publisher in the database, as mentioned in section 3.5. The procedure to obtain these variables is now explained. After the Realtime Database SDK has been imported to Unity and the JSON file has been added, two Scripts were created so that each subprocess is independent: the first was used to control the animation, and the second to download the data from the base. The two scripts were programmed in the C# programming language using Visual Studio 2019. For the download script the Firebase libraries were imported, the JSON file was called and the value of the queried variable was requested honoring the structure of the nodes; in the case of the second script, the data obtained from the first script was requested, the conditions for each animation were received and assigned, it was saved in Unity and exported to a mobile device as an augmented reality app, as can be seen in Figure 6.

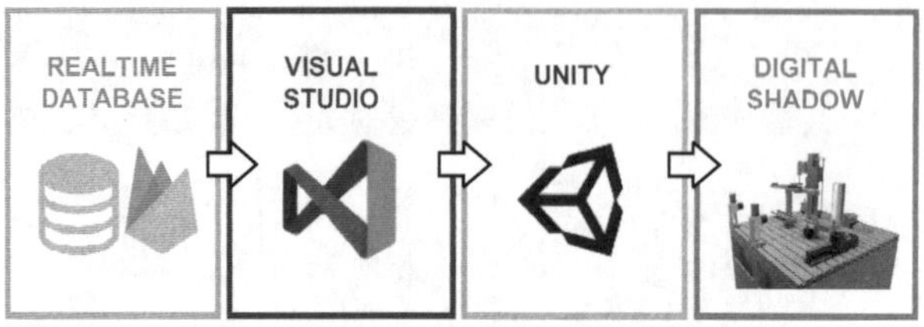

Figure 6. Process for downloading the subscriber data

4. RESULTS

4.1 Evaluation of the Station Model

The environment modeled from the digital twin needs to be understandable and efficient. For this reason, a survey with 5 questions was conducted on 25 people with prior experience in the MPS laboratory; these included graduates, students working in their theses and electronic engineering professionals, because they can be considered as potential operators. The aim was to determine if they considered that the digital shadow fulfilled the requirements formulated in the questions.

The questions were stated as follows: 1.- How would you rate the presented distribution station model? 2.- How do you consider the scaling of the station elements? 3.- How would you rate the realism and definition of the model? 4.- How understandable was the design? 5.- Based on the features observed, how likely is that you recommend the use of the model presented? The responses to questions 1-4 ranged from 1 (Excellent) to 5 (Very Poor), whereas the response to question 5 was in the same range, but 1 represented Extremely Likely and 5 represented Not Likely.

Figure 7 shows the percentage results. It is observed that the station model is accepted, since 66.4% of the respondents rate it as excellent, 27.2% as very good and 6.4% as good; the very poor and regular ratings obtained 0%.

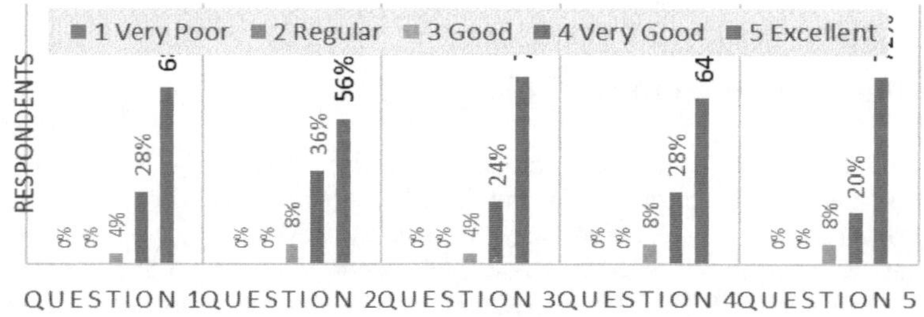

Figure 7. Survey results graph

4.2 Latency of the Publisher and Subscriber according to the Firebase Performance Tool

The data provided by the Firebase Performance tool were considered for a precise analysis. These data included upload and download times for the publisher and subscriber respectively, and relevant statistics and plots, as shown in Figure 8.

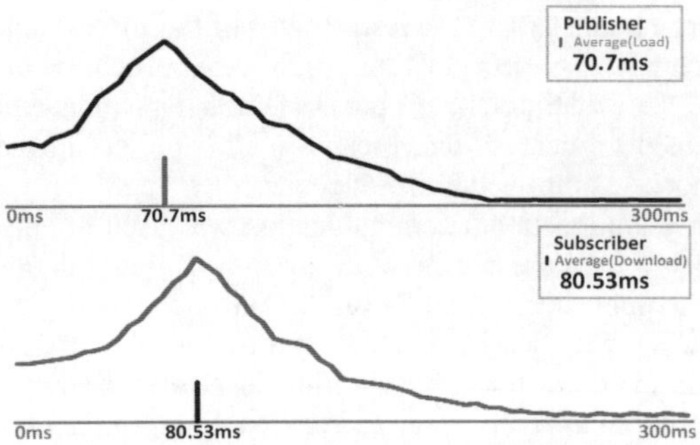

Figure 8. Latency Analysis using Firebase Performance

The total latency of the system is given by the sum of the publisher upload time plus the subscriber download time, which verifies the level of the automation pyramid it belongs to (Mustafa et al., 2019). For the test it was used an IPV4 network with a bandwidth of 20 Mbps, and the subscriber had a Galaxy J7 with Android 7.1 OS, a 1.5GHz processor and a 2.4GHz Wi-Fi connectivity under the 802.11b/g/n standard.

4.3 Performance of the Physical Twin and of the Digital Shadow

The test mentioned in the previous section is now presented. In such test it was verified if the behaviors of the digital environment and the physical twin are synchronized. It was observed that there is an evident delay from the digital shadow; this delay or latency is analyzed in Figure 9. Later, the delay went unnoticed due to a physical effect of the station when, in the physical twin, the exchanger module leaves the cylinder in the elevator module; then, the digital shadow stays ahead and both environments become synchronized again.

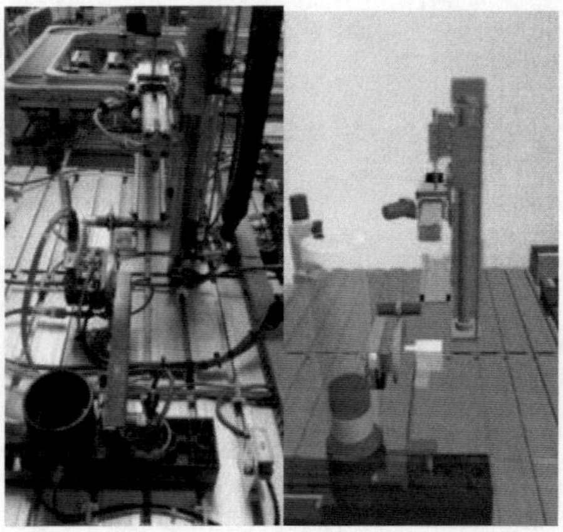

Figure 9. Synchronization of the physical twin and of the digital shadow

5. CONCLUSION

Based on the publisher-subscriber unidirectional communication method described, from the MPS 500 distribution station and the Raspberry Pi board, a digital shadow system was developed that enabled monitoring its performance using augmented reality. The methods employed were developed based on the important contribution of bibliographic material that was collected and analyzed, related to digital shadows for industrial environments. This enabled considering and discarding different alternatives; likewise, the model built in the Blender software enabled that the environment and behavior of the physical twin were precisely designed to obtain the digital environment, such that there is an agreement with the process.

Based on the acceptance obtained from the respondents of the survey conducted, it is important to remark that features such as precision, correct scaling, high design quality and similarity with its physical counterpart, yielded that 72% of the potential operators further recommended to use the way in which the model was built; this enabled to increase the research of this project for another possible application with other station, other laboratory or simply other machinery.

The publisher-subscriber unidirectional communication was used to obtain an agreement in the process, and mainly for synchronizing the behavior between the physical and digital twins. As shown in Figure 8, latencies of 70.7 ms for the publisher and 80.53 ms for the subscriber were obtained; this analysis became relevant when the total latency was classified and related to a level of the automation pyramid. Specifically, this total latency of 151.23 ms corresponds to the third level or supervision level, that is characterized by performing functions such as data supervision, acquisition and storage; thus, it is evident that the process meets the standards associated to monitoring, which is the main purpose.

REFERENCES

Alam, T. (2020). Cloud Computing and its role in the Information Technology. IAIC Transactions on Sustainable Digital Innovation (ITSDI), 1(2), 108–115.

Bergs, T., Gierlings, S., Auerbach, T., Klink, A., Schraknepper, D., & Augspurger, T. (2021). The concept of digital twin and digital shadow in manufacturing. Procedia CIRP, 101, 81-84.

Caiza, G., & García, M. (2017). Implementation of low cost distributed system under iec-61499 estandard, in classification and handling station of mps-500. Ingenius. Revista de Ciencia y Tecnología, 18, 40–46.

Castillo, M. A., & Guerrero, D. F. (2020). Automatización y monitoreo para planta festo mps-500 del laboratorio de fabricación flexible de UPS-G.

Ciffolilli, A., & Muscio, A. (2018). Industry 4.0: national and regional comparative advantages in key enabling technologies. European Planning Studies, 26(12), 2323–2343.

Cortés, C. B. Y., Landeta, J. M. I., & Chacón, J. G. B. (2019). El entorno de la industria 4.0: implicaciones y perspectivas futuras. Conciencia Tecnológica, 54, 33–45.

Davis Randall y King, J. (2019). An overview of production systems.

Diegmann, P., Schmidt-Kraepelin, M., Eynden, S., & Basten, D. (2015). Benefits of augmented reality in educational environments-a systematic literature review.

Guo, J., Zhao, N., Sun, L., & Zhang, S. (2019). Modular based flexible digital twin for factory design. Journal of Ambient Intelligence and Humanized Computing, 10(3), 1189–1200.

Hamid, M. A., Rahman, S. A., Darmawan, I. A., Fatkhurrokhman, M., & Nurtanto, M. (2021, November). Performance efficiency of virtual laboratory based on Unity 3D and Blender during the Covid-19 pandemic. In Journal of Physics: Conference Series (Vol. 2111, No. 1, p. 012054). IOP Publishing.

Hermann, P. T. y O. B. (n.d.). Design Principles for Industrie 4.0 Scenarios 2016. 49th Hawaii International Conference on System Sciences (HICSS).

Jiang, Q., Yan, X., & Huang, B. (2019). Review and perspectives of data-driven distributed monitoring for industrial plant-wide processes. Industrial & Engineering Chemistry Research, 58(29), 12899–12912.

Martinez, E. M., Ponce, P., Macias, I., & Molina, A. (2021). Automation pyramid as constructor for a complete digital twin, case study: A didactic manufacturing system. Sensors, 21(14), 4656.

Mustafa, J., Sandström, K., Ericsson, N., & Rizvanovic, L. (2019). Analyzing availability and QoS of service-oriented cloud for industrial IoT applications. 2019 24th IEEE International Conference on Emerging Technologies and Factory Automation (ETFA), 1403–1406. https://doi.org/10.1109/ETFA.2019.8869274

Requena, J. M. (2018). Diseño de un sistema de automatización de una planta de lavado de zanahoria de 10 t/h.

Sepasgozar, S. M. (2021). Differentiating digital twin from digital shadow: Elucidating a paradigm shift to expedite a smart, sustainable built environment. Buildings, 11(4), 151.

Villacreses Pita, A. A. (2021). Diseño e implementación de un sistema de medición y supervisión de eficiencia productiva de una máquina FESTO MPS-500 del laboratorio de flexible utilizando TVC.

Zhao, X., Liu, C., Xu, Z., Zhang, L., & Zhang, R. (2020). SSVEP stimulus layout effect on accuracy of brain-computer interfaces in augmented reality glasses. IEEE Access, 8, 5990-5998.

FACTORS INFLUENCING THE INTEGRATION OF SOCIAL GRANTS INFORMATION SYSTEMS IN THE NAMIBIAN GOVERNMENT: ACTOR-NETWORK THEORY ANALYSIS

Filippus Nafuka and Irja Shaanika
Namibia University of Science and Technology, Namibia

ABSTRACT

The government of Namibia strives to alleviate poverty by providing social grants to its citizens. Some of the social grant schemes provided by the Namibian government include old-age pensions, disability grants, orphans and vulnerable children state maintenance grants and veterans' monthly subventions. The government is currently faced with challenges in the administration and provision of social grants. The challenges include data duplications, beneficiaries' inclusion and exclusion errors and beneficiaries' payment irregularities such as duplicate payments, payment into wrong accounts, payment rejections, and over and underpayment are attributed to the silo information systems which are used by Ministries in the administration of social grants. The challenges above call for the integration of social grants information systems, as a measure to solve them. Otherwise, the challenges will persist which will negatively keep affecting the government's provision of social grants to the citizens. Therefore, this study primarily aims to investigate and understand the factors that can impact the integration of the social grants' information systems among the ministries.
Two cases, the Ministry of Gender Equality, Poverty Eradication and Social Welfare, and the Ministry of Defence and Veterans Affairs, were qualitatively studied. Data was collected through semi-structured interviews and documentation technique. Actor-Network Theory's moments of translation was employed as a lens to help examine and understand the technical and non-technical factors that can impact the integration of the social grants information systems. Nine factors namely: payment irregularities, eligibility check mechanisms, non-distributed systems setup, data migration challenges, system development skills shortage, systems in-house support and maintenance, un-documented systems, and memorandum of understanding were found to impact the integration of the social grants information system.

KEYWORDS

Social Grants, Information Systems, Actor-Network Theory, Information Systems Integration, Namibia

1. INTRODUCTION

Namibia is one of the developing countries with a widespread and comprehensive social grants system that is mandatorily integrated into the annual national government budget (Schade et al., 2019). The various types of social grant schemes in Namibia include old-age pensions, disability grants, orphans and vulnerable children state maintenance grants and veterans' monthly subventions (Dempers, 2016; Social Protection Policy 2021-2030, 2021). Wiman et al. (2016) asserted that the Namibian social grant types such as an old-age pension, orphans and vulnerable children maintenance and special maintenance grants were inherited and continued from the South African colonial regime.

The provision of social grants has proven to have a positive effect on alleviating poverty and reducing inequality in post-independence Namibia, as a larger portion of the population benefits directly or indirectly (Schade et al., 2019). The benefits of social grants' provision include promoting the local market economy, an increase in children's school enrolment and completion, and an improvement in beneficiaries' food and financial security (Granlund & Hochfeld, 2020). These positive impacts have overall helped the vulnerable groups' integration and participation in the socio-economic stand of Namibia.

Various Ministries in Namibia are mandated to oversee the management, administration, and provision of national social grants (Social Protection Policy 2021-2030, 2021). Each of the ministries has developed and implemented disparate social grant information systems. These information systems are to help with the administration, processing, and provision of these social grants to the registered beneficiaries.

An information system is defined as a set of interrelated components that function together to collect, process, store and disseminates information to automate organisational processes and support decision-making (Bourgeois et al., 2019). This makes information systems essential and critical to the operation of organisations because they make it easier for people to perform their organisational functions and improve service delivery and earn a competitive advantage (Nguyen, 2019).

However, the implementation of information systems in organisations is often associated with various challenges. Faris (2019) explained that organisations are constantly faced with the challenges of maintaining information systems over time, securing, and aligning them with the organisational needs and business strategies. The vast and ever-changing technology, pressures organisations to integrate information systems to operate efficiently and effectively to solve the above-mentioned challenges and effectively manage changes (Yu et al., 2021). According to Ngoepe and Mello (2021), the integration of information systems within the organisation and among their business partners is critical for the effective and efficient organisational operation and streamlined access to information. However, the ministries' social grants information systems are not integrated, contributing to a lack of streamlined services.

Information systems integration is the process of bringing multiple systems or subsystems together to communicate and perform a particular function beyond what each system would perform individually (Hamatwi, 2018). Information systems are integrated to form an organised coherent composition of multiple information systems to share and exchange data (Koen, 2019). Therefore, within the Namibian government, social grants information systems integration is essential to enable data sharing and exchange among the stakeholders. This is critical to minimise and eventually eradicate the social grants mismanagement and provision irregularities caused by the use of disparate social grants information systems. Furthermore, this would be essential for ministries to cut operational and administration costs that would be incurred from the irregularities of using as disparate social grants information systems.

System integration is a complex process that needs to be scrutinised and managed to ensure its success. The complexity of the process is attributed to the many actors that are involved in the administration of social grant information. In the Namibian environment, the factors influencing the social grants information systems integration are not known. Thus, this study aims to address the research question: what are the factors that can impact the integration of the social grants' information systems among the ministries? In order to gain a better understanding of the factors, Actor-Network Theory's moments of translation phases are employed. The findings from the study will guide and inform the Ministries embarking on the social grants' information systems integration projects.

This study is divided into seven sections. The first section introduces the study. The second section provides an overview of the Actor-Network Theory. Section three covers the literature review on the keywords of the study. The research approach about how the study was carried out is covered in section four. Section five covers the use of the Actor-Network Theory for analysis, while section six discusses the results of the findings. Lastly, section seven concludes the study.

2. ACTOR-NETWORK THEORY (ANT): OVERVIEW

ANT is a relational and materialistic research underpinning theory that illustrates phenomena as a system of diverse interacting socio-technical actors (Yusuf et al., 2020). Luscombe and Walby (2017) added that the aim of actor-network theory as an underpinning theory is to analytically trace, empirically reconstruct and describe actor-networks relationships and associations. This means that ANT is based on the principle concepts of agency and symmetry and its moments of translation to reconstruct a phenomenon (Tummons, 2021). Agency and symmetry deal with treating all human and non-human actors in the actor network as equals, as they both influence each other to maintain and sustain the actor-networks stability (Cresswell, 2019). This means that actor-networks' stability results from constant and iterative successful negotiations and alignment of the heterogeneous actors' interests (Gebre-Mariam & Fruijtier, 2018).

The moments of translation phases are composed of four iterative phases, namely: problematization, interessment, enrolment and mobilization, as depicted in figure 1 below (Birke & Knierim, 2020)

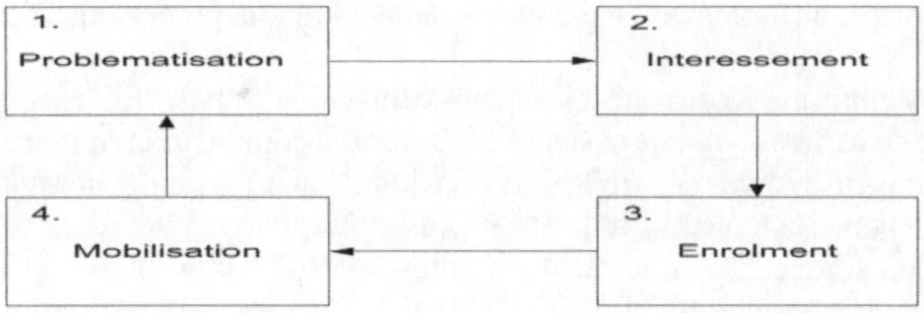

Figure 1. ANT's moments of translation phases (Nehemia-Maletzky et al., 2018)

The problematisation phase deals with the introduction of the identified problem, its impact, and suggested solutions to the identified key actors of a phenomenon by the focal actor (Benqatla et al., 2017). It is then followed by the interessment phase where the focal actor continues to interest the identified key actors to be part of the actor network to provide a solution to the identified problem (Dedeke, 2017). This involves all the strategies and tools used by the focal actor to align the key actors' interests to the problem (Benqatla et al., 2017). The successful interessment phase leads to the enrolment phase, where roles are created, defined, and assigned to each respectively identified actor based on the actors' interests (Altabaibeh et al., 2020). The actors accept the assigned roles, form alliances, and agree to the solution to the problem (Aka, 2019). The actors then take up and execute their assigned roles in the mobilisation phase where resources are mobilised for the actors to perform their roles and to maintain the actor-networks' stability (Dedeke, 2017). A spokesperson is also identified as the representative of the actor network to the outside world (Luscombe & Walby, 2017).

ANT depicts actor networks as a system of diverse heterogeneous socio-technical actors (Yusuf et al., 2020). The social and technical actors of a phenomenon are intertwined and should therefore be studied together as equals to prevent and avoid biased research outcomes (Boychenko et al., 2020; Cresswell, 2019). That is why ANT is applied in information systems studies to unpack and analyse the various heterogeneous actors involved in the development, implementation, management, and use of information systems within a phenomenon (Nehemia-Maletzky et al., 2018).

3. LITERATURE REVIEW

The number of social grants' recipients has been increasing globally, as countries in both parts of the world adopt social grant programmes as means of achieving social development and improving social welfare (Fisher et al., 2017). Granlund and Hochfeld (2020) stated that over seventeen million South African individuals received social grants in 2017. While in Namibia, 170 386 individuals received the old age grant while 41 061 received the disability grant and 344 055 received the child grant in the 2017/2018 fiscal year (Schade et al., 2019). These numbers rise over the years as more beneficiaries become eligible and different social grants are introduced (Dempers, 2016).

Literature has ascertained that the provision of social grants is indeed beneficial, and the main benefit of social grants is that it reduces the poverty rate, with Dempers (2016) stating that the Namibian poverty rate officially declined from 69.3% to 28.7% as a direct result of social grants. Social grants also lift the vulnerable groups' coping strategies by securing food security, financial security, and psychological welfare to end intergenerational poverty (Granlund & Hochfeld, 2020; Fisher et al., 2017). Fisher et al. (2017) further added that the provision of social grants has boosted agricultural and livestock production as recipients invest in agricultural technologies and supplies to supplement traditional farming methods. Social grants also positively impact the educational sector as grants' recipients can afford school fees, which enables scholars to stay in school and complete their education (Mackett, 2020).

The provision of social grants in Namibia is carried out by various ministries, which are the Ministry of Gender Equality, Poverty Eradication and Social Welfare and the Ministry of Defence and Veterans Affairs. The administration and provision of social grants by various ministries have caused process fragmentation hence the duplication of effort. Fragmentation is a result of similar processes being carried out by different ministries, leading to duplication of efforts. Applicants for social grants, who may qualify for multiple grants and at different ministries, are forced to submit documents to these multiple entities. This leads to the duplication of data and efforts to maintain this data by the different entities. Each ministry has developed and implemented an information system to help with the administration, processing, and provision of social grants to beneficiaries.

Information Systems are known to be socio-technical systems. Eljaoued et al. (2020) defined a socio-technical system as "a large-scale system that features a combination of human-intensive organisational systems and technological systems" (p. 2626). As a socio-technical system, information systems require a high degree of interaction between humans and the technical aspects to operate successfully and optimally (Ryan et al., 2021). The technical aspects of information systems include hardware and software resources which are coupled with information structures (Mazhar et al.,2019). The interactions between the different actors are necessary, as they are dependent on each other to carry out business processes and achieve business goals. For different actors to interact seamlessly in a computing environment, information systems integration is vital.

Information systems integration is defined by Hietajärvi et al. (2017) as the process of combining and standardising information systems (data elements, knowledge, and processes) through a common or compatible system element to perform a particular function beyond what each system would perform individually. Nguyen (2019) described information systems integration as the process of allowing interactions of disparate information systems to act as a unified system. According to Naki et al. (2018), the integration allows multiple disparate information systems to communicate. A disparate information system is defined by Koen (2019) as "an information management system that is unable to freely communicate with other information management systems" (p. 29). This is because of its implementation as a standalone system.

Information system integration is very beneficial. That is why Schade et al. (2019) recommended for the integration of the ministries' policies, information systems and social grants provision mechanisms for an efficient social grants provision in Namibia. The integration of the information systems prevents and minimises manual data entry and redundancy by automating business processes (Abbas et al., 2018). Ngoepe and Mello (2021) stated that the automation of business processes, as a result of integration, leads to reduced paper handling and labour, minimises loss of transactional data, increases productivity and return on information systems' investment. Furthermore, the maintenance of integrated information systems is cheaper as opposed to the individual systems' maintenance (Koen, 2019). As the licencing and subscription fees reduce which in turn reduces the maintenance costs (Subiyakto, 2018). Thus, integrating disparate social grant information systems will be valuable to the beneficiaries and organisations managing the provision of social grants. The integration will harmonise and consolidate the fragmented social grants provision, improve the communication between the social grants provider and stakeholders and help eliminate fraud by ensuring beneficiaries' details are correct and up to date (Barca, 2017; Transform, 2017).

4. RESEARCH APPROACH

This study is qualitative. Qualitative research strategy captures the meanings and qualities that are not quantifiable such as feelings, thoughts and experiences which are captured in a form of words, phrases, sentences, and narrations (Kilani & Kobziev, 2016). It is an approach that answers the what, how, when and where questions to understand a phenomenon in its natural environment (Basias & Pollalis, 2018).

Two (2) cases were studied. The first case study is the Ministry of Defence and Veterans Affairs, and the second case was the Ministry of Gender Equality, Poverty Eradication and Social Welfare. The cases have been chosen and studied because they provide social grants to the Namibian citizenry and use disparate social grants information systems for the administration, management, and provision of social grants. The semi-structured interviews and documentation technique were used to acquire data from the selected cases and ensure adequate qualitative data was collected for thorough data analysis. The semi-structured interview was used as the primary data collection technique for both cases, because it gave freedom to the researcher and participants to instantly probe on what they did not understand during the interview session (Zortea et al., 2019). While the documentation technique was used to acquire critical documentations that provide information to further understand and provide insight into the provision of social grants phenomenon (Wakhidah & Erman, 2022).

Interview guiding questions were set up for the data collection process. The interview guiding questions enabled the researcher to maintain uniformity and consistency throughout the data collection process. Interviews were conducted at the participants' places of work, and some through Zoom Meetings.

5. ANT FOR DATA ANALYSIS

ANT was selected as a socio-technical theory to underpin this study for three reasons. Firstly, to guide the identification of all the relevant actors involved in the provision of social grants. The provision of social grants is a construct of multiple diverse actors, who are entangled and interconnected to form the actor networks (Aka, 2019). Therefore, ANT's generalized symmetry allows the study of these actors despite their size and influence (Vickers et al., 2018). The social grants provision is viewed and thought of as an assembly of various actors which include information systems, personnel, financial institutions, policies and so on, who work together to provide social grants to beneficiaries. ANT thus facilitates researchers to uncover the various actors involved and expose the motivations and actions of various human actors (Gunawong & Gao, 2017).

Secondly, ANT was selected to gain a deeper understanding of the disparate social grants' information systems design, development and implementation process and activities. The moments of translation help scholars relive and re-construct the formation of a phenomenon and its components (Dedeke, 2017). The properties of a phenomenon, in this case, the provision of social grants, are not innate but gradually emerge during the translation phase (Lukka & Vinnari, 2017). According to Rudnicki (2017) ANT examines the process of building networks as composed of human and nonhuman actors that leads to new objects or modification of an existing object. The re-enactment of the social grants' provision through the moments of translation would hence provide insight into how the actors' relationships and interactions have been formed. This would thus help in tracing the design, development, and implementation of the disparate social grants information systems.

Lastly, to examine and understand the actors' relationships and interactions that take place in the provision of social grants. According to Boychenko et al. (2020), ANT enabled the researchers to elaborate on the interactions of how actors are organized and connected to influence each other's behaviour in the provision of social grants to beneficiaries. This provides insight into how the involved actors function and operate to achieve their respective objectives of successfully (Dedeke, 2017). The understanding of the actors and their relationships allows the exploration of the effects of implementing new technology and why they fail or succeed after implementation (Cresswell, 2019). It thus provides feedback on how the involved actors will react towards the implementation of new technology, in this case, the integrated social grants information system.

The use of ANT as an underpinning theory for this research study hence provided an understanding of how people, technologies and processes work together to achieve the social grants provision objectives. It further provided insight into how the social grants information systems may be integrated as a collective accomplishment, by outlining the common grounds for deciding when, how and what to integrate.

6. RESULTS DISCUSSION

As discussed above the analysis was guided by ANT's moments of translation. Based on the analysis that was carried out, factors that influence the provision, management, and administration of government social grants were found. The findings are interpretively discussed to gain a deeper understanding of the identified technical and non-technical factors. These factors include payment irregularities, eligibility check mechanisms, non-distributed systems setup, data migration challenges, system development skills shortage, systems in-house support and maintenance, un-documented systems, and memorandum of understanding. These factors are interdependent as illustrated in Figure 2 below. The discussion of the factors is presented below.

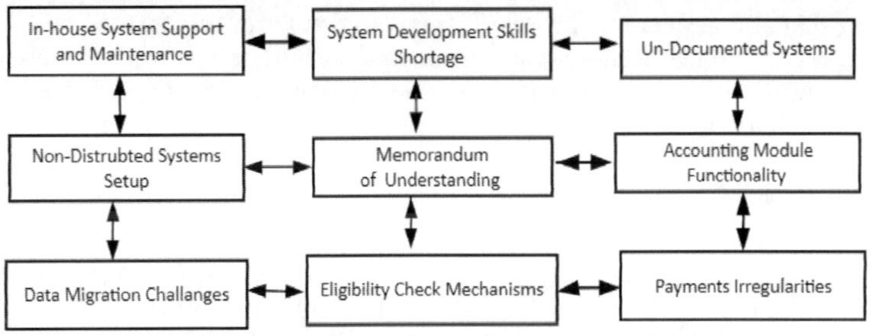

Figure 2. The impacts of unintegrated information systems on social grants provision

6.1 Payment Irregularities

There are payment irregularities identified within the social grants provision. These payment irregularities include double or duplicate payments of beneficiaries, delayed payments, payments of social grants into a wrong account, continuous payments into a deceased beneficiary's account, and paying a person that earns a taxable income as prescribed. These payment irregularities are caused by technical and non-technical factors.

First of all, the use of un-integrated social grants information systems in managing and sustaining the social grants service is one of the contributing aspects. As each ministry is respectively using a standalone social grant information system, there is no systematic data sharing and exchange between the information systems with the stakeholders and business partners. According to Ngoepe and Mello (2021), the use of un-integrated information systems leads to an inefficient exchange and sharing of data, data disparities and inconsistency. Therefore, without data sharing, the verification and validation of the beneficiaries' data are hindered and limited. This has therefore made it difficult to identify ineligible grants' beneficiaries efficiently and smoothly.

On the other hand, the transition from manual to computerized payment methods is another aspect that caused payment irregularities. This is because data was lost during the information systems' transitioning processes. The data is usually lost when the migration process is not sufficiently planned for or carried out without a data migration plan (Rai & Talawar, 2022). Therefore, it was hard and at certain levels impossible to distinguish the beneficiaries that have already been paid from the unpaid beneficiaries. This led to double payments of certain beneficiaries whose payment records were lost during the transition process.

The efficient and smooth distribution of social grants to beneficiaries is greatly hampered by payment irregularities and inconsistencies. One of the main effects is the high cost as the ministries continue to spend more money on social grants than they could have on other government programs. To cut down on payment irregularities and inconsistencies, the ministries have implemented eligibility check mechanisms.

6.2 Eligibility Check Mechanisms

To guarantee that applicants and recipients of the provided social grants are eligible, the ministries have implemented eligibility check mechanisms. These are both manual and computerized eligibility check mechanisms to help with guarding against erroneous social grant payments and guarantee all beneficiaries' eligibility. This is to ensure the efficiency in social grants provision to beneficiaries.

The manual eligibility check mechanisms included attestation, vetting social grant applicants, and carrying out the certificate of existence (CoE). With the attestation method put in place by the Ministry of Gender Equality, Poverty Eradication, and Social Welfare, eligibility is ensured as the administrative officers fill in the social grants' application forms on behalf of the applicants. This ensures that the applicant answers truthfully as the condition of the applicant is observed during the process. The method also ensures that all the mandatory fields of the application forms are filled in precisely and correctly. Additionally, beneficiary vetting is carried out by the Ministry of Defence and Veterans Affairs to ensure that the veteran applicants have been persistently and consistently involved in the liberation struggle (Veterans Act (Act 2 of 2008)). Based on the findings of the vetting procedure, the veteran's status is assigned to the applicant. This ensures that only eligible applicants as per the Veterans Act are given the veteran's status and subsequently the social grants. Furthermore, a CoE is carried out by the ministries to certify that the beneficiaries are still alive and eligible for the grants.

The electronic mechanisms included the implementation of database triggers during application data entry and the performance of the preliminary pay-run. These electronic mechanisms validate whether a beneficiary has valid personal details such as full name, date of birth, id number or birth certificate number, marital status, and whether the beneficiary earns above the prescribed amount. The database triggers are enforced during the insertion and deletion of beneficiaries' records. This means that for every insertion or deletion of beneficiaries' records, the triggers ensure that it meets the set standards for the respective beneficiary to be paid. The set standards include the insertion of mandatory fields, fields containing the right length and required data type, the right grant and amount are assigned and the prevention of deleting an applicant with a paid transaction.

6.3 Non-Distributed System Setup

The social grants information systems are implemented and hosted through a non-distributed system setup. A non-distributed system setup is a computing environment in which all parts of an information system are only accessible at one physical location (Usman et al., 2020). This means that an information system is set up at different autonomous computers connected to a single centralised database over a local area network.

The non-distributed system setup has led to the social grants provision processes being partially manual. This is because the social grants information systems are only accessible at head offices and not at the regional offices. Therefore, the regional staff members do not have access to the information systems. This has led to manual operation for all the processes carried out at the regional and constituency offices

The implications caused by the partially manual processes as a result of using non-distributed information systems are delays, high costs, and risks of transporting the application forms and attached documents to the head offices for registration onto the systems. This leads to overworking the head office administrative officers while underworking the regional administrative officers. It also deprives the regional staff members of information on the beneficiaries of the social grants, which may hamper timely responses to queries from the beneficiaries as they visit their offices.

6.4 Data Migration Challenges

Data migration is the process of transferring data from one storage system to another (Saranya et al., 2021). The data migration process usually takes place when organisations are moving or transitioning from one information system to another or changing database management systems. The social grants ministries were required to migrate data as they had to move from using an old system to a new system. Upon migrating data, challenges were faced by the social grants ministries in successfully migrating data.

Some of the data migration challenges faced included data loss and duplicate payments. The Ministry of Gender Equality, Poverty Eradication, and Social Welfare experienced data loss as they moved from the mainframe system onto the currently used client-server system. while, the Ministry of Defence and Veterans Affairs implemented a computerised system, Veterans Administrative System, and had to move all data from the manual payment processing onto the new system. In both instances, the migration process led to payments duplication due to the duplicate creation of beneficiaries' accounts and the loss of payment records and receipts for certain beneficiaries.

6.5 System Development Skills Shortage

Medvedeva and Umpleby (2022) asserted that having personnel with the right skills and self-management is important and determines the quality of information systems. However, there is a shortage of system development skills within the social grants ministries. The lack of system development skills is due to two reasons. The first reason is that the Ministry of Defence and Veterans Affairs had a vacant position for an analyst programmer. The analyst programmer is required to have programming skills within their IT subdivision. On the other hand, the Ministry of Gender Equality, Poverty Eradication, and Social Welfare did not have a provision for any analyst programmer in their IT structure to efficiently create, support, and manage the social grants information systems. System development skills are a vital requirement in an IT department.

To develop and maintain information systems, a variety of system development abilities are needed. These abilities include understanding programming languages, such as Java, having expertise in creating and managing databases, and knowledge of system documentation. These competencies ought to be prerequisites for the hire as the ministries search for suitable employees to manage social grants information systems.

6.6 Systems In-house Support and Maintenance

The ministries responsible for social grants have been faced with the challenge of heavily relying on OPM and IT Consultants to provide social grants information system support and maintenance. This is because the ministries do not have the personnel capacity to maintain the social grants information systems.

There are implications with the reliance on OPM and consultants to support and maintain the social grants systems. The major implication is the speed on attending to and resolving system issues on time, which impacts end-users' productivity. OPM or the IT Consultant only act on the requests only after the elongated channel of communication and formal agreement is reached between the parties.

6.7 Accounting Module Functionality

The social grants information systems do not have an accounting functionality for doing financial calculations to assist with assigning the grants to the beneficiaries. The functionality was never incorporated into the social grants systems as it was not part of the initial system's requirements at the beginning of the development phase.

Without the accounting module functionality, the grants calculations for the inheritance payments and division of orphans and vulnerable children's grants are done manually. The manual calculations of the social grants are thus susceptible to human errors and mistakes, which may as well lead to over or underpayment of beneficiaries which are among the payment irregularities. It is thus important that an accounting module or functionality is implemented to eradicate human errors of under-or over-assigning social grant amounts and overall reduce social grants complaints. According to Jangkholam and Singh (2021) an information system should incorporate an accounting functionality that allow the organisation to confidently manage its finances

6.8 Un-Documented Systems

System documentation is a practice in system development whereby the developers and designers of a system develop artefacts to convey information about the system they are developing (Hashemi et al., 2020). System documentation provides a reference point for an easier understanding of a system's design and development.

Unfortunately, the social grants information systems were not documented. Some of the unavailable documents due to undocumented processes includes user requirements documents, source code documents, system design documents, user manuals, and database schema design and configuration documentation.

Without the various kinds of documentation, it is difficult to understand and maintain the source codes, improve the functionality of the system, as well pose a security threat to an organisation as there is no documentation on how a system is protected (Wallace, 2021). This led to difficulties in upgrading the functionality of the social grants information systems, as new developers find it hard to understand the legacy source codes. Therefore, the social grants information systems have not had major functional changes since their implementation and thus led to the information systems running on legacy platforms and facing challenges such as weakened security, high system maintenance, data migration challenges, and inability to integrate.

6.9 Memorandum of Understanding

The social grants ministries do not have a memorandum of understanding (MoU) with their stakeholders and business partners. A MoU is a document signed between organisations to allow collaboration towards a common objective (Moreby, 2020). A memorandum of understanding will officially establish and enforce partnerships between the ministries, the relevant stakeholders and business partners to provide social grants to recipients efficiently and effectively.

Without the MoU between the social grants providing ministries and their respective stakeholders the social grants provision is negatively affected. The major effect is that there is no direct systematic sharing and exchanging of data between the ministries, and the ministries with their external stakeholders. Currently, data exchange and sharing is done on a need-be basis, which is not ideal for accurate and consistent data leading to irregularities. These irregularities are not handled promptly as without the MoU in place, the long formal route of communication has to be taken, as opposed to having a direct dedicated point of contact.

7. CONCLUSION

The study employed ANT primarily to guide the analysis of data and provide insight and understanding of how people, technologies and processes work together to achieve the social grants provision objectives. Based on the analysis, technical and non-technical factors that could influence the integration of social grants information systems within the Namibian government. Nine major factors were derived and discussed in detail to provide an understanding about how they impact the integration of social grants information systems. These factors were derived through the re-enactment of the social grants provision through ANT's moments of translation. The study will be beneficial to the management and IT personnel within the social grants' ministries. As this study provides knowledge and understanding of how they can manage the factors that would impact the integration of social grants. Furthermore, the study significantly contributes to the academics' body of knowledge. As the study adds to the literature on the use of Actor-Network Theory as a tool for data analysis in information systems studies. Clearly indicate advantages, limitations, and possible applications.

REFERENCES

Abbas, W. F., Ismail, S. H., Haron, H., & Hariri, W. N. A. W. (2018). Enterprise Integration of Employee Onboarding Process Using Zachman Framework. International Journal of Engineering and Technology, 7(January), 46–51. https://doi.org/10.14419/ijet.v7i4.31.23340

Aka, K. G. (2019). Actor-network theory to understand, track and succeed in a sustainable innovation development process. Journal of Cleaner Production, 225, 524–540. https://doi.org/10.1016/j.jclepro.2019.03.351

Altabaibeh, A., Caldwell, K. A., & Volante, M. A. (2020). Tracing healthcare organisation integration in the UK using actor–network theory. Journal of Health Organization and Management, 34(2), 192–206. https://doi.org/10.1108/JHOM-12-2019-0339

Barca, V. (2017). Integrating data and information management for social protection: social registries and integrated beneficiary registries (Issue October). https://www.dfat.gov.au/about-us/publications/Pages/integrating-data-information-management-social-protection

Basias, N., & Pollalis, Y. (2018). Quantitative and Qualitative Research in Business & Technology: Justifying a Suitable Research Methodology. Review of Integrative Business and Economics Research, 7(1), 91–105.

Benqatla, M. S., Chikhaoui, D., & Bounabat, B. (2017). Actor network theory a framework of IT collaboration. 2017 International Conference on Wireless Networks and Mobile Communications (WINCOM), 1–6. https://doi.org/10.1109/WINCOM.2017.8238192

Birke, F. M., & Knierim, A. (2020). ICT for agriculture extension: actor network theory for understanding the establishment of agricultural knowledge centers in South Wollo, Ethiopia. Information Technology for Development, 26(3), 591–606. https://doi.org/10.1080/02681102.2020.1727826

Bourgeois, D., Smith, J. L., Wang, S., & Mortati, J. (2019). Information Systems for Business and Beyond (2019). Saylor Academy. https://opentextbook.site/exports/ISBB-2019.pdf

Boychenko, K., Teixeira, F. F., Kuzovkova, T., & Boychenko, I. (2020). Role of interactive space in social relationships through actor-network theory. 2020 International Conference on Engineering Management of Communication and Technology, EMCTECH 2020 - Proceedings, 1–6. https://doi.org/10.1109/EMCTECH49634.2020.9261525

Cresswell, K. (2019). Using Actor-Network Theory to Study Health Information Technology Interventions. Studies in Health Technology and Informatics, 263, 87–97. https://doi.org/10.3233/SHTI190114

Dedeke, A. N. (2017). Creating sustainable tourism ventures in protected areas: An actor-network theory analysis. Tourism Management, 61, 161–172. https://doi.org/10.1016/j.tourman.2017.02.006

Dempers, U. (2016). Social Protection in Namibia: A Civil Society Perspective (Issue September).

Eljaoued, W., Yahia, N. Ben, & Ben Saoud, N. B. (2020). A Qualitative-Quantitative Resilience Assessment Approach for Socio-technical Systems. Procedia Computer Science, 176, 2625–2634. https://doi.org/10.1016/j.procs.2020.09.305

Faris, S. (2019). Common Problems in Management Information Systems. Small Business. Chron. http://smallbusiness.chron.com/common-problems-management-information-systems-63376.html

Fisher, E., Attah, R., Barca, V., O'Brien, C., Brook, S., Holland, J., Kardan, A., Pavanello, S., & Pozarny, P. (2017). The Livelihood Impacts of Cash Transfers in Sub-Saharan Africa: Beneficiary Perspectives from Six Countries. World Development, 99, 299–319. https://doi.org/10.1016/j.worlddev.2017.05.020

Gebre-Mariam, M., & Fruijtier, E. (2018). Countering the "dam effect": the case for architecture and governance in developing country health information systems. Information Technology for Development, 24(2), 333–358. https://doi.org/10.1080/02681102.2016.1214808

Granlund, S., & Hochfeld, T. (2020). 'That Child Support Grant Gives Me Powers'–Exploring Social and Relational Aspects of Cash Transfers in South Africa in Times of Livelihood Change. Journal of Development Studies, 56(6), 1230–1244. https://doi.org/10.1080/00220388.2019.1650170

Gunawong, P., & Gao, P. (2017). Understanding e-government failure in the developing country context: a process-oriented study. Information Technology for Development, 23(1), 153–178. https://doi.org/10.1080/02681102.2016.1269713

Hamatwi, M. F. (2018). Implementation of an Integrated Traffic Fine Information System for Namibia. Namibia University of Science and Technology.

Kilani, M. Al, & Kobziev, V. (2016). An Overview of Research Methodology in Information System (IS). OALib, 03(11), 1–9. https://doi.org/10.4236/oalib.1103126

Koen, P. I. (2019). Improving operational efficiencies through integrated information systems [University of Johannesburg]. http://hdl.handle.net/102000/0002

Lukka, K., & Vinnari, E. (2017). Combining actor-network theory with interventionist research: present state and future potential. Accounting, Auditing and Accountability Journal, 30(3), 720–753. https://doi.org/10.1108/AAAJ-08-2015-2176

Luscombe, A., & Walby, K. (2017). Theorizing freedom of information: The live archive, obfuscation, and actor-network theory. Government Information Quarterly, 34(3), 379–387. https://doi.org/10.1016/j.giq.2017.09.003

Mackett, O. (2020). Social grants as a tool for poverty reduction in South Africa? A longitudinal analysis using the NIDS survey. African Studies Quarterly, 19(1), 41–64.

Mazhar, S., Wu, P., & Rosemann, M. (2019). Designing complex socio-technical process systems - the airport example. Business Process Management Journal, 25(5), 1101–1125.

Medvedeva, T. A., & Umpleby, S. A. (2022). Advancing Social System Development through Organizational Change. Cybernetics and Systems, 0(0), 1–13. https://doi.org/10.1080/01969722.2022.2093696

Moreby, N. (2020). Treeconomics has signed a memorandum of understanding with Dutch firm Pius Floris Boomverzorging. Arboricultural Journal, 42(2), 127–127. https://doi.org/10.1080/03071375.2020.1784665

Naki, A., Boucher, D., & Nzewi, O. (2018). A framework to mitigate water billing information systems integration challenges at municipalities. 2018 IST-Africa Week Conference, IST-Africa 2018, 1–11.

Nehemia-Maletzky, M., Iyamu, T., & Shaanika, I. (2018). The use of activity theory and actor network theory as lenses to underpin information systems studies. Journal of Systems and Information Technology, 20(2), 191–206. https://doi.org/10.1108/JSIT-10-2017-0098

Ngoepe, M., & Mello, V. (2021). Integration of records management systems at a South African water utility company. Global Knowledge, Memory and Communication, ahead-of-p(ahead-of-print). https://doi.org/10.1108/GKMC-08-2020-0125

Ryan, B., Golightly, D., Pickup, L., Reinartz, S., Atkinson, S., & Dadashi, N. (2021). Human functions in safety - developing a framework of goals, human functions and safety relevant activities for railway socio-technical systems. Safety Science, 140(April), 105279. https://doi.org/10.1016/j.ssci.2021.105279

Saranya, N., Brindha, R., Aishwariya, N., Kokila, R., Matheswaran, P., & Poongavi, P. (2021). Data Migration using ETL Workflow. 2021 7th International Conference on Advanced Computing and Communication Systems (ICACCS), 1661–1664. https://doi.org/10.1109/ICACCS51430.2021.9441840

Schade, K., La, J., & Pick, A. (2019). FINANCING SOCIAL PROTECTION IN NAMIBIA OECD DEVELOPMENT Financing Social Protection in Namibia By Klaus Schade, Justina La and Alexander Pick. Oecd, April. https://www.oecd.org/countries/namibia/SPSR_Namibia.pdf

Social Protection Policy 2021-2030, Pub. L. No. 4th/23.03.21/009 (2021).

Subiyakto, A. (2018). Assessing Information System Integration Using Combination of the Readiness and Success Models. Bulletin of Electrical Engineering and Informatics, 7(3), 400–410. https://doi.org/10.11591/eei.v7i3.1182

Transform. (2017). Management Information Systems and Approaches to Data Integration - Manual for a Leadership and Transformation Curriculum on Building and Managing Social Protection Floors in Africa. https://socialprotection.org/sites/default/files/publications_files/TRANSFORM Full Document - MIS.pdf

Tummons, J. (2021). Ontological Pluralism, Modes of Existence, and Actor-Network Theory: Upgrading Latour with Latour. Social Epistemology, 35(1), 1–11. https://doi.org/10.1080/02691728.2020.1774815

Usman, B. U., Ambursa, F. U., Egwan, J. O., & Tanimu, J. J. (2020). Virtual Machine Migration Techniques in Cloud Computing Environment: A Review of Load Balancing Algorithms. International Journal of Artificial & Computational Intelligence, 1(4).

Veterans Act (Act 2 of 2008), (2008).

Vickers, D. A., Moore, A., & Vickers, L. (2018). Performative narrative and actor-network theory – a study of a hotel in administration. International Journal of Organizational Analysis, 26(5), 972–983. https://doi.org/10.1108/IJOA-03-2018-1385

Wakhidah, N., & Erman, E. (2022). Examining environmental education content on Indonesian Islamic religious curriculum and its implementation in life. Cogent Education, 9(1). https://doi.org/10.1080/2331186X.2022.2034244

Wallace, G. L. (2021). Ethics in Technology: Heroes Assemble! 2021 International Conference on Computational Science and Computational Intelligence (CSCI), 1085–1090. https://doi.org/10.1109/CSCI54926.2021.00229

Wiman, R., Helenius, H.-M., & Masabane, P. (2016). Universal Social Protection: The Basic Social Grant for all older persons in Namibia. http://www.social-protection.org/gimi/gess/RessourcePDF.action?ressource.ressourceId=53959

Yu, H. Y., Ogbeyemi, A., Lin, W. J., He, J., Sun, W., & Zhang, W. J. (2021). A semantic model for enterprise application integration in the era of data explosion and globalisation. Enterprise Information Systems. https://doi.org/10.1080/17517575.2021.1989495

Yusuf, M., Adams, C., Dingley, K., Muntasa, A., Agustiono, W., & Oseni, K. O. (2020). Actor-Network Theory (ANT) for Indonesia e-Government implementation. 2020 6th Information Technology International Seminar (ITIS), 280–285. https://doi.org/10.1109/ITIS50118.2020.9321043

Zortea, T. C., Dickson, A., Gray, C. M., & O'Connor, R. C. (2019). Associations between experiences of disrupted attachments and suicidal thoughts and behaviours: An interpretative phenomenological analysis. Social Science and Medicine, 235, 112408. https://doi.org/10.1016/j.socscimed.2019.112408

AGENT-BASED MODEL FOR THE CONTROL AND MONITORING OF KPI IN A CURRICULUM: CIVIL ENGINEERING DEGREE IN INFORMATION TECHNOLOGY

Marcos Lévano[1] and Billy Peralta[2]

[1]*Departamento de Ingeniería Informática, Universidad Católica de Temuco, Av. Manuel Montt 56, 4780000, Chile*

[2]*Departamento de Ciencias de la Ingeniería, Universidad Andrés Bello , Antonio Varas 880, piso 6, Providencia, Región Metropolitana, Chile*

ABSTRACT

The present work proposes an intelligent agent model for the control and monitoring of KPI (key performance indicator) that impacts on the profile of professional exit. The intelligent agent allows to verify the performance of KPIs that impacts on professional performance in a civil engineering career in computing at UC Temuco, Chile. It can be seen that the development of KPIs obeys the integral control panel where the agent behaves. In this work we have worked with 8 KPI for the control and monitoring in a curriculum of undergraduate training.

KEYWORDS

Intelligent Agent, Control, KPI, Curriculum, Professionals

1. INTRODUCTION

Training by competencies, why? These are the questions asked by the team of academics of the Civil Engineering degree in Computer Science at the Catholic University of Temuco in Chile during the years 2008 - 2009 (Lévano et al, 2016; Herrera et al, 2009) with a focus on the need to answer challenges that lead to the training of professionals with tools in computing. It was enough a series of participatory works in cloisters, work meetings, attendance to congresses, consultations to the student medium, business environment, consultations to specialists and graduates, that allowed to build the paths to develop the formation of computing in the career of Computer Engineering. Responding like this, to the current challenges of the new millennium. Where it seeks to promote and intend the graduation profile, to respond to the demands and demands of the labor market with respect to computer technologies based on general and specific competences (Lévano and Herrera, 2012; Tobón, 2007; Lévano, 2020).

UCT Educational Model: In our university, we define competence as: "to know how to behave, using our own means and outside resources in order to solve real problems in an effectively and ethically responsible manner". We also distinguish two kinds of competences or skills, the generic competences, which are shared among all the programs and the specific competences which are directly related to the areas of study of each program. The educational model in our university (Lévano and Albornoz, 2016; Lévano, 2020), is based on five axes.

1.1 Problem

Decision makers have to adapt to the constant problems of dynamic complex context in the development of a University. Changes as for example: why the approval rate in such level, of such generation has fallen in this year?, Why the students do not manage to be titled opportunely ?, Why the students defect in the initial process ?, Why the do students drop out by the third year? How can we achieve quality according to the demands of the education ministry? How do we monitor that the learning outcomes are being achieved?, among others.

1.2 Proposal

Through this work we propose an intelligent agent model for the control and monitoring of KPI (key performance indicator) (Kovacevic and Reynoso, 2017; Porter, 1987; Norton and Kaplan, 2000; Medne, Lapina and Zeps, 2022; Leiber, 2022), in a curriculum for an undergraduate degree, such as the Civil Engineering degree in Computer Science at the Catholic University of Temuco (Lévano and Herrera, 2012; Lévano and Albornoz, 2016).

This work is composed of the following sections, the introduction that exposes the context, the problem, the proposal and the fundamentals of agents, section 2 describes the hypotheses proposed, section 3 describes the architecture of the agent-based model, the strategic map of agent behavior, KPI's integral scorecard that allow to measure the behavior of the agent, in section 4 the results are exposed, then the conclusions and references.

1.3 Agent-Based Model

Agent-based models (ABMs) are particularly suitable for studying. Complex adaptive systems (CAS) (Bankes, 2002a; Canessa, 2002). In general terms, a CAS is one where numerous elements, parties or agents. (homogeneous or not) interact in a non-linear way. The one with the other and with its environment, such that its properties can be modified as a result of these interactions (Canessa and Riolo, 2003). Traditional approaches to studying CAS (Canessa and Riolo, 2003) often limit our ability to understand the complete complexity of these systems, in part because the CAS characteristics (eg, dependent on the dynamic route) violate many of the presumptive statistics needed to use those approaches (ie, survey research, controlled experiments, game theory) (Bonabeau, 2002).

The distinctive feature of ABMs is that they are constructed "from the bottom up", defining the model in terms of entities and dynamics at the micro level, that is, at the level of individual actors and their interactions with each other and with the environment. (Bankes, 2002a; Canessa, 2002).

An ABM consists of one or more types of agents, and possibly a non-agent environment (for example, in a prey predator ABM, the environment could be the food of the prey, example: if the prey is sheep and predators are the wolves The environment could be the grass. Agent definitions include the specification of their capabilities to determine particular behaviors, as well as the decision-making norms and other mechanisms that agents use to choose their own behaviors.

2. HYPOTHESIS

In this section, we expose two hypotheses related to KPI (key performance indicator) (Kovacevic and Reynoso, 2017; Porter, 1987; Norton and Kaplan, 2000; Medne, Lapina and Zeps, 2022; Leiber, 2022), organizational climate and demand according to labor market competencies, seeing how it impacts the decisions of the university organization at lower levels.

2.1 Effect of Organizational Climate on the KPI

The KPIs (Kovacevic and Reynoso, 2017; Porter, 1987; Norton and Kaplan, 2000; Medne, Lapina and Zeps, 2022; Leiber, 2022) are the key business indicators that help to account for the efficiency and productivity of the actions, thus responding to the tasks planned in the set of projects designed to achieve the objectives based on goals and the realization of the strategic plan (Norton and Kaplan, 2000).

Regarding the organizational climate we can specify it as an organizational climate (CO) i with dimension N, where we define that there is a greater increase in CO if the variability is lower, otherwise the CO degree will be smaller and the variability is greater or distant. Thus, we can observe how the KPI is disturbed in its performance. Therefore we can summarize the following hypothesis:

H1: The higher the organizational climate, the greater the wealth of KPI performance.

2.2 Effect of Competency Demands on the Labor Market in the KPI

The demand for requirements in skills or abilities come from the labor market, leading to unique attributes that are grouped in soft skills, hard competition or semi-hard competitions. The demand obeys to the different areas of computing in technical and scientific knowledge.

The current behavior in the case of Chile, the demand for programmers at different levels with focus on the line of software development. There is also the line of information and communication technologies very highly demanded. We can specify that the demand of labor market competences (ECML) and with dimension N, where we define that there is a higher degree of ECML, if the variability is lower and in another case the ECML degree will be lower and the variability is greater or distant.

In this way, a KPI achieves its expected value E(KPI), if the ECML is of lesser degree and remains in time. On the other hand, a KPI does not achieve its expected value E(KPI), if the ECML is of a higher degree and does not remain in time.

H2: Greater demand for skills in the labor market, the lower the wealth of the KPI's performance.

3. INTELLIGENT AGENT DIAGRAM

This section describes the conceptual framework and mechanisms as a physical problem, and the hypotheses are described in sections 1 and 2 (Figure 1).

The representation of our organizational system, which is a university educational entity, is treated as a conceptual scheme that connects the business perspectives (such as customer, financial, process, growth, and innovation) with a focus on quality in teaching and learning.

The system can be treated as a case of data clustering in an n-dimensional space (Lévano and Nowak, 2009). The objective is to find optimal clusters that represent a strong interaction between the effective communication (*ce*) of the agents, and for this there are x_i agents (data) and y_j points called nodes. Clusters are sought by minimizing the quadratic distance between data and nodes, which will be called energy,

$$E_{ij} = \frac{1}{2} | x_i - y_j |^2$$

The total energy of the system will be given by,

$$E = \sum_i \sum_j P_{ij} E_{ij}$$

Where P_{ij} is an unknown probability of finding a given data point i with node j at position y. How do we find the node positions and the probability that minimizes the energy E? This is solved by putting the system in a thermal reservoir at different temperatures. This contact maximizes for a given temperature the entropy or minimizes the Helmholtz free energy (Nowak and Haeussler, 2013; Lévano and Nowak, 2009).

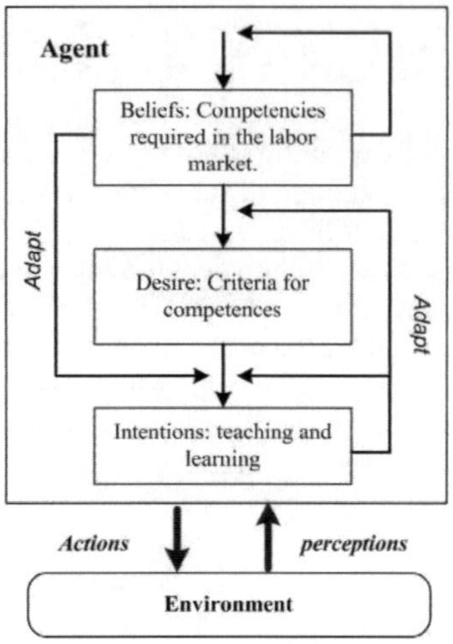

Figure 1. Agent-based model schema

3.1 Strategic Map of the Career Where the Agent Behaves

Strategic focus: Academic excellence in the training of computer professionals, with an identity in the assessment and respect for diversity and social responsibility.
Therefore, based on the strategic career map, the following perspectives are formulated, reflecting the agent's performance.

Perspective of client (PC): in this perspective the objectives are to strengthen the extension and link with other public and private institutions (C1). Improve the student's bond (C2).
KPI performance measures are:

a) KPI 1: Impact activities related to the career N° activities with impact evaluation in the middle. # (unit of measurement)
b) KPI 2: Institutional positioning of the career. Percentage of participation of subjects related to computing. % (unit of measurement)

Financial perspective (FP): In this perspective, the objectives are, Manage the resources to support the planned activities, allowing sustainability (F1).

a) KPI 3: Retention rate (A/B)*100, A= number of students admitted in the year they enrolled, B= number of students admitted in the year by admission cutoff. % (unit of measurement)
b) KPI 4: Timely Graduation Rate (Number of students who graduated in 5 or 6 years) / (Total number of admissions court), % (unit of measurement)

Process perspective (PP): in this perspective the objectives are to strengthen the curricular program for student development (P1).

a) KPI 5: Support workshops for critical courses Cumulative Nominal. # (unit of measure)
b) KPI 6: Annual percentage of wellness service coverage. (A/B)*100, A= wellness services coverage B= Wellness service. % (unit of measurement)

Perspective of learning and growth (PA): in this perspective the objectives are, To consolidate the formation of the educational development in the undergraduate (A1).

a) KPI 7: percentage of self-evaluations applied in the career to teachers. (A / B) * 100, A = N° of self evaluations carried out, B = Number of teachers evaluated planned. % (unit of measurement)
b) KPI 8: Accreditation of the race A = A + X, A = number of successful years of accreditation in the race X = No of years of accreditation. # (unit of measurement)

4. DISCUSSION AND RESULTS

To check the behavior of the agent, a descriptive statistical study of qualitative aspects was carried out. For the discussion of H1 hypothesis, the following sample of 24 graduates from a population of 82 professionals graduated at the national level, Observation Year 2014, was designed. Among the questions that were consulted were:

- Did the degree from which he graduated and the Catholic University of Temuco have a good placement policy and graduates? What he gave as a result: that 14% strongly disagree, 29% said they disagreed, 43% agreed, and 14% strongly disagreed.
- There an efficient process of the university or career to track graduates and graduates? What resulted was that 27% strongly disagreed, 32% said they disagreed, 27% said they agreed, and 14% strongly disagreed.
- Does the university currently offer alternatives for improving or updating its graduates and graduates? What resulted was that 26% strongly disagree, 36% said they disagreed, 32% said they agreed, and 9% strongly disagreed.

It can be observed from the race that the tools taught during the race are well valued and that they are adapted to face the labor field. The weakness is in improving the process of monitoring the graduate. In the part A, regarding the performance of KPIs against H1 hypothesis, we can have evidence of the behavior of the agent according to the architecture (Figure 1).

4.1 Behavior of the Agent Against Hypothesis H1

Case 1: The higher the organizational climate, the greater the wealth of the KPI performance, if only when the time is shorter, where CO is higher and the variance is lower, then E (KPI) has good performance, but because of the short time the KPI must change, which implies that the agent must adapt.

Case 2: The greater the organizational climate, the greater the wealth of the performance of the KPI, if only when the time is less, where CO is lower and the variance is greater then the E (KPI) does not perform well.

Case 3: The greater the organizational climate, the greater the wealth of the performance of the KPI, if only if, when the time is greater, where CO is greater and the variance is lower then the E (KPI) has good performance.

Case 4: The higher the organizational climate, the greater the wealth of the KPI performance, if only when the time is longer, where CO is lower and the variance is greater then the E (KPI) has a regular performance.

This shows that the KPI indicators that the agent model has are key to the performance of teaching in the career, so much so that it demonstrates the effectiveness and productivity of the actions carried out, thus responding to the tasks planned in the set of projects designed to achieve the objectives based on the goals and improvement plan. For this agent, they show that with a lower variance, the organizational climate is higher or indicates a good performance of the KPIs (part A). In other cases there is no good performance or performance is not achieved, or there is a good performance but short durability, which leads to generate new reformulations of KPI, resulting in economic losses and redesigns in operational activities in an organization.

Regarding the hypothesis H2, to check the behavior of the agent, a descriptive statistical study of qualitative aspects was carried out. For the discussion of hypothesis H2, the following sample of 16 employers from a population of 37 employers at national level was designed, the year of observation was 2014. Among the questions that were consulted were respects in criteria referring to the specific and general competences of the career of civil engineering in computer science, such questions were:

- You. Do you think that the abilities related to applying engineering sciences are observable and demonstrate that they apply deductive logical reasoning to address problems of technological systems? What he gave as a result: that 7% said regular, and 93% said good.
- You. Do you believe that the capabilities related to modeling and applying compilation science procedures are observable and demonstrate that they apply computer science procedures to address problems of technological systems in information technologies and software development? What he gave as a result: that 13% said regular, and 83% said good.
- You. Do you believe that the capabilities related to the management of information technologies are observable and are demonstrated in that it manages systems that involve the use of hardware and software in an organization for the automation of management systems and production processes? What he gave as a result: that 6% said regular, 6% said bad, and 88% said good.
- You. Do you think the capabilities related to software development are observable and are shown in developing software solutions appropriate to one or more application domains using an engineering approach? What he gave as a result: that 13% said regular, and 87% said good.
- You. Do you believe that the capacities related to the assessment and respect for diversity are concerned with the development of the other in its human dimension, understanding that social, religious, gender, cultural and capacity differences enrich coexistence? What he gave as a result: that 25% indicates regular, and 75% indicates good.
- You. Do you believe that the capacities related to ethical action, is demonstrated ethical sense based on principles, values of justice, common good and the absolute dignity of the human person that translates into attitudes and actions at the service of society? What he gave as a result: that 13% indicates bad, 25% indicates regular, and 63% indicates good.

It can be observed that the general and specific competences (Lévano and Herrera, 2012) taught during the career are well valued, and they are adapted to face the labor field. The weakness lies in improving the process of monitoring the behavior of the labor market according to the economy of the country and the world. In the part B, regarding the performance of the KPIs versus the H2 hypothesis, we can have evidence of the behavior of the agent according to the architecture (figure 1).

4.2 Behavior of the Agent Against Hypothesis H2

Case 1: Greater demand for skills in the labor market, the lower the wealth of the performance KPI, if and only if, the time is constant, where labor market competition demand (ECML) is lower and the variance is lower then the E(KPI) presents good performance.

Case 2: Greater demand for labor market skills, less wealth of the performance of the KPI. If and only if, the time is constant, where labor market competition (ECML) is lower and the variance is higher, then the E(KPI) presents good performance.

Case 3: Greater demand for skills in the labor market, less wealth is the performance of the KPI., If and only if, the time changes, where demand labor market competition (ECML) is higher and the variance is lower, then the E(KPI) does not achieve performance.

Case 4: Greater demand for skills in the labor market, less wealth will be the performance of the KPI. If and only if, the time changes, where demand labor market competition (ECML) is higher and the variance is higher, then the E(KPI) does not achieve performance.

5. CONCLUSIONS

The training of professionals in a training model by competences leads to generate a series of KPI as part of the teaching and learning process in order to validate the specific and general competences in training.

We believe that the analyzes made possible by an ABM can provide a guide for empirical research efforts and to support hypotheses about the relationships between variables associated with KPI, which can then be evaluated using other research methods.

We can also conclude that when it is not possible to obtain the wealth of the KPI in its expected value, this leads to an instability in the system, which causes losing focus and generating downtime and economic losses.

REFERENCES

______(2008). Generic competences for the integral formation of socially responsible citizens. Chile, Temuco: Universidad Católica de Temuco.

Bankes, S.C. (2002a). Agent Based Modeling: A revolution. PNAS 99(3): 7199–7200.

Bonabeau, E. (2002). Agent Based Modeling: Methods and techniques for simulating human systems, PANAS 99(3): 7280–7287.

Canessa, E. (2002). Computer Mediated Communication and Organizational Culture: A survey based study and agent based simulation model, Ph.D. Thesis, Rackham Graduate School, University of Michigan.

Canessa, E. and Riolo, R.L. (2003). The Effect of Organizational Communication Media on Organizational Culture and Performance: An agent based simulation model, Computational and Mathematical Organization Theory 9(2): 147–176.

David Norton, Robert Kaplan. El cuadro de mando integral: The balanced scorecard. Editor Gestión 2000. Harvard Business Review.

H. Nowak, P. Haeussler, Energy–entropy dispersion relation in DNA sequences, Physica A: Statistical Mechanics and its Applications, Volume 392, Issue 19, 2013, Pages 4688-4700, ISSN 0378-4371, https://doi.org/10.1016/j.physa.2013.06.018.

Herrera, O. Lévano, M., Mellado, A., Schindler, M., Donoso, G., and Contreras, G. (2009). Profile of the Civil Engineering Degree in Computer Science. UCT, Temuco: School of Computer Engineering

Kovacevic A. y Reynoso, A. (2017). El diamante de la Excelencia Organizacional: una propuesta para mejorar la implementación de la estrategia. M´exico, D.F.: Cengage Learning Editores S.A.

Leiber, T. (2022). Justifying, contextualising and operationalising performance indicators of learning and teaching: the role of theories and practice of learning and teaching. Quality in Higher Education, 28(1), 120-140.

Lévano, M. and Albornoz, A. (2016): Findings in professional training: computer engineering Science program, UCTemuco. 12th International CDIO Conference. CDIO, Turku, pp. 528-537.

Lévano, M. and Herrera, O. (2012). Validation Strategies of Competences in a Computer Science Curriculum. In IEEE (Ed.), 31st International Conference of the Chilean Computer Science Society (pp. 9–11). Valparaso: Pontificia Universidad Cat´olica de Valparaíso.

Lévano, M., Herrera, O., Mellado, A., Rojas, J., Contreras, G., Peralta, B., and Caro, L. (2016). Profile of the Civil Engineering Degree in Computer Science. Chile, Temuco: School of Computer Engineering UCTemuco.

Lévano, M., Nowak, H. (2009). New Aspects of the Elastic Net Algorithm for Cluster Analysis. In: Palmer-Brown, D., Draganova, C., Pimenidis, E., Mouratidis, H. (eds) Engineering Applications of Neural Networks. EANN 2009. Communications in Computer and Information Science, vol 43. Springer, Berlin, Heidelberg. https://doi.org/10.1007/978-3-642-03969-0_26

M. A. Levano, "Customization of self-regulation in the use of ICT for the learning process with continuous improvement. Catholic University of Temuco, Chile," 2020 11th International Conference on Information, Intelligence, Systems and Applications (IISA, 2020, pp. 1-7, doi: 10.1109/IISA50023.2020.9284344.

M. A. Lévano, "Effects of Cycle Evaluation on Peer Learning: Competency Assessment, Case Study, Catholic University of Temuco, Chile," 2020 11th International Conference on Information, Intelligence, Systems and Applications IISA, 2020, pp. 1-6, doi: 10.1109/IISA50023.2020.9284369.

Medne, A., Lapina, I., & Zeps, A. (2022). Challenges of Uncertainty in Sustainable Strategy Development: Reconsidering the Key Performance Indicators. Sustainability, 14(2), 761.

Porter, Michael, (1987) Ventaja Competitiva. Creación y sostenimiento de un desempeño superior, México: Editorial Compañía Editorial Continental 1982, reimpresión 2005.

Tobón, S. (2007). Metodología sistémica de diseño curricular por competencias. Bogota: Grupo cife.ws. UCT. (Ed.).

OMNICHANNEL ADOPTION IN HEALTH INFORMATION SYSTEMS FOR PATIENT FOLLOW-UP

Ailton Moreira and Manuel Filipe Santos
ALGORITMI Research Centre / LASI
Azurém Campus, University of Minho, Guimarães, Portugal

ABSTRACT

The evolution of technology and health information systems has allowed patients in home-based care to receive continuous medical monitoring without the necessity to be in-person at the care unit. This evolution brings to discussion many challenges that the care provider faces and must overcome, but on the other side, it brings a lot of benefits to them both patients, health professionals, care providers and to the society in general. Omnichannel strategy in healthcare services is in its early adoption, but it has the potential to overcome many burdens that care providers are facing currently regards remote patient follow-up. This article aims to present the adoption of omnichannel strategy in health information systems regarding remote patient follow-up in home-based care. The omnichannel strategy has the potential to increase the organization's footprint in society, as this type of interaction aims to fill the gap between organizations and their peers.

KEYWORDS

Omnichannel in Healthcare, Remote Monitoring, Patient Follow-Up, Personalized Care Services, Health Information Systems

1. INTRODUCTION

Lately, healthcare institutions have increasingly focused on an omnichannel interaction model in the various services they provide to their patients. Thus, this adoption has brought positive gains for both the healthcare institutions that implemented it, as well as for the patient who enjoys the new healthcare service without having to be in-person at the care unit to receive it (Burri, 2013). The omnichannel strategy adoption has a huge potential in healthcare services, as it would integrate different channels with different services provided to patients and enables the interaction among patients and health professionals more seamlessly (Annis et al., 2020; Moreira et al., 2020). Furthermore, it can automate the collection process and patient clinical data sharing with health professionals remotely as mentioned previously, without the physical presence of the patient at the care unit. With these processes, the data collected can be sent through different channels to health professionals according to their preferences (Cruz et al., 2014; Oleshchuk and Fensli, 2011).

The remote patient follow-up is a practice that has been increasingly adopted in healthcare, especially in patients with implanted pacemakers and implantable cardioverter defibrillators (ICDs) (Varma et al., 2021; Varma and Ricci, 2013) at home-based care. Although this practice has been practiced for some time, it still has many limitations both at a technological and human level, especially in terms of patient compliance (Abdolkhani et al., 2019). Until now all patient health monitoring was carried through a single channel. Generally, patients use a body sensor that retrieves the data and shares it with health professionals and care providers (Lupu et al., 2009). The omnichannel interaction intends to present a solution where there is not only one channel of interaction, but multiple channels of interaction between patients and health professionals, as was the case until now. This approach specifies the existence of several interaction channels all interconnected with each other, in which patients can choose any of these channels to interact with health professionals (Moreira and Santos, 2020). This is a very recent approach, so more studies are still needed to better understand the impact it has on both patients and healthcare professionals (Moreira et al., 2021).

Due to the workload that health professionals have daily, the adoption of an omnichannel strategy in health information systems to follow-up patients in home-based care can have a significant role to play in this situation. The omnichannel strategy has the potential to solve many challenges that health professionals face regarding manual patient monitoring. It will release these health professionals from these manual and exhausting tasks regarding patient monitoring. With the patient clinical data collected from the body sensors, it can be loaded and uploaded through an interaction channel to the care provider where health professionals will analyze the gathered data and make their clinical decision. Thus, the research question identified in this article is: **to what extent can the adoption of an omnichannel interaction strategy for remote patient follow-up translate into more effective and efficient communication between patients and healthcare professionals?**

With the research question identified, this article aims to assess the possibility of the existence and implementation of omnichannel interaction solutions for remote patient follow-up and to study the impact that it may have on the communication process between the different actors.

2. BACKGROUND

Omnichannel interaction is an evolution of multichannel interaction. Currently, omnichannel interaction has already been applied in several areas mainly in retail industry, marketing, and e-commerce. The fast pace of advancement of technologies and information systems has continuously allowed the appearance of new and innovative models and solutions for omnichannel interaction in healthcare services (Moreira et al., 2020; Moreira and Santos, 2020). An interesting model of multichannel interaction was proposed by Ailton M. (2020) which is based on three different tiers. These tiers are the patient tier, coordination tier, and care provider tier. Each of the tier has a set of actors/roles to play on the overall model proposed (Moreira et al., 2020). Many retail organizations have been developing and improving their omnichannel interaction models to offer a seamless user experience to their customers across all interaction channels without interruption. Besides, several concepts and techniques were adopted from the retail organization as they shown some maturity regarding the implementation and interaction with customers through multiple channels of interaction continuously.

Many authors have presented several solutions to try to overcome the lack of efficiency in the interaction between patients and health professionals, but the solutions that have been proposed are not easy to implement, and most of the time they didn't have the result that was expected, in a way to make these solutions unfeasible (Archip et al., 2016; Prabhakar and Rajaguru, 2017; Varma et al., 2021). On the other hand, the process of implementing the omnichannel interaction strategy in the different health services has been growing at a very fast pace and with visible results both for the hospitals that implemented this strategy as well as for the patients who started to take advantage of this strategy in their interactions with health professionals. Considering the impact that the multichannel interaction has demonstrated in the healthcare services where they were applied, the same could be perfectly applied in the interaction between health professionals and patients who are in home-based care, to assess the impact that this strategy has in the process of interaction between them.

3. OMNICHANNEL PATIENT FOLLOW-UP

Several authors present in their article different solutions for remote patient monitoring, which are exclusively based on wearable devices or in-body implantable devices that collect clinical data from patients autonomously and automatically and share this data with health professionals (Cruz et al., 2014; Oleshchuk and Fensli, 2011). This practice brought several benefits as it made it possible to monitor patients remotely without having to physically be in hospital units. On the other hand, several limitations that this practice presents were also identified, namely in terms of technology infrastructure and issues related to privacy and security of patients' clinical data.

Data collected through patient remote follow-up automatically by body sensors can be sent over multiple channels of interaction on a scheduled basis from the patient's home to health professionals, thus avoiding the unnecessary in-person visit to the care provider. This is very convenient both for patients and health professionals that are monitoring these patients. Patient follow-up in home-based care has a lot of challenges that care providers that decided to implement it still need to overcome yet. Besides, it has a huge benefit to care providers, health professionals, and patients. Table 1 presents the main challenges and benefits identified regarding remote patient follow-up in home-based care (Abdolkhani et al., 2019; Anwar et al., 2015; Health Services Research, 2011; Hjelm, 2005; Mohammadzadeh and Safdari, 2014; Neslin et al., 2006; Stone et al., 2002; Ventola, 2014).

Table 1. Challenges and Benefits of Remote Patient Follow-up

Challenges	Benefits
Channels integration	Reduction of workload of health practitioners
Data standardization and synchronization across different channels	Better quality of data across multiple channels
Data sharing across multiple interaction channel	Autonomous patient clinical data recording
Patients' device battery life	Improve communication among patients and care practitioners
Legacy systems integration in an omnichannel services	Continuous patient health monitoring without in-person appointment
Ethical issues regarding data access	Timely decision making by health practitioners based on data gathered

4. OMNICHANNEL PROCESS

The introduction of an omnichannel process in health information system for home-based care can have a significant impact on improving the way that health practitioners interact with patients, by integrating multiple channels of interaction with healthcare systems that are collecting patient clinical data. But, before its implementation care provider must address each of the steps of the omnichannel process first. Following the concepts of the retail industry, in the healthcare field, the same steps can be applied. Figure 1 shows the omnichannel process presented and its cycle process.

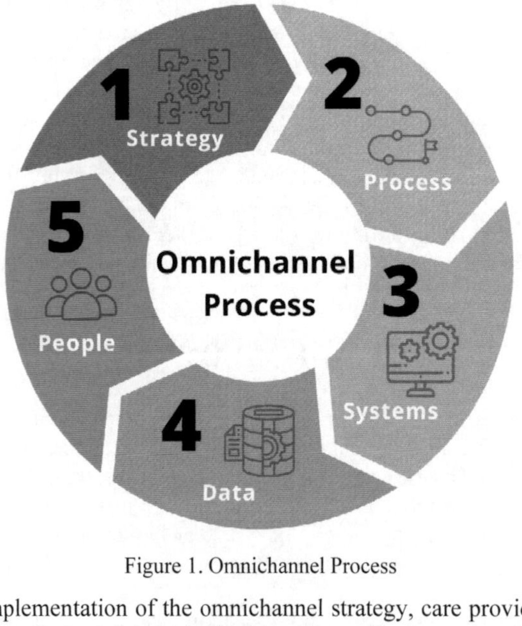

Figure 1. Omnichannel Process

To have a successful implementation of the omnichannel strategy, care providers should study and learn from the omnichannel process that retail industry had implemented. An explanation of each step is provided below (Mike, 2021; Valos, 2009; Vincle, 2019):

- **Strategy** – are the goals and objectives that care providers aim to achieve with omnichannel implementation. The challenges also should be considered when defining the omnichannel strategy.
- **Process** – are all the procedures and workflow regarding the adoption of the omnichannel strategy. It must be designed to be adequately and proactive instead of reactive.
- **Systems** – are all the information and technology necessary to enable to omnichannel strategy to happen. The systems can make or break the care provider adoption successful or unsuccessful.
- **Data** - are all the clinical data exchanged among different channels and healthcare systems.
- **People** – are all the actors that somehow will belong to the interaction process, these actors may include patients and their relatives, nurses, physicians, technicians, administrative staff, etc.

Regarding the patient remote follow-up in home-based care, the care provider should define the right strategy with the right process and systems to be able to get clinical data from patients and share it with health professionals. Successful implementation of the omnichannel strategy in healthcare service still has a long way to go, but the present omnichannel process aims to help care providers adopt the omnichannel strategy in their activities and make these processes less painful. The following section will present a brief discussion regarding the omnichannel adoption in health information system for remote patient follow-up.

5. DISCUSSION

Patients in home-based care need continuous medical follow-up from caregivers. Omnichannel strategy can play an important role in the interaction between patients in home-based care and health professionals, by automatizing the process of collecting clinical data and sending it to care providers which will be processed and presented to a health professional. Thus, this will reduce the workload from health professionals who isn't needed to manually contact the patient to collect patient clinical data, or the patient moves the caregiver for health professionals to collect the data. The omnichannel adoption in healthcare will give a huge relief for health professionals from some repetitive tasks and free up the patient from the need to be physically at care provider to health professionals collect their clinical data.

Besides, patients can use any of the different channels available to them to interact continuously with health professionals. Through the data exchange across omnichannel interaction, it will be processed before it is presented to health professionals. Thus, with the omnichannel strategy, the caregiver will be present with useful information that can help them in their decision-making process. The Figure 2, presents an illustration of omnichannel strategy adoption in healthcare services for remote patient follow-up.

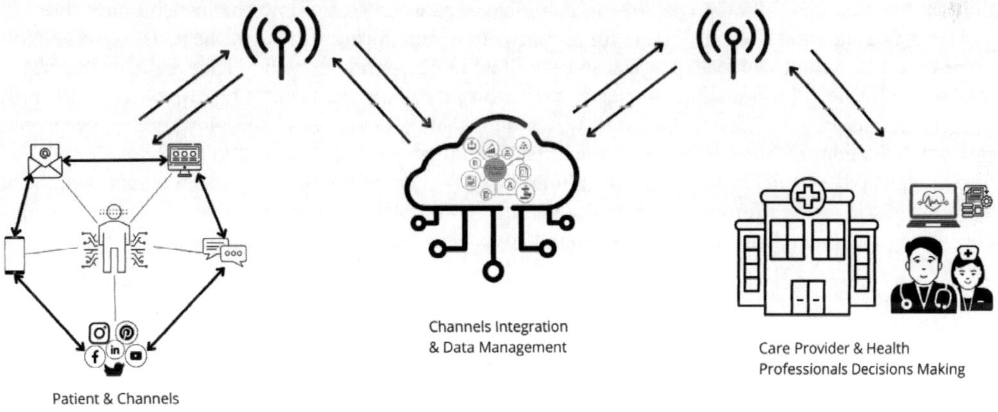

Figure 2. Omnichannel Interaction in Remote Patient Follow-up

The omnichannel strategy enables patient monitoring across multiple interaction channels (see Figure 2) and gives the care professionals more data and options to analyze the collected data and consequently improve the timing that they can take their clinical decision.

A SWOT analysis regarding the adoption of omnichannel interaction in healthcare services for remote patient follow-up is presented below (Caldwell, 2021; Cunha et al., 2020; Mohammadzadeh and Safdari, 2014; Rangaswamy and Bruggen, 2005; Ventola, 2014; Wan et al., 2018).

Table 2. SWOT Analysis of Omnichannel strategy for remote patient follow-up

Strengths	**Weaknesses**
Patient clinical data available across multiple channels of interaction	Lack and poor of preparation of health professionals to use new technologies to interact with patients in home-based care
Reduce health professional's workload and tasks	Poor implementation of omnichannel strategy
Increase the quality-of-care services provided to patients in home-based care	Data inconsistence across channel can be a huge problem and can make health professionals decision-making even harder
Opportunities	**Threats**
Improve interaction among patient and health practitioners	Law and regulation regard patient clinical data
Care practitioners can make timely decision-making based on data available in different channels of interaction	Data security and privacy
Improve the quality of work of health professionals	Third-party entities

Following the analysis provided in Table 2 combined with Figure 2, it seems plausible to affirm that the omnichannel strategy can be a viable solution in remote patient follow-up. The adoption of an omnichannel strategy in health information systems for remote patient follow-up can remove many burdens that health professionals face daily and reduce their workload and tasks regarding patient clinical data collection and interaction. Alongside, this strategy brings a new opportunity to health professionals concerning the way that they can monitor and follow-up patients in home-based care across multiple channels of interaction.

Thus, this adoption of omnichannel for remote patient monitoring will allow the patients to be involved and more enrolled in the treatments process and they feel more confident as they have a direct channel to use to interact with a health professional to clarify their worries without the need to be in-person at care provider to interact with a health professional. Currently, the omnichannel strategy in health information systems still is in the early adoption in care services, but it is already demonstrated its potential to care provider who adopts it. The impact and potential of this strategy in home-based care monitoring can be even bigger with the adoption of it, but it will require further research and maturity of omnichannel solutions to take better advantage of it concerning the interaction and communication between patients and health practitioners.

5.1 Results

This paper presents a more theoretical concept of omnichannel interaction in healthcare services, but there are some previous studies already carried out with the implication of multichannel interaction in healthcare services. Omnichannel interaction services are an evolution of multichannel interaction services that aims to combine all available channels of interaction in a single touchpoint to present to its users. To support the work presented in this paper, several studies are referred to in this paper such as A Conceptual Model for Multichannel Interaction in Healthcare Services, and Health Professionals' Decision-Making Based on Multichannel Interaction Services which are already published and available online. Also, some preliminary studies regarding omnichannel interactions in healthcare services are highly encouraging since they open a brand-new window for patient involvement with health professionals in healthcare services that are provided to them. Additionally, this kind of interaction has a big impact on the activity of health professionals as well as resource allocation and management in health institutions, which is a very flattering indication of the impact of omnichannel approach in health information systems.

6. CONCLUSION

The concepts of omnichannel interaction for health information systems in home-based care for remote patient follow-up presented in this article are a theoretical study of how the omnichannel strategy can be used and impact remote patient follow-up. Besides, the concepts introduced here are still in their very early stage of development and adoption which requires more studies to assess the different topics proposed and discuss in this article to evaluate the impact of omnichannel interaction health information systems in home-based care with the more practical use case. As stated before, the adoption of the omnichannel strategy in home-based care still has a very long way ahead that must be addressed both by researchers and care providers who decide to adopt it. On the other hand, this adoption will bring to discussion more issues that care providers still need to overcome such as data protection and privacy of patients in home-based care, among many other ethical issues related to omnichannel interaction in general and in healthcare field. As the proposed research question to this article, it aimed to study the viability of omnichannel strategy adoption in health information systems for home-based care and how this approach can contribute to a better and more effective interaction between the different actors involved and to the society. So far, was possible to address and accomplished the proposed research questions, but more studies should be carried out with more practical use cases to address the presented practice and take more lessons from omnichannel in home-based care.

ACKNOWLEDGEMENT

The work has been supported by FCT – Fundação para a Ciência e Tecnologia within the Project Scope: UID/CEC/00319/2020.

REFERENCES

Abdolkhani, R., Gray, K., Borda, A., DeSouza, R., 2019. Patient-generated health data management and quality challenges in remote patient monitoring. JAMIA Open 2, 471–478. https://doi.org/10.1093/JAMIAOPEN/OOZ036

Annis, T., Pleasants, S., Hultman, G., Lindemann, E., Thompson, J.A., Billecke, S., Badlani, S., Melton, G.B., 2020. Rapid implementation of a COVID-19 remote patient monitoring program. Journal of the American Medical Informatics Association 1326–1330. https://doi.org/10.1093/jamia/ocaa097

Anwar, M., Joshi, J., Tan, J., 2015. Anytime, anywhere access to secure, privacy-aware healthcare services: Issues, approaches and challenges. Health Policy Technol. https://doi.org/10.1016/j.hlpt.2015.08.007

Archip, A., Botezatu, N., Şerban, E., Herghelegiu, P.C., ZalĂ, A., 2016. An IoT based system for remote patient monitoring. Proceedings of the 2016 17th International Carpathian Control Conference, ICCC 2016 1–6. https://doi.org/10.1109/CARPATHIANCC.2016.7501056

Burri, H., 2013. Remote follow-up and continuous remote monitoring, distinguished. Europace 15. https://doi.org/10.1093/europace/eut071

Caldwell, A., 2021. What Is Omnichannel? Benefits and Strategies [WWW Document]. URL https://www.netsuite.com/portal/resource/articles/ecommerce/omnichannel.shtml

Cruz, J., Brooks, D., Marques, A., 2014. Home telemonitoring in COPD: A systematic review of methodologies and patients' adherence. Int J Med Inform 83, 249–263. https://doi.org/10.1016/J.IJMEDINF.2014.01.008

Cunha, C., Gomes, J.P., Fernandes, J., Morais, E.P., 2020. Building smart rural regions: challenges and opportunities. Advances in Intelligent Systems and Computing 1161, 579–589. https://doi.org/10.1007/978-3-030-45697-9

Health Services Research, 2011. Health services research: helping tackle Europe's health care challenges.

Hjelm, N.M., 2005. Benefits and drawbacks of telemedicine. J Telemed Telecare 11, 60–70. https://doi.org/10.1258/1357633053499886

Lupu, R.G., Stan, A., Ungureanu, F., 2009. Patient monitoring: Wearable device for patient monitoring. Lecture Notes in Electrical Engineering 39 LNEE, 659–668. https://doi.org/10.1007/978-90-481-2311-7_56

Mike, P., 2021. Building an Omnichannel Healthcare Strategy.

Mohammadzadeh, N., Safdari, R., 2014. Patient monitoring in mobile health: Opportunities and challenges. Acta Informatica Medica. https://doi.org/10.5455/aim.2014.22.263-267

Moreira, A., Guimarães, T., Santos, M.F., 2020. A conceptual model for multichannel interaction in healthcare services, in: Procedia Computer Science. Elsevier B.V., pp. 534–539. https://doi.org/10.1016/j.procs.2020.10.074

Moreira, A., Miranda, R., Santos, M.F., 2021. Health Professional's Decision-Making Based on Multichannel Interaction Services. Procedia Comput Sci 184, 899–904. https://doi.org/10.1016/J.PROCS.2021.03.112

Moreira, A., Santos, M.F., 2020. Multichannel Interaction for Healthcare Intelligent Decision Support, in: Procedia Computer Science. https://doi.org/10.1016/j.procs.2020.03.074

Neslin, S.A., Grewal, D., Leghorn, R., Shankar, V., Teerling, M.L., Thomas, J.S., Verhoef, P.C., 2006. Challenges and opportunities in multichannel customer management. J Serv Res. https://doi.org/10.1177/1094670506293559

Oleshchuk, V., Fensli, R., 2011. Remote Patient Monitoring Within a Future 5G Infrastructure. Wireless Pers Commun 57, 431–439. https://doi.org/10.1007/s11277-010-0078-5

Prabhakar, S.K., Rajaguru, H., 2017. Development of Patient Remote Monitoring System for Epilepsy Classification. IFMBE Proc 61, 80–87. https://doi.org/10.1007/978-981-10-4220-1_16

Rangaswamy, A., Bruggen, G.H. van, 2005. Opportunities and challenges in multichannel marketing: An introduction to the special issue. Journal of Interactive Marketing 19, 5–11. https://doi.org/10.1002/dir.20037

Stone, M., Hobbs, M., Khaleeli, M., 2002. Multichannel customer management: The benefits and challenges. Journal of Database Marketing & Customer Strategy Management 10, 39–52. https://doi.org/10.1057/palgrave.jdm.3240093

Valos, M.J., 2009. Structure, people and process challenges of multichannel marketing: Insights from marketers. Journal of Database Marketing and Customer Strategy Management 16, 197–206. https://doi.org/10.1057/dbm.2009.21

Varma, N., Love, C.J., Michalski, J., Epstein, A.E., 2021. Alert-Based ICD Follow-Up: A Model of Digitally Driven Remote Patient Monitoring. JACC Clin Electrophysiol 7, 976–987. https://doi.org/10.1016/J.JACEP.2021.01.008

Varma, N., Ricci, R. pietro, 2013. Telemedicine and cardiac implants: What is the benefit? Eur Heart J 34, 1885–1893. https://doi.org/10.1093/EURHEARTJ/EHS388

Ventola, C.L., 2014. Mobile devices and apps for health care professionals: uses and benefits. P T 39, 356–64.

Vincle, 2019. 7 advantages of an omnichannel strategy | Vincle.

Wan, J., Gu, X., Chen, L., Wang, J., 2018. Internet of Things for Ambient Assisted Living: Challenges and Future Opportunities, in: Proceedings - 2017 International Conference on Cyber-Enabled Distributed Computing and Knowledge Discovery, CyberC 2017. https://doi.org/10.1109/CyberC.2017.83

CHALLENGES FACED IN TRANSITIONING FROM TRADITIONAL BUSINESS ANALYSIS TO AGILE BUSINESS ANALYSIS: AN ACTOR-NETWORK PERSPECTIVE

Augustine Iyamu and Lisa F. Seymour
Department of Information Systems,
University of Cape Town,
Cape Town, South Africa

ABSTRACT

There seems to be a lack of understanding of organisations' challenges when transitioning to agile business analysis, which has prohibitive effects in the process. This paper therefore provides clarifications by describing the challenges faced during the transition from traditional business analysis to agile business analysis. As a way of dealing with this gap, this paper uncovered theoretical evidence on the challenges faced by organisations while transiting to agile business analysis methods. This paper uses Actor-Network Theory (ANT) as a lens to address these challenges. Through the lens of ANT, an understanding of the challenges faced by organisations in transitioning from traditional business analysis to agile business, analysis is gained. Although ANT has been employed in many studies, it is very important to establish and explain the challenges, from a social perspective, the challenges that organisations faced during the transition from traditional business analysis to agile business analysis.

KEYWORDS

Agile Method, Agile Business Analysis, Traditional Business Analysis, Actor-Network Theory

1. INTRODUCTION

In today's business environments, the practice of transforming business activities and optimisation, business analysis as a discipline played a key role in determining business requirements and assisted in finding the best possible solution for businesses (Gobov et al., 2020). The Project Management Institute (2017) stated that the most important factors that caused software development project failures are forty-one percent (41%), which were the result of changes in organisations' priorities. Of which 39% were because of errors in the requirements elicitation stage, 36% were a result of changes in project goals and objectives, and 30% of project failures were caused by poor project vision. All the issues highlighted here are a consequence of inadequately organised business analysis activities. This challenging phenomenon can be explained by the fact that currently, business analysis roles have been reduced to business solution requirements management (Gobov et al., 2020).

Additionally, the distribution of skills, methods, practices, and techniques for executing business analysis activities in a project has resulted in a need to describe the concept and framework required for the performance of business analysis activities (Pastor, 2016). Thus, many organisations explore alternative to traditional business analysis approach, and found the agile method suitable (Kose, 2021). Based on the current research, it's not a surprise that agile is changing business analysis. In the past five years, the transition to agile business analysis has increased across many sectors and has transformed the way organisations practice business analysis works (De Gregorio, 2021). The traditional business analysis approach is outdated in the sense it is rigid and inflexible. While modern organisations require a greater need for agility, flexibility, and adaptability (Pastor, 2016).

Although the agile is considered suitable and dynamic for many organisations, there exist challenges in their attempts to transit from the current (traditional business analysis) to the future (Gill, Henderson-Sellers & Niazi, 2018; Bose & Thakur, 2013). The challenges do not seem clear or known, empirically. Hence this paper poses the question: what are the challenges faced by organisations during this transitioning process? Based on existing literature, there is prima facie evidence that the challenges affecting transitioning from the use of traditional business analysis to agile business analysis are more of non-technical (non-technology) than technology factors (Kanabar, 2022; Boehm & Turner, 2005). The non-technical factors include processes, people (employees and stakeholders), and skill set.

Some individuals and groups in many quarters include academic studies have tried to examine the challenges but have proven to be difficult to understand. Hence, a different approach is needed. Thus, the actor-network theory (ANT) as a lens is applied to underpin the study. This means that theory is used to examine perspective on what, how, and why things occur in the manner they do during the transitioning from traditional business analysis to agile business analysis.

In terms of structure, this paper first introduces business analysis practices. It then describes Agile business analysis followed by challenges faced in the transitioning process. It then uses ANT as lens to address the challenges that were identified.

2. BUSINESS ANALYSIS

Business analysis as a discipline has grown significantly in recent decades. The growth of business analysis roles certainly shows an increasing awareness in businesses of the values of such a role (Milani, 2019). There are various interpretations of what business analysis is and what the duties of a business analyst are. Although there have been many interpretations, many of them are centered around the implementation of solutions that provide business value for stakeholders (Milani, 2019). Business analysis is the process of facilitating change in an organisational by describing requirements and proposing solutions that will deliver benefits to stakeholders (Brandenburg, 2017). The main components of business analysis include people, processes, tools, and methods (Milani, 2019). Some of the factors which are identified as challenges faced in the transitioning from traditional business analysis to agile business analysis persist primarily because the challenges have not been properly discussed.

3. AGILE BUSINESS ANALYSIS

When we talk about agile business analysis, firstly we need to reflect on the processes of the current system, and pain points and only then think about the implementation of agile methods (Gunda, 2020). Agile business analysis is mostly about improving and delivering business value to the stakeholder (owner) of the product that is being developed. Agile business analysis is in line with the values and principles of the Agile Manifestos (IIBA, 2015).

In agile business analysis, a set of tools, practices, and methodologies such as scrum, backlogs, Sprint Planning and Execution are used to elicit, analyse, document, communicate, validate, and manage requirements (IIBA, 2015). In agile business analysis, the agile team members are involved in eliciting and defining all product requirements (Prakash & Agarwal, 2013).

Agile business analysis is about making sure that the correct information is available to the development team at the correct detail level at the right time, so the correct product can be developed (IIBA, 2015). Girvan and Paul (2017) stated that an agile approach in business analysis is relevant in two aspects, namely, the business analyst's role in aiding business agility by using agile approaches and philosophy as well as promoting the use of agile methods through business improvement and software development projects.

In agile business analysis, the agile team requires the business analyst to correctly explain and communicate the detailed requirements (user stories). The success of a business analyst in an agile project relies on requirements being defined incrementally and by working collaboratively with the rest of the agile team throughout the project's lifecycle (Prakash & Agarwal, 2013). In a traditional project, the business analyst is responsible for requirements elicitation, analysis, communication, and validation of all changes to the business's processes, and policies.

4. CHALLENGES FACED IN TRANSITIONING FROM TRADITIONAL BUSINESS ANALYSIS TO AGILE BUSINESS ANALYSIS

The introduction and transitioning to agile business analysis practice is difficult and occasionally comes with unique challenges (Dikert et al., 2016; De Gregorio, 2021; VersionOne Inc., 2019). It needs a change to be made in the whole organisational culture and senior management support is required (Paasivaara & Lassenius, 2016). In order to perform quality business analysis work, there is a need for all team members to recognise and understands the tasks completed by other team members and the methodology employed to achieve a common objective in the transitioning process (Beecham et al., 2014). Human factors cannot be ignored when transitioning from traditional business analysis to agile business analysis. Digital transformation is a strategic organisational transformation involving bringing cross-organisational changes, operations of several digital technologies, and obtaining new skills at a human level (Milani, 2019). The agile approach had introduced digital transformation, which is rapidly initiating significant changes in most sectors (Kettunen & Laanti, 2017; Uludag et al., 2018). Agile approaches have therefore been adopted to address the changes presented by the digital transformation.

5. THE LENS OF ACTOR-NETWORK THEORY

According to Shiga (2007), ANT is a social theory that relates to human and non-human actors, which represent networks. ANT stems from the discipline of technology and sociology, but it has been embraced by other disciplines, in order to examine and explain various phenomena. Previous ANT studies concentrated more on human-related elements of systems development, but recently, ANT studies have included the contribution of non-human setups to illustrate balancing the human and non-human actors (Wernick et al., 2008). ANT is viewed as comprising the organisation of network components such as technology, humans, objects, institutions, and organisations (Hanseth et al., 2004). The human and non-human elements play a crucial role in the transition from traditional business analysis to agile business analysis. There are few studies from an ANT perspective that have combined human and non-human factors when transitioning to agile business analysis and therefore, there is a requirement for further research to be done from that perspective (Beecham et al., 2014; Kettunen & Laanti, 2017).

The social-technical focus of ANT makes the theory suitable to help actors to investigate the social context, which in turn requires having the capacity to make a difference; association between the actors, which is the basis of communication, roles, activities, and processes in the transitioning from traditional business analysis to agile business analysis. Luoma-aho and Paloviita (2010) stated that the occurrence of an act is influenced by related factors such as the environment, human beings, entities, and policies. Table 1 shows the principles of ANT, which provide explanations for the terms used in the theory of networks, as described by ANT. The primary principles of ANT contain Actor and Network.

Table 1. ANT Tenet's tools (Mitra & Campoy, 2009)

Tenets	Description
Actor or (actant)	Both human and non-human actors such as technology components.
Actor-network	A mixed network of aligned interests, for example, people, organisations, and values.
Enrolment and Translation	Forming a body of allies, human and non-human, around a process of translating and aligning their interest with the actor-network.
Delegates and Inscription	Delegates are actors who "speak for" a specific view that has been inducted into them.
Irreversibility	The degree for which is hardly impossible to go return to a point where a different possible is.
Black box	A solid network component, often with assets of irreversibility.
Immutable mobile	Network component with solid assets of irreversibility, and effects that exceed time and space.

Actors inside the network have the duties of working as a team to achieve the ultimate objective which is to successfully transition from traditional business analysis to agile business analysis. Regardless of whether the actor is an entity, human, or organisation it is similarly crucial to the network. On the perception of why applications perform in the manner that they do require individuals to provide clarification to more actors, whether actors are in a similar network or not. According to William-Jones and Graham (2003), ANT can be beneficial in studying the connection between technical and social components that are concerned with the development and implementation latest technologies. Cho et al. (2008) argued that ANT is viewed as a method for examining how several actors are collectively placed and connected within a larger network.

Many actors are engaged in the transition to agile business analysis, within organisations. The actors' participation in the transitioning from traditional business analysis to agile business analysis, unavoidably brings negotiation, in order to achieve a common objective for the benefit of the organisation. The lens, being the moment of interpretation is extremely important from the ANT perspective, during the bargaining process. The interpretation moments contain four elements, problematisation, intersegment, enrolment, and mobilisation, and are centered on collaboration, bargaining, and modification of actions. There are few studies from an ANT perspective that have combined human and non-human factors when transitioning to agile business analysis and therefore, there is a requirement for further research to be done from that perspective (Beecham et al., 2014; Kettunen & Laanti, 2017). The moments of translation are briefly discussed below.

5.1 Problematisation

According to Mpazanje (2009), the problematisation stage is where the main actor may feel like changing how things are performed. Therefore, the main actor's interests are shown and distributed to prospective actors and then they seek to build relationships with other actors with related aims. However, power formation within the network may influence some actors' ability to resist the problematisation of the adoption of the technology (William-Jones & Graham, 2003).

5.2 Interessement

Interessement at this stage, the main actor attempts to enforce their identity on other actors that have become components of the alliance (Callon,1986). Interessement may include certain types of negotiation, and convincing in order for the actors to be interested in the positions proposed to them. William-Jones and Graham (2003) stated that the power formation within the network additionally impacts certain actors who were against the preliminary problematisation. This then obliges the actors to join the network. This is referred to as the obligatory passage point.

5.3 Enrolment

Only the network actors who accept the positions described for them in the preceding phrase will take part in the network (Macome, 2008). Actors are required to complete tasks that have been allocated to them, as agreed with the main network actor. Luoma-aho and Paloviita (2010) stated that communication plays a crucial part in the enrolment phase because it explains what is required from the actors and what activities need to be implemented.

5.4 Mobilisation

According to Callon, (1986). The appointed representative in the mobilisation stage represents other actors within the network activities. A quality representation helps to strengthen the network. Greenhalgh and Stones (2010) stated that the task of the appointed representatives is to involve other actors to conduct their duty and to develop connections with other actors within the network. In order to perform as a unit, it is crucial for trust to be developed between network actors and to support other networks.

6. DEALING WITH THE CHALLENGES FACED IN THE TRANSITION TO AGILE BUSINESS ANALYSIS USING AN ANT LENS

In using the ANT lens to address the challenges faced in transitioning to agile business analysis; several actors were identified, as shown in Table 2.

Table 2. Identified Actors in the Network

Actor	Roles Description
Senior management	The of setting organisational goals and objectives lies with senior management. Senior Management also has the responsibilities of managing and coordinating activities in the functional departments, for example, finance, IT, and HR (Gobov et al., 2020).
IT heads	Manage organisations' information requirement through technology; and ensures that the technology organisations have allowed them to achieve their objectives (Dikert et al., 2016)
Business unit head	A business unit head manages a specific department within an organisation. The business unit head is responsible for managing the daily operations of the business unit and ensuring that the unit meets its objectives (Dikert et al., 2016)
Senior Business Analyst Manager	A senior business analyst manager is responsible for managing other business analysts within an organisation (Gobov et al., 2020).
Product Specialists (Boxed)	Product specialists work with a product team to ensure excellent product delivery. Product specialists recommend improvements, identify opportunities, and increase revenue (Dikert et al., 2016).
Business Analyst (Boxed)	Elicits business requirements map business processes and produces functional specifications. In an agile environment a business analyst documents user stories (Gobov et al., 2020).
Scrum master	Manages the system development lifecycle using agile methodologies (Beecham et al., 2014).
System Developer (Boxed)	Codes the required system functionalities as per business requirements. A developer produces working software (Beecham et al., 2014).
Application owner	Owns the business application within an organisation (Kettunen & Laanti, 2017).

6.1 Barriers to the Transitioning Agile Business Analysis

Like any change, business analysts who are comfortable with traditional business analysis methods, act as barriers to change in adopting the business analysis method. The literature illustrates eight main reasons for this challenge (Figure 1), including cultural issues, resistance to change, lack of knowledge, wrong mindset, and lack of collaboration. (Dikert et al., 2016; De Gregorio, 2021; Paasivaara & Lassenius, 2016; VersionOne Inc., 2019; Gandomani & Nafchi, 2016). The challenges for the acceleration of systems and product delivery and competition because of digital transformations demand that organisations must quickly adapt to new ways of working (Dikert et al., 2019; Kettunen & Laanti, 2017). If these challenges are not dealt with, they might impact the smooth transition to agile business analysis within organisations (VersionOne Inc., 2019). For the transition to agile business analysis to be successful, organisations need to identify and acknowledge these challenges and look for ways to address them.

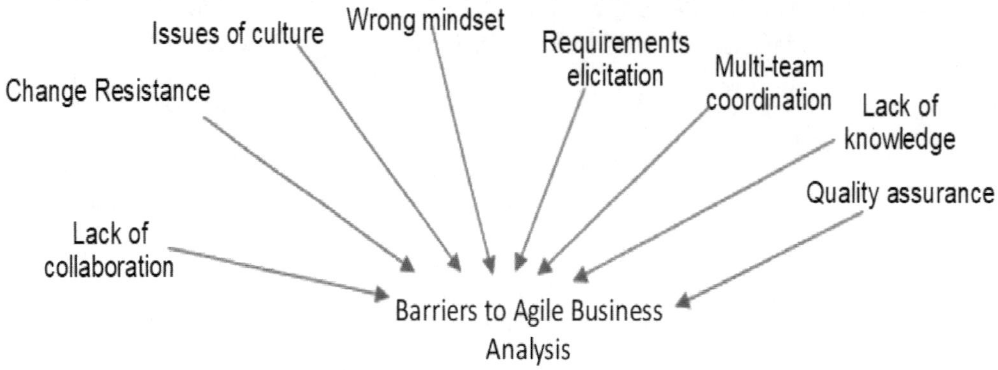

Figure 1. Challenges faced in transitioning to agile identified from the literature

6.2 Problematisation in the Transitioning to Agile Business Analysis

Problematisation arises when a senior business analyst manager enforces their identity on the business analysts to start thinking about better ways of eliciting business requirements in order to deal with issues around consistency, quality, and efficiency (William-Jones & Graham, 2003). According to William-Jones and Graham (2003), a senior business analyst manager, the main actor, makes sure that the problem is recognised by all business analysts. William-Jones and Graham (2003) further stated that the attempt for a senior business analyst manager to form an alliance with all members of a business analysts' team, in response to the main actor problematisation. the business analysts may attempt to develop a requirements elicitation methodology which might be unsuccessful (Mpazanje, 2009). Some actors may try to grab that opportunity to promote their personal interests (Mpazanje, 2009) This is a strong signal that problematisation is not working for them.

According to Girvan and Paul (2017), during the transitioning journey, it is important to mention that the traditional business analysis approach had small or no opposition in the network and hence, at this stage the fairly, powerful actor within the network. The traditional business analysis approach managed to problematise its interests as an actor in the network (Girvan & Paul, 2017). The failure of problematisation could be because there are contradictory interests between human and non-human actors in the network that could complicate the issue (Mpazanje, 2009). It is challenging for the main actor to deal with the interests of human actors over those of non-human actors in the network.

6.3 Interessement

As indicated by Callon (1986), interessement is persuading actors to become interested and become part of the network. Callon (1986), according to, Callon (1986), the success of interessement lead to enrolment. Several approaches can be employed in the interessement stage (Gandomani & Nafchi, 2016) For instance, the senior business analyst manager includes the business analysts' team to come up with an approach that is appropriate for dealing with requirements elicitation challenges. Scrum can be seen as a potential solution to these challenges (VersionOne Inc.,2019). By attempting to move the business requirements documentation towards a leaner approach, through lightweight documentation. This is a form interessement. Upon the official introduction of the scrum, some resistance to change should be expected from some members of the business analysts and development teams (Gandomani & Nafchi, 2016), The actors opposing the introduction of scrum and how they should be handled are discussed below.

6.3.1 Business Analysts' Resistance

The business analysts, as can be seen in the problematisation attempt, opposed lean documentation because they did not think it was feasible. Some business analysts still want to produce thirty pages of business requirements documents (VersionOne Inc., 2019; Gandomani & Nafchi, 2016).

6.3.2 Experienced Employees Resistance

This is a group of employees who had several years of experience in the traditional business analysis approach. The group does not see any value in unlearning the traditional business analysis approach and learning scrum method (VersionOne Inc., 2019; Gandomani & Nafchi, 2016), especially when they only have a few years to go for their retirement.

6.3.3 Dealing with Change Resistance

In addressing change resistance, some Interessement approaches will need to be employed. Corridor salesmanship, driven by an agile practitioner, can be employed. Corridor salesmanship has a responsibility to ensure that agile operations are extensively discussed within the entire organisation by starting conversations about agile business analysis, to spark informal conversations within the organisation (Mpazanje, 2009). The aim is to create an opportunity for Interessement to explain the misconceptions. Another popular action of the Interessement approach is to ensure that all actors attend agile methods training sessions (formal or informal) After the agile training, the business analysts and developers, who were resistant to changing to lean documentation, are trained on how the documentation is done in an agile system (VersionOne Inc., 2019). To address the resistance, the agile practitioner should keep on highlighting the need for the team to stay focused on the required functionality but not all functionalities (Gandomani & Nafchi, 2016). The agile practitioner will need to indicate the importance of having sufficient documentation to get the needed functionality into working shape (VersionOne Inc., 2019).

The agile practitioner will need to draw the attention of the team to prioritise requirements (VersionOne Inc., 2019). Business analysts will thereby be made to understand the expected business value and should then ensure that they produce sufficient documentation (Gandomani & Nafchi, 2016). These actions thus demonstrate acts of Interessement on the business analysts who were change resistant. The objective of the agile practitioner will be to get all actors to be able to understand agile methodology This is according to Vaagaasar (2006), who highlighted the importance of agreement between stakeholders who have become network actors and are then able to translate their interests into enrolment.

6.4 Enrolment

Enrolment the process whereby roles are proposed or forced on each actor by the main actor is (Macome, 2008). According to Gandomani & Nafchi, (2016), There are two important parts of enrolment in a network; in the challenges faced in the transition to agile business analysis: (1) the transition involves people with influence within the organisation's hierarchy, and (2) the transition may have increased strength because some actors within the network strongly believe in agile business analysis.

A strong and stable network makes it difficult for any actor not to become a participant in the network, as not participating will make actors feel isolated (Macome, 2008). Since they understand that agile business analysis will be implemented with or without their involvement. The business analyst's team members are enrolled because of their team responsibilities. (Gandomani & Nafchi, 2016), With the assistance of an agile practitioner, business analysts will need to understand the new business analysis methods that are applied in their positions, and ultimately, they will become enrolled (VersionOne Inc., 2019). The roles traditional business analysts occupy will need to be re-defined, and they will need to accept the fact that lengthy documentation will no longer be required from them (Gandomani & Nafchi, 2016).

6.5 Mobilisation

Mobilisation is the last stage of ANT translation and is the stage where the main actor is represented by negotiators appointed to speak on behalf of other actors (Greenhalgh & Stones, 2010) All actors who speak against the network are silenced, and thereby, the network is stabilised and strengthened. The objective is to ensure that actors remain focused on the primary objective of the network (Callon,1986). The level of mobilisation determines the level of success of the transition. The agents of mobilisation in the network are discussed below.

6.5.1 The Agile Practitioner

In the transition process, an agile practitioner will be the most obvious spokesperson in the network (De Gregorio, 2021). Agile practitioners must give guidance and direction as to what is required in the transition process (VersionOne Inc., 2019). An agile practitioner will also make suggestions on how best to implement agile business analysis and he will also coach, the business analysts, and the developer's team on agile methodologies.

6.5.2 The Senior Business Analyst Manager

The senior business analyst manager is another spokesperson who is influential in the mobilisation of the network actors (Pastor, 2016). The objective of the senior business analyst manager is to discuss challenges and to share new developments that relate to agile business analysis methodology (Prakash & Agarwal, 2013).

7. CONCLUSION

The objectives of this paper were to provide an understanding of the challenges faced when transitioning from traditional business analysis to agile business analysis from an ANT perspective. ANT was used primarily because of itsfocus and strength on complex relationships between actors within network. This prove useful as the theory assisted in providing a comprehensive method for tracking the manner in which the interests of actors are aligned and executed. For examples, without the use of ANT, it would have been difficult or impossible to deeper understand on how the challenges when transitioning to agile business analysis relate to people and the organisational culture they operate in; and how the challenges manifest themselves in social context, to manipulate processes and activities.

Based on the challenges that are revealed, this paper contributes significantly, from both theory and practice perspectives. Theoretically, the challenges identified in this paper can be examined further and adds to the existing literature. From practical perspective, the paper provides a front on how organisations need to manage the transition from traditional business analysis approaches, in a more carefully and productive manner. This includes taking cognisance of the importance of getting employees' buy-in, to successfully transition to agile business analysis

For future study, it would be beneficial to develop a framework that will make it easy for organisations to address these challenges. This framework will decrease the risks of failure when transitioning to agile business analysis. Organisations are moving away from the traditional business analysis approach to the agile business analysis approach. While some organisations may want to adopt this type of change, the challenges to such a change include a lack of practical evidence as to what processes have been followed by other organisations.

REFERENCES

Beecham, S., Noll, J., and Richardson, I. (2014). Using agile practices to solve global software development problems -- a case study. 2014 International conference on global software engineering workshops (pp. 5-10). The Institute of Electrical and Electronics Engineers, Inc.

Boehm, B., and Turner, R. (2005). Management challenges to implementing agile processes in traditional development organizations. IEEE software, 22(5), 30-39.

Bose, L., and Thakur, S. (2013). Introducing Agile into a Non Agile Project: Analysis of Agile Methodology with its Issues and Challenges. International Journal of Advanced Research in Computer Science, 4(1), 305-311.

Brandenburg, L. (2017). BA Roles and Responsibilities, Plan Your Business Analysis Approach, Bridging the Gap. Available on: http://www.bridging-the-gap.com/business-analysis-proces [09 March 2022].

Callon, M. (1986). Some elements of a sociology of translation: Domestication of the scallops and the fishermen of St Brieux bay. Power, action, and belief: A New sociology of knowledge, 196–223.

Cho, S., Mathiassen, L., and Nilsson, A. (2008). Contextual dynamics during health information systems implementation: an event-based actor-network approach. European Journal of Information Systems, 17(1), 614–630.

De Gregorio, B. (2021). The states of agile in South Africa [Report]. IQ Business, Available on: http://iqbusiness.net/wp-content/upload/2021/21/Agile-state-of-Agile-Africa-2021-Report.Pdf[Accessed:15August 2022]

Dikert, K., Paasivaara, M., and Lassenius, C. (2016). Challenges and success factors for large-scale agile transformations: a systematic literature review. Journal of Systems and Software, 119, 87-108.

Gandomani, T.J., and Nafchi, M.Z. (2016). Agile transition and adoption human-related challenges and issues: A grounded theory approach. Computers in Human Behavior, 62, 257-266.

Gill, A. Q., Henderson-Sellers, B., and Niazi, M. (2018). Scaling for agility: A reference model for hybrid traditional-agile software development methodologies. Information Systems Frontiers, 20(2), 315-341.

Girvan, L., and Paul, D. (2017). Agile and Business Analysis: Practical guidance for IT professionals The Chartered Institute for IT ISBN: 9781780173245

Gobov, D., Maliarcuk, C., Kunanets, N., and Oliinyk, Y. (2020). Approaches for the Concept "Business Analysis" Definition in IT Projects and Frameworks. Available on: https://www.researchgate.net/publication/344886792 [Accessed:15 June 2022]

Greenhalgh, T., and Stones, R. (2010). Theorising big IT programmes in healthcare: Strong structuration theory meets actor-network theory. Social Science & Medicine, 70(9), 1285–1294.

Gunda, S. (2020). Business Analysis Life Cycle & IT- Business Analyst Role in Traditional, Digital, and Agile World. Gurucool Publishing ISBN: 978-93-88435-73-4 First Edition – 2020.

Hanseth, O., Aanestad, M., and Berg, M. (2004). Guest editors' introduction Actor-network theory and information systems. Information Technology & People, 17(2), 116–123.

International Institute of Business Analysis (IIBA) (2021), Business Analysis Body of Knowledge, [Online], Available on: http://www.pdfdrive.com/Agile-Extension-to-the BABOK-Guide -Agile Alliance - PDF Drive [06 July 2022].

Kanabar, V. (2022). Integrating Agile Development Approaches and Business Analysis Foundational Knowledge into a Project Management Course. In International Conference on Computer Science and Education in Computer Science (pp. 233-244). Springer, Cham.

Kettunen, P. and Laanti, M. (2017). Future software organizations–agile goals and roles. European Journal of Futures Research, 5(1), 1-15.

Kose, B. O. (2021). Agile Business Analysis for Digital Transformation. In Handbook of Research on Multidisciplinary Approaches to Entrepreneurship, Innovation, and ICTs (pp. 98-123). IGI Global.

Luoma-Aho, V., and Paloviita, A. (2010). Actor networking stakeholder theory for today's corporate communications. Corporate Communications: An International Journal, 15(1), 49–67.

Macome, E. (2008). On Implementation of an information system in the Mozambican context: The EDM case viewed through ANT lenses. Information Technology for Development, 14(2), 154–170.

Milani, F. (2019). Digital Business Analysis. Springer, Cham. https://doi.org/10.1007/9778-3-030-05719-0

Mitra, A., and Campoy, L. (2009). Evolution of an IS development effort; An ANT interpretation. Journal of Systems and Information Technology, DOI 10.1108/13287260910955110.pp150-167

Mpazanje, F.T.H. (2009). Towards understanding as-lived experiences in information systems projects: An actor-network theory perspective. Unpublished masters.

Paasivaara, M., and Lassenius, C. (2016). Scaling scrum in a large globally distributed organization: a case study. Proceedings of the 11th IEEE international conference on global software engineering (pp. 74-83). The Institute of Electrical and Electronics Engineers, Inc.

Pastor, O. (2016). A capability-driven development approach for requirements and business process modeling. International Conference on Conceptual Modeling, pp.3-8. Springer, Cham. DOI: 10.1007/s00766-007-0043-3.

Prakash, R., and Agarwal, N. (2013). Managing Business Analysis for Agile Development International Journal of Modern Engineering Research, ISSN: 2249-6645. Pp 1393-1395

Project Management Institute (PMI) (2017): Success Rates Rise–Transforming the High Cost of Low Performance. Available on: https://www.pmi.org › pulse-of-the-profession-2017 [Accessed: 15 June 2022].

Shiga, J. (2007). Translations: Artifacts from an actor-network perspective. Artifact, 1(1). Available on: https://www.researchgate.net/publication/249047084 [Accessed: 20 August 2022].

Uludag, Ö., Kleehaus, M., Caprano, C., and Matthes, F. (2018). Identifying and structuring challenges in large-scale agile development based on a structured literature review. In 2018 IEEE 22nd International Enterprise Distributed Object Computing Conference (EDOC) (pp. 191-197).

Vaagaasar, A.N. (2006). From tool to actor: How a project came to orchestrate its own life and that of others. Available on: https://www.researchgate.net/publication/277291618 [Accessed: 20 August 2022].

VersionOne Inc. (2019). The 13th annual state of agile report. [Report]. Available on https://www.stateofagile.com/#ufh-i-521251909-13th-annual-state-of-agile-report/473508 [Accessed: 30 August 2022].

Wernick, P., Hall, T., and Nehaniv, C.L. (2008). Software evolutionary dynamics modelled as the activity of an actor-network. The Institution of Engineering and Technology, 2(4), 321–336.

William-Jones, B. and Graham, J.E. (2003). Actor-network theory: A tool to support ethical analysis of commercial genetic testing. New genetics and society, 22(3), 271–296.

CUSTOMER SWITCHING: A REVIEW OF THE LITERATURE

Kamel Rouibah
College of Business Administration, Kuwait University
Kuwait University, Shuwaikh Campus, 13055 Kuwait

ABSTRACT

While there are many studies that review prior studies in different technology adoption, prior studies that review the switching behavior are lacking. To overcome this gap, this study reviews 53 studies about switching in different technology. The main questions that this study answered are: What countries where the subject of witching behavior studies? What dimensions of switching were studied? Do prior swithcing studies focused on intention to swithcin or on current switching behavior? What consequences of switching factors where studied? Who were the participants in the switching behavior? What studies did invetigate switching behavior after introduction of Mobile Number Portability (MNP)? Do pior studies focused on switchers or stayers or on mixed? What theories were used to investigate switching behavior? This study provides answers to these questions and points to their main findings.

KEYWORDS

Switching Intention, Customer Retention, Switching Costs, Satisfaction, Loyalty

1. INTRODUCTION

1.1 Research Background

Since June 16, 2013, the National Technology Enterprise Company (www.ntec.com.kw) has developed mobile number portability (MNP) between telecommunication mobile service providers (TMSP) to allow customers to freely switch (without paying any extra cost) between the three operators of TMSPs in Kuwait while retaining their mobile phone numbers. This is not new as many countries have already taken steps in this direction and initiated such a service long ago (table 1), and more countries continue to do so (see Xconnect 2021; MNP2021). For example, 13.31 million Brazilian consumers have changed carriers without changing their identification numbers between 2008 and 2011 (RCR wireless 2021).

The ultimate goal of implementing MNP is to promote competition among TMSP companies, and customers will definitely win in the implementation of this technology. However, it presents both risks and opportunities for TMSPs. From a customer perspective, MNP is expected to bring several benefits as they experience improvement in the quality of mobile service, decrease of service costs, and get more advanced and innovative products/services. And therefore customers can freely switch to any TMSP whom they think offer the best services. In addition, the market will become mature, with more improvements in network infrastructure as TMSPs will invest in order to offer better services and keep their base of customers. Unlike customers, MNP may present risks for TMSPs who will face more competitive marketing campaigns, severe market competitiveness, potential reduction in their market share, costs associated with improve existing technologies and keeping their brand and customers as churn rate may increase. After years of following offensive strategies to attract new customers, the introduction of MNP leads TMSPs to follow defensive strategies in order to retain their existing customers and prevent them from switching to their competitors, and keep them loyal.

Table 1. MNP in a subset of countries

Year	Countries
1997	Singapore
1999	Hong Kong, the UK, the Netherlands
2000	Switzerland, Spain
2001	Denmark, Sweden, Norway, Portugal, Australia
2002	Italy, Belgium, Germany
2003	Finland, France, Austria, Greece, Ireland, Island, Luxembourg
2004	Lithuania, South Korea, USA, Slovenia, Cyprus, Poland, Hungary, Taiwan
2005	Estonia, Latvia, Malta
2006	Slovakia, Czech Republic, Japan, West Africa
2007	Canada
2008	Brazil
2009	China
2011	Colombia
2012	Chile, Panama
2013	Republic of Moldova, Honduras
2014	Bangladesh
2015	El Salvador, Senegal
2016	Iran, Maldives
2017	Tanzania
2018	Vietnam, Bangladesh
2019	Ukraine
2020	Palestine

1.2 Research Question and Importance

In order to retain existing customers and to avoid losing them for companies that provide more attractive and innovative services, this study aims to answer the following research question: ***What key potential factors may lead customers to switch to other service providers?***

This main question was split into the following sub questions that the SLR will answer

Q1: What countries where the subject of witching behavior studies? And what dimensions of switching were studied?

Q5: Do prior swithcing studies focused on intention to swithcin or on current switching behavior

Q6: What consequences of swithing factors where studiesd ?

Q2: What studies investigate switching in TMSP and what approaches they used: Quantitative, qualitative or mixed? And what were the panticipants in the switching behavior (students vs. real customers)?

Q3: What studies did invetigate switching behavior after introduction of MNP?

Q4: Do pior studies focused on swithcers or stayers or mixed?

Q7: What theories were used to investigate switching behavior?

Q8: Do prior studies included switching cost factors as independent factor vs. mediating factors ?

Q9: Do switching costs (financial switching cost, perceived switching barriers, and customer lock-in) matter, i.e., do they have an impact on customer retention (loyalty vs. switching)?

This is an important search question facing executives of TMSPs in order to propose strategies to keep customers' loyalty and deter them from switching to competitors. This is in line with past studies that have shown that customer switching is an important research area for three main reasons (Parthasarathy and Bhattacherjee, 1998; Fan and Suh, 2014). *First*, for market share and revenues, both the number of new adopters and discontinuers at any period are regarded as significant. *Second*, evidence shows that negative interpersonal influence by service discontinuers is generally more influential than positive interpersonal influence from continuing customers. In addition, new adopters might be influenced against subscribing (e.g. Mizerski, 1982; Mahajan et al., 1984) despite positive influence from other sources (Reichheld et al., 1990). *Third*, it is well known in marketing that it costs six times more to get a new customer than to keep and maintain existing clients.

The research question we investigate is the first phase of a larger project conducted by the researcher with the objective to identify factors that lead to customer retention (loyalty and switching) while the second phase consists to design and test a customer retention model (that includes both loyalty and switching) in a telecommunication context with MNP.

Before achieving the objective of the phase 2 (development of retention model), this current study aims to conduct a systematic literature review (SLR) on customer retention (loyalty and switching) in order to derive relevant guidelines to complete the second phase of the research project. The following sections present the method to implement the SLR, the result findings and discussion, and conclusions.

2. METHOD OF CONDUCTING THE SLR

2.1 Selected Databases for the SLR Search

For more than three decades, many studies have focused on the end-users switching behavior in both the marketing and the information system usage literature. This study identified scientific journals studies in four famous and well-known scientific databases: ProQuest Direct, ScienceDirect, ACM Digital Library, and Google Scholar.

2.2 Search Descriptors

To identify studies on switching behavior, we used the following descriptors "switching", "IT switching", "mobile service switching", "loyalty and switching", and "satisfaction and switching" that were to be found in the title or abstract of the paper. We retained published studies that fulfilled the three criteria: empirical research (qualitative and quantitative), peer-reviewed journals, and available in full text and. We excluded studies published in other language than English, conference studies and non-peer-reviewed papers. We limited the search to the years 2001–2020. After searching we succeeded to identify 104 studies but only 53 studies did successfully meet the requirements of the study.

3. FINDINGS

3.1 What is Switching?

There are several definitions of switching (Table 2). Based on this table this study, we define switching behavior as "the process or decision by which a customer decides to end his relationship with a servive provider, for whatever reason, and enter or establish the same relationship with another one" (Rouibah, 2017).

Table 2. A subset of definitions of switching behavior

Authors	Definition
Holland (1984) in Bansal (1997)	Brand changing
Carpenter and Lehmann (1985)	Movement of buyers from one product to another
Kasper (1988) in Bansal (1997)	Non-repeat purchase behavior
Reichheld and Sasser (1990) in Bansal (1997)	Customer defections
Bucklin and Srinivasan (1991)	Inter brand substitutability
Morgan and Dev (1994) in Bansal (1997)	Changes in brand choice
Keaveney (1995)	The loss of continuing service customer
Sambandam and Lord (1995)	Inconsistency of brand choice from purchase to purchase
Yi and Zeithaml (1990); Sing 1990, in Colgate and Norris (2001)	The voluntary termination of an exchange relationship
Bansal et al (2004)	Termination of the relationship between customer and the service provider
Bansal et al (2005)	Consumers move from one country (service provider) to another.
Lopez et al (2006)	Losing a customer (from the firm's point of view)
Shin and Kim (2008)	Migrating of customers from one provider to another

3.2 Main Results

These studies have investigated different factors affecting intention to use, current use, continuous use, satisfaction, loyalty and switching/retention behavior. The literature review includes 53 studies focused on different sectors, including the IT sector, services, and telecommunication, which include a type of switching cost either as independent, latent or dependent variables. Based on the previous literature review, we can infer the following remarks and observation.

Answer to Q1: Tthe literature review reveals that switching behavior was studied in some countries including the United States (Shin, 2006), Australia (Gray et al., 2012), New Zealand (Ecommerce Commission New Zealand, 2012), Korea (Geong and Park, 2003; Yuan and Choi, 2003; Kim et al., 2004; Park and Kim, 2007), Germany (Gerpott et al., 2001), China (When-Hua and Jing-Yi, 2010), Finland (Smura, 2004; Björkroth, 2005), India (Gupta and Sharma, 2009), Pakistan (Iqbal, 2010), Taiwan (Chen et al., 2007), and Central America (Garcia-Murillo, 2007). But we found only four studies focused on factors that affect switching behavior after MNP was introduced such as in China (Shi, Zhou, and Liu, 2010), USA (Shin 2006), South Korea (Lee, Kim, Lee and Park, 2006) and Ghana (Nimako, Ntim and Mensah, 2014) while another study discussed the process of introducing MNP in Japan (Otsuka and Mitomo, 2013). In addition, while most reviewed studies focused on switching behavior in developing countries, we found very few were carried out in less developed countries (Nimako, Ntim, and Mensah, 2014; Iqbal, 2010) and Arab countries (Bashir, 2011). We found several dimension of switching were studied under different names including switching cost, satisfaction/dissatisfaction, trust, perceived value, switching experience, financial switching cost, procedural switching cost, relational switching cost, switching benefit, perceived switching value, switching cost, expected switching benefits, expected switching cost, expectation, disconfirmation, product quality, overall mobile provider service quality, mobile device quality, mobile software quality, overall mobile product quality, and network quality.

Answer to Q2: We found that prior studies mainly focused on intention to switch (Liu, 2015; Hsu, 2014; Raitani, 2014; Peng, Scott, and Prybutok, 2014; Fan and Suh, 2014; Hsu, 2014; Bhattacherjee et al., 2012; Gray et al., 2012; Pookulangara, Hawley, Xiao, 2011; Han, Kim, and Hyun, 2011; Shi, Zhou, and Liu, 2010; Zhang, Lee, Cheung, and Chen, 2009; Coulter, 2009; Hou, Chern, Chen, and Chen, 2009; Min and Wan, 2009; Yoo, Kim, Hong, 2008; Shin and Kim, 2008; Anton et al., 2007; Hu and Huang, 2006; Kim et al., 2006; Whitten and Wakefield, 2006; Low and Johnston, 2006; Kim, Shin, and Lee, 2006; Bansal, Taylor, and James, 2005; Harvir and Taylor, 2004; Jones, Taylor, Becherer, and Halstead, 2003; Bansal and Taylor, 1999, Keaveney, 1995). While those that included current switching behavior are lacking.

Answer to Q3: There are many studies that integrated different forms of switching factors, either as independent or mediating variables, and switching conseuquences in term of: (i) customer satisfaction (Jones, Taylor, Becherer, and Halstead, 2003); (ii) customer complaints (Chapa, Hernandez, and Wang, 2014); (iii) customer loyalty in TMSPS (Edward, George, and Sark, 2010; Min and Wan, 2009) and customer loyalty in other technologies (Blut, Beatty, Evanschitzky, and Brock, 2014; Chebat, Davidow, and Borges, 2011; Wang, Cheng, Hui Lin, and Wang, 2011; Kheng, Mahamad, Ramayah, and Mosahab, 2010; Chou and Shan, 2009); Lee, Lee, and Feick, 2001); (iv) customer retention, i.e. both intention to switch and loyalty (Baksi and Parida, 2012; Ranaweera and Prabhu, 2003; Patterson and Smith, 2003). But there are fewer studies that focused solely on switching behavior as a dependent variable (e.g. Dwivedi et al., 2010; Min & Wan, 2009; Ranganathan, Seo, and Babad, 2006). In addition, prior studies on intention to switch have included switching factors either as independent variables (e.g. Deng, Lu, Wei and Zhang, 2010; Blut, Beatty, Evanschitzky and Brock, 2014; Şahin, and Kitapci, 2013; Baksi and Parida, 2012; Wang, Wu, Lin and Wang, 2011; Chebat, Davidow, Borges, 2011; Edward, George, and Sark, 2010; Chou and Shan, 2009; Pae and Hyun, 2006; Ranaweera and Prabhu, 2003) or as mediating and moderating variables (e.g. Matzler, Strobl, Thurner and Füller, 2015; Park and Ryoo, 2013; Huang and Hsieh, 2012; Chang and Chen, 2008; Kim, Park and Jeong, 2004; Lee, Lee, and Feick, 2001) (Sharma and Patterson, 2000).

Answer to Q4: Among the reviewed studies only a few (8) focused on switching between mobile service providers (TMSPs) and used quantitative approach (Peng, Scott, and Prybutok, 2014; Şahin, Hin and Kitapci, 2013, Gray, Alessandro, and Carter, 2012; Morgan, 2012; Bashir, 2011; Anton, Camarero and Carrero, 2007; Low and Johnston, 2006; Lee, Kim, Lee and Park, 2006), while studies that approached the problem from a qualitative approach are lacking. In addition, most studies have tried to understand the switching behavior using a single research approach (quantitative-based questionnaires or qualitative-based interviews). But to the best of our knowledge, and with the exception of Gray et al. (2012), no study has used the mixed or combined approaches. In addition, many studies used samples composed of students (Patterson and Smith, 2003; Bansal, Taylor, and James, 2005; Lee, Kim, Lee, and Park, 2006; Min and Wan, 2009; Bhattacherjee, Limayem, and Cheung, 2012; Park and Ryoo, 2013; Peng, Scott, and Prybutok, 2014; Fan and Suh, 2014) while the rest of the studies focused on general customers.

Answer to Q5: We have noticed fewer studies focused on switching behavior after a trigger took place such as the introduction of MNP. We were able to identify only five studies that focused on switching after MNP implementation has started (Otsuka & Mitomo, 2013; Bashir, 2011; Shin, 2006; Lee, Kim, Lee & Park, 2006; Nimako, Ntim & Mensah, 2014).

Answer to Q6: We found very few studies (8) that focused on mix sample of switchers and stayers (Gray et al., 2012; Dwivedi et al., 2010; Min & Wan, 2009; Shin and Kim, 2008; Shin, 2006; Ranganathan, Seo & Babad, 2006; Keaveney and Medhavan, 2001; Ganesh, Arnold & Reynolds, 2000) while the majority focused on intention to switch by one type of users (those who intend to switch) (e.g. Bhattacherjee et al., 2012). However, exploring both groups and their retention (in terms of staying –loyalty or switching) within each of the two categories (stayers and switchers) with the effect of demographic variables (level of education, gender, brand name, use of call centers, awareness of MNP, type of service (prepaid vs. postpaid), etc.) did not receive due attention. The causal relationship between these variables is a must as marketers need causal models to understand the cause and effect of switching behavior. This is important in order to keep their clients and avoid losing them compared to more proactive TMSP companies.

Answer to Q7: Several theories were used to investigate different issues related to switching and loyalty issues including the following: theory of planned behavior—TPB (Nimako, Ntim, and Mensah, 2014; Pookulangara, Hawley, and Xiao, 2011), technology acceptance model—TAM (Larkotey, Ansong, Damoah, Abandoh-Sam, 2012), expectation disconfirmation theory—ECT (Fan and Suh, 2014; Ganesh, Arnold, and Reynolds, 2000), innovation diffusion theory-IDT (Huang and Hsieh, 2012), Push, pull and Mooring's migration model (Gray, Alessandro, and Carter, 2012; Bashir, 2011; Hou, Chern, Chen, and Chen, 2009; Hou, Chern, Chen, and Chen, 2009; Bansal, Taylor, and James 2005), unified theory of acceptance and use of technology- UTAUT (Bhattacherjee, Limayem, and Cheung, 2012), value-based decision model (Hsu, 2014; Park and Ryoo, 2013), social movement theory (Lee, Trimi, and Yang, 2014), theory of motivation (Park and Ryoo, 2013), transaction cost theory and social exchange theory (Whitten and Wakefield, 2006), commitment theory (Harvir and Taylor, 2004; Sharma and Patterson, 2000), transactional/relational continuum (Garbarino and Johnson, 1999), cultural model of Hofsteded (Chapa, Hernandez, and Wang

2014). Other studies used non-theory models. This is the case of Shin (2006) who built their model based Kim et al. (2004). In addition, while much studies focused on the antecedent of loyalty that lead to retention of customers, including trust, perceived value, habit and commitment (Sanchez-Franco et al., 2009), we found out the existing literature ignored the important role of other variables such as service quality and system quality which are two important variables that affect the continuous use and system success of different technologies (DeLone and McLean, 2003). We also noticed that while some items of these two constructs did not use reliable and validated items such as "SERVQUAL" of Parasuraman et al. (1988), none switching study did include this construct despite the fact that some studies included fewer items (Dwivedi et al., 2010). We have also observed another limitation. We did not find any past study that integrates and combines some of the well-known behavioral theories in the information system field, including ECT, SERQUAL, and information system success). Those that used a specific model theory did not have enough rationale for the choice of selected theory. The use of these theories is necessary to allow a comparison of findings across studies. Last, we did not find any prior study that provided a rationale for the chosen model.

Answer to Q8: There was also a conflict of results with regard to whether switching costs (financial switching cost, perceived switching barriers, and customer lock-in) have direct impact customer retention (loyalty vs. switching). Existing knowledge are conflicting with regard to this issue (Fan and Suh, 2014; Hsu, 2014; Park and Ryoo, 2013; Zhang et al., 2009; Shin and Kim, 2008; Kim et al., 2006; Bansal et al., 2005; Kim et al., 2004).

4. CONCLUSION

This study conducted of literature review of 53 studies related to switching and customer retention. The main achieved findings were the following:

- The literature review reveals that switching behavior was studied more in developed countries compare to developing countries
- We found several dimension and factors affect intention to switching behavior
- Most prior studies used a quantitative approach to study the intention to switch, while very few have a mixed method research (quantitative and qualitative). Also most prior studies have used mainly students as the participants, and no study has used the mixed or combined approaches.
-
- Fewer studies focused on switching behavior after a trigger took place such as the introduction of MNP.
- Very few studies focused on mix sample of switchers and stayers while the majority focused on intention to switch by one type of users (those who intend to switch).
- While switching costs are important driver toward switching, results revealed mixed results. They were studied either as independent variables or as mediating and moderating variables. Switching costs were studied as independent or mediating variables and their consequences in term of: customer satisfaction; or customer loyalty (Edward, George, and Sark, 2010; Min and Wan, 2009), or customer retention, i.e. both intention to switch and loyalty.
- Most studies have approached the switching behavior using well-known theories including TPB, TAM, ECT, IDT, Push, pull and Mooring's migration model, UTAUT, but others have also used non-theory models. However, studies that integrate and combine some of the well-known behavioral theories in the information system field, including ECT, SERQUAL, and information system success are lacking.
- Many factor lead to customer retention (loyalty vs. switching). However, prior studies ignored the important role of other variables such as service quality and system quality.
- There was a conflict of results with regard to the effect of switching costs (financial switching cost, perceived switching barriers, and customer lock-in) on customer retention (loyalty vs. switching)/.

ACKNOWLEDGEMENT

This research was funded by Kuwait Foundation For the Advancement of Science, Research Grant KFAS 2013-1110-0.

REFERENCES

Anton, C; Camarero, C; and Carrero, M. Analysing firms' failures as determinants of consumer switching ontentions: The effect of moderating factors. European Journal of Marketing, 41, 1/2 (2007), 135-158.

Bansal, H; Irving, P; and Taylor, S. A three component model of customer commitment to service providers. Journal of the Academy of Marketing Science, 32, 3 (2004), 234-250.

Bansal, H; Taylor, S; and James, Y. Migrating to new service providers: Toward a unifying framework of consumers' switching behaviors. Academy of Marketing Science, 33, 1 (2005), 96-115.

Bansal, HS and Taylor, SF. The service provider switching model (SPSM): A model of consumer switching behavior in the services industry. Journal of Service Research 2, 2 (1999), 200–218.

Bhattacherjee, A; Limayem, M; and Cheung, C. User switching of information technology: A theoretical synthesis and empirical test. Information & Management, 49, 7/8 (2012), 327-333.

Chang, HH and Chen, SW. The impact of customer interface quality, satisfaction and switching costs on e-loyalty: Internet experience as a moderator. Computers in Human Behavior, 24, 6 (2008), 2927-2944.

Chou, PF and Lu, CS. Assessing service quality, switching costs and customer loyalty in home-delivery services in Taiwan. Transport Reviews, 29, 6 (2009), 741-758.

Deng, Z; Lu, Y; Wei, KK; and Zhang, J. Understanding customer satisfaction and loyalty: An empirical study of mobile instant messages in China. International Journal of Information Management, 30, 4 (2010), 289-300.

Dwivedi, UK, Papazafeiropoulou, A., Brinkman, W., and Lal, B., Dwivedi, UK; Papazafeiropoulou, A; Brinkman, W; and Lal, B. Examining the influence of servicande quality and secondary influence on the behavioral intention to change internet service provider. Information System Frontiers, 12, 2 (2010), 207-217.

Edward, M and Sahadev, S. Role of switching costs in the service quality, perceived value, customer satisfaction and customer retention linkage. Asia Pacific Journal of Marketing and Logistics 23, 3 (2011), 327-345.

Fan, L and Suh, Y. Why do users switch to a disruptive technology? An empirical study based on expectation-disconfirmation theory. Information & Management, 51, 2 (2014), 240-248.

Ganesh, J; Arnold, M; and Reynolds, K. Understanding the customer base of service providers: An examination of the differences between switchers and stayers. Journal of Marketing, 64, 3 (2000), 65-87.

Gerpott, TJ; Rams, W; and Schindler, A. Subscriber retention, loyalty, and satisfaction in the German mobile cellular telecommunications market. Telecommunications Policy 25, 4 (2001), 249–269.

Gray, D; D'Alessandro, S; Johnson, L; and Carter, L. Inertia in services: causes and consequences for switching. Journal of Services Marketing, 31, 6 (2017), 485-498.

Han, H; Kim, W; and Hyun, S. Switching intention model development: Role of service performances, customer satisfaction, and switching barriers in the hotel industry. International Journal of Hospitality Management, 30, 3 (2011), 619-629.

Hou, A; Chern, C; Chen, H; and Chen, Y-C. Migrating to a new virtual world: Exploring MMORPG switching through human migration theory. Computers in Human Behavior 27, 5 (2011), 1892-1903.

Hsu, J. Understanding the role of satisfaction in the formation of perceived switching value. Decision Support Systems, 59, 1 (2014), 152-162.

Huang, L and Hsieh, Y. Consumer electronics acceptance based on innovation attributes and switching costs: The case of e-book readers Electronic Commerce Research and Applications, 11, 3 (2012), 218-228.

Keaveney, S. Customer switching behavior in service industries: An exploratory study. Journal of Marketing, 59, 2 (1995), 71-82.

Keaveney, SM and Parthasarathy, M. Customer switching behavior in online services: An exploratory study of the role of selected attitudinal, behavioral, and demographic factors. Journal of the Academy of Marketing Science, 29, 4 (2001), 374-374.

Kim, G; Shin, B; and Lee, HG. A study of factors that affect user intentions toward email service switching. Information & Management, 43, 7 (2006), 884-893.

Kim, H; Chan, HC; and Gupta, S. Value-based adoption of mobile internet: An empirical investigation. Decision Support Systems, 43, 1 (2007), 111–126.

Kim, M; Park, M; and Jeong, D. The effects of customer satisfaction and switching barrier on customer loyalty in Korean mobile telecommunication services. Telecommunications Policy 28, 2 (2004), 145–159.

Lee, J; Kim, Y; Lee, J; and Park, Y. Estimating the extent of potential competition in the Korean mobile telecommunications market: Switching cost and number portability. International Journal of Industrial Organization, 24, 1 (2006), 107-124.

Lee, J; Lee, J; and Feick, L. The impact of switching costs on the customer satisfaction-loyalty link: Mobile phone service in France. Journal of Services Marketing, 15, 1 (2001), 35-48.

Li, Y; Liu, H; Lim, ET; Goh, JM; Yang, F; and Lee, MK. Customer's reaction to cross-channel integration in omnichannel retailing: The mediating roles of retailer uncertainty, identity attractiveness, and switching costs. Decision Support Systems, 109, May (2018), 50-60.

Lin, H and Wang, Y. An examination of the determinants of customer loyalty in mobile commerce contexts. Information & Management 43, 3 (2006), 271–282.

Lin, K-Y; Wang, Y-T; and Hsu, H-YS. Why do people switch mobile platforms? The moderating role of habit. Internet Research, 27, 5 (2017), 1170-1189.

Liu, C; Guo, YM; and Lee, C. The effects of relationship quality and switching barriers on customer loyalty. International Journal of Information Management, 31, 1 (2011), 71–79.

Matzler, K; Strobl, A; Thurner, N; and Füller, J. Switching experience, customer satisfaction, and switching costs in the ICT industry. Journal of Service Management, 26, 1 (2015), 117-136.

Min, D and Wan, L. Switching factors of mobile customers in Korea. Journal of Service Science, 1, 1 (2009), 105-120.

MNP (2021) Mobile number portability 2021, https://en.wikipedia.org/wiki/Mobile_number_portability and http://www.mnportability.com/en/pages/news/pn/1

Park, S and Ryoo, S. An empirical investigation of end-users' switching toward cloud computing: A two factor theory perspective. Computers in Human Behavior, 29, 1 (2013), 160-170.

Patterson, P and Smith, T. A cross culture study of switching barriers and propensity to stay with service providers. Journal of Retailing, 79, 2 (2003), 107-120.

Peng, X; Scott, R; Prybutok, V; and Sidorova, A. Product quality vs. service quality in the mobile industry: Is there a dominant driver of customer intention to switch providers? Operations Management Research, 7, 3-4 (2014), 63-76.

Ping, RA. The effects of satisfaction and structural constraints on retailer exiting, voice, loyalty, opportunism, and neglect. Journal of Retailing 69, 3 (1993), 320-352.

Ranaweera, C and Prabhu, J. The influence of satisfaction, trust and switching barriers on customer retention in a continuous purchasing setting. International Journal of Service Industry Management, 14, 4 (2003), 374-395.

Ranganathan, C; Seo, DB; and Babad, Y. Switching behavior of mobile users: Do users' relational investments and demographics matter? European Journal of Information Systems, 15, 3 (2006), 269-276.

RCR wireless (2021). Number portability: more than 5 million Brazilian switched operators in 2011, URL: www.rcrwireless.com/americas/20120110/carriers/number-portability-more-than-5-million-brazilian-switched-operators-in-2011/# accessed 22.12.2021

Rouibah K. (2017). Switching Factors In the Mobile Service Providers: A qualitative study. Advances in Economics, Business and Management Research (AEBMR), volume 37 pp. 68-8, ISBN= 978-94-6252-405-7, ISSN: 2352-5428, DOI: doi:10.2991/ictim-17.2017.2 Proceedings of the International Conference on transformation and innovation in management (ICTIM-17), Shanghai, China 9-10 September 2017

Salo, M and Makkonen, M. Why do users switch mobile applications? Trialing behavior as a predecessor of switching behavior. Communications of the Association for Information Systems, 42, 14 (2018), 1-21.

Sharma, N and Patterson, P. Switching costs, alternative attractiveness and experience as moderators of relationship commitment in professional, consumer services. International Journal of Service Industry Management, 11, 5 (2000), 470-490.

Shin, D. Study of mobile number portability effects in the United States. Telematics and Informatics 24, 1 (2007), 1-14.

Shin, DH and Kim, WY. Forecasting customer switching intention in mobile service: An exploratory study of predictive factors in mobile number portability. Technological Forecasting and Social Change, 75, 6 (2008), 854-874.

Wang, YS; Wu, SC; Lin, HH; and Wang, YY. The relationship of service failure severity, service recovery justice and perceived switching costs with customer loyalty in the context of e-tailing. International Journal of Information Management, 31, 4 (2011), 350-359.

Whitten, D and Wakefield, RL. Measuring switching costs in IT outsourcing services. Journal of Strategic Information Systems, 15, 3 (2006), 219-248.

Xconnect (2021). Countries with Mobile Number Portability. URL: https://www.xconnect.net/countries-with-mobile-number-portability/ accessed 11 December 2021

Zhang, KZK; Lee, MKO; Cheung, CMK; and Chen, H. Understanding the role of gender in bloggers' switching behavior. Decision Support Systems, 47, 4 (2009), 540-546.

UNDERSTANDING HYBRID AGILE APPROACH: A CONCEPTUAL FRAMEWORK

Majid Alsubaie and Hamed Sarbazhosseini
University of Canberra, Australia

ABSTRACT

Hybrid agile approach involves combining both agile and non-agile techniques in managing projects within organizations. While hybrid agile is an emerging approach that is gaining popularity, its nature is not well-defined, and there is limited research on the outcomes of this approach in areas such as project success, people skills, and IT project management. This study aims to address these gaps by developing a conceptual framework and conducting case studies to examine hybrid agile from various perspectives. The findings suggest that the hybrid agile approach is more effective than pure agile due to its flexibility in utilizing a variety of approaches, frameworks, and practices while also addressing both internal and external success measures. The study also highlights the importance of people culture and an agile mindset in building effective teams. By leveraging the flexibility of the hybrid agile approach, organizations can tailor their project management strategies to meet their specific needs. The proposed conceptual framework can be applied to evaluate any project management approach and offer insights to overcome challenges within organizations.

KEYWORDS

Hybrid Agile, Information Systems, Success Measures, Project Management

1. INTRODUCTION

Hybrid Agile is a combination of agile and non-agile practices used in project management (Hartman, 2017). The use of this approach has been considered effective in IT projects and is claimed to increase the success of project outcomes compared to traditional methods (Copola Azenha et al., 2021; Digital.ai, 2021; Gemino et al., 2021; Serrador & Pinto, 2015). The recent research has mostly focused on identifying the agile practices with little research on exploring how organizations can effectively combine different approaches with purpose of achieving results (Copola Azenha et al., 2021). However, there is limited research on how organizations can effectively use the Hybrid Agile approach to manage IT projects. Also, hybrid agile is an emerging approach that combines traditional agile methodologies with other project management approaches, such as waterfall or Lean. While hybrid agile is gaining popularity in various industries and organizations, there is still limited research on its outcomes in areas such as project success, team dynamics, and overall project management effectiveness (Gou et al., 2021; Ranganath et al., 2021; Manikas & Hansen, 2018). This approach allows organizations to customize their project management processes to suit their specific needs and goals. Hybrid agile recognizes that different projects and teams require different levels of flexibility and structure, and it seeks to find a balance between the two.

The importance of hybrid agile lies in its ability to provide organizations with the best of both worlds. It combines the flexibility and adaptability of agile with the structure and control of traditional project management approaches. This allows organizations to better manage risk, meet deadlines, and deliver high-quality products or services.

Despite its increasing popularity, there is still a gap in researching the outcomes of hybrid agile. While there are some studies that have explored the effectiveness of hybrid agile, there is still limited research on its outcomes in areas such as project success, team dynamics, and overall project management effectiveness. As a result, there is a need for more research on hybrid agile to better understand its impact and effectiveness.

This research aims to explore hybrid agile from an Information Systems perspective by examining its frameworks, tools, techniques, success measures, and people skills. The study of hybrid agile management has been a recent focus for researchers and the development of a conceptual framework for it can provide structure and standardization to the field. This research will first provide background on hybrid agile and its need for conceptualization, then develop a framework for it and apply it in the research design. The findings from the case studies will conclude the paper.

2. BACKGROUND

Hybrid agile approach is a combination of agile and non-agile practices that has been increasingly adopted in IS projects. The adoption of hybrid agile is driven by the need to leverage the benefits of agile while considering the constraints that large organizations face (Zasa et al., 2020). The integration of non-agile practices with agile environment enhances the effectiveness of agile implementation (Gill et al., 2018). The studies have shown that the hybrid-agile methods lead to better project outcomes and success (Serrador & Pinto, 2015).

However, there are several challenges in effectively managing agile projects, including the inability to support requirement changes during a project and lack of project predictability at the initial phase of a project (Kasauli et al., 2021; Heeger & Nielsen, 2018). The implementation of hybrid-agile processes enables project predictability and supports requirement changes during a project (Islam & Storer, 2020). Furthermore, while hybrid approaches aim to integrate traditional and agile project management methods, there is a lack of clarity on how this integration should be done and what the most effective strategies are for ensuring successful implementation (Bhattacharya, 2020).

In hybrid agile environment, it requires effective communication and stakeholder management to succeed. However, there is a need for further research on how to effectively communicate and manage stakeholders in hybrid project management environments, especially in complex or large-scale projects as well as the need for new metrics and performance measurements methods to accurately assess project progress and success (Gupta et al., 2021). Also, it requires effective team collaboration and coordination. However, there is a need for further research on how to promote and sustain team collaboration in hybrid project management environments, especially when team members come from diverse backgrounds and may have different ways of working (Bhattacharya, 2020).

Several studies have highlighted the importance of understanding the outcomes of hybrid agile in project management. For example, Ranganath et al. (2021) found that hybrid agile methods can have a positive impact on project performance in the IT industry. However, there is still a lack of research on the outcomes of hybrid agile in other industries and contexts.

Furthermore, Gou et al. (2021) conducted a systematic mapping study of hybrid agile software development and found that there is limited research on the effectiveness of hybrid agile in areas such as team dynamics, project success, and overall project management effectiveness. This highlights the need for more research on hybrid agile to better understand its impact and effectiveness in project management.

Manikas and Hansen (2018) also conducted a review of the literature on hybrid agile project management approaches and found that there is still a lack of understanding of the optimal approach to hybrid agile. They emphasized the need for further research to identify best practices and effective ways to implement hybrid agile in project management.

3. DEVELOPMENT OF CONCEPTUAL FRAMEWORK

The call for investigating hybrid agile approach is demonstrated in the previous sections and by many researchers. This paper tries to develop a conceptual framework that looks at hybrid agile from several angles in order to provide a comprehensive understanding about the phenomena.

The conceptual framework for understanding hybrid agile approach in IT project management is developed based on a literature review of existing studies and research in the field. The framework aims to provide clarity and completeness in understanding the concept of hybrid agile and how it can be successfully implemented in organizations. The framework consists of several elements, including the approaches and frameworks that make up hybrid agile, the practices, tools, and techniques used in implementing hybrid agile, the benefits and challenges of adoption, and the success measures used to evaluate the success of hybrid agile delivery. The conceptual framework seeks to fill the gap in the existing knowledge about hybrid agile and provide a basis for further primary studies on the topic.

The conceptual framework development is derived from the literature review of agile environments and referring to IT project management concepts to better examine hybrid agile approaches. Below we discuss the elements and concepts which construct the conceptual framework.

3.1 Hybrid Agile Conceptual Framework

The development of a conceptual framework for understanding hybrid agile approaches aims to formalize a theory to explore a less researched concept. The framework is based on two main areas: factors of benefits and challenges of hybrid agile, and the exploration of how organizations can successfully implement hybrid agile through practices, tools and techniques, success measures, and people factors. The framework aims to clarify and complete the understanding of hybrid agile, by exploring why it is selected, the benefits and challenges of adoption, and how it can be successfully implemented. The conceptual framework includes elements such as the kind of frameworks and approaches that make up hybrid agile, practices, tools, and techniques, benefits and challenges of adoption, success measures, and people factors. The framework is based on existing studies and the importance of understanding these elements in building a successful hybrid agile environment. The conceptual framework is shown in figure 1.

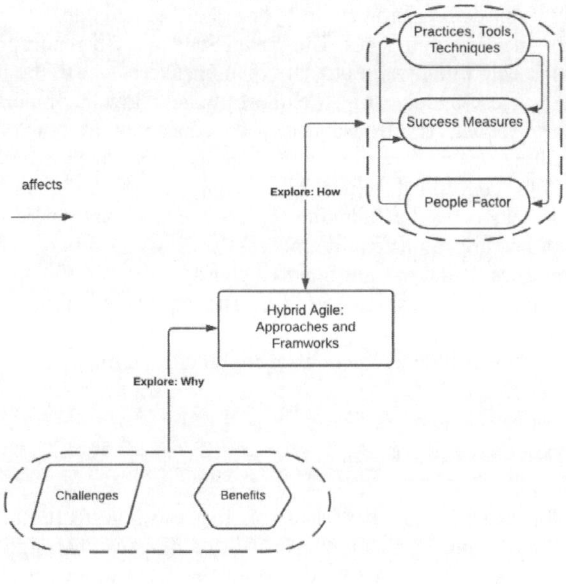

Figure 1. Hybrid Agile Approach Conceptual Framework

There are two characteristics for the conceptual framework which can make it unique and useful for understanding hybrid agile use in organisations. The characteristics of the conceptual framework are clarity and completeness. Clarity is derived from understanding why hybrid agile can be selected in organisation as their management approach by understanding the benefits of the adoption of hybrid agile and the challenges of such adoption. By understanding such two important things about hybrid agile, it can clarify to whomever would like to implement and adopt the same approach and framework.

In relation to completeness, the decision of choosing the practices, tools and techniques, success measures, and people factor can also enrich the understanding of the concept of hybrid agile and contribute to the completeness of our understanding of the new concept. Such clarify and completeness would justify the importance of the conceptual framework in investigating the hybrid agile concept to help in successfully management of IT projects.

In terms of practices, tools, and techniques, each approach and framework have a set of practices, tools, and techniques that help in following it. It is important to cover the practices, tools, and techniques that help in following hybrid agile approaches. Currently, a wide range of tools support agile techniques and practices, so it is important to understand which tools could be associated with hybrid agile. The importance of identifying such information is aligned with studies such as the State of Agile report, which shows which agile techniques are used among practitioners when following the agile methodology.

The benefit of adopting hybrid agile approaches is another element that our conceptual framework consisted of. The rationale behind including the benefits of hybrid agile adoption is derived from studies like (Digital.ai, 2021). It is very important to understand hybrid agile adoption to understand the successful hybrid agile environment. The studies of the benefits of agile in the literature are extensive, and that added extra importance to the necessity of this element in our conceptual framework.

The challenges of hybrid agile approaches are another element of our conceptual framework. Such identification could help us to understand the hybrid agile adoption consequences. It adds to the value of understanding the successful hybrid agile environment. The importance of identifying the key challenges that organizations face when adopting hybrid agile is derived from the literature around agile challenges in studies such as (Digital.ai, 2021). The two elements (benefits and challenges) are recommended to be the subjects of further primary studies evaluating agile hybrids and project management to benefit agile research (Hoda et al., 2017).

Another element of this conceptual framework is success measures. Understanding how organizations measure the success of hybrid agile delivery is important. Many studies have focused on success measures and factors. Therefore, the success measures help to understand the hybrid agile environment and build an image around how to successfully deliver projects in hybrid agile environments, as well as the success measures around specific frameworks and approaches. The annual State of Agile report provides the significant measures that organizations use in determining agile transformation success. Also, the literature review analyzed other papers that looked at the success factors of agile: those studies show the importance of identifying the success measures around any project delivery. Consequently, the conceptual framework includes the success measures that could be used in assessing and determining the success of hybrid agile delivery.

The last element of the conceptual framework is people factors. Agile is known for being people-focused, and studies on people factors in the literature underscore the importance of including people factors to understand a successful hybrid agile environment as well as the kind of people factors associated with frameworks and approaches. Agile has put more emphasis on people factors, and one of the sections of the Agile Manifesto is about people, as explained earlier. The importance of identifying people factors that can be associated with successful hybrid agile environments was derived from the fact that agile is people-focused, and the Agile Manifesto puts people interactions over process and tools.

4. RESEARCH METHOD

The research design for this study is a case study approach to investigate the implementation of the hybrid approach in organizations. Figure 2 presents an overview of the research design utilized in this study, providing a visual summary of its key components. The study includes three case studies from government and non-government organizations, with 19 participants interviewed and more than eight documents reviewed. The participants included the following roles: program manager, scrum master, agile coach, product owner, system analyst and senior project manager.

The data was collected using semi-structured interviews and document review. The four criteria tests in social sciences, construct validity, internal validity, external validity, and reliability, were addressed by using techniques such as establishing a chain of evidence, structural coding, content analysis, thematic coding, and inter-coder reliability. The research questions were developed using both means-ends and framework perspectives, focusing on three parts. The first part is an introduction to the interview to provide a convenient environment. The second part covers why organizations apply the hybrid approach, and how the manage their hybrid agile environment. The third part of the interview protocol covers how organizations measure project success, and what team and people requirements affect the success of hybrid-agile projects. The developed framework was used to structure the research project and evaluate the literature.

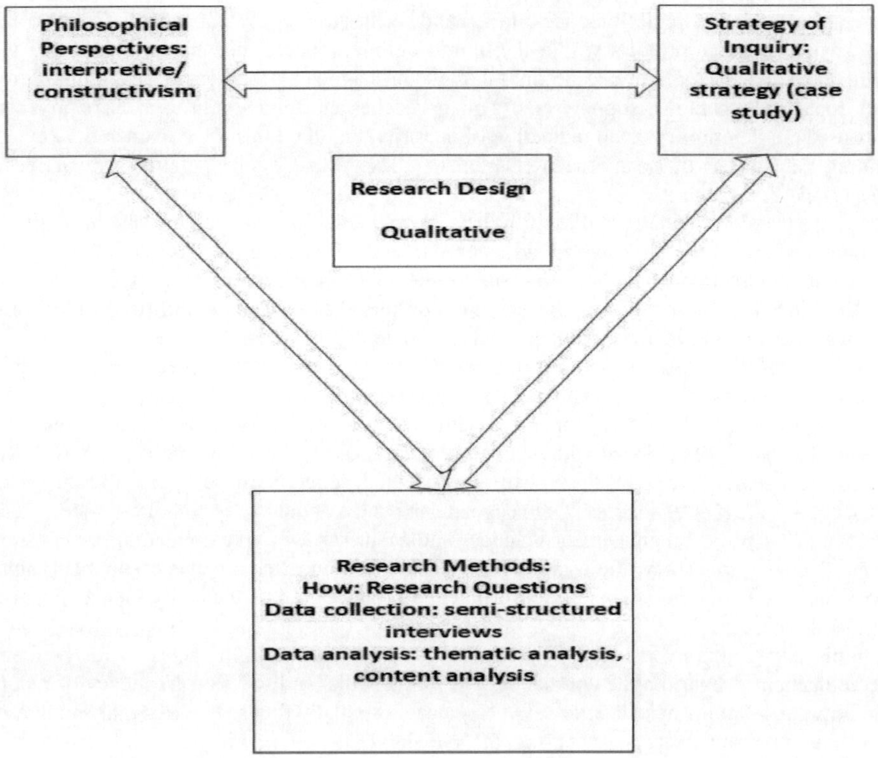

Figure 2. Framework for design: the interconnection of worldviews, strategy of inquiry, and research methods for this study

5. RESULTS AND DISCUSSION

The study collected data from three large case studies and expert interviews to explore themes in hybrid agile environments. The study identified five main themes: agile, hybrid agile, scaled agile, structured frameworks, and lean principles. The most common combination of approaches and frameworks in hybrid agile were the scrum framework, in-house hybrid agile approach, and SAFe. Success in hybrid agile was focused on both internal and external measures, with agile metrics, customer and user satisfaction, product scope, and triple constraint as the most cited success measures. People themes emphasized the importance of an agile mindset and culture, continuous improvement and learning, and team member soft skills. Adopting hybrid agile brings benefits such as clear requirements, customer satisfaction, and team development satisfaction. Common barriers to adopting hybrid agile include change in scope, lack of integration of non-development functions, and lack of documentation.

The five main themes of approaches and frameworks identified in this study which construct the hybrid agile environment are agile, hybrid agile, scaled agile, structured frameworks, and lean principles. Each theme consists of one or more approaches or/and frameworks. For example, Scrum and Kanban are considered under the agile theme. The agile theme is combined with all of the other themes which can lead to the fact that scrum and Kanban are the basic of hybrid agile approach. The hybrid agile theme consists of approaches and frameworks which are represented as an in-house built hybrid agile framework and Prince2 agile framework combinations. The scaled agile frameworks consist of SAFe, LeSS, Nexus, and Spotify. However, SAFe is the most common one. The structured frameworks are the waterfall and Prince2 frameworks. Finally, the lean principles are found common to be combined with constructing the approaches and frameworks in hybrid agile.

The concept of hybrid agile practices, tools, and techniques in the conceptual framework provides the specific ways to manage projects within the hybrid agile approach. In our study, there are twenty themes describing the practices, tools, and techniques in the hybrid agile environment. As explained before, the use of practices, tools, and techniques support the use of approaches and frameworks to manage projects. Further, the practices used are determined as an indication of maturity, and the tools are considered a key component for determining the success of an approach (Digital.ai, 2021). Most of the practices are derived from scrum practices and SAFe practices.

There are several combinations of approaches and frameworks that construct hybrid agile. However, the scrum framework, in-house built hybrid agile approach, and SAFe are the most common combinations. The importance of the mentioned approaches and frameworks is based on their popularity. The variety of combinations in hybrid agile indicates the flexibility of hybrid agile. The flexibility can allow organisations to leverage what suits them best to serve their needs in managing their projects.

The list of how organisations measure success in hybrid agile includes a spectrum of internal and external factors as well as addressing project management success and product success. The internal and external factors mean the driver's context of these factors and whether the business benefits identification that will result if the investment objectives are achieved and who can be influenced by such outcomes (Gomes & Romão, 2016). The project management success is the type of success which concern time, cost, quality, and satisfaction while product success is the type of success which concerns the value of outcomes. The pre-defined success measures can assist in better project management practices and ensure an effective impact on project success (Gomes & Romão, 2016). In this study, the use of agile metrics is the most common measurement metrics in hybrid agile environment. Customer and user satisfaction and product scope are equally seen as important measures of hybrid agile success.

It can be claimed that hybrid agile delivery success is focused on agile metrics with the metrics linked to every combination of hybrid agile approaches and frameworks and the high frequency of reporting them. It also can be argued that the hybrid agile delivery success is equally focused on external and internal measures, with the most cited success measures and the one linked to every kind of combination of hybrid agile approaches and frameworks. It is focused on agile metrics, customer and user satisfaction, product scope, and triple constraint. The focus on internal and external measures indicates the uniqueness of hybrid agile because it focuses on external measures in agile (Digital.ai, 2021). The focus of the success measures also includes both project management success and product success.

The people themes explored the importance of team characteristics and important for building effective teams around the hybrid agile environment. Amongst the nine themes, agile mindset and culture factors are the most important factors. The concepts of continuous improvement and learning, soft skills, openness to change, and organisation support are seen as equally important factors for team members.

The hybrid agile adoption presents various benefits that are achievable in organisations. The list of themes associated with the most important reasons and benefits for adopting hybrid agile include the ability to build quickly, having clear requirements, having customer satisfaction, and gaining team development satisfaction. The benefits that organizations gain when adopting hybrid agile approach can show that stakeholders inside and outside the organization are benefiting out this the developed product.

The reasons that encourage organisations to adopt hybrid agile indicate the ability of organisations to meet their goals. The reasons span from the ability to build quickly to clear requirements. Both are critical to ensure the right product is successfully delivered. The ability to respond to change quickly is evidently critical since we live in a pandemic. It can be claimed that organisations can address their goals in hybrid agile adoption. The reasons customer satisfaction and team satisfaction and development focus on the alignment of the happiness of the customer and team members plays an important role in rapidly changing working environments. Additionally, the satisfaction of the customer and team members can play a critical role in ensuring the success of hybrid agile adoption.

On the other hand, the most common barriers and challenges when adopting hybrid agile approach are the change in scope, integration of non-development function, and lack of documentation. It is evident that organizations are frustrated with change in project scope while the purpose of using agile techniques is to initiate the project where there is a little clarity and scope. It seems that the change particularly in the hybrid environment, organisations require better understanding of scope and planning. In addition, the lack of documentation and lack of quality metrics are discovered as major challenges where hybrid approach requires clear quality metrics and detailed documentation.

In summary, there are number of different approaches that can been taken into consideration in hybrid management. In this study we reported on analyzed data for explored tools and techniques, success, and people requirements. We believe the conceptual framework benefits organization by providing a clear and complete picture of how they can consider the hybrid agile approach for achieving better outcomes. This can be extended to assess any other project management approach or any work settings.

6. CONCLUSION

This paper explored the hybrid-agile domain, which is a complex and evolving field in the project management. To address these challenges, the paper proposed a conceptual framework to structuring the study and applies it to organizational analysis. The study adopts a critical realist perspective to identify the socially, materially, and discursively real aspects of the phenomenon under investigation. The paper presents a framework that can be used to formulate research questions, design and collect data, and analyze findings. The contributions of the paper include a new method for conceptualizing management domains and an approach to conducting research that is particularly useful for complex problem areas.

The study provides valuable insights into hybrid agile approaches and frameworks and their implementation in organizations. It highlights both the benefits and challenges of adopting this approach and provides recommendations for organizations looking to adopt hybrid agile. The paper also highlights the need for further research to establish evidence-based practices for hybrid-agile management. The limitations of the paper include the small sample size and the limited scope of the study. Future research could benefit from larger sample sizes, additional data sources, and more comprehensive analyses. Another limitation can be the reliance on conceptualization approach. The paper relies heavily on the use of the conceptualizing approach for the analysis of the hybrid-agile domain. This could limit the validity and reliability of the findings if the approach is not applied correctly or if there are limitations in the approach itself.

Overall, the paper provides a valuable contribution to the study of hybrid-agile management and offers a new conceptual framework to research and analysis in complex problem areas. Future research also should focus on understanding the impact of hybrid agile in different industries and contexts, identifying best practices for its implementation, and exploring its effectiveness in areas such as team dynamics, project success, and overall project management effectiveness.

ACKNOWLEDGEMENT

We extend our gratitude to all individuals who participated in every phase of this study.

REFERENCES

Adelakun, O., Garcia, R., Tabaka, T., & Ismail, R. (2017). *Hybrid project management: Agile with discipline.* Paper presented at the International Conference on Information Resources Management (CONF-IRM).

Bhattacharya, S. (2020). Hybrid project management: A review of the literature. Journal of Modern Project Management, 8(3), 32-49.

Copola Azenha, F., Aparecida Reis, D., & Leme Fleury, A. (2021). The role and characteristics of hybrid approaches to project management in the development of technology-based products and services. *Project Management Journal, 52*(1), 90-110.

Cram, W. A., & Marabelli, M. (2018). Have your cake and eat it too? Simultaneously pursuing the knowledge-sharing benefits of agile and traditional development approaches. *Information & Management, 55*(3), 322-339.

Digital.ai. (2021). 15th State of Agile Report.

Dybå, T., & Dingsøyr, T. (2008). Empirical studies of agile software development: A systematic review. *Information and Software Technology, 50*(9-10), 833-859.

Fleetwood, S., & Ackroyd, S. (2004). *Critical realist applications in organisation and management studies* (Vol. 11): Psychology Press.

Gemino, A., Horner Reich, B., & Serrador, P. M. (2021). Agile, traditional, and hybrid approaches to project success: Is hybrid a poor second choice? *Project Management Journal, 52*(2), 161-175.

Gill, A. Q., Henderson-Sellers, B., & Niazi, M. (2018). Scaling for agility: A reference model for hybrid traditional-agile software development methodologies. *Information Systems Frontiers, 20*(2), 315-341.

Gomes, J., & Romão, M. (2016). Improving project success: A case study using benefits and project management. *Procedia Computer Science, 100*, 489-497.

Gregor, S. (2006). The nature of theory in information systems. *MIS quarterly*, 611-642.

Gou et al. (2021). "Hybrid Agile Software Development: A Systematic Mapping Study." IEEE Access, 9, 84926-84939.

Gupta, et al. (2020). Hybrid project management framework: A systematic review. Journal of Modern Project Management, 8(2), 36-53.

Hartman, B. (2017). What is hybrid agile, anyway? *Agile Alliance, Portland, OR, White Paper*.

Heeager, L. T., & Nielsen, P. A. (2018). A conceptual model of agile software development in a safety-critical context: A systematic literature review. *Information and Software Technology, 103*, 22-39.

Hoda, R., Salleh, N., Grundy, J., & Tee, H. M. (2017). Systematic literature reviews in agile software development: A tertiary study. *Information and Software Technology, 85*, 60-70.

Islam, G., & Storer, T. (2020). A case study of agile software development for safety-Critical systems projects. *Reliability Engineering & System Safety, 200*, 106954.

Kasauli, R., Knauss, E., Horkoff, J., Liebel, G., & de Oliveira Neto, F. G. (2021). Requirements engineering challenges and practices in large-scale agile system development. *Journal of Systems and Software, 172*, 110851.

Manikas & Hansen (2018). "Hybrid Agile Project Management Approaches: A Review of the Literature." International Journal of Project Management, 36(2), 327-340.

Nerur, S., Mahapatra, R., & Mangalaraj, G. (2005). Challenges of migrating to agile methodologies. *Communications of the ACM, 48*(5), 72-78.

Noll, J., & Beecham, S. (2019). *How agile is hybrid agile? an analysis of the helena data.* Paper presented at the International Conference on Product-Focused Software Process Improvement.

Ranganath et al. (2021). "Exploring the Relationship between Hybrid Agile Methods and IT Project Performance." Journal of Enterprise Information Management, 34(4), 938-958.

Sekaran, U., & Bougie, R. (2016). *Research methods for business: A skill building approach*: john wiley & sons.

Serrador, P., & Pinto, J. K. (2015). Does Agile work?—A quantitative analysis of agile project success. *International journal of project management, 33*(5), 1040-1051.

Sommer, A. F., Hedegaard, C., Dukovska-Popovska, I., & Steger-Jensen, K. (2015). Improved product development performance through agile/stage-gate hybrids: The next-generation stage-gate process? *Research-Technology Management, 58*(1), 34-45.

Theocharis, G., Kuhrmann, M., Münch, J., & Diebold, P. (2015). *Is water-scrum-fall reality? on the use of agile and traditional development practices.* Paper presented at the International Conference on Product-Focused Software Process Improvement.

Wideman, R. M. (2002). Comparing PRINCE2® with PMBoK®. *AEW Services, Vancouver, BC, Canada*, 13-16.

Yin, R. K. (2017). *Case study research and applications: Design and methods*: Sage publications.

Zasa, F. P., Patrucco, A., & Pellizzoni, E. (2020). Managing the hybrid organization: How can agile and traditional project management coexist? *Research-Technology Management, 64*(1), 54-63.

AN EXPERT VIEW ON CHALLENGES IN MANAGING IT COSTS IN THE DIGITAL AGE

Constanze Riedinger[1] and Melanie Huber[2]

[1]*Konstanz University of Applied Sciences, Alfred-Wachtel-Straße 8, 78462 Konstanz, Germany*

[2]*BITCO³ GmbH, Max-Stromeyer-Straße 116, 78467 Konstanz, Germany*

ABSTRACT

In the digital age, information technology (IT) is a strategic asset for organizations. As a result, the IT costs are rising, and the cost-effective management of IT is crucial. Nevertheless, organizations still face major challenges and former studies lack comprehensiveness and depth. The goal of this paper is to generate a deep and holistic view on current management challenges of IT costs. In 15 expert interviews, we identify 23 challenges divided into 7 categories. The main challenges are to ensure transparency on IT cost information, to demonstrate the business impact of IT as well as to change the mindset for the value of IT and overcoming them requires attention to their interactions. Hence, this paper leads to a better understanding of the issues that IT cost management (ITCM) faces in the digital age and builds a base for future research.

KEYWORDS

IT Cost Management, Expert Interviews, Challenges, IT Governance, COBIT Components

1. INTRODUCTION

The increasing demands on companies in terms of digitalization require companies to make strategic investments in technology (Capgemini, 2022). As a result, IT costs have been rising steadily in recent years and are forecast to increase by a further 5.1% in 2023 (Gartner Inc., 2022b). This necessitates IT responsible to choose the right digital initiatives and thereby achieve cost-effectiveness (Gartner Inc., 2022a). Cost-effective use of IT is a goal of IT Governance (Weill & Ross, 2004) and requires a functioning IT cost management (ITCM). It ensures that organizations control IT costs, support decisions on IT investments, IT outsourcing, and IT innovation, and establish a cost-effective IT deployment (Egle, 2008). However, a study of 501 IT managers in 2022 states that 81% of the respondents still have difficulties to ensure spend-efficiency and avoid waste (Flexera, 2022). This is why we aim to understand the specific challenges that organizations face in the digital age when managing IT costs.

The exchange with practice is substantial for academia in order to create knowledge and develop new theoretical approaches that address existing challenges (Strecker & Kargl, 2009). Earlier studies investigate integration deficits between practice and theory in the field of IT cost management: Strecker and Kargl (2009) as well as Walter and Spitta (2004) show that existing research either does not cover the problem or lack application in practice. Recent research develops new approaches on cloud costs and chargeback (Ajeh et al., 2014; Stefanov et al., 2012) and the pricing of new collaboration models or platforms (Grytz et al., 2020). However, it does not face the challenges of the cost management discipline in times of digital transformation. We therefore conduct expert interviews to generate a deep and holistic view on the management challenges of IT costs. Thereby, we contribute to scientific research by shedding light on current challenges and consequently, by highlighting future research directions to solve these challenges. Additionally, practitioners gain awareness through the holistic view of the challenges.

This paper is structured as follows: First, we introduce the research field of ITCM. We then show our research method, which comprises expert interviews and a qualitative analysis. Finally, we present our findings, posit propositions for future research and draw a conclusion.

2. EVOLVING FIELD OF IT COST MANAGEMENT

The discipline of ITCM has a long research history reacting to different challenges often triggered by external influences or transformations such as increasing portions of IT costs (Berghout & Renkema, 2001) or the evolving IT landscape (Drury, 1998; Grytz & Krohn-Grimberghe, 2018b). In the last decade, researchers especially focused on the identification of root causes and drivers of IT costs (Glissmann & Ludwig, 2013; Hamel et al., 2012; Riedinger et al., 2022), the pricing of digital goods and cloud services (Ajeh et al., 2014; Huang & Sundararajan, 2011) as well as the development of cost allocation mechanisms for BI&A systems (Grytz et al., 2020). In order to identify research directions and react to transformations, researchers focus on expert opinions and perform interviews with multinational business groups to determine ITCM requirements (Hamel et al. 2011) or conduct surveys to identify the major challenges in BI&A cost accounting (Grytz & Krohn-Grimberghe, 2018a). Thus, they focus on specific company sizes or subsections of ITCM lacking a holistic perspective of the discipline and the current management challenges. In contrast, latest practical studies (Flexera, 2022; Foundry, 2022) identify the challenges and trends for IT management using quantitative surveys. They include questions on challenges in ITCM but are limited to a predefined subset of questions and assessment scales which impedes acquiring more detailed and in-depth information (Adams & Cox, 2012). "As the pace of change accelerates" (Flexera, 2022) in the digital age, organizations need to gain a deep insight in IT and IT spend in order to keep up. However, the research community lacks a deep and holistic investigation of the current challenges from a broad practical perspective to derive relevant directions for the discipline in the digital age. These shortcomings lead to the research question of this paper: *what are the challenges of IT cost management in the digital age?*

3. RESEARCH METHOD

Academics apply expert interviews to obtain a comprehensive picture of a phenomenon in practice (Saunders, 2019). To understand the changes and challenges of ITCM in practice, we carried out 15 expert interviews (Meuser & Nagel, 2009; Saunders, 2019). The interviews were semi-structured and in-depth (Meuser & Nagel, 2009; Saunders, 2019) to have the opportunity to ask more detailed follow-up questions during the conversation. The leading question was: *which challenges do you currently face in the management of IT costs?* We wanted to cover a broad spectrum of people and functions in the interviews to get as comprehensive an overview as possible. The interviewed persons (P) have various backgrounds coming from different industries, consultancies, platform vendors or academia. As decisive criterion for the selection of the interviewees, we specified that each of the interviewees must have a relevant responsibility and job description. All interviewees were either already part of the network of the research team or were acquired in the network of *VOICE Bundesverband der IT Anwender e.V.*. The interviews were performed by the first author via Microsoft Teams in German language. Finally, we recorded, transcribed, and anonymized all interviews. Table 1 shows an overview of all interviewees (chronological listing based on the date of the interview).

After the interview phase, we conducted qualitative coding (Corbin & Strauss, 2015) for the data analysis, using the tool MAXQDA, which supports researchers during the qualitative content analysis (Santos et al., 2021). In doing so, we assigned respective codes to the data in several iterations. We applied guidelines for open coding to identify challenges (Corbin & Strauss, 2015). In a selective coding, we assigned the challenges to categories aligned to COBIT components. COBIT as established IT governance framework encompasses seven relevant components to build a governance system and achieve management objectives (ISACA, 2018). Through the alignment of the challenges to the categories, we ensure the link to an existing framework (Saunders, 2019) and the holistic view on the ITCM discipline as part of IT governance (ISACA, 2018). In two further iterations, the research team, consisting of four researchers, reviewed and adjusted the coded challenges and their connection to the categories. We identified 23 challenges referring to the following seven categories: (1) People, Skills, and Competencies, (2) Services, Infrastructure, Applications, (3) Information, (4) Culture, Ethics and Behavior, (5) Organizational Structure, (6) Processes, (7) Principles, Policies and Frameworks.

Table 1. Overview Interviewees

ID	Function	Workplace	ID	Function	Workplace
P1	Director IT Governance Global	Multi Industry, 11.250 employees (EMP)	P9	Sales Manager	ITCM Platform Vendor, 1.000 EMP
P2	Chief Information Officer (CIO)	Electrical Engineering, 400 EMP	P10	Process Owner Global Risk and Compliance	Automotive Sector, 172.500 EMP
P3	Project Manager	IT Consultancy, 50 EMP	P11	Head of Global IT Controlling	Transportation, 30.000 EMP
P4	CIO	Construction Sector, 1.850 EMP	P12	Head of IT Governance	Multi Industry, 4.300 EMP
P5	Head of ITCM	Automotive Sector, 172.500 EMP	P13	Head of IT Governance	Financial Services & Insurance, 350 EMP
P6	TBM Advisor	IT Consultancy, 1.000 EMP	P14	CIO	Fashion Industry, 1.300 EMP
P7	CIO	Financial Services & Insurance, 3.000 EMP	P15	Professor	University of Applied Sciences, Business Information Technology
P8	Head of IT Governance	Automotive Sector, 157.500 EMP			

4. FINDINGS AND DISCUSSION

In the following, we answer our research question: *what are the challenges of IT cost management in the digital age?* To do so, we present the different challenges for the management of IT costs and discuss them in the context of their relevance to the experts and their interrelations.

4.1 Practical Challenges in the Management of IT Costs in the Digital Age

In this subsection, we describe the different challenges for the management of IT costs in detail based on the seven categories introduced above. Table 2 shows an overview of all identified challenges.

Table 2. Overview of challenges in managing IT costs

Category	Challenges
People, Skills, and Competencies	• Enhance Awareness of IT Costs and Cost Drivers (P3, P4, P5, P6, P11, P12, P15) • Establish General IT Know-How (P1, P3, P5, P6, P7, P8, P12, P15) • Improve Management Competencies According to Role of IT (P1, P8, P14)
Services, Infrastructure, Applications	• Realize Adequate Tool Support for ITCM (P2, P3, P5, P6, P9, P10, P11, P14) • Ensure Technical Data Supply for ITCM (P1, P5, P7, P8, P10, P11)
Information	• Specify Clear Objective of ITCM (P1, P3, P5, P11, P15) • Provide a Clear and Consistent Definition of IT Costs (P3, P5, P6, P12, P15) • Ensure Transparency of Consistent IT Cost Information (P1, P2, P3, P5, P6, P7, P9, P10, P12, P13) • Demonstrate Business Impact of IT Costs (P1, P3, P5, P6, P7, P9, P10, P11, P12, P13) • Conduct Stakeholder-Oriented Reporting (P5, P8, P10) • Ensure Comparability of IT Costs Internally and Externally (P1, P4, P5, P12)
Culture, Ethics and Behavior	• Establish a Common Language (P3, P6, P8, P9, P10, P15) • Change Mindset about Value of IT (P1, P5, P6, P7, P8, P9, P10, P11, P12, P15) • Accept IT Department as Equal Partner (P1, P6, P9, P11, P12) • Foster Honest and Transparent Cost Discussion (P1, P5, P8)
Organizational Structure	• Overcome Isolated Units (P3, P5, P6) • Establish Dialogue Structure (P3, P5, P6, P12) • Ensure Formal and Informal Decisions Structures (P1, P5, P6, P8, P9, P10, P15)
Processes	• Execute Processes Efficiently (P1, P3, P5, P8, P10, P11) • Ensure Transparent and Complete Processes for ITCM Execution (P1, P11) • Ensure Process Follow-Up (P5, P6, P11)
Principles, Policies and Frameworks	• Provide a Uniform Data Model (P1, P2, P3, P5, P8, P12) • Enable Policy Enforcement (P1, P5)

IT is a critical success factor for business processes in the digital age and its efficient management becomes a competitive advantage (Urbach et al., 2019). **People, skills and competencies** are "required for good decisions, execution of corrective action and successful completion of all activities" (ISACA, 2018). However, experts identify issues concerning IT know-how and competencies relevant for the efficient management of IT costs. They see a challenge in *enhancing the awareness of IT costs and cost drivers*: especially business employees lack understanding the origin of IT costs and how to link them to the value chain and their consumption behavior (P3, P6, P12, P5). This impedes the ability to use cost as a strategic control variable and for long-term decision-making (P11, P15). The skills "to bring cost information and decisions closer together" (P15) and to use cost driver models for more awareness should be built up to counteract the challenge (P6). Furthermore, experts face a lack of competencies to adapt classical controlling mechanisms on ITCM especially because functioning and complexity of IT relations are not known beyond the IT department (P1, P5, P7, P8, P12). The challenge is to *establish this general IT know-how* to perform target-oriented controlling of IT costs and outline the interrelation between cost and provided service (P3, P6, P15). Furthermore, experts see the challenge to *improve management competencies* even if they are required to efficiently make decisions under cost pressure (P14) and in a long-term perspective (P1). This strategic perspective, however, often cannot be fulfilled as IT personnel lacks management skills (P8) and decision competencies (P1).

Services, infrastructure and applications provide organizations with technology for IT processing and management (ISACA, 2018). The finance discipline makes use of tools and methods of data processing and analysis for improved data quality and decision-making (Rikhardsson & Yigitbasioglu, 2018). The experts agree on challenges concerning the infrastructure, technology and applications (ISACA, 2018) for ITCM related to tool support and technical data supply. First, organizations face the issue to *realize adequate tool support for ITCM*: experts state that they still base their ITCM completely or partly on Microsoft Excel as it is well-known, flexible and no change is needed, however they experience the lack of scalability und integrity (P5, P10, P12). Classical cost management tools miss specificity and therefore cannot support the complexity of IT services (P6, P9). Specific ITCM tools require high effort and cost in customizing to display a company's cost structure (P3) and enable cost recording within the system (P14). Those tools need a consistent and clear data supply in order to support management decisions and foster transparency. However, organizations struggle to *ensure technical data supply for ITCM* by establishing an encompassing master data management as single source of truth (P5, P8). On the contrary, there is inconsistent (P7) and inefficient (P11) data capturing as well as a lack of interfaces for data exchange (P1, P10).

In the digital age, IT is a strategic asset (Urbach et al., 2019). Consequently, the management of IT costs must adopt a strategic character (Urbach & Ahlemann, 2019). A strategic orientation in cost management means using cost information to develop and identify overarching strategies and support decision-making that ensures the long-term perspective of a company (Hansen & Mowen, 2006). According to ISACA (2018) **information** is pervasive throughout any organization. It is required for the effective functioning of the governance system of the enterprise and better cost information allows managers to achieve strategic objectives (Cooper & Kaplan, 1988). However, for ITCM the provision and delivery of information poses major challenges, starting with a clear and company-wide *specification of the objective of ITCM*. "Without target, IT costs can be captured but not managed" (P12). However, experts mention this lack of goal as an inhibitor to execute ITCM (P3, P6) and control the effect of the management discipline (P5, P15). In addition, organizations face a challenge to *provide a clear and consistent definition of IT costs* (P11): "IT costs are those allocated to the IT department, but the fact is that many more are costs for IT and digitalization" (P5). Organizations lack this unambiguous demarcation from other cost types (P1, P15) and thereby lose transparency (P3, P5). The effective management and strategic decision-making (P10) requires cost information. However, interviewees mention a challenge *ensuring transparency of consistent IT cost information*: Data is consolidated and aggregated, losing clarity (P9). As a result, information is not always traceable (P1), and a total cost of ownership analysis is not possible (P6). In addition, personnel costs in IT are not differentiated, which hampers their allocation to individual services (P2, P5, P12). Transparency also lacks for cloud costs, as these occur in both business units and the IT department and are not handled in a uniform manner (P3, P13). This lack of transparent information also hinders organizations to *demonstrate the business impact of IT costs* (P9, P10). Experts state that "it is crucial to understand what we spend money on" (P7) and to directly relate IT costs with content (P1, P5, P12, P13) and strategic topics (P11). However, organizations face an issue to transparently illustrate value (P6), the relation between cost and value (P3, P6) and constructively discuss this business impact through IT investments (P5). ITCM discipline aims to deliver supporting information to enable the responsible persons to make the right decisions. However, interviewees mention the challenge to *conduct* *stakeholder-oriented reporting* and deliver the necessary information to them (P5). "The multitude of offered dashboards is error-prone" (P8) and organizations are not able to continuously prove the IT cost for IT services to the stakeholders and thereby offer transparency (P10). Furthermore, interviewees find it also challenging to *ensure comparability of IT costs internally and externally*. Internally, missing harmonization of data hampers comparability (P1) and the relation between cost and impact is not transparent in order to benchmark (P5, P12). On the other hand, external benchmarks require standards for cost types and models that are currently insufficiently developed (P4).

"**Culture, ethics and behavior** of individuals and of the enterprise are often underestimated as factors in the success of management activities" (ISACA, 2018). Culture influences strategic decision-making as well as the collaboration between business and IT (Riedinger et al., 2022). Both are relevant for the efficient management of IT costs (Egle, 2008). However, experts display issues on the behavior of employees concerning IT costs or related to the discussion culture within organizations. Several interviewees mention the lack of a *common language* (P3, P8) that prevents business and IT from establishing a constructive discussion culture and "building a bridge between technological and commercial world" (P9). Instead, they face issues in commonly understanding delivered cost information (P10, P15) and through that taking data-based decisions (P6, P9). Furthermore, IT is often still labeled as cost factor and IT leaders face cost-cutting measures (P1, P5). The challenge is to *change the mindset within organizations about the value of IT* (P5, P11, P12). This mindset change "should move beyond numbers and data" (P6, P9). Currently, the "focus is on money instead of content" (P15) or value add (P7), and interviewees mention a low acceptance of IT costs in business when it comes to chargeback (P1, P8, P10). There is a lack of dialog at "eye level" (P9) which stresses the challenge of *IT departments being seen as equal partner in discussions* (P6, P12). IT is seen as a by-product (P11) and the IT department accordingly does not have the power to make decisions (P1). The behavior of all stakeholders also counts as success factor for management activities (ISACA, 2018). However, experts experience dishonesty and manipulation, especially connected to misallocation of IT costs in chargeback mechanisms (P8) and hidden IT budgets (P5). A challenge therefore is to *encourage honest and transparent IT cost discussion* and thereby overcome disregarded specifications (P1) and the pursuit of non-transparent peer support (P5).

Digitalization drives the demand in IT for more flexibility, faster modifications, and a proximity to the business (Urbach & Ahlemann, 2019). This impacts **organizational structures** as key decision-making entities in organizations (ISACA, 2018). The set-up and execution of the roles and responsibilities for decisions relevant for ITCM pose issues for the interviewees. First, the challenge is to *ensure formal and informal decision structures*. Some organizations lack clear governance and thereby formal decision-making entities (P9), others define organizational structures but do not execute them (P10). They cannot ensure those informal decision structures and "power seems to be in the wrong place" (P15). The responsibility then lies with people who do not have the power of control (P5, P8) or especially business executives do not take accountability for their IT-related decisions afterwards (P6, P9). The conversation about IT costs "is only possible together with IT department and business executives" (P6). The isolated consideration of the IT unit (P5) as well as the separation of IT and finance departments hampers the management of IT costs (P5). A challenge for the experts is to *overcome isolated units* and open up rigid organizational structures for a holistic view (P3, P6). They mention that the decision-making parties act individually, even if "a dialogue only works if we can bring business, IT department and finance together at the same table" (P3). However, experts still see the difficulty in *establishing a functioning dialogue structure* throughout their whole organization (P3, P5, P6).

"**Processes** describe an organized set of practices and activities to achieve certain objectives and produce a set of outputs that support achievement of overall IT-related goals (ISACA, 2018)." If these processes are not defined and harmonized for ITCM (P1) or there is no common process understanding throughout the company (P11), there is a challenge to *ensure transparent and complete processes for ITCM execution*. Furthermore, the *efficient execution of ITCM processes* is an issue: the high number of manual activities are error-prone and slow and require additional effort (P1, P10). Often, this effort is invested into detailed cost allocation and reporting instead of strategic ITCM which hampers an efficient ITCM process (P3, P5, P11). In addition, organizations undertake a detailed planning of targets (P11) and „elaborate business cases that are not tracked" (P5). Therefore, they hamper to *ensure a process follow-up* to close the gap through target performance comparison and by taking measures (P6).

The diffusion of IT and the accelerating adoption of new technologies (IBM Corporation, 2021) lead to a continuously growing IT spend partly managed outside the IT department (Harvey Nash & KPMG, 2020). For a holistic view, organizations need a uniform framework to perform ITCM throughout the whole organization. **"Principles, policies and frameworks** translate desired behavior into practical guidance for day-to-day management (ISACA, 2018)". However, experts mention the challenge to *provide a uniform costing model* as basis for transparency and comparability (P1): costing models lack a detailed mapping of the company structures (P12) or cost types (P5). Therefore, models only partly reflect total IT costs and services cannot be ordered by users at constant prices (P2, P3, P8). Another challenge is to *enable policy enforcement*. Experts describe a defined central governance which then lacks implementation and enforcement (P1, P5). "Central policies of the IT department are not respected" (P1) such as the deregistration of not needed licenses which lead to increasing IT costs (P5).

4.2 Relevance and Interrelations between ITCM Challenges

In this subsection, we discuss the presented challenges in ITCM in the digital age based on their relevance for the practitioners. Therefore, we compare all categories concerning the number of experts and frequency of mentions. We also include in the heatmap in Figure 1 all challenges on a range from "least mentioned" in white color to "most mentioned" in black color. Furthermore, we examine the interrelations of the challenges.

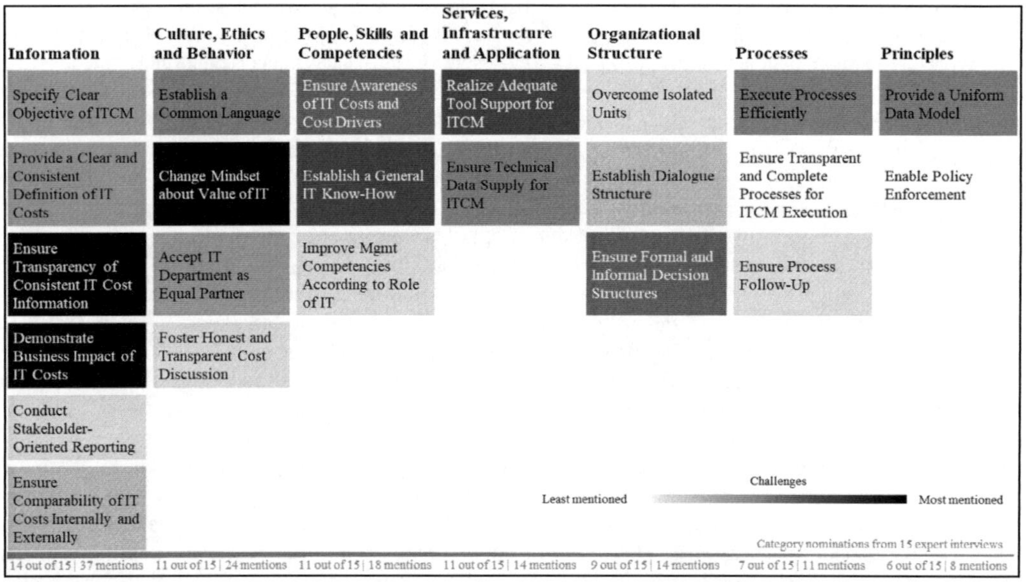

Figure 1. Heatmap of Practitioner Challenges in ITCM

Most practitioners mention challenges concerning **information**. Especially, transparency as well as the presentation of relevant cost information and their impact pose issues for the experts. On the one hand, experts relate those issues in transparent presentation with a lack of tool support or data supply concerning **services, infrastructure, and applications**. On the other hand, most of the experts agrees that the categories **culture, ethics, and behavior** as well as **people, skills, and competencies** have a greater influence on the efficient management of IT costs. As outlined above, the increasing complexity of the IT landscape and greater responsibility in business influence the importance of know-how and cultural change. In addition, required collaboration leads to changes in **organizational structures** and many experts also experience organizational issues for the efficient management of IT costs.

Literature states that the seven used categories do not only individually contribute to a successful management of IT but also interact with each other requiring a holistic perspective (ISACA, 2018). Our results confirm this for a successful management of IT costs. During the interviews, it became clear that the identified issues in ITCM are highly interrelated and overcoming the most mentioned challenges first requires solving other issues. The most mentioned challenges are to *ensure transparency on IT cost information*, *demonstrate the business impact of IT* as well as *change the mindset for the value of IT*. For the *change of the mindset on value of IT*, **organizational structures** need to support collaboration between business and IT (P6) through *formal and informal decision-making* (P15) to foster changes in **culture, ethics and behavior**. Furthermore, the mindset change requires a clear understanding and *demonstration of the business value of IT* (P1, P10). However, the findings show that experts often mention difficulties connecting IT costs with content and explaining their direct link to the added value. They require *transparency of IT cost information* on the one hand (P5) and the *awareness of IT cost and cost drivers* on the other hand (P15) to demonstrate the value. Studies outline that the awareness of cost drivers enhances a better understanding of IT cost and business value of IT (Riedinger et al., 2022), however the interviews show that organization still face issues ensuring this awareness. Furthermore, the experts often mention a lack of transparency when it comes to consistent IT cost information. In order to overcome **information** challenges, experts agree on the need of a consistent presentation through an adequate tool (P10), and stakeholders with the competencies to interpret the information to ensure transparency (P7). The experts, however, acknowledge the challenge to *realize adequate tool support for ITCM.* As prerequisite for the appropriate tool the stakeholders need the general IT know-how to make use of the supporting ITCM tool (P5) and to interpret the presented information for decision-making (P6). *Establishing general IT know-how* represents another major challenge for the experts in ITCM. Adequate skill training supports organizations to overcome challenges in both components: **services, infrastructure and applications** as well as **people, skills, and competencies** (ISACA, 2018). The consideration of challenges thus requires focusing on interrelations in a holistic approach.

5. CONCLUSION

Digitalization and increasing IT spend urge ITCM for the effective and efficient management of IT costs. Nevertheless, several challenges arise in the management of IT costs. A deep and holistic overview and discussion of these challenges in the digital age does not yet exist in academia. Therefore, the goal of this publication is the identification and analysis of challenges for practitioners. To reach this goal, we conduct expert interviews and discuss the findings. The mapping to the seven COBIT components ensures a holistic perspective of the 23 challenges. The number of mentions show challenges especially in the categories **information**, **culture, ethics, and behavior** as well as **people, skills, and competencies**. Experts face major issues ensuring transparency on IT cost information, demonstrating the business impact of IT as well as changing the mindset for the value of IT. However, the categories and underlying challenges are interrelated and overcoming the challenges requires a holistic approach involving these interactions.

This paper makes a theoretical contribution by providing a deep and holistic view on current management challenges of IT costs from an expert perspective, and thus by identifying potential future research directions. Moreover, practice gains insight into challenges during ITCM in the digital age from several practitioners' perspectives and the interrelation between those challenges.

However, the study itself has limitations. First, we only interviewed 15 German-speaking experts. We mitigated these limitations by including experts with diverse backgrounds and from different industries and company sizes. Although we cover as broad a spectrum as possible with these experts, further interviews with experts in various roles around the world could enrich the current research findings, add even more validity, and provide the basis for a holistic analysis of different stakeholder group perspectives or differentiated view on organization sizes or industries. Second, we focus on the expert perspective to identify the challenges in the management of IT costs. A comparison of these challenges with the literature enables a broader insight and the identification of integration deficits between theory and practice. In summary, future research should now seek to analyze ITCM research to enhance or develop solutions to overcome the identified challenges.

REFERENCES

Adams, A., & Cox, A. L. (2012). Questionnaires, in-depth interviews and focus groups. In P. Cairns & A. L. Cox (Eds.), Research methods for human-computer interaction (2nd ed., pp. 17–34). Cambridge Univ. Press.

Ajeh, D. E., Ellman, J., & Keogh, S. (2014). A Cost Modelling System for Cloud Computing. In 14th International Conference on Computational Science and Its Applications (74-84). IEEE.

Berghout, E., & Renkema, T.-J. (2001). Methodologies for investment evaluation: a review and assessment. Information Technology Evaluation Methods and Management, 78–97.

Capgemini (Ed.). (2022). Studie IT Trends 2022: IT wird Kern der Wertschöpfung.

Cooper, R., & Kaplan, R. S. (1988). Measure costs right: make the right decisions: Use activity-based costing to guide corporate strategy. Harvard Business Review, 66(5), 96–103.

Corbin, J. M., & Strauss, A. L. (2015). Basics of Qualitative Research: Techniques and Procedures for Developing Grounded Theory (4th ed.). Sage Publications, Inc.

Drury, D. H. (1998). Temporal Analysis of Information Technology Chargeback Systems. Information Resources Management Journal, 11(2), 5–13.

Egle, U. (2008). IT-Kostenmanagement: Studie zum Kostenmanagement und zur IT bei Schweizer Unternehmen (1st ed.). GRIN-Verlag.

Flexera (Ed.). (2022). State of Tech Spend Pulse.

Foundry (Ed.). (2022). State of the CIO Report: Rebalancing Act: CIOs Operationalize Pandemic-Era Innovation.

Gartner Inc. (2022a). 2023 CIO Agenda. 4 Actions to Ensure Your Tech Investments Pay Digital Dividends.

Gartner Inc. (Octobre 2022b). Gartner Forecasts Worldwide IT Spending to Grow 5.1% in 2023. Gartner IT Symposium/Xpo™ 2022 [Press release]. Orlando.

Glissmann, S., & Ludwig, H. (2013). Value cost impact analysis: Estimating the IT cost impact of business developments. In 2013 IEEE Int. Symposium on Integrated Network Management.

Grytz, R., & Krohn-Grimberghe, A. (2018a). Business Intelligence & Analytics Cost Accounting: A Survey on the Perceptions of Stakeholders. In Hawaii International Conference on System Sciences 2018: HICSS - 51.

Grytz, R., & Krohn-Grimberghe, A. (2018b). Business Intelligence & Analytics Cost Accounting: Review and Synthesis of the Literature. In PACIS 2018 Proceedings, Japan.

Grytz, R., Krohn-Grimberghe, A., & Müller, O. (2020). Business Intelligence & Analytics Cost Accounting: An Action Design Research Approach. In ECIS 2020 Research Papers.

Hamel, F., Herz, T. P., Uebernickel, F., & Brenner, W. (2012). Towards a Better Understanding of IT Cost Drivers of Asset Management Companies. In Conf-IRM 2012, Vienna, Austria.

Hansen, D. R., & Mowen, M. M. (2006). Cost management: Accounting and control (5. ed.). Thomson.

Harvey Nash, & KPMG. (2020). CIO Survey 2020: Everything Changed. Or Did It?

Huang, K.-W., & Sundararajan, A. (2011). Pricing Digital Goods: Discontinuous Costs and Shared Infrastructure. Information Systems Research, 22(4), 721–738.

IBM Corporation. (2021). 2021 CIO Study: The CIO Revolution: Breaking barriers, creating value (C-suite Study). IBM Institute for Business Value.

ISACA. (2018). COBIT 2019®: Framework: Introduction and Methodology. ISACA.

Meuser, M., & Nagel, U. (2009). Das Experteninterview - konzeptionelle Grundlagen und methodische Anlage. In S. Pickel, G. Pickel, H.-J. Lauth, & D. Jahn (Eds.), Methoden der vergleichenden Politik- und Sozialwissenschaft (pp. 465–479). VS Verlag für Sozialwissenschaften.

Riedinger, C., Huber, M., Prinz, N., & Rentrop, C. (2022). Towards a Taxonomy of Strategic Drivers of IT Costs. In 19th European Mediterranean & Middle Eastern Conference on Information Systems (EMCIS 2022), 21-22 December 2022, online.

Rikhardsson, P., & Yigitbasioglu, O. (2018). Business intelligence & analytics in management accounting research: Status and future focus. Int. Journal of Accounting Information Systems, 29, 37–58.

Santos, N., Monteiro, V., & Mata, L. (2021). Using MAXQDA in Qualitative Content Analysis: An Example Comparing Single-Person and Focus Group Interviews. In M. C. Gizzi & S. Rädiker (Eds.), The Practice of Qualitative Data Analysis (pp. 35–53). MAXQDA Press.

Saunders, M. (2019). Research Methods for Business Students (8th ed.). Pearson.

Stefanov, H., Jansen, S., Batenburg, R., van Heusden, E., & Khadka, R. (2012). How to Do Successful Chargeback for Cloud Services. In K. Vanmechelen, J. Altmann, & O. Rana (Eds.), Economics of Grids, Clouds, Systems, and Services (Vol. 7150, pp. 61–75). Springer.

Strecker, S., & Kargl, H. (2009). Integration Deficits of IT Controlling. Business & Information Systems Engineering, 1(3), 204–212.

Urbach, N., & Ahlemann, F. (2019). It Management in the Digital Age: A Roadmap for the IT Department of the Future. Management for Professionals. Springer.

Urbach, N., Ahlemann, F., Böhmann, T., Drews, P., Brenner, W., Schaudel, F., & Schütte, R. (2019). The Impact of Digitalization on the IT Department. Business & Information Systems Engineering, 61(1), 123–131.

Walter, S. G., & Spitta, T. (2004). Approaches to the Ex-ante Evaluation of Investments into Information Systems. WIRTSCHAFTSINFORMATIK, 46(3), 171–180.

Weill, P., & Ross, J. W. (2004). IT Governance on One Page. Massachusetts Institute of Technology.

DATA GOVERNANCE, ENTERPRISE ARCHITECTURE AND ENTERPRISE AGILITY

Tarek Kaddoumi[1] and Torben Tambo[2]
[1]Independent Information Systems Professional
Villa 334, Street 26, Amaranta 2, Villanova, Dubai, United Arab Emirates
[2]Dept. Business Development and Technology, Aarhus University
Birk Centerpark 15, 7400 Herning, Denmark

ABSTRACT

The purpose of this paper is investigating the relationship between data, enterprise architecture (EA) and agility in corporate information technology services. Data is represented by the Chief Data Office(r). The underlying assumption is an assumed disconnectedness between CDO and EA functions. Where CDO is assumed to monitor and exploit data but might lack of connectedness to other relevant business and technology functions in order to released the potentials of the data-driven enterprise. Especially data semantics seems strongly affected by recent health and geopolitical situations. The study is organized based on grounded research especially use of the Gioia method to guide and code semi-structured interview with ten CDO professionals worldwide. Findings pertain to indications of business benefits of connecting CDO and EA functions and responsibilities in ideas of co-ownership of enterprise data resources. The over-arching rationale of this is velocity of change as represented by agile thinking. This is well-known in software development but must be considered broader and in a more committed form connecting enterprise and data in a proposed Enterprise Data Agility. A key practical implication is that the CDO function have been established to exploit data but are more tasked with data governance in form of reporting, integrity assurance, privacy, access policies and similar. The proposed agile thinking suggests more proactive and change-oriented actionability. In other words, changes in data semantics are the best indicators for risks and potentials of the enterprise. By assuring agility in both EA and CDO, changes can be accommodated faster and with more timely risk mitigation.

KEYWORDS

Enterprise Data Agility, Enterprise Architecture, Chief Data Office(r), Data, Agility

1. INTRODUCTION

Enterprises are concerned with extracting and realizing value from their data (Rashed and Drews, 2020). Many practices and organization programs exist to leverage their capabilities in grasping benefits from their data (Jagals, 2021; Fadler & Legner, 2021; Karkošková, 2022). This focus on upskilling enterprise data practices and comes at the same time when enterprises are more motivated to explore more agile ways in architecting their enterprises, business models, and technology platforms. However, there is a topical issue and a question about how connected are enterprises' efforts in implementing agile methodologies in their enterprise architecture management, with their efforts to respond to the increasing data velocity and the need to have more agile data practices (van de Wetering, 2021). In this paper we analyze the dynamics of data and the subsequent data management roles in order to understand the need, limitations and opportunities of agile enterprise architecture (Gong and Janssen, 2021).

The motivation of this paper is led by seeing rapid changes in business dynamics as first and foremost reflected in changes in data semantics. The recent years have induced a range of incidents, e.g., pandemic, supply chain disruptions, materials scarcity, price fluctuations, armed conflicts, tightened regulatory demands, where enterprise IT and architecture have been in the center of solutioning, however systems are not being architected for these purposes. This has led to data as the key change indicator.

Per the explained motivation, and with a goal to contribute to the domains of data, enterprise architecture (EA) and agility in corporate information technology services, we investigate agile enterprise architecture by exploring the need of embedding a proposed Enterprise Data Agility practice as a necessary Agile Enterprise Architecture practice. We question the "ownership" model of the enterprise data agility mainly in the light of the mutual relationship between the Chief Data Office (CDO) (Brenneman, 2018) and the Enterprise architecture management (EA/EAM) (Ahlemann et al., 2021). "Ownership" is in the remainder of this paper the aggregate of organizational and technological factors determining the key governance responsibility and decision power of data in the organization.

The paper is thus identifying the challenges that enterprises might face toward empowering their enterprise data with more agile practices. Which leads to the following research questions:

- Question 1: What is the perception of Chief Data Office stakeholders about the Enterprise Data Agility?
- Question 2: What Chief Data Office stakeholders perceive as main challenges toward achieving Enterprise Data Agility?
- Question 3: How do Chief Data Office stakeholders see the mutual relationship with Enterprise Architecture toward achieving Enterprise Data Agility?

2. THEORETICAL BACKGROUND

The academic literature that documents the agile nature of the enterprise architecture management is scarce, and that empirical ground in particular is missing (Hauder et al., 2013; Schelp & Stutz, 2007), however the topic of applying agile principles and methods in enterprise architecture started to attract studying and research in the recent years (Rouhani et al., 2008; Buckl et al., 2011; Alzoubi et al., 2015; Kaddoumi and Watfa, 2016; Kaddoumi and Watfa, 2021). Defining enterprise architecture has been the subject of multi-faceted publications and research initiatives. However, there are many definitions of the enterprise architecture, no one single agreed definition over all the literatures (Cameron and McMillan, 2013). Achieving the alignment between the business and the IT processes was the main area to highlight in the Systems & Software Consortium definition. Other researchers refer to the enterprise architecture as a set of models and definitions, with description of the structure of the enterprise, the enterprise divisions and the relationships existing between them, and the relationships with the external environment (Engesmo & Panteli, 2021; Alaeddini and Salekfard, 2013). Another perspective has been presented by (Ullrich et al., 2022; Bente et al., 2012) by introducing the enterprise architecture as an architectural thinking to simplify the management of a complex enterprise IT landscape, by defining the IT strategy, modeling the architecture, evolving the IT landscape, assessing and developing capabilities, and developing and enforcing standards and guidelines. Other researchers (Cameron and McMillan, 2013) refer to EA as a blueprint for the system and the project that develops it. Enterprise architecture scope includes the enterprise technology, enterprise information, enterprise processes, and enterprise people; the relationships between these elements and their external environments are also part of the EA scope (Ullrich et al., 2022; Bente et al., 2012).

Enterprises have started recognizing agile methodologies as evolutionary methods in the field of technology development and management specifically and in the fields of business administration and management in general (Kaddoumi and Watfa. 2016; Kaddoumi et al., 2018). There is an interest in adopting the agile principles in enterprise practices, e.g. production management, marketing, strategy execution, etc. This interest can be justified by the ability of Agile methods to introduce incremental, iterative, and change embracing development and management enabling better risk management (Hoda et al., 2008).

Agile methods are considered as counterparts to the traditional waterfall methods. As per (Borad and Rajput, 2015) the waterfall method gives the complete software at the end of its cycle while agile methods work in sprints and provide the repetitive outcomes after each cycle and complete the implementations as per the customer's requirements. The waterfall methodology is a sequential method that follows the step by step model, and it considers a phase as done and completed whe progress moves to the next step. Waterfall method is known for the difficult ability to go back to previous steps (Hoda et al., 2008). On the other hand, the agile methods satisfy the customers and offer most value in a shorter time, by being focused towards customer satisfaction, and allowing for changes through repetitive and incremental development where only needed functionalities are focused on. Agile methods promote the "Just In Time" principle by owning the tasks needed to be achieved in one iteration, which leads to easier ability to modify functionalities when and if needed (Hoda et al., 2008). To embed Agile methods and practices in their change management, decision making architecture and making processes, and more naturally technology change and management, Enterprises have been exploring, piloting, and adopting the Agile Enterprise Architecture (AEA) as a potential Enterprise Architecture adaptation to address Enterprise Architecture complexity (Hauder et al., 2013; Schelp & Stutz, 2007). Agile enterprise architecture is considered as a new method that can solve the challenge of the complex enterprise architecture frameworks and explain aspects and different viewpoints of a busy and complex enterprise completely which is influenced by unexpected changes in functions and technologies (Rouhani & Kharazmi, 2012). Agile enterprise architecture faces many challenges, mainly when it comes to its ability to ensure early and periodical enterprise architecture deliverables and to be able to adapt to the volatile business environment with changing criteria for goal fulfillment (Buckl et al., 2011). This is due to the fact that enterprise architects dedicate most of their time and efforts attempting to document enterprise architecture artifacts and follow enterprise architecture frameworks. This has created an obstacle toward achieving the main goals and values of enterprise architecture. Per (Buckl et al., 2011) the lengthy nature of enterprise architecture is expected to take a minimum of two years so EA and enterprise teams can realize the full-scale benefits of EA management, this also comes with high cost which leads to dissatisfied information providers who regard their efforts as wasted. According to (Rouhani & Kharazmi 2012), agile enterprise architecture is a new suggested method that might address and solve the challenge of the complex enterprise architecture frameworks, "agile EA is a method that explains aspects and different viewpoints of a busy and complex enterprise completely which is influenced by unexpected changes in functions and technologies a lot" (Rouhani & Kharazmi 2012). Agile enterprise architecture might address the studied challenge, seeing "Agile EA is result oriented and mostly concentrated on people's gumption. The most important advantage of agile EA is that it is faster, cheaper and better in people's relationships" (Rouhani & Kharazmi 2012). In the listing of the characteristics of the future enterprise architecture it is insisted on having the "architecture for agile business" as one of the core pillars of such futuristic enterprise architecture. Additionally, in one of his articles in the website of the association of enterprise architects, Allen Brown (President and CEO of the Open Group) appreciated the agile capability in adapting with the constantly changing business requirements by stating, "Agile software development has emerged as one of the ways for IT developers to adapt to the requirements of constant change". He also suggested that "adopting the adaptation of the twelve principles of Agile Development to the discipline of Enterprise Architecture would be an interesting place to start" (Brown 2014).

The Data Management Body of Knowledge identifies data management as the development, execution and supervision of plans, policies, programs and practices that control, protect, deliver and enhance the value of data and information assets (Brackett and Early, 2009). However, the data management practices are not free of challenges, the data management strategies implementations tend to be challenged with traditional and documentation-heavy mindset which results in onerous, bureaucratic strategies that more often than not struggle to support the goals of your organization (PMI, 2022). Moreover, it is reported that enterprises often apply data driven approaches, from predictive systems to AI-driven automation, sporadically throughout the organization, which leaves the value that enterprises anticipate on the table and creates inefficiencies, this has been reasoned by the fact that problems still get solved through traditional approaches and take months or years to resolve (McKinsey, 2022). According to (Lee et al., 2014) leading organizations have learned an important lesson that seemingly tedious data problems are often fundamentally business problems, which can reflect weaknesses in business strategy and operations. To address the need to solve data issues and ongoing concerns, a large number of enterprises established an enterprise-level, executive-rank Chief Data Office (Lee et al., 2014). Enterprises might have different expectations from the Chief Data Office role. Commonly they expect the function to define the enterprise data strategy and priorities, to identify new data business products and offerings, and to position the data as an enterprise strategic asset. Although multiple studies highlight the critical mutual relationship between the data and enterprise architecture either by identifying the data as a key product of the enterprise architecture management practices (Sessions, 2017; Kurniawan, 2013; The Open Group, 2022), or as a supporting asset toward achieving better enterprise architecture. However, aside from having studies addressing the agility of very specific and technical data practices e.g. data science (Närman et al., 2011; Journey, 2017) and data warehouse (Hughes, 2012; Corr and Stagnitto, 2011), there is little material in the academic literature that documents the application of the agile principles and methods on the enterprise data assets, mainly by being part of studying the agile enterprise architecture, and the implementation of the agile methodologies on the enterprise architecture.

3. RESEARCH DESIGN

It has been realized and recognized during and after conducting the literature review phase for this research that there is very little academic literature around the CDO and Enterprise Agility, and - per our limited research capability - nothing about Enterprise Data Agility. With such a situation we decided to use the Grounded Theory method, which is a method that is appropriate when little is known about a phenomenon with an aim to produce or construct an explanatory theory that uncovers a process inherent to the substantive area of inquiry (Chun Tie et al., 2019). The grounded theory method is concerned with the generation of theory, or theorization (Glaser and Strauss, 2017). The most prominent characteristic of grounded theory is that it should be applied to infer new theory strictly by analyzing the primary data. Thus, Grounded Theory is most accurately described as "a qualitative research method that uses a systematic set of procedures to develop an inductively derived grounded theory about a phenomenon" (Strauss and Corbin, 1998).

The Gioia methodology is one implementation of the Grounded Theory approach, which is specifically designed to generate grounded theory, so the emergent theory rooted in the data constitutes the theory. According to Gioia, "Theory is a statement of concepts and their interrelationships that shows how and/or why a phenomenon occurs" (Corley and Gioia, 2011). Relatedly, theoretical contributions arise from the generation of new concepts and/or the relationships among the concepts that help us understand phenomena. The concepts and relationships developed from inductive, grounded theorizing should reflect principles that are portable or transferable to other domains and settings.

The position of this paper is rooted in enterprise architecture. A motive is to reach out of CDOs to consider professional "partnerships".

3.1 Sampling and Sampling Strategy

Data for this research is acquired using case methodology based on a global professional services company. The professional services work is project or program oriented that serves the needs of external clients and customers rather than internal management (Stumpf et al., 2002). Our research case study company is a well established professional services firm with a long history in the field. The company has established their Chief Data Office for more than five years. The Chief Data Office structure has global and local presence by having a Global level Chief Data Office, and local entities Chief Data Offices. The research sample group of our study from the case study firm is a representation of the firm's CDO team representing leadership, management, and functional roles and representation. We interviewed 10 informants with the criteria that interviewees should be part of the Chief Data Office team for the last three years, with not less than 10 years in the professional services domain. The sample is sparse but selected from is strong character of experience and global connect.

Table 1. Expert informants of CDO

Informant Code	Role	Location	Experience (yrs)
Inf1	Senior Business Analyst	US	10
Inf2	Director, Data Management	UK	20
Inf3	Products Owner	India	10
Inf4	Director Products Management	US	20
Inf5	Operational Account Manager	Canada	20
Inf6	Technical Business Architect	UK	15
Inf7	Data Products Lead	US	10
Inf8	Data Protection Officer	UK	20
Inf9	Director Data Engineering	US	20
Inf10	Director Data Governance and Strategy	UK	20

3.2 Data Collection

The data collection method followed during the interviews is individual semi-structured in-depth interviews organized around a set of predetermined open-ended questions, with other questions emerging from the dialogue between interviewer and interviewee. The interviews have been conducted virtually using the remote connectivity application Zoom due to the pandemic situation, the social distancing considerations, the recent working from home preferences, and the multiple geographical locations. The interviews lasted for a period between 30 to 45 min. The noting method employed during the interviews are note-taking and voice-recording with permission given by interviewed informants at the start of each call to record audio. We started each interview by requesting the interviewed informant to describe his/her role and to describe his/her responsibilities in their team. After that interviewed informants have been requested to answer the following questions:

1. How do you perceive the Enterprise Data Agility? necessary, desired, not desired? Why.
2. Considering the role of your company Chief Data Office, do you perceive Enterprise Data Agility as one of the Chief Data Office objectives/goals? Why.
3. Do you see your role participating in achieving Enterprise Data Agility? Why? Can you provide some examples?
4. What are the main challenges your company CDO, and/or you, face toward achieving the Enterprise Data Agility.
5. How do you describe the relationship / interaction between the Chief Data Office and the Enterprise Architecture function (alternatively the 'central enterprise (IT) planning' function)?
6. Do you consider your company and / or the Enterprise Architecture function sufficiently responsive to data? Can you support with examples?

These questions have been utilized as a driver of the interview discussion, many follow up and deep dive questions have been raised and discussed.

3.3 Data Analysis and -Structure

Recorded interviews transcripts were downloaded and analyzed. Per Gioia et al. (2013), authors should revisit the data in iterations of discussions, and develop decisions about how to code terms. The authors performed coding as per the Grounded Theory methodology (Gioia et al., 2013; Charmaz, 2014) and applied the ideas of Thematic Analysis which is a process to encode qualitative input to be used as part of qualitative methodologies (Boyatzis, 1998). The coding process was conducted in different phases: Phase 1: The authors read all transcripts and generated codes, where codes are terms used by interviewees or a reflection of authors on the meaning and the language of interviewees (Strauss and Corbin, 1998; Gioia et al., 2013). Phase 2: Generating first-order categories. Authors grouped the codes from Phase 1 in higher-level concepts per similarities. Step 3: Generating second-order themes. Authors used the axial coding as per (Strauss and Corbin, 1998) to link the first-order codes and to group them in higher-order themes.

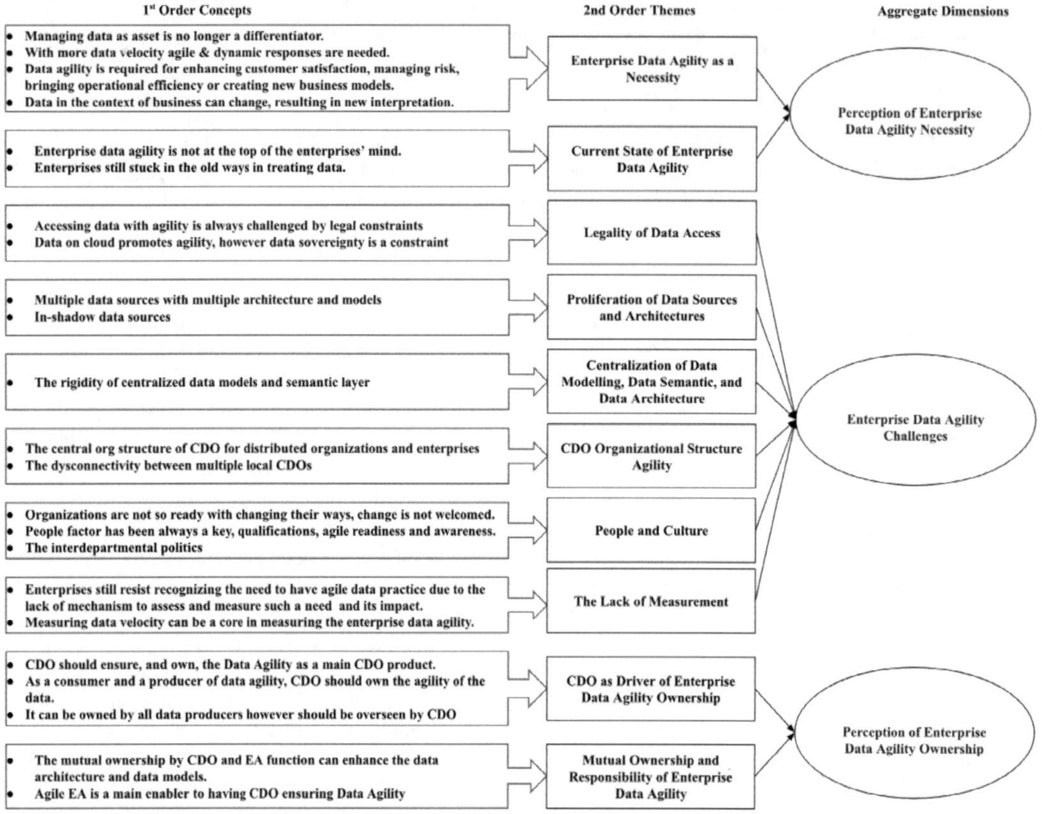

Figure 1. Casuality of data, architecture and agility derived from the interviews

4. FINDINGS

4.1 Perception of Enterprise Data Agility

4.1.1 Enterprise Data Agility as a Necessity

The majority of the interviewed informants highlighted that enterprise data agility is a necessity. The necessity of enterprise data agility has been reasoned by multiple drivers and motivators. First, "*enterprise data agility plays a critical role in addressing the important role of data as an asset toward having businesses more able to reflect on business changes*". Second, it was highlighted that "*enterprise data agility is necessary due to the dynamic business environment, which leads to more data velocity due to vibrant data sourcing and more data created and requested for analytics and insight products*". Third, informants advised that "*enterprise data agility is required due to the current changing nature of the data that is evolving with a variety of data schemas and formats*". Fourth, it has been underlined that "*anytime a new data source, data shape or form is recognized, agile & dynamic responses are needed*". Third, during the interviews, some informants reported that "*enterprise data agility is required for enhancing customer satisfaction, managing risk, bringing operational efficiency or creating new business models*". Fifth, informants reflected on the need to have the enterprise capable of coping with "*the agile meaning of data, mainly the same data, in the context of business keeps changing, and new challenges such as pandemic, divisiveness, geopolitics, healthcare challenges etc. are resulting in new interpretation of data in many cases*".

In reviewing the interviews, ideas, suggestions, and desires have been evaluated as it was convenient answers rather than answers based on shortcomings in existing business designs. Here informants generally were well-argumented on the positions. As such necessity is not just "nice", but a matter of sense-making on value-creation of data, management and architectural resources.

4.2 Enterprise Data Agility Challenges

Six common themes have been extracted from the discussions with the informants in regards to the enterprise data agility challenges.

4.2.1 Legality of Data Access

First, it has been identified by many informants that data access and legal constraints and obligations to facilitate the data access and movement is a main challenge that informants and their Chief Data Office teams face while trying to access data and improve the agility state of their data practices. Multiple cases have been given as examples during the interviews, e.g. cross territories access of data, cross entities access of data, and data privacy and laws related constraints.

4.2.2 Proliferation of Data Sources and Architectures

Second, the rapid, diversified, and ungoverned introduction and addition of data sources to the enterprise data architecture has been identified by most of the informants as a main challenge that ensuring enterprise data agility because of the lack of identification and awareness of these data sources the Chief Data Office data modeling and architecture practices face.

4.2.3 The Centrality of Data Modelling, Data Semantic, and Data Architecture

Third, it was reported by many informants that the state of having enterprise data models and data semantic layers owned and maintained by the Chief Data Office is among the main challenges that data consumers and citizens report always while expressing their struggle with being able to access the data in a more agile way. This has been illustrated with use cases where multiple business teams ad data citizens groups with multiple business perspectives request to access data and they have to adapt their request to be compatible and aligned with the Chief Data Office driven enterprise data models and semantic layers; although the informants have recognized the criticality of these enterprise data architecture artifacts (i.e. data models and semantic layers), however they raised the fact that these models are usually static, outdated, and not able to reflect the very fast moving need to have models and semantic layers able to cope with the business changes and the multiple perspectives, meanings, and contexts the enterprise data citizens might have.

4.2.4 CDO Organizational Structure Agility

Fourth, and one of the most widely reaching challenges that have been proposed, informants who work for Chief Data Office teams in geo-distributed enterprises highlighted the lack of agility in the organizational setup and implementation of the Chief Data Office organizational structure. This is one of the challenges that enterprises face while attempting to establish more agile state of the enterprise data. This challenge has been elaborated with details related to having a central Chief Data Office for multiple territories organizations with or without local CDOs, where central Chief Data Office acts as a single version of control over Chief Data Office products and services leading toward slow and unresponsive state of data.

4.2.5 People and Culture

Fifth, almost all informants raise the issue of people and enterprise's culture in accommodating and being ready for change. It has been agreed upon that the journey towards agile enterprise data is not an easy journey, and it requires people and enterprise culture shift to accept, adopt, enable, and promote the agile data state and its practices. However, similar to any agile transformation journey, this has the potential to be resisted by cultural resistance and inter-departmental politics and conflicts. Examples have been given mainly in relation to the multiple stakeholders involved in managing data, specially when it comes to stakeholders who have been traditionally involved in owning and managing enterprise data (e.g. Information Technology) and Chief Information Office team.

4.2.6 The Lack of Measurement

Interesting insights have been extracted from a few interviews where the issue of the lack of measuring enterprise data agility, and enterprise architecture agility in general has been raised. Related to the previous challenge, i.e. People and Culture, it was pinpointed that to shake a current state, where enterprise data agility is not appreciated as a necessity or recognized a critical enterprise need, chief data office team would struggle to deliver well measured argument about the need for more data agility without having measured impact on the current state and/or a well measured assessment of return on investment in the efforts required to transform into a more enterprise agile data state. Velocity of data has been nominated as a core element to build an index upon by categorizing the enterprise department use cases per data velocity and assigning a data velocity index value to each case and/or category, and then assigning data agility index in form of As-Is index value and To-Be index value to identify the prioritization and efforts needed to address, enhance, and achieve the data agility of each category and/or use case.

4.3 Enterprise Data Agility Ownership

Informants reflected on the enterprise agility and highlighted the ownership as a main area to focus on, and every informant identified the Chief Data Office organization as a main owner of the enterprise data agility, however with nominating one or more co-owner along with the Chief Data Office. It has been emphasized that the Chief Data Office organization is expected to own, ensure, and consider data agility as a main Chief Data Office product. Informants suggested that collaborative ownership is expected as well, by proposing that enterprise data agility can be owned by many or/and all data producers however such ownership should be overseen and maintained by the Chief Data Office function within the enterprise. Enterprise architecture function/team has been identified by many informants as one of the potential co-owner of the enterprise data agility; the co-ownership between the two functions (i.e. Chief Data Office and enterprise architecture) has been proposed as a leverage to address more than one areas, first the lack of communication and collaboration between the two functions in regards to the overlapping areas, e.g. enterprise data modeling, enterprise data semantic layer, the effectiveness of data implementations between application layer and Chief Data Office products. Some informants also recognized that agile enterprise architecture can be an enabler toward having more efficient ownership of the enterprise data agility by the Chief Data Office team.

5. DISCUSSION

The aforementioned findings encourage us to propose that enterprises should recognize the need to introduce, embed, and adopt Enterprise Data Agility to achieve the motivators suggested by the informants. The three research questions that we raised in the beginning of this research are:

1. What is the perception of Chief Data Office stakeholders about the Enterprise Data Agility.
2. What Chief Data Office stakeholders perceive as main challenges toward achieving Enterprise Data Agility.
3. How do Chief Data Office stakeholders see the mutual relationship with Enterprise Architecture toward achieving Enterprise Data Agility.

On RQ1, the research data collection, analysis, and findings led to the following results. All interviewed informants, who presented their professional services industry Chief Data Office team agreed on the necessity of having the enterprise data agility. Not as the phenomena of 'agile' but due to the increasing need to recognize data as an asset and in order to have enterprises more capable to reflect on the objectively more changing business environments. Informants however highlighted that their Chief Data Office teams face challenges and are not capable of providing and maintaining the needed level of agility of the enterprise data.

On RQ2, the informants raised many "challenges" (i.e. business risks and workloads) during the interviews, the four common themes of these challenges were about: 1) Legal constraints of accessing data, 2) Proliferation of data sources and architectures, 3) Centralization of data modeling, data Semantic, and data architecture, 4) Chief Data Office organizational structure agility، 5) People and Culture, and 6) The Lack of Measurement.

On RQ3, according to the interviewed informants, it has been established that Chief Data Office is the main owner of enterprise data agility in enterprises, and data agility should be considered as one of the main products and deliverables of the Chief Data Office practice. Informants also recommended and encouraged having co-ownership of the enterprise data agility, mainly between the Chief Data Office and Enterprise Architecture team. A secondary co-ownership model was suggested between the Chief Data Office and the data owners, consumers, and citizens.

This study has been conducted in professional services industries. The viewpoint of respondents covers global operations and business process services to clients across most industries. This provides a perspective of common drivers and obstacles across most business. Furthermore, it provides an aspect of methodological triangulation. Information technology organizations are often regarded a homogeneous viewed from outside, this paper contributes to matters of multiple strands of governance that often contradict and establishes IT governance more heterogeneous. This paper suggests for strengthen and explicit "co-ownership" across data resources.

6. DELIMITATION

This study has the general limitations of any qualitative research. We are aware of the industry specificity limitation in this research by focusing only on the professional services industry. Additionally, we are aware of the limitation of not including enterprise architecture practitioners in this study, although many informants stated they have general or specific experience in the enterprise architecture domain; these two limitations can be addressed in further studies by extending the research community and population by including more industries in the data gathering scope and practitioners from more domains insights.

7. CONCLUSION

Enterprises have started recognizing agile methodologies as evolutionary methods in the field of technology development and management specifically and in the fields of business administration and management in general (Kaddoumi and Watfa. 2016; Kaddoumi et al., 2018). There is an interest in adopting the agile principles in enterprise practices, e.g. production management, marketing, strategy execution, etc. This expansion of agile practices, frameworks, and methodologies from the technology domain of an enterprise to the business and operation domains raises the challenge of having better enterprise agility mainly when it comes to the data of the enterprise as a foundational platform between technology and business. In light of the lack of literature review, professional content, and professional practices around the identification and assessing the need and the ownership of an agile state of the enterprise data, this paper has set a contour of Enterprise Data Agility as a necessity driven by a close relationship between enterprise data semantics, the CDO roles and responsibilities, and the volatile, uncertain, complex and ambiguous context of business. Here core enterprise systems – in some ways represented by the enterprise architecture management – establishes a less agile state of data in the enterprise. The paper highlighted the overlapping area between the Chief Data Officer team and the Enterprise Architecture Management teams in term of owning the agile state of enterprise data, and concluded that there is a potential opportunity to have the enterprise data agility led by the Chief Data Officer team, yet co-owned by both Chief Data Officer team and the enterprise architecture teams. Moreover, the research confirmed that the enterprise data agility faces a set of challenges that the Chief Data Office should be aware of toward owning, delivering, and maintaining the agile state of the enterprise data.

REFERENCES

Ahlemann, F., Legner, C., & Lux, J. (2021). A resource-based perspective of value generation through enterprise architecture management. *Information & Management*, *58*(1), 103266.

Alaeddini, M., & Salekfard, S. (2013). Investigating the role of an enterprise architecture project in the business-IT alignment in Iran. *Information Systems Frontiers*, *15*(1), 67-88.

Alzoubi, Y. I., Gill, A. Q., & Al-Ani, A. (2015). Distributed Agile Development Communication: An Agile Architecture Driven Framework. *J. Softw.*, *10*(6), 681-694.

Bente, S., Bombosch, U., & Langade, S. (2012). *Collaborative enterprise architecture: enriching EA with lean, agile, and enterprise 2.0 practices*. Newnes.

Borad, A., & Rajput, I. (2015). Software engineering-Agile methodology using SCRUM. *International Journal for Innovative Research in Science & Technology*, *1*(12), 175-189.

Boyatzis, R. E. (1998). *Transforming qualitative information: Thematic analysis and code development*. Sage Publications.

Brackett, M., & Earley, P. S. (2009). The DAMA Guide to The Data Management Body of Knowledge (DAMA-DMBOK Guide).

Brenneman, K. (2018). What a Chief Data Officer Needs to Know. *Information Management*, *52*(5), 44-45.

Buckl, S., Matthes, F., Monahov, I., Roth, S., Schulz, C., & Schweda, C. M. (2011). Towards an agile design of the enterprise architecture management function. In *2011 IEEE 15th International Enterprise Distributed Object Computing Conference Workshops* (pp. 322-329). IEEE.

Cameron, B. H., & McMillan, E. (2013). Analyzing the current trends in enterprise architecture frameworks. *Journal of Enterprise Architecture*, *9*(1), 60-71.

Charmaz, K. (2014). *Constructing grounded theory*. Sage Publications.

Chun Tie, Y., Birks, M., & Francis, K. (2019). Grounded theory research: A design framework for novice researchers. *SAGE open medicine*, *7*, 2050312118822927.

Glaser, B. G., & Strauss, A. L. (2017). *The discovery of grounded theory: Strategies for qualitative research*. Routledge.

Corley, K. G., & Gioia, D. A. (2011). Building theory about theory building: what constitutes a theoretical contribution?. *Academy of management review*, *36*(1), 12-32.

Corr, L., & Stagnitto, J. (2011). *Agile data warehouse design: Collaborative dimensional modeling, from whiteboard to star schema*. DecisionOne Consulting.

Engesmo, J., & Panteli, N. (2021). Digital leaders and the transformation of the IT function. *Scandinavian Journal of Information Systems*, *33*(1), 4.

Fadler, M., & Legner, C. (2021). Toward big data and analytics governance: redefining structural governance mechanisms. In *Proceedings of the 54th Hawaii International Conference on System Sciences* (p. 5696).

Gioia, D. A., Corley, K. G., & Hamilton, A. L. (2013). Seeking qualitative rigor in inductive research: Notes on the Gioia methodology. *Organizational research methods*, *16*(1), 15-31.

Gong, Y., & Janssen, M. (2021). Roles and capabilities of enterprise architecture in big data analytics technology adoption and implementation. *Journal of theoretical and applied electronic commerce research*, *16*(1), 37-51.

Hauder, M., Schulz, C., Roth, S., & Matthes, F. (2013). Organizational factors influencing enterprise architecture management challenges. In *21st European Conference on Information Systems (ECIS), Utrecht, Netherland.*

Hoda, R., Noble, J., & Marshall, S. (2008). Agile project management. In *New Zealand computer science research student conference* (Vol. 6, pp. 218-221).

Hughes, R. (2012). *Agile data warehousing project management: business intelligence systems using Scrum*. Newnes.

Inghirami, I. (2012). Taming Corporate Data (2021). ITAIS 2021 Proceedings. 4. https://aisel.aisnet.org/itais2021/4

Jagals, M. (2021). Expanding Data Governance Across Company Boundaries–An Inter-organizational Perspective of Roles and Responsibilities. In *IFIP Working Conference on The Practice of Enterprise Modeling* (pp. 245-254). Springer, Cham.

Jurney, R. (2017). *Agile data science 2.0: Building full-stack data analytics applications with Spark*. O'Reilly Media, Inc.

Kaddoumi, T., & Watfa, M. (2016). A proposed agile enterprise architecture framework. In *2016 Sixth International Conference on Innovative Computing Technology (INTECH)* (pp. 52-57). IEEE.

Kaddoumi, T., & Watfa, M. (2021). A foundational framework for agile enterprise architecture. *International Journal of Lean Six Sigma*. 13. 136-155.

Kaddoumi, T., Elhabashy, K., Diab, M., & Watfa, M. K. (2018). The impact of knowledge engineering and cloud computing adoption on business driven IT. International Journal of Machine Learning and Computing. 8, 460–465.

Karkošková, S. (2022). Data Governance Model To Enhance Data Quality In Financial Institutions. *Information Systems Management*, 1-21.

Kurniawan, N. B. (2013). Enterprise Architecture design for ensuring strategic business IT alignment (integrating SAMM with TOGAF 9.1). In *2013 Joint International Conference on Rural Information & Communication Technology and Electric-Vehicle Technology (rICT & ICeV-T)* (pp. 1-7). IEEE.

Närman, P., Holm, H., Johnson, P., König, J., Chenine, M., & Ekstedt, M. (2011). Data accuracy assessment using enterprise architecture. *Enterprise Information Systems*, *5*(1), 37-58.

PMI (2022). Data Management – Disciplined Agile. Project Management Institute. https://www.pmi.org/disciplined-agile/process/data-management

McKinsey (2022). The data-driven enterprise of 2025. McKinsey & Company, Inc. https://www.mckinsey.com/capabilities/quantumblack/our-insights/the-data-driven-enterprise-of-2025).

Rashed, F., & Drews, P. (2020). Supporting the development and realization of data-driven business models with enterprise architecture modeling and management. In *International Conference on Business Information Systems* (pp. 264-276). Springer, Cham.

Sessions, R. (2007). A comparison of the top four enterprise-architecture methodologies. *Houston: ObjectWatch Inc*.

The Open Group (2022). *The TOGAF Standard - 10 Edition.* The Open Group.

Rouhani, B. D., Shirazi, H., Nezhad, A. F., & Kharazmi, S. (2008). Presenting a framework for agile enterprise architecture. In *2008 1st International Conference on Information Technology* (pp. 1-4). IEEE.

Schelp, J., & Stutz, M. (2007). A balanced scorecard approach to measure the value of enterprise architecture. Journal of Enterprise Architecture. 3, 8-14.

Strauss, A., & Corbin, J. (1998). Basics of qualitative research technique: Grounded theory procedures and techniques. Sage Publications, Inc.

Stumpf, S. A., Doh, J. P., & Clark, K. D. (2002). Professional services firms in transition: Challenges and opportunities for improving performance. *Organizational Dynamics*, *31*(3), 259-279.

Ullrich, A., Bertheau, C., Wiedmann, M., Sultanow, E., Körppen, T., & Bente, S. (2021, October). Roles, tasks and skills of the enterprise architect in the VUCA world. In *2021 IEEE 25th International Enterprise Distributed Object Computing Workshop (EDOCW)* (pp. 261-270). IEEE.

van de Wetering, R. (2021). Understanding the Impact of Enterprise Architecture Driven Dynamic Capabilities on Agility: A Variance and fsQCA Study. *Pacific Asia Journal of the Association for Information Systems*, *13*(4), 2.

SOCIAL NETWORKING SITES USE CONTINUANCE IN ORGANIZATIONS: INSIGHTS FROM A SUB-SAHARAN AFRICAN COUNTRY

Bangaly Kaba
Ph.D., Athabasca University, Faculty of Business
1 University Drive, Athabasca, AB T9S 3A3, Canada

ABSTRACT

Social networking sites (SNSs) could offer tremendous advantages to organizations, especially in sub-Saharan African organizations, but their use is unsustainable. Our proposed research aims to understand the psychological factors behind SNSs' use continuance by explaining them through a model. We used structural equation modeling to examine the collected data, and we found that habits are the main driver of SNSs use continuance. The practical and theoretical implications were presented as well.

KEYWORDS

SNS, Use Continuance, Organization

1. INTRODUCTION

In several Sub-Saharan Africa countries such Guinea, non or under use of emergent information technologies to achieve organizational performance is not an exception. In these countries, most often, social network sites (SNS) tend to be used as tools to handle marketing and product promotion related activities. With some exceptions, it is overlooked how SNS could be used sustainability to enhance the overall organizational performance (Kaba, 2021). Indeed, Leornadi et al. (2013) showed SNS can be used in an organizational setting to improve work processes, collaborate and share knowledge. SNS's use in work setting could even contribute to a country's economic performance through collaboration enhancement within the workplaces (Leonardi, 2015). Unfortunately, it has been clearly argued that we lack a deeper understanding of the psychosocial factors that predict people's use of SNS in the workplace (Kane, 2017; Leonardi, 2017).

Despite the potential benefits of SNS, there are a few studies explaining its use, especially in Sub-Saharan Africa (Pelling et al., 2009; Treem & Leonardi, 2012). Although the fact SNS is an enterprise social networking sites (ESNS), its acceptance and use in the organizations is still in its early stages. Subsequently, a great number of SNS are abandoned over time because users stop using them (Baer, 2018). As the usefulness of SNS goes further than the personal setting, many scholars such as Leonardi (2017) urge to research SNS use in the workplace. This study is one such effort to investigate SNS use beyond typical personal settings in a region with great potential for using the technology for productivity and performance increase. Therefore, knowing the factors driving the workers' use of SNS would represent a significant advantage for businesses in Guinea and similar African countries. Kaba and Toure (2014) indicated that there are places like Sub-Saharan Africa in which conventional ICT adoption and use models do not play out. This implies that the models may offer different outcomes in distinct places (Roztocki & Weistroffer, 2017; Mengesha & Garfield, 2018; Duffett, 2015, Venkatesh & Zhang, 2010, Kaba, 2021).

Our study's aim is to explain the factors of SNSs' sustained use in a Guinean's workplace through a model. Undertaking this study is vital because it is not only adopting a technology that offers gains, but it is using it frequently that results in sustainable success. (Zhang, Lu, Gupt, & Gao, 2015).

2. RESEARCH HYPOTHESES

Hsieh et al. (2008) advocated that the theory of planned behavior (TPB) becomes a foundational theory for a study examining information technology (IT) use continuance. Alternatively, Bhattacherjee (2001) proposed a model explaining ICT use continuance after the initial adoption by individuals. Since TPB and other related theories explain mainly ICT pre-adoption factors, in this study, our proposed model merges the theory of Bhattacherjee (2001) and TPB after operating some adjustments to fully consider SNS's use continuation influenced by pre-adoption and adoption behaviors. Indeed, according to Kaba, Meso, N'Da & M'Barika (2009), in a study in an African state, attitude does not impact an individual's ICT use behavior. Thus, we will exclude attitude in the research model. On another front, we included pleasure in the model since it significantly affects users' satisfaction and use continuance intentions (Lowry et al., 2015). Furthermore, since most of the SNS use is done voluntarily without explicit coercion, especially in the context of this study, we add voluntariness to the model. In the next sections, we present the study's hypotheses.

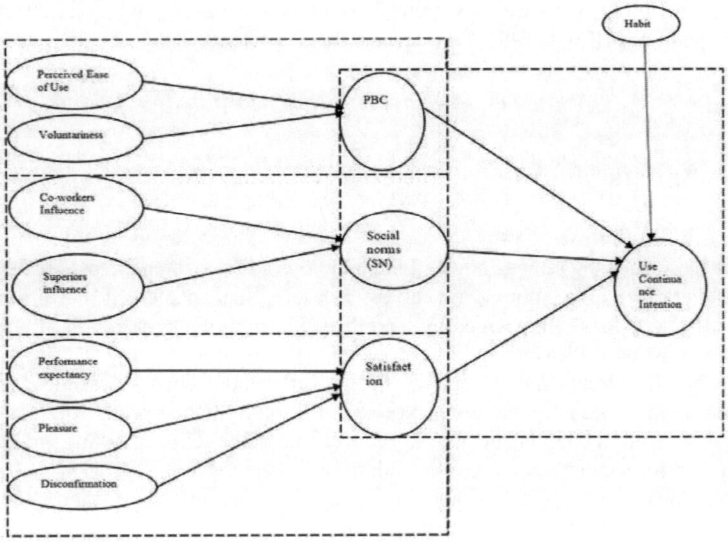

Figure 1. Research Model

2.1 Behavioral Intention

Behavioral intention determines the power of one's intention to take a given action (Ajzen, 1991). According to the theory of reasoned action (TRA), the individual's behaviors are powered by intention (i.e., behavioral intention (BI)). Intention was confirmed by many studies as a predictor of ICT upcoming use (Liao, et al., 2009; Venkatesh et al. 2012). SNS provide potentially tremendous benefits to organizations in Guinea, where there is limited ICT to enhance the overall organizational performance (Kaba, 2021). Indeed, Leonardi et al. (2013) showed that SNS could be used in an organizational setting to improve work processes, collaborate, and share knowledge, facilitate workers' access to expertise within the enterprise and improve cooperation among them. It also offers social benefits and access to required information, expands social capital, obtains feedback, and solves problems (Leonardi et al., 2013). In contrast to other communication technologies, SNS possesses attributes enabling sharing and dissemination of knowledge among employees (Leonardi, 2017) through open communication and easy tracking (Leonardi, 2015). When the necessary resources and other facilitating conditions are offered to workers who are sensitive to normative influence from their referent groups (Kaba, N'Da, Meso, & Mbarika, 2009; Kaba, 2015; Kaba, 2018), they will be willing to use SNS to support their work activities to benefit all the advantages the technology offers. Hence, we stipulate these hypotheses.

***H1a**: SNS users' perceived behavioral control (PBC) influences positively their continued-use intention.*
***H1b:** SNS users' perceived social norms influence positively their continued-use intention.*
***H1c**: SNS users' satisfaction influences positively their continued-use intention.*

2.2 Drivers of Perceived Behavioral Control (PBC)

PBC is one's assessment of the existence of or not means, abilities, and prospects necessary to perform a particular action. According to Hsieh et al. (2008), PBC is a multidimensional factor including three facets: self-efficacy (SE), availability, and perceived ease of use (PEOU). All these three facets may depend on the type of technology. SNS is a user-friendly technology easily accessible and affordable when allowed by an organization's policy and managers compared to an ERP system. Thus, we will consider PEOU and voluntariness as drivers of PBC in this study. Generally, the utilization of SNS by workers is free of effort. When the work environment allows them to use it without any constraints, they will form beliefs of having skills and a sense of autonomy to use the system. This will reflect developing a perception of behavioral control or facilitating conditions (Davis, 1989; Dhir et al. 2018). Hence, we state these hypotheses.:
***H2a**: SNS users' perceived ease of use will positively influence PBC.*
***H2c**: SNS users' perceived voluntariness will positively influence PBC.*

2.3 Drivers Satisfaction

Satisfaction toward an ICT use refers to its potential to bring value to someone. When people are satisfied with ICT by getting the value they desire, they will intend to use it to a greater extent. The values that bring an ICT are essential due to its usefulness, perceived pleasure, and perceived performance confirmation or disconfirmation. Usefulness is the perception that the utilization of a system will provide an extrinsic reward that is valuable to the user. Pleasure is the perceived happiness of using an ICT (Venkatesh & Brown, 2001), and it is among the strong salient drivers of a user's satisfaction (Krasnova, et al. 2017). Finally, disconfirmation is the difference between expected ICT performance prior to its usage and post-adoption performance (Churchill & Suprenant, 1982; Liao et al., 2009; Oliver, 1980), and its positive effect on satisfaction and performance has been consistently proven (Lowry et al., 2015). SNS use brings value to users by helping them to connect with co-workers in the organization and get the information needed to perform a job, and maintain professional tight and business relationships. Besides, the Numerous interactive features of a SNS make it a system of fun, enjoyment, and playfulness (Al-Azawei, 2018). Casaló, et al. (2017) showed pleasure as a predominant factor influencing a SNS user's satisfaction and untimely intention to use it.Thus, we state the hypotheses:
***H3a**: SNS users' usefulness will positively influence their satisfaction.*
***H3b**: SNS users' pleasure will positively influence their satisfaction.*
***H3c**: SNS users' disconfirmation will positively influence their satisfaction.*

2.4 Drivers of Social Norms (SN)

SN is the most accepted behavior in each society or group (Rogers, 2003). SN may be referential to direct or influence individuals' actions or behaviors (Ajzen & Fishbein, 1980). Rogers also supports that new ICT is adopted by following a referent's actions. Anandarajan et al. (2002) and Kaba, N'Da, Meso, and Mbarika (2009) have indicated that SN is among the most significant drivers of ICT use in the African environment. The choice and use of communication technology are determined, on the one hand, by objective processes of evaluation and, on the other hand, by SN. Individuals develop socially acceptable behaviors that are justified by norms shared with those around them, which leads to a social consensus on the appropriate use of communication technologies. People are inclined to get information from and rely upon the persons they know personally and are more likely to trust, have seen before, and are familiar with (Leonardi, 2017; Behringer et al. (2017). In addition, in the organizational setting, the pairs and the supervisors play the role of the referent groups. According to Taylor and Todd (1995), the distinction between these two categories of actors is crucial in the context of ICT implementation in organizations. Thus, peers and supervisors can influence potential users, but sometimes this influence is antagonistic. The management team may be in favor of adopting an ICT while, at the same time, peers show opposition. Hence, when a worker receives a positive recommendation from a referent peer or supervisor about using SN because of several opportunities it provides, he or she will develop a positive attitude toward the system and then form the intention to use it if the normative believe remains relevant. Therefore, we can postulate the hypotheses as follows:

H4a*: SNS users' perceived influence by peers will positively impact SN.*

H4b*: SNS media users' perceived influence by superiors will positively impact SN.*

2.5 Habit

According to Hsiao et al. (2016), habit is defined as ''learned sequences of acts that become automatic responses to specific situations, which may be functional in obtaining certain goals or end states" (Verplanken & Wood, 2006; Hsiao et al., 2016). Habits are repetitive behaviors occurring subconsciously (Shiau & Luo, 2013). In information systems, habit refers to using an ICT subconsciously frequently (Hsiao, Chang, & Tang, 2016). The role of habits is beyond routine usage in specific instances, but it is a force driving users' intentions to sustainably perform an action or behavior (Liu et al., 2018; Shiau & Luo, 2013). Several studies have established its influence on ICT, especially on SNS's use continuance (Hsiao et al., 2016). Habit positively impacts SNS's use continuance (Liu, Shao, & Fan, 2018). Individuals use SNS daily in their personal life for different purposes. These routines make them familiar with the system and reinforce subconscious behaviors toward it to the point they instantly once they are exposed to it at the workplace without any prior normative beliefs or mercantile calculation. Thus, we stipulate the following hypotheses:

H5*: SNS users' habitual behavior will influence positively behavioral use continuance.*

3. METHODOLOGY

This section will cover the method and instruments used to achieve the aim of our research. In particular, we describe the process that led to the questionnaire development and the strategy to collect the data we needed.

3.1 Data Collection

We believe there is no database publicly accessible to find Internet subscribers in Guinea. Considering the above shortfall, we used direct contact to recruit the respondents in this study. We recruited about eight familiar and trained investigators to conduct a survey. They were made aware of the requirements of precision and consistency in this study. To complete the questionnaires, the researchers and the investigators looked for respondents across the country with a focal point of Conakry, the living place of most Internet users.

3.2 Results Analysis

We used 183 responses to assess the research's hypotheses. Next, we ran SPSS to perform descriptive statistics and the partial least squares (PLS) for assessing our assumptions (Chin & Todd, 1995; Ringle et al., 2005; Wixom & Watson, 2001). According to Nitzl and Chin (2017), PLS has been criticized by a few researchers (e.g., Aguirre-Urreta & Rönkkö, 2018; McIntosh et al., 2014; Rönkkö, et al., 2016).

Moreover, contrary to covariance-based structural equation modeling methods like LISREL, the variance-based method as PLS approach has fewer retractions in terms of the sample size and distribution (Bhattacherjee & Premkumar, 2004, Gefen et al. 2011; Gefen, et al. 2000). Finally, because explaining use continuance through behavioral intention requires anticipation of future behavior, the research model we developed should take a predictive-oriented approach. In this case, PLS was a more appropriate assessment technique we adopted in our study (Nitzl & Chin, 2017).

3.3 Descriptive Statistics

Demographic variables are: age, gender, experience, income, and level of education. Indeed, 65.5% of the individuals are men compared to 34.5% of women. Persons surveyed are pretty young, with nearly 90.6% 40 years old or younger. Finally, 85% of the respondents are well educated (above secondary school). 64.5% of the respondents are employed in the service sector; among these, 4% are the CEO or owner, 4% are managers, and the remaining are regular employees.

3.3.1 Tests for Validity

Three tests, namely reliability, convergent, and discriminant validity, are required to assess a given instrument's suitability prior to hypotheses testing (Nunnally, 1967; Fornell & Larcker, 1981; Wixom & Watson, 2001; DeVellis, 1991).

3.3.2 Reliability and Convergent Validity of Measurements

We used composite reliability coefficients to test the reliability and the variance extracted (AVE) to assess the convergent validity of the measurement of the variables. Indeed, the former should be above the threshold value of 0.7 (Nunnally, 1978), and the later needs to be higher than 0.5 (Fornell & Larcker, 1981; Wixom & Watson, 2001). As shown in Table 1, only two variables, voluntariness and PBC, are not meeting the reliability and convergent validity tests requirement. Therefore, these two variables will be excluded from the subsequent analysis.

Table 1. Reliability and average variance extracted (AVE)

Constructs	*AVE*	*Composite Reliability*
Disconfirmation	**0.822**	**0.933**
PBC	0.393	**0.750**
Habit	**0.726**	**0.913**
PeerInfluence	**0.929**	**0.963**
PerceivedEasyuse	**0.543**	**0.777**
PerceivedPleasure	**0.700**	**0.872**
SNS	**0.804**	**0.925**
Satisfaction	**0.882**	**0.957**
SuperiorInfluence	**0.956**	**0.978**
UseContinuanceIntention	**0.736**	**0.893**
Usefulness	**0.747**	**0.898**
Voluntariness	0.609	0.179

3.3.3 Discriminant Validity

The discriminant validity test reveals that the study's variables are different from one another. The model variables satisfy the test if the square root of the AVE of each variable is higher than the correlation it shares with other variables in the model (Fornell & Bookstein, 1982). As seen in Table 2, the square root of the AVE of each variable is better than the variable's correlations. Consequently, all variables satisfy the discriminant validity requirements.

Table 2. Discriminant Validity

Construct	Disc.	Habit	PInfl	PEOU	Pleas.	SN	Satisf.	SupInf	Int.	Usef
Disc.	.90									
Habit	.68	.85								
Peer influence	.40	.39	.96							
PEOU	.31	.39	.23	.74						
Perceived pleasure	.57	.58	.33	.36	.84					
SN	.52	.38	.33	.31	.41	.90				
Satisfaction	.66	.70	.24	.38	.60	.38	.94			
Superior influence	.60	.45	.49	.23	.42	.46	.40	.98		
Use continuance intention	.40	.41	.15	.48	.38	.24	.37	.25	.86	
Usefulness	.73	.50	.39	.41	.47	.58	.43	.53	.41	.87

3.3.4 Research Model Assessment or Tests of Hypotheses

In addition, the PLS procedure, especially bootstrapping, was completed to appraise the research's hypotheses by using T-statistics (Ringle et al., 2005). The results of a two-tailed T-test appear in Table 3, with the threshold values of 1.645, 1.96, and 2.576 standing as the key T significance levels corresponding to (p-values) of 0.1, 0.05, and 0.01, respectively (Chin & Todd, 1995; Nunnally, 1978; Ringle et al., 2005; Wagner, 1992).

Table 3. Path analysis

Paths	Path Coefficients	Sample Mean	Standard Deviation	t-Statistics
Disconfirmation -> Satisfaction	**0.622**	**0.615**	**0.107**	**5.799*******
Habit -> Use Continuance Intention	**0.275**	**0.286**	**0.088**	**3.115*******
Peer Influence -> SNS	0.138	0.140	0.094	1.472
Perceived Pleasure -> Satisfaction	**0.332**	**0.334**	**0.075**	**4.447*******
SN-> Use Continuance Intention	0.082	0.081	0.088	0.933
Satisfaction -> Use Continuance Intention	0.146	0.143	0.118	1.245
Superior Influence -> SNS	**0.391**	**0.392**	**0.083**	**4.718*******
Usefulness -> Satisfaction	**-0.186**	**-0.177**	**0.093**	**2.002****

Path coefficient is significant at: ***$p < 0.01$, **$p < 0.05$

4. DISCUSSION

This study examines the predictors of SNS' continuance use intention. The main objective is to find the drivers explaining SNS use continuance in the workplace from users' perspectives. The results of the hypothesis tests are discussed below.

4.1 Influence of the Antecedent of Intention to Continue to Use SNS

Only habit positively predicts use continuance intention among the other predictors we defined on the research model (see Table 3).

The effect of satisfaction is not significant for the users of SNS. That result is inconsistent with earlier results that repeatedly found the impact of satisfaction on users' intention to continue using SNS. The fact that satisfaction has no impactful effect on users' continuance intention was unaligned with our assumption as well as with earlier studies. It may be possible that this group of users did not effectively appraise or were not aware of the benefit of using SNS in work related setting.

Previous research has many times showed that SN is a main driver explaining persons' intention to use a new ICT in an African environment (Kaba, 2009). The outcome of this research of SNS use in the workplace seems to disconfirm the long-established view point of the role of SN in influencing use continuance behavioral intention. Even though most ESNS use can be regard as voluntary on the surface, we may find situations where social influence can end up creating social pressure; SN use may appear as a menace (Gruzd, et al. 2012). This unwelcome view of the media in the workplace could generate stressful situation for workers (Gruzd et al., 2012). Thus, we would expect this to have a harmful, constructive, or neutral impact on normative beliefs because workers may feel persuade against using SNS that may perhaps contribute to performing their duties. A general feeling is that involvement in online digital technology as SNS may not be welcomed by some companies (Kirkup, 2010; Gruzd et al., 2012) since in a few extreme situations, companies might opt not to allow their staff's use of SNS, even though take severe disciplinary actions against offenders (Gruzd et al., 2012).

The data showed that habit positively affects respondents' intention to continue using SNS (see Table 3). Indeed, these results implied that respondents' SNS's past experience with the tool in a personal setting plays a role in their willingness to use it in the workplace sustainably. When the respondents have the opportunity, skills, and resources to use SNS in their personal life frequently, they will develop a favorable predisposition toward the technology and become outfitted to use it in an organizational setting when required. Previous familiarity with the tool becomes an indicator of a favorable behavioral intention. When a behaviour is routinized over time, it becomes difficult to change it without the risk of deploying extra efforts and resources by adopting new alternatives.

4.2 Influence of the Antecedents of Satisfaction

We conjectured that usefulness positively impacts SNS users' satisfaction. Unexpectedly, the results of the data analysis indicated a significant relationship between both variables, but it was negative. It is a surprising outcome since it has been shown in many studies that usefulness or performance expectancy is the major driver of any of ICT use's outcomes.

The effect of pleasure on satisfaction was insignificant, aligning with our theorization and several previous studies that support the notion that people use an ICT for perceived pleasure. However, this finding contradicts some previous studies like Hsieh et al. (2011), confirming the decreasing effect of pleasure over time. These studies argue that when an individual starts using a new (ICT), the perceived pleasure decrease over time due to its routine use. At this time, it will take new or innovative skills to provide further enjoyment.

The results corroborated the positive association between disconfirmation and users' satisfaction we theorized. The respondents are further satisfied after concretely using SNS and observing its actual positive outcomes, leading to a stronger instrumental perception of the SNS during the post-adoption period. The respondents of this study are well equipped with strong digital skills. This observation corroborates the finding of Yu et al. (2017), who showed that high information literacy positively affected ICT use continuance behavior over time.

4.3 Influence of the Antecedents of SN

We conjured that peers and superiors influence SNS users' SN. As it appears in Table 3, superiors' perceived normative beliefs have a greater influence than those of peers. Overall, this result aligns with the previous findings who confirmed the predominant influence of one's manager in ICT adoption and use in the African environment. This study went further by highlighting that superiors benefit from more influential roles in the workplace regarding using SNS for handling professional duties.

5. PRACTICAL CONTRIBUTION

From the study's results, there were several factors influencing respondents' continuance intentional behavior. Taken as a whole, 47% of the variance of users' continuance intention can be explained by the research model. One most important result of this research is to demonstrate that habit is the strongest driver of SNS use continuance. Therefore, companies and their leaders need to consider offering workers opportunities to be familiar with SNS. SN did not positively affect users' continuance intention as theorized. Still, superiors' influence appeared to be the dominant factor in impacting one's normative beliefs regarding SNS's use continuance at the workplace. Indeed, it will be advised to find methods that help managers boost workers' awareness of SNS use within the company.

6. THEORETICAL CONTRIBUTION

Addressing Benbasat and Barki (2007)'s call to use TPB as theoretical foundation in studying ICT's use continuance, we integrated TPB and expectancy theory as the theoretical base of this research. This research is among fewer studies that combine four relevant beliefs and their drivers to study SNS use continuance from the individuals' perspectives in a non-Western organizational context.

The model elaborated and assessed in this study found that SNS use continuance is explained primarily by habit to a greater extent. If users are to make frequent use of SNS, they will be used to it, and it will be easier for them to get accommodated utilizing the system in an organizational setting. Moreover, how often they use the tool, how much time they spend on using it, the more favorable attitude they will form toward it. Therefore, the acquaintance of SNS use in the workplace needs to be promoted in contexts like that of this study. The results will contribute to understanding the sustained use of SNS in Guinea, an African country. Gaining such an understanding is vital because SNS can serve companies' needs, improve the potential market, enlighten attractiveness, increase customers' loyalty, give local businesspeople an opportunity to develop professional networks, ease entry into the marketplace, and fall other advertising-related costs.

This research outlines a good direction in comprehending SNS use by the individual in the organization using a grounded approach. The finding of this study will address the often cited need to understand the complexities of SNS's sustainable use in the workplace (Kane, 2017; Leonardi, 2017). SNS are affecting the workplace in diverse fashions, and the impact on knowledge dissemination management is the most important piece. SNS overcomes many limitations of former generations of knowledge management systems (Kane, 2017).

7. CONCLUSION

This study investigated employees' behavior in post-implementation continued-use intentions toward SNS. We elaborated and assessed a theoretical model. Habit is the most prominent factor explaining SNS use continuance. The traditional drivers such as SN and satisfaction were not validated in this study. As Kaba and Toure (2014) showed, the traditional adoption models did not apply to SNS's use in an African context. Besides, the role of SN indicated as the most predominant driver of ICT use in an African context seems to be lessened in this research. Our research findings on SNS continued use intention in a distinct socio-cultural setting are challenging the established view of the role of SN and satisfaction by showing that these established drivers are not shaping people's behavioral intention. The findings revealed that traditional models do not stand in all adoption and may not be used elsewhere without necessary adjustments (Kaba & Toure, 2014). This result is valuable as it tells Information Systems researchers and practitioners to be vigilant in their use of acceptance and use models within an international context, giving due consideration to cross-cultural validity and context-sensitive issues. The findings might help ensure better success in ICTs' use in sub-Saharan African countries with a comparable context to the Guinean context. Finally, the results will be in the interest of Western organizations operating in developing countries to better comprehend the factors governing how employees react to SNS; gaining that knowledge will contribute to its success.

ACKNOWLEDGEMENT

The author is grateful for the financial support from Athabasca University (AU) through the research incentive grant (RIG). Any opinions, findings, conclusions, or recommendations expressed in this material are those of the author and do not necessarily reflect the views of AU. The authors also the research assistant Daniel Wilton for his editing work and Colleen Haubrich for helping reshape the chart. Finally, he thanks the anonymous reviewers for their time and suggestions that amended the paper.

REFERENCES

Ajzen, I. (1991). The theory of planned behavior. *Organizational behavior and human decision processes*, Vol. 50, 179-211.

Ajzen, I. et Fisbein, M. (1980). *Understanding Attitudes and predicting social Behavior*. Englewood cliffs (USA): Prentice Hall.

Al-Azawei, A. (2018). Predicting the adoption of social media: An integrated model and empirical study on Facebook usage. *Interdisciplinary Journal of Information, Knowledge and Management*, Vol. 13.

Aguirre-Urreta, M., & Rönkkö, M. (2018). Statistical inference with PLSc using bootstrap confidence intervals. *MIS Quarterly*, Vol. 42, No.3, pp. 1001-1020.

Anandarajan et al. (2002). IT acceptance in a less-developed country: A motivational factor perspective. *International journal of information management*, Vol. 22, pp. 47-65.

Behringer, N et al. (2017). Knowledge contribution in organizations via social media: The interplay of identification and perceived usefulness. *Journal of Personnel Psychology*, Vol. 16, No. 1, pp. 12-24.

Benbasat, I., & Barki, H. (2007). Quo vadis, TAM? *Journal for the Association of Information Systems*, Vol. 8, No. 4, pp. 211-218.

Bhattacherjee, A. (2001). Understanding information systems continuance: An expectation-confirmation model. *MIS quarterly*, Vol. 25, No. 3, pp. 351-370.

Bhattacherjee, A., & Premkumar, G. (2004). Understanding changes in belief and attitude toward IT usage: A theoretical model and longitudinal test. *MIS Quarterly*, Vol. 28, No. 2, pp. 229-254.

Casaló, L. et al. (2017). Understanding consumer interaction on Instagram: The role of satisfaction, hedonism, and content characteristics. *Cyberpsychology, Behavior, and Social Networking*, Vol. 20, No. 6, pp. 369-375. doi: 10.1089/cyber.2016.0360

Chin, W. W., & Todd, P.A. (1995). On the use, usefulness, and ease of use of structural equation modeling in MIS research: A note of caution. *MIS Quarterly*, Vol. 19, No. 2, pp. 237-246.

Churchill, G. A., & Suprenant, C. (1982). An investigation into the determinants of consumer satisfaction. *Journal of Marketing Research*, Vol. 19, pp. 491-504.

Davis, F. D. (1989). Perceived usefulness, perceived ease of use, and user acceptance of information technology. MIS Quarterly, Vol.13, No. 3, pp. 318-343.

Dhir, A. et al. (2018). Why do young people tag photos on social networking sites? Explaining user intentions. *International Journal of Information Management*, Vol. 38, No. 1, pp. 117-127. doi: 10.1016/j.ijinfomgt.2017.07.004

DeVellis, R. F. (1991). *Applied social research methods series*, Vol. 26. Scale development: Theory and applications. Thousand Oaks, CA: Sage Publications, Inc.

Duffett, R.G. (2015). The influence of Facebook advertising on cognitive attitudes amid Generation Y. *Electronic Commerce Research*, Vol.15, No. 2, pp. 243-267.

Fornell, C., & Larcker, D. (1981). Evaluating structural equation models with unobservable variables and measurement error. *Journal of Marketing Research*, Vol. 18, No.1, pp. 39-50.

Fornell, C. & Bookstein, F.L. (1982) Two Structural Equation Models: LISREL and PLS Applied to Consumer Exit-Voice Theory. *Journal of Marketing Research*, Vol. 19, 440-452.

Gefen, D. et al. (2011). An update and extension to SEM guidelines for administrative and social science research. *MIS Quarterly*, Vol. 35, No. 2, pp. 2-3.

Gefen, D. et al. (2000). Structural equation modeling and regression: Guidelines for research practice. Communications of the Association for Information Systems, Vol.4, No.7, pp. 1-70.

Gruzd et al. A. (2012). Connected scholars: Examining the role of social media in research practices of faculty using the UTAUT model. *Computers In Human Behavior*, Vol. 28, No. 6, pp. 2340-2350.

Hsiao et al. (2016). Exploring the influential factors in continuance usage of mobile social Apps: Satisfaction, habit, and customer value perspectives. *Telematics and Informatics*, Viol. 33, pp. 342-355.

Hsieh, J.J., et al. (2008). Understanding digital inequality: Comparing continued use behavioral models of the socio-economically advantaged and disadvantaged. *MIS Quarterly*, Vol. 32, No. 1, pp. 97-126.

Hsieh, J.J., et al. (2011). Addressing digital inequality for the socioeconomically disadvantaged through government initiatives: Forms of capital that affect ICT utilization. *Information Systems Research*, Vol. 22, No. 2, 233-253.

Kaba, B. (2015). Heterogeneous reactions to digital opportunities: A field study to test our assumptions. International Conferences on Information Systems (ICIS), Fort Worth, Texas, USA, December 13-16.

Kaba, B. (2018). Information and communication technology use continuance behavioral intention: Differential effect based on socio-economic status. The Hawaii International Conference on System Sciences (HICSS), Hawaii, USA, January 3-6.

Kaba, B., et al. (2009). Micro factors influencing the attitudes toward and the use of a mobile technology: A model of cellular phones use in Guinea. *IEEE Transactions on Professional Communication*, Vol. 52, No. 3, pp. 272-290.

Kaba, B. & Toure. B-S. 2014. Understanding Information and Communication Technology Behavioral Intention to use: Applying the UTAUT Model to Social Networking Site Adoption by Young People in a Least Developed Economy. *Journal of the Association for Information Science and Technology (JASIST),* Vol. 65, No. 8, pp. 1662-1674.

Kaba, B. 2021. Explaining social networking sites' use continuance from employees' perspectives. *Journal of System and Information Technology*, Vol. 23, pp. 2, pp. 171-198

Kane, G. C. (2017). The evolutionary implications of social media for organizational knowledge management. *Information and organization*, Vol. 27, pp. 37-46.

Kirkup, G. (2010). Academic blogging: Academic practice and academic identity. *London Review of Education*, Vol. 8, No.1, pp. 75-84.

Krasnova, et al. (2017). Why men and women continue to use social networking sites: The role of gender differences. *Journal of Strategic Information Systems*, Vol. 26, pp. 261-284.

Leonardi, P. M. (2015). Ambient awareness and knowledge acquisition: Using social media to learn "who knows what" and "who knows whom". *MIS Quarterly*, Vol. 39, No. 4, pp. 747-762.

Leonardi, P. M. (2017). The social media revolution: Sharing and learning in the age of leaky knowledge. *Information and Organization*, Vol. 27, pp. 47-59.

Leonardi, et al. (2013). Enterprise Social Media: Definition, History, and Prospects for the Study of Social Technologies in Organizations. *Journal of Computer-Mediated Communication*, Vol. 19, No. 1, pp. 1-19.

Liao, C., et al. (2009). Information technology adoption behavior life cycle: Toward a technology continuance theory (TCT). *International Journal of Information Management*, Vol. 29, pp. 309-320.

Liu, Q., et al. (2018). The impact of users' sense of belonging on social media habit formation: Empirical evidence from social networking and microblogging websites in China. *International Journal of Information Management*, Vol. 43, pp. 209-223.

Lowry, P. B., et al. (2015). Proposing the multimotive information systems continuance model (MISC) to better explain end-user system evaluations and continuance intentions. *Journal of the Association for Information Systems*, Vol. 16, No.7, pp. 515-579.

McIntosh, C. N., et al. (2014). Reflection on partial least squares path modeling. *Organizational Research Methods*, Vol. 17, pp. 210-251.

Mengesha, G.H., & Garfield, M. J. (2018). A contextualized IT adoption and use model for telemedicine in Ethiopia. *Information Technology for Development*. doi: 10.1080/02681102.2018.1461057

Nitzl, C., & Chin, W. W. (2017). The case of partial least squares (PLS) path modeling in managerial accounting research. *Journal of Management Control*, Vol. 28, pp. 137-156.

Nunnally, G. (1978). *Psychometric theory*. New York, NY: McGraw-Hill.

Oliver, R. L. (1980). A cognitive model for the antecedents and consequences of satisfaction. *Journal of Marketing Research*, Vol. 17, pp. 460-469.

Pelling, E. L., et al. 2009. The Theory of Planned Behavior Applied to Young People's Use of Social Networking Web Sites, *Cyberpsychology & behavior*, Vol. 12, No. 6, pp. 755-759.

Ringle, C. M. et al., A. (2005). SmartPLS 2.0 beta. Hamburg, Germany:Accessed November 10, 2011 from http://www.smartpls.de

Rogers, E. M. (2003). *Diffusion of innovation*, 5th edition. New York, NY: The New Press.

Rönkkö, M., et al. (2016). *Partial least squares path modeling: Time for some serious second thoughts. Journal of Operations Management*, Vol. 47-48, pp. 9-27.

Roztocki, N., Soja, P., & Weistroffer, H. R. (2017). Enterprise systems in transition economies: Research landscape and framework for socioeconomic development. *Information Technology for Development*. Vol. 26, No.1, pp. 1-37.

Shiau, W-L., & Luo, M-M. (2013). Continuance intention of blog users: The impact of perceived enjoyment, habit, user involvement and blogging time. *Behaviour & Information Technology*. Vol. 32, No. 6, pp. 570-583.

Taylor, S., & Todd, P. A. (1995). Understanding information technology usage: A test of competing models. *Information Systems Research*, Vol. 6, No.2, pp. 91-108.

Treem, J.W., & Leonardi, P. M. (2012). Social media use in organizations: Exploring the affordances of visibility, editability, persistence, and association. *Communication Yearbook*, Vol. 36, pp. 143-189.

Venkatesh, V., & Brown, S. A. (2001). A longitudinal investigation of personal computers in homes: Adoption determinants and emerging challenges. *MIS Quarterly*, Vol. 25, No.1, pp. 71-99.

Venkatesh, V., Morris, M. G., Davis, G. B., Davis, F. G. (2003). User acceptance of information technology: Toward a unified view. *MIS Quarterly*, Vol. 27, No.3, pp. 425-478.

Venkatesh, V. et al. (2012). Consumer acceptance and use of information technology: Extending the unified theory of acceptance and use of technology. *MIS Quarterly*, Vol. 36, No. 3, pp. 157-178.

Venkatesh, V. & Zhang, X. (2010). Unified Theory of Acceptance and Use of Technology: U.S. Vs. China. Journal of Global. *Information Technology Management*, (13)1, 5-27.

Verplanken, B., & Wood, W. (2006). Interventions to break and create consumer habits. *Journal of Public Policy Marketing*. Vol. 25, No.1, pp. 90-103.

Wixom, B. H., & Watson, H. J. (2001). An empirical investigation of the factors affecting data warehousing success. *MIS Quarterly*, Vol. 25, No.1, pp. 17-41.

Yu, T. K., et al., (2017). Understanding factors influencing information communication technology adoption behavior: The moderators of information literacy and digital skills. *Computers in Human Behavior*, Vol. 7, No. 1, pp. 196-208.

Zhang, H., et al. (2015). Understanding group-buying websites continuance: An extension of expectation confirmation model. *Internet Research*, Vol. 25, No. 5, pp. 767-793.

AUTOMOBILE SALES FORECAST USING SOCIAL LISTENING AND CONDITIONS TO FORECAST SALES

Hisaki Goto[1] and Yukiko Goto[2]
[1]*Nagoya Gakuin Univercity, Japan*
[2]*Enconnect Inc., Japan*

ABSTRACT

The amount of information created by end-users has become massive; it is often referred to as an 'information explosion', and social media is a typical tool for gathering that information. We gathered and analyzed tweets related to automobiles in Japan from June 2018 to May 2020, attempting to create a formula to forecast future automobile sales through content posted on Twitter. We found that forecasting the sale of automobiles is possible when the number of tweets for a model is large, which indicates that social media can be beneficial as alternative data to forecast product sales. Although we could successfully make a sales forecast on certain models with a large number of tweets, all the models were not possible to forecast. However, we propose a hypothesis that forecasting sales using Twitter is possible only after a product enters the so-called 'cash cow' phase under the Product Portfolio Matrix developed by Boston Consulting Group, which creates business strategy using market growth rates and relative markets.

KEYWORDS

Twitter, Alternative Data, Social Listening, Automobile Sales Forecasts

1. INTRODUCTION

In our previous study we had analyzed national elections in Japan through social listening by gathering and utilizing text data posted on Twitter (Goto, 2018, Goto, 2019). 2,009,520 tweets were gathered for the election analyses (Goto, 2019), making the study uniquely valuable because other previous studies had only used several hundred thousand tweets. We found that social media is a useful tool to make predictions about elections under the proportional representation system and that it can replace conventional prediction methods such as the RDD (Random Digit Dialing) method at low cost with frequency.

As Figure 1 shows, Japan's Twitter population is ranked as the second following the U.S. Considering the U.S. population is 2.6 times large as that of Japan (329,500,000 in the U.S. and 125,800,000 in Japan in 2020), it is easy to understand how large the proportion of Twitter population is in Japan. TPS (Tweets Per Second) numbers also show the Japanese love of Twitter: Akimoto (2011) mentions that New Year's tweets in Japanese in 2011 made the world record of 6,939 TPS, and 143,199 TPS during the broadcast of the animation movie 'Castle in the Sky' on August 2, 2013 renewed the world record. Also, the majority of top 10 TPS come from Japan. In this study, we attempted to forecast automobile sales in Japan by taking advantage of the Japanese love of Twitter.

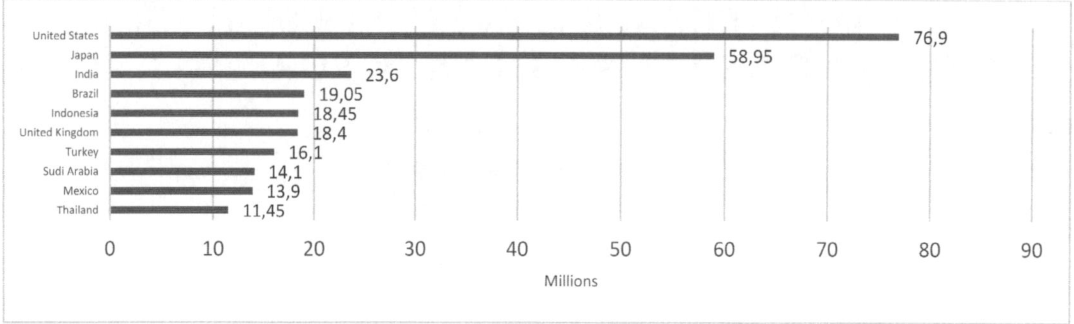

Figure 1. Leading countries based on number of Twitter users as of January 2022
Source : Statista (2022), <https://www.statista.com/statistics/242606/number-of-active-twitter-users-in-selected-countries/>Retrieved on April 29, 2021

2. LITERATURE REVIEW

Previous studies that forecast product sales using social media include Dijkman, Ipeirotis & Aertsen (2015), Wijnhoven & Plant (2017) and Pai & Liu (2018). The study by Dijkman, Ipeirotis & Aertsen (2015) showed that commodities that receive less attention on social media did not show similar results as shown in books or movie tickets. This case study classified tweets into three type of tweet: the type of tweet, the type of user who posted the tweet, and the sentiment of the tweet in four countries. Their analysis suggested that positive tweets by persons may be useable to predict sales and that there was a relation between a peak in the number of positive tweets and an increase in sales in the following weeks. However, they pointed out that the relation between tweets and sales was not necessarily a causal relation but may be affected by a third factor for the sales. Wijnhoven & Plant (2017) explored the usefulness of sentiment analysis and Google Trend for automobile sales forecasts. They analyzed half a million postings related to the eleven automobile models on social media using linear regression models. Also, the study compared its results to Google Trends for predictability. The study concluded that sentiment analysis on social media showed little predictability on automobile sales, while Google Trends data and social mention volume showed meaningful results. Pai & Liu (2018) employed social media data, stock market values and time-series models to predict monthly sales of automobiles in the U.S. Sentiment analysis of tweets, stock market values and hybrid data were used for the analysis to forecast the total monthly sale of automobiles in the U.S. The study concluded that the values from social media and the stock market were essential for the monthly sales forecast and that the exclusion of seasonal variability improved the forecast of precise monthly sales. As such, most sales forecasts using Twitter have not seen success yet.

Our study gathered tweets related to 12 vehicle models sold in Japan for two years, from June 2018 to May 2020. The total number of tweets gathered was 3,247,796, quite large compared to other previous studies.

3. METHODS FOR THE STUDY

The study analyzed Twitter data of 12 automobile models and actual sales data published by Japan Automobile Dealers Association (JADA). In this chapter we discuss the methods for social listening and how the social listening data was analyzed.

3.1 Vehicle Models Subject for the Study

JADA publishes previous month's sales by models, and we selected the 25 top sold vehicle models published in May 2018. Those model names were searched by keywords on Real-Time search by Yahoo! Japan(1), and models that cannot be identified due to homonyms were excluded (for example, when searching for Toyota 'AQUA'('Prius C' is the international name), non-related words such as 'aquarium' were excluded). Among 25 models, we selected twelve models after having removed model names with many homonyms (Table 1).

Table 1. Models subjected for study

Prius	VOXY	SIENTA	COROLLA
C-HR	Vitz	IMPREZA	VEZEL
ALPHARD	STEP WGN	X-TRAIL	DEMIO

Figure 2 is the sales record of the 12 models from June 2018 to May 2020 published by JADA. Toyota's models are always high on the list of the chart. Especially, Toyota Prius had been the most sold model since January 2019, but a Higashi-Ikebukuro runaway car accident (2) on April 19, 2019 damaged the sales, and after August 2019 the sales dropped to 1/3 of its peak. On the other hand, Toyota Yaris has become the top seller since May 2020. Honda came second on the number of sales. Nissan had held the second ranking on the sales for a long time, but after the arrest of the former Nissan CEO Carlos Ghosn on charges of fraud related to the executive compensation, its sales dramatically plummeted, and although the Nissan X-TRAIL was subject to the research, the sales dropped by half during the data gathering.

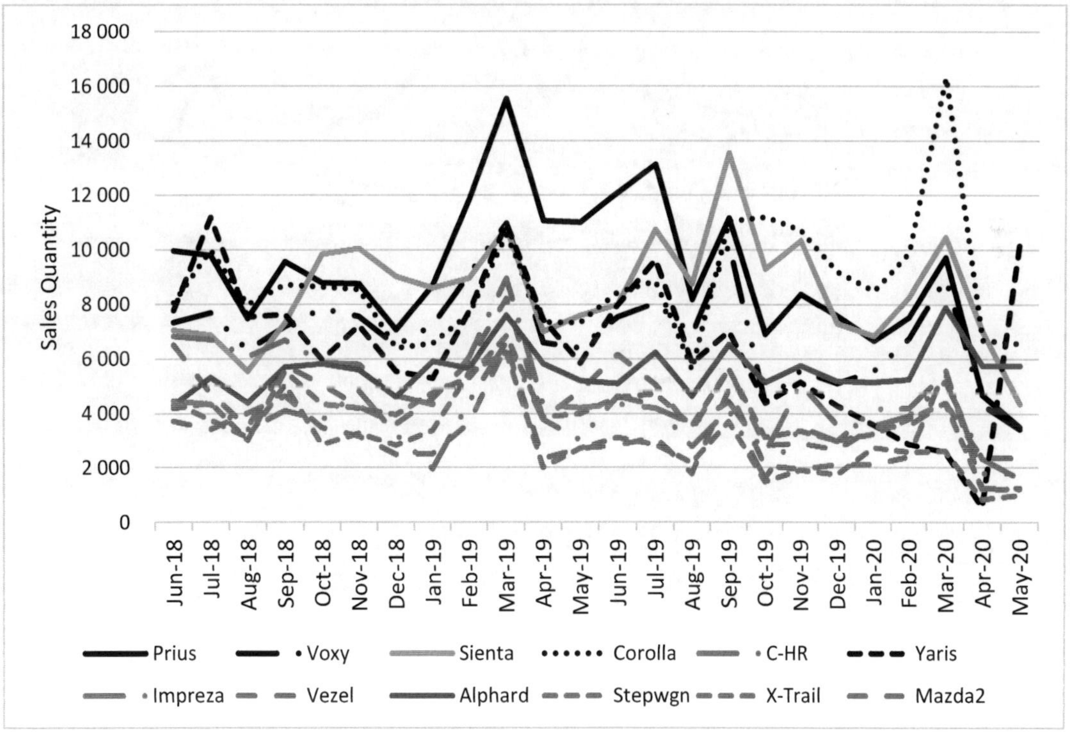

Figure 2. Sales by models
Source : JADA (2018-2020),<http://www.jada.or.jp/data/month/m-r-hanbai/m-r-type>
Retrieved on April 29, 2021. (Vits and Demio were renamed Yaris and Mazda 2, respectively.)

3.2 Methods for Social Listening

We obtained data on vehicle models for social listening through the real-time search provided by Yahoo! Japan. Through the real-time search, Japanese tweets that are written in Japanese and are not set in private can be searched. Therefore, tweets written overseas (for example, tweets from Honolulu, Hawaii, which has a 19 hour time-difference to Japan) are also included in the data. We believed that gathering Twitter information by key words makes the information volume bigger and more precise than gathering hash-tagged information.

Figure 3 is the number of tweets on each model. This shows only positive tweets identified through sentiment analysis, of which criteria of 'negative' and 'positive' are set by Yahoo. Also, since Japanese anime characters occasionally take after Japanese car model names, words related to anime characters had to be excluded when researching Yahoo! Japan. For example, when searching a model name 'Sienta', key words for search looks like this: 'Sienta -Sientaris -Senisienta -Sienta Super Beast -Enamel Made Sienta' ('-' means 'to exclude'). The figure shows that tweets about Toyota Prius increase around every January. The reason for the increase is because Toyota announces minor changes to the model during that period. Also, as Figure 4 shows, the previously mentioned Higashi-Ikebukuro runaway car accident brought the fire on Twitter; thus, we decided to use only positive tweets for the analysis. The tweets on Toyota Prius gradually took a downhill slide since April 2019 shown in Figure 3, while tweets on Toyota Yaris showed rapid increase.

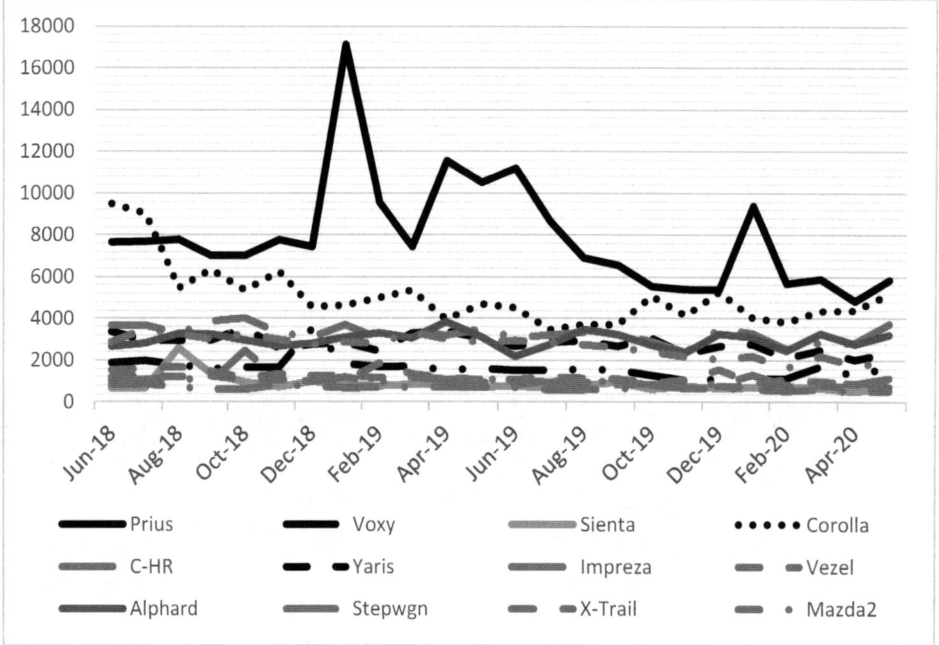

Figure 3. Positive tweets by month

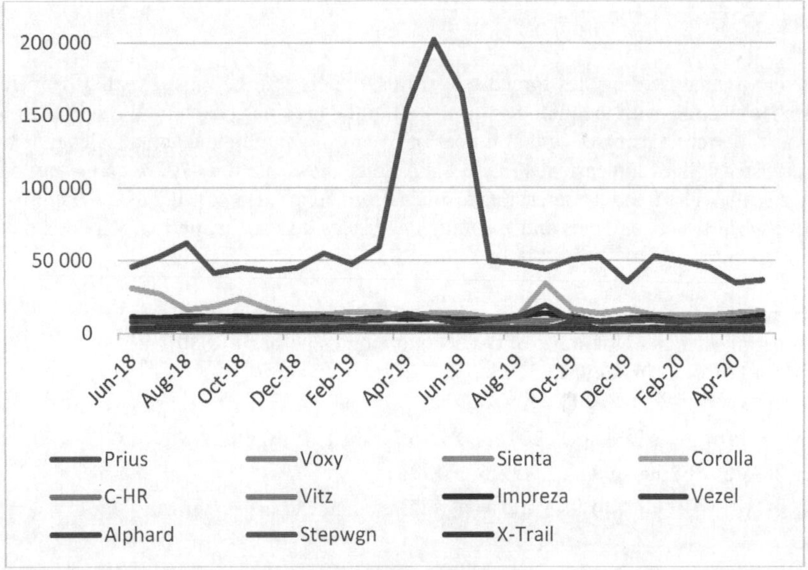

Figure 4. Tweets by month

3.3 Methods for Analysis

Because the data used for the study is time-series data, we first performed a cross correlation calculation for the models to measure time-lag between tweets and actual sales. Analysis was performed after the time-lag was adjusted.

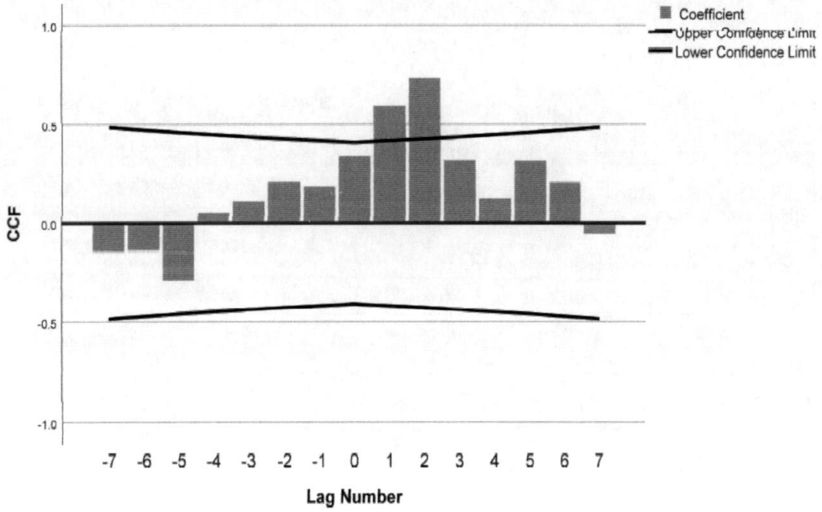

Figure 5. Prius Twitter with Prius Sales Quantity

Figure 5 is a cross correlation graph between the number of tweets on Prius and its actual sales. The cross-correlation coefficient is the highest at the lag value of 2. This means the leading index is two months ahead of actual sales, which means two months of time-lag exists between the tweets and actual sales. This time-lag can be justified, because in Japan brand-new cars are assembled after a sales contract, and actual delivery takes 2 to 3 months after the contract.

4. ANALYSIS

In this chapter we analyze the sales forecast for Prius, which was the most tweeted from June 2018 to May 2020 (1,516,016 tweets), with the methods discussed in the previous chapter. We set up a regression formula by creating a scatter chart using the total number of tweets of a month and actual sales two months after those tweets were posted. Sales forecast was made for August and September 2020, using the regression formula. Figure 6 is a scatter chart and a regression formula from June 2018 to May 2020. Figure 7 is a correlation coefficient between tweets on Prius and the number of sales during that period, which is the mark of 1% and is significant.

From the regression formula:
The number of sales=0.87×number of tweets two months before +1,830
Sales forecast of Prius in August 2020 is:
Number of tweets in June 2020: 5,309
Sales forecasts of Prius in August 2020: 0.87×5,309+1,830 = 6,448.8
Number of sales of Prius in August 2020: 6,429
Relative error: (6,429-6,449) ÷6,449 = -0.3%

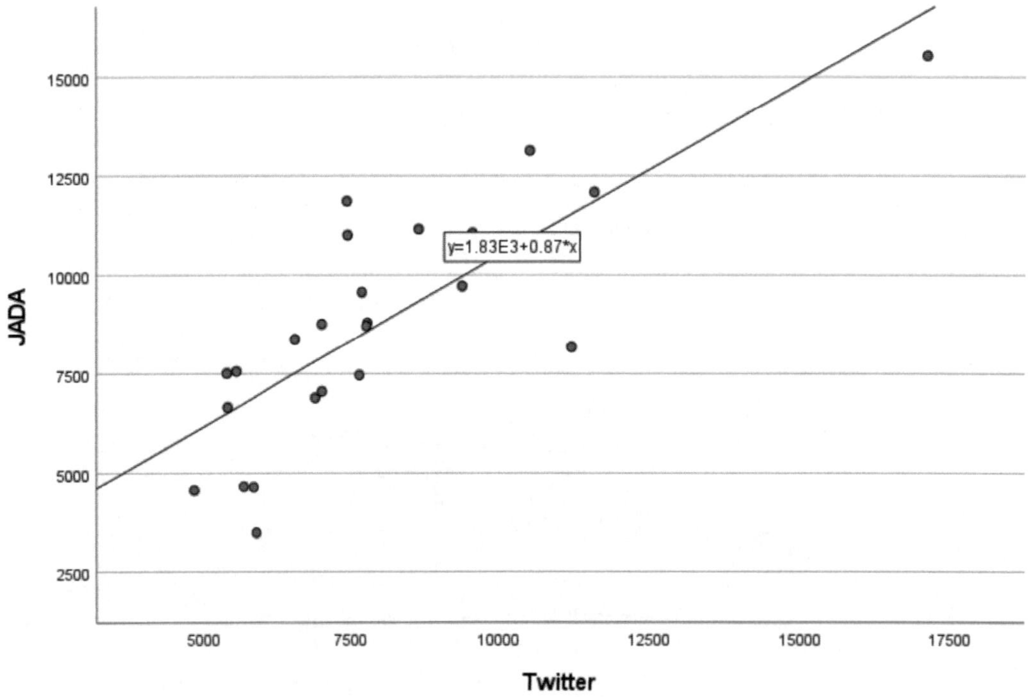

Figure 6. Scatter chart and regression formula for tweets on Prius

Correlations

		JADA	Twitter
JADA	Pearson Correlation	1	.796**
	Sig. (2-tailed)		<.001
	N	24	24
Twitter	Pearson Correlation	.796**	1
	Sig. (2-tailed)	<.001	
	N	24	24

**. Correlation is significant at the 0.01 level (2-tailed).

Figure 7. Correlation coefficient of number of tweets and sales for Prius

Sales forecast of Prius in September 2020 is:
Number of tweets in July 2020: 4,943
Sales forecasts of Prius in September 2020: 0.87×4,943+1,830＝6,130.4
Number of sales of Prius in September 2020: 5,818
Relative error: （5,818-6,130） ÷6,130＝-5.1%

Next, we discuss Corolla, which had the second largest number of tweets during the 24 months of data gathering. According to Toyota, Corolla went on the market in 1966 in Japan. The model was sold 0.4 million units at its peak in the 70s, but recently sells less than 0.1 million (Toyota, 2022). However, outside Japan its annual sales is over one million since 2000, and repeating minor changes contribute to the accumulated total sales of over 50 million so far. The total number of tweets about Corolla was 393,523, which was 26% of Prius', and the sales forecast of the model was not possible.

The model with the third highest number of tweets was Vits (currently Yaris). Its sales volume has been rapidly increasing after renaming to Yaris in February 2020. The number of tweets about Vits has been increasing since the spring of 2020. The forecast was not successful with the current data, but we expect that the forecast will be possible with more Twitter data. Forecasts for other models were not successful either.

Table 2. Number of tweets on each model

Prius	Voxy	Sienta	Corolla	C-HR	Vitz
1,516,016	96,697	68,470	393,523	54,468	204,176
Impreza	Vezel	Alphard	Stepwgn	X-Trail	Mazda2
250,772	65,692	231,582	89,675	78,066	198,658

Now we discuss each model. According to the sales data published by JADA (Figure 2), Prius was in the transition period from a maturity stage to a decline stage, Corolla was in a decline stage in Japan, and Yaris was in a growth stage. When those stages were applied to the PPM (Product Portfolio Management) Model(3) by BCG (Boston Consulting Group) (Henderson, 1979), Prius was in a transitional period from 'star' to 'cash cow' and then to 'dog', and Yaris was in a transitional period from 'star' to 'cash cow'. To confirm that, we created matrix diagrams for the models applying PPM. Figure 8 is a matrix by models in the first half of 2019. The vertical axis shows a growth rate (an increase or decrease of the total automobile sales) from the latter half of 2018 to the first half of 2019, and the horizontal axis is a share of each model in the first half of 2019. The size of the circle indicates the sales of each model. Figure 9, 10 and 11 are created in the same manner.

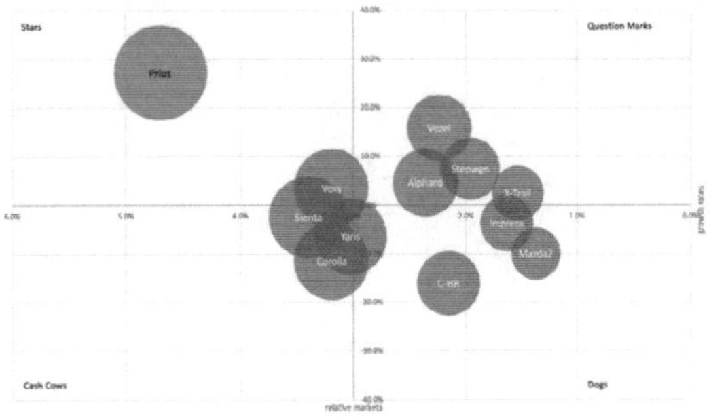

Figure 8. PPM in the 1st half of 2019 by models

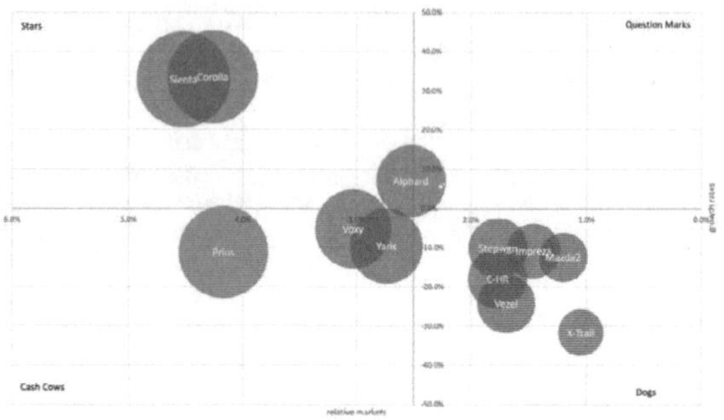

Figure 9. PPM in the 2nd half of 2019 by models

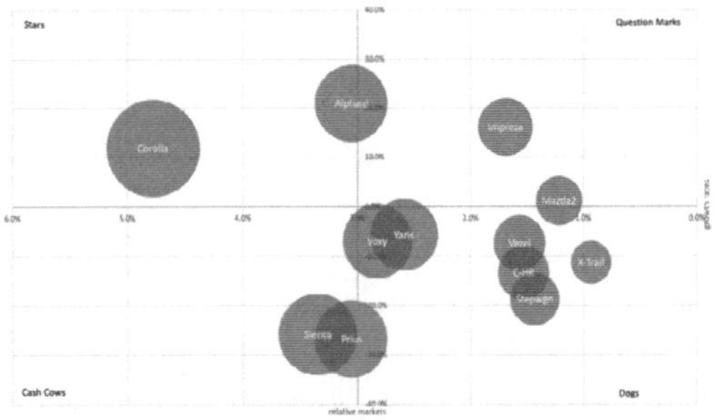

Figure 10. PPM in the 1st half of 2020 by models

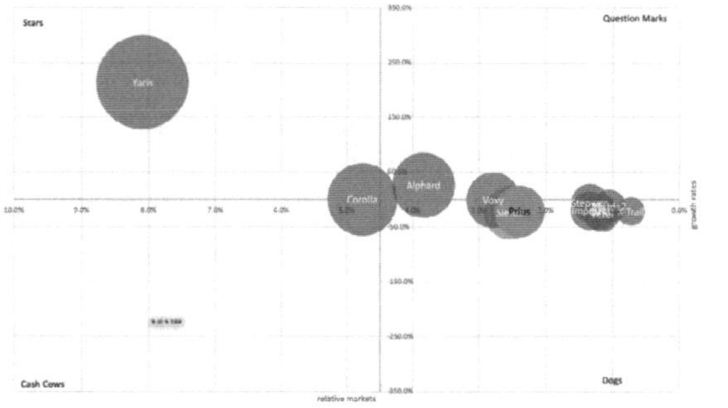

Figure 11. PPM in the 2nd half of 2020 by models

As these figures show, Prius was in the position of star in the first half of 2019 but shifted to cash cow in the latter half of the year. The model was in the transitional period to dog in the first half of 2020 and positioned in dog in the latter half of the year. Other models transition in random order.

From the above, we assumed that although a number of tweets are necessary to make sales forecast through social listening, it is important for products to undergo the four stages of life cycle, which consist of introduction, growth, maturity and decline, to be forecast. In other words, forecast through social listening is not possible on products which shift to decline stage straight after introduction stage.

It is likely that sales forecast is possible during the process of products shifting from cash cows to dogs after positioning as stars and that the products in stars and dogs phases are difficult to forecast sales. This is because people are less likely to write about products in question mark and dog phases. There is a possibility that both a large number of tweets and the product being shifted from cash cows to dogs after positioning as star contributed to the correct sales forecast of Prius.

5. CONCLUSION

In this study we gathered tweets related to automobile models in Japan and used them as alternative data for social listening to forecast the sales of each model. A cross correlation between the number of tweets and the actual number of sales published by JADA showed two month of time-lag. In Japan brand-new cars are assembled after a sales contract, and actual delivery takes two to three months after the contract; thus, this time-lag is deemed accurate. However, models with a lower number of tweets were unforecastable and a versatile sale forecast model which can be applied to all models has not been built yet. For this study we gathered 3,247,796 tweets from June 2018 to May 2020, and Prius accounted for 1,516,016 tweets. This large number of tweets contributed to the correct sales forecast of Prius. In addition, after a PPM analysis, we came to think that the fact that Prius shifted from cash cow to dog after positioning in star may be also a factor for the forecast. Hence, we propose a hypothesis that sales forecast is possible for products whose life cycle undergoes the growth, maturity, and decline; in other words, sales can be forecast during the process of products shifting from cash cows to dogs after positioning in stars. Our future task is to find the number of tweets necessary for forecast and to establish a versatile model which takes into account life cycle's stage changes in the PPM analysis model caused by various factors such as sales decline due to negative tweets and change of sales price.

ACKNOWLEDGEMENT

This work was supported by Nagoya Gakuin University.

NOTES

(1). Real-time search is an internet search that reflects and adds postings on the real-time web service like Twitter on the second-by-second basis. Google initiated the services in October 2009, but halted the service in July 2011 due to the expiration of the access provision contract with Twitter. Yahoo! Japan started the real-time research services on June 14, 2011. Yahoo! in the U.S. does not provide the real-time search services.

(2). The Higasi Ikebukuro runaway car accident is the fatal car accident which occurred in Tokyo on April 19, 2019 caused when a driver mistakenly stepped on the accelerator instead of the brake, resulting in two deaths and nine injuries. The driver, who was a retired elite public bureaucrat and was 87 years old at that time, was driving Prius and insisted that its brake pedal did not work. There were several factors why the number of tweets increased. There were criticism about Prius itself, but also his status as a retired elite public bureaucrat helped the number of tweets related to Prius increase. Toyota announced that its driving record showed no brake pedal was hit right before the accident, and he was sentenced to five years in jail. This accident caused many elders to surrender their driver's license.

(3). PPM is also called the growth-share matrix, BCG-matrix or Boston matrix. Crainer (1998)

REFERENCES

Akimoto, A. (2011). *Japan, the Twitter nation*. The Japan Times. May 18th. Retrieved June 3, 2021, from http://tony-silva.com/eslefl/miscstudent/downloadpagearticles/twitterinjapan-jt.pdf

Crainer, S., (1998). Key Management Ideas: Thinkers that Changed the Management World, Financial Times Pitman Pub.

Dijkman, R., Ipeirotis, P., Aertsen, F., & van Helden, R. (2015). Using Twitter to Predict Sales: A Case Study. *arXiv preprint arXiv:1503.04599*.

Goto, H & Goto, Y. (2018). Analysis of Elections Using Social Listening in Japan. *51st Hawaii International Conference on System Sciences*. pp.1742-1751

Goto, H. & Goto, Y. (2019). Regression Analysis of National Elections in Japan Using Social Listening. *IADIS*. 2019.

Henderson, B. D., (1979). *Henderson on Corporate Strategy*, Harpercollins College Div.

Pai, P. F., & Liu, C. H. (2018). Predicting vehicle sales by sentiment analysis of Twitter data and stock market values. *IEEE Access*, *6*, 57655-57662.

Toyota (2022). 'カローラ累計販売台数 (English Translation: Accumulated sales volume of Carolla)', https://global.toyota/jp/corolla50th/history/by_the_numbers/sales_results_01/, retrieved in June 3, 2021

Wijnhoven, F., & Plant, O. (2017). Sentiment Analysis and Google Trends Data for Predicting Car Sales. *ICIS*.

THE TAXONOMICAL DISTINCTION BETWEEN THE CONCEPTS OF SMALL DATA AND BIG DATA

Wandisa Nyikana and Tiko Iyamu
Cape Peninsula University of Technology
Cape Town, Western Cape, South Africa

ABSTRACT

The differentiation between big data and small data is growing in confusion, in both academic and business domains. The confusion is endorsed by studies, by consistently arguing that the difference between big data and small data is not about size. The confusion between big data and small data is increasingly prohibitive for many organisations including students. As a result of the confusion and its associated implications, there are many costly decisions by individuals and groups in organisations. Consequently, productivity and quality of service are affected, which negatively reflect in competitiveness and sustainability. Thus, it is critically essential to address these growing challenges while the consequences are manageable. The objective of the study was to develop a taxonomy that distinguishes small data from big data, to remove the confusion, which often hinder understanding and affect the use for business enhancement. From the interpretivist approach perspective, the qualitative methods were employed in the study.

KEYWORDS

Big Data, Confusion between Small and Big Data, Taxonomic, Small Data

1. INTRODUCTION

Many organisations are increasingly realising the importance and value of data. The realisation triggers organisations, to gain better understanding and exploit the usefulness of their data from different angles, for effective business decisions (Ugur & Turan, 2020). The academic domain, too, are increasingly conducting studies, to gain experimental and empirical studies, to contribute to the developmental and usefulness of data (Cockcroft & Russell, 2018). In doing so, both business and academic domains characterise data into two main categories, small data and big data (Minami & Ohura, 2021; Gelhaar, Groß & Otto, 2021; Rengarajan et al., 2022). The categorisation has infused confusion for many people in both business and academics (Uğur & Turan, 2020).

Small data often refers to data or normal data. Small data is often viewed and explained as a concept that uses tiny clues and specific attributes to uncover huge trends (Rengarajan et al., 2022). Kitchin and Lauriault (2015) argue that small data is characterized by limited volume, non-continuous collection, and narrow variety. From scientific angle, Ferguson et al. (2014) explain how the small data is a collective representation of entities for various purposes. Without contradiction, small data has been used for many years by businesses, to produce meaningful insights (Kitchin & Lauriault, 2015) and to make operational decisions (Cekerevac et al., 2016).

Big data is defined by its characteristics known as the 4 V's volume, velocity, veracity, and variety (Sun et al., 2018; Osman, 2019). According to Barham (2017), Volume refers to size, which entails the scale of data. Velocity is the speed at which data travels, including how the data or set of data is streamed and flows in exchanges (Iyamu, 2018). Veracity is the complexity and uncertainty of data (Lam et al., 2017). Variety refers to the different forms of data (Barham, 2017). According to Bariki et al. (2017), value is another characteristic that defines big data, which depends on the importance that an organisation associated with it. Small data on the other hand is the sample data retrieved by using sampling methods to understand certain problems (Cheng et al., 2018). It is characterised by its limited volume and narrow variety (Kitchin & Lauriault, 2015).

There are obvious and unclear similarities and differentiation between small data and big data. The differentiation can be clarified and put into perspectives by an understanding of the taxonomies of the concepts, which include their nomenclature. Nomenclature is the systematic way that we use to name things (Hugenholtz et al., 2021), or the rules that we use to form these names or terms (Sterner & Franz 2017). Its purpose is to provide unambiguous clear meaning of names so that there are no misunderstandings or confusion (Hawksworth, 2013). Sterner and Franz (2017) argue that nomenclature goes beyond an understanding the information that surrounds the usage of those names. Thus, standard nomenclature is required for small data and big data that can be used by both humans and machines, to gain better understanding of the concepts, idiosyncratically.

This study does not concentrate on redefining small data and big data, rather, it focuses on the confusion and distinction the concepts pose to individuals and organisations. Primarily, the confusion remains because the concepts, small data and big data are not understood, distinctively. The confusion can be attributed to lack of clarification of the taxonomies including the nomenclature of the concepts. This problem does not get easier because many studies either concentrate on big data or small data. Thus, it is hard to find studies that focus on both concepts, to increase their distinctiveness towards usefulness by organisations and stakeholders. Therefore, this study focuses on defining and establishing the taxonomies of small data and big data, for organisational purposes. This will help to provide clarity of the two concepts, eliminate the confusion and increase their usefulness.

The objective of the study was to develop a taxonomy that distinguishes small data from big data, to remove the confusion, which often hinder understanding and affect the use for business enhancement. In achieving the objective, two steps were followed in examining the phenomenon. In the first step, the nomenclatural and the differences between small data and big data were examined. Through the second step, the scope and boundaries of each concept, small data and big data were understood better. This helps to gain better understanding to, what big data is if it is not about the size. From this understanding a distinction is established.

2. PROBLEMATISATION OF THE CONCEPTS

In many organisations, the term and concept of big data remain a bass word. This is attributed to the fact that many employees or stakeholders of organisations do not seem to observe or believe that there is difference between small (normal) data and big data. In some organisations, small data is often mistaken for big data, vice versa. Consequently, this type of confusion has negative effect and influence on data structuring, management and planning for business enhancement. For example, despite the similarities, tools for big data analysis are purchased for small data purposes. In such an instance, two prohibitive things happen: (1) the cost of purchasing the tools for analysis or analytics and scarce skill required; and (2) inappropriate tool is employed, which yields undesirable results.

The small data contains some of the big data characteristics (Kitchin & Lauriault, 2015). Hence Cheng (2018) claims that big data comes from small data but did not draw boundary or distinction between the two concepts. Also, the data analytics tools used to analyse big data can also be applied to small data to extract information and gain useful insight. The overlapping of the two concepts brings confusion hence it is important to understand the nomenclature for big data and small data.

Yet, the characteristics including the nomenclature of both small data and big data are the same (Katal, Wazid & Gouda, 2013; Faraway & Augustin, 2018). Faraway and Augustin (2018) explain how the confusion makes it difficult for the data analyst/scientists to be skilled and be confident that they understand both. For examples, some organisations are challenged with pricing the services of their data because they cannot differentiate big from small; and organisations duplicate analytics tools because of lack of clarity.

3. LITERATURE REVIEW

This section presents the review of literature conducted. It focuses on the core aspects of the study, which are the small data, big data, including the differentiation between the small and big data, and the concept of taxonomy.

3.1 Small Data in Organisations

Small data is defined by Kitchin and Lauriault (2015) as sample data that is focusing at answering specific questions. It consists of structured data sets. Ahmed et al. (2017) suggest that small data is characterised by low volumes, quantified velocities, and structured varieties. Because of its manageable volumes, small data can be understood without the use of analytics (Dhaliwal & Shojania, 2018). However, low or size can be subjective if there is no universal definition or measurable agreement. Such subjectivism allows an enterprise to decide on volume (big or small) in isolation. The emergence of big data invoke contrast in the category and boundary including differentiation between the two concepts (Faraway & Augustin, 2018). Thus, it is essential to understand the characteristics and usefulness of the concepts in organisations towards to enhancing activities and improving competitiveness.

Small data focuses on discovering and understanding what causes things to happen rather than the prediction (Faraway & Augustin, 2018). Hence, it is used to determine current situations and conditions. Academic institutions specifically the researchers use small data for the intervention of the research studies. Many organisations use it to produce meaningful results and solutions (Vargas, 2018) and to discover new useful insights (Dhaliwal & Shojania, 2018). According to Cekerevac et al. (2016), organisations use it because it is properly developed and has been used for a long time. Also, it enables organisations to make key business decisions (Necsulescu, 2017). This could be attributed to the fact that small data is granular and insightful.

Small data faces challenges with machine learning algorithms from analysis perspective because small data are overfitting (Li et al., 2020; Kong et al., 2020). The machine learning algorithms do not provide robustness when applied to smaller data sets and this leads to poor performance, expensive and complex process (Kennedy et al., 2017; Vecchi et al., 2022). Also, other methods available for analysis of small data have limited effectiveness and require skilled personnel (Kong et al, 2020). On the other hand, Kennedy et al. (2017) claim that since small data is using sample data, it does not have the ability to fully represent the large data sets. Furthermore, small data focuses on answering specific questions or queries. Hence, it is difficult to apply its findings to large groups of events and activities (Ravi, 2021).

3.2 Big Data in Organisations

Big data comes from various sources with several types of data formats and structures. It is collected using different devices (Iyamu, 2020). Big data contains large, structured, semi structured, and unstructured data sets (Oussous et al., 2018). The concept is concerned with capturing, storing, analysing, and evaluating the data that is created by human beings and devices using computer technologies (Herschel & Miori, 2017).

Big data has become a crucial and useful resource to the organisations. Cockcroft and Russell (2018) highlight big data as an asset in many organisations. It is recognised in many sectors and by different professionals such as scientists and healthcare practitioners (Iyamu, 2020). Some of the organisations use it to address their processes and strategies (Barham,2017). While others use it for sustainability, efficiency, and competitiveness (Iyamu, 2018). Also, big data helps the organisations to improve decision making, to achieve their goals (Sivarajah, 2017). Moreover, it assists the organisations to understand their operations Ahmed et al. (2017) and to cut costs (Grable & Lyons, 2018). Cekerevac et al. (2016) adds that the organisations use big data to gain new insights and for prediction. Financial institutions use the big data to detect fraud (Cockcroft & Russell, 2018). While pharmaceutical companies use it to trace defects on new products (Barham, 2017).

Big data presents some challenges to organisations regardless of its usefulness. One of those challenges is the complexity with integration of the data (Barham, 2017). This is due to different data structures that big data has and the high speed in which it flows (Barham, 2017; Samsudeen & Haleem, 2020). Also, some of the organisations still have data in legacy databases and this makes it difficult to gain value from big data (Nunu,2019). According to Mgudlwa and Iyamu (2018), processing data is complex because of the large size of the data. Moreover, it is complicated to process the big data using traditional data processing applications. Nyikana and Iyamu (2022) highlight other challenges as storage, skills, searching, security, and privacy violation. On the other hand, the infrastructure for big data is inadequate and expensive, according to Sivarajah et al. (2017). Furthermore, the synchronisation of large data sets is another challenge.

3.3 Small Data and Big Data

The confusion in differentiation between small data and big data is growing and affects logic and value associated to them (Kitchin & Lauriault, 2015). Sacristán and Dilla (2015) suggest that organisations struggle in achieving the potentiality of big data because the small data are not differentiated from each other by the users. Letouzé, Areias and Jackson (2016) the dichotomy between small data versus big data does not capture the complexity of their structure and ecosystems. According to Aversa, Doherty and Hernandez (2018), currently, there seems to be no consensus on the determinants of the small data and big data. Kitchin and Lauriault (2015) posit that the term 'big' is misleading as big data are characterized by much more than volume, and 'small' data can be large, such as national censuses.

Small data and big data are usually distinguished from each other using several factors, which include scope and volume. The capability, requirements and support mechanism for small data is different from big data (Davenport, Barth & Bean, 2012). The differences draw its inferences from factors such as accessibility, conciseness, and workability. Furht and Villanustre (2016) argue that there is distinction between the small data and big data but did not detail the differences. Wang (2017) highlights heterogeneity as one of the differences between the concepts of small and big data.

3.4 The Concept of Taxonomy

It is important to categorise and classify the concept of big data and small data, which can be done through taxonomy. Rizk et al. (2018) define taxonomy as the process of classification used in scientific fields. Gelhaar et al. (2021) explain that taxonomies provide a structure and organised knowledge that can be used by the researchers to understand and analyse complex areas. Hence, developing the taxonomy of big data and small data would benefit both academics and the business domains, in gaining better insights and understanding of the existing knowledge about the concepts. Furthermore, taxonomy helps to develop rigour theory.

Taxonomies are used in the literature of information systems (IS) to analyse and classify complex phenomenon (Azkan et al., 2020). Also, to understand relationships among concepts (Rizk et al., 2018). According to Nickerson et al. (2013), there is a method that has been developed for IS researchers to use for taxonomy development to classify artifacts. Maslin (2002) explains that without taxonomy in biology, it is not easy to communicate and exchange information about organisms. Also, when the taxonomy is poorly defined, all the information linked to those defined names will be incorrect.

Taxonomy is widely used in different fields. Bloom's taxonomy is a well-known taxonomy used in the academic domain for the classification of educational learning objectives (Anindītya et al., 2019). In chemistry, periodic table is another example where taxonomy has been used to understand the elements (Oberlander et al., 2019). While in the field of IS, taxonomy has been used for the classification of digital technologies such as the internet of things, cloud computing and social media (Berger et al., 2018; Szopinski et al., 2019). Health care uses taxonomies to classify diseases and medication to improve diagnosis (Haendel et al., 2018; Seyhan & Carını, 2019). Furthermore, in health research, taxonomy is used to categorise the results of clinical trials, to improve knowledge discovery, which makes it easier for trials in the registries and databases (Dodd et al., 2018).

4. RESEARCH METHODOLOGY

Qualitative method was employed in this study. Primarily, this is because qualitative method seeks to understand why things are the way that they are (Al-Ababneh, 2020) and the study focuses on quality rather than quantity (Iyamu & Shaanika, 2022). The method is suitable because the study seeks to understand the distinction between big data and small data, which is based on experiences, opinions, and views. That distinction cannot be discovered by using the quantitative method as the method focuses more on numbers. Another reason for using qualitative method is because it is exploratory by nature (Sovacool et al., 2018). Hence, it was used to explore the characteristics of big data and small to eliminate the confusion between the two concepts. Thus, from the perspective of qualitative, a design is selected.

Document analysis was employed in the data collection, primarily because of wide-coverage and historical purposes. According to Lakay and Iyamu (2022), documentation focuses on collecting the existing data that is stable and may sometimes not be noticeable. Furthermore, it helps to provide broad knowledge and extensive coverage of the phenomenon being studied. Iyamu, Nehemia-Maletzky and Shaanika (2016) argue that documentation helps to provide historical background of over a period. Hence, it has been adopted for the study to gain extensive and historical knowledge about small data and big data.

Criteria was set, consisting of two factors, source and period, to guide the collection of data. First, the use of academic databases, to ensure credibility and reliability of the data. Second, a period of ten years, to ensure extensive coverage of the meanings and attributes that have been associated with the concepts, historically. The data was collected from academic databases which include Google Scholar, AIS, and Ebscohost. The coverage was on articles published between 2012 and 2022. As shown in Table 1, a total of 41 articles were collected, of which 17 were for small data and 24 for big data. The Table depicts the types of materials that were collected.

Table 1. Data collection

	Journal	Conference Proceedings	Book chapter	Book	Others (e.g., white papers)	Total
Small data	8	4		1	2	15
Big data	16	5		1	1	23
Total	24	9		2	3	38

5. ANALYSING THE QUALITATIVE DATA

We are aware that conducting analysis of data in a qualitative study can be cumbersome in that there is no specific guidelines or method, as revealed and discussed in literature (Dufour & Richard, 2019; Lester, Cho & Lochmiller, 2020). Thus, we carefully and methodologically employ interpretivist approach, from whose perspective the hermeneutics approach is applied to analyse the data in this study. It was methodological in that the analysis involves a process of describing, classification and interpretation of the data, to provide relevance, and useful meaningful information (Taherdoost, 2022; Cassell & Bishop, 2019).

Hermeneutics approach is concerned with understanding and interpretation of data (Lakay & Iyamu 2022). According to Nigar (2020), the hermeneutics approach focuses on digging deep into text, to find new knowledge. Furthermore, it allows the researcher's own understanding and interpretation of the text. According to Nyikana and Iyamu (2022), the use of the hermeneutics circles helps to gain deeper understanding of the meanings that are associated with things, through repeated reading of the texts. The circles mean continuous interrogation of the text, by going forward and back until a satisfactory point where the researchers feels that a better understanding is gained.

Based on the focus of the hermeneutics, the approach is most appropriate for this study, primarily for two reasons. First, the data is not firs-hand. Existing materials (literature) are used as data in the study, as discussed in section 6.3. This means that the researcher needs to be thorough so as to gain deeper insights of the authors of the literature's perspectives. Second, the focus of the study, which is to determine differentiation between small data and big data is unwieldly. Therefore, it requires unfathomable details, to achieve the goal of the study. Thus, reading of the 38 (see Table 1) related materials in circles, is inevitable.

The analysis of the data is conducted in accordance with the objectives of the study, which are, to, (1) examine the nomenclature and differences between small data and big data; and (2) understand what big data is if it is not about the size.

6. DISCUSSION OF THE OUTCOME

From the analysis, there are two main outcomes, which are (1) the nomenclatural and differences between small data and big data; and (2) gain better understanding of what big data is since it is not about the size. The outcomes are presented in the remainder of this section.

6.1 The Nomenclatural and Differences between Small Data and Big Data

In understanding the nomenclature of both small data and big data, their attributes were identified, as tabulated in Table 2.

Table 2. The nomenclature

Attribute	Small data	Big data
Database	Relational Database. Data is managed and accessed using Sequel Query Language (SQL).	Non-Relational Database. Data is managed using No Sequel Query Language (No SQL)
Data Warehouse	Centralised architecture with structured datasets.	Distributed architecture with structured, semi-structured and unstructured datasets.
Data storage	Uses data marts to store the information of particular function in a single place.	Uses data lakes to store raw data from the various sources.
Data Analysis	The analysis occurs after the event. Uses statistical and business intelligence tools.	The analysis occurs in real time. Uses Big data analytics tools.

This will help to understand the scope and boundaries of each concept, small data and big data. One of the similarities is that both big data and small data contribute value to the organisations. According to Faraway and Augustin (2018), clearly, big data and small data are generated using the same sources, which include technological, business, and societal factors. Small or big data drives innovation and productivity of the businesses including decision making (Hassani & Silva, 2015). According to Jin et al. (2015), big data can enhance the competitive advantage of organisations, economic growth of countries, and help to predict the future of enterprises. Doesn't small data provide the same capability? The differences seem to hide within each other, small data and big data.

6.2 Understand what Big Data is if it is not about the Size

Table 3 provides a distinction between small data and big data, which explains the trajectory of the concepts. The distinction shows that the differences between the concepts is beyond size.

Table 3. The characteristics

Characteristic	Small data	Big data
Volume	The data is in the range of up to hundreds of gigabytes.	The data is more is in terabytes or more.
Velocity	The data is regulated, and constantly, it flows. The aggregation of the data is slow.	The data arrives at unprecedented high speeds, and large volumes of data aggregation in a short time.
Variety	It has narrow variety of data sets which include records, files and tabular data.	It consists of numerous data set, which include tabular data, text, audio, images, video, logs, JSON.
Veracity	The data comes from reliable sources.	The data comes from several sources with complex, less reliable, bias and noise data sets.
Value	The data is used to produce insights, drive innovation, productivity and improve decision making.	The data is used to drive innovation and productivity, enhance economic growth, improve decision making and gain competitive advantage.
Structure	The data is structured, often in tabular format with fixed schema (relational).	The data is structured, semi structured, and unstructured data sets with dynamic schema (non- relational)
Discover trends/insights	The data uses tiny clues and specific attributes to discover meaningful insights. The data is current. It focuses on what causes things to happen.	The data is used to discover insights. It focuses on what causes things to happen and predict what could happen in future.
Drives decision making	The data is granular. It answers specific questions.	The data increases organisational outputs and profits.
Optimisation	The data can be optimized manually (human effort)	The data requires machine learning techniques for optimization of the data.

Based on the aim of the study which is to develop a taxonomy that distinguishes small data from big data, an in-depth investigation was conducted. The investigation focused on removing the confusion that exist between the two concepts. Thus, the two concepts, small data and big data were investigated in two phases.

First, the concepts were investigated separately. Second, the concepts were mapped against each other. This approach helps to detect the similarities and differences, towards removing the confusion between small data and big data using its characteristic, as shown in Table 3. In addition, the approach will help to gain an understanding of how factors transform to form the taxonomies of each concept.

7. CONCLUSION

The study develops a taxonomy that distinguishes small data from big data, to remove the confusion that currently exists between the two concepts. This has immense significance for business, in conducting transaction that are dependent on data and assessing value. The study is significant in IT specialists, which include managers and data architects, as they strive to support and enable organisation's aim and objectives. Through better understanding of the distinction between the concepts, data architects can design a less complex architecture from both business and technology perspectives. A fewer complex data architecture is intended to increase competitiveness and sustainability, for an organisation.

The study provides two distinctives entities, nomenclature and characteristics between small data and big data. From academics' viewpoints, each of these entities is a foundation for further development. From this perspective, the study contributes to the body of knowledge, which researchers and students, particularly, postgraduates can access for better understanding and clarifications concerning small data and big data.

The study provides clarity of an area that has been most confusing and conflict through its categorisation of the attributes and characteristics of small data and big data. This enables individuals such as data scientists and manager, data architects and organisations at large to have better understanding of the dimensions and myriad in carrying out activities such as analysis and computing of small data or big data. This can be used to define the value and contributions of either the small data or big data in an organisation. From academic viewpoint, the study can be used as baseline for developing a framework for data attribution platform. The platform will focus on business related services and value-creating mechanisms, to increase effective and efficient use of data in an organisation.

Although the study provides useful clarification for the confusion that exist between small data and big data, the work can be extended. For further studies, it will be useful and relevant to both academic and business domain, if a model is designed for the evaluation of the concepts.

REFERENCES

Ahmed, V. et al, 2017. The future of big data in facilities management: opportunities and challenges. *Facilities*, Vol. 35, No. 13, pp 725-745.

Al-Ababneh, M.M., 2020. Linking ontology, epistemology and research methodology. *Science & Philosophy*, Vol. 8, No.1, pp 75-91.

Aninditya, A. et al, 2019. Text mining approach using TF-IDF and naive Bayes for classification of exam questions based on cognitive level of bloom's taxonomy. In *International Conference on Internet of Things and Intelligence System (IoTaIS)*. Bali, Indonesia, pp. 112-117.

Aversa, J. et al, 2018. Big data analytics: "The new boundaries of retail location decision making". *Papers in Applied Geography*, Vol. 4, No. 4, pp 390-408.

Azkan, C. et al, 2020. A Taxonomy for Data-Driven Services in Manufacturing Industries. In *Twenty-Fourth Pacific Asia Conference on Information Systems*. Dubai, UAE, pp.1-14.

Barham, H., 2017. Achieving competitive advantage through big data: A literature review. In *Portland international conference on management of engineering and technology (PICMET)*. Portland, USA, pp.1-7.

Bariki, L. et al, 2017. Big data analytics: Challenges, research issues, tools and application survey. *International Journal of Engineering Sciences & Research Technology,* Vol. 6, No. 1, pp 548-554.

Berger, S. et al, 2018. The Nature of Digital Technologies-Development of a Multi-Layer Taxonomy. In *Twenty-Sixth European Conference on Information Systems*. Portsmouth, UK, pp.1-18.

Cassell, C. and Bishop, V., 2019. Qualitative data analysis: Exploring themes, metaphors and stories. *European Management Review*, Vol. 16, No. 1, pp 195-207.

Cekerevac, Z. et al, 2016. Big vs small data in micro and small companies. *Communications-Scientific letters of the University of Zilina*, Vol.18, No. 3, pp 34-40.

Cheng, J. et al, 2018. Thoughts on the problem of small data. In *IOP Conference Series: Materials Science and Engineering*. Nanjing, China, pp. 012029.

Cockcroft, S. and Russell, M., 2018. Big data opportunities for accounting and finance practice and research. *Australian Accounting Review*, Vol. 28, No. 3, pp 323-333.

Davenport, T. et al, 2012. How 'big data' is different. *MIT Sloan Management Review*, Vol. 54, No. 1, pp 21-25.

Dhaliwal, G. and Shojania, K.G., 2018. The data of diagnostic error: big, large and small. *BMJ Quality & Safety*, Vol. 27, No. 7, pp 499-501.

Dodd, S. et al, 2018. A taxonomy has been developed for outcomes in medical research to help improve knowledge discovery. *Journal of clinical epidemiology*, Vol. 96, No. 2018, pp 84-92.

Dufour, I.F. and Richard, M.C., 2019. Theorizing from secondary qualitative data: A comparison of two data analysis methods. *Cogent Education*, Vol. 6, No: 1-15.

Faraway, J.J. & Augustin, N.H., 2018. When small data beats big data. *Statistics & Probability Letters*, Vol. 136, No. 2018, pp 142-145.

Ferguson, A.R. et al, 2014. Big data from small data: data-sharing in the'long tail'of neuroscience. *Nature neuroscience*, Vol. 17, No. 11, pp 1442-1447.

Furht, B., and Villanustre, F., 2016. *Introduction to big data. In Big data technologies and applications*. Springer, Cham.

Gelhaar, J. et al, 2021. A taxonomy for data ecosystems. In *Proceedings of the 54th Hawaii International Conference on System Sciences*. Hawaii, USA, pp. 6113 - 6122.

Grable, J.E. and Lyons, A.C., 2018. An Introduction to Big Data. *Journal of financial service professionals*, Vol. 72, Vol. 5, pp 17-20.

Haendel, M.A. et al, 2018. Classification, ontology, and precision medicine. *New England Journal of Medicine*, Vol. 379, No. 15, pp 1452-1462.

Hassani, H. and Silva, E.S., 2015. Forecasting with big data: A review. *Annals of Data Science*, Vol. 2, No. 1, pp 5-19.

Hawksworth D. L., 2013. *Encyclopedia of Biodiversity*. Academic Press, Waltham, Vol. 2, No. 5, pp :547-559.

Herschel, R. and Miori, V.M., 2017. Ethics & big data. *Technology in Society*, Vol 49, No. 2017, pp 31-36.

Hugenholtz, P. et al, 2021. Prokaryotic taxonomy and nomenclature in the age of big sequence data. *The ISME Journal*, Vol. 15, No. 7, pp 1879-1892.

Iyamu, T. et al, 2016. The overlapping nature of business analysis and business architecture: What we need to know. *Electronic Journal of Information Systems Evaluation*, Vol.19, No. 3, pp 169–179.

Iyamu, T., 2018. A multilevel approach to big data analysis using analytic tools and actor network theory. *South African Journal of Information Management*, Vol. 20, No. 1, pp 1-9.

Iyamu, T., 2020. A framework for selecting analytics tools to improve healthcare big data usefulness in developing countries. *South African Journal of Information Management*, Vol. 22, No. 1, pp 1-9.

Iyamu, T. and Shaanika, I., 2022. Assessing Business Architecture Readiness in Organisations. In *Proceedings of the 24th International Conference on Enterprise Information Systems*. Online Steaming, pp. 506-514.

Jin, X. et al, 2015. Significance and challenges of big data research. *Big data research*, Vol. 2, No. 2, pp 59-64.

Katal, A. et al, 2013. Big data: issues, challenges, tools and good practices. In *2013 Sixth international conference on contemporary computing*. Nodia, India, pp. 404-409.

Kennedy, O. et al, 2017. Small data. In *2017 IEEE 33rd International Conference on Data Engineering*. San Diego, CA, 1475-1476.

Kothari, C.R., 2020. Research methodology methods and techniques. 2nd ed. Daryaganj: New Age International, New Delhi.

Kitchin, R. and Lauriault, T.P., 2015. Small data in the era of big data. *GeoJournal*, Vol. 80. No. 4, pp 463-475.

Koseleva, N. and Ropaite, G., 2017. Big data in building energy efficiency: understanding of big data and main challenges. *Procedia Engineering*, Vol.172, No. 2017, pp 544-549.

Kong, S. et al, 2020. Conservative Generalisation for Small Data Analytics–An Extended Lattice Machine Approach. In *2020 International Conference on Machine Learning and Cybernetics*. Adelaide, Australia, pp. 99-104.

Kumar, R. 2018. *Research methodology: A step-by-step guide for beginners*. 5th ed. Sage Publications, London.

Lam, S.K. et al, 2017. Leveraging frontline employees' small data and firm-level big data in frontline management: An absorptive capacity perspective. *Journal of Service Research*, Vol. 20. No. 1, pp 12-28.

Lakay, D. and Iyamu, T., 2022. Examining academic performance through ant towards rpa-based system in South Africa. Education and Information Technologies, Vol. 27, No. 2022, pp 9437–9454.

Alhajj. R. and Rokne.J., *Encyclopedia on Social Network Analysis and Data Mining*. Springer, New York.

Lester, J.N. et al, 2020. Learning to do qualitative data analysis: A starting point. *Human Resource Development Review*, Vol.19, No. 1, pp 94-106.

Bamberger, M. et al, 2015. *Dealing with complexity in development evaluation: A practical approach*. SAGE. pp 221–250.

Li, Z. et al, 2020. Learning with small data. In *Proceedings of the 13th International Conference on Web Search and Data Mining*. Houston, ACM, pp 884-887.

Maslin, B.R., 2002. The role and relevance of taxonomy in the conservation and utilisation of Australian acacias. *Conservation Science Western Australia*, Vol. 4, No. 3, pp. 1-9.

Minami, T. and Ohura, Y., 2021. Small data analysis for bigger data analysis. In *2021 Workshop on Algorithm and Big Data*. Fuzhou, China, pp. 1-8.

Mgudlwa, S. and Iyamu, T., 2018. Integration of social media with healthcare big data for improved service delivery. *South African Journal of Information Management*, Vol. 20, No. 1, pp 1-8.

Mukherjee, S.P., 2019. *A guide to research methodology: An overview of research problems, tasks and methods*. CRC Press, Boca Raton.

Nigar, N., 2020. Hermeneutic phenomenological narrative enquiry: A qualitative study design. *Theory and Practice in Language Studies*, Vol. 10, No. 1, pp 10-18.

Necsulescu, N., 2017. Focusing on small data to drive big results. *Applied Marketing Analytics*, Vol. 2, No. 4, pp 296-303.

Nickerson, R.C. et al, 2013. A method for taxonomy development and its application in information systems. *European Journal of Information Systems*, Vol. 22, No. 3, pp 336-359.

Nyikana, W. and Iyamu, T., 2022. A Guide for selecting big data analytics tools in an organisation. In *Proceedings of the 55th Hawaii International Conference on System Sciences*. Hawaii, USA, pp. 5451-5461.

Nunu, K., 2019. A big data framework to improve government service delivery in South Africa. Unpublished Thesis, Cape Peninsula University of Technology, Cape Town. http://hdl.handle.net/20.500.11838/2962 [23 October 2019].

Oberländer, A.M. et al, 2019. Taxonomy research in information systems: a systematic assessment. In *27th European Conference on Information Systems*. Stockholm, Sweden, pp. 1 – 17.

Osman, A.M.S., 2019. A novel big data analytics framework for smart cities. *Future Generation Computer Systems*, Vol. 91, No. 2019, pp 620-633.

Oussous, A. et al, 2018. Big Data technologies: A survey. *Journal of King Saud University-Computer and Information Sciences*, Vol. 30, No. 4, pp 431-448.

Rengarajan, S. et al, 2022. Data strategies for global value chains: Hybridization of small and big data in the aftermath of COVID-19. *Journal of Business Research*, Vol. 144, No. 2022, pp 776-787.

Rizk, A. et al, 2018. Towards a taxonomy for data-driven digital services. In *Proceedings of the 51st Hawaii international conference on system sciences*. Hawaii, USA, pp. 1076-1085.

Sacristán, J. A. and Dilla, T., 2015. No big data without small data: learning health care systems begin and end with the individual patient. *Journal of evaluation in clinical practice*, Vol 21, No. 6, pp 1014-1017.

Samsudeen, S.N. and Haleem, A., 2020. Impacts and challenges of big data: a review. *International Journal of Psychosocial Rehabilitation*, Vol. 24, No. 7, pp 479-487.

Seyhan, A.A. and Carini, C., 2019. Are innovation and new technologies in precision medicine paving a new era in patients centric care?. *Journal of translational medicine*, Vol. 17, No. 1, pp 1-28.

Sivarajah, U., 2017. Critical analysis of big data challenges and analytical methods. *Journal of Business Research*, Vol. 70, No. 2017, pp 263-286.

Sterner, B. and Franz, N.M., 2017. Taxonomy for humans or computers? Cognitive pragmatics for big data. *Biological Theory*, Vol. 12, No. 2, pp 99-111.

Sovacool, B.K., 2018. Promoting novelty, rigor, and style in energy social science: Towards codes of practice for appropriate methods and research design. *Energy Research & Social Science*, Vol. 45, No. 2018, pp 12-42.

Sun, Z., 2018. Big data with ten big characteristics. In *Proceedings of the 2nd International Conference on Big Data Research*. Weihai, China, pp 56-61.

Szopinski, D., 2019. Because Your Taxonomy is Worth IT: towards a Framework for Taxonomy Evaluation. In *27th European Conference on Information Systems*. Stockholm, Sweden, pp 1 – 20.

Taherdoost, H., 2022. Different types of data analysis; data analysis methods and techniques in research projects. *International Journal of Academic Research in Management*, Vol. 9, No. 1, pp 1-9.

Uğur, N.G., 2020. Understanding Big Data. In Big Data Analytics for Sustainable Computing, *IGI Global*, pp 1-29. DOI: 10.4018/978-1-5225-9750-6.ch001

Vargas, L. 2018. Smart media: Museums in the new data terroir. In The Routledge Handbook of Museums, Media and Communication. Drotner, k., Dziekan, v., Parry, R. & Schrøder, K.C. (ed.). 261– 73. Routledge International Handbooks. Abingdon: Routledge: 261-273.

Vecchi, E. et al, 2022. eSPA+: Scalable Entropy-Optimal Machine Learning Classification for Small Data Problems. *Neural Computation*, Vol. 34, No. 5, pp 220-1255.

Wang, L., 2017. Heterogeneous data and big data analytics. *Automatic Control and Information Sciences*, Vol. 3, No. 1, pp 8-15.

INFORMATION MANAGEMENT IN CARBON EMISSIONS QUANTIFICATION

Lai Ke En, Nafisah Abdul Rahiman and Kherun Nita Ali
Faculty of Built Environment and Surveying, Universiti Teknologi Malaysia
Johor, Malaysia

ABSTRACT

Global warming is a critical problem that resulted from excessive greenhouse gas emissions and 97% of the greenhouse gases are carbon emissions. The current carbon quantification methods involved massive information and deemed to have low productivity and the accuracy of the quantified carbon emissions is debatable. Thus, the effectiveness of mitigation efforts to reduce carbon emissions is lowered due to the simplification and assumptions during the quantification process. This paper aims to review the potential of Internet of Things (IoT), Building Information Modelling (BIM), and blockchain to quantify the lifecycle carbon emissions. Literature review using synthesis method is adopted to identify the state-of-art for the application of IoT, BIM, and blockchain for carbon emissions quantification. The review concluded that IoT, BIM, and blockchain have the potential to reduce human errors and speed up the real-time carbon emissions quantification. IoT is capable to extract real-time data from the physical environment, BIM can reduce document errors, enhance the collaboration between the stakeholder, and improve the workflow across the supply chain, and Blockchain is well-known for its tamper-proof characteristic which increases the reliability and security of the data stored. These technologies are complementary to each other and able to enhance the reliability and accuracy of carbon emissions quantification. In short, the integration of the technologies can increase the credibility in quantifying the carbon emitted and facilitate the selection of the most appropriate retrofit scenarios for emissions reduction.

KEYWORDS

Carbon Emissions Quantification, Internet of Things (IoT), Building Information Modelling (BIM), Blockchain

1. INTRODUCTION

Global warming and climate change are some of the severe problems which can be resulted from greenhouse gas (GHG) emissions and the construction industry is the main contributor. The construction industry consumes 40% of the total energy consumption and emits 33% of the related global GHG (Chau et al., 2015; Li et al., 2020; Zabalza Bribián et al., 2009). According to Li et al. (2020), 97% of GHG emissions are made up of carbon emissions. The studies in reducing carbon emissions have indeed been extensively carried out and many more similar studies are still underway. Although many studies have been carried out, the results have not yet resolved some basic issues which are the accuracy of carbon footprint estimates and feasibility of methods and techniques introduced. This is because the energy consumption and carbon emissions are subject to uncertainties due to the different computational methods (Ingrao et al., 2018). Ingrao et al. (2021) reviewed and highlighted the need to have accurate life cycle assessment for quality, reliable, and reproductive inventories data.

Traditionally, carbon emissions are measured by adding all the emission output from different phases in the construction supply chain. This will cause missing data when tracking the carbon emission (Resch et al., 2019) and affect the accuracy of the data collected due to manual effort and potential human error. The accuracy of the assessment will be greatly reliant on the quality of the data collected. However, data in the existing assessment methods are collected manually and do not satisfy real-time and dynamic requirements (Tao et al., 2014). Real-time monitoring of carbon emissions is essential to governance the use of clean energy and improve environmental performance (Liu et al., 2020). Wu et al. (2014) also conclude that real-time data can ensure a more precise calculation and comparison in energy estimation and carbon emissions. Nonetheless, monitoring real-time and automation in carbon quantification is still minimal due to a scarcity of trustworthy inventories and models (Liu et al., 2020). Therefore, the accuracy of energy consumption and carbon footprint needs to be enhanced to facilitate the selection of the most appropriate retrofit scenarios for emissions reduction.

The calculation of life cycle carbon emission is complicated and thus simplification and approximation are common in LCA practice (Yang et al., 2018). Thus, these make the process of collecting and tracking reliable data for life cycle carbon emission strenuous across the building life cycle (Fenner et al., 2020; Zhang et al., 2020). Besides, the quality of the data is debatable as existing data available from different locations will be used at locations that lack local data (Anand & Amor, 2017). This is because the construction products in different countries may have different energy consumption and emissions due to many factors including the diversity of fuels and methods in generating electricity (Song et al., 2021). Typically, LCA in Malaysia is conducted by using databases from other countries as Malaysia does not have local inventory data (Moayedi et al., 2017). Thus, it reduces the reliability of the carbon emissions measured.

This research identifies the gap and review the potential of integrating relevant technologies to measure and record real-time carbon emissions to solve issues related to the accuracy and accountability of the data for carbon emission quantification. The next section of paper discussed the existing carbon emissions quantification in the construction industry followed by the background of IoT, BIM, and blockchain. Further discussions were made to explore the potential of integration IoT, BIM, and blockchain for carbon quantification.

2. CARBON EMISSIONS QUANTIFICATION

Life cycle carbon emission comprises embodied carbon and operational carbon. Embodied carbon is generated throughout the upstream material production, transportation, and construction with the downstream maintenance and demolition stage. Meanwhile, operational carbon is created from the energy consumed during the use stage for heating, cooling, lighting, air-conditioning, machinery, and plant operation, and so forth (Chau et al., 2015; Pan & Teng, 2021). Operational carbon has been found to dominate the fractions in studies related to carbon footprints due to the continuous emissions throughout the building lifecycles (Fenner et al., 2020). Operational emissions are the energy required to maintain the comfort of the indoor environment by the operation process such as air conditioning, lightings, equipment, and appliances (Biswas & Gupta, 2019; Ibn-Mohammed et al., 2013). Moreover, operational emissions are relying on the occupants (Ibn-Mohammed et al., 2013), building location, occupation type (Fenner et al., 2018, 2020), climate condition, degree of comfort demanded, and operating schedule (Yang et al., 2018). Operational emissions are accumulated over the building lifespan and will be influenced by the effective life of the building (Dixit et al., 2010; Ibn-Mohammed et al., 2013). Meanwhile, embodied carbon is the summation of the GHG emissions excluding the operational phase emissions (Opher et al., 2021). It includes the emissions from extraction of the natural resources, manufacturing of the construction materials, transportation to the construction site, construction, maintenance, and demolition at the end of life (Chau et al., 2015; Opher et al., 2021). Embodied emissions are largely affected by material selection and primary energy sources (Dixit et al., 2010; Ibn-Mohammed et al., 2013). It is important to quantify carbon emission accurately to further plan relevant actions to net-zero carbon. Technologies such as IoT, BIM, and blockchain have great potential to enhance the reliability and accuracy of carbon emissions quantification.

3. IOT, BIM, AND BLOCKCHAIN

IoT, BIM, and blockchain have great potential to improve the current practice in the built environment (Alvarez et al., 2021; Siountri et al., 2020). Blockchain is able to support BIM technology through smart contracts and integration of these technologies is able to establish clear responsibilities among stakeholders. On the other hand, the integration of blockchain and IoT is able to enhance security in the centralized database (Zhong et al., 2020). The combination of IoT, BIM, and blockchain technologies has been used for various purposes yet integration of these technologies for carbon emissions estimation is relatively novel. Brandín & Abrishami (2021) investigate the synergy between IoT and blockchain in a BIM environment for off-site manufacturing management across the supply chain. The authors concluded that the synergies between blockchain and IoT are able to improve the transparency and immutability of the system while the integration of IoT, BIM, and blockchain is able to guarantee the quality of data. Alvarez et al. (2021) highlighted the advantages and challenges of adopting distributed ledger systems, BIM, and IoT for airport pavement management. Meanwhile, Siountri et al. (2019) integrate the technologies for information management in smart building and highlight the capabilities of the integration to assure data integrity. Siountri et al. (2020) also concluded that integration of IoT, BIM, and blockchain are complimentary and the collaboration between the technologies can secure the storage and management of data while at the same time improve the IoT services.

3.1 Internet of Things (IoT)

Internet of things (IoT) is an interconnection of sensing devices that give real-time data to assist the designer to make better decisions (Carneiro et al., 2018). It connects all real-life and virtual devices and allows them to interact in the same network (Carneiro et al., 2018). It is also able to collect and analyze data automatically by using sensors, radio-frequency identification (RFID), or Near Field Communication (NFC) (Isikdag, 2015). A study by An et al. (2021) on the IoT-based LCA platform of wind turbines has proven that the accuracy of the assessment can be ensured by using a real-time collection of energy consumption and carbon emissions data spawned by the physical environment. The author also suggested the use of blockchain technology for the authenticity and credibility of data for future research directions. Tao et al. (2014) employed IoT for LCA for energy-saving and emission-reduction and highlighted the potential of IoT in the whole life cycle of a product. Ingrao et al. (2021) concluded that using sensors in IoT technology is capable to increase the effectiveness of LCA evaluation and demonstrated the difference between data calculated from mathematical models and data collected from the direct measurement from sensors. Zuo et al. (2018) developed an IoT and cloud-based method for real-time energy consumption monitoring and analysis for green and sustainable manufacturing.

3.2 Building Information Modelling (BIM)

Building information modelling (BIM) has been utilized to solve sustainability issues in recent years. BIM is a 3D modelling that provides a great amount of information including geometric and semantic information (Carneiro et al., 2018). Moreover, Crippa et al. (2018) integrates BIM and LCA for embodied carbon estimation on wall systems and concluded that the integrations improvise the building carbon footprint quantification. Kaewunruen & Lian (2019) uses 6D BIM to optimize the life cycle management for the railway turnout system. Ding et al. (2020) developed a BIM-based carbon emission measurement system for prefabricated residential buildings for a more precise measurement of carbon footprint. Lu et al. (2019) conducted research for BIM-based LCA for hospital building and summarized that carbon emitted throughout the operational stage are the highest due to geographical location and the characteristic of the hospital building. Gan et al. (2018) present a framework that uses BIM to analyze the effect of various envelope designs on building carbon emissions. Sun & Park (2020) built a BIM-based performance evaluation system to compute the carbon footprint and provide a strategy to manage the carbon emissions effectively by converting them into the cost. Asare et al. (2020) concluded that integrating BIM and LCA is able to aid the designers in selecting more eco-friendly materials and products. Yang et al. (2018) develop a BIM-enabled LCA method to facilitate low carbon design and increase the credibility of LCA data. In short, various research has proven the advantages of integrating BIM and LCA but mainly focused on embodied carbon measurements. This is because BIM is often used as a source to acquire the material properties and characteristics which can reduce the manual input of quantified materials and shorten the time for the estimation procedure (Tushar et al., 2021).

The integration of BIM and IoT is focusing on the field of facility management (Chang et al., 2018; Cheng et al., 2020; Evjen et al., 2020), safety (Chen et al., 2021; Chen et al., 2018; Cheung et al., 2018; Ding et al., 2021), and energy management (Bapat et al., 2021; Birgonul, 2020). Atazadeh et al. (2019) concluded that BIM can assist in the process to understand legal ownership of the data collected through IoT sensors.

3.3 Blockchain

Blockchain is a decentralized and distributed ledger system that stores all the transactions (Manglekar & Dinesha, 2018). It is a tamper-proof database that can ensure the security and accuracy of the data recorded by autonomous verification through a consensus algorithm (Biswas & Gupta, 2019; Rodrigo et al., 2020; Xu et al., 2018). Besides, it can perform transactions without centralized third parties (Liu et al., 2019) which makes data sharing easier across a large network (Xu et al., 2018). Blockchain technology was originally used to transfer digital money, but it was adopted widely in other applications lately including Construction Supply Chains (CSCs) (Shemov et al., 2020; Sivula et al., 2020; Tezel et al., 2020), information management (Sheng et al., 2020; Zhong et al., 2020), procurement (Tezel et al., 2020), asset management (Götz et al., 2020), transportation (López & Farooq, 2020), etc.

Blockchain has been widely employed in the construction supply chain to strengthen the traceability of the supply chain. Wang et al. (2021) concluded that blockchain can solve the transparency and provenance problems in the supply chain. Wang et al. (2021) developed a smart contract in blockchain to improve traceability and shareability in the agricultural food supply chain. Wang et al. (2021) suggested that integration of blockchain and supply chain can enhance the collaboration in the supply chain by information sharing and automation by the blockchain system. Carbon emissions are measured across the construction supply chain. Since many researchers have highlighted the advantages of incorporating blockchain system in the supply chain, optimizing blockchain system in carbon emissions calculation have the potential to increase the accuracy and credibility of the measurement. Rodrigo et al. (2020) have examined the potential of adopting blockchain systems in embodied carbon estimation in the construction supply chain and conclude that blockchain systems are able to increase the accuracy of the estimation. The automation in data collection is able to prevent data error by human factors. However, the centralized database is vulnerable to attack (Zhong et al., 2020). Arif et al. (2020) concluded that blockchain is able to enhance the data security, confidentiality, and integrity of smart homes. Cho et al. (2021) developed a blockchain network to provide transparent and reliable management of IoT data for fine dust reduction measures. Thus, an integration of IoT and decentralized blockchain systems is necessary to ensure the information in the databases is secured. Besides, the information by IoT can be recorded automatically when the condition in the smart contract by blockchain is triggered. Therefore, automation in life cycle carbon emission collection can be performed by integrating IoT and blockchain.

Integrating blockchain and BIM is able to establish clear responsibility and contractual relationships among the stakeholders (Liu et al., 2019; Zhong et al., 2020). Suliyanti & Sari (2021) and Zheng et al. (2019) integrate BIM and blockchain for information exchange and enhance information security. Xue & Lu (2020) integrates BIM and blockchain to reduce the information redundancy issues that arise due to the integration process.

3.4 Integrating IoT, BIM, and Blockchain for Carbon Quantification

The traditional manual methods in estimating the carbon emissions are exhaustive and require a mass amount of fragmented data to complete the quantification. The manual and repetitive nature of completing the estimation can result in loss of data. To overcome the issues, the carbon emitted at various construction phases can be collected by using IoT-based sensing devices in real-time. The data can then be integrated into the BIM platform for visualization and be used further for sustainability analysis and recorded in a tamper-proof blockchain system. IoT will be the source of real-time data which collects the information automatically. The data can be collected from the physical environment automatically through IoT sensor and thus reduces errors due to human factors. The carbon emissions recorded is able to fulfill the real-time requirement and increase the accuracy and reliability of the data collected. Meanwhile, BIM will act as a platform to visualizes the information from various parties and stages. Besides, BIM is a great tool to assist in the calculation of embodied carbon by multiplying the quantity of the material used with the carbon factors of the building material. Traditionally, the quantity of material used will be extracted manually from the bill of quantity (BQ). BIM can assist in extracting the precise quantity of material in the form of an excel file and reduces omission errors. Various research has been conducted and proven the use of BIM in increasing the accuracy of embodied carbon emission measured (Asare et al., 2020; Gan et al., 2018; Sun & Park, 2020, Yang et al., 2018). Whereas blockchain will act as a core to record data, which solves the information authenticity and information sharing simultaneously (Zhong et al., 2020). Beforehand, simplification and assumption are common when calculating carbon emissions. Blockchain is also able to ensure all the carbon emission across the supply chain is collected. This is because blockchain is well-known for its transparent and tamper-proof nature that is able to secure the accuracy of data collected. The decentralized system of blockchain enables it to operate without the need for third-party control. The carbon emissions can be recorded automatically once the predefined conditions in the smart contract are triggered.

In short, integrating IoT, BIM, and blockchain is able to ensure the carbon emissions quantified are of higher accuracy as compared to the traditional manual method. The integration of these technologies is able to increase the reliability of the carbon emissions quantification as these technologies are complementary to each other.

4. CONCLUSION

This paper reviews the potential of integrating IoT, BIM, and blockchain into quantifying carbon emissions. The integration has the potential to promote automation in carbon quantification and increase the accuracy and traceability of the carbon emission due to real-time data obtained from IoT, the capability to reduce manual input and potential human errors from BIM, and the tamper-proof characteristics of blockchain. The study examines the role of each technology in quantifying carbon emissions and how the technology is complementary to each other. IoT is the source of real-time data that collects the information automatically. Meanwhile, BIM is the platform that visualizes the information from various parties and stages and blockchain is the core which is to record data and solve the information authenticity and information sharing simultaneously. Integrating BIM and IoT is able to promote automation in real-time data collection which is hard across the construction supply chain. Blockchain is able to solve the information authenticity issues from BIM and the security issues that arise from IoT. The findings of the paper are expected to create a novel way to quantify carbon emissions and broaden the use of IoT, BIM, and blockchain. However, the integration of IoT, BIM, and blockchain technologies is still at an early stage and are more applicable to the carbon emissions quantifications of operational phase than of the construction phase, where many of site issues have to be considered. Also, the input mechanism of blockchain data is relatively weak despite its tamper proof structure. Thus, future research is suggested to focus to study the feasibility to integrate IoT, BIM, and blockchain.

ACKNOWLEDGEMENT

This work was funded and supported by the Ministry of Higher Education (MoHE) Malaysia under Fundamental Research Grant Scheme (FRGS/1/2020/SSI02/UTM/02/2) and Universiti Teknologi Malaysia. The authors would like to express their appreciation for the assistance of the sponsors.

REFERENCES

Alvarez, A.P. et al. (2021) 'Opportunities in airport pavement management: Integration of BIM, the IoT and DLT', Journal of Air Transport Management, 90. Available at: https://doi.org/10.1016/j.jairtraman.2020.101941.

An, J. et al. (2021) 'An IoT-based life cycle assessment platform of wind turbines', Sensors (Switzerland), 21(4), pp. 1–22. Available at: https://doi.org/10.3390/s21041233.

Anand, C.K. and Amor, B. (2017) 'Recent developments, future challenges and new research directions in LCA of buildings: A critical review', Renewable and Sustainable Energy Reviews, 67, pp. 408–416. Available at: https://doi.org/10.1016/j.rser.2016.09.058.

Arif, S. et al. (2020) 'Investigating Smart Home Security: Is Blockchain the Answer?', IEEE Access, 8, pp. 117802–117816. Available at: https://doi.org/10.1109/ACCESS.2020.3004662.

Asare, K.A.B. et al. (2020) 'BIM-based LCA and energy analysis for optimised sustainable building design in Ghana', SN Applied Sciences, 2(11), pp. 1–20. Available at: https://doi.org/10.1007/s42452-020-03682-2.

Atazadeh, B. et al. (2019) 'Utilizing a building information modelling environment to communicate the legal ownership of internet of things-generated data in multi-owned buildings', Electronics (Switzerland), 8(11). Available at: https://doi.org/10.3390/electronics8111258.

Bapat, H., Sarkar, D. and Gujar, R. (2021) 'Application of integrated fuzzy FCM-BIM-IoT for sustainable material selection and energy management of metro rail station box project in western India', Innovative Infrastructure Solutions, 6(2), pp. 1–18. Available at: https://doi.org/10.1007/s41062-020-00431-7.

Basbagill, J. et al. (2013) 'Application of life-cycle assessment to early stage building design for reduced embodied environmental impacts', Building and Environment, 60, pp. 81–92. Available at: https://doi.org/10.1016/j.buildenv.2012.11.009.

Birgonul, Z. (2020) 'A receptive-responsive tool for customizing occupant's thermal comfort and maximizing energy efficiency by blending BIM data with real-time information', Smart and Sustainable Built Environment [Preprint]. Available at: https://doi.org/10.1108/SASBE-11-2020-0175.

Biswas, B. and Gupta, R. (2019) 'Analysis of barriers to implement blockchain in industry and service sectors', Computers & Industrial Engineering, 136, pp. 225–241. Available at: https://doi.org/10.1016/j.cie.2019.07.005.

Brandín, R. and Abrishami, S. (2021) 'Information traceability platforms for asset data lifecycle: blockchain-based technologies', Smart and Sustainable Built Environment [Preprint]. Available at: https://doi.org/10.1108/SASBE-03-2021-0042.

Cabeza, L.F. et al. (2021) 'Embodied energy and embodied carbon of structural building materials: Worldwide progress and barriers through literature map analysis', Energy and Buildings, 231. Available at: https://doi.org/10.1016/j.enbuild.2020.110612.

Carneiro, J. et al. (2018) 'BIM, GIS, IoT, and AR/VR Integration for Smart Maintenance and Management of Road Networks: A Review', in 2018 IEEE International Smart Cities Conference, ISC2 2018. Available at: https://doi.org/10.1109/ISC2.2018.8656978.

Chang, K.M., Dzeng, R.J. and Wu, Y.J. (2018) 'An automated IoT visualization BIM platform for decision support in facilities management', Applied Sciences (Switzerland), 8(7). Available at: https://doi.org/10.3390/app8071086.

Chau, C.K., Leung, T.M. and Ng, W.Y. (2015) 'A review on life cycle assessment, life cycle energy assessment and life cycle carbon emissions assessment on buildings', Applied Energy, 143(1), pp. 395–413. Available at: https://doi.org/10.1016/j.apenergy.2015.01.023.

Chen, H. et al. (2021) 'Development of BIM, IoT and AR/VR technologies for fire safety and upskilling', Automation in Construction, 125(January). Available at: https://doi.org/10.1016/j.autcon.2021.103631.

Chen, X.S., Liu, C.C. and Wu, I.C. (2018) 'A BIM-based visualization and warning system for fire rescue', Advanced Engineering Informatics, 37(October 2017), pp. 42–53. Available at: https://doi.org/10.1016/j.aei.2018.04.015.

Cheng, J.C.P. et al. (2020) 'Data-driven predictive maintenance planning framework for MEP components based on BIM and IoT using machine learning algorithms', Automation in Construction, 112(January), p. 103087. Available at: https://doi.org/10.1016/j.autcon.2020.103087.

Cheung, W.F., Lin, T.H. and Lin, Y.C. (2018) 'A real-time construction safety monitoring system for hazardous gas integrating wireless sensor network and building information modeling technologies', Sensors (Switzerland), 18(2). Available at: https://doi.org/10.3390/s18020436.

Cho, S. et al. (2021) 'Blockchain-based network concept model for reliable and accessible fine dust management system at construction sites', Applied Sciences (Switzerland), 11(18). Available at: https://doi.org/10.3390/app11188686.

Crippa, J. et al. (2018) 'A BIM–LCA integration technique to embodied carbon estimation applied on wall systems in Brazil', Built Environment Project and Asset Management, 8(5), pp. 491–503. Available at: https://doi.org/10.1108/BEPAM-10-2017-0093.

Ding, L., Jiang, W. and Zhou, C. (2021) 'IoT sensor-based BIM system for smart safety barriers of hazardous energy in petrochemical construction', Frontiers of Engineering Management, pp. 1–15. Available at: https://doi.org/10.1007/s42524-021-0160-6.

Ding, Z. et al. (2020) 'A building information modeling-based carbon emission measurement system for prefabricated residential buildings during the materialization phase', Journal of Cleaner Production, 264. Available at: https://doi.org/10.1016/j.jclepro.2020.121728.

Elghaish, F., Abrishami, S. and Hosseini, M.R. (2020) 'Integrated project delivery with blockchain: An automated financial system', Automation in Construction, 114. Available at: https://doi.org/10.1016/j.autcon.2020.103182.

Evjen, T.Å. et al. (2020) 'Smart Facility Management: Future Healthcare Organization through Indoor Positioning Systems in the Light of Enterprise BIM', Smart Cities, 3(3), pp. 793–805. Available at: https://doi.org/10.3390/smartcities3030040.

Fenner, A.E. et al. (2020) 'Embodied, operation, and commuting emissions: A case study comparing the carbon hotspots of an educational building', Journal of Cleaner Production, 268. Available at: https://doi.org/10.1016/j.jclepro.2020.122081.

Gan, V.J.L. et al. (2018) 'Holistic BIM framework for sustainable low carbon design of high-rise buildings', Journal of Cleaner Production, 195, pp. 1091–1104. Available at: https://doi.org/10.1016/j.jclepro.2018.05.272.

Götz, C.S., Karlsson, P. and Yitmen, I. (2020) 'Exploring applicability, interoperability and integrability of Blockchain-based digital twins for asset life cycle management', Smart and Sustainable Built Environment [Preprint]. Available at: https://doi.org/10.1108/SASBE-08-2020-0115.

Ingrao, C. et al. (2021) 'The contribution of sensor-based equipment to life cycle assessment through improvement of data collection in the industry', Environmental Impact Assessment Review, 88. Available at: https://doi.org/10.1016/j.eiar.2021.106569.

Isikdag, U. (2015) 'BIM and IoT: A synopsis from GIS perspective', International Archives of the Photogrammetry, Remote Sensing and Spatial Information Sciences - ISPRS Archives, 40(2W4), pp. 33–38. Available at: https://doi.org/10.5194/isprsarchives-XL-2-W4-33-2015.

Jiang, Y. and He, X. (2020) 'Overview of Applications of the Sensor Technologies for Construction Machinery', IEEE Access, 8, pp. 110324–110335.

Kaewunruen, S. and Lian, Q. (2019) 'Digital twin aided sustainability-based lifecycle management for railway turnout systems', Journal of Cleaner Production, 228, pp. 1537–1551. Available at: https://doi.org/10.1016/j.jclepro.2019.04.156.

Li, D. et al. (2020) 'Driving factors of total carbon emissions from the construction industry in Jiangsu Province, China', Journal of Cleaner Production, 276. Available at: https://doi.org/10.1016/j.jclepro.2020.123179.

Liu, G. et al. (2020) 'Cyber-physical system-based real-time monitoring and visualization of greenhouse gas emissions of prefabricated construction', Journal of Cleaner Production, 246. Available at: https://doi.org/10.1016/j.jclepro.2019.119059.

Liu, Z. et al. (2019) 'Building information management (BIM) and blockchain (BC) for sustainable building design information management framework', Electronics (Switzerland), 8(7), pp. 1–15. Available at: https://doi.org/10.3390/electronics8070724.

López, D. and Farooq, B. (2020) 'A multi-layered blockchain framework for smart mobility data-markets', Transportation Research Part C: Emerging Technologies, 111(June 2019), pp. 588–615. Available at: https://doi.org/10.1016/j.trc.2020.01.002.

Lu, K. et al. (2019) 'Development of a carbon emissions analysis framework using building information modeling and life cycle assessment for the construction of hospital projects', Sustainability (Switzerland), 11(22), pp. 1–18. Available at: https://doi.org/10.3390/su11226274.

Manglekar, S. and Dinesha, H. (2018) 'Block Chain: An Innovative Research Area', in Proceedings of the Fourth International Conference on Computing Communication Control and Automation. Pune, India.

Mataloto, B. et al. (2021) '3D IoT System for Environmental and Energy Consumption Monitoring System', Sustainability, 13(1495).

Moayedi, F. et al. (2017) 'Quantification of Carbon Footprint From Major Construction Materials for Office Projects in Malaysia', Science International, 29(1), pp. 19–23.

Pan, W. and Teng, Y. (2021) 'A systematic investigation into the methodological variables of embodied carbon assessment of buildings', Renewable and Sustainable Energy Reviews, 141(February). Available at: https://doi.org/10.1016/j.rser.2021.110840.

Perera, S. et al. (2020) 'Blockchain technology: Is it hype or real in the construction industry ?', Journal of Industrial Information Integration, 17. Available at: https://doi.org/10.1016/j.jii.2020.100125.

Resch, E. et al. (2019) 'An analytical method for evaluating and visualizing embodied carbon emissions of buildings', Building and Environment [Preprint]. Available at: https://doi.org/10.1016/j.buildenv.2019.106476.

Rodrigo, M.N.N. et al. (2020) 'Potential Application of Blockchain Technology for Embodied Carbon Estimating in Construction Supply Chains', Buildings, 10(140), pp. 1–13.

Shemov, G., Garcia de Soto, B. and Alkhzaimi, H. (2020) 'Blockchain applied to the construction supply chain: A case study with threat model', Frontiers of Engineering Management, 7(4), pp. 564–577. Available at: https://doi.org/10.1007/s42524-020-0129-x.

Siountri, K., Skondras, E. and Vergados, D.D. (2019) 'Towards a Smart Museum using BIM, IoT, Blockchain and Advanced Digital Technologies', in ACM International Conference Proceeding Series. Available at: https://doi.org/10.1145/3387168.3387196.

Siountri, K., Skondras, E. and Vergados, D.D. (2020) 'Developing Smart Buildings Using Blockchain, Internet of Things, and Building Information Modeling', International Journal of Interdisciplinary Telecommunications and Networking, 12(3), pp. 1–15. Available at: https://doi.org/10.4018/ijitn.2020070101.

Sivula, A., Shamsuzzoha, A. and Helo, P. (2020) 'Requirements for Blockchain Technology in Supply Chain Management: An Exploratory Case Study', Operations and Supply Chain Management: An International Journal, 14(1), pp. 39–50. Available at: https://doi.org/10.31387/oscm0440284.

Song, Y., Zhang, H. and Mo, H. (2021) 'A LCA-based Optimization Method of Green Ecological Building Envelopes: A Case Study in China', in IOP Conference Series: Earth and Environmental Science. Available at: https://doi.org/10.1088/1755-1315/696/1/012023.

Suliyanti, W.N. and Sari, R.F. (2021) 'Blockchain-based implementation of building information modeling information using hyperledger composer', Sustainability (Switzerland), 13(1), pp. 1–21. Available at: https://doi.org/10.3390/su13010321.

Sun, H. and Park, Y. (2020) 'CO2 emission calculation method during construction process for developing BIM-based performance evaluation system', Applied Sciences (Switzerland), 10(16). Available at: https://doi.org/10.3390/app10165587.

Tao, F. et al. (2014) 'Internet of Things and BOM-Based Life Cycle Assessment of Energy-Saving and Emission-Reduction of Products', IEEE Transactions on Industrial Informatics, 10(2), pp. 1252–1261. Available at: https://doi.org/10.1109/TII.2014.2306771.

Tezel, A. et al. (2020) 'Preparing construction supply chains for blockchain technology: An investigation of its potential and future directions', Frontiers of Engineering Management, 7(4), pp. 547–563. Available at: https://doi.org/10.1007/s42524-020-0110-8.

Tushar, Q. et al. (2021) 'An integrated approach of BIM-enabled LCA and energy simulation: The optimized solution towards sustainable development', Journal of Cleaner Production, 289. Available at: https://doi.org/10.1016/j.jclepro.2020.125622.

Wang, L. et al. (2021) 'Smart Contract-Based Agricultural Food Supply Chain Traceability', IEEE Access, 9, pp. 9296–9307. Available at: https://doi.org/10.1109/ACCESS.2021.3050112.

Wang, M. et al. (2021) 'Blockchain and supply chain management: A new paradigm for supply chain integration and collaboration', Operations and Supply Chain Management, 14(1), pp. 111–122. Available at: https://doi.org/10.31387/oscm0440290.

Wang, Y., Chen, C.H. and Zghari-Sales, A. (2021) 'Designing a blockchain enabled supply chain', International Journal of Production Research, 59(5), pp. 1450–1475. Available at: https://doi.org/10.1080/00207543.2020.1824086.

Wu, W. et al. (2014) 'A Real-Time Recording Model of Key Indicators for Energy Consumption and Carbon Emissions of Sustainable Buildings', Sensors, 14, pp. 8465–8484. Available at: https://doi.org/10.3390/s140508465.

Xu, X. et al. (2018) 'Designing Blockchain-based Applications A Case Study for Imported Product Traceability', Future Generation Computer Systems, pp. 399–406. Available at: https://doi.org/10.1016/j.future.2018.10.010.

Xue, F. and Lu, W. (2020) 'A semantic differential transaction approach to minimizing information redundancy for BIM and blockchain integration', Automation in Construction, 118(May), p. 103270. Available at: https://doi.org/10.1016/j.autcon.2020.103270.

Yang, X. et al. (2018) 'Building-information-modeling enabled life cycle assessment, a case study on carbon footprint accounting for a residential building in China', Journal of Cleaner Production, 183, pp. 729–743. Available at: https://doi.org/10.1016/j.jclepro.2018.02.070.

Zabalza Bribián, I., Aranda Usón, A. and Scarpellini, S. (2009) 'Life cycle assessment in buildings: State-of-the-art and simplified LCA methodology as a complement for building certification', Building and Environment, 44(12), pp. 2510–2520. Available at: https://doi.org/10.1016/j.buildenv.2009.05.001.

Zhang, A. et al. (2020) 'Blockchain-based life cycle assessment: An implementation framework and system architecture', Resources, Conservation and Recycling, 152. Available at: https://doi.org/10.1016/j.resconrec.2019.104512.

Zheng, R. et al. (2019) 'BcBIM: A Blockchain-Based Big Data Model for BIM Modification Audit and Provenance in Mobile Cloud', Mathematical Problems in Engineering, 2019. Available at: https://doi.org/10.1155/2019/5349538.

Zhong, B. et al. (2020) 'Hyperledger fabric-based consortium blockchain for construction quality information management', Frontiers of Engineering Management, 7(4), pp. 512–527. Available at: https://doi.org/10.1007/s42524-020-0128-y.

Zuo, Y., Tao, F. and Nee, A.Y.C. (2018) 'An Internet of things and cloud-based approach for energy consumption evaluation and analysis for a product', International Journal of Computer Integrated Manufacturing, 31(4–5), pp. 337–348. Available at: https://doi.org/10.1080/0951192X.2017.1285429.

S-ISFMF: SOCIAL NETWORK AND IMAGE SHAPE FEATURE MATRIX FACTORIZATION

Takuya Tamada[1], Mingtian Gao[2] and Ryosuke Saga[1]
[1]*Osaka Metropolitan University, Graduate School of Informatics, Sakai, Japan*
[2]*Osaka Prefecture University, Graduate School of Humanities and Sustainable System Sciences, Sakai, Japan*

ABSTRACT

Recommender system is a useful tool to help users to select the best item in today's information-overloaded society. Probabilistic Matrix Factorization (PMF) is one of successful recommender system methods that introduces a probabilistic algorithm to matrix factorization. Various auxiliary information can be used in PMF. However, there is no example of using images and social networks at the same time. In this paper, we describe a model that extracts information from images and social networks and incorporates it into PMF. In our method, we extracted contour information from item images and optimized the user and item matrix in matrix factorization. We further optimized the user matrix using explicit and implicit social networks among users. As a result, we achieved an accuracy improvement of 0.75%~7.25% on three real world datasets compared to existing methods.

KEYWORDS

Recommender System, Machine Learning, Matrix Factorization, Deep Learning

1. INTRODUCTION

Recommender System is a useful tool for presenting appropriate information to users from among a large amount of information in today's information-overloaded society(Saga et al., 2008; Saga & Duan, 2018). Especially in recent years, with the development of online review sites such as Amazon and Yelp, referring to the ratings of items that one is considering purchasing has become a natural part of everyday consumption. In addition, people often rely on the opinions of others, such as close friends and family members, to help them decide on the purchase of an item. In recommender systems, collaborative filtering, which makes recommendations based on the preference information of similar users, is a widely used technique (Resnick et al., 1994; Su & Khoshgoftaar, 2009).

Matrix factorization has been used successfully in rating prediction tasks. Among the collaborative filtering methods, Probabilistic Matrix Factorization (PMF), which employs a stochastic model to matrix factorization, works well on sparse and unbalanced datasets and contributes to solving the cold start problem (Salakhutdinov & Mnih, 2007). PMF decomposes the rating matrix obtained from the user's rating information into two matrices, a user matrix and an item matrix, which represent the characteristics of each user and item, respectively. There are other examples of attempts to improve accuracy by using auxiliary information in matrix factorization to solve the cold start problem(Kim et al., 2016; Lu et al., 2021; Ma et al., 2008; Saga & Duan, 2018; Tamada & Saga, 2022; Wang et al., 2019). For example, ConvMF is a typical example of research that uses text information in matrix factorization to improve recommendation accuracy (Kim et al., 2016). In this method, features are extracted from the text representing the features of the item using CNN and incorporated into PMF. Among the various auxiliary information, images and social networks are considered particularly useful in the recommender system (Li et al., 2015; Lu et al., 2021; Ma et al., 2008, 2008, 2008; McAuley et al., 2015; Saga & Duan, 2018; Wang et al., 2019).

One of recommender systems using images is the method by McAuley (McAuley et al., 2015). It used image information to compute models of higher-level relationships between objects and to recommend complementary clothing. There are also models that extract features from images and apply collaborative filtering. Verma tried to understand the preferences of individual users and to take into account user evaluation information using image information for collaborative filtering(Verma et al., 2020). It was method to construct a visual preference model by inputting several images that represent user preferences. One method that incorporates image information into PMF is ISFMF(Saga & Duan, 2018). In this method, item contour information is captured by CNN and incorporated into the item vector V in the PMF to improve accuracy. In Bi-ISFMF, the user vector U, which is not considered in ISFMF, is also incorporated into PMF by capturing features based on the items purchased by users in the past (Lu et al., 2021). our proposed method uses Bi-ISFMF model in image feature extraction.

Social networks have long been used in recommender systems. Generally, when we purchase an item, we often ask friends and acquaintances for their recommendations. Because we usually share interests and tastes with our friends and acquaintances. Social networks include explicit social ties such as friendships, siblings, superiors, and subordinates, and implicit social ties are those with users who share common interests; similarity calculations show they are related. Therefore, research has been conducted to systematically leverage explicit social networks among users to make recommendations (Ma et al., 2008, 2009). Ma et al. proposed an MF method that takes into account social trust among users (Ma et al., 2008) and a method that takes into account not only trust but also distrust between users (Ma et al., 2009). Li et al. proposed a method that calculates similarity from scoring data and builds an implicit social network to be incorporated into the recommendation system, claiming that it is only slightly inferior to a recommender system that uses an explicit social network in terms of recommendation accuracy, but has the advantage of being less prone to accuracy degradation when scoring data increase (Li et al., 2015). Recommender systems that consider social network and textual information have also emerged. Wang et al. proposed a method that incorporates explicit social network and review information into the PMF (Wang et al., 2019).

As we have seen, there have been researches that have incorporated images and social networks into PMF independently to improve their accuracy, however no research has clarified the effectiveness of using images and social networks at the same time. In this paper, we propose *Social network and Image Shape Feature Matrix Factorization* (S-ISFMF) which incorporates image shape information and social relationships into PMF for fields where visual information and social relationships are important, such as apparel and restaurants.

The contributions of this paper are as follows:

- S-ISFMF, which incorporates image shape information and social relationships into PMF, achieves improvements on three datasets over other models that add auxiliary information to matrix factorization.
- We used two types of social relationships—explicit social networks derived from real-world friendships and acquaintances, and implicit social networks derived from the degree of similarity between users and examined the difference in effectiveness between these two types of relationships.

2. METHOD

2.1 Probabilistic Matrix Factorization

Salakhutdinov et al. proposed a recommendation method called PMF, which is a matrix factorization method (Salakhutdinov & Mnih, 2007). PMF assumes users N, items M, an arbitrary integer D, and a scoring matrix $R \in \mathbf{R}^{N\times M}$ obtained from the user's rating information. The PMF is a matrix factorization R into a user matrix $U \in \mathbf{R}^{D\times N} = \{u_1, u_2, ..., u_N\}$ and an item matrix $V \in \mathbf{R}^{D\times M} = \{v_1, v_2, ..., v_M\}$. The measured score r_{ij} is made by user i for item j. In this case, R is expressed by the following equation.

$$p(R|U,V,\sigma^2) = \prod_i^N \prod_j^M \left[N(r_{ij}|u_i^T v_j, \sigma^2)\right]^{I_{ij}} \quad (1)$$

where σ is the Gaussian noise of R. I_{ij} is the indicator function that is equal 1 if user i rated item j and equal to 0 otherwise. The optimal matrix U, V minimizes the loss function ε, as shown in the following:

$$\min \mathcal{E}(U,V) = \sum_i^N \sum_j^M \frac{I_{ij}}{2}(r_{ij} - u_i^T v_j)^2 + \frac{\lambda_U}{2}\sum_i^N \|u_i\| + \frac{\lambda_V}{2}\sum_j^M \|v_j\| \quad (2)$$

where λ_u and λ_v are the L_2 regularization terms derived from the Gaussian noise of R, U, and V, and I_{ij} is an indicator function of 1 if user i evaluated item j and 0 otherwise.

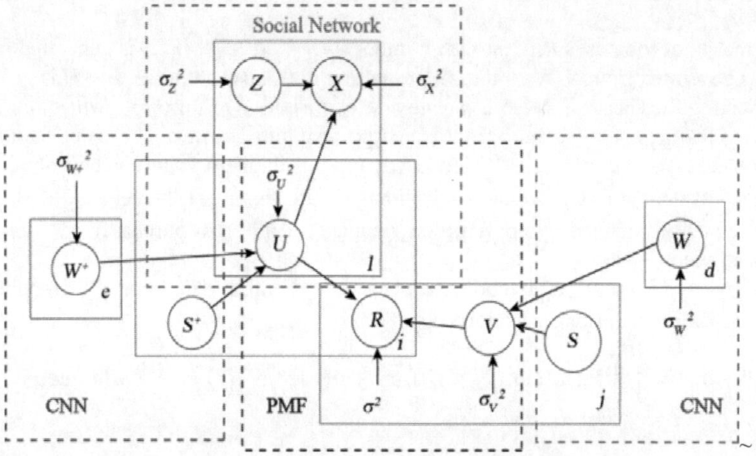

Figure 1. Graphical model of S-ISFMF

2.2 Overview of *S-ISFMF*

S-ISFMF is a model that incorporates images and social networks into PMF at the same time, referring to Bi-ISFMF (Lu et al., 2021), which extracts and integrates shape information from images representing item and user features into PMF, and SoRec (Ma et al., 2008), which incorporates social networks into PMF.

Figure 1 shows an overview of the probabilistic model of S-ISFMF, which integrates CNN and social networks that capture image contour information into PMF. As shown in this figure, S-ISFMF requires as data, in addition to the evaluation matrix R required by the PMF, the image of the item (S, S^+) and also X representing the social network. Then, features are extracted from these matrices and data and integrated to build a latent model of U and V. Specifically, to capture image contour information, we detect contours from item images and incorporate those features into the item matrix V in the PMF. In addition, we consider that the images of items purchased by the user in the past represent the user's characteristics, and we assume that those characteristics have an impact on the user matrix U and the item matrix V. We also consider that the social relationship matrix X is decomposed by the latent social network matrix $Z \in \mathbf{R}^{D\times N} = \{z_{k1}\, z_{k2}, \dots, z_{kN}\}$ and U, just as the evaluation matrix R is decomposed by U and V. These elements are combined and adjusted U and V to finally decompose the evaluation matrix R by its U and V. However, there are cases where the social relationship matrix may or may not exist as explicit data. If an explicit network exists, then an adjacency matrix X can be constructed based on the relationships. For example, X is constructed by an adjacency matrix that represents directed graphs representing follow/follower relationships such as Yelp and Twitter, and undirected graphs representing friendship relationships such as Facebook. If the social network does not exist as data, then we assume that the social network is hidden in the user's purchase history, etc. (i.e., an implicit social network exists), and we represent the network by calculation and use it as X.

2.3 Mathematical Model of *S-ISFMF*

In this section, the mathematical model of S-ISFMF, is explained. In Figure 1, $S = \{s_1, s_2, \dots, s_M\}$ is the set of images of items, and W is the weight vector of the CNN architecture of items. $S^+ = \{s^+_1, s^+_2, \dots, s^+_N\}$ is the set of images of items the user has purchased in the past. X represents the social network matrix, where x_{ik} takes the value 1 if a social relationship exists between user i and user k, and 0 otherwise. Z is also the latent social network matrix, and U and Z are obtained by decomposing X.

Then, from a probabilistic point of view, X can be expressed by the following equation and by R shown in Equation (1):

$$p(X|U,Z,\sigma_X^2) = \prod_i^N \prod_k^N [N(x_{ik}|u_i^T z_k, \sigma_X^2)]^{X_{ik}} \quad (3)$$

Next, the matrix decomposes *R*, *X* into latent models *U, V, Z*. In PMF, *R* is generated from *U, V*, and σ. In S-ISFMF, *V* is generated from *S*, W, and σ_V representing the Gaussian noise, and *U* is generated from S^+, W^+ and σ_U representing the Gaussian noise. *Z* can also be expressed in terms of σ_Z, which represents the Gaussian noise. The shape features of the image are then incorporated into *U* and *V*. The shape features of the image are denoted as $cnn(w, s_j)$ and $cnn(w^+, s_i^+)$. Here, $cnn(w, s_j)$ is the item feature vector obtained by applying the product image s_j of item *j* to a CNN that extracts image shape features (Shen et al., 2015), and $cnn(w^+, s_i^+)$ is the user feature vector obtained by applying the image s_i of the item purchased by user *i* in the past to the previously mentioned CNN.

When $cnn(w, s_j)$, $cnn(w^+, s_i^+)$, and σ_Z are used, *V, U*, and *Z* in the PMF probability model can be expressed by the following prior distribution equations:

$$p(U|W^+,S^+,\sigma_U^2) = \prod_i^N N\left(u_i|cnn(W^+,s_i^+),\sigma_U^2 I\right), p(V|W,S,\sigma_V^2) = \prod_j^M N\left(v_j|cnn(W,s_j),\sigma_V^2 I\right) \quad (4,5)$$

$$p(Z|\sigma_Z^2) = \prod_k^N N(z_k|0,\sigma_Z^2) \quad (6)$$

where *I* is the diagonal matrix.

The weights w_d and w_e for each of *W* and W^+ can be expressed by the following two prior distribution formulas:

$$p(W|\sigma_W^2) = \prod_d N\left(w_d|0,\sigma_W^2\right), p(W^+|\sigma_{W^+}^2) = \prod_e N\left(w_e^+|0,\sigma_{W^+}^2\right) \quad (7,8)$$

Equations (4) to (8) can be rewritten as follows:

$$p\left(U,V,Z,W,W^+ \mid R,X,S,S^+,\sigma^2,\sigma_X^2,\sigma_U^2,\sigma_V^2,\sigma_Z^2,\sigma_W^2,\sigma_{W^+}^2\right)$$
$$\propto p(R \mid U,V,\sigma^2)p(X \mid U,Z,\sigma_X^2)p(U \mid W^+,S^+,\sigma_U^2)p(V \mid W,S,\sigma_V^2)p(Z \mid \sigma_Z^2)p(W \mid \sigma_W^2)p(W^+ \mid \sigma_{W^+}^2) \quad (9)$$

To optimize (9), we use the following maximum a posteriori estimation:

$$\max_{U,V,Z,W,W^+} p\left(U,V,Z,W,W^+ \mid R,X,S,S^+,\sigma^2,\sigma_X^2,\sigma_U^2,\sigma_V^2,\sigma_Z^2,\sigma_W^2,\sigma_{W^+}^2\right)$$
$$= \max_{U,V,Z,W,W^+} [p(R \mid U,V,\sigma^2)p(X \mid U,Z,\sigma_X^2)p(U \mid W^+,S^+,\sigma_U^2)p(V \mid W,S,\sigma_V^2)p(Z \mid \sigma_Z^2)p(W \mid \sigma_W^2)p(W^+ \mid \sigma_{W^+}^2)] \quad (10)$$

By taking the negative algorithm in (10), we can reformulate it as follows:

$$\min \varepsilon(U,V,Z,W,W^+) = \sum_i^N \sum_j^M \frac{I_{ij}}{2}\left(r_{ij} - u_i^T v_j\right)^2 + \frac{\lambda_X}{2}\sum_i^N \sum_k^N I_{ik}(x_{ik} - u_i^T z_k)^2 + \frac{\lambda_Z}{2}\sum_k^N \|z_k\|^2 + \frac{\lambda_V}{2}\sum_j^M \left\|v_j - cnn(W,s_j)\right\|^2$$
$$+\frac{\lambda_W}{2}\sum_d^{|W_d|}\|w_d\|^2 + \frac{\lambda_U}{2}\sum_i^N \|u_i - cnn(W^+,s_i^+)\|^2 + \frac{\lambda_{W^+}}{2}\sum_e^{|W_e^+|}\|w_e^+\|^2 \quad (11)$$

$\lambda_X, \lambda_Z, \lambda_V, \lambda_W, \lambda_U,$ and λ_{W^+} are the regularization terms derived from the Gaussian noise in *X, Z, V, U, W*, and W^+, respectively. Partial differentiation of (11) by *U* and *V* respectively yields the following equation:

$$u_i = (VI_iV^T + \lambda_X Z I_i^X Z^T + \lambda_U)^{-1}(VR_i + \lambda_U cnn(W^+,s_i^+) + \lambda_X Z x_i) \quad (12)$$

$$v_j = \left(UI_jU^T + \lambda_V I\right)^{-1}\left(UR_j + \lambda_V cnn(W,s_j)\right), z_k = (\lambda_X U I_k^X U^T + \lambda_Z I)^{-1}(\lambda_X U x_k) \quad (13,14)$$

where I_i is a diagonal matrix whose diagonal components are the evaluation vectors $\{I_{i1}, I_{i2}, \dots, I_{i1}\}$ that indicate whether user i evaluated each item. Similarly, I_j is a diagonal matrix whose diagonal components are the evaluation vectors $\{I_{1j}, I_{2j}, \dots, I_{Nj}\}$ that indicate whether item j was evaluated each user. Furthermore, I_i^X is a diagonal matrix with the vector $x_i = \{x_{i1}, x_{i2}, \dots, x_{iN}\}$ representing the social relationship with each user of user i in its diagonal components. I_k^X is also a similar diagonal matrix for user k.

On the basis of (12), (13), and (14), U, V, and Z are updated by stochastic gradient descent to obtain the optimal user matrix U, item matrix V, and social network matrix Z. However, W and W^+ cannot be optimized in the same ways as U, V, and Z because they are closely related to the features of CNN architecture, such as the max pooling layer and nonlinear activation function. Therefore, we temporarily fix U, V, and Z, and use the error backpropagation method to estimate W and W^+.

$$\varepsilon(W) = \frac{\lambda_V}{2}\sum_{j}^{M} \left\|v_j - cnn(W, s_j)\right\|^2 + \frac{\lambda_W}{2}\sum_{d}^{|W_d|} \|w_d\|^2 + constant, \quad (15)$$

$$\varepsilon(W^+) = \frac{\lambda_U}{2}\sum_{i}^{N} \|u_i - cnn(W^+, s_i^+)\|^2 + \frac{\lambda_{W^+}}{2}\sum_{e}^{|W_e^+|^2} \|w_e^+\|^2 + constant \quad (16)$$

3. EXPERIMENT

In this section, we compare the performance of the proposed and existing methods using three real-world datasets. We also discuss how the performance of the proposed method changes when the parameters are varied. First, we describe experiment settings, including the details of the dataset, evaluation index, and parameter settings. Then, we discuss the experiment results.

3.1 Experiment Settings

For this experiment, we used two Amazon datasets, namely, Clothes and Accessories, for the apparel sector (McAuley et al. 2015). For the restaurant dataset, we used data from the Yelp dataset for the British Columbia region. These datasets include rating information, images of each item, and user reviews. The Yelp dataset has an explicit social network, but the Amazon dataset does not. For this reason, an implicit social network was created in the Amazon dataset by calculating the cosine similarity derived from the user's rating history and assuming that a network exists between users whose relationships are above a threshold value. The evaluation value for each dataset was taken from 1 to 5. This experiment used image data; thus, items without an image were excluded from these datasets. Users with fewer than two evaluations were deleted because they could not be divided into training data and test data, and thus could not be evaluated properly. The statistics for each dataset as a result of these processes are shown in Table 1. In actual experiments, 80% of these datasets were divided randomly into training data, 10% into validation data, and the remaining 10% into test data. The best values, λ_U, λ_V and λ_Z were obtained in advance using the validation data, and the test data were evaluated using these parameters.

In this experiment, we adopted root mean square error (RMSE) as an evaluation index and took an average of five trials to ensure reliability. We compared our proposed method with following models. PMF (Salakhutdinov & Mnih, 2007), ConvMF (Kim et al., 2016), SRCMF (Wang et al., 2019), ISFMF (Saga & Duan, 2018), Bi-ISFMF (Lu et al., 2021). In addition, we performed grid search for λ_U, λ_V and λ_Z in the range [0.1,1,10,20,30,40,50,60,70,80,90,100] to find best parameters. We set other parameters as follows: Dimensionality D of the user matrix U and the item matrix V is set to 50. The size of the item image is set to 45×45. The images representing the user's characteristics were images of two previously purchased items. The cosine similarity threshold was 0.5 when using implicit social networks. These parameters were chosen because they were the optimal values when comparing accuracy in prior experiments.

Table 1. Detailed statistics of the datasets

Dataset	**Users**	**Items**	**Ratings**	**Density**
Clothes	12062	14182	29547	0.0173%
Accessories	4049	4503	8824	0.0484%
Food	53391	2634	224461	0.160%

3.2 Experiment Results

3.2.1 Comparing the Proposed Method with Existing Methods

Table 2 shows the RMSE of each model. Here, S-ISFMF with I is a model that uses implicit social network, S-ISFMF with E is a model that uses explicit social network, and Improve is the percentage improvement between our proposed method and the best value of the compared methods. This table indicates that the best accuracy is obtained by the proposed method S-ISFMF in any dataset. This result suggests that incorporating image contour information and social network into PMF at the same time is useful. For each dataset, we achieved an improvement of 7.25% for the Amazon Clothes dataset, 6.97% for the Amazon Accessories dataset, and 0.75% for the Yelp dataset. Improvement was lower in the Yelp dataset than in the other two datasets possibly because textual information such as item descriptions and user reviews is as important as image information in restaurant recommendations. In fact, the next most accurate model after the proposed method was the SRCMF, which uses text and social networks. However, both the proposed method and SRCMF use social networks. This finding indicates that using social networks together with other auxiliary information is effective. As can be seen from Table 2, the RMSE for the Yelp dataset with explicit social networks was 1.451, while the accuracy with implicit social networks was 1.454. The explicit social network works slightly better than the implicit social network, but the difference is not very large. Therefore, we believe that implicit social networks can be used in the same way as explicit social networks.

Table 2. Overall RMSE on each dataset

Dataset	**Clothes**	**Accessories**	**Food**
PMF	1.781	1.761	1.834
ConvMF	1.514	1.422	1.654
SRCMF	1.336	1.239	1.462
ISFMF	1.394	1.372	1.526
Bi-ISFMF	1.255	1.233	1.521
S-ISFMF with I	**1.164**	**1.147**	1.454
S-ISFMF with E	-	-	**1.451**
Improve	7.25%	6.97%	0.75%

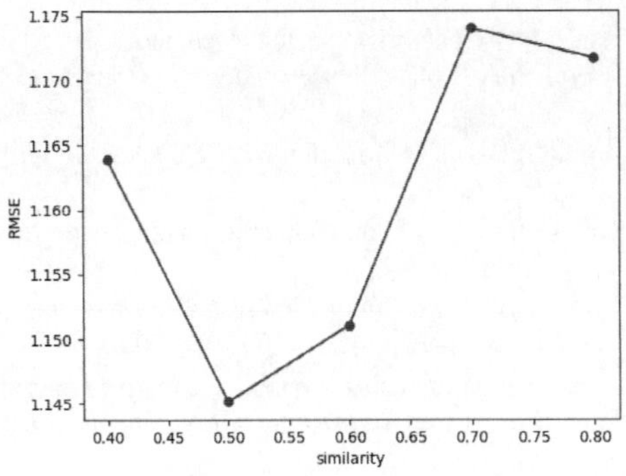

Figure 2. Impact of the similarity on implicit social network

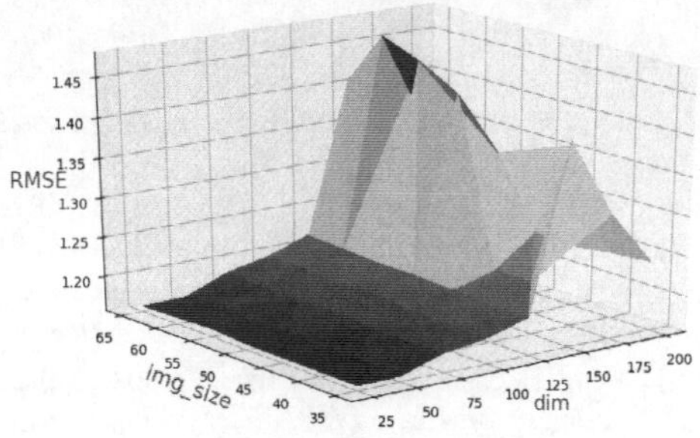

Figure 3. Impact of the dimension and image size

3.2.2 Parameter Analysis

The previous experiment showed the usefulness of using an implicit network. In this section, we first discuss the threshold in the creation of that implicit network. Figure 2 shows the relationship between similarity on threshold of implicit social network and RMSE. if the threshold is too high, then the accuracy of similarity determination will increase, but the accuracy will also decrease because the density of the social network will be smaller. Next, experiments were conducted to examine the robustness of the latent matrix U, V by changing the number of dimensions D and the size of the images used as input. Figure 3 shows the relationship between RMSE when changing D and image size using the best parameters (λ_U:100, λ_V:10, λ_Z:0.1) obtained using validation data in Amazon Clothes. This figure shows that the overall trend is that the accuracy worsens as the number of dimensions D increases. When D is sufficiently large, the accuracy worsens as the image size increases. However, when D is sufficiently small, the image size has no effect on accuracy.

3.3 Experiment Summary

Experimental results on the Amazon product dataset and the Yelp dataset yield the following findings:

- The proposed S-ISFMF obtains better results than those of existing methods.
- The predicted results are best when the similarity threshold for creating an implicit social network is 0.5.
- Implicit social networks can be used in the same way as explicit social networks.
- As U and V dimensions increase, the experimental results gradually deteriorate, with abrupt changes and fluctuations occurring in higher dimensions.
- Image size is stable and highly accurate when U and V are low dimensional. When U and V are high dimensional, the accuracy is affected by the image size.

These are some of the useful details and characteristics of the S-ISFMF that we have identified.

4. CONCLUSION

In this paper, we proposed S-ISFMF, which extracts contour information features from images that represent item and user features and incorporates them into a matrix factorization method with social networks. The proposed method achieves an improvement of 0.75% to 7.25% on three real-world datasets over other existing models that add auxiliary information to matrix factorization. The effectiveness and robustness of the implicit social network compared with the explicit social network are also discussed.

One of the current challenges is that we are not able to consider features such as item descriptions and user reviews, which are highly likely to represent item and user characteristics. Future work will include clarifying the effectiveness of extracting features from other auxiliary information, such as textual information, and incorporating them into matrix factorization.

REFERENCES

Kim, D., Park, C., Oh, J., Lee, S., & Yu, H. (2016). Convolutional Matrix Factorization for Document Context-Aware Recommendation. *Proceedings of the 10th ACM Conference on Recommender Systems*, 233–240. https://doi.org/10.1145/2959100.2959165

Li, Y., Song, M., & E, H. (2015). Recommender System Using Implicit Social Information. *IEICE TRANSACTIONS on Information and Systems*, *E98-D*(2), 346–354.

Lu, Y., Gao, M., & Saga, R. (2021). Apparel Recommender System based on Bilateral image shape features. *ArXiv:2105.01541 [Cs]*. http://arxiv.org/abs/2105.01541

Ma, H., Lyu, M. R., & King, I. (2009). Learning to recommend with trust and distrust relationships. *Proceedings of the Third ACM Conference on Recommender Systems*, 189–196. https://doi.org/10.1145/1639714.1639746

Ma, H., Yang, H., Lyu, M. R., & King, I. (2008). SoRec: Social recommendation using probabilistic matrix factorization. *Proceedings of the 17th ACM Conference on Information and Knowledge Management*, 931–940. https://doi.org/10.1145/1458082.1458205

McAuley, J., Targett, C., Shi, Q., & van den Hengel, A. (2015). Image-Based Recommendations on Styles and Substitutes. *Proceedings of the 38th International ACM SIGIR Conference on Research and Development in Information Retrieval*, 43–52. https://doi.org/10.1145/2766462.2767755

Resnick, P., Iacovou, N., Suchak, M., Bergstrom, P., & Riedl, J. (1994). GroupLens: An open architecture for collaborative filtering of netnews. *Proceedings of the 1994 ACM Conference on Computer Supported Cooperative Work*, 175–186. https://doi.org/10.1145/192844.192905

Saga, R., & Duan, Y. (2018). Apparel Goods Recommender System Based on Image Shape Features Extracted by a CNN. *2018 IEEE International Conference on Systems, Man, and Cybernetics (SMC)*, 2365–2369. https://doi.org/10.1109/SMC.2018.00406

Saga, R., Hayashi, Y., & Tsuji, H. (2008). Hotel recommender system based on user's preference transition. *2008 IEEE International Conference on Systems, Man and Cybernetics*, 2437–2442. https://doi.org/10.1109/ICSMC.2008.4811660

Salakhutdinov, R., & Mnih, A. (2007). Probabilistic Matrix Factorization. *Proceedings of the 20th International Conference on Neural Information Processing Systems*, 1257–1264.

Shen, W., Wang, X., Wang, Y., Bai, X., & Zhang, Z. (2015). DeepContour: A deep convolutional feature learned by positive-sharing loss for contour detection. *2015 IEEE Conference on Computer Vision and Pattern Recognition (CVPR)*, 3982–3991. https://doi.org/10.1109/CVPR.2015.7299024

Su, X., & Khoshgoftaar, T. M. (2009). A Survey of Collaborative Filtering Techniques. *Advances in Artificial Intelligence*, *2009*, e421425. https://doi.org/10.1155/2009/421425

Tamada, T., & Saga, R. (2022). Book Recommender System Using CNN Capturing Feature of Synopses and Reviews. In J. Y. C. Chen, G. Fragomeni, H. Degen, & S. Ntoa (Eds.), *HCI International 2022 – Late Breaking Papers: Interacting with eXtended Reality and Artificial Intelligence* (pp. 518–530). Springer Nature Switzerland. https://doi.org/10.1007/978-3-031-21707-4_37

Verma, D., Gulati, K., & Shah, R. (2020). Addressing the Cold-Start Problem in Outfit Recommendation Using Visual Preference Modelling. *2020 IEEE Sixth International Conference on Multimedia Big Data (BigMM)*. https://doi.org/10.1109/BigMM50055.2020.00043

Wang, X., Yang, X., Guo, L., Han, Y., Liu, F., & Gao, B. (2019). Exploiting Social Review-Enhanced Convolutional Matrix Factorization for Social Recommendation. *IEEE Access*, *7*, 82826–82837. https://doi.org/10.1109/ACCESS.2019.2924443

SOFTWARE EFFORT ESTIMATION WITH METAHEURISTIC OPTIMIZED ENSEMBLE FOR SOFTWARE CROWDSOURCING

Anum Yasmin and Wasi Haider Butt
Department of Computer & Software Engineering
National University of Sciences & Technology (NUST), Islamabad, Pakistan

ABSTRACT

Software crowdsourcing (SWCS) is rapidly growing from past decade due to its flexible work environment. Software effort estimation (SEE) is already renowned field in traditional software engineering, utilized in preliminary resource planning, budget, and time. SWCS platform can suffer from schedule, cost, and human resource uncertainty, which can be attained by estimating effort consumed on crowdsourced tasks. With more advent in SEE, ensemble effort estimation (EEE) is emerged providing unbiased results across different datasets. Recently, intelligent methods such as metaheuristic algorithms are used for ensemble by assigning optimal weights. This study aims to utilize prediction accuracy of EEE and metaheuristics on SWCS tasks to established accurate effort estimation model. In this work, ensembles are created using high predictive solo machine learning algorithms (RF, SVM, NeuralNet), whose weights are optimized with MO. TopCoder is selected as target SWCS platform, and this is first work to utilize TopCoder Design category tasks and contributes in dataset formation with relevant crowdsourced designing features. Results of proposed scheme clearly show that Metaheuristic-weight learning is giving more accurate ensembles with approximately 60% performance improvement compared to solo ML and other EEE techniques, proving it more suitable SEE technique for SWCS.

KEYWORDS

Software Effort Estimation, Crowdsourcing, Machine Learning, Ensemble Effort Estimation, Metaheuristic Optimization

1. INTRODUCTION

Software Crowdsourcing (SWCS) is new and emerging filed and known as distributed problem-solving platform for complex computations. SWCS mostly works by open-call format in competitive environment, to exploit collective crowd intelligence. Platforms enable SWCS services included oDesk, vWorker, eLance, Guru, TaskCity, and Taskcn and TopCoder. Among these platforms, TopCoder has the largest developer community and immensely utilized by researchers and practitioners (Sarı et al., 2019). The community decides whether to perform tasks by attending competitions which mainly influences by offered price of task. Currently, no SWCS platform has certain cost assignment mechanism. Decision to adopt a task can be largely impacted by effort required by the SWCS tasks, which can lead to justified task selection criteria.

SEE is already established field in traditional software engineering to estimate effort spent on software project. SEE is crucial since under and overestimation may lead unclear assumption about project's time and resources. Due to the need and challenges of SEE, multiple techniques are developed in past including expert judgement (Jørgensen et al., 2010), algorithmic methods (Effendi et al., 2018) and machine learning (ML). Among these, ML-based SEE is popular since they handle complex, non-linear relationship between effort and software features. However, researchers agree that no single SEE technique outperformed in every context. Ensemble Effort Estimation (EEE) is explored for eliminating instability issues which predictions of more than one single SEE technique to improve accuracy. An SLR on SEE is conducted by (Idri et al., 2016) according to which, EEE outperformed in general single predictive approaches. EEE techniques are categorized into: (1) Homogeneous ensemble (HM), which work by combining more than two configurations of the same single SEE technique, and (2) Heterogeneous ensemble (HT) which combine at least two different SEE techniques via some combination rule. In SLR conducted by idri. et al HT comparatively accurate EEE. However, performance of HT ensemble majorly depends on method for combining single predictions. Weight assignment is one method of creating HT which assigns appropriate weights to predictions of single SEE techniques. Accurate weight learning is very critical in weighted HT since single SEE technique may induce its own bias in results. Metaheuristic optimization (MO) is recently investigated field in ML for catering optimization problems. In SEE, MO is utilized in dataset feature selection and hyperparameter tunning of ML algorithms. For HT ensemble weights learning, MO are rarely utilized (Palaniswamy et al., 2021; Song et al., 2019).

In this work, we are analyzing the impact of EEE for estimating effort of crowdsourced tasks. Study determines effectiveness of MO in HT weighted ensemble on our crowdsourced dataset. Ensemble is created by optimal weights obtained from MO algorithms. TopCoder is selected as target SWCS platform. Reason being, TopCoder is supporting highly skilled developers' community and tendency of researchers adopting TopCoder for analysis is high (Alelyani et al., 2017; Mao et al., 2013). Crowdsourced designing tasks on TopCoder platform are used for further analysis. Moreover, this is the first work to present any analysis on TopCoder tasks of "Design" category.

Proposed work attempts to address following research questions:

RQ1: What performance improvement is shown by ensemble models compared to solo ML model for effort estimation on SWCS dataset?

RQ2: Which EEE techniques are giving good results either homogenous (HM) ensembles or heterogenous (HT) ensembles in software effort estimation for SWCS dataset?

RQ3: What is the performance of ensemble created with metaheuristic optimization for predicting effort, and which metaheuristic technique provides best estimation?

Main contributions of the study are:

- Constructing crowdsourced designing task dataset, with highly relevant features for accurately estimating effort and establishing effort estimation scheme for SWCS designing perspective.
- Exploring the power of metaheuristic algorithms for optimal weights to heterogenous ensemble.
- Comparison of solo ML algorithms, homogenous and heterogeneous ensembles to provide most appropriate effort estimation solution for SWCS designing tasks.

Structure of the paper is as follows: Section 2 presents literature of previous SWCS and EEE work, Section 3 represents brief details of techniques used for proposed scheme implementation. Section 4 contains proposed scheme procedure, and Section 5 and Section 6 contains results and conclusions of this study.

2. LITERATURE REVIEW

Work done by (Mao et al., 2013) was the first study to address the pricing issue for TopCoder SWCS. 490 TopCoder projects with 16 cost drivers are extracted. Cost estimation is made using LogR, LReg, C4.5, CART, QUEST, KNN, NNet and SVMR. Study verified that ML estimation surpass the random guessing and parametric model (COCOMO). However, the attribute selection is not practical since some attributes are not directly participating in effort and some attributes require information about previous phase, not available for all tasks. This issue is tackled by (Alelyani et al., 2017) with context-based pricing on TopCoder with 6 pricing factors, analyzed from task descriptions and 7 classification models (LDA, LR, kNN, CART, Naive Bayes, SVM and NNet). Although the study work on limited information, but aspects related to developer's ability, task and technology complexity are not considered.

Ensemble effort estimation (EEE) is frequently explored in SEE. (Idri et al., 2016) performed SLR of 24 past EEE studies published between 2000 to 2016. SLR concluded that 17 studies used homogenous ensemble, making them most frequently utilized ensemble models. For single base learners, 12 studies choose ANNs and DTs. Overall, EEE models produce accurate results, compared to their base leaners. HT is explore by 9 studies, which yielded better performance compared to their constituent ML techniques (with MMRE=62.48%, Pred(25)=43.35%, and MdMRE=26.80%).

Work of (Elish et al., 2013) implemented various HM and HT ensembles with different hybrid optimization techniques and implementation is done on 5 datasets of PROMISE repository. Results revealed that performance of ensemble is higher than solo models.

Similarly (Hussain et al., 2021) incorporated enhanced SVR for recursive feature elimination. RF is used as ensemble and experimentation is performed on COCOMO and NASA93 datasets. Results have shown improve performance in terms of MMRE MMER, MBRE, MIBRE error measures.

Work of (Shukla et al., 2019) used ensembles of Multi-Layer Perceptron Neural Network (MLPNN), including Ridge-MLPNN, Lasso-MLPNN, Bagging-MLPNN, and AdaBoost-MLPNN to improve effort estimation. Results are evaluated on Desharnais dataset (PROMISE) concluded that ensemble MLPNN has 82.213% increased accuracy. (Palaniswamy et al., 2021) utilized Particle Swarm Optimization (PSO) and Genetic Algorithms (GA) for tuning hyperparameters of stacking ensemble. Hyperparameters of MLP, RF, SVM and AdaBoost are tuned on ISBSG dataset and identified that stacking with hyperparameter tuning provides better accuracy.

Metaheuristics is explored frequently in past researchers for various optimization problems. However, for SEE, MO mostly utilized in hyperparameters tunning while a little work on ensemble weight optimization is tackled to get best estimation results. Known MO techniques included: GA, PSO, Artificial bee colony (ABC), Firefly algorithm (FFA) and Bat algorithm (BA) (Kaushik et al., 2019).

From the literature review, it is concluded that no previous SEE work has utilized crowdsourcing projects for SEE experimentation. Most frequently used repositories are PROMISE, ISBSG or other private projects. Also, EEE domain is not much explored in SWCS domain. This work combines prediction accuracy of EEE, more specifically metaheuristic optimized weighted ensemble (MO-WE) on SWCS tasks to established accurate effort estimation model.

3. METHODOLOGY USED

This section includes the different algorithms used to build effort estimation models on SWCS dataset. Effort is predicted using, solo ML algorithms, Homogenous ensembles and Heterogenous ensembles to assess more accurate prediction. Details of algorithms used in this study are described in Table 1.

Table 1. Description of SEE techniques used in study

Type	SEE technique	Description
ML algorithms	RF	combines several DTs with bagging, performs better with inter-correlated features, work with both numerical and categorical variables.
	SVM	deals with linearly separable data and works both for classification and regression problem.
	NeuralNet	Fast learning and is simple to implement and represent complex relationships between dependent and independent variables.
Homogenous ensemble (HM)	Bagging	ensemble algorithm works by creating separate samples of training datasets (bootstrap), model is trained for each sample, and then, results are combined (average) to find the final output.
	Gradient boosting machine (GBM)	incorporates different regularization techniques to maintain under-over fitting
Heterogenous ensemble (HT)	Majority Voting	implemented by creating two or more models with output combined by taking mean or mode.
	Stacking	multiple sub-models are created and combined with a meta-model to predict effort.
	Manually Weighted ensemble (MA-WE)	Manual weights assigned and highest weight given to best performing model in 2:1:1 ratio.
	GLM-based weighted ensemble (GLM-WE)	Assigned ensemble weights are coefficients of GLM model, trained using solo ML models' prediction.
	NeuralNet based weighted ensemble (NN-WE)	ensemble weights are learned using NeuralNet model.

RF, SVM and NeuralNet are selected as solo learners. Both categories of ensemble, HM and HT are used for experimentation. Bagging and Gradient boosting machine (GBM) are used as HM. For HT, multiple forms are used i.e., non-weight-based ensembles (Majority Voting, Stacking), weight-base ensemble (with manual, Generalized linear model (GLM) and NeuralNet based weights). In this study, MO weights learning of our solo ML models is included to form ensemble and assign optimal weights for solo ML predictions. For this, MO techniques are: GA, PSO, FFA and BA.

4. PROPOSED SCHEME

This section describes proposed scheme of this study. First, TopCoder designing task dataset is created with crowdsourced design-relevant features, along with regression analysis to ensure regression significance of features. Details of dataset are discussed in Section 4.1. After this, effort estimation is done on crowdsourced dataset (described in Section 4.2).

4.1 Dataset

This section describes the details of the dataset used in this study. As SWCS platform, TopCoder is selected. For dataset, 1500 tasks from TopCoder "Design" category are crawled, from Oct 31, 2019, to Aug 13, 2021 and sorted according to their posting time. For simplicity, only those tasks are included having 70% above submissions score with 1 winner. After applying elimination criteria, 200 tasks are finalized to be part of the dataset. Profile details of all task winners (referred as "designer" in this work) are also collected. Careful selection of TopCoder designing features is made while preparing dataset, ensuring all features are highly relevant for SEE without any dependability on previous phase. Finalized dataset can be found at 1. Total 18 input design features and one output feature as "Effort" are gathered, grouped into 5 categories (shown in Table 1). Brief description of input features is as follows:

- ***Task characteristics (TSCH)*** represent task or challenge characteristics particular to designing i.e., kind of application and design required in tasks (i.e., UI/UX or data visualization) Features of this category: APPT, DREQ, DSCH.
- ***Personnel Metrics (PERS)***, includes the details related to designer's capabilities. i.e., designer's winning and submission trend, previous performance, skills and experience. Features are: WINP, SBRT, SSCR, AVGP, TSCR, EXPR.
- ***Requirement Complexity (RCPX)*** shows business requirements complexity i.e., rounds, screens and platform constrains. Features included are: ROUN, STOC, SCRN, FEAT, ECNS.
- ***Artifact complexity (ACPX)*** includes helping material provided with task, their helping level, required documents by task and their overhead level. Features included are: ASST, DLVB.
- ***Quality parameters (QLTY)***, capturing quality aspects while delivering the output. Features included: FFIX, JUDG.

$$Effort = 91.5 + 75.5\,(\text{APPT}) + 25.3\,(\text{DREQ}) + 59.4\,(\text{DSCH}) - 8.7\,(\text{WINP}) - 9.3\,(\text{SBRT}) - 5.1\,(\text{SSCR}) - 4.8\,(\text{AVGP}) - 1.8\,(\text{TSCR}) - 24.8\,(\text{EXPR}) + 15.9\,(\text{ROUN}) + 2.5\,(\text{STOC}) + 31.5\,(\text{SCRN}) + 6.9\,(\text{FEAT}) + 23.5\,(\text{ECNS}) + 45.8\,(\text{ASST}) + 36.1\,(\text{DLVB}) + 2.7\,(\text{FFIX}) + 28.3\,(\text{JUDG}) \quad (1)$$

Datatypes assigned to features are Ordinal or Numerical. Ordinal features are assigned 6 levels depending upon their complexity and impact on effort as, "very low", "low", "nominal", "high", "very high" and "extra High" and values assigned to each level from 1 to 6 (1 assigned to "very low" while 6 to "extra High"). Effort is dependent feature of the dataset and measured based on task duration in hours and reflected in person-hours (PH) unit. Table 1 also showing regression analysis details for dataset features. Regression is performed on dataset with significance level ρ-value < 0.05. Overall model statistics are: R2 = 0.93, Standard Error = 0.38, F-Statistics = 128.5. Regression analysis shows that all feature are significant at $\rho = 0.1$ in performing regression and estimating effort. However, features like DREQ, SSCR, EXPR, FEAT, DLVB are not showing significance at $\rho = 0.05$. Regression equation for the dataset features is given in Eq. (1). Features of APPT, DREQ, DSCH, ROUN, STOC, SCRN, FEAT, ECNS, DLVB, FFIX and JUDG put an increasing impact (having positive β) on effort consumed on task. Similarly features like WINP, SBRT, SSCR, AVGP, TSCR, EXPR and ASST possess negative β, i.e., effort decreases by enhancing the values of these features.

[1] https://drive.google.com/drive/folders/12uBPa-KyUcZ6hj5uoSUrYkzCzynqSKXW?usp=sharing

Table 2. Descriptive statistics and regression details dataset features

Category	Features	Description	Data Type	Min	Max	Mean	β	τ-value	ρ-value
Task characteristics (TSCH)	APPT	Kind of application under design (web/android/iOS)	Ordinal	1	6	3.67	75.5	6.74	2.10e-10
	DREQ	Kind of design required (UI/ high or low fidelity etc.)	Ordinal	1	6	3.56	25.34	0.29	0.07
	DSCH	Required designing new application or adjustment in previous design	Ordinal	2	4	3.52	59.35	2.39	0.02
Personnel Metrics (PERS)	WINP	Win percentage	Numerical	0.47	100	11.12	-8.72	-2.36	0.02
	SBRT	Submission rate	Numerical	23.9	100	83.87	-9.27	-2.06	0.04
	SSCR	Screening success rate	Numerical	54.5	100	98.83	-5.06	-0.43	0.08
	AVGP	Average placement	Numerical	1	154.8	14.05	-4.80	-3.51	0.0005
	TSCR	Count of designer's acquired skills	Numerical	1	19	9.88	-1.81	-1.39	2.10e-10
	EXPR	Designer's experience in years	Numerical	0.08	13.16	7.96	-24.83	-2.49	0.07
Requirement Complexity (RCPX)	ROUN	No. of rounds in task	Ordinal	1	5	2.86	15.94	0.36	0.02
	STOC	Stock photography allowed	Ordinal	2	4	2.46	13.25	2.16	0.02
	SCRN	No. of screens required to design	Ordinal	1	5	2.55	31.50	4.05	0.04
	FEAT	No. of features required to design	Ordinal	1	5	2.47	6.97	1.25	0.09
	ECNS	Environmental constraints	Ordinal	2	6	3.88	23.51	1.67	0.0005
Artifact complexity (ACPX)	ASST	Assets provided with task for help	Ordinal	2	6	3.49	-45.76	-1.02	2.10e-10
	DLVB	Deliverable required with task	Ordinal	1	6	4.11	36.11	2.09	0.07
Quality parameters (QLTY)	FFIX	Final fixes required	Ordinal	2	4	2.95	2.66	1.41	0.018
	JUDG	Judgement criteria for design	Numerical	1	6	4.05	28.25	2.82	0.02

4.2 Effort Estimation Framework

In this section, effort estimation scheme is established for SWCS dataset, explained in Section 4.1. Figure 1 represents proposed framework. As solo models RF, SVM and NeuralNet are used to create ensemble. For weight optimization, GA, PSO, FFA and BA are used as MO. Optimal weights for each solo algorithm are obtained with lowest RMSE as fitness criteria. Optimal weights are used to created Metaheuristic optimized weighted ensemble (MO-WE) to obtain final prediction. Following steps are included in proposed framework:

1) Divide dataset into training and testing samples with 70:30 ratios.

2) For training dataset, train data separately with three solo algorithms (RF, SVM, NeuralNet).

3) Acquire predictions from three trained models on training dataset.

4) Obtain weights of predictions with MO (GA, PSO, FFA, BA) with fitness = minimum RMSE

5) On 30% remaining test data, repeat step 2-3 and acquire testing predictions.

6) Predict final outcome on testing data by creating MO-WE i.e., assign optimal weights (obtained from MO in step 4) to testing data predictions in step 5.

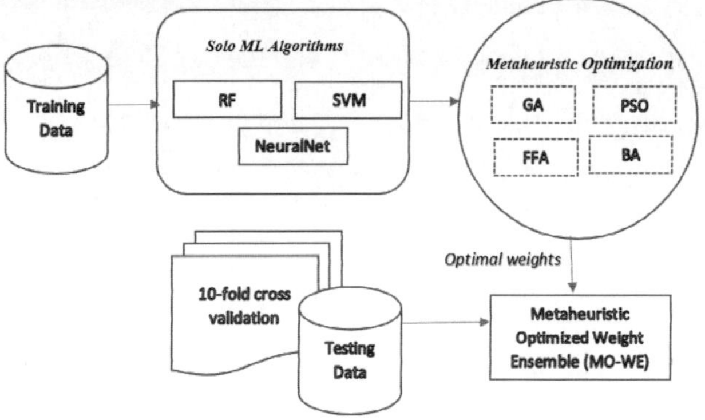

Figure 1. Overview of proposed MO-WE framework

4.3 Experimental Setup

For comparison, all models are trained on dataset (Table 2) by randomly dividing dataset into 70-30 ratio with 10-fold cross validation (10-fold-CV). All experiments are executed in RStudio. 5 performance evaluation metrices are used in this study represented in Eq. (2)- Eq. (7).

$$MSE = \frac{1}{T}\sum_{t=1}^{T}(Effort_{actual} - Effort_{estimated})^2 \quad (2)$$

$$RMSE = \sqrt{\frac{1}{T}\sum_{t=1}^{T}(Effort_{actual} - Effort_{estimated})^2} \quad (3)$$

$$MRE = \left|\left(\frac{Effort_{actual} - Effor_{estimated}}{Effort_{actual}}\right)\right| \quad (4)$$

$$MMRE = \frac{1}{T}\sum_{t=1}^{T} MRE_t \quad (5)$$

$$MdMRE = median(MRE_t)\ t \in \{1 \cdots T\} \quad (6)$$

$$PRED(d) = \frac{100}{T}\sum_{t=1}^{T}\begin{cases}1 \text{ if } MRE \leq d \\ 0 \text{ otherwise}\end{cases} \quad (7)$$

Where $t \in [1 \cdots T]$ is SWCS task from dataset T. Model having higher performance exhibit lower values of MSE, RMSE, MMRE, MdMRE, and higher PRED.

5. RESULTS AND DISCUSSION

This section presents the results of implementing SEE models (mentioned in Section 3 and Table 1) and reported in Table 3. Results of proposed MO-WE is also compared with other models. MO-WE created with GA, PSO, FFA and BA are referred as: GA-WE, PSO-WE, FFA-WE and BA-WE respectively.

Table 3. Evaluation metrices results of SEE techniques

SEE Techniques	RMSE	MMRE	MdMRE	PRED
RF	26.59	22.97	0.68	56.7
SVM	39.60	35.52	1.05	51.7
NeuralNet	37.49	25.82	0.46	71.2
Bagging	26.21	22.85	0.67	55.0
GBM	25.60	20.51	0.65	60.0
Majority Voting	34.26	26.22	0.51	63.9
Stacking	28.39	24.04	0.56	56.9
MA-WE	40.73	29.30	0.60	56.8
GLM-WE	41.09	34.87	0.77	62.1
NN-WE	36.65	31.23	0.84	61.4
GA-WE	24.16	18.63	0.41	80.0
PSO-WE	24.04	19.04	0.45	75.0
FFA-WE	22.71	17.09	0.33	80.0
BA-WE	22.60	16.98	0.30	81.7

Table 3 shows the performances of implemented SEE techniques to predict effort on our dataset using 5 performance metrices mention in Section 4.3.

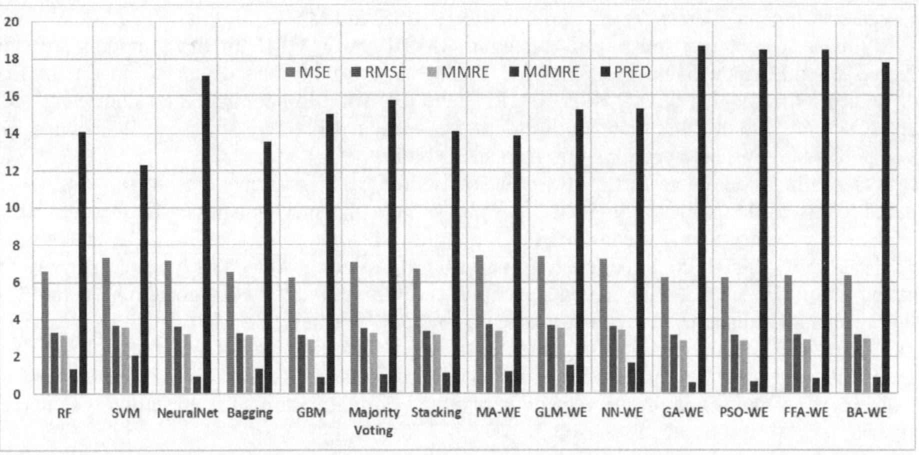

Figure 2. Performance comparison of SEE techniques

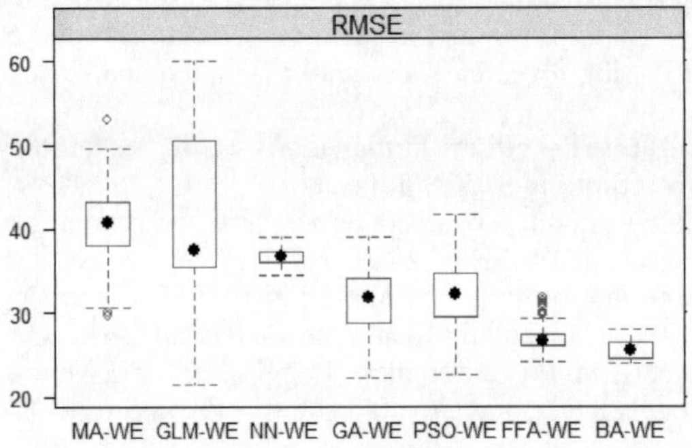

Figure 3. RMSE boxplot for weighted ensemble methods

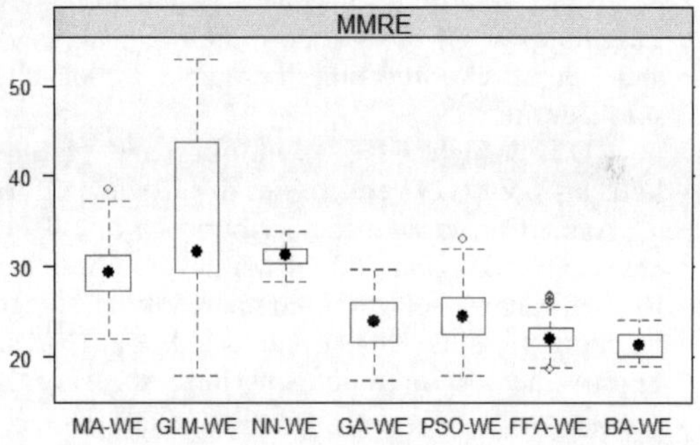

Figure 4. MMRE boxplot for weighted ensemble methods

- Solo algorithms (RF, SVM, NeuralNet) did not performance better compared to ensembles like bagging and GBM. However, compared to HT, RF is only solo algorithm performed better in RMSE and MMRE. SVM, is least performing solo algorithm. However, no solo algorithm surpassed any MO-WE (GA-WE, PSO-WE, FFA-WE, BA-WE). Overall, MO based ensembles has outperformed all models, in all performance metrices.
- Analyzing all ensembles, Bagging and GBM are better performing after MO-WE, compared to other HT ensemble.
- Among non-weight ensembles, Stacking has shown least amount of error while predicting effort. For HT, MA-WE and GLM-WE induced largest error and could not surpassed any other model.
- Overall, weighted HT ensembles (not using MO), have not shown performance improvement, compared to non-weight-based ensembles (Majority Voting, Stacking).
- MO-WE outperformed all HM and HT and solo techniques. Also, MO weight learning gives better results compared to other weight learning methods (NN-WE and GLM-WE).
- BA-WE has shown least amount of error among all models, after which FFA-WE proved better for predicting SWCS task effort, reflects, BA-WE has better weight learning ability for SWCS dataset.

Figure 2 shows performance comparison of all models using 5 metrices. Decreasing trend in error can be seen in MO-WE ensembles. PRED of MO-WE is also on increasing side, reflecting better learning capability of metaheuristics. Error bars of GLM-WE and MA-WE are higher among all, showing poor performance of algorithms on dataset. Figure 3 and Figure 4 represent boxplot of all weighted ensembles showing their RMSE and MMRE performance respectively. As it can be seen, GA-WE, PSO-WE, FFA-WE and BA-WE have lower mean, compared to MA-WE, GLM-WE, and NN-WE, giving better estimate of effort.

Furthermore, error distribution in GLM-WE is varied as it shows longer range, while FFA-WE and BA-WE show even distribution of error for effort prediction. RMSE and MMRE of GA-WE, PSO-WE, FFA-WE and BA-WE almost at center of the boxes, reflecting RMSE and MMRE for these models are symmetrically distributed around the medians. The FFA-WE and BA-WE boxes are shorter and have narrower ranges of values, which indicates that their RMSE, MMRE have less variation compared to other weighted ensembles (except NN-WE). Small number of outliers can be seen in FFA-WE and PSO-WE, while GA-WE and BA-WE possess no outliers in resultant performance values.

Results accumulated above can confirm that individual ML algorithms are not showing credible results, compared to ensemble, particularly GBM. This shows boosting mechanism can be fruitful effort prediction mechanism for datasets under-consideration, having both numerical as well as categorical features. Ensembles with averaging combination rule (i.e., Majority Voting, MA-WE) are not appropriate choice for estimating effort in SWCS dataset, since simply combining individual algorithms (without any weight learning mechanism) can negatively affect the performance. Further, non-MO weight learning i.e., GLM and NN can surpass in manual weight assignment, but due to learning limitations, optimal solution cannot be achieved. MO are good weight learning solution for our dataset. Reason is, MO are better for non-linear multi-objective problems and presence of numerical and ordinal features in dataset tends to make regression non-linear.

Here we can answer the research questions

RQ1: What performance improvement is shown by ensemble models compared to solo ML model for effort estimation on SWCS dataset?

Ans1: According to Table 3 ensemble models show considerable results compared to solo ML models. Ensembles with MO-WE show approximately 27% to 63% improvement in performance than solo RF, SVM and NeuralNet while other ensemble models show 13% improvement in overall results compared to their solo algorithms.

RQ2: Which EEE techniques are giving good results either homogenous (HM) ensembles or heterogenous (HT) ensembles in software effort estimation for SWCS dataset?

Ans2: Considering the performance of HT ensemble (without metaheuristic weights), both homogenous ensembles (Bagging and GBM) have outperformed, showing RMSE of 26.21 and 25.60 respectively. Both RMSE values are lower compared to best and worst performing non-metaheuristic HT ensemble i.e., Stacking (RMSE 28.39) and GLM-WE (RMSE 41.09) respectively. This shows overall 36% and 9% improvement in prediction performance. For Metaheuristic HT ensembles, Bagging and GBM are not showing any improvement, in fact, all of MO-WE models have shown overall 7% to 11% improved RMSE results.

RQ3: What is the performance of ensemble created with metaheuristic optimization for predicting effort, and which metaheuristic technique provides best estimation?

Ans3: MO-WE models are better than all comparing models in prediction. BA-WE is showing better performance with RMSE 22.60, after which FFA-WE is getting accurate results with RMSE 22.71. GA-WE is showing least performance among all MO-WE with RMSE 24.16. However, overall, GA-WE and PSO-WE is getting almost similar results while FFA-WE and BA-WE are giving similar performance values.

6. CONCLUSION AND FUTURE WORK

Software crowdsourcing (SWCS) is well researched field in software engineering domain but not explored much in effort estimation perspective. In this work, SWCS is analyzed particularly in crowdsourced designing perspective for analyzing effort consumed on crowdsourced task. For this, TopCoder tasks data is collected with highly effort-relevant and readily available features. Ensemble effort estimation is applied on collected dataset with three solo ML algorithms (RF, SVM, NeuralNet). Further, impact of metaheuristic optimization is explored in regard of assigning optimal weights to ensemble. This is the first work to utilized crowdsourced designing task data for analyzing effort. Results of our model reflect that for SWCS dataset, metaheuristic algorithms provide efficient mechanism in assigning optimal weights to ensemble, which significantly improve prediction accuracy in comparison with other ensemble techniques.

As future work, we intend to extend the study for other crowdsource categories i.e., development, testing and QA. Furthermore, other crowdsourced and open-sourced software development platforms are to be evaluated for metaheuristics and effort estimation perspective.

REFERENCES

Alelyani, Turki, Mao, Ke, & Yang, Ye. (2017). Context-centric pricing: early pricing models for software crowdsourcing tasks. Paper presented at the *Proceedings of the 13th International Conference on Predictive Models and Data Analytics in Software Engineering.* doi:https://doi.org/10.1145/3127005.3127012

Effendi, Yutika Amelia, Sarno, Riyanarto, & Prasetyo, Joco. (2018). Implementation of Bat Algorithm for COCOMO II Optimization. Paper presented at the *2018 International Seminar on Application for Technology of Information and Communication.* doi:https://doi.org/10.1109/ISEMANTIC.2018.8549699

Elish, Mahmoud O, Helmy, Tarek, & Hussain, Muhammad Imtiaz. (2013). Empirical study of homogeneous and heterogeneous ensemble models for software development effort estimation. *Mathematical Problems in Engineering, 2013.* doi:https://doi.org/10.1155/2013/312067

Hussain, Azath, Raja, Maheswari, Vellaisamy, Pandimurugan, Krishnan, Sangeetha, & Rajendran, Lakshminarayanan. (2021). Enhanced framework for ensemble effort estimation by using recursive-based classification. *IET Software, 15*(3), 230-238. doi:https://doi.org/10.1049/sfw2.12020

Idri, Ali, Hosni, Mohamed, & Abran, Alain. (2016). Systematic literature review of ensemble effort estimation. *Journal of Systems and Software, 118*, 151-175. doi:https://doi.org/10.1016/j.jss.2016.05.016

Jørgensen, Magne, & Halkjelsvik, Torleif (2010). The effects of request formats on judgment-based effort estimation. *Journal of Systems Software, 83*(1), 29-36. doi:https://doi.org/10.1007/s41870-019-00339-1

Kaushik, Anupama, & Singal, Niyati. (2019). A hybrid model of wavelet neural network and metaheuristic algorithm for software development effort estimation. *International Journal of Information Technology*, 1-10. doi:https://doi.org/10.1007/s41870-019-00339-1

Mao, Ke, Yang, Ye, Li, Mingshu, & Harman, Mark. (2013). Pricing crowdsourcing-based software development tasks. Paper presented at the *2013 35th International Conference on Software Engineering (ICSE).* doi:https://doi.org/10.1109/ICSE.2013.6606679

Palaniswamy, Sampath Kumar, & Venkatesan, R (2021). Hyperparameters tuning of ensemble model for software effort estimation. *Journal of Ambient Intelligence Humanized Computing, 12*(6), 6579-6589. doi:https://doi.org/10.1007/s12652-020-02277-4

Sarı, Aslı, Tosun, Ayşe, & Alptekin, Gülfem Işıklar (2019). A systematic literature review on crowdsourcing in software engineering. *Journal of Systems Software, 153*, 200-219 doi:https://doi.org/10.1016/j.jss.2019.04.027

Shukla, Suyash, Kumar, Sandeep, & Bal, Pravas. (2019). Analyzing Effect of Ensemble Models on Multi-Layer Perceptron Network for Software Effort Estimation. Paper presented at the *IEEE World Congress on Services (SERVICES).* doi:https://doi.org/10.1109/SERVICES.2019.00116

Song, Liyan, Minku, Leandro L, & Yao, Xin (2019). Software effort interval prediction via Bayesian inference and synthetic bootstrap resampling. *ACM Transactions on Software Engineering Methodology, 28*(1), 1-46. doi:https://doi.org/10.1145/3295700

VIRTUAL FEEDBACK, A POWERFUL LEVER IN TEAMS: A SYSTEMATIC LITERATURE REVIEW

Luisa Koloch[1], Paul Goldmann[2] and Björn Schäfer[3]
[1]*Organizational Theory and HRM, University of Eichstätt-Ingolstadt, Germany*
[2]*Organizational Theory and HRM, University of Applied Sciences Zwickau, Germany*
[3]*Organizational Theory and HRM, Free University of Bozen-Bolzano, Italy*

ABSTRACT

Virtual collaboration has become more widespread in recent years making virtual feedback an indispensable means for individual and team success. Throughout the last decades, many researchers examined how virtual feedback is received, processed and whether it even has desired effects, e.g., accounting for effects of distortions in electronic communication. Unfortunately, there is no comprehensive review that structures and summarizes the disparate literature on virtual feedback. We undertake a systematic review of 88 articles on virtual feedback published between 1986 and 2022 in peer-reviewed academic journals in Business, Management, and Psychology Sciences. By drawing on Ilgen et al.'s (1979) feedback process model as a theoretical framework, we analyze the articles due to the multidimensional nature of virtual feedback and address the process by which virtual feedback influences behavior. This work has three major contributions. First, we identify the aspects of virtual feedback from the literature that influence (a) the way it is perceived, (b) its acceptance by the recipient, (c) the willingness of the recipient to respond to the feedback, and (d) the recipients' behavior. This results in a context-specific application of Ilgen et al.'s (1979) feedback process model. Second, this systematic organizing of the literature allows us to identify blind spots in current literature that have not received sufficient scholarly attention and, thus, to propose related future research directions. Third, our implications at both individual and team level demonstrate guidelines for communicating feedback virtually to reduce misunderstandings, promote feedback acceptance, and foster desired effects of virtual feedback.

KEYWORDS

Computer-Mediated Communication, Virtual Collaboration, Virtual Team, Feedback, Feedback Process Model

1. INTRODUCTION

Organizations are increasingly using virtually collaborating teams to support major strategic initiatives in digital transformation (Bartsch et al., 2021). As the importance of teams working remotely increased tremendously due to the COVID-19 pandemic, virtual feedback (also known as digital feedback or computer-mediated feedback) has been playing a crucial role in ensuring team collaboration in a virtual work environment (Karl et al., 2022). Feedback is a powerful intervention for individuals and teams to improve learning, development, and task performance. In this vein, feedback has received considerable research attention as a determinant of individual and team behavior (Gabelica et al., 2014).

The sheer volume of studies on virtual feedback might suggest that research has reached a mature stage of theoretical development. For instance, studies address virtual feedback using various theoretical lenses e.g., by focusing on individual's cognitive processes when receiving virtual feedback (He et al., 2017), and diverse effects of virtual feedback at an individual and team level (Adamovic, 2018). Further, various studies demonstrate that virtual feedback is more limited compared to in-presence feedback due to distortions in electronic communication (e.g., a lack of nonverbal behaviors such as gestures, facial expressions, head nods, and tone of voice) which might hinder to achieve desired effects (Parker & Grote, 2020). Virtual feedback is transmitted by information and communication technologies (ICTs) and refers to information about actual performance of a system used to control the future actions of a system (Hertel et al., 2005). Hence, Johnson & Connelly (2014) argue that "We also cannot be completely certain that informal feedback functions the same in an online versus a face-to-face context" (p.1284). Referring to this previous work, it seems that individuals process feedback differently when communicated in a virtual work environment than in an in-person conversation. Consequently, in-presence feedback might not be fully transferrable to virtual feedback due to existing challenges salient in the virtual context, e.g., distractions in electronic communication.

Despite the growing body of literature on virtual feedback, clear questions about what research has been conducted, what it has found, what is missing, and what should be further explored and examined to advance the literature related to virtual feedback are yet to be answered. In addition, factors influencing individuals' cognitive processes and behavior when receiving feedback by computer mediated communication remain unclear.

These are issues best addressed by conducting a systematic literature review. As a comprehensive overview on virtual feedback is still missing in the literature, we undertake a systematic review of 88 articles on virtual feedback published between 1986 and 2022 in peer-reviewed academic journals in Business, Management, and Psychology. We draw on Ilgen et al.'s (1979) feedback process model to analyze the articles by addressing the multidimensional nature of feedback as well as the process by which feedback influences behavior. Due to distortions in electronic communication and contradictory findings in the literature, we need to understand the factors affecting a feedback recipient's information processing in a virtual work environment.

Such a systematic literature review is worthwhile for at least three reasons. First, we contribute to existing works by revealing the aspects of virtual feedback that influence (a) the way it is perceived, (b) its acceptance by the recipient, (c) the willingness of the recipient to respond to the feedback, and (d) the recipients' behavior. This results in a context-specific application of Ilgen et al.'s (1979) feedback process model that demonstrates the model's elements examined in the virtual context and those elements which are still lacking empirical investigation. Second, we pave the way for future research by identifying gaps in the literature and proposing related directions for future research. Third, we derive implications for scholars and practitioners on both individual and team level to advance understanding of virtual feedback.

2. THEORETICAL FRAMEWORK

Grounded in environmental psychology, the stimulus-organism-response (SOR) model provides the theoretical basis for explaining individual behavior (Mehrabian & Russell, 1974). This framework demonstrates that clues (stimulus) perceived from the environment can trigger an individual's internal assessment state (organism), which in turn leads to a specific behavior (response) (Mehrabian & Russell, 1974). For instance, a stimulus is the influencing factor of an external environment which affects an individual's cognitive and emotional states and, thus, produces approach or avoidance responses (Bigne et al., 2020). Ilgen et al. (1979) developed the feedback process model for explaining individual behavior stimulated by feedback, which is depicted in figure 1. The model includes factors relating to the entities involved in the feedback delivery, namely, the provider, the message, the recipient as well as the underlying cognitive processes that explain the recipient's reactions to feedback (Ilgen et al., 1979). As Ilgen et al. (1979) established a foundation for subsequent research on feedback, this framework provides a sound basis for organizing and integrating literature on virtual feedback (Wang et al., 2014).

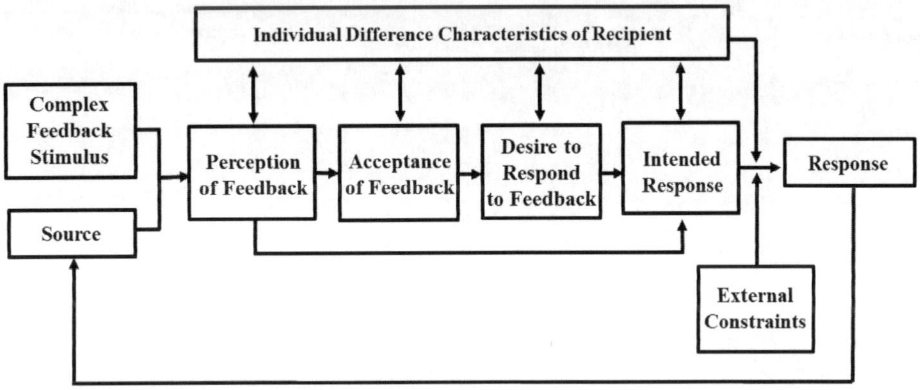

Figure 1. Feedback process model (Ilgen et al., 1979)

3. METHODOLOGY

To ascertain the state of the academic discussion about virtually communicated feedback in teams in the business and management context, the authors performed a systematic review and a content analysis. Therefore, this article adopts a systematic approach as explained by Petticrew & Roberts (2008) for reviewing the literature. Finally, by drawing on Ilgen et al.'s (1979) feedback process model we code and analyze the literature to reveal elements related to the source, the message, the recipient as well as the underlying cognitive processes that explain the recipient's reactions to virtual feedback in computer mediated communication. The authors base the description of the methodological approach on the RAMESES scheme, which provides guidelines for conducting a meta-narrative review (Wong, Greenhalgh, Westhorp, Buckingham, & Pawson, 2013). Referring to the databases Web of Science, EBSCO, and Google Scholar, we screened the existing literature and related fields to identify works addressing computer-mediated feedback in virtual teams. We depict the literature review process in figure 2.

Using an extensive list of relevant search terms, we search journals in the fields of Management, Business, and Psychology. At this stage, we also corrected for inter-category and inter-database doublets with and between both databases, leading to a total of 5,732 published articles.

In the second step, we screened titles and abstracts of the articles, each applying pre-defined in- & exclusion criteria. We excluded articles with contextual misfit, thus, excluding all articles not focusing on virtual collaboration in teams. Further, all articles with search terms part of a formulation with different meaning were excluded, e.g., social information space and online feedback forums. Afterward, we screened all titles of the articles applying these criteria resulting in 1,584 papers. Of these articles, we excluded 1,470 papers by screening all abstracts of the articles applying these criteria.

This process left the author with 114 papers to analyze. Of these articles, the authors excluded another 26 at a later stage because six articles did not fit to language and 20 articles were inaccessible and after directly contacting the authors. These steps lead to an overall 88 articles included and analyzed in-depth in this literature review.

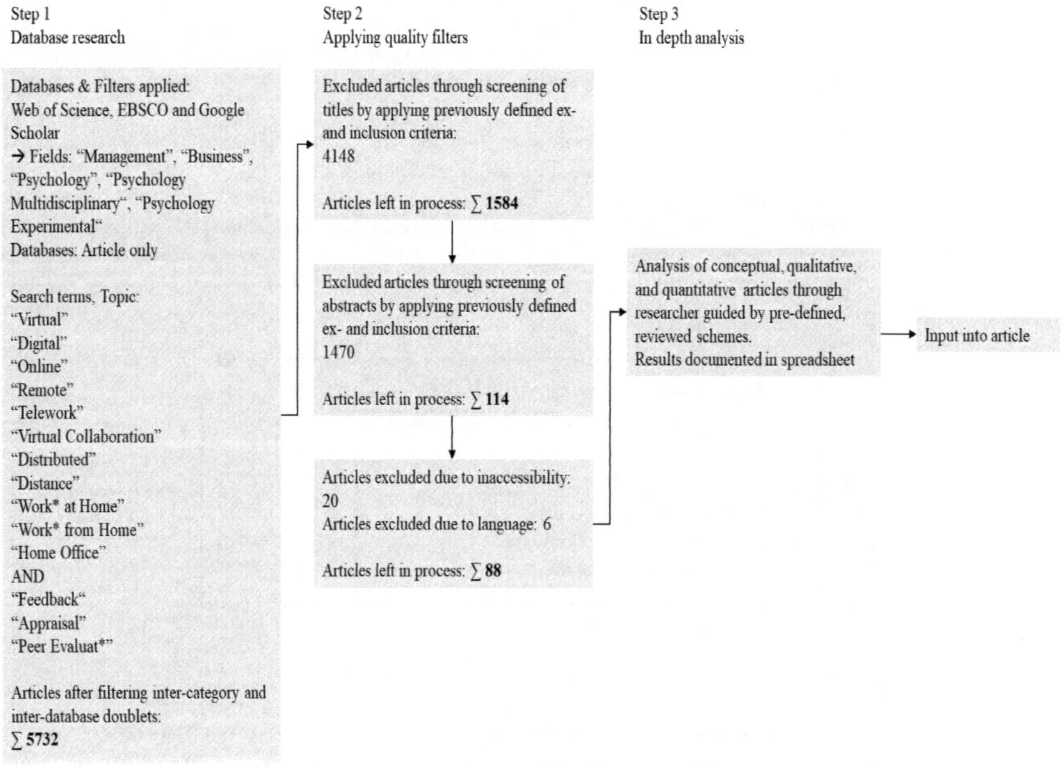

Figure 2. Literature review process

The authors analyzed the content of the articles due to their a) theoretical and b) methodological approach, and c) elements of Ilgen et al.'s (1979) feedback process model.

4. RESULTS

We integrate the components of Ilgen et al.'s (1979) feedback process model into the SOR model to visualize the stimuli of virtual feedback, which then influence individual's cognitive states and, thus, lead to a response at an individual and team level. This results in a conceptual framework that provides a sound basis for organizing and integrating the literature on virtual feedback in teams. This approach helps us to identify gaps in the literature and to suggest future fields of research. Figure 3 depicts our conceptual framework that reveals the elements examined in literature on virtual feedback.

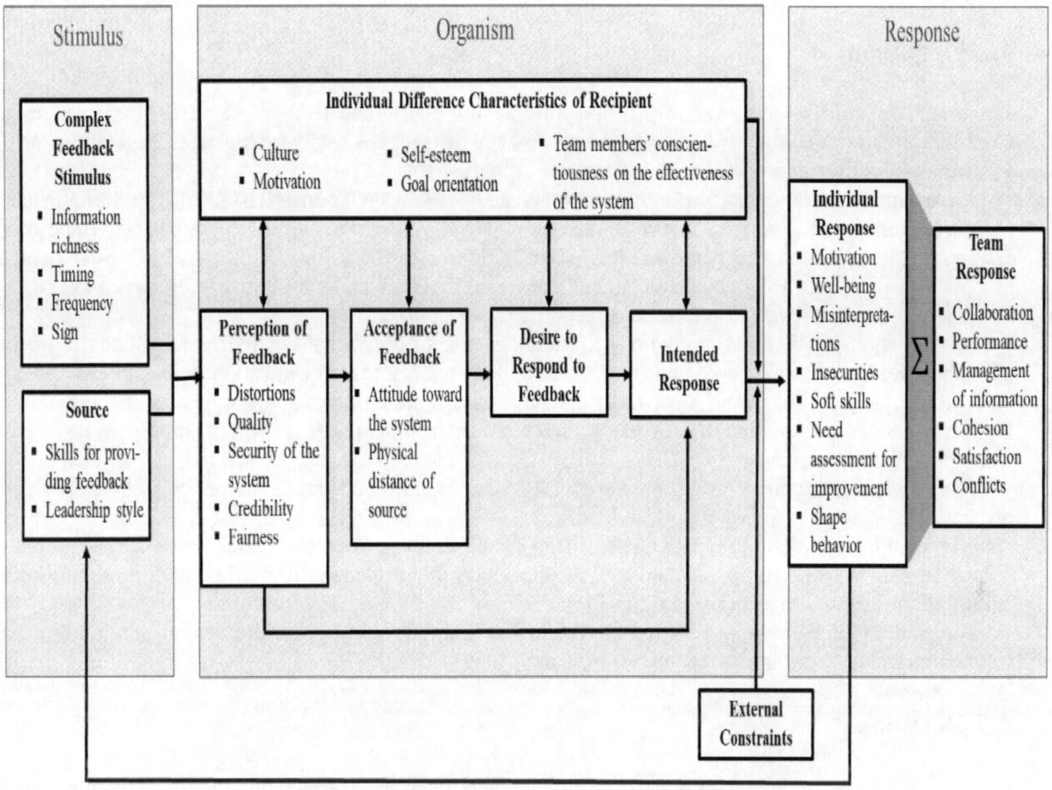

Figure 3. Conceptual framework of virtual feedback in teams

4.1 Stimulus

We demonstrate the complex feedback stimulus and source as stimuli in the environment influencing an individual's cognitive processes to explain the recipient's reactions to feedback. The complex feedback stimulus was examined by researchers due to its sign, information richness, timing, and frequency. For example, literature on virtually communicated feedback reveals that the sign of the feedback message is rather positive or negative. Whereas a positive sign refers to a positively worded feedback message and can signal an individual's or team's adequate behavior, a negative sign relates to a negatively worded feedback message and can signal an individual's or team's inadequate behavior (Kahai & Cooper, 2003).

In terms of information richness, media vary based on the capacity to transmit cues and facilitate shared meaning within a given time interval (Daft & Lengel, 1986). Thus, Eisenberg et al. (2021) demonstrate that rich feedback is enabled by media that is rich in cues e.g., face-to-face and video conferencing allowing immediate verbal and non-verbal interactions, such as facial expressions, gesture, head nods, and tone of voice. In contrast, feedback that is lean in cues is written media e.g., e-mail or instant messaging by containing fewer verbal and non-verbal cues (Eisenberg et al., 2021). Thus, Friedman & Currall (2003) show that the richness of feedback diminishes in e-mail compared to personal conversations because nonverbal behaviors are reduced in electronic communication.

Researchers addressed the source regarding the skills for providing feedback virtually as well as the leadership style. On the one hand, individuals should feel comfortable when giving feedback virtually, which implies their adequate use of ICTs (Payne et al., 2009). On the other hand, feedback providers should have the skills to offer both, positive and negative feedback in a constructive way and friendly manner (Breuer et al., 2020).

4.2 Organism

The organism explains the effect of stimuli on an individual's and team's response. Literature on virtual feedback reveals perception of feedback and acceptance of feedback as cognitive states to demonstrate "how" a stimulus leads to a response.

For example, literature on virtually communicated feedback demonstrates such distortions in terms of perceived bandwidth limitations (Powers et al., 2011). When bandwidth is limited in video-mediated communication, recipients perceive an audio-visual delay in feedback (Powers et al., 2011). Such delays vary in their strength as they might be small and not consciously perceived by individuals, or they might be obvious and lead to increased levels of interrupted speech (Powers et al., 2011).

Driskell et al. (2003) mention that the physical distance of individuals in a virtual team environment may affect how feedback is evaluated. Feedback is more likely to be accepted from sources that are psychologically closer to the recipient than from those more distant. Thus, the researchers suggest that recipients might accept feedback less readily from individuals in a virtual team environment who are seen as more remote or removed from the immediate social setting (Driskell et al., 2003).

Our analysis of literature on virtual feedback revealed that no article addressed an individual's desire to respond and intended response to virtual feedback.

Further, a recipient's individual characteristics influence these cognitive states. For example, in culturally diverse teams, the same computer-mediated feedback was interpreted in different ways depending on national culture of the team members (He et al., 2017).

The analysis of literature on virtual feedback revealed that no article addressed an individual's external constraints which might influence the response to virtual feedback.

4.3 Response

Researchers have examined the effects of virtually communicated feedback on individual and team response. On an individual level, effects of virtual feedback are demonstrated in terms of motivation, well-being, misinterpretations, insecurities, soft skills, need assessment for improvement and shape behavior (Sardeshmukh et al., 2012, Martínez-Argüelles et al., 2015; Powers et al., 2011). The results regarding outcomes of virtual feedback on a team-level can be described as mixed. Besides intensely investigated topics, such as the effects of virtually communicated feedback on team collaboration and performance, further effects of virtual feedback like the management of information, cohesion, satisfaction, and conflicts have been addressed by researchers (Gerards et al., 2020; Chen et al., 2019; Johnson & Connelly, 2014).

5. RESEARCH OPPORTUNITIES MOVING FORWARD

In the prior section, "Results" we addressed the literature on virtually communicated feedback for moving this research stream forward – connecting the diverse works due to the dimensions of Ilgen et al.'s (1979) feedback process model. This provides a comprehensive way to specify theoretical overlaps of related studies by focusing on all entities involved in the feedback process. Our results demonstrate that previous works mostly addressed the complex feedback stimulus, the recipient's perception of the message as well as effects of feedback on an individual and team level. Thus, it seems surprising that further cognitive variables which are of strong relevance for processing feedback, such as acceptance of feedback, desire to respond to feedback, intended response and external constraints were slightly or not addressed in research on virtually collaborating teams. Figure 4 depicts opportunities for future fields of research on virtually communicated feedback in teams. Here we discuss these opportunities for further research, again reviewing extant literature where relevant.

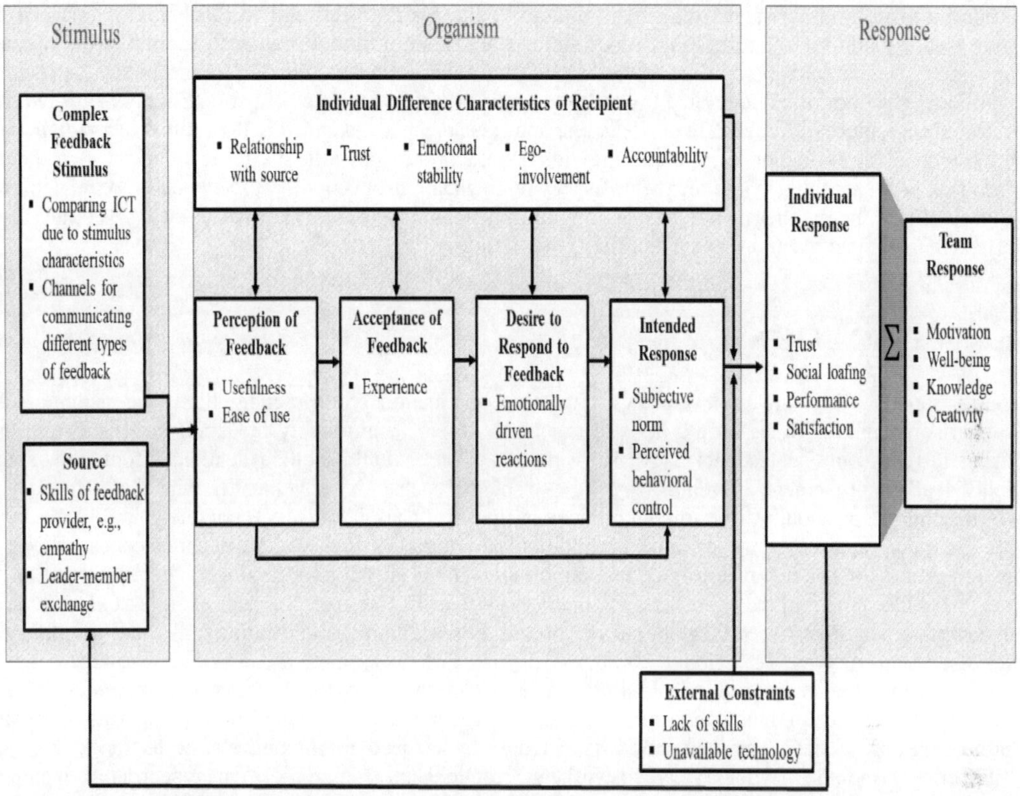

Figure 4. Future fields of research for virtually communicated feedback in teams

Studies have investigated stimuli in the environment influencing an individual's cognitive processes to understand the recipient's reactions to virtual feedback. However, comparing diverse ICTs, e.g., videoconferencing, Metaverse, and email for communicating virtual feedback due to their effects on individual's cognitive processing of the feedback is uncharted territory. Whereas the comparison of different channels for communicating feedback is not new, researchers have so far focused solely on effects of feedback when being rated with an online feedback system compared to a traditional paper-and-pencil system (see Payne et al., 2009). Due to contradictory findings in previous research (see Johnson & Connelly, 2014), diverse channels for communicating virtual feedback might have different effects on individuals' cognitive processes, e.g., in the perception and acceptance of feedback. Therefore, there are many questions that need to be answered: For example, which ICTs should be chosen by virtual team members to communicate positively or negatively framed feedback in order to be accepted and used by the recipient? Depending on the variety of ICTs, what is the adequate timing and frequency for communicating feedback to be accepted? This would allow scholars and practitioners to select contextually appropriate channels to deliver diverse types of feedback.

As acceptance of feedback is a cognitive variable of strong relevance for processing feedback, we encourage researchers to investigate individual's acceptance of virtually communicated feedback to help advance this underexplored area. For instance, future studies should address if an individual's previous experiences with feedback might influence a recipient's acceptance of digital feedback. Thus, an employee might not accept virtual feedback if such feedback has not led to a desired result in the past, e.g., due to a lack of resources in terms of digital skills or digital infrastructure.

As no article addressed an individual's desire to respond to virtual feedback in our analysis of literature, we call for more investigations on this cognitive factor. This would enhance scholars' understanding of the feedback process in a virtual work environment. As the desire to respond to feedback is described as the individual's willingness to react to the received feedback, it seems that this cognitive step is strongly based on an individual's rationality in Ilgen et al.'s (1979) feedback process model. Consequently, it seems that emotional reactions of an individual towards the received virtual feedback are still strongly neglected. As the effect of acceptance of feedback to desire to respond was not yet investigated in the context of a virtual working environment, we lack knowledge on an individual's reaction towards the digital feedback if, e.g., the digital feedback is not accepted by the recipient. Especially in situations when virtual feedback is not related to work aspects but to the recipient's personality, e.g., in developmental feedback, virtual feedback might provoke affective emotional reactions of the recipient when being misunderstood.

6. IMPLICATIONS

Our systematic literature review draws important implications for practice. First, we recommend that supervisors and employees should be well-trained to provide high-quality feedback to their co-workers by using ICTs and online feedback systems. Virtual feedback should include detailed information about an individual's improvement, as well as ways how to achieve such an improvement (Payne et al., 2009).

Second, teams should strive to communicate virtual feedback frequently, concretely, and timely both on the individual and the group level. This is particularly important due to the disconnectedness among team members and lack of rich face-to-face interaction inherent to virtual team settings, where information about the goal achievement of the other team members is more difficult to receive (Hertel et al. 2005). This can be accomplished by setting specific guidelines regarding feedback frequency, meeting times, and specific agendas for discussion (Kayworth & Leidner, 2000).

Third, we recommend supervisors and co-workers to choose adequate ICTs to communicate feedback virtually due to the communication needs. Whenever group discussions, e.g., on critical issue in a software project, require a rich communication channel due to the need for immediacy of feedback, high group interactions, and the need to view co-workers' reactions on comments in a synchronous manner, we recommend using media that is rich in cues e.g., video conferencing. This would allow immediate verbal and non-verbal interactions, such as facial expressions, gesture, head nods, and tone of voice to reduce risks for misunderstandings, and to lead to feedback acceptance and desired outcomes. In contrast, e-mail might be effectively used for communication needs requiring less interaction among co-workers as well as less immediate feedback (Kayworth & Leidner, 2000).

Forth, distortions in terms of bandwidth limitations should be eliminated when communicating feedback virtually. To reduce misinterpretations of the feedback message and conflicts caused by delayed feedback, supervisors and employees should be aware of possible distortions and, thus, react quickly to appearing bandwidth limitations. For example, the video function in video conferences should be switched off when bandwidth limitations appear to reduce audio-visual delay.

7. CONCLUSION

Throughout the last decades, researchers addressed virtual feedback under various theoretical lenses. Due to distortions in electronic communication and contradictory findings in the literature, virtual feedback might be processed differently by individuals than feedback communicated in person. To synthesize and comprehensively structure the disparate literature, we undertook a systematic review of 88 articles on virtual feedback published between 1986 and 2022 in peer-reviewed academic journals in Business, Management, and

Psychology Sciences. We draw on Ilgen et al.'s (1979) feedback process model to analyze the articles by addressing the multidimensional nature of feedback as well as the process by which feedback influences behavior. This work has three major contributions. First, we identify the aspects of virtual feedback from the literature that influence (a) the way it is perceived, (b) its acceptance by the recipient, (c) the willingness of the recipient to respond to the feedback, and (d) the recipients' behavior. This results in a context-specific application of Ilgen et al.'s (1979) feedback process model. Second, this systematic organizing of the literature allows us to identify blind spots in current literature that have not received sufficient scholarly attention and, thus, to propose related future research directions. Third, our implications at both individual and team level demonstrate guidelines for communicating feedback virtually to reduce misunderstandings, promote feedback acceptance, and foster desired effects of virtual feedback.

REFERENCES

Adamovic, M. 2018. An employee-focused human resource management perspective for the management of global virtual teams. *The International Journal of Human Resource Management,* Vol 29, No. 14, pp. 2159-2187.

Bartsch, S. et al, 2021. Leadership matters in crisis-induced digital transformation: how to lead service employees effectively during the COVID-19 pandemic. *Journal of Service Management, Vol.* 32, No. 1, pp. 71-85.

Bigne, E. et al. 2020. Pictorial content, sequence of conflicting online reviews and consumer decision-making: the stimulus-organism-response model revisited. *Journal of Business Research*, Vol. 115, pp. 403-416.

Breuer, C. et al, 2020. Trust in teams: A taxonomy of perceived trustworthiness factors and risk-taking behaviors in face-to-face and virtual teams. *Human Relations*, Vol. 73, No. 1, pp. 3-34.

Chen, Q. et al, 2019. Collective firm-internal online idea development: Exploring the impact of feedback timeliness and knowledge overlap. *European Journal of Innovation Management*, Vol. 23, No. 1, pp. 13-39.

Daft, R. L., & Lengel, R. H. 1986. Organizational information requirements, media richness and structural design. *Management Science,* Vol. 32, No. 5, pp. 554-571.

Driskell, J. et al. 2003. Virtual teams: Effects of technological mediation on team performance. *Group Dynamics: Theory, Research, and Practice,* Vol. 7, No. 4, pp. 297-323.

Eisenberg, J. et al, 2021. Multicultural virtual team performance: The impact of media choice and language diversity. *Small Group Research,* Vol. 52, No. 5, pp. 507-534.

Friedman, R. A., & Currall, S. C. 2003. Conflict escalation: Dispute exacerbating elements of e-mail communication. *Human relations*, Vol. 56, No. 11, pp. 1325-1347.

Gabelica, C. et al, 2014. The effect of team feedback and guided reflexivity on team performance change. *Learning and Instruction*, Vol. 34, pp. 86-96.

Gerards, R. et al, 2020. Do new ways of working increase informal learning at work? *Personnel Review*.

Golden, T. et al, 2009. Implications of virtual management for subordinate performance appraisals: A pair of simulation studies. *Journal of Applied Social Psychology*, Vol. 39, No. 7, pp. 1589-1608.

He, H. et al, 2017. Two Sides to Every story: Mitigating intercultural conflict through automated feedback and shared self-reflections in global virtual teams. Proceedings of the *ACM on Human-Computer Interaction, 1*(CSCW), pp. 1-21.

Hertel, G. et al, 2005. Managing virtual teams: A review of current empirical research. *Human resource management review*, Vol. 15, No. 1, pp. 69-95.

Ilgen, D. et al, 1979. Consequences of individual feedback on behavior in organizations. *Journal of applied psychology,* Vol. 64, No. 4, pp. 349-371.

Johnson, G., & Connelly, S. 2014. Negative emotions in informal feedback: The benefits of disappointment and drawbacks of anger. *Human Relations,* Vol. 67, No. 10, pp. 1265-1290.

Kahai, S. S., & Cooper, R. B. 2003. Exploring the core concepts of media richness theory: The impact of cue multiplicity and feedback immediacy on decision quality. *Journal of management information systems,* Vol. 20, No. 1, pp. 263-299.

Karl, K. et al, 2022. Virtual work meetings during the COVID-19 pandemic: The good, bad, and ugly. *Small Group Research,* Vol. 53, No. 3, pp. 343-365.

Kayworth, T., & Leidner, D. 2000. The global virtual manager: A prescription for success. *European Management Journal*, Vol. 18, No. 2, pp. 183-194.

Martínez-Argüelles et al. 2015. Usefulness of feedback in e-learning from the students' perspective. In European Conference on e-Learning (ECEL), Vol. 11, No. 4, pp. 283-292.

Mehrabian, A., & Russell, J. A. 1974. An approach to environmental psychology. Cambridge, MA: MIT Press.

Parker, S. K., & Grote, G. 2022. Automation, algorithms, and beyond: Why work design matters more than ever in a digital world. *Applied Psychology,* Vol. 71, No. 4, pp. 1171-1204.

Payne, S. et al, 2009. Comparison of online and traditional performance appraisal systems. *Journal of Managerial Psychology,* Vol. 24, No. 6, pp. 526-544.

Petticrew, M., & Roberts, H. 2008. Systematic reviews in the social sciences: A practical guide. John Wiley & Sons.

Powers, S. et al. 2011. The effect of video feedback delay on frustration and emotion communication accuracy. *Computers in Human Behavior,* Vol. 27, No. 5, pp. 1651-1657.

Sardeshmukh, S. et al, 2012. Impact of telework on exhaustion and job engagement: A job demands and job resources model. *New Technology, Work and Employment,* Vol. 27, No. 3, pp. 193-207.

Tavoletti, E. et al, 2019. The impact of peer evaluation on team effort, productivity, motivation and performance in global virtual teams. *Team Performance Management: An International Journal*, Vol. 25, No. 5, pp. 334-347.

Wong, G. et al, 2013. Rameses publication standards: Meta-narrative reviews. BMC Medicine, 11.

A MULTI-SENSOR APPROACH TO BUSINESS PROCESS MANAGEMENT: APPLICATION FOR THE HEALTH CARE FIELD

Syrine Khalfallah[1], Asma Daassa[2,3] and Sonia Ayachi Ghannouchi[1,4]
[1]*University of Sousse, Higher Institute of Management of Sousse, Sousse, Tunisia*
[2]*University of Tunis El Manar, Engineering School of Tunis, Tunis, Tunisia*
[3]*University of Monastir, Electronics and Microelectronics Laboratory, Faculty of Sciences, Monastir, Tunisia*
[4]*University of Mannouba, ENSI, RIADI Laboratory, Mannouba, Tunisia*

ABSTRACT

Since the global health disaster of COVID-19, the health professionals have been looking for new technologies to monitor and mitigate the number of patients affected by this pandemic. Through this research work, we seek to optimize the healthcare process of the infectious disease department of a hospital through the proposal of an approach that integrates IoT devices into the care process model. More generally, we propose the integration of a set of sensors in business processes and analyze their effect to improve their performance.

To reach our objective we developed a Framework intended for the doctor which aims to group together the different measurements from the different IoT devices that can be used during COVID-19 health care. We tested the approach by collecting two different measures which are oxygen saturation and heart rate. These measurements were obtained thanks to an oximeter. Our approach is valid for a multi-sensor solution with several measured data. We have adopted an analysis through the decision tree which is one of the data mining techniques in order to facilitate the diagnosis and improve the process of care against the COVID-19 pandemic.

KEYWORDS

E-health, Internet of Things, Business Process Management, Covid-19, Multi-Sensor Approach, Decision Tree

1. INTRODUCTION

Business Process Management (BPM) is a mature discipline, involving the identification, discovery, analysis, design, implementation, execution, monitoring and evolution of business processes (Janiesch et al., 2020).

The trend of the Internet of Things (IoT) has also become very common, helping to automate data collection. It is a revolutionary technology, which constitutes a networked object world, in which everything is interrelated and has a virtual form of expression (Pascual et al., 2011). Through the combination of the Internet, radio frequency identification, real-time positioning, embedded sensors and other emerging technologies, objects in daily life are transformed into intelligent objects that can perceive, interpret and respond to the environment (Vermesan fries, 2013).

The internet of things and BPM are considered to be two independent topics in research and practice. On the other hand, the Internet of Things provides an improvement of the current state of traditional BPM processes (Janiesch et al., 2020). The combination of Internet of Things technology and BPM method has brought great benefits in various fields, especially in the field of medical care. More precisely, nowadays, coronavirus causes many symptoms for infected people. These symptoms can be detected through a set of medical sensors.

This work combines the internet of things technology and BPM technology to effectively control the popularity of covid-19. Section 2 describes some of the work in the literature that combines BPM and the Internet of Things. Section 3 describes the recommended approach. Prototypes and experiments are presented in section 4 and 5. Then we give an analysis of the data collected from the existing executions of COVID-19 health care processes and we present the corresponding result in section 7. Finally, the conclusion of the article is presented in section 8.

2. RELATED WORKS

In literature, we find a certain number of works on the integration of BPM and the Internet of Things in various fields, especially in the field of health, among which we cite the works below.

The paper of (Fernandez et al., 2017) proposes a new model based on BPM strategy, internet of things and remote sensing to solve the problems of low efficiency of chronic disease clinical process and lack of integration of medical staff, patients and the process itself.

Research of (Antonius Dachyar, 2020) aims to develop a remote patient heart monitoring system (RPM) to improve the hospital's heart service. Through business process reengineering (BPR) and management information system (MIS), the Internet of Things (IoT) is used to reduce emergency response time and outpatient treatment time.

This paper of (Al-jamal et al., 2017) proposes an improved process model of monitoring system for heart disease patients, which simplifies the patient tracking process, realizes remote monitoring, reduces costs and shortens treatment time. The system uses the Internet of Things technology to help doctors monitor patients with heart disease remotely and in real time.

This work (Domingos et al., 2020) focuses on reliability, and suggests using the random workflow reduction (SWR) method to calculate the reliability of BPMN healthcare processes compatible with the Internet of Things. This method treats hypertension patients by integrating the BAN (body area network sensor) sensor connected to the patient's body.

These related work deal with diseases other than COVID-19. Moreover, they do not use data mining techniques for data analysis.

In this context, our contribution in this work is to adopt a combination of BPM and the Internet of Things, using various medical Internet of Things sensors in the process of treating COVID-19 disease, and using data mining for the analysis of the generated patients' data.

3. PROPOSED APPROACH

The basic idea of our approach is to present a way to manage the presence of several IoT sensors in the BPMN model of the process in the health field. More exactly, the process of monitoring people affected by COVID-19 is considered, while taking into account the specification of the two domains (IoT and BPM) and providing the data from the IoT in a compatible way with the process. For that we have developed a general model of a multi-sensor approach for business process management. This model, shown in Figure 1, is represented as a BPMN model, which gives it clarity and makes it easy to evolve. It has 5 main steps which are step1: choose and model the process, step2: Associate Sensors, step3: Implement the solution, step4: Execute the process and step5: Analyze the recorded data.

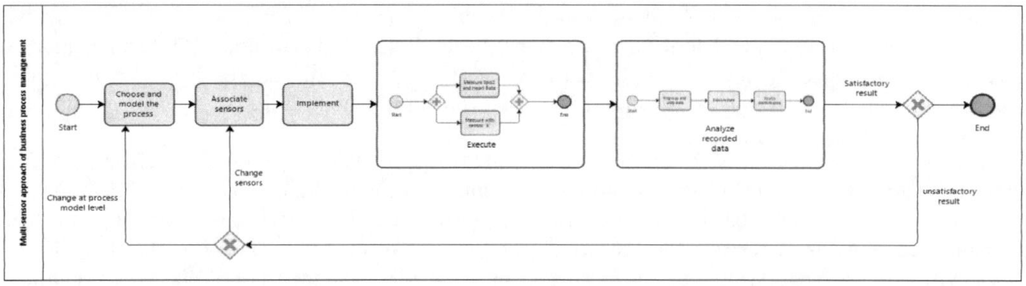

Figure 1. General model of a multi-sensor approach for business process management

We applied this model as a way to describe our approach to modeling and executing health care processes. We aim to provide in a first step a process model that includes the integration of IoT elements which are the main source of data (step 1). The purpose is to provide a coordinated course of care which ensures the safety of patients who need medical supervision.

In the design phase, the IoT elements in the BPMN model can be positioned as an actor. They can be called "IoT devices", whose main task is to provide specific information in the model to be integrated (step 2). Once the model has been presented, the next step is the implementation (step 3). We need to use technical tools to help us implement the "To-be Process" model. In the configuration and execution step of the BPM approach (step 4), the focus is on selecting tools that allows the exchange of data with the IoT sensors. Next, we need to run the BPMN model. Next, we need to run the BPMN model. Once the process is executed, the analysis phase can take place (step 5). During this phase, we make sure that the connected objects are working correctly, it is possible to check whether there are anomalies in the data exchange (example: slowness or erroneous data), then ensure a uniform structure for the data recorded by the connected objects and explore them. Finally, performance is evaluated. This phase ultimately leads to improvements to make, if the results are not satisfactory. Among these improvements, the association of new sensors or changes at the level of the process model will make it possible to achieve a better performance.

In this work, we consider medical IoT devices such as sensors and actors placed on wireless resources with limited human intervention. Each of them has measurements generated in a specific application interface for each sensor. This data can be used in an E-Heath ecosystem to track a patient's physical condition and digitally monitor vital signs of the body.

Our approach is a multi-sensor approach, especially recommended for doctors. In this approach, the aim is, for example, to measure the oxygen level and the heart rate of a patient affected by the COVID-19 pandemic. These two values can be obtained using a connected oximeter.

In our work we have collected two different measurements which are the oxygen saturation and the heart rate thanks to an IoT device which is the oximeter. Our approach is valid for a multi-sensor solution with several measured data.

4. PROTOTYPE FOR MONITORING PATIENT AFFECTED BY THE COVID-19 PANDEMIC

It is difficult to treat patients contaminated by COVID-19 pandemic, especially because such patients need to be isolated and one meter from them should be kept. Given the delicacy of this disease, it is imperative to provide an improved service and adapt the classic COVID-19 healthcare process. More precisely, we conducted a case study in the infectious diseases Department of Farhat Hached University Hospital in Sousse, Tunisia. The main actors involved in this process are administrative agents, doctors and nurses. Administrative agents are responsible for registering patients and giving them appointments. Doctors and nurses carry out medical tasks such as PCR tests, measurement of SpO2, heart rate and body temperature. They are also in charge of monitoring hospitalized patients affected by COVID-19.

In order to realize our proposed solution, we developed a prototype, which is mainly composed of the Covid-19 disease monitoring framework using the "Symfony" framework in which, patients can be added as well as all the information necessary for the doctor to make the diagnosis. This Framework is developed in order to store the oximeter data generated by the "SPO2 assistant" application delivered with the oximeter, in the database, and also to keep the history of the measurements of each patient and group them all in the same space. Each doctor has his own profile in this Framework, in which he will save the list of patients who have symptoms of covid-19 and consult this doctor. When the measurement is finished, the doctor saves the data in a CSV file then imports this file into the Framework. These measurements become instantly available in the COVID-19 disease monitoring framework. Each new measurement will be added in the table displayed on the screen, sorted by decreasing date and also displayed in the form of a statistical curve. After acquiring the data, the Framework will save the data to the MySQL DBMS system.

Upon connection, the first interface is displayed (figure2). If it's a former patient, the doctor will look for it. He can search either by: last name/first name or by age or by gender or by chronic disease or by more than one variable at the same time. Additionally, the list of all registered patients is displayed.

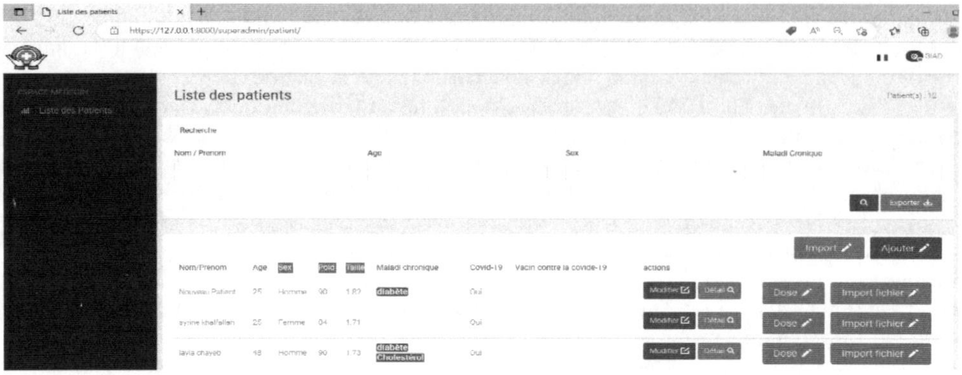

Figure 2. Patient search and list interface

For each patient the doctor can add his last name, first name, gender, weight, height as well as the names of the chronic diseases by which the patient is infected and the name of the COVID-19 vaccine taken by the patient as well as the number of doses taken. Also the doctor can import the different measurements from the different IoT devices that can be used during an assignment by COVID-19. The imported measurements can be viewed by clicking on the "Detail" button in the form of a table and they can also be generated in the form of a statistical curve as shown in figure 3.

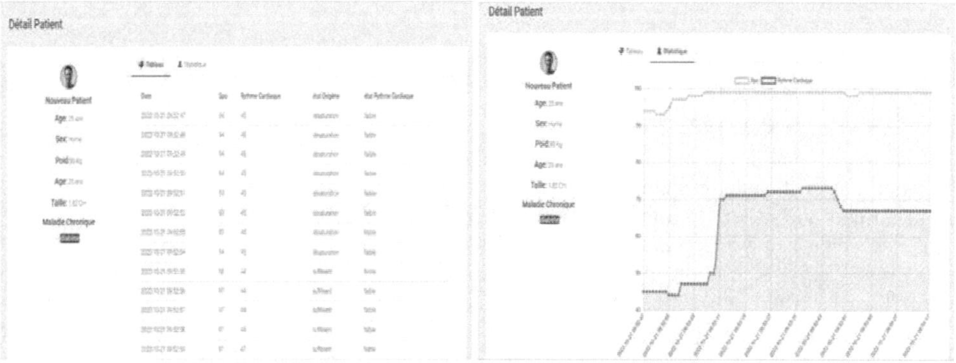

Figure 3. Presentation of SpO2 and heart rate measurements over time in two different forms

5. EXPERIMENTATION OF THE PROPOSED APPROACH

We tested our proposed approach by respecting the various phases of the BPM cycle. We have chosen to apply the model of (Weske, 2019). We have chosen as a concrete case the COVID-19 department of the Farhat Hached University Hospital. Since the treatment of patients contaminated by the COVID-19 pandemic is delicate, especially since this disease requires isolation and requires keeping a distance of one meter from a sick person, we have chosen that the improvement will concern the minimization of the contact between the doctor and the affected patient using one or more connected sensors at a distance of at least one meter and also we have given an analysis study which helps in the diagnosis of the patient's condition, according to the values of the SpO2 and the heartbeat. Then it is possible to predict whether the patient is affected by COVID-19 or not without doing a PCR. Changes and improvements must occur to better facilitate the classic process of treating COVID patients presented by the BPMN model in Figure 4 which we have called the "As-Is model".

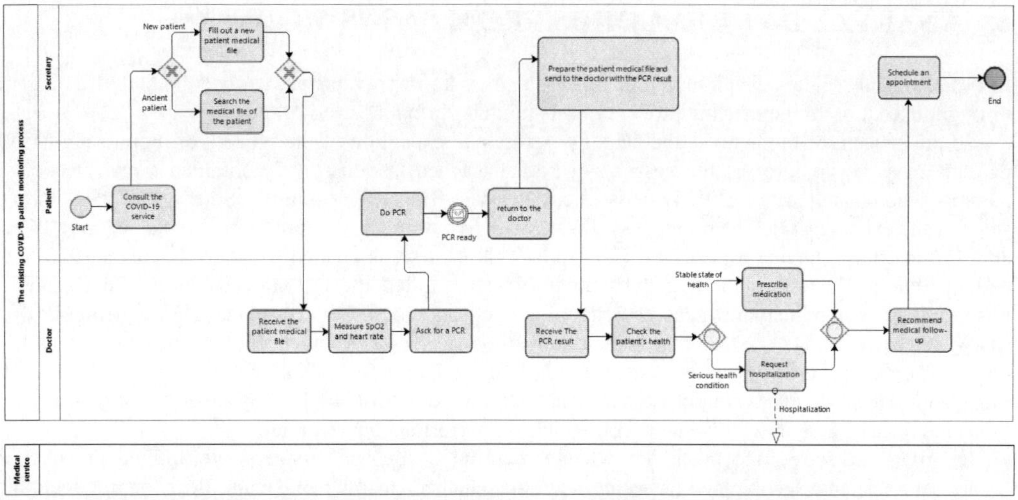

Figure 4. As-Is model: the existing COVID-19 patient monitoring process

This model is triggered when the patient visits the infectious disease department of the hospital and prescribes it for an appointment. The secretary fills out the patient's medical file and then sends it to the doctor, who in turn begins the consultation and monitors the patient's state of health. He/she will first measure the SpO2 level and the heart rate, and then he asks for doing a PCR. If the patient status is very critical, he can decide to hospitalize him/ here before obtaining the result of the PCR. The patient will in turn make an appointment for the PCR, wait for the result for a certain period of time, then he/she returns to the consulting room with the result of the PCR, gives it to the secretary who in turn sends it back to the doctor.

Following this result, the doctor can monitor the patient's condition and specifies medication if the patient's condition is not serious. If the case is critical, he/she asks for hospitalization. In these two cases, the doctor may recommend one or more appointments depending on the improvement in the patient's state of health.

Our contribution will help doctors make decisions based on SpO2 value and heart rate without using PCR.

According to the analysis results of the existing COVID-19 monitoring process, we decided to automate the tasks of filling out medical files and measuring the oxygen level and heart rate using a connected object which is an oximeter, which is placed on the fingertip and measures the oxygen saturation as well as the heart rate. Then we developed an application using the "symfony" framework, we chose to name it "COVID-19 disease monitoring framework". The improved "To-Be process" is presented in figure 5; it allows managing automatic actions.

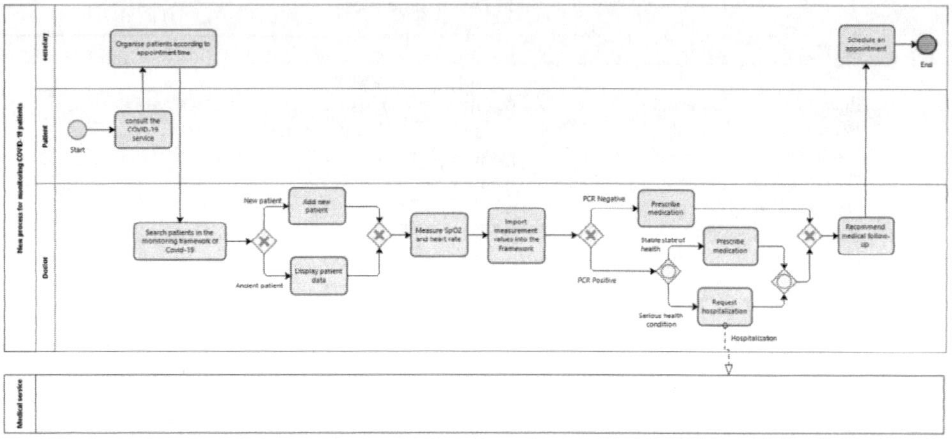

Figure 5. To-Be Model: Improved COVID-19 patient monitoring process

6. ANALYZE DATA RECORDS FROM "AS-IS MODEL"

In order to analyze the behaviour of the process and make improvements, we use the stored data generated throught execution of the existing process (As-Is model) during a period of time.

So our objective is to analyze the actual progress and execution of the process of monitoring COVID-19 patients in its initial form, at the hospital of Farhat Hached in Sousse. We obtained a real Data Set about patients who consulted the COVID department at Farhat Hached Hospital in Sousse and went through the steps of the existing COVID care process. IT includes 64 instances of people who have a negative PCR result and 438 instances, having a positive PCR result. This data set is created between the years 2020 and 2021 and include all the information of the patients who consulted the COVID service of the Farhat Hached hospital in Sousse, namely the measurements of oxygen saturation (SpO2) and cardiac frequency (Pulse).

We cleaned the Data set obtained, by eliminating all the lines which contain missing values (missing data). To obtain a more logical analysis, we balanced the number of people with a negative PCR result with those with a positive PCR. Finally we obtained a structured data set of 152 instances, among which we have 74 negative cases and 78 positive cases, on which we performed our learning.

In order to discover the useful knowledge required by decision-makers, we applied the data mining algorithm to the data set obtained from Sousse Farhat Hached Hospital. We chose decision tree technology as one of the most popular classification technologies. One of the biggest benefits is that it is easy to use and understand even by non-experts.

We were able to extract knowledge from our Data set by the software "Sipina" using the "A Limited search induction tree algorithm" method which led to the construction of the decision tree shown in Figure 6.

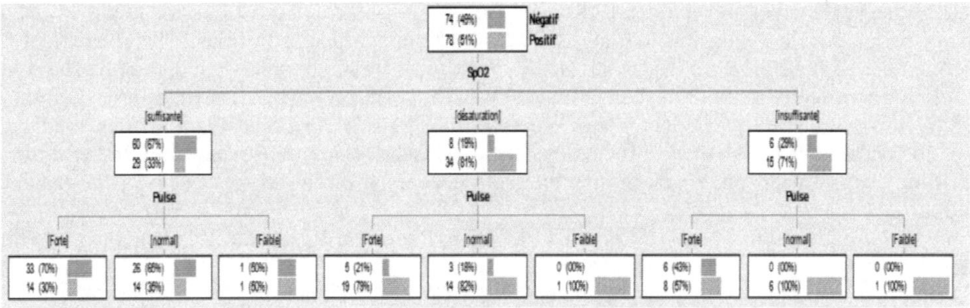

Figure 6. Decision Tree for PCR Result of Patients with COVID-19 Symptoms

We describe the results obtained following the application of the decision tree technique for each value of oxygen and heart rate by the decision rules presented in table 1.

Table 1. Decision rules

SpO2	Pulse	PCR
Enough	Strong	Covid negative (70% cases)
Enough	Normal	Covid negative (65%)
Enough	weak	Patients may be Covid positive/negative (50% of each case)
Desaturation	Strong	Covid positive (79% of cases)
Desaturation	Normal	Covid positive (82%)
Desaturation	weak	Covid positive (100% cases)
Insufficient	Strong	Covid positive (57%)
Insufficient	Normal	Covid positive (100% cases)
Insufficient	weak	Covid positive (100% cases)

The extracted rules corresponding to the decision tree have been validated by a medical expert.

7. EXPERIMENTAL RESULT

According to the results obtained through learning from the real Data Set of the Farhat Hached hospital in Sousse, we were able to propose improvements on the basis of which we defined an improved version of the process. The improvements we propose concern both the patient and the doctor.

In order to facilitate the diagnosis without loss of time, we first propose to minimize the use PCR tests for patients when possible. Given the delicacy of this disease, it will be helpful to eliminate the effort of PCR testing, and mitigate the risk of spreading this pandemic.

Moreover, we offer a decision support system that allows the doctor to make the right choice regarding the patient's state of health without wasting time waiting for the PCR result.

Following the results of the analysis established on the data acquired by the execution of the process in its initial form at the COVID-19 department of the Farhat Hached hospital in Sousse, we have developed a process model based on the analysis of the data of the decision tree shown in Figure 7.

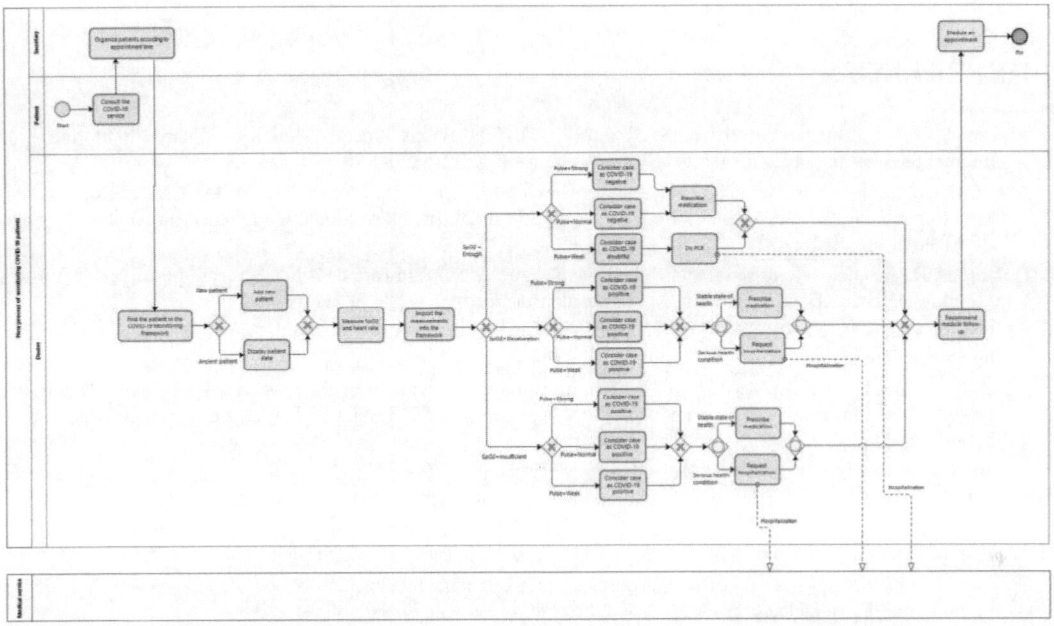

Figure 7. Enhanced COVID-19 patient monitoring process model

In this model, we decided to replace the fragment including the task of PCR detection, wait for the results and return to the consulting room so that the doctor can make his diagnosis according to the result of the PCR and determine the patient's health. All these tasks will be replaced in a way that allows decreasing the waiting time and offering a quick diagnosis to the affected patient without wasting time.

Indeed, the doctor's decisions based on the PCR result have been replaced in the new model by a set of XOR-type gateways, based on the evaluation of the values of oxygen saturation (SpO2) and heart rate (Pulse), in accordance with the obtained decision tree. This made it possible to automate decision-making relating to the patient's state of health without the need, in most cases, to perform a PCR test.

8. CONCLUSION

We have proposed a general model that integrates IoT sensors into the BPM model, and we described the approach according to the business process management life cycle proposed by Weske. Then we applied this model in the field of health particularly in the diagnosis of COVID-19 disease.

We also modeled our approach with BPMN. Then we carried out our approach by developing a prototype consisting essentially of a COVID-19 disease monitoring framework intended for doctors. Finally, we took advantage of learning methods to make decision-making automatic in the proposed process. We propose in this context an analysis through a technique of Data Mining.

Our result is especially valid for people who do not have a chronic disease and have presented symptoms of COVID-19 and not by other diseases which can influence the severity of COVID-19 and their state of health. Our analysis can be complemented by adding other variables from measurements of other chronic disease sensors and studying their effects on COVID-19 symptoms and severity.

This work remains a modest contribution to improving business processes and treating patients infected with COVID-19. It presents multiple perspectives to better optimize, complement and perfect our proposed approach. As future work proposals, we suggest to establish interaction with various connected objects. We can also integrate chronic disease measurement sensors to study the impact of these on COVID-19 and vice versa. Our prototype can also be improved by including a dashboard through which visualizations of data mining and process mining results will be displayed and help in decision making.

REFERENCES

Al-Jamal, D. Y., Eshtaiwi, M. H., & Syed, L. (2017). IOT Based Process Model for Heart Monitoring Process. International Journal of Computer and Systems Engineering, 11(6), 783-788.

Antonius, N., & Dachyar, M. (2020, October). The Internet of Things (IoT) Design for Cardiac Remote Patient Monitoring using Business Process Re-Engineering. In 2020 3rd International Conference on Applied Engineering (ICAE) (pp. 1-7). IEEE.

Domingos, D., Respício, A., & Martinho, R. (2020). Reliability of IoT-aware BPMN healthcare processes. In Virtual and Mobile Healthcare: Breakthroughs in Research and Practice (pp. 793-821). IGI Global.

Dr. Ovidiu Vermesan and Dr. Peter Friess, "Internet of Things: Converging Technologies for Smart Environments and Integrated Ecosystems", River Publishers, 2013 - 364 pages.

Janiesch, C., Koschmider, A., Mecella, M., Weber, B., Burattin, A., Di Ciccio, C., ... & Zhang, L. (2020). The Internet of Things Meets Business Process Management: A Manifesto. IEEE Systems, Man, and Cybernetics Magazine, 6(4), 34-44.

Pascual J,Sanjua´n O,CuevaJM,PelayoBC,A´lvarez M and Gonza´ lez A., "Modeling architecture for collaborative virtual objects based on services", Journal of Network and Computer Applications 2011;34(5):1634–47

Ruiz-Fernández, D., Marcos-Jorquera, D., Gilart-Iglesias, V., Vives-Boix, V., & Ramírez-Navarro, J. (2017). Empowerment of patients with hypertension through BPM, IoT and remote sensing. Sensors, 17(10), 2273.

Weske, M. (2019). Business process management architectures. In Business Process Management (pp. 351-384). Springer, Berlin, Heidelberg.

MANAGEMENT OF CODE REVIEWER RECOMMENDATION USING OPTIMIZATION ALGORITHM, NSGA-III

Zaeem Anwaar and Wasi Haider Butt
Department of Computer and Software Engineering, College of Electrical and Mechanical Engineering (CEME), National University of Sciences and Technology (NUST)
Islamabad, Pakistan

ABSTRACT

Code review is considered as efficient and effective practice to improve software quality, identify and remove defects before integration. Code reviewers having right expertise, experience and apt amount of knowledge with the code being reviewed leads to successful code processes, fewer bugs and less maintenance cost. With the growing size of distributed development teams, picking suitable reviewers is a challenging task. However, due to less resources and shorter deadlines, the management of code reviews and appropriate recommendation of code reviewers based on three objectives consecutively is an ambitious task to be considered as aim of this research. This paper addresses the formulation for managing and recommending code reviewers based on multi conflicting objectives (i.e., availability, expertise and collaboration) simultaneously. Non-sorting genetic algorithm-III (NSGA-III) is used as optimization algorithm to find the most suitable reviewers while keeping expertise and availability ratio high and less collaboration between reviewers and developers. The results were implemented and validated on three (medium to large size) open-source projects named as LibreOffice, Qt and Open-Stack. We calculated precision, recall, mean reciprocal rank (MRR), accuracy for all 3 projects on average. The results from our proposed approach accurately recommended the code reviewers with the precision up to 80%, 86% of recall, 82% MRR and 84% accuracy by improving state-of-the-art. NSGA-III recommended the reviewers in less execution time and better fitness values in comparison to NSGA-II in all experimental sets. The proposed approach could be practical to Modern Code Review (MCR) in order to help developers while recommending suitable code-reviewers in less time and resources to speed up the review process.

KEYWORDS

Code-Reviewer Recommendation, Modern Code Review, Software Development, Multi-Objective Algorithm, NSGA-III

1. INTRODUCTION

Software code review is an integral part of software development and has been in practice for more than three decades. It involves identifying and fixing the defects i.e., logical errors or bugs in a software system, to ensure code quality. A reviewer is requested to review the change and identify the issues with the change, and then recommend further actions to the software developer responsible for the code (Asthana et al., 2019). A series of meetings between the reviewer and the developer are taken place, to ensure a mutual understanding of the change made and the review feedback. The drawback of this manual process of code review is time-consuming and expensive; as the time, effort and experience of the reviewers are not judiciously and efficiently utilized. The purpose is to get a code check-in the shortest possible time as the author/company needs to release the new version of the modified code as early as possible. Thus, a suitable code reviewer is required to serve the purpose of code review. Such a reviewer should possess thorough knowledge, experience and expertise needed for the job and shouldn't be over-committed as well. Only, the reviewer with the requisite expertise and appropriate time may contribute toward efficient examination of the code changes and defects (Chouchen, Ouni, Mkaouer, Kula, & Inoue, 2021).

Over the period, the manual process of assigning a reviewer has evolved into an informal, fully automated, structured and documented approach. It has progressed to a lightweight, quicker and tool-based process named Modern Code Review (Balachandran, 2013). MCR is also known as change-based code review. MCR is a collaborative, quicker and automated approach that ensures that both author and code reviewer follow the standards of code review in a literal manner. Here, the reviewer is assigned to review a specific code, based on certain logic and certain credentials, in an automated manner. Some of the benefits of choosing the reviewer in an automated manner are: **1)** Reviewer is automatically assigned as per certain credentials in a much shorter time frame without compromising other projects. **2)** Human factor / biases which may result in a selection of inappropriate reviewers is eliminated. **3)** All the reviewers share the optimized load. **4)** The selection of the right reviewer (as-per requisite skills, experience and commitment) enhances the quality of the review (Chouchen et al., 2021), (Balachandran, 2013).

This paper proposes to articulate the selection of peer code reviewers as a multi-objective problem using an optimization algorithm 'NSGA-III' (Bhesdadiya, Trivedi, Jangir, Jangir, & Kumar, 2016), (Deb, 2014). Multi-objective optimization is defined as "to find the trade-off balanced optimization between more than one objective". Usually, it is difficult to find such a solution that provides multi-objective optimization because the objectives in the problem are mostly conflicting. To find and propose such solutions, mostly Genetic Algorithms are used. These algorithms consider certain credentials i.e., reviewer's profile, experience, workload, expertise and commitment status, etc. to recommend reviewers. These credentials are termed 'Objectives' and an algorithm may use a single objective, may incorporate multiple objectives, or may utilize many objectives to suggest a reviewer. For example, an algorithm considering only one objective (i.e., experience) may be termed a single objective utilization algorithm. The algorithm that takes into account two or three objectives is termed a multi-objective optimization algorithm and an algorithm taking into account more than three objectives, while deciding on a reviewer, is termed a many-objective algorithm.

The research motivation is to recommend/choose the right reviewers for the code review process more quickly and accurately to save time and resources. Moreover, we validated our approach on 3 open-source projects to confirm its efficiency and accuracy to comparison to the state of the art. The major objectives of the research are as follows: **1)** To reform and organize 3 different open-source project data-sets, that are to be used for Code reviewer recommendation (CRR). **2)** To perform a detailed literature review of the recent research on CRR. **3)** Explore Multi-objective optimization search algorithms. **4)** Propose an approach that navigates between three different proportions/credentials by providing multiple non-dominant peer reviewer recommendations instead of one solution. **5)** Analyzing and validating the precision, recall, MRR and Accuracy of the proposed approach. **6)** Comparison of the results with state-of-the-art.

The rest of the paper is followed as; Section II presents the literature of the related studies. Section III proposes the approach used in the research. Section IV discuss and presents the results. Lastly the paper is concluded.

2. LITERATURE REVIEW

To highlight some related researches, existing work or research that has been done concerning the proposed domain by worthy researchers is analyzed.

Authors (Chouchen et al., 2021) introduced multi-objective search-based approach 'Who-Review' to find the best suitable reviewers for code changing using IBEA (Indicator-Based Evolutionary Algorithm). The recommendation was based on two factors; experience and workload on reviewers. Validation on four open-source projects resulted in an average precision of 68% and recall of 77%.

Researchers (Thongtanunam et al., 2015) proposed 'Rev-Finder' to help developers in finding appropriate reviewers using a file-location based approach. Recommendation was based on finding similarity with the previously reviewed files. The approach was evaluated on 4 different data sets that resulted in accurately recommended 79% of reviews.

In (Balachandran, 2013), an automatic static analysis approach was introduced by authors named 'Review Bot'. It uses various static analysis tools as output to automate the process of checking coding standard violations. A user study was taken into account to validate the tool. The tool also recommended reviewers based on change history of the code. Results showed recommendation accuracy better than the method based on file change history.

'RevRec' (Ouni, Kula, & Inoue, 2016) a search-based approach to suggested reviewers and also to support in decision making for code change submitter was proposed by authors. Genetic algorithm was used to perform the research aim based on their expertise and past collaborations. Authors evaluated the approach on 3 opensource projects and resulted in 59% of precision and 74% of recall.

The most recent and relevant literature to our approach is presented in (Rebai, Amich, Molaei, Kessentini, & Kazman, 2020). The authors formulated the recommendation of code reviewers as a multi-objective search problem to balance the conflicting objectives of expertise, availability, and history of collaborations. Authors used NSGA-II genetic algorithm in their study. 9 open-source projects were used to validate their study. The motivation for our approach is gathered from this study (Rebai et al., 2020) where we have updated the optimization algorithm by using NSGA-III. The authors from an open-source framework 'Pymoo' (Blank & Deb, 2020) for multi-objective optimization in python (Deb & Jain, 2013), (Jain & Deb, 2013) claim that NSGA-II is not much better in optimization of multi-objective (more than two objectives) as compare to NSGA-III (Blank, Deb, & Roy, 2019).

To deal with a large number of possible reviewers for multiple pull requests in terms of multi-objective context is a problem that is under-studied in the research literature. This management process requires handling multiple competing criteria including expertise, availability and previous collaborations with the owners and reviewers.

3. PROPOSED METHODOLOGY

In this section, the recommendation of a most appropriate set of reviewers is presented for pull requests to be reviewed as a framework/approach by using the NSGA-III optimization algorithm. The proposed approach consists of data collection, data pre-processing, main components of the approach, detailed knowledge about NSGA-III (i.e., high-level pseudo-code) algorithm, solution representation, fitness functions and change operators. The high-level diagram for proposed approach is shown in Figure 1. The methodology starts with a project's new pull request to be reviewed is received. The data is collected from the project in terms of its previous pull request information (newly opened, under-review, closed), reviewers' and developers' information, etc.

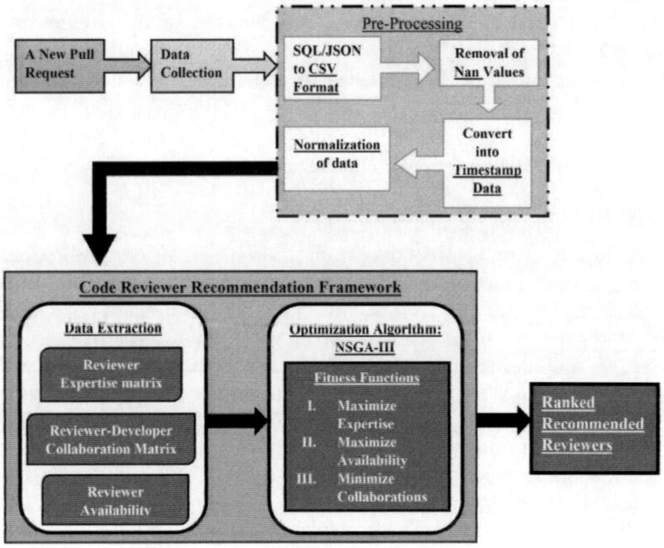

Figure 1. Proposed Approach

3.1 Data Pre-Processing

The data is collected from the link shared by the authors in the literature available at Mining Code Review Repositories (kin-y.github.io) in SQL format. None of the literature shared the data in CSV format. The gathered SQL data was converted into CSV format as it is faster to handle, a standard format and easy to parse. Removal of Not-a-Number (NaN) values from the data was performed by replacing it with zero. The purpose of doing NaN removal was because optimization algorithm's performance and accuracy can't be made sure on NaN data. Also, the data was normalized by doing Min-Max scaling from 0 to 1 so that any outliers from the data-set should be removed. The pre-processed data in CSV format is shared at https://drive.google.com/file/d/1CiZWHc0z_JFZ_Tg7pewTfNZb91o9XzIg/view?usp=sharing as shown in Table 1.

Table 1. Project's Information

Project name	Repository link	Project Duration	Num of pull request (Closed)	Num of pull request (New-Past 7 days)	Num of reviewers
LibreOffice	https://git.libreoffice.org/core	07/2014~12/2021	28030	12	934
Qt	https://code.qt.io/cgit/qt/qtbase.git/	05/2011~11/2021	115888	25	1437
OpenStack	https://opendev.org/openstack	07/2011~12/2021	173749	52	5091

3.2 Code Reviewer Recommendation Framework

This section presents the framework in two steps. Step 1 explains the data extraction from the CSV and step 2 explains the optimization algorithm i.e., NSGA-III and fitness functions (Rebai et al., 2020).

3.2.1 Data Extraction

Three type of matrix formation is implemented to extract data that is required in our approach. Reviewer-Expertise Matrix, Reviewer-Developer Matrix and Reviewer Availability Matrix. Reviewer-Expertise Matrix represents the expertise of the reviewer based on previous commits that has been reviewed by reviewer. The number of times a reviewer is familiar/reviewed a same type of file is counted as his/her expertise. Reviewer-Developer is basically a collaboration matrix for the times when both collaborated on the same files i.e., closed pull requests. Lastly the reviewer availability matrix is formed according to the workload/files being reviewed on current time by the reviewer.

3.2.2 Fitness Functions

Since we are working on a multi-objective optimization so in our approach, we intend to provide optimization on three fitness functions. These three objective functions are Expertise, Availability, and Collaboration. Availability is defined as the inverse of approximated wait until reviewers from their workload (already working on a set of file S) become available. Expertise is estimated by the rank of a reviewer in the set of pool between other reviewers for reviewing a file. Lastly, Collaboration is the summation of all associates between the recommended reviewers chosen to work with a selected set of developers.

We aim to maximize the formulation of expertise and availability of the reviewers while minimizing the fitness function of collaboration due to socio-technical aspects of reviewers and developers in the hope to reduce human biases. The fitness functions are kept the same to literature studies so that a healthy comparison could be brought out of it. The formulas for calculating fitness functions can be explored at (Rebai et al., 2020). All these three-fitness function first values would be collectively passed to NSGA-III a best solution from all of them. The high-level pseudo-code of NSGA-III is available at (Bhesdadiya et al., 2016). The proposed approach is implemented in Python Language on Jupiter Lab (3.0) using Pymoo Library (Blank & Deb, 2020) in our case. While defining problem and Pymoo algorithm library, the change or genetic operators are used. We applied Das-Dennis (Bhesdadiya et al., 2016) approach to define reference points. The rest of the genetic operator used in results are explained in Table 2. The literature results are computed using random selection (to compare with state of the art), we have used tournament selection in one experiment (to give a new horizon for future comparison). We used 'Uniform ('real ux', 'bin ux', 'int ux') Crossover' and 'Polynomial ('real pm', 'int pm') Mutation' to explore and exploit the search space.

Table 2. Experimental Genetic Operators

Experiment Number	Pop Size	Selection Operator	Crossover Operator	Crossover Probability	Mutation Operator	Mutation rate	Number of Generation
Exp. 1	50	Random	Uniform	0.5	Polynomial	0.01	500
Exp. 2	50	Random	Uniform	0.6	Polynomial	0.1	450
Exp. 3	100	Random	Uniform	0.8	Polynomial	0.2	550
Exp. 4	200	Random	Uniform	0.5	Polynomial	0.1	550
Exp. 5	200	Random	Uniform	0.8	Polynomial	0.05	600
Exp. 6	100	Tournament	Uniform	0.85	Polynomial	0.2	500

4. RESULTS AND DISCUSSION

Precision, recall, Mean Reciprocal Rank (MRR) and average accuracy were calculated to compare our results with state-of-the-art.

$$Pricision@Exp = \frac{TP}{TP + FP} \quad (1) \qquad Recall@Exp = \frac{TP}{TP + FN} \quad (2)$$

In equation (1) and (2), TP (True Positive) corresponds to the number of top-k reviewers recommended by the approach and also actual reviewers. FP (False Positive) corresponds to the number of top-k reviewers recommended by the approach, but not actual reviewers; FN (False Negative) corresponds to the number of actual reviewers, that are not among the top-k reviewers recommended by the approach.TN (True Negative) corresponds to the number of not actual reviewers, that are also not among the top-k reviewers recommended by the approach.

MRR (Mean Reciprocal Rank): The average rank of correct reviewers in the recommendation list. Given a reviewers recommendation lists R, the score MRR is calculated with the help of equation (3).

$$MRR = \frac{|\Sigma \forall r \epsilon R| rank(r)}{|R|} \quad (3)$$

where rank(r) is the rank score of the first reviewer in the recommendation list r. The higher is the MRR score, the better is the recommendation rank approach.

Average Accuracy of Projects: The projects accuracy is determined as average accuracy in terms of number of experiments performed in that project. The average accuracy Equation. (4) is determined as:

$$Average\ Accuracy = \frac{\Sigma Accuracy(E1 + E2 \ldots EN)}{N} \quad (4)$$

Where E1 is the accuracy of experiment 1, E2 is the accuracy of experiment 2 till last Experiment. The N is the total number of Experiments used in a project.

The efficiency and precision to identify relevant code reviewers by using of our proposed approach i.e., NSGA-III is confirmed on pull requests from 3 different projects are resulted in table III IV and figure no 2 & 3. Tables 3 and 4 shows the precision and recall in context to every experiment result separately. For example, LibreOffice has a precision ranging from 51% to 67% for all experiments. It has a recall range from 52% to 75%. Qt project has precision range of 50% to 69% and recall rate ranging from 58% to 73%. Whereas Open-Stack project has the highest precision value of 80% and recall ranging from 69-86%. Due to large number of reviewers in the projects (i.e., Qt, LibreOffice) the precision rate of 50% or 51% in projects could also be considered acceptable. Also, some of the highest recall scores are obtained in Open-Stack as some pull request require more than one code reviewer. The highlighted/bold results in both the tables are the best ones identified.

Table 3. Precision Comparison with literature

Project Name	Experiment number	Precision@Exp.					
		Proposed Approach (NSGA-III)	**AEC (NSGA-II)**	**RevRec (GA)**	**Who Review (IBEA)**	**RevFinder**	**ReviewBot**
LibreOffice	**Exp. 1**	**0.64**	N/A	0.52	0.61	0.48	0.38
	Exp. 2	**0.59**	N/A	0.45	0.54	0.4	0.36
	Exp. 3	**0.57**	N/A	0.50	0.56	0.42	0.40
	Exp. 4	0.52	N/A	0.41	**0.53**	0.32	0.32
	Exp. 5	**0.51**	N/A	0.39	0.46	0.3	0.23
	Exp. 6	**0.67**	N/A	N/A	N/A	N/A	N/A
Qt	**Exp. 1**	**0.66**	0.58	0.49	0.58	0.3	0.22
	Exp. 2	**0.62**	0.51	0.42	0.53	0.27	0.19
	Exp. 3	**0.57**	0.54	0.45	0.55	0.29	0.13
	Exp. 4	**0.55**	0.52	0.41	0.43	0.21	0.10
	Exp. 5	**0.50**	0.46	0.34	0.48	0.16	0.09
	Exp. 6	**0.69**	N/A	N/A	N/A	N/A	N/A
OpenStack	**Exp. 1**	**0.74**	0.70	0.59	0.62	0.32	0.24
	Exp. 2	**0.69**	0.64	0.57	0.55	0.27	0.2
	Exp. 3	**0.67**	0.65	0.51	0.59	0.30	0.22
	Exp. 4	**0.63**	**0.63**	0.43	0.54	0.25	0.16
	Exp. 5	**0.57**	0.54	0.46	0.48	0.21	0.11
	Exp. 6	**0.80**	N/A	N/A	N/A	N/A	N/A

Table 4. Recall Comparison with literature

Project Name	Experiment number	Recall@Exp.					
		Proposed Approach (NSGA-III)	**AEC (NSGA-II)**	**RevRec (GA)**	**Who Review (IBEA)**	**RevFinder**	**ReviewBot**
LibreOffice	**Exp. 1**	**0.67**	N/A	0.34	0.48	0.32	0.18
	Exp. 2	**0.62**	N/A	0.48	0.52	0.38	0.22
	Exp. 3	**0.59**	N/A	0.57	0.56	0.42	0.20
	Exp. 4	0.59	N/A	0.58	**0.61**	0.45	0.31
	Exp. 5	**0.69**	N/A	0.59	0.68	0.49	0.38
	Exp. 6	**0.75**	N/A	N/A	N/A	N/A	N/A
Qt	**Exp. 1**	**0.58**	0.56	0.41	0.44	0.14	0.09
	Exp. 2	**0.62**	0.60	0.50	0.45	0.27	0.16
	Exp. 3	**0.68**	0.66	0.55	0.58	0.30	0.20

	Exp. 4	**0.72**	0.68	0.59	0.60	0.35	0.24
	Exp. 5	**0.73**	0.70	0.65	0.64	0.43	0.30
	Exp. 6	**0.67**	N/A	N/A	N/A	N/A	N/A
OpenStack	**Exp. 1**	**0.69**	0.59	0.31	0.46	0.15	0.12
	Exp. 2	**0.70**	0.68	0.39	0.49	0.29	0.2
	Exp. 3	**0.78**	0.76	0.52	0.59	0.37	0.32
	Exp. 4	**0.80**	0.75	0.54	0.60	0.46	0.39
	Exp. 5	**0.82**	0.80	0.66	0.63	0.50	0.41
	Exp. 6	**0.86**	N/A	N/A	N/A	N/A	N/A

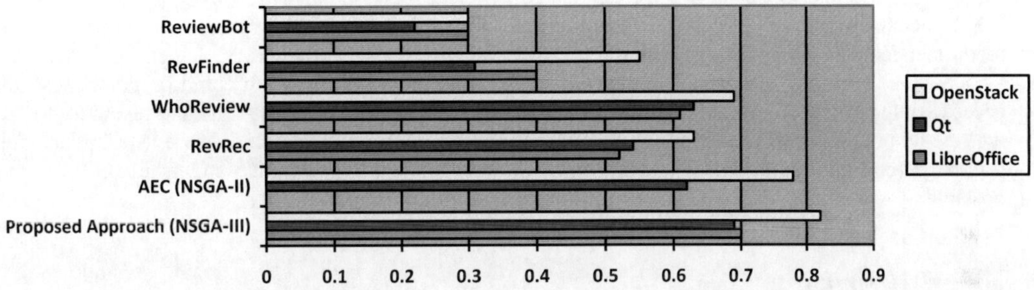

Figure 2. Mean Reciprocal Rank Chart

Figure 2 shows the MRR values that NSGA-III was able to efficiently rate the recommended code reviewers. The best resulted solution of the last population obtained in the last iteration of GA are copied in a single pool. Then, the rank of each reviewer corresponds to his frequency count in the pool. That is, reviewers that are recommended in many solutions are ranked first. The proposed approach shows the MRR values better than all other presented in literature. LibreOffice came up with 70%, Qt with 69% and Open-Stack with highest 82% MRR scores. The efficiency for ranking the reviewers is measured by this parameter so the outcomes of MRR are very important. Additionally, it is one of the main motivations of this proposed approach as ranking is directly related to availability and collaboration of code reviewers.

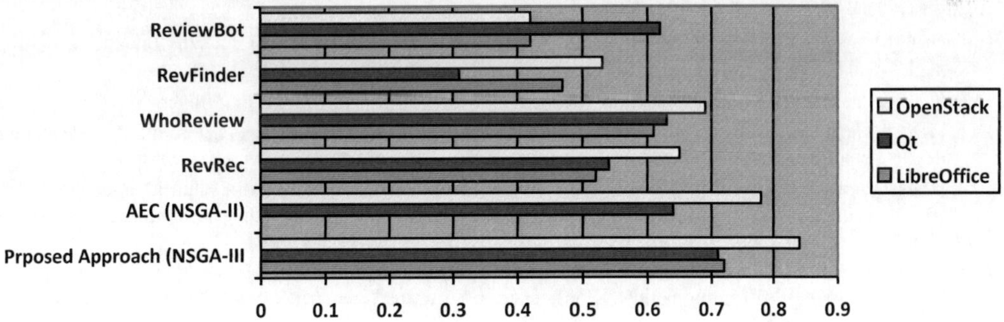

Figure 3. Average Accuracy Chart

Figure 3 presents the average accuracy of our approach on experiments. The accuracy of each experiment is calculated separately and then average of accuracy's is calculated as discussed in equations 9 and 10. LibreOffice came up with 72%, Qt with 71% and Open-Stack with highest 84% Average Accuracy scores which are better than all others approach.

Most importantly our proposed technique doesn't have a bias towards the projects that are used for validation as we used average values of mean reciprocal rank and accuracy. Out of 3 open-source projects, our proposed approach performed well on Open-Stack pull requests. The accuracy, MRR, precision and recall of the project was good in comparison to other projects.

5. CONCLUSION

In this research, we have proposed a multi objectives problem to manage and recommend code reviewers by adopting an optimization algorithm that is NSGA-III. The purpose is to recommend the best trade-off reviewers between three conflicting objectives i.e., maximizing the availability and expertise of reviewers and minimizing the collaboration between developers and reviewers to lessen the human biases factor. We implemented and evaluated our approach on three (medium to large size) open-source projects named as LibreOffice, Qt and Open-Stack. We calculated efficiency on our approach by finding precision, recall, MRR, accuracy for all 3 projects on average. The results from our proposed approach accurately recommended the code reviewers with the precision up to 80%, 86% of recall, 82% mean reciprocal rank and 84% average accuracy by improving state-of-the-art. The proposed approach could be practical to MCR in order to help developers while recommending suitable code-reviewers in less time and resources to speed up the review process. This research highlighted the importance of managing code reviews to reduce delays in review process in less time and resources while confirming high expertise and availability as much as possible.

REFERENCES

Asthana, S., Kumar, R., Bhagwan, R., Bird, C., Bansal, C., Maddila, C., ... Ashok, B. (2019). *WhoDo: automating reviewer suggestions at scale.* Paper presented at the Proceedings of the 2019 27th ACM Joint Meeting on European Software Engineering Conference and Symposium on the Foundations of Software Engineering.

Balachandran, V. (2013). *Reducing human effort and improving quality in peer code reviews using automatic static analysis and reviewer recommendation.* Paper presented at the 2013 35th International Conference on Software Engineering (ICSE).

Bhesdadiya, R. H., Trivedi, I. N., Jangir, P., Jangir, N., & Kumar, A. J. C. E. (2016). An NSGA-III algorithm for solving multi-objective economic/environmental dispatch problem. *3*(1), 1269383.

Blank, J., Deb, K., & Roy, P. C. (2019). *Investigating the normalization procedure of NSGA-III.* Paper presented at the International Conference on Evolutionary Multi-Criterion Optimization.

Blank, J., & Deb, K. J. I. A. (2020). Pymoo: Multi-objective optimization in python. *8*, 89497-89509.

Chouchen, M., Ouni, A., Mkaouer, M. W., Kula, R. G., & Inoue, K. J. A. S. C. (2021). WhoReview: A multi-objective search-based approach for code reviewers recommendation in modern code review. *100*, 106908.

Deb, K. (2014). Multi-objective optimization. In *Search methodologies* (pp. 403-449): Springer.

Deb, K., & Jain, H. J. I. t. o. e. c. (2013). An evolutionary many-objective optimization algorithm using reference-point-based nondominated sorting approach, part I: solving problems with box constraints. *18*(4), 577-601.

Jain, H., & Deb, K. J. I. T. o. e. c. (2013). An evolutionary many-objective optimization algorithm using reference-point based nondominated sorting approach, part II: Handling constraints and extending to an adaptive approach. *18*(4), 602-622.

Ouni, A., Kula, R. G., & Inoue, K. (2016). *Search-based peer reviewers recommendation in modern code review.* Paper presented at the 2016 IEEE International Conference on Software Maintenance and Evolution (ICSME).

Rebai, S., Amich, A., Molaei, S., Kessentini, M., & Kazman, R. J. A. S. E. (2020). Multi-objective code reviewer recommendations: balancing expertise, availability and collaborations. *27*(3), 301-328.

Thongtanunam, P., Tantithamthavorn, C., Kula, R. G., Yoshida, N., Iida, H., & Matsumoto, K.-i. (2015). *Who should review my code? a file location-based code-reviewer recommendation approach for modern code review.* Paper presented at the 2015 IEEE 22nd International Conference on Software Analysis, Evolution, and Reengineering (SANER).

MULTIMODAL DIGITAL ASSISTANT FOR A SMART FOOD PROCESSOR: A DESIGN SCIENCE APPROACH

Amitrajit Sarkar[1], Nicholas Leslie[2], John Ascroft[2], Ralph Bergmann[3], Lilly Heindl[3] and Markus Westner[4]
[1]*ARA Institute of Canterbury, New Zealand*
[2]*Jade Software Corporation, New Zealand*
[3]*BSH Hausgeräte GmbH, Germany*
[4]*OTH Regensburg, Germany*

ABSTRACT

This paper presents the results of a comprehensive research project on the integration of an alternative human-computer interaction interface in home appliances, using a design science research approach. The outcome of the project is a user interface concept and prototype with a focus on multimodal design that incorporates voice commands and manual interaction to reduce friction and improve user experience. The paper presents the design and development of an offline natural language processing (NLP)-based application for a food processor, which allows users to interact with the appliance through voice-based interaction. The research and testing of offline NLP solutions is detailed, and the results of research into alternative user interfaces for smart home appliances are presented. The findings suggest that external application programming interface (API) solutions such as Google's should be used for conversational API services, and that natural language understanding service implementations can be extended to provide additional functionality. The results illustrate an alternative novel and effective approach to user interaction with smart home appliances.

KEYWORDS

Digital Assistant, Design Science Research, Design Artifact Development, Innovation, Artificial Intelligence

1. INTRODUCTION

Nowadays, digital assistants that are primarily operated through voice commands, have become a part of daily interaction of users with computer systems (Fernandes and Oliveira, 2021). Popular and commonly used assistants are provided by the global technology companies such as Amazon ("Alexa"), Apple ("Siri"), or Google. Aside from those appliance- or phone-related assistants, voice-based human-computer interaction, also plays a significant role in other application scenarios, such as cars (Scates, 2022). Another field for, partially artificial intelligence (AI)-based, digital assistants are home appliances.

In 2020/2021 we had an opportunity to be part of an international virtual collaboration project. The multinational project involved two business organizations, and two academic institutions, with equal representation from Germany and New Zealand.

Based on the generic user story of our artifact development we will here narrate the scenario which is like the scenario described by Maedche et al. (2019): It is an illustration of a digital assistant powered by AI interacting in the scenario of a smart kitchen. When cooking in the kitchen, a user can activate a food processor without touching the appliance's switch by interacting with a speech-based conversational agent (such as Alexa or Siri). The AI-powered digital assistant uses the audio recordings as input, analyzes the speech, and attempts to comprehend the language. The anticipated action is chosen as part of dialogue management (e.g., the food processor is turned on via the connected smart sensors). Finally, text-to-speech synthesis is used to produce and convey a confirming answer to the user.

Current interactions with the system are achieved by the front panel touch display. This display shows cooking information and helps guide the user through the cooking process. The food processing system has 140 recipes included and more can be downloaded. The system can then give step-by-step instructions displayed on the panel. The goal of this project is to rethink the user interaction process of the smart home appliance and research the viability of integrating alternative human-computer interaction into home appliances. The project stakeholders have stated four questions concerning rethinking the user interaction process of home appliances:

1. "Can we speed up the setting process by telling the appliance what we need and want?"
2. "How can we easily configure the user settings instead of reading manuals and complicated menus?"
3. "How can we find relevant functions quickly?"
4. "How can we interact with the UI manually and via voice command?"

The primary goal of this paper is to inform the community of researchers and practitioners of how we have conducted, evaluated, and present design science research. The output of this project is to produce a user interface (UI) concept and prototype with a focus on a multimodal design (traditional touch interactions and a new voice-based interaction). This prototype will include voice commands along with manual interaction.

This will have the benefit of offering alternative methods of interacting with the food processor, increase the speed at which the appliance takes to set up, ease configuration, reduce the need for traversing complicated menus, and reduce the need for reading product manuals. This will take the user to the relevant menu quickly and efficiently, and help the user reach their goal quickly allowing them to be up and cooking with little friction.

2. RESEARCH APPROACH

In this research, we adhere to the design-science paradigm (Hevner et al., 2004) which aims to push the boundaries of human and organizational capabilities by creating new and innovative artifacts. According to Hevner et al., 2004, design science paradigm is a problem-solving paradigm: Based on the identification of a problem, a potential solution is derived based on the combination of existing knowledge and new ideas. The potential solution is subsequently iteratively implemented and evaluated and, ultimately, contributes to and extends the current body of knowledge. Hevner et al., 2004, define seven ideas that can guide design science-driven research. We will briefly outline the seven ideas and mention how we implement those in our research.

1. Design Science Research aims at a real result (artifact). This can be a method, a model, or a product. The artifact designed must achieve a practical use. In our project we develop a speech interface for a home appliance.

2. Problem Relevance: The result must solve an existing and current practical problem. In our project, we examine how speech recognition and control can be attached to a device lacking this functionality.

3. Design evaluation: Whether the result solves the problem must be evaluated in a methodologically clean way. The literature provides numerous established methods that can be applied for this purpose - from user testing to case studies to controlled usability lab tests. In the paper at hand, we relied on user testing.

4. Research Contributions: In addition to the artifact solving the practice problem, there must also be a generally applicable contribution. In the paper at hand, we generate the lessons learnt from the use of the artifact in a particular industry or domain and generalize the artifact itself.

5. Research rigor: Correctly apply established methods from the literature in developing and evaluating the outcome. In our paper, we follow proven software development and testing methods.

6. Design as an optimization problem: With Design Science Research, the result is incrementally developed in search of the "perfect" solution that satisfies all constraints. While, due to capacity constraints, we could not strive for the "perfect" solution, we evaluated several solution problems and iterated towards the most effective solution.

7. Communication: The research contribution must be made accessible to the professional public. This is achieved by the publication at hand.

3. DESIGN OF AN ARTIFACT

3.1 Natural Language Processing (NLP) Background

Spoken dialogue systems are an example of an advanced application of spoken language technology. Dialogue systems represent an interface between the user and a computer-based application that allows for interaction with the application in a natural manner based on NLP (Cenek, 2005). NLP was one of the fundamental aspects of the project and one of the cornerstone pieces needed for project success. NLP is concerned with how human language is interpreted by a computer. NLP includes speech recognition (speech to text transcriptions), natural language understanding (the machine's reading comprehension), and natural language generation (turning data into natural, human-like language). Natural language generation was not included in this project. NLP is what makes up the conversational chatbot service at the center of this application.

Speech recognition is the process of transforming spoken language (in our case, recorded audio recorded after triggering the assistant service) into text. This text transcription is used by the later steps in the NLP process.

Natural Language Understanding (NLU) is inferring intent and comprehending what the input text is saying. Text is analyzed to determine things such as concepts, entities, keywords, relationships, and what the purpose of the text is (IBM, 2022). Effectively, NLU leads to a computer understanding what you have said.

These concepts are put into practice to produce any dialogue system where the applications that can perform tasks such as answering questions and can have conversations with humans. For example, a user could ask a dialogue system to update their address stored in the database. The dialogue system in response would be able to comprehend the request, ask follow-up questions such as, "What is your new address?", and forward the request to the appropriate services.

3.2 NLP Terminology

The following paragraphs provide an overview of relevant NLP terminology used in this paper.

Intent: What the user wants to do. For example, alter the screen's brightness or change the current system language.

Entities: Variables that are part of a request sent to the chatbot and extract from a sentence. For example, in the statement, "decrease screen brightness by 50", the entities that would be extracted are "decrease" and "50". These entities can be used by the system later, along with the current intent, "change screen brightness", to alter the screen brightness.

Utterances: These are the phrases the dialogue service is trained upon and uses to determine intent. They are different ways to say the same thing. For example, for the "change screen brightness" intent, the utterances could be "decrease screen brightness", "alter screen brightness", "dim the screen", "reduce brightness".

3.3 Artifact Design Steps

During the development phase of this project, many applications and options were investigated. We created a system that utilized all-online services, such as Google's APIs, but later transitioned the entire project to all-offline.

The application was developed in two components. One was the backend; the section that would handle the applications settings, supply the audio recording and playback features, support the Speech-to-Text (STT), NLU, and Text-to-Speech (TTS) processes, and query external APIs. The front-end was developed as a separate application to decouple it from the backend.

Communication between the two applications was formed through Socket.IO, a WebSocket technology used for real-time communication between a server and a client (Socket.IO, 2022). This allowed for two-way communication between the applications. When a setting was altered from the backend, it would emit an event to the frontend informing it of the change, and vice-versa.

The application supports switching between online-only services and offline-only services, as well as a hybrid of the two. For example, taking advantage of the accuracy of Google's STT allow with the speed provided from the offline NLU and TTS.

The backend was developed using TypeScript and NodeJS. Hotword detection provided by Snowboy, Speech-to-Text provided by Google's STT and Mozilla DeepSpeech, NLU/Chatbot services provided by Google's Dialogflow and NLP.js, Text-to-Speech provided by Google's TTS and Espeak, Authorisation service provided by ExpressJS.

The backend has been developed to ensure modularity. This ensures that all features can be replaced with alternatives. This helped ease the development process when transitioning from online to offline.

It displays a recreation of the pre-existing UI found on the food processor. The UI was created using TypeScript and VueJS 2, along with Vue-i18n (for internationalization support). Special attention was made to ensure the front end mimicked the existing UI in as much detail as possible. This includes animations, loading screens, page transitions, dropdown menus, and icons.

The UI was created using web technologies, as opposed to developing it with Qt (a UI framework for C++ currently used for the food processor), due to the speed at which we could develop the UI with VueJS. The development team did not have experience with C++ or the Qt framework, and since the speed of development was important, the development team decided to focus on what they knew as opposed to learning new technology.

Each screen, found on the Food Processor, was recreated on the UI concept, with focus made on the Recipes page and Settings page.

The UI introduced an "Assistant" pop-up, like the Siri animation on iPhones. This was provided by the graphics department at one of the participating organisations. When the user activates the assistant, either from the backend or frontend, an animated ring appears in the middle of the screen. This is to inform the user that the assistant is listening and provides feedback when the assistant has stopped listening. Figure 1 shows the completed UI screen examples.

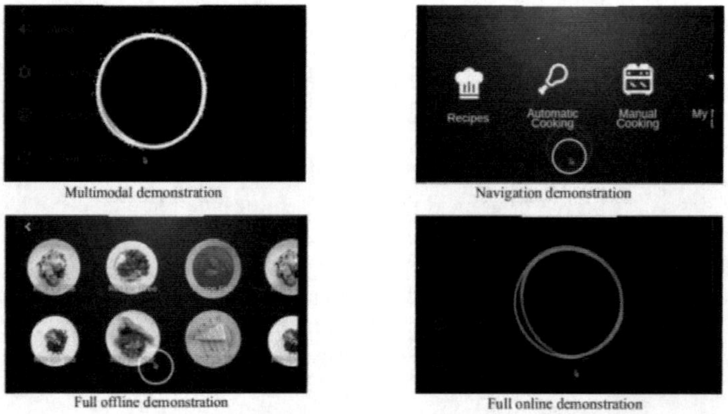

Figure 1. UI Screen examples

A minimal investigation was performed when developing the original, online-only, application. This was based on the recommendations of the industry supervisor. Since they had experience with online technology from previous projects, they recommended utilized the Google Cloud APIs. These included Google's Speech-to-Text, Google's Dialogflow, and Google's Text-to-Speech.

These three services provided the underlying chatbot services. The user would speak into a microphone, it would be recorded and streamed to the Google Speech-to-Text API. A response would be returned to what the user said. This transcription would be forwarded to Dialogflow. Dialogflow is an NLU service provided by Google. From here, an intent was inferred, entities extracted, and returned to the application. If Dialogflow required more information, it would trigger the Text-to-Speech service. This would turn a follow-up request from Dialogflow into an audio file that would be played to the user. This would prompt the user to continue speaking so Dialogflow could get all the information required. From here, the request would alter the system settings, update the current screen, or query the Home Connect service.

During the implementation of these processes, we discovered that remote users (the testers in Germany) needed to recreate the cloud infrastructure on their end, due to the security issues arising from transmitting the Google credentials files (a file used to ensure you are a valid user that can call that Google services. This file is unique to an organization and losing track of it could cause the particular organisation to infer increased costs of these cloud services). Sharing this file is considered “bad practice” (Steffres, 2018).

What was done to remedy this situation was to create “API-middlemen”. API-middlemen are small servers that handle incoming requests, from a user, and make the request to a service on behalf of that user. The small server knows the credentials needed to access that service and can then return the results from that service. These small servers could be full, traditional servers hosted on a computer somewhere, or (in our case) cloud functions.

Cloud functions are a serverless framework that automatically runs the backend code when a request is made to it and deactivates the backend after a short period (Firebase, n.d.). This works like traditional servers but is designed for small, lightweight processes. This would be perfect for something that would just forward the user’s requests and return results. We used Firebase Cloud Functions for these ephemeral API-middleman servers.

Dialogflow also supports a streamlined process of providing it with an audio file, it will be able to transcribe that into text, process it through the Dialogflow chatbot, and return an audio file in response. This process was implemented to speed up the online processes and reduce the need for querying three different online services. This increased performance substantially but couples the solution to one service. This is an option that can be picked if needed.

Before we transitioned to all-offline, we spent numerous weeks researching and testing different offline solutions. For the Speech-to-Text solutions, we investigated Mozilla’s DeepSpeech, Kaldi, and PocketSphinx by Carnegie Mellon University. For the NLU service, we investigated NLP.js by AXA, and Botpress from Botpress, Inc. For the Text-to-Speech service, we investigated Espeak, Flite, Picotts, Nanotts, MaryTTS, and Mozilla Voice TTS.

For the Speech-to-Text, we investigated multiple options but decided upon Mozilla’s DeepSpeech. This was chosen for its ease of installation, the large development community, ease of extension to support new languages and new language models, and its overall accuracy during testing. Mozilla’s DeepSpeech has issues with the provided language models. These models are, mostly, trained on audio provided by American males in quiet environments (Morais, 2020). This will need to be considered if this service was to be used in future iterations of the application.

For the NLU service, NLP.js was chosen. This was picked because NLP.js was easy to install, open-source, extensive documentation, lightweight and performant for low-computational environments (such as a Raspberry Pi), easy to use and implement new intents and entities, and come with an optional UI that could be added in, if needed. The benefit of having the UI be an optional extra meant it wouldn’t take up resources in an already constrained environment. The offline NLU service performed similarly to Google’s Dialogflow and worked exceptionally well for our use case.

For the Text-to-Speech, Espeak was chosen. Espeak was picked for its ease of installation and low computational overhead. Espeak is not as human as the online version (Google’s Text-to-Speech), but most on-device options were poor quality to reduce the computational power required. Mozilla’s TTS was investigated but due to the lack of documentation, it was discarded.

During the development of this application, we contributed to three open-source repositories. These changes have been merged into the master codebase or waiting for pull-request to be integrated.

Improvements were made to the “Dialogflow-NLP-to-nlpjs”, an application to convert a Dialogflow chatbot into a format that can be read by NLP.js. Improvements to defensive checks of input data ensured any language could be selected and ensured that asynchronous code was called correctly.

Additional code was added to “bumblebee-hotword-node”, a NodeJS package used to listen to hotwords uttered by a user. Changes were made to ensure an audio device could be selected for Unix operating systems (Leslie, ncpleslie/bumblebee-hotword-node, 2020).

Further contributions to the open-source community were made with “node-speaker”, a NodeJS package for playing audio through a hardware speaker. Contributions were made to their TypeScript declarations to ensure all features were supported when in a TypeScript environment.

The extensive focus was made to ensure all services support both English and German languages, at a minimum.

The assistant and backend processes, including STT, NLU, TTS, can support multiple languages. The total number of languages each service can support is discussed in Findings and Recommendations. The bottleneck for language support will be the NLU process. This is due to having to create custom chatbot intents, entities, and responses for each language. The STT and TTS will support a large assortment of languages out of the box or will require updating their models to support more languages. Adding new languages to the NLU chatbot service is documented in the guides provided with the source code and is as simple as adding new intents to the chatbot service.

Frontend internationalization currently supports only the German and English languages. This is facilitated by provided language files along with the UI. The process of adding new languages is documented in the documentation provided with the code. Switching the displayed language can be triggered by tapping the preferred language in the settings menu, or through the voice assistant by saying, "Change language". This will refresh the UI and display the newly selected language.

4. FINDINGS AND RECOMMENDATIONS

Hotword recognition is a low-power, low-cost process. The findings of the hotword detection services we investigate (Snowboy and Porcupine) were both fast enough to provide instant activation. The major differences between the two services were:

Snowboy offered custom hotword support but must be manually trained, with large datasets (500 instances for English, 2000 instances for German (Snowboy, 2022). That means that the custom wake words will require voice recordings of the hundreds of different people in multiple sound environments. This is fine for personal projects, but for commercial products, this could be expensive and bothersome. Snowboy can run on many architectures. We developed with Snowboy on an ARM processor, but it also tested on an x86 processor.

Porcupine offers out-of-the-box universal hotwords (will support many user's voices). These phrases include "bumblebee", "grasshopper", "porcupine", and "hey, Edison", and will work on most device architectures (ARM and x86). This will work well for personal projects but not excellent for commercial products. Porcupine does offer custom wake words, but due to the costs involved with training custom hotwords for ARM processors, their custom wake word service was unable to be tested (Picovoice, 2022). This option could be explored if a commercial product is to be released.

We investigated and implemented two speech-to-text options, Google's STT and Mozilla's DeepSpeech. We found that both were able to perform the task of speech-to-text on the Raspberry Pi. The quality of their transcriptions was vastly different.

Mozilla DeepSpeech performed the worst of the two, with the accuracy of transcriptions far below Google's offering. During testing, phrases were repeated to the device and DeepSpeech would detect differing statements, even though the same sentence was said. When the phrase, "Decrease screen brightness by 50" was uttered to the device, the results returned would include phrases such as, "Dennis, screen brighter bye thief tee". This is most likely caused by the voice models being trained on American male voices and lacking support for New Zealand accents. The DeepSpeech models can be extended and trained if additional voice data is provided. Considerations will have to be made for each new language and country Bosch wished to ship the product. The English voice model is over 1 gigabyte in size (Steffres, 2018).

Google's Speech-to-Text service provided excellent transcription will minimal computation required on the device. Google's STT service can provide transcriptions in 71 different languages and 127 different locales (Barnes, 2020), including New Zealand English, Indian English. This will reduce the need to train custom models or rely on the open-source community to train them for you.

Considerations will need to be made with data privacy. Since DeepSpeech is all performed on-device, data is kept on the device. Google's STT services do log data, but "no logging" and on-premises options are available where data privacy is required (Google Cloud, n.d.).

Our recommendation is to use an external API, such as Google. It will provide a well-trained conversational API, will support multiple languages, will use low computational power, and provide accuracy of their service. But an "on-prem" solution could be considered if data privacy is paramount.

We implemented two NLU services in this application, Google's Dialogflow and AXA's NLP.js. In terms of the accuracy of intent detection, we found similar results between the two.

The major differences between the two come down to how you extend the functionality of the NLU services. Since Google's Dialogflow is an online service, extending it can be simply down through the browser. This has the benefit of updating the service for all users using the service. NLP.js will need to be provided with an update to support new intents. New functionality for NLP.js can be included by updating a JSON file included with the source code.

Google's Dialogflow can support all the processes required to make a functioning chatbot service. This includes Speech-to-Text, NLU, and Text-to-Speech. This will reduce the processing times but couple the chatbot service to one solution.

Our recommendations are to pick whichever option is the most convenient. Both options perform exceptionally well, require low computation overhead, and can be upgraded relatively simply. Considerations will need to be made with Google's services as data logging will occur.

During development, we investigated multiple Text-to-Speech options. These included Google's Text-to-Speech, Mozilla's TTS, Espeak, Flite, Picotts, Nanotts, MaryTTS. We concluded that all on-device offerings we of much lower quality (less human-sounding) than those options offered by Google's Text-to-Speech.

Google's TTS was fast and high quality, with life-like voices (Google Cloud, 2022). It also supports more languages than any of the other services we investigated. Google supports over 40 languages and 220 different voices.

Of the on-device TTS options that were investigated: Mozilla TTS, Espeak, Flite, Picotts, Nanotts, MaryTTS, one was difficult to install (Mozilla) and the rest were low quality and robotic sounding. The research we made determined that high-quality, humanlike TTS would require large computational power. Some research said that the Raspberry Pi could be six times slower than real-time (Stoker, 2020), well beyond any practical use.

Although Speech-to-Text is not a large component of the application, only being required when follow-up information is required or providing feedback on the current cooking process, it is still part of the process to give the user a pleasant experience. If high-quality is required, we recommended using Google's STT services.

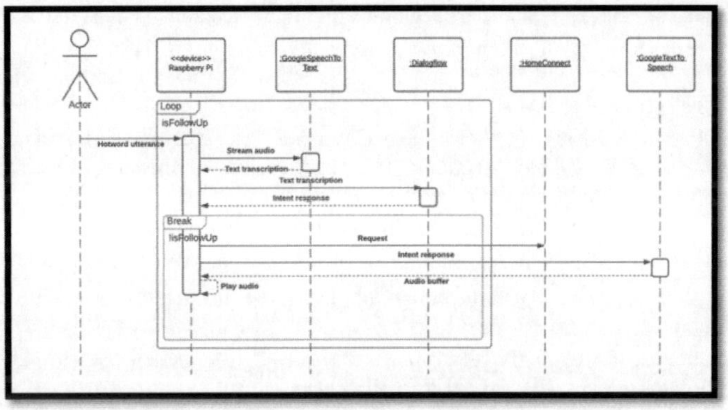

Figure 2. Sequence of the assistant process and how it updates the UI

Although everything can be performed on the device, these details mentioned previously should be considered. To continue further with our recommendations, considerations should be made, when calling external APIs (Google Cloud, etc), for latency. During development, we found that calling these APIs would introduce delays in response. Some queries could take upwards of five seconds to complete. This was due to how we called these external services. Each external query would be sent back to the Raspberry Pi before being sent off to the next external service. This introduced some latency. Hosting the entire application in the cloud could reduce this latency. This would reduce the need of having API middlemen, reduce latency since it will share tenancy with the external APIs it needs, and reduce the need to provide updates to the device should you want to extend the functionality of the service. A simple API call could be made on the device and return a response. These services we investigated, such as STT and TTS, require some computational power. The Raspberry Pi could keep up with them, but research showing it is slower than the cloud offerings provided by Google. If performing these services all on-device is required, this could increase the cost of the hardware shipped with every Food Processor. Figure 2 represents a Sequence diagram of the current system's flow of a general request, from hotword utterance, updating the Home Connect API and responding to the user through the speaker.

5. CONCLUSION

This study investigated how to rethink the user interaction process of smart home appliances and examined the potential of incorporating alternative human-computer interfaces into these devices. The results showed that the implementation of speech-based interaction provided a more efficient and alternative way of interacting with home appliances. The research also looked at two hotword recognition services, Snowboy and Porcupine, and two speech-to-text options, Google's STT and Mozilla's DeepSpeech. Based on the results, it was suggested that for conversational API services, external API solutions such as Google's should be used to handle numerous languages, offer accuracy, and require less processing capacity. Finally, NLU service implementations such as Google Dialogflow and AXA's NLP.js can be extended to provide additional functionality. Overall, the study presents a novel user interaction process for smart home appliances that can provide an efficient and user-friendly experience.

ACKNOWLEDGEMENT

The authors acknowledge the highly effective collaboration between the two industry partners and the two academic institutions. We also acknowledge the use of ChatGPT and DeepL Write for improving the fluency and clarity of the text regarding language.

REFERENCES

Barnes, C., 2020. *Enhanced Models And Features Now Available in New Languages on Speech-to-Text*. Retrieved from https://cloud.google.com/ blog/products/ai-machine-learning/new-features-models-and-languages-for-speech-to-text.

Cenek, P., 2005. *A Framework for Rapid Multimodal Application Design*. In *Text, Speech and Dialogue*, Hutchison, d. et al. (Eds.). Lecture Notes in Computer Science. Springer, Berlin, Heidelberg, pp. 393–403. DOI: https://doi.org/10.1007/11551874_51.

Fernandes, T. and Oliveira, E., 2021. *Understanding Consumers' Acceptance of Automated Technologies in Service Encounters. Drivers of Digital Voice Assistants Adoption*. Journal of Business Research, Vol. 122, pp. 180–191. DOI: https://doi.org/10.1016/j.jbusres.2020.08.058.

Google Cloud, 2022. *Text-to-Speech*. Retrieved from https://cloud.google.com/text-to-speech.

Hevner, A. et al., 2004. *Design Science in Information Systems Research*. MIS Quarterly, Vol. 28, No. 1, pp. 75–105.

IBM, 2022. *Watson Natural Language Understanding*. Retrieved from https://www.ibm.com/cloud/watson-natural-language-understanding.

Maedche, A. et al., 2019. *AI-Based Digital Assistants*. Business & Information Systems Engineering, Vol. 61, No. 4, pp. 535–544. DOI: https://doi.org/10.1007/s12599-019-00600-8.

Morais, R., 2020. *DeepSpeech 0.9.0*. Retrieved from https://github.com/mozilla/DeepSpeech/releases/tag/v0.9.0.

Picovoice, 2022. *Procupine*. Retrieved from https://github.com/Picovoice/porcupine.

Scates, K., 2020. *How Mercedes Benz's MBUX Voice Control Revolutionizes the User Experience*. Retrieved from https://www.soundhound.com/voice-ai-blog/how-mercedes-benzs-mbux-voice-control-revolutionizes-the-user-experience/.

Snowboy, 2022. *Snowboy Hotword Detection - Hey Bosch*. Retrieved from https://snowboy.kitt.ai/hotword/54265.

Socket.IO, 2022. *What Socket.IO is*. Retrieved from https://socket.io/docs/v4/.

Steffres, 2018. *Best Practice to Share Google Drive API Credentials for Being Used by a Script*. Retrieved from https://security.stackexchange.com/ questions/186329/best-practice-to-share-google-drive-api-credentials-for-being-used-by-a-script.

Stoker, N., 2020. *Installing Mozilla TTS on a Raspberry Pi 4*. Retrieved from https://levelup.gitconnected.com/installing-mozilla-tts-on-a-raspberry-pi-4-e6af16459ab9.

TOWARDS ACTIONABLE INFORMATION SYSTEM ETHICS: REQUIREMENTS ANALYSIS AND NON-MALEFICENCE

Dimitrius Keykaan
School of Computer Science and Information Systems, North-West University
11 Hoffman Street, Potchefstroom, South Africa

ABSTRACT

Unethical Software development is the cause of many harms that emanate from information systems. This paper proposes the explicit use of the non-maleficence bioethical principle, to assess whether system requirements may have ethical implications. The assessment takes place before the requirement advances to a following phase in the software development life cycle. Some harm caused by unethical Information systems will be highlighted to show the reality of the harm caused. An unethical software development scenario is then created, and a systems requirement of the system is formulated. A single bioethical principle is then used, as criteria, to determine whether a particular system requirement may be advanced to the design and implementation phases of the information systems development life cycle. The chosen approach has indicated usefulness in working towards actionable ethics that are not simply a long list of rules and principles. This research advises on the exact point in the development process, where ethical considerations can be made. It also guides the developer on how to determine whether a system could potentially cause harm or not. The actionability of the approach is also considered beneficial because takes place during the design process instead of after the design stages, where little can be done to influence ethicality.

KEYWORDS

Ethics, Information Systems, Non-Maleficence, Harm, Requirements Analysis

1. INTRODUCTION

Organizations often implement information systems to improve effectiveness, efficacy and to assist in reaching organizational goals (Hevner *et al.*, 2004). These goals generally include but are not limited to sustainability, growth and profitability that can enhance an organizations competitive ability (Abualoush *et al.*, 2018). As a result of growing organizations and new technologies, information systems are implemented though the use of software processes i.e. software engineering and software development, which enables keeping up with evolving organizational needs (Gregg *et al.*, 2001). Going forward, for the purpose of this paper, this implementation will simply be referred to as information systems (IS). The implementation of IS has been adopted by various industries in modern / e-society i.e., health (Eltajoury *et al.*, 2021), accounting (Darma, 2018), transport (Shmeleva *et al.*, 2019) and hospitality (Sever & Kağnıcıoğlu, 2019), just to mention a few. Over time it has been seen that IS can indeed contribute to reaching organizational goals and to have reasonably improved effectiveness and efficacy. Despite these successes, concerns of harm causing IS have also been raised (Pirkkalainen & Salo, 2016). This study views harm of any kind, to human beings, society as a whole or the environment as unethical and therefore any act of harm that comes from the use or implementation of IS is also considered unethical.

To mitigate this problem, ethical intervention in the software development process is proposed.

The Association for Computing Machinery (ACM), in its *ACM Code of Ethics and Professional Conduct*, has pointed out that ethical issues in IS can be addressed by software developers (Gotterbarn *et al.*, 2018). However, it does not explicitly guide the developer on when or at what point of development ethics should be considered. This paper proposes the sole and explicit use of a single bioethical principle, *non-maleficence*, to be used as criteria on determining whether a given *system requirement* should advance to the *design and implementation phases* of the software development life cycle, or not. The *non-maleficence* principle considers the potential harm that can be caused on the basis of a particular choice made. The intended contribution of this paper is to make ethics in IS actionable by simplifying the ethical considerations of the developer and providing guidance on how to minimize the potential harm that may emanate from the implementation of an IS. Therefore, the following research question has been formulated:

How can non-maleficence, as a bioethical principle, be used to address the potential harm that information systems may cause?

The remainder of this paper will be structured as follows: In Section 2, examples of unethical behavior in information systems will be presented. In Section 3, the software development process will be considered to emphasize where ethics can be used. Existing ethical approaches will then be considered in Section 4 and Section 5 will detail the proposed approach to using *non-maleficence* in the development of IS software. Some limitations will be considered in Section 6 and then following a brief reflection, the paper will be concluded in Section 7.

2. UNETHICAL BEHAVIOUR IN INFORMATION SYSTEMS

Harm caused by information systems (IS) is not limited to human beings, unethical behavior of IS also extends to the environment. In this section, unethical behavior of IS will be discussed in terms of harm caused to people and the environment, examples of each will be presented. The examples do not seek to serve as a literature review, it is only to demonstrate the reality of unethical behavior in IS.

2.1 Harm on Human Beings

The use of IS in organizations, though popular today, is not a recent practice. In 1985 the US and Canadian governments implemented a system called *Therac-25*, in their respective healthcare departments (Leveson & Turner, 1993). This system was intended to assist in contributing benefit to the patients who it served and healthcare professionals who depended on it. Leveson and Turner (1993) however, reveal that the system contained software design problems that led to grievous harm, including the death of 4 patients and serious injury of 2 others. Since its occurrence, this incident has received a lot of attention and has been cited in many research studies (McQuaid, 2012; Porrello, 2012; Silvis-Cividjian, 2021; Zelkowitz, 2012). Despite software professionals having become aware of possible harm, recent reports confirm that this problem is still found in IS implementations. Different views on whether the developers of *Therac-25* were deliberately negligent when programming the system have been shared. However, a common view is that the harm caused was avoidable by design.

Recent implementations of harmful IS include persuasive information systems (PIS) that persuade people into doing things they would not normally have done such as repeated and dangerous online gambling (Benner *et al.*, 2021). In PIS the developers deliberately design a system that will persuade individuals in a certain way, without considering the harm it may cause the gambler or their families. Another implementation is that of addictive information systems (AIS) that employ psychological tactics to ensure users continue using the system (Cemiloglu *et al.*, 2020). Examples of AIS include Facebook that has caused people to present with behavioral addiction symptoms such as mood modification, withdrawal, too much focus on the IS which can lead to job loss etc. (Turel, 2015). Addiction that results in the loss of a job leads to financial difficulty in the individual's life which causes harm to the individual and involved family members. An IS is therefore considered to have unethical effects if it is designed in a way that would harm human beings in the above-mentioned ways. Sometimes the negative effects of IS extend further than just individuals or groups of society, though they are also affected. The next subsection will show how IS harm can also affect the environment.

2.2 Harm on the Environment

Much research has been able to point out how unethical IS causes harm in the lives of human beings. In addition to human harm, research has shown that the environment can also be harmed by the implementation of IS.

Examples of this is covered in the emergence of a term often referred to as *green IS* (Gholami *et al.*, 2013) that address environmental issues such as energy consumption by IS, sustainability and related environmental challenges etc. (Dao *et al.*, 2011; vom Brocke *et al.*, 2013).

A very famous example of environmental harm deliberately caused by an unethical IS is the case of an automobile manufacturer (Volkswagen), that employed software designed to present false results during an emissions test (Mansouri, 2016). In 2015 Volkswagen was found to have designed its software in a way that it would disable certain emission control measures, making it seem as if the engine is emitting less harm causing gasses into the environment (Contag *et al.*, 2017). The act was unethical in the sense that it presented false values that would keep Volkswagen out of trouble with the Environmental Protection Agency (EPA) but also because of the environmental damage it caused with its excessive amount of nitrogen oxides and carbon monoxide released into the environment (Klier & Linn, 2016).

Volkswagen admitted that it knowingly had unethical software designed and installed in their engines and they paid a criminal penalty of $2.8 billion (Rogerson *et al.*, 2017). If this kind of software was not designed, then VW would not have been able to cheat. This research, therefore, contends that unethical software should be identified and stopped in the development process. In the next section, the information system development lifecycle will be discussed and an area for the consideration of ethical software development will be identified. Once the area for ethical considerations is established, ethical approaches to the problem can be looked at.

3. INFORMATION SYSTEMS DEVELOPMENT LIFE CYCLE

The information systems development life cycle (SDLC), also called the software development life cycle, is the process of creating and maintaining information systems. To date, various approaches to the SDLC exist (Kute & Thorat, 2014). In this study, the two majorly recognized approaches will be covered to demonstrate that different approaches are, in principle very much the same, in terms of collecting requirements from various stakeholders, before designing a system. The first approach is known as the *traditional approach* and the second approach is known as the *agile approach* (Leau *et al.*, 2012).

3.1 Traditional SDLC Approach

The traditional approach, also known as the waterfall approach (Kisielnicki & Misiak, 2017), is one with six phases. The phases must be followed in a sequential fashion, one phase must be completed before the next one is started with, and the phases must always be followed in the same order (Sinha & Das, 2021).

The phases in the traditional approach are:

- Requirements: user requirements for the system are gathered from stakeholders.
- Design: planning program architecture and logical flow of program before implementation.
- Implementation: actual coding of the software system, based on requirements and design.
- Verification: testing the software against the requirements that were documented in phase one.
- Deployment: deployment of the system, into production environment.
- Maintenance: fix production bug(s)/defect(s) and push further build in production with cleaner code

All the phases are completed only once, then after deployment, only maintenance is possible, this approach does not allow for the return to any prior phase,

3.2 Agile SDLC Approach

The major difference between the traditional and the agile approaches is that the agile approach allows for the return to previous phases. The development team meets with the stakeholders often and are able to deliver a small part of the final program. The team then has the customer review that small iteration, and subsequently return to implement changes for a newer version of the same system. This is obtained by splitting a large project into a set of smaller subprojects that are completed in short time periods (Usman & Ogwueleka, 2018). Simply put, the agile approach can follow the same phases of the traditional approach with the exception that, after implementation, it can be returned to requirements and design and iterate through those phases until all stakeholders are satisfied.

3.3 Post Requirements Ethical Considerations

From looking at the different approaches to the SDLC it is clear that, irrespective of the chosen approach, requirements are gathered from the stakeholder before coding is finalized. The design and implementation phases of the system are based on the IS requirements gathered i.e., functional, and non-functional requirements. This points to the fact that requirements determine how IS behave, therefore it is argued that unethical behavior stems from collected system requirements. On the basis of this argument, this paper proposes that there be a pause for ethical considerations of each requirement before it is allowed to advance to the design and implementation phases.

Figure 1 shows how each requirement, that would normally go directly from the requirements phase to the design phase, now first needs to go through a form of ethical consideration. Should the requirement not meet the given criteria, whatever the criteria may be, the requirement should be reviewed before advancing to the design and implementation phases. This new phase, for the purpose of this paper will be referred to as the ethical considerations phase (ECP).

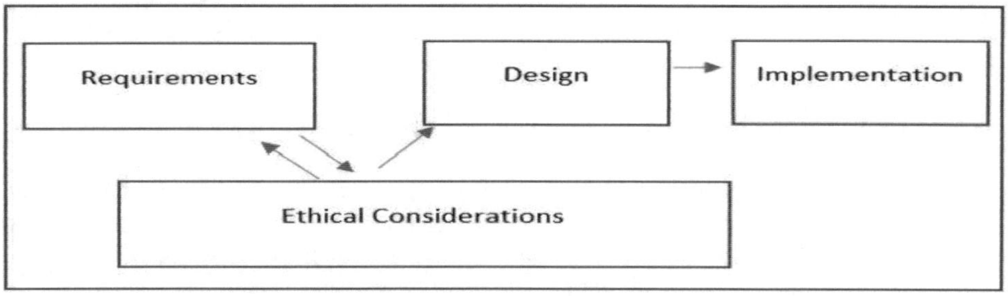

Figure 1. Post requirements ethical considerations phase (ECP)

In the next section various ethical principles or approaches will be discussed and one of those principles will be used as criteria in the ECP.

4. ETHICAL PRINCIPLES

To date, several attempts have been worked on to ensure ethical software development. One of the most famous efforts is found in the ACM code of conduct for software professionals (Gotterbarn *et al.*, 2018). The code of conduct lists a variety of principles that a software developer should follow to produce ethical software. In principle, the code of conduct addresses most ethical concerns that one may have, but it seems the code of conduct is not actionable. McNamara *et al.* (2018) did a research study on a large group of students and IT professionals (participants) and found that the explicit instructing of participants, to use the ACM code of conduct, had no effect. This code of conduct will therefore not be considered as criteria. The code of conduct also does not guide the developer to the point of the development process, where ethics should be applied. It also fails to, clearly, guide on the order in which the code should be followed. Such undetailed and lengthy codes of conduct or practice may be the reason why its ethical guidance is not actionable. It is the view of this research that minimal ethical principles may lead to actionable ethics for IS.

Out of the many minimal or less complex sets of ethical principles that exist, and have been applied in multiple fields, is bioethical principles. Among other fields, bioethics has been used in education (Nunes *et al.*, 2015), legal matters (Kirillova *et al.*, 2020) and in politics (Pelluchon, 2016).

In the absence of another IT related set of minimal or ethical principles or code of conduct, bioethical principles will be considered as criteria for the ethical considerations phase (ECP).

According to Kuhse and Singer (1998) Bioethics is a set of principles derived from the Hippocratic oath which is normally taken by medical professionals. Healthcare professionals often use these principles to guide them in making ethics related decisions. The four ethical principles of bioethics are beneficence, non-maleficence, justice, and autonomy. Each of the four principles can be summarized as follows:

(Aksoy & Elmali, 2002)

- Beneficence: doing good and promoting the welfare of others
- Non-maleficence: avoid causing harm unto others
- Justice: be fair to all party's involved
- Autonomy: value the freedoms and individual worth of others

Each of the four principles serves its own purpose and that is why they are initially listed as separate principles. This paper, however, contends that the principle of *non-maleficence* is an implicit and underlying idea in the remaining three bioethical principles. If this principle is adhered to then it will be difficult to go against any of the others. If one avoids causing harm to others (*non-maleficence)* it will be difficult to be unfair (*justice*), deprive others of their individual freedom (*autonomy)* or to deliberately disregard the welfare of others (*beneficence)*. Based on this reasoning and an attempt to make information systems ethics actionable, through simplification, only the principle of *non-maleficence* will be used as criteria. It can then be determined whether system requirements have the potential to cause harm.

In the next section a system requirement will be judged using the criteria of non-maleficence. A summary of the required action will then be given, and this can be applied to other requirements as well.

5. NON-MALEFICENCE POST REQUIREMENTS CONSIDERATION

Due to page constraints the application of the non-maleficence principle will only be done based on one requirement of an IS that has already been discussed in section 2. The Volkswagen case of having developed software, that deliberately lies about the amount of harm causing gases released into the environment. It is assumed that one of the system requirements was similar to:

Display correct emissions only if it is below the legal limit, else manipulate the results to display emissions below the legal limits. Do this even if emissions are higher than the legal limit.

If a developer is faced with a requirement such as this one, using the non-maleficence principle, the developer must consider the following criterion question:

Will the use of this requirement possibly cause harm to any of the stakeholders or the environment?

The developer must then refer to the list of all the stakeholders (normally defined in the requirements phase) and consider whether this requirement can potentially harm any of them or the environment.

If, after consideration, the answer to the question is "NO", then the requirement may be advanced to the next SDLC phase. If the answer is "YES" or the answer cannot be "NO" for sure, then the requirement must be reviewed and may not be advanced to the next phase. This would mean that the requirement must stay in the requirements phase, where alternative avenues are discussed with stakeholders, until a newer version of the requirement is ready for another round of ethical consideration. Honest and comprehensive consideration of the criterion question is likely to increase the effectiveness of this approach. The answer will not always be a simple "yes" or "no", some alternatives may include "possibly", "maybe", "sometimes" etc., all of these responses are also not "NO" for sure and therefore the related requirement will need to be reviewed until the answer is "NO".

In the case of the assumed requirement above, the answer to the criterion question is "YES" because the environment will be harmed if emissions above the legal limit are released into it. The developer(s) must thus return the requirement to the requirements phase and alternatives must be considered.

6. LIMITATIONS

Actionable information systems ethics are expected to contribute to the minimizing of harmful software, however, optimal results would rely on more research in future. At this early stage of research on the topic, there are some limitations that can be addressed in future work. The process, though simplified and actionable, requires a software developer to be honest about the potential harm that a system requirement is likely to cause.

If the developer does not consider all stakeholders and the environment, then the process may be less effective. This study currently only focuses on the assessing of individual system requirements, which are allowed to advance to the design and implementation phases. There exists a possibility that the combination of two requirements, which were individually considered not to cause potential harm, may lead to unexpected unethical consequences once in design or implementation. This possibility, though unlikely, should also be considered and researched in future.

7. CONCLUSION

If not acted upon, from an ethical point of view, IS caused harm may be perpetuated for years to come. Based on this reasoning, a research question was formulated in Section 1, and it will now be readdressed:

> *How can non-maleficence, as a bioethical principle, be used to address the potential harm that information systems may cause?*

In Section 2 it was shown that unethical IS does cause harm and that the harm caused can be serious. This makes it necessary to avoid IS related harm as far as possible. In Section 3, the post requirements phase of the SDLC was identified as an effective area for the use of ethical considerations. Section 4 presented non-maleficence as an ethical principle that covers concerns addressed in other bioethical principles and for that reason it was selected as the principle that will be used as criteria for system requirements. In Section 5 it was demonstrated that non-maleficence can be used to determine whether a particular system requirement is likely to cause harm to stakeholders or the environment. A non-maleficence criterion question was asked and based on the answer, the requirement will advance to the next SDLC phase, else it will be reviewed until it satisfies the criterion question. The advantage of this approach is that it is not complex or tedious, it is actionable due to its simplicity and the precise indication of where it should be applied.

This study has shown that the use of a single bioethical principle is useful in moving toward actionable ethics in IS. As actionable ethics for IS is still at a very early stage, possible application of the contribution made in this paper would be to serve as a basis for future research but also to supplement existing attempts in raising awareness of the harms caused by unethical IS. Future work will include actionable ethics in IS teaching and learning. Furthermore, actionable ethics in data management for Machine learning applications as well as more ethical approaches to IS development will also be investigated.

REFERENCES

Abualoush, S. H., et al. 2018. The role of employees' empowerment as an intermediary variable between knowledge management and information systems on employees' performance. *VINE Journal of Information and Knowledge Management Systems,* 48(2):217-237.

Aksoy, S. and Elmali, A. 2002. The core concepts of the four principles of bioethics as found in Islamic tradition. *Med. & L.,* 21(1):211-224.

Benner, D., et al. 2021. It is only for your own good, or is it? Ethical Considerations for Designing Ethically Conscious Persuasive Information Systems. In Proceedings of the *27th Americas Conference on Information Systems (AMCIS)*: Association for Information Systems, pp. 1-10.

Cemiloglu, D., et al. 2020. Towards ethical requirements for addictive technology: The case of online gambling. In Proceedings of the *2020 1st Workshop on Ethics in Requirements Engineering Research and Practice (REthics)*: IEEE, pp. 1-10.

Contag, M., et al. 2017. How they did it: An analysis of emission defeat devices in modern automobiles. In Proceedings of the *2017 IEEE Symposium on Security and Privacy (SP)*: IEEE, pp. 231-250.

Dao, V., et al. 2011. From green to sustainability: Information Technology and an integrated sustainability framework. *The Journal of Strategic Information Systems,* 20(1):63-79.

Darma, J. 2018. The role of top management support in the quality of financial accounting information systems. *Journal of Applied Economic Sciences,* 13(4):1009-1020.

Eltajoury, M. W., et al. 2021. Physicians' Attitudes towards Electronic Prescribing Software: Perceived Benefits and Barriers. In Proceedings of the *International Conference on Data Science, E-learning and Information Systems 2021*, pp. 47-53.

Gholami, R., et al. 2013. Senior managers' perception on green information systems (IS) adoption and environmental performance: Results from a field survey. *Information & management,* 50(7):431-438.

Gotterbarn, D., et al. 2018. Acm code of ethics and professional conduct.

Gregg, D. G., et al. 2001. Understanding the philosophical underpinnings of software engineering research in information systems. *Information systems frontiers,* 3(2):169-183.

Hevner, A. R., et al. 2004. Design science in information systems research. *MIS quarterly*:75-105.

Kirillova, A., et al. 2020. Bioethical and legal issues in 3D bioprinting. *International Journal of Bioprinting,* 6(3).

Kisielnicki, J. and Misiak, A. M. 2017. Effectiveness of agile compared to waterfall implementation methods in IT projects: Analysis based on business intelligence projects. *Foundations of Management,* 9(1):273-286.

Klier, T. and Linn, J. 2016. Comparing us and eu approaches to regulating automotive emissions and fuel economy. *accessed April,* 16:2018.

Kuhse, H. and Singer, P. 1998. What is bioethics? A historical introduction. *A companion to bioethics,* 2:1-3.

Kute, S. S. and Thorat, S. D. 2014. A review on various software development life cycle (SDLC) models. *International Journal of Research in Computer and Communication Technology,* 3(7):778-779.

Leau, Y. B., et al. 2012. Software development life cycle AGILE vs traditional approaches. In Proceedings of the *International Conference on Information and Network Technology*, pp. 162-167.

Leveson, N. G. and Turner, C. S. 1993. An investigation of the Therac-25 accidents. *Computer,* 26(7):18-41.

Mansouri, N. 2016. A case study of Volkswagen unethical practice in diesel emission test. *International Journal of Science and Engineering Applications,* 5(4):211-216.

McNamara, A., et al. 2018. Does ACM's code of ethics change ethical decision making in software development?, In Proceedings of the *Proceedings of the 2018 26th ACM joint meeting on european software engineering conference and symposium on the foundations of software engineering*, pp. 729-733.

McQuaid, P. A. 2012. Software disasters—understanding the past, to improve the future. *Journal of Software: Evolution and Process,* 24(5):459-470.

Nunes, R., et al. 2015. Education for values and bioethics. *Springerplus,* 4(1):1-8.

Pelluchon, C. 2016. Taking Vulnerability Seriously: What Does It Change for Bioethics and Politics?, *Human Dignity of the Vulnerable in the Age of Rights*: Springer, pp. 293-312.

Pirkkalainen, H. and Salo, M. 2016. Two decades of the dark side in the information systems basket: Suggesting five areas for future research. In Proceedings of the *24th European Conference on Information Systems*: European Conference on Information Systems, pp. 1-16.

Porrello, A. M. 2012. Death and denial: The failure of the therac-25, a medical linear accelerator. *Death and Denial: The Failure of the THERAC-25, AMedical Linear Accelerator*.

Rogerson, S., et al. 2017. Information systems ethics–challenges and opportunities. *Journal of Information, Communication and Ethics in Society*.

Sever, M. M. and Kağnıcıoğlu, C. H. 2019. A new information system for inventory management in hospitality industry. *İşletme Araştırmaları Dergisi,* 11(1):64-71.

Shmeleva, A. G., et al. 2019. Transport logistics management information system. In Proceedings of the *2019 IEEE Conference of Russian Young Researchers in Electrical and Electronic Engineering (ElConRus)*: IEEE, pp. 1471-1473.

Silvis-Cividjian, N. 2021. Awesome bug manifesto: Teaching an engaging and inspiring course on software testing (position paper). In Proceedings of the *2021 Third International Workshop on Software Engineering Education for the Next Generation (SEENG)*: IEEE, pp. 16-20.

Sinha, A. and Das, P. 2021. Agile Methodology Vs. Traditional Waterfall SDLC: A case study on Quality Assurance process in Software Industry. In Proceedings of the *2021 5th International Conference on Electronics, Materials Engineering & Nano-Technology (IEMENTech)*: IEEE, pp. 1-4.

Turel, O. 2015. An empirical examination of the "vicious cycle" of Facebook addiction. *Journal of Computer Information Systems,* 55(3):83-91.

Usman, A. V. and Ogwueleka, F. N. 2018. SDLC Models as Tools in the Development of MIS: A Study. *IUP Journal of Information Technology,* 14(4).

vom Brocke, J., et al. 2013. Green information systems: Directives for the IS discipline. *Communications of The Association for Information Systems,* 33(1):30.

Zelkowitz, M. V. 2012. What have we learned about software engineering? *Communications of The Acm,* 55(2):38-39.

IT-COMPLIANCE IN SME - A METHOD FOR THE ADAPTED USE OF FRAMEWORKS

Nico Deistler
KIPS, HTWG Konstanz, Konstanz, Germany
Alfred-Wachtel-Straße 8, 78462 Konstanz

ABSTRACT

The digital transformation of business processes and the integration of IT systems leads to opportunities and risks for small and medium-sized enterprises (SMEs). Risks that can result in a lack of IT Governance, Risk and Compliance (GRC). The purpose of this paper is to present the Design and Evaluation phase of creating an artefact, to reduce these risks. With this, the Design Science Research approach based on Hevner is using. The artefact will be developed by selecting relevant existing frameworks and the identification of SME-specific competencies. The method enables IT-GRC managers to transfer or adapt the frameworks to an SME organizational structure. The results from ten interviews and further three feedback loops showed that the method can be applied in practice and that a tailoring of established frameworks can take place. Contrary to the previous basic orientation of the research, this paper focuses on the concretization of approaches.

KEYWORDS

IT-Compliance, GRC, SME, Design-Science Research

1. INTRODUCTION

Small and medium-sized enterprises (SMEs) are known for their innovative strength and are increasingly confronted with the challenges of digitalization. In order to maintain or expand their competitive advantages, they are forced to actively address this development. The digital transformation of business processes and the greater integration of IT systems bring both, opportunities, and risks. Risks can lead to a lack of IT governance, Risk, and Compliance (GRC), for example with regard to information security and data protection.

A literature review conducted (Deistler and Rentrop 2020) found that existing best practice approaches and frameworks are largely not suitable for SMEs and are therefore not widespread among SMEs. The results of a survey of IT-GRC managers show that the reasons for this status quo are too high costs for IT, limited staff resources, lack of know-how and frameworks that do not fit SME structures. This leads to companies not implementing a holistic approach, but only individual technological measures. In addition, digitalization, cloud applications and cybersecurity already play a major role as drivers (Deistler and Rentrop 2022a). Due to the heterogeneity, it is not reasonable to adapt one of the common standards for all SMEs (Beißel 2017). Instead, general SME-relevant competencies should be abstracted, and a guideline for the selection of appropriate standards should be provided.

The aim of this paper is to develop an artefact for the selection of standards by adapting SME-relevant competencies and existing frameworks to the defined criteria.

In the following chapter, the status quo is presented, from which the problem is specified, and the research question is derived. Subsequently, the research approach with the applied design science methodology is discussed. Next, the case studies are discussed, and the steps and measures developed to design the artefact are outlined and the evaluation of the final methodology is shown. Finally, the results are discussed and implications for practice and research are presented with a summary.

2. STATUS QUO

First, a systematic review of previous research on IT-Compliance was conducted (Deistler and Rentrop 2020). Contributions focus on the topics of IT risk management, IT security, cloud computing, IT governance and the implementation of reference models. Particularly in the case of the contributions in connection with SMEs, it is apparent that these relate almost exclusively to the topics of digitalization and compliance management systems. However, the willingness in companies to actively address measures for IT-Compliance and IT security is low despite an increasing perception of risk (Hillebrand et al. 2017). The reasons and motives for this are, on the one hand, the perceived high costs of external expertise or building up in-house staff, who are also still scarce on the labor market (Deistler and Rentrop 2022a). In addition, the frameworks do not fit the structures in SMEs, which was also described by Johannsen and Kant (2020).

Barriers to implementation exist in small and medium-sized enterprises, especially with more complex frameworks such as COBIT. These lie in the fact that parts of the approach still have to be largely specified by SMEs, and comprehensive requirements and process recommendations have to be handled (Beißel 2017).

Recent empirics show different approaches for SMEs. Henschel and Heinze (2016) present a GRC approach for SMEs, but this largely ignores the specific requirements and the extent of digital transformation that has now also reached SMEs. Knoll and Strahringer (2017, p. 2) define IT-GRC as an integrated planning and control view of a company's opportunities and risks arising from the use of information as a production factor in the age of digitalization. Their approach provides a good orientation, but still requires "tailoring" for SMEs. Beißel (2017) uses the example of IT risk to show how existing frameworks can be meaningfully differentiated. Johannsen and Kant (2020) developed a competency-based approach to perceive, measure, and manage IT governance, risk, and compliance management in SMEs.

The goal of this paper is to develop an artefact for selecting appropriate standards by abstracting SME-relevant competencies and tailoring existing approaches and standards to the defined characteristics. Based on the problem definition and the state of research, the following research question can be derived: How can an IT GRC approach be designed to leverage existing frameworks and address specific needs of SMEs?

3. RESEARCH APPROACH

This chapter describes the methodological approach for developing and evaluating the artefact for selecting appropriate standards in SMEs.

The work has been conducted according to the design science research approach of Hevner (Hevner et al. 2004). The goal is to develop and evaluate an artefact in order to address the research question. First, in the Problem Identification & Objectives phase, a literature review and expert interviews were used to identify and clearly describe the relevant IT problem and to demonstrate the research gap. This is followed by the Design & Demonstration phase, in which an artefact, in this case a method, is developed to adequately implement IT-Compliance in SMEs. This initial approach was presented, discussed and adaptations directly incorporated. Further evaluation was conducted with the help of two case studies by practice partners, which are discussed in the next section. Here, the artefact was deployed and tested for functionality, quality, and effectiveness. The two phases of design & demonstration and evaluation run iteratively until the final artefact is developed.

3.1 Conducting the Case Studies

The ideal type of an evaluation of an artefact consists of its complete application in practice (Pries-Heje et al. 2008). However, this does not take place in the context of this work. For pure practicality reasons, the author lacks access to an IT organization with the authority necessary for an organizational design. The limited duration and resources of the work also stand in the way of such an ideal-typical approach to evaluation. Therefore, conducting comparative case studies according to Yin (2014) was chosen to evaluate the artefact. Accordingly, expert interviews are conducted, with the help of which a broad expertise, which the experts have acquired from their professional practice, is queried, and presented in a representative manner.

Furthermore, the instrument of triangulation was applied (Yin 2014). The interviews took place in the period from August to October 2022 and had different target groups and objectives as their purpose.

On the one hand, the methodological approach was to be evaluated. For this purpose, ten experts from compliance-relevant positions in small and medium-sized companies, scientists, and consultants from the field of business informatics were interviewed (see Chapter 4.5).

Second, the implemented design object was to be evaluated. In order to keep the number of cases manageable for the scope of the work, these were limited to four, one SME per archetype and one external consultant (see Chapter 4.6).

4. A METHOD FOR THE ADAPTED USE OF FRAMEWORKS IN SME

Starting from the Problem Identification & Objectives phase, this chapter presents the development and evaluation of the artefact. The methodological procedure is shown graphically in Figure 1. An essential component are the structural elements as well as SME relevant competencies. These were selected based on existing literature and serve as structure-giving elements for the artefact. The derivation and definition are explained in advance.

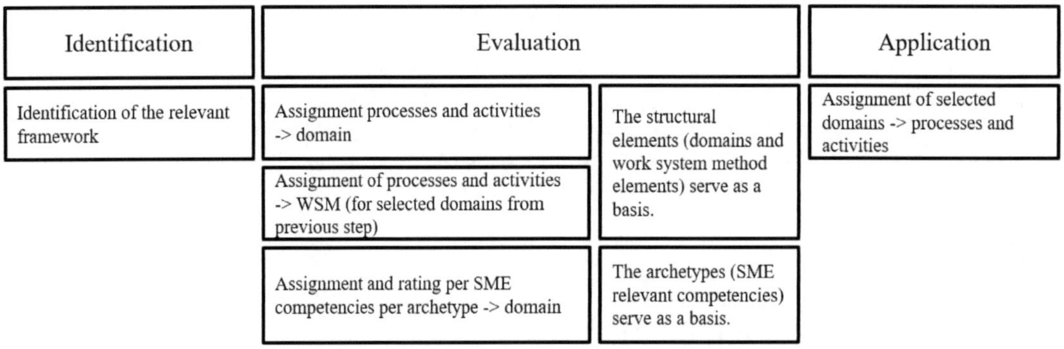

Figure 1. Methodical Approach

4.1 Definition of the Structural Elements

With the help of the structural elements, the individual processes and activities are to be brought into a uniform comparative structure, detached from the respective focus of a framework. In order to derive the appropriate elements, it is necessary to take a look at the strategic alignment of business and IT, which is regarded as an essential prerequisite for IT to contribute to business success. Henderson and Venkatraman have developed a model for this purpose to clarify how alignment works. This is divided into an external and internal perspective and contains, among other things, the positions Infrastructure, Processes, Capabilities, Competencies, Governance, and Scope (Henderson and Venkatraman 1989). Weill & Ross propose the differentiation into IT Principles, Architecture, Infrastructure, Business requirements, and Investments (Weill and Ross 2004). However, this proves to be not granular enough in practice, as the area of infrastructure is very comprehensive. Accordingly, Rentrop (Rentrop 2022) proposes a division into seven domains: IT Principles (subdomain: Stakeholders, Strategic Role, Fundamental Alignment of IT), Governance of IT (subdomain: Strategy, Budgeting, Investment Decisions, Cost Management), Architecture (subdomain: Design of the Development Plan, Standardization, Data Governance), Sourcing (subdomain: Sourcing Strategy, Supplier Selection, Relationship Design), Security, Risk & Compliance, Organization and Personnel (subdomain: IT in the Enterprise, IT within, Personnel Decisions) and IT Services.

The domains mentioned cover all areas and are therefore suitable as structure-giving elements for the further steps.

However, a further structural element is necessary, which takes into account in particular the aspect that SMEs have specific challenges, for example with regard to employees and costs. In addition, there are differences by industry and by small and medium-sized enterprises (Deistler and Rentrop 2022b).

For this reason, Alter's Work System Method (WSM) is suitable to differentiate and classify them. The Work System Method is an approach to analyzing systems in organizations, whether or not IT plays a significant role. This method is more broadly applicable than techniques designed to specify detailed software requirements, and it is more prescriptive and powerful than domain-independent system analysis methods such as the Soft System Method (Alter 2002). For this paper, we do not use all the elements Alter uses in his model but limit ourselves to the coherent elements of processes and activities, people, information, and technology that are relevant to us. These are explained below.

Processes and activities: Steps by which work is performed within a work system. In our case, these map to the relevant Objectives (COBIT 2019 and ISO/IEC 27001:2013) and Practices (ITIL4).

People (P): the people who perform at least some of the work in the business process are the people of the work system.

Information (I): Information includes codified and non-codified information that is used and created as people perform their work.

Technologies (T): Technologies include the tools and techniques used by the people of the work system as they perform their work (Alter 2002).

4.2 Definition of SME Relevant Competencies

In a next step, a further classification is made according to SME-relevant competencies. To this end, a classification of company sizes within SMEs must be made first, as this has a significant influence on the design of an IT GRC approach. This is based on a common understanding of the term. According to this, a company with fewer than 9 employees is defined as a micro enterprise, with 10 to 49 employees as a small enterprise, and with 50 to a maximum of 249 employees as a medium-sized enterprise (EU Commission 2005). However, this classification does not go far enough for an IT GRC approach. The presence of technology in the company also has a significant influence. It can be assumed that there is a correlation between the design or maturity of the technology and the number of stakeholders. In order to incorporate this into the model, three archetypes are developed based on Rohlfing and Funck (2002) and COBIT2019 Focus Area SMEs (ISACA 2018), according to which a differentiation within SMEs is possible and thus the different characteristics in SMEs are taken into account, as shown in Table 1.

Table 1. Archetypes

Archetype	Competencies
1	small enterprise, IT mainly outsourced, no clear responsibility for the IT, limited in-house IT skills/capacity, relative high-risk tolerance, because of their low-risk capacity, simple command structure and limited organizational structures in place
2	small enterprise, IT mainly in-house, IT department in place, outsource more complex tasks, limited in-house IT skills and/or capacity, relative high-risk tolerance, because of their low-risk capacity, simple command structure and limited organizational structures in place
3	medium-sized enterprise, heterogeneous IT-landscape, and IT department in place, aim more to buy (and potentially tailor) than to build themselves, outsource more complex tasks

Furthermore, current trends and developments are to be considered from the Problem Identification & Objectives phase. These are Information Security Awareness, Cybersecurity, Cloud Compliance and Data Protection (Deistler and Rentrop 2022a).

After describing the structure-giving elements that serve as a basis, the next step is the identification, evaluation, and application phases. It should be added at the outset that in this work, not one framework but three widely used frameworks were selected and evaluated due to their greater informative value (Deistler and Rentrop 2022a). Therefore, the next step, the mapping of the selected frameworks can be seen as optional for the actual method.

4.3 Mapping of the Selected Frameworks

The established and continuously revised COBIT 2019 framework serves as a reference framework, which is used for structuring and mapping other standards. Mappings from COBIT 2019 to ITIL4 (Hartawan and Suroso 2017) and ISO/IEC 27001:2013 (Yasin et al 2020) have already been performed. This was done using the ArchiMate Language according to Lankhorst. ArchiMate is an open and independent modeling language for enterprise architecture that can represent the description, analysis, and visualization of architecture within and between business units in an unambiguous manner (Lankhorst 2009). Thus, a comparability of the different frameworks was worked out, which is shown in Figure 2 (part "Mapping COBIT2019, ITIL4, ISO/IEC 27001:2013" of the table).

4.4 Step 1: Identification of the Relevant Frameworks

For the identification of the relevant frameworks, the complete existence of the individual framework, in particular the respective requirements, which are also called objectives, practices, or scope, is relevant.

ISO/IEC 27001:2013 and COBIT 2019 are both frameworks that address how organizations manage and monitor their IT systems. COBIT has clearly defined objectives and governance structures, while ISO/IEC 27001:2013 requires that information security objectives related to confidentiality, integrity and availability be defined according to organizational context. The difference between these two standards is that ISO/IEC 27001:2013 focuses mainly on security, while COBIT 2019 looks at IT as a whole and takes a functional perspective. In ITIL4, the focus is on the operational view and assessment of the security process, with an emphasis on information security. ITIL4 and ISO 27001:2013 primarily define how requirements should be implemented, COBIT 2019 primarily defines what should be implemented. COBIT 2019 is therefore at a higher level. In highly simplified terms, ITIL4 and ISO/IEC 27001:2013 are operational and tactical, while COBIT 2019 is more strategic.

4.5 Step 2: Evaluation of the Relevant Frameworks

In the evaluation phase, the processes and activities are first assigned to domains and based on this, the selected domains are assigned to the WSM elements. In the last step, the assignment is made to the domains with the help of a rating of the SME competencies per archetype. These assignments and the procedure were evaluated in the case studies and are presented in detail below.

In order to perform an assignment of the processes and activities to the defined seven domains in the first step, techniques of the ArchiMate Language (Lankhorst 2009) and the evidence suggested from the case study research (Yin 2014), such as manuals, process models and service catalogs, were used. In detail, all processes and activities from the frameworks were individually sifted and assigned to the respective domain. Multiple assignments are possible (see marked green in Figure 2). The ten experts reviewed and supplemented the results of this preliminary stage. The data collection procedure used for each interview partner was based on the specific assignment of processes and activities to domains in the form of a matrix prepared in advance. Deviations were identified, re-evaluated, and adjusted.

On this basis, the next step was to assign the selected processes and activities and associated domains to the WSM elements of people, information, and technology. For a better understanding, for the activity and process EDM01 from COBIT 2019, a domain mapping to IT principles was developed. As a result, it must be evaluated for this domain whether people, information or/and technology are required to achieve the objective. Multiple assignments may occur. For example, a process, such as APO05 from COBIT 2019, may require multiple processes and activities, such as IT principles, management of IT, and architecture. This results in multiple people being required for these processes, and thus multiple assignments to people. The personal intensity to cover this process is thus reflected. The result of these assignments is shown with an "x" in Figure 2.

In the final step, the three archetypes were evaluated based on their proficiencies and assigned to the corresponding domains. A two-level scoring model was used: high (h; +1) for indicating that this domain is appropriate and important to express and should be mapped as a priority, and low (l; -1) for indicating that this domain should not be included. No rating means that the domains are neutral for these proficiencies and thus a rating of 0 is assigned. For example, for the expression "IT mainly outsourced" in archetype 1, the domain Sourcing was rated as high because it can be assumed that the topics such as strategies of IT (cloud application, integration) and selection of suppliers/vendors can be classified as an important characteristic for this. The IT services domain, however, can be considered irrelevant, as the operation of the IT systems (with its sub-areas such as: change management, software development) is primarily the responsibility of the service provider in the case of outsourcing. Due to these qualitative measurements, we have a subjective interpretation here. However, in order to achieve high validity, this was discussed and adjusted several times with all ten interviewees. The summarized result is shown in the following table for archetype 1 in full and the results for archetypes 2 and 3 in the bottom row.

Table 2. Assignment and Rating to Archetype 1 in Detail and Archetype 2 and 3 in Summary

Archetype 1	**IT Principles**	**Management of IT**	**Architecture**	**Sourcing**	**Security, Risk & Compliance**	**Organization and Personal**	**IT Services**
small enterprise	l	h	l	h	h	l	l
IT mainly outsourced				h			l
no clear responsibility for the IT		h					
limited in-house IT skills/capacity						l	
relative high risk tolerance, because of their low-risk capacity					h		
simple command structure and limited organizational structures in place					h	l	
Information Security Awareness, Cyber Security, Cloud Compliance and Data protection					h		
Result Archetype 1	**-1**	**2**	**-1**	**3**	**4**	**-3**	**-2**
Result Archetype 2	**0**	**2**	**-1**	**3**	**4**	**-3**	**2**
Result Archetype 3	**0**	**2**	**1**	**4**	**3**	**-2**	**4**

Finally, each interviewee assigned the relevant processes and activities per archetype. The final step is the application of the relevant framework.

4.6 Step 3: Application of the Relevant Frameworks

In the further procedure, the final assignments were made based on the ratings from Table 1. Domains with a rating greater than 0 (see "Result" in Table 1) were classified as relevant and included in the target object (highlighted in blue in Figure 2), domains with a rating below 0 were considered as not relevant for this archetype. If a process such as EDM02 covers multiple domains, such as the domain IT Principles and Management of IT, which were rated -1 and +2, this business process was included because the relevance was clearly highlighted with +2. However, if a process such as BAI01 is assigned to two domains and one of them is Organization & Personal, which was rated -3 in archetype 2, this process has not been included because it is assumed that this is difficult to apply. This process was performed for all three archetypes.

Subsequently, three experts who had already been involved in the implementation, customization and operation related to COBIT2019/ITIL/ISO27001:2013 in their organization and could describe the operation and background based on their recollection and experience were interviewed. In doing so, each expert represented an archetype. The data collection procedure used for each case was based on a guideline. A pilot case study with a consultant was also incorporated to improve the data collection process. The entry point was formed by general questions about the framework of the organization and the project/implementation of the relevant framework. In this context, collected experiences of the respondents should be identified. In the next step, the target object (artefact per archetype) was mirrored to the experiences of the expert and feedback on feasibility was requested. A positive/negative test was also carried out, for example, it was checked whether the target object of archetype 1 was suitable, but it was also checked whether archetype 2 or 3 would also be suitable. Accompanying the expert interviews, a triangulation of the information thus collected was performed. At Expert A, for example, the documentation of an internal audit was inspected, and it was seen which processes and activities from the ISO standard were assessed as not effective. Likewise, project presentations were viewed at Expert C, which manifested the statement that personnel-intensive processes were minimized, and projects were set up to automate them with the help of IT applications. Each interviewee was interviewed a second time to confirm the results and to clarify the descriptions.

Relevance Archetype 1	Relevance Archetype 2	Relevance Archetype 3	Mapping COBIT2019, ITIL4, ISO/IEC 27001:2013			IT Principles			Management of IT			Architecture			Sourcing			Security,Risk,Compliance			Organization and Personal			IT Services		
			COBIT2019 Objectives	ITIL4 Practices	ISO/IEC 27001:2013 Scope	P	I	T	P	I	T	P	I	T	P	I	T	P	I	T	P	I	T	P	I	T
			EDM01 - Ensured Governance Framework setting and Maintenance	n/a	A.5 Information Security Policies, A.6 Organization of Information Security	x	x																			
x	x	x	EDM02 - Ensured Benefits Delivery	n/a	A.5 Information Security Policies, A.6 Organization of Information Security	x	x		x	x																
x	x	x	EDM03 - Ensured Risk Optimization	Risk Management	A.5 Information Security Policies, A.6 Organization of Information Security													x	x	x						
x	x	x	EDM04 - Ensured Resource Optimization	n/a	A.5 Information Security Policies, A.6 Organization of Information Security		x		x	x	x						x				x					
			EDM05 - Ensured Stakeholder Engagement	n/a	A.5 Information Security Policies, A.6 Organization of Information Security	x	x																			
			APO01 - Managed I&T Framework Management	n/a	n/a	x	x	x																		
x	x	x	APO02 - Managed Strategy	Strategy Management	n/a	x	x		x	x	x			x		x		x	x	x	x					x
		x	APO03 - Managed Enterprise Architecture	Architecture Management	n/a							x	x	x												
	x	x	APO04 - Managed Innovation	n/a	A.14 System Acquisition, Development and Maintenance		x		x	x				x												
x	x	x	APO05 - Managed Portfolio	Portfolio Management	n/a		x		x	x				x												
x	x	x	APO06 - Managed Budget and Cost	Service financial management	n/a				x	x	x															
			APO07 - Managed Human Resources	Workforce and talent management	A.7 Human resource security																x	x				
			APO08 - Managed Relationships	Relationship Management	n/a		x														x	x				
	x	x	APO09 - Managed Service Agreements	Service catalogue management, Service level management	n/a																			x	x	x
x	x	x	APO10 - Managed Vendors	Supplier management	A.15 Supplier Relationships										x	x										
			APO11 - Managed Quality	n/a	n/a		x														x	x				
x	x	x	APO12 - Managed Risk	Risk Management	n/a													x	x							
x	x	x	APO13 - Managed Security	Information security management	A.14 System Acquisition, Development and Maintenance, A.18 Compliance													x	x							
		x	APO14 - Managed Data	Business analysis	A.12 Operations security, A.14 System Acquisition, Development and Maintenance							x	x	x												
		x	BAI01 - Managed Programs	Portfolio Management	n/a																x	x		x		x
	x	x	BAI02 - Managed Requirements Definition	Business analysis, Service design, Service level management	n/a																			x	x	
	x	x	BAI03 - Managed Solutions Identification and Build	Service design, Software development and management	n/a																				x	x
	x	x	BAI04 - Managed Availability and Capacity	Capacity and performance management, Availability Management	n/a																			x		x
	x	x	BAI05 - Managed Organizational Change	Organizational change management	n/a																			x		
	x	x	BAI06 - Managed IT Changes	Change enablement	n/a																			x		x
	x	x	BAI07 - Managed IT Change Acceptance and Transitioning	Release Management, Service validation and testing, Deployment management	n/a																			x		x
			BAI08 - Managed Knowledge	Knowledge Management	n/a																x	x				
	x	x	BAI09 - Managed Assets	IT asset management	A.8 Asset management									x												x
	x	x	BAI10 - Managed Configuration	Service configuration management	n/a									x										x	x	x
		x	BAI11 - Managed Projects	Project Management	n/a																x	x		x		
	x	x	DSS01 - Managed Operations	Monitoring and event management, Infrastructure and platform management	A.12 Operations security																			x		x
	x	x	DSS02 - Manage Service Requests and Incidents	Incident management, Service desk, Service request management	n/a																			x		x
	x	x	DSS03 - Managed Problems	Problem Management	n/a																			x		x
	x	x	DSS04 - Managed Continuity	Service continuity management	A.17 Information security aspects of Business Continuity Management																			x	x	x
x	x	x	DSS05 - Managed Security Services	Information security management	A.9 Access control, A.10 Cryptography, A.11 Physical and Environmental Security, A.12 Operations security, A.13 Communication Security, A.16 Information security incident management														x	x	x	x		x		x
x	x	x	DSS06 - Managed Business Process Controls	n/a	n/a													x		x						x
x	x	x	MEA01 - Managed Performance and Conformance Monitoring	Measurement and reporting	n/a		x		x	x	x							x		x						
x	x	x	MEA02 - Managed System of Internal Control	n/a	n/a													x	x							
x	x	x	MEA03 - Managed Compliance with external Requirements	n/a	A.18 Compliance													x	x							
x	x	x	MEA04 - Managed Assurance	n/a	A.12 Operations security													x	x							

Figure 2. Results per Archetype

5. DISCUSSION OF RESULTS

If the number of assignments of the WSM elements, personal (47), information (42) and technology (33) in the initial state of the framework are considered and these are compared with the assignments in the developed archetypes, the following results can be determined. For archetype 1, the result of assignments of people (22), information (22), and technology (15) that correspond to the characteristics of this archetype. The WSM assignments for archetype 2 and 3 also confirm a reduction in the human element relative to the baseline condition. This addresses the problem of lack of employee resources in SMEs. Furthermore, the element Technology (32) has the highest number of assignments in archetype 3, which correlates with the characteristics of this archetype. The same issue can be seen with the number of relevant processes and activities, so of the 40 relevant processes and activities in the baseline condition, 15 have been evaluated as relevant in archetype 1, 29 in archetype 2, and 33 in archetype 3.

The results are seen as consistently helpful among interviewees. The method enables those responsible for IT-GRC to transfer or adapt the frameworks to an SME organizational structure. By focusing on SME-relevant competencies in the developed method, processes and activities are prioritized. Risks can thus be reduced because the (missing) capacities are used in a more goal-oriented manner. Finally, the flexibility and innovative capacity for which SMEs are known should be maintained and not imposed on processes and activities that are easy to implement for large companies but bureaucratize SMEs.

The steps outlined examined the utility, quality, and effectiveness of the method developed (Hevner et al. 2004). The successful simulation in the three archetypes proves the usefulness of the method. This can be seen in the execution of each step (Peffers et al. 2008) and in the evaluation of each case by the experts involved. With the final design, the research question can be answered.

Contrary to the basic orientation of the research so far, this paper focuses on the concretization of approaches. Thus, the results contribute to the extension of the literature as it is based on basing approaches and generates a possibility to evaluate them. Moreover, the criteria of the evaluation are independent of technology and organizational structure.

6. CONCLUSION

The results of ten interviews and further three feedback loops showed that the method can be applied in practice, that established frameworks can be "tailored", and that it provides SMEs with recommendations for action to achieve a certain level of IT-Compliance. In addition, the method can be carried out with little effort.

However, the selection of cases could have limitations. Generalization could be improved by studying even more cases from other industries and with a different organizational structure. In addition, a full application could be tested in practice. It can also be assumed that there is a certain bias towards positive extreme cases, as it can be assumed that such companies agreed to participate where the projects are seen as successful. Moreover, our study is based exclusively on qualitative data, as allocations are difficult to quantify.

In addition to the described competencies, a company may need to consider other individual characteristics that may lead to a further archetype and thus change the result. Furthermore, the omission of processes and activities should be critically reviewed again by each company to see if they are really not necessary, as the frameworks usually represent a holistic approach. We are sure that this work will contribute to theory and practice in the field of IT-Compliance in SMEs.

In summary, the paper can be an impetus for SMEs to raise their awareness with regard to IT GRC and provides recommendations for action for an adapted minimum level of IT-Compliance.

REFERENCES

Alter, S. 2002. The Work System Method for Understanding Information Systems and Information Systems Research. In: *Communications of the Association for Information Systems*, Vol. 9, Article 6.

Beißel, S. 2017. Differenzierung von Rahmenwerken des IT-Risikomanagements. In: *HMD Praxis der Wirtschaftsinformatik*, Vol. 1, S. 54:37–54.

Deistler N., Rentrop C. 2020. IT-Compliance in KMU – State of the art. In *HMD Praxis der Wirtschaftsinformatik*, Vol. 57, pp 1047-1057.

Deistler, N., Rentrop, C. 2022a. IT-Compliance in KMU – Experteninterviews zum Status quo. In *Wirtsch Inform Management,* https://doi.org/10.1365/s35764-021-00380-5.

Deistler, N., Rentrop, C., 2022b. A Method for an IT-GRC Approach in SMEs – Design Phase. In *PACIS 2022 Proceedings*. 316.

EU-Commission, 2005. Definition of SMEs. https://eur-lex.europa.eu/legal-content/DE/TXT/PDF/?uri=CELEX:32003H0361&from=EN. Access on: 11.02.2022

Hartawan, F., Suroso, J. 2017. Information Technology Services Evaluation Based ITIL V3 2011 and COBIT 5. In *Center for Data and Information. In Intelligent Information and Database Systems*. 9th Asian Conference.

Henderson, J. C., Venkatraman, N. 1989. Strategic alignment. A framework for strategic information technology management. In: *CISR WP No. 190*. Massachusetts, USA.

Hevner, A., Salvatore M., Jinsoo P., Sudham R. 2004. Design Science in Information Systems Research. In: *MIS Quarterly* (28:1), S. 75-105.

Hillebrand A, et al, 2017. Aktuelle Lage der IT-Sicherheit in KMU.WIK https://www.wik.org/fileadmin/Sonstige_Dateien/ IT-Sicherheit_in_KMU/ __2_.pdf. Access on: 28. Nov. 2020.

Henschel T., Heinze I. 2016. Governance, Risk und Compliance im Mittelstand, Praxisleitfaden für gute Unternehmensführung. Erich Schmidt Verlag, Berlin, Deutschland.

ISACA 2018 Cobit 2019: Einführung und Methodik. ISACA.org, USA.

Johannsen A., Kant D. 2020. IT-Governance, Risiko- und Compliance-Management (IT-GRC) – Ein Kompetenz-orientierter Ansatz für KMU. In: *HMD Praxis der Wirtschaftsinformatik*, Vol. 57, S. 1058–1074.

Knoll M., Strahringer S. 2017. IT-GRC-Management im Zeitalter der Digitalisierung. In: *Knoll M, Strahringer S (Hrsg) IT-GRC-Management –*. Springer Vieweg, Wiesbaden, Deutschland, S. 1–24.

Lankhorst, M. 2009. Enterprise Architecture at work. In *The Enterprise Engineering*, Springer Berlin, Deutschland.

Peffers, K., Tuunanen T., Rothenberger A., Chatterjee S. 2008. A Design Science Research Methodology for Information Systems Research. In: *Journal of Management Information Systems* (24:3), S. 45-77.

Pries-Heje, J., Baskerville, R., Venable, J. 2008. Strategies for Design Science Research Evaluation. In: *Proceedings of the ECIS 2008 conference*, Galway, Ireland.

Rentrop C. 2022. IT-Governance. Erfolgsfaktor für die digitale Transformation. Erich Schmidt, Berlin, Deutschland.

Rohlfing, M., Funck, D., 2002. SMEs Kritische Diskussion quantitativer und qualitativer Definitionsansätze. In: *IMS-Forschungsberichte Nr.7*. Universität Göttingen. Deutschland.

Weill, P., Ross, J. W. 2004. IT governance. How top performers manage IT decision rights for superior results. In: *Harvard Business School*. Boston, Massachusetts. USA.

Yasin, M., et al. 2020. Designing Information Security Governance Using COBIT 2019 Framework and ISO 27001:2013. In *14th International Conference on Telecommunication Systems, Services, and Applications (TSSA)*.

Yin, R. K. 2014. Case study research: Design and methods (5th ed.), Los Angeles, CA: Sage Publications.

ONTOLOGIES FOR SMART FARMING

Mohd Firdaus Sulaiman[1], Mohammad Nazir Ahmad[1], Liew Kok Leong[2,3], Ummul H. Mohamad[1], Nik Mohd Habibullah Nik Mohd Nizam[1] and Azrulhizam Shapii[2]

[1]*Institute of IR4.0, Universiti Kebangsaan Malaysia, 43600 Bangi, Selangor, Malaysia*

[2]*Faculty of Information Science & Technology, Universiti Kebangsaan Malaysia, 43600 Bangi, Selangor, Malaysia*

[3]*ARB Berhad, Level 22, Menara Exchange 106, Lingkaran TRX, Tun Razak Exchange, 55188, Kuala Lumpur, Malaysia*

ABSTRACT

Smart Farming (SF) includes the integration of Information and Communication Technologies (ICT) into farming equipment and sensors for use in crop cultivation and food production systems. In this advanced technical era, the Internet of Things (IoT) and various electronic instruments (such as robots and artificial intelligence components) with data transformation and signaling facilities are now revolutionizing the agriculture sector. Nowadays, farmers can leverage IoT to enhance their farming conditions such as in areas like irrigation and fertilization, as well as increase the efficiency by using data from harvesting information, and projecting climate forecasts to improve their decision making. One of the key challenges in this essence is to deal with the semantic heterogeneity from multiple data sources. As such, ontology is regarded as one of the normative tools that is suitable to solve the semantic interoperation problem by describing, extracting, sharing, and making the domains' knowledge explicit. In the field of smart farming, several ontologies have been developed. For example, soil-based farming methods have been further developed to represent and store the essential knowledge of aquaponics. Unfortunately, how these ontologies support the SF context is not well understood. This article reviews the recent available ontologies for smart farming. From the review, we discuss some key points from an ontology engineering point of view on the state-of-the-art ontologies for SF that should be designed and developed. Moreover, we add some key important remarks on the direction to further explore potential areas of ontologies for supporting smart farming operations.

KEYWORDS

Agriculture, Data Management, Farming Data, Ontology, Smart Farming

1. INTRODUCTION

The agricultural sector has experienced a revolution from traditional agriculture to the era of modern agriculture. Agricultural becomes more modernize to transform to smart farming era align with the advancement of many ICT technologies such as the Internet of Things (IoT), big data analytics and mixed reality together with using of latest equipment such as sensors, robot and satellite on farming environment. Nowadays farmers can leverage IoT to enhance their farm efficiency such as irrigation, fertilization, harvesting information, and climate forecast by monitoring with sensors to improve their decision making. Several ontologies have been developed to support SF operation. An ontology that is regarded as one of the normative tools solves the semantic interoperation problem by describing, extracting, and sharing the domains' knowledge.

This section covers the comparison of traditional and modern agriculture, using ICT for Precision Agriculture, data management issues in smart farming and significance of using ontology on smart farming. Section II provide literature review on ontologies use on smart farming. In Section III we discuss research findings and finally in Section IV we give conclusion.

1.1 Agriculture: Traditional vs Modern

Agriculture is the industry that supports the most basic life need, which is food. Hence, it is regarded as one of the crucial sectors that ensure the sustainability and the livelihood for the maximum number of people, and also contribute to the climate change (Singh and Singh, 2017). Traditional agriculture is a primitive style of farming that involves the intensive use of indigenous knowledge, traditional tools, natural resources, organic fertilizer and cultural beliefs of the farmers (Rathnayake et al, 2021). Some common type of traditional agriculture includes slash and burn agriculture, agroforestry and crop rotation. Meanwhile, modern agriculture uses technically advanced tools and machinery, the farming method includes fertilization, pest control handling and fulfillment of crop growth requirements by depending heavily on the farmers' knowledge and experience. The aid for agriculture with the upcoming technologies helps in increasing the speed of work and thus ensures smart work in few hours of time (Kalaiselvi and Keerthana, 2018). Some common types of modern agriculture include indoor vertical farming, farm automation, hydroponic farming and large-scale greenhouse. To add, modern agriculture aims to revolutionize the agriculture sector using several advanced techniques such as precision agriculture (smart farming) technology, GPS technology and soil sensor technology to meet the growing needs for food safety of the global population. Table 1 compared the characteristics of traditional and modern agriculture

Table 1. Comparison of Traditional vs Modern Agriculture

Parameters	Modern Agriculture	Traditional Agriculture
Techniques	Mono-cropping, precision agriculture, indoor vertical farming, farm automation.	Crop rotation, agroforestry, slash and burn cultivation
Fertilizers	Chemical fertilizers, pesticides.	Manure, vegetable waste, ash
Input	Higher input of seeds, irrigation, fertilizers, and agrochemicals.	Lower input required
Knowledge system	Scientific knowledge system	Traditional knowledge system
Species	Few commodity species	Many species, including 'neglected and underutilized species
Value Chain	Global value chains and specialized actors	Value chains primarily local to regional
Seed System	Formal seed system, including private sector	Informal seed system, often exchanged for free through social networks

Source: (Rudebjer et al., 2021)

1.2 ICT for Precision Agriculture (Smart Farming)

Smart farming has progressed rapidly with the advancement of many ICT technologies such as the Internet of Things (IoT), big data analytics, mixed reality, cloud computing, and mobile applications (Balafoutis et al, 2020). Navarro and Pereira (2020) mentioned that IoT technology often integrates with several types of sensors to ease the collection and communication of data over the network, while it revolutionizes the hardware to be more compact-sized and optimizes power consumption in a smart farming setting. Meanwhile, big data analytics technology serves to capture, analyze, and provide insights from the voluminous data which can then be used for farming operational decisions (Wolfert et al, 2017). Mixed reality technology, which encompasses virtual and augmented reality, has carved the path towards increasing farming efficiency, reducing supervisory needs, as well as providing guidance for farming operations and visualizations of plant growth (Hurst et al, 2021). Besides that, Zammora-Izquierdo et al. (2019) explained that cloud computing allows smart farming data to be stored in cloud servers where accessibility, privacy, and data security can be efficiently monitored. Other than that, ICT technology has realized the use of autonomous robots and drones to inspect the health of agricultural production (Tripicchio et al, 2017). The presence of a mobile or web-based platform, on the other hand, allows farmers and smart farm owners to effectively monitor their smart farm processes and operations, regardless of the location and time, as reported by Sinha and Dhanalakshmi (2022). Nevertheless, with the availability and applicability of these many ICT technologies for smart farming, smart farming has its challenges with data management, as these technologies also consume, process, store, and accumulate data.

1.3 Data Management Issues in Smart Farming

In smart farming, data comes from a variety of sources, formats and complexity. Some issues like heterogeneity can cause data management to become hard and challenging. These different datasets create enormous challenges to integrate them into a workable system (Ngo et al, 2018). In the context of smart farming, cloud data storage become the main platform for how these data are saved. Chukkapalli et al. (2020) mention that large data collected from the sensors in the farm can be stored in the cloud for faster computation which helps in uniform decisions. However, the relationship of these data is important and the way this data is stored and accessed by various users in smart farming requires a mechanism so that all this data is always efficiently synchronized for the decision-making support process. Therefore, among other important challenges in data management is focused on data synchronization where data resides in the cloud storage must be always synchronized and relate meaningfully.

Data synchronization is the ongoing process of synchronizing data between two or more devices and updating changes automatically between them to maintain consistency within systems. While the sheer quantity of data afforded by the cloud presents challenges, it also provides the perfect solution for big data.

1.4 An Ontology and Why Ontology?

Wolfert et al. (2017) explained that smart farming is a development that emphasizes the use of ICT in the cyber-physical farm management cycle. Recent technologies such as the Internet of Things and Cloud Computing are expected to leverage this development and introduce more robots and artificial intelligence (AI) in farming. This is encompassed by the phenomenon of Big Data, massive volumes of data with a wide variety that can be captured, analyzed and used for decision-making. However, all these data require semantics. Semantics can be explained by giving the meaning of the data, understanding the relationship among them, making data explicit, structuring data, establishing data standardization and putting data into meaningful information and knowledge for assisting decision making and right actions. Gruber (1993) explains an ontology is a conceptual model and is prominently recognized as a promising conceptual tool to capture, organize, structure, and represent knowledge. In SF-context, ontology can be used to represent SF-related knowledge at a semantic level and make sense of SF-related data which is generated in substantial amounts from daily smart farming operations.

2. ONTOLOGIES IN SMART FARMING: AN OVERVIEW

A variety of ontologies have been created and used in smart farming. From food cultivation to sales and marketing, ontology helps farmers in many ways, especially in decision making. A number of papers have studied the usage of ontologies on smart farming. This section presents a detailed overview of these studies.

Sivamani et al. (2013) propose a Vertical Farm Ontology (VFO) which is designed to focus on the service-based vertical farm without any human intervention. The ontology model is designed using OWL based on RDF and implemented in Protégé 4.0. By emphasizing vertical farming, VFO is proposed to enable semantic interoperability between the internet of things (IoT) that operated for vertical smart farming. With the proposed model, the information from the Internet of things is recomposed as context information and made understandable for the other systems. For the sake of agriculture, the authors hoped that the proposed model will pave a great path for the development of smart and intelligent agricultural services, or generally for ubiquitous computing.

Chukkapalli et al. (2020) develop a smart farming ontology to implement an Attribute Based Access Control (ABAC) to help farmers create and enforce access control rules for their smart farms. The ontology model is a combination of context and platy ontology that conform to the ABAC is written using Semantic Web Language (SWRL). A smart farm ecosystem architecture is created consisting of physical entities that contain smart sensors and machines, digital twins that monitor the data authorized to be shared and to what extent to maintain security policies and a representation graph including nodes and edges that represent and monitor interactions between various cyber-physical systems on the smart farm. This ontology is used to determine access control in the smart farm architecture where access decisions are dynamically computed using an entity's fine grained attributes. With the implementation of ABAC using an ontology, the authors strived to prevent cyber-attack and vulnerabilities in smart farming.

Burlacu et al. (2016) introduce a Farm Management Information System (FMIS) Ontology to support farmers in decision-making regarding land and crop management. The ontology was built through Protégé editor, using the OWL Full version. FMIS framework is developed to focus on performing data acquisition, mapping, making the spatial distribution, productivity and profit maps based on information that is stored on a platform together with the information from the various external web services. Web services are to enable communication, interoperability and data exchange between applications such as Variable Rate Technologies (VRT), Remote Sensing, GIS and Global Positioning System (GPS) so that the system purposes some possibilities from its knowledge base, through which the farmer can decide on land or crops. In the future, the authors intended to develop a platform that will integrate this ontology and external services, and then effectively test the proposed FMIS for precision agriculture.

Abbasi et al. (2021) provide a knowledge model as a framework using ontology to support the parametric design automation in an indoor aquaponics system with the notion of automatically determining the design parameter of grow bed based on crop selection. The framework consists of three primary stages including knowledge generation, extraction and application depict the complete lifecycle of the decision-making process. An ontology model known as AquaONT is developed by acquiring knowledge from farm and domain experts and unifying it as domain concepts to represent aquaponics knowledge. The ontology is designed based on OWL develop using Protégé 5.5. AquaONT then extracts inferred knowledge about crop characteristics and grow bed design features using Apache Jena API 1 and SPARQL query language. MySQL Workbench2 is used to import and organize extracted knowledge into a MATLAB database with various mathematical equations utilized to develop a graphical user interface (GUI). The results (design features) obtained from GUI are exported to SOLIDWORKS for parametric modeling of the final grow bed design. For future works, the author aimed to incorporate intelligent techniques such as machine learning, deep learning, and computer vision to make the system smart and autonomous.

Bhuyan et al. (2021) proposed a lattice structure in knowledge representation for smart farming. The lattice structure is created from spatio-temporal data retrieved from sensors. It used panel data both homogeneous model (same set model parameters) and heterogeneous model (different set model parameters) to organize the data. A series of definitions that contained function was created based on panel data and formal interpretation. Later, several agglomeration algorithms were created in order to form a knowledge representation in terms of a lattice for smart agriculture. Finally, some rules were generated based on the properties of the lattice for reasoning. In the future, the authors intend to collect real-time data from sensors and implement the same algorithms as described.

Chukkapalli et al. (2020) developed an architecture of a smart farming cooperative ecosystem that defines sensors and their communication among different entities along with cloud supported co-op hub. To support the ecosystem, the author introduced two types of ontologies which are member farm ontology and cooperative agriculture ontology. Member farm ontology contained several classes such as individual owner, worker, hub and others with a different relationship to describe various interactions that happened on an individual member farm. Meanwhile, cooperative agriculture ontology was created based on the co-op ecosystem that details interactions like how co-op resources were shared between individual member farms. This ontology contained different classes such as member farm, unit, agreement and it captured data from various interactions of the relationship between them. This ontology was utilized to describe various operations of the co-op with the help of use cases in selected scenarios. The author also presented various AI applications in different domains which would integrally benefit individual member farm owners that are part of a co-op.

Symeonaki et al. (2022) described an architecture of an Integrated Farm Management (IFM) system utilizing IoT middleware as an ontology approach for smart livestock farming. IFM consisted of three main layers of architecture which was the perception layer, middleware layer and application layer and its integration into a cloud platform. All the functional elements in the layer of the architecture coped with the context, while context awareness was achieved in the cloud-based distributed middleware that formed the core of the whole system and acted as the decision support system (DSS) in the backend. The proposed ontology-based context modeling structure consisted of five core ontologies including Thing Ontology, Event Ontology, Time Ontology, Location Ontology and Rule Ontology. These ontologies were developed using OWL 2.0 and implemented using XML Language. The consolidation of the ontology-based IoT middleware was expected to create a unique framework for livestock management that will depend on the types of devices, the services available, or the complete design of the system. For future work, the authors will include an in-depth performance evaluation of the middleware by incorporating multiple livestock farming environments with different specifications and at different locations.

Ngo et al. (2018) highlighted a framework of knowledge for an agriculture ontology known as ArgiOnt for smart agriculture systems. It included four thematic subdomains which were agriculture, geographical, IoT and business subdomain. The agricultural subdomain included basic classes in the agriculture domain, such as Farm, Crop, Product, Fertilizer or Condition. Meanwhile, the IoT subdomain was connecting sensor systems and links to observed objects. The geographical subdomain included two main administrative levels (Country and Sub country classes) and free control locations. Business subdomain linked agricultural subdomain and IoT subdomain to monitor production. In short, ArgiOnt aimed to tackle the challenges in pre-processing and analyzing real-world agriculture datasets. It was stored as linked data and applied data analytics techniques to make a semantic framework. The proposed ontology was able to assist the process of integrating, harmonizing and transforming raw agriculture data efficiently.

Fonou-Dombeu et al. (2021) described an ontology for the Climate Smart Agriculture (CSA) domain namely OntoCSA. OntoCSA ontology can be used to integrate and facilitate the interoperability of subsystems of scientists, academics, agro foresters and many more. The OntoCSA ontology was developed in web ontology language (OWL) with Protégé. OntoCSA ontology was validated with the HermiT reasoner within Protégé. OntoCSA ontology can be used to develop ubiquitous systems to store relevant CSA data that can serve to draw various statistical analyses for research and decision-making. It can also be integrated with existing agriculture ontologies to develop more comprehensive and up-to-date ontologies of the agriculture domain. For future direction, the author will enhance OntoCSA ontology so that it can be incorporated with machine learning techniques to predict various trends in CSA uptake to date.

Ingram and Gaskel (2019) constructed a user-centered ontology in the development of search engines. It aimed to help agriculture practitioners in the field of agriculture and forestry to find research outputs that responded to their specific queries. The development of ontology involved three phases which are analyses of the design, validation and evaluation phases. The construction of the ontology was to improve the structuring of knowledge for the specific agriculture domains according to the context of the users, create a shared vocabulary between experts and stakeholders to allow users to express questions and answers, annotate digital documents in a document base and provide a semantic index so that best-matching documents to answer a query could be found. The co-constructing ontologies also contribute to a deeper theoretical understanding of shared concepts and meanings in the context of digital communications. Analysis showed how involving users in the design of the user-centered ontology moved the search engine from an information processing synaptic capacity to a semantic capacity (beyond current web semantic abilities) where common meaning concerning specific agricultural domains can be represented and shared.

Kaewboonma et al. (2020) proposed an ontology-based big-data analysis system that provided recommendations based on the environmental factors to improve orchid production. The ontology model was designed using OWL based on RDF and implemented in HOZO ontology editor to describe the scope of knowledge and relationships with SPARQL query to retrieve the measurement and assessment results for orchids data. Ontology was divided into two sub-domains of ObjectType (domain ontology) which consisted of the concepts, attributes and instances of orchids and Measurement (information ontology) which describes knowledge objects such as Measure_Day, Measure_Sensor and Temperature_Value. The ontology process consisted of defining the scope, investigating the existing ontologies and plan to reuse, defining terms and their relations, creating instances, and implementing and evaluating. The authors aimed to include the evaluation of new orchid ontology by orchid specialists, and the evaluation of the recommendation system based on an orchid farmer survey for the future work.

Fuentes et al. (2021) mentioned on a Dairy Cattle Performance Ontology (DCPO) to provide decision support systems to dairy farmers to help them adapt to the new realities. DCPO reconciled the complex structure to the heterogeneous nature of dairy data within a unified framework that ensured extensibility to external data. The ontology was designed using UML-based OWL based on RDF to capture the current state of elicited knowledge and design decisions. SPARQRL was implemented as query-based approach on the data collected. DCPO will embody knowledge across six distinct perspectives over dairy production that include breeding (pedigree), genetics, production and milk quality control, environment, health and nutrition. It divided the ontology according to the different aspects of the dairy process such as core, production and quality control, testing, breeding and genetic evaluation. Moreover, the authors intended to exploit ontology design patterns such as integration with OBO ontologies and enhancing the data-centered ontology with knowledge discovered from the data by mining tools as future direction.

Table 2. Ontologies in Smart Farming

References	Type of SF	Ontology name	Role of ontologies	Tools	Ontology Languages	ICT systems	Research Issues
Sivamani et al. (2013)	Vertical farm	Vertical Farm Ontology (VFO)	To support semantic interoperability	Protégé 4.0	OWL, RDF	Ubiquitous computing	service automation and smart service application in the vertical farm environment
Chukkapalli et al. (2020)	Both (vertical and horizontal)	Ontology for ABAC system	To create and enforce access control rules for smart farms.	Not mentioned	SWRL	Smart farm ecosystem, specifically on the access control system. Cybersecurity	Security issues on smart farming cyber-attack and vulnerabilities.
Burlacu et al. (2016)	Horizontal Farm	Farm Management Information System (FMIS)	To support decision-making regarding land and crop management	Protégé	OWL full version	Management Information System	- Decision-making in smart farming - Data management
Abbasi et al. (2021)	Vertical Farm	AquaONT	To support parametric design automation	Protégé 5.5	OWL, Apache Jena API 1 and SPARQL	Aquaponic system (combination of hydroponic and aquaculture unit).	- To deal with semantic heterogeneity of multiple data resources in aquaponic system - Data management
Bhuyan et al. (2021)	Both (vertical and horizontal)	Knowledge representation of Smart Farming	To capture and perform reasoning on spatio-temporal agricultural data	Not mentioned	Not mentioned	Precision Agriculture	Not mentioned
Chukkapalli et al. (2020)	Horizontal farm	Member Farm Ontology and Cooperative Agriculture Ontology	To support AI application in cooperative Smart Farming Ecosystem	Not mentioned	Not mentioned	Artificial Intelligence, Cyber-physical system, Precision Agriculture	- Exploit the applications of AI and Internet-connected devices in the co-op ecosystem. - Data management
Symeonaki et al. (2022)	Horizontal farm	Thing Ontology, Event Ontology, Location Ontology, Time Ontology, Rule Ontology	To support real-time remote monitoring and control of livestock facilities	Phyton, Microsoft Azure Platform	OWL 2.0, XML,	Internet of Thing, Middleware, Smart Farming	facilitating the management, processing, and sharing of the vast and heterogeneous data points generated in livestock facilities

References	Type of SF	Ontology name	Role of ontologies	Tools	Ontology Languages	ICT systems	Research Issues
Ngo et al. (2018)	Horizontal farm	ArgiOnt	To support agricultural data links between a farmer from different data resources	Not mentioned	Not mentioned	Precision Agriculture, Semantic Framework	- Integration of different datasets from different IoT systems of organizations into a workable system. - Data management
Fonou-Dombeu et al. (2021)	Horizontal farm	OntoCSA	To integrate and facilitate the interoperability of subsystems of scientists, academics, agro foresters and many more.	Protégé	OWL	Semantic Web	building a knowledge-based ontology for the climate-smart agriculture (CSA) domain.
Ingram and Gaskel (2019)	Both (vertical and horizontal)	user-centered ontology	To help agriculture practitioners in the field of agriculture and forestry find research outputs that respond to their specific queries	Not mentioned	Not mentioned	Semantic Web	Limited for the practitioners who are dealing with multi-faceted and context-related issues while using computer-aided search engines.
Kaewboonma et al. (2020)	Horizontal farm	Ontology-based big data	To improve orchid production	HOZO editor	OWL, RDF and SPARQL	Precision Agriculture	higher costs of production while selling price remains the same or goes lower
Fuentes et al. (2021)	Horizontal farm	Dairy Cattle Performance Ontology (DCPO)	To provide decision support systems to dairy farmers	Not mentioned	OWL, RDF and SPARQL	Precision Agriculture	Data management issues on data imprint from different stakeholders (farmers, managers, consultants)

3. DISCUSSION

Smart Farming includes a combination of various technologies in cyber-physical farm management and equipment for use in crop cultivation and food production system. Use of these technologies will produce a large volume of data and all these data require semantics. Semantics can be explained by giving the meaning to the data, understanding relationships among them, making data explicit, structuring data, establishing data standardization and putting data into meaningful information and knowledge for assisting decision making and right actions. In SF-context, ontology can be used to represent SF-related knowledge at a semantic level and make sense of SF-related data. This ontology enables the monitoring and managing of various devices deployed on the smart farm at any given time (Chukkapalli et al, 2020).

According to Table 2, most ontologies are developed using ontology web language (OWL) based on RDF and implemented in Protégé (Sivamani et al, 2013; Burlacu et al, 2016; Abbasi et al, 2021; Fonou-Dombeu et al, 2021). Semantic Web Language (SWRL) also can be used to develop ontologies (Chukkapall et al, 2020). HOZO ontology editor is another application to implement ontology using OWL based on RDF (Kaewboonma et al, 2020). Most applications used SPARQRL as a query language-based approach to the data collection method.

Ontology can capture, organize, structure, and semantically represent data. It can support semantic interoperability (Sivamani et al, 2013) between applications and technologies or from different data resources (Ngo et al, 2018). Ontologies also can integrate and facilitate the interoperability of systems and subsystems (Ngo et al, 2018; Chukkapalli et al, 2020; Fonou-Dombeu et al, 2021). Organized data can make it easier in decision-making regarding the land and crop management or for dairy farmers (Fuentes et al, 2021). Eventually, this will improve plant production (Kaewboonma et al, 2020).

According to Table 2, most ontologies fell under domain ontologies type. Guarino (1998) mentioned that the domain ontology described, respectively, the vocabulary related to a generic domain (like medicine, or automobiles), by specializing in the terms introduced in the top-level ontology. Ontologies that are from domains ontology type includes ArgiOnt (Ngo et al, 2018), Ontology for ABAC system (Chukkapall et al, 2020), OntoCSA (Fonou-Dombeu et al, 2021), Ontology-based big data (Kaewboonma et al, 2020) and Dairy Cattle Performance Ontology (DCPO) (Fuentes et al, 2021). Other than that, application ontology type is also used as ontologies to support SF. These ontologies included Farm Management Information System (FMIS) (Burlacu et al, 2016), Member Farm Ontology and Cooperative Agriculture Ontology (Chukkapalli et al, 2020) and Ontology-Based IoT Middleware Approach (Symeonaki et al, 2022). Application ontology described concepts depending on both particular domain and task, which were often specializations of both related ontologies. These concepts often corresponded to the roles played by domain entities while performing a certain activity, like replaceable units or spare components.

Most ICT application is applied in conjunction with ontological support for SF. According to Table 2, most ontologies applied precision agriculture as ICT application on developing ontologies (Ngo et al, 2018; Bhuyan et al, 2021; Chukkapalli et al, 2020; Kaewboonma et al, 2020; Fuentes et al, 2021). It assists management decisions by using high-technology sensors and analysis tools. Moreover, ICT application such as the semantic web (Fonou-Dombeu et al, 2021; Ingram & Gaskel, 2019) and ubiquitous computing (Sivamani et al, 2013) were most likely to apply to ontologies that deals with data management. A Management Information System (Burlacu et al, 2016) can be applied to ontologies that deal with decision-making and data management. Other ICT applications that supported ontologies for SF included Cyber-Security, Artificial Intelligence and the Internet of Things depend on ontologies being developed.

The ontologies model seemed to be widely used in SF. The main objective of using ontologies in SF is to facilitate major problems or issues related to the operation of smart farming itself. According to Table 2, ontologies were mostly used to solve or support semantic interoperability (Ngo et al, 2018; Sivamani et al, 2013; Abbasi et al, 2021; Fonou-Dombeu et al, 2021) of data between data resources, service applications, system and subsystems. By using or creating these ontologies, it makes data more understandable between parties involved.

Several farmers also faced issues related to the decision-making with regard to the operation of smart farming. Ontologies were used as the perfect model to solve this issue of land or crop management (Burlacu et al, 2016) or dairy farmers (Fuentes et al, 2021). Use of various technologies such as Artificial Intelligence and remote sensing make smart farming became more sophisticated. Therefore, the ontologies model can also be used to integrate these technologies (Chukkapalli et al, 2020; Symeonaki et al, 2022). Some other issues or problems that can be solved using ontologies were access control rules for smart farming and improvement to the farming production.

Data management is a common issue in smart farming. According to Table 2, ontology was used to solve issues such as information coming from various sources such as sensors to assist farmers in the decision-making of agriculture business (Burlacu et al, 2016). Moreover, the ontology model helped to deal with the semantic heterogeneity of multiple data resources in aquaponics systems (Abbasi et al, 2021). Also, ontologies were used to solve the integration of different datasets from different IoT systems, applications of AI and Internet-connected devices in the co-op ecosystem of organizations into a workable system (Ngo et al, 2018; Chukkapalli et al, 2020). Data management issues on data imprints from different stakeholders for decision-making (Fuentes et al, 2021) can also be solved using ontology. In the context of smart farming, cloud data storage become the main platform for how these data are saved and organized. **However, to the best of our knowledge, no recent examples have been found on how ontology can support data synchronization in cloud computing for SF context.**

AquaONT (Abbasi et al, 2021) was one of the ontologies that support hydroponics. It supported the parametric design automation in an indoor aquaponics system with the notion of automatically determining the design parameter of grow bed based on crop selection. AquaONT was developed by acquiring knowledge from farm and domain experts and unifying it as domain concepts to represent aquaponics knowledge. The ontology was designed based on OWL develop using Protégé 5.5.

4. CONCLUSION

Ontologies play a significant role in the SF operation. Ontologies acted as a conceptual tool that can be used to capture, organize, structure, and represent knowledge on SF. SF generates huge data. All these data must be synchronized to support the decision-making process. Therefore, making sense of data for SF is crucial, hence, ontologies are significant to be developed to assist in the SF context. Even more, to design ontologies for SF is a task that is challenging, yet must be investigated further due to its potential in SF.

With advancements in the field of SF this leads to more data being used. These data come in a variety of formats and forms. These data should be uniform among various parties that use SF to enable SF to be used more efficiently. The synchronization of data between devices and its use among the parties involved is important to ensure that this SF operation runs smoothly. Besides that, cloud data storage became the main platform of storage to store and save data from different devices. The relationship of these data is paramount and the way this data is stored and accessed by various users and platforms in smart farming is essential to be understood well and important for the decision-making support process. Ontology can play a role by ensuring that the data stored in this cloud storage is always synchronize and available for use by any party involved. Therefore, further investigation on data management especially on data synchronization on cloud storage will help ease the operation of SF to become more efficient.

ACKNOWLEDGEMENT

This research is supported by ARB Industrial Grant, Vot. No: ZG-2022-003. We highly appreciate the enormous support received for this research project.

REFERENCES

Abbasi, R. et al, 2021. An ontology model to support the automated design of aquaponics grow beds, *Science Direct*, No. 100, pp. 55-60.

Balafoutis, A. T. et al, 2020. Smart farming technology trends: Economic and environmental effects, labor impact, and adoption readiness, *Agronomy,* Vol. 10, No. 5, pp. 743.

Bhuyan, B. P. et al, 2021. An ontological knowledge representation for Smart Agriculture, *IEEE International Conference on Big Data (Big Data)*, pp. 3400-3406.

Burlacu, G. et al, 2016. A conceptual model of Farm Management Information System for decision support, *Technological Innovation for Collective Awareness Systems*, Vol. 423, No. 423, pp. 47-54.

Chukkapalli, S. S. L A. et al, 2020. A Smart-Farming ontology for Attribute Based Access Control, *IEEE 6th Intl Conference on Big Data Security on Cloud (BigDataSecurity), IEEE Intl Conference on High Performance and Smart Computing, (HPSC) and IEEE Intl Conference on Intelligent Data and Security (IDS).*

Chukkapalli, S. S. L. et al, 2020. Ontologies and artificial intelligence systems for the Cooperative Smart Farming Ecosystem, *IEEE Access*, No, 8, pp. 164045-164064.

Fonou-Dombeu, J. V. N. et al, 2021. OntoCSA: A Climate-Smart Agriculture Ontology, *International Journal of Agricultural and Environmental Information Systems,* Vol. 12, No. 4.

Fuentes, V. et al, 2021. Toward a Dairy Ontology to Support Precision Farming, *International Conference on Biomedical Ontologies*, pp 24-35.

Gruber, T.R., 1993. A translation approach to portable ontology specifications, *Knowledge Acquisition,* Vol. 5, pp. 199-220.

Guarino, N., 1998. Formal Ontology and Information System, *Proceedings of FOIS'98*, pp 3-15.

Hurst, W. et al, 2021. Augmented Reality in Precision Farming: Concepts and Applications, *Smart Cities*, Vol. 4, No. 4, pp. 1454–1468.

Ingram, J. and Gaskel, P., 2019. Searching for meaning: Co-constructing ontologies with stakeholders for smarter search engines in agriculture, *NJAS: Wageningen Journal of Life Sciences*, Vol. 90-91, No. 1, pp. 1-13.

Kaewboonma, N. et al, 2020. Ontology-based big data analysis for orchid smart farming, *Library and Information Science Research E-Journal*, Vol. 29, No. 2, pp. 91-98.

Kalaiselvi, V. K. G. and Keerthana, B., 2018. Modern agriculture aid, *International Journal of Engineering & Technology*, Vol. 7, No. 2.33, pp 580-582.

Navarro, E. et al, 2020. A systematic review of IoT solutions for smart farming, *Sensors*, Vol. 20, No. 15, pp. 4231.

Ngo, Q.H. et al, 2018. Ontology Based Approach for Precision Agriculture, *Multi-disciplinary Trends in Artificial Intelligence,* No. 1124812, pp. 175-185.

Rathnayake, I. et al, 2021. Preliminary Study of Perception on Traditional Agriculture among Young Generation in Anuradhapura District, *SSRN Electronic Journal,* 10.2139/ssrn.4171206.

Rudebjer, P. et al, 2021. Teaching agrobiodiversity for food and agriculture: a curriculum guide for higher education.

Singh, R. and Singh, G. S., 2017. Traditional agriculture: A climate-smart approach for sustainable food production, *Energ. Ecol. Environ*, Vol. 2, No. 5 pp 296–316.

Sinha, B. B. and Dhanalakshmi, R., 2022. Recent advancements and challenges of Internet of Things in smart agriculture: A survey, Future Generation Computer Systems, Vol. 126, pp. 169–184.

Sivamani, S. et al, 2013. A smart service model based on Ubiquitous Sensor Networks using Vertical Farm Ontology, *International Journal of Distributed Sensor Networks*, Vol. 9, No. 12, pp. 1-8.

Symeonaki, E. et al, 2022. Ontology-Based IoT middleware approach for Smart Livestock Farming toward Agriculture 4.0: A case study for controlling thermal environment in a pig facility, *Agronomy*, Vol. 12, pp 750.

Tripicchio, P. et al, 2015. Towards smart farming and sustainable agriculture with drones, *International conference on intelligent environments*, pp. 140–143.

Wolfert, S. et al, 2017. Big data in smart farming–a review, *Agric Syst*, Vol. 153, pp. 69–80.

Zamora-Izquierdo, M. A. et al, 2019. Smart farming IoT platform based on edge and cloud computing, *Biosyst Eng,* Vol. 177, pp. 4–17.

A SYSTEMATIC REVIEW OF THE NEW PMI® PROJECT MANAGEMENT BEST PRACTICES GUIDE (PMBOK® 7TH EDITION) AGAINST THE PREVIOUS ONE (PMBOK® 6TH EDITION): USING INFORMETRIC ON THEIR ORGANIZATION AND CHAPTER STRUCTURE

João Carlos Boyadjian and Nilo Sergio Maziero Petrin
SENAC University Center, Brazil

ABSTRACT

This article evaluates the change made by the PMI® - Project Management Institute, in its most recent guide of best practices and project management standards, a substantial change in the organization and structure of its content compared to the previous guide.

A quantitative analysis was carried out on the volume of citations of terms related to five evaluation perspectives: 1) project management approaches; 2) areas of knowledge; 3) process groups; 4) management principles; 5) performance domains, between the two most recent publications of PMI® project management standards and best practices guides (the 6th and 7th editions of the PMBOK® guide).

The result showed us that the predictive, adaptive and hybrid approach, with some variations in their individual percentages in each version of the guides, maintained, in general, a similar proportion between them, without significant changes. On the other hand, it is important to note the emphasis placed on team and stakeholder management in the latest edition of the PMBOK® Guide.

KEYWORDS

Quantitative Analysis, Project Management Approaches, Areas of Knowledge, Process Groups, Management Principles, Performance Domains

1. INTRODUCTION AND CONTEXT

Periodically, volunteer members of the PMI® Project Management Institute, the world's largest project management institute, with more than one million members, come together to update their guide to best practices and management standards of projects, with the most recent edition (PMBOK® -7th edition) being published in July 2021 (PMI®, 2021).

Updates are required to align with new global project management perspectives and updated approaches to realizing benefits and generating valuable outcomes for organizations and their stakeholders.

Previous editions from the first, edited in 1996, to the 6th edition (PMI®, 2017-a), were based on five (5) process groups (Initiating; Planning; Execution; Monitoring and Control; Closing) and ten (10) knowledge areas (Integration; Scope; Schedule; Cost; Quality; Resources; Communication; Risks; Procurement; Stakeholders). Publication number 7 broke with this pattern and brought another organization, based on twelve (12) project management principles (Stewardship; Team; Stakeholders; Value; Systems Thinking; Leadership; Tailoring; Quality; Complexity; Risk; Adaptability & Resilience; Change) and eight (8) performance domains (Stakeholders; Team; Development Approach and Lifecycle; Planning; Project Work; Delivery; Measurement; Uncertainty).

This represents a shift of paradigm.

2. OBJECTIVE

The objective of this article is to present an analysis of the most representative terms in the structure of the two most recent publications of the PMBOK® guide (6th and 7th editions): agile approach; management principles; performance domains; process groups; knowledge areas; in order to be able to compare them in relevance and continuity of use of these terms and analyze the result from the new perspective of management proposed by PMI®.

3. METHODOLOGY

This study is classified as an applied and descriptive research, with the use of quantitative analysis procedures about quotations of terms of reference selected in the two latest guides of project management best practices: PMBOK® 7th edition (PMI®, 2021) and its previous version - PMBOK 6th edition (PMI®, 2017-a).

Descriptive research aims to carry out a detailed analysis of something that already exists and is known to deepen the theme, analyzing data collected without interference from the researcher to obtain a statistical view, detailing the results (Gil, 1999).

The analysis of the presence and relevance of terms in a text requires a collection and analysis methods. There are some types of methods to analyze the use of words or terms in texts.

One of them is to use morphology, initially proposed as a decomposition matrix of a problem by the Swiss astronomer Fritz Zwicky (1898 – 1974). This solution allows associating words in a text and obtaining a better understanding from natural language processing and the probability of the word in question being used for a certain purpose (Bender, 2013).

Another method is the co-occurrence of keywords, which implies recognizing that a word has a high probability of being present in a text simply because there is another word that is often associated with the first one (Inomata, 2015).

Bibliometrics can be used also to track production, compare, classify the state of knowledge with graphs and maps (Godin, 2006). It is a quantitative technique for measuring the production and dissemination of scientific knowledge.

Finally, we have the Informetric (Judit-Bar, 2008), which is a subfield of bibliometrics, and allows quantitatively measuring aspects of information. It uses the "words behavior" to map information flows and elucidate the structures of ideas and other problems represented in appropriate sets of documents.

In this way, for the preparation of this content analysis work in view of the structural change made by PMI® using the texts of the PMBOK® 7th edition (PMI®, 2021) and PMBOK® 6th edition (PMI®, 2017-a) guides, the technique of Informetric was chosen. The informetric percentage representativeness were performed by simply summing the number of terms found in each edition.

The analyze were elaborated under the prism of five (5) different representative perspectives in relation to the chapter structures of the current and previous PMBOK® guides.

4. LITERATURE REVIEW: PMBOK® GUIDES ORGANIZATION AND CHAPTER STRUCTURE

The PMBOK® Guide 6th edition (PMI®, 2017-a) is structured in process groups and knowledge areas, while the new PMBOK® Guide 7th edition (PMI®, 2021) is based on project management principles and domains of performance (Figure 1).

Before starting a project, it is necessary to determine which management approach should be used, depending on the delivery cadence and the possibility or not of many changes in requirements throughout the project (PMI®, 2017- b).

Projects with little change and single delivery should follow a predictive approach, also known as waterfall or traditional. In this approach, the scope, the time, and the budget are determined at the beginning of the project.

For projects that require continuous deliveries, or changes in requirements throughout the development effort, an adaptive approach should be adopted, such as the agile model.

Projects can also be managed in a hybrid way, that is, parts following the predictive approach and parts following the agile approach (PMI®, 2017-a).

The project management landscape continues to evolve and continually adapt. Projects not only produce outputs but enable those outputs to generate results that add value to organizations and stakeholders. In this way, the greater focus should be directed to the results that can be obtained and less on the generation of deliveries themselves.

Process-only standards are prescriptive in nature. Reflecting the expected value of a project's results can no longer be guaranteed with process-based guidance alone (PMI®, 2021). In this way, the new standard will be more centered on principles to support the project manager to act in order to seek the intended results. A statement of principles makes project management more effective in the pursuit of value creation. The process approach, however, remains relevant in the new context, with many professionals and organizations finding it useful to guide their resources in project management.

In this sense, the new guide proposes a vision of project management systems, aligned with the delivery of value, that is, the outputs need to generate results that add value to organizations and stakeholders.

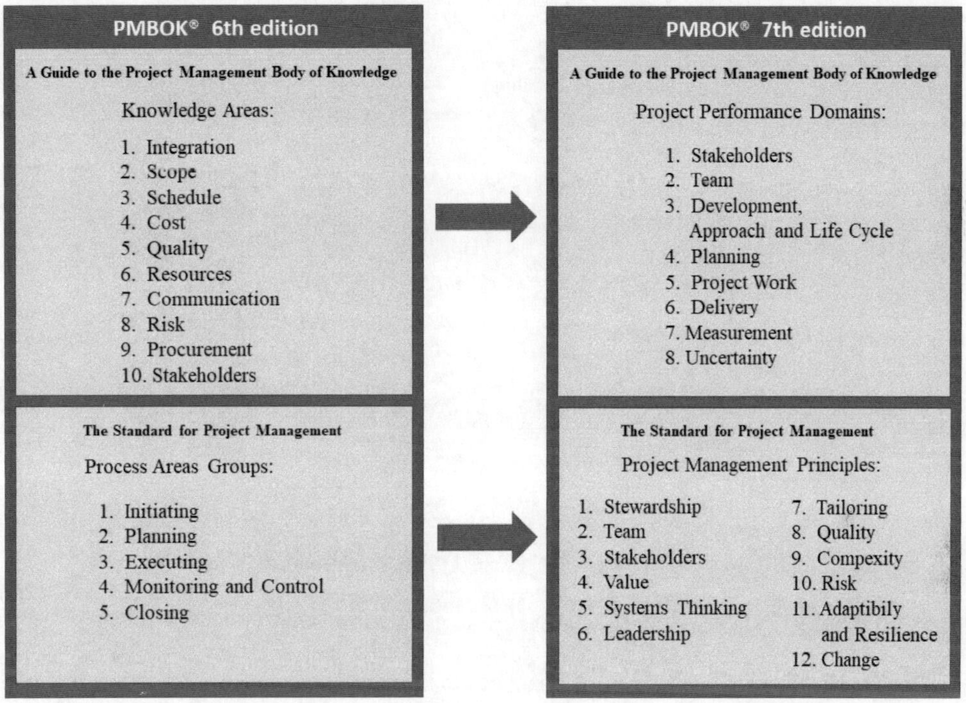

Figure 1. PMBOK® , 6th and 7th edition chapters structure. source: adapted from (PMI®, 2021, p. XIII)

5. RESEARCH APPLICATION

The present research took place in the period of September to November 2022, with the collection of data on the cited guides and corresponding quantitative and comparative analysis under five significant perspectives for study: Management Approaches, (Figure 2), Areas of knowledge (Figure 3), Process Groups (Figure 4) Management Principles (Figure 5) and Performance Domains (Figure 6).

5.1 Management Approach Perspective

In this collection, were selected the terms "adaptive"; "hybrid", "predictive", and the possible variations of the latter one, such as "cascade", and "traditional".

The adaptive/agile approach in essence, began to be used after 2001, with the emergence of agile thinking and the publication of the Agile Manifesto (Agile Alliance, 2001), a declaration of principles created to guide software development, but which expanded and is now used in other types of industry. From then on, the PMBOK® Guide in its 3rd edition (PMI®-2004) began to be labeled by a portion of project management practitioners as a guide aimed at managers and professionals who worked only using the predictive approach projects.

However, as shown in Figure 2, it is noted that even on the 6th edition version, the term "adaptive" has a higher percentage of appearance (61%) than the term "predictive" itself, which appears in (24%) of the total citations, contrary to the common thinking of the paragraph above, what represented a little surprise.

In the same reasoning, the guide on the 7th edition, which is a guide considered to be directed to all approaches, shows that the adaptative approach, despite being the most cited on that guide, appears less than on the 6th edition (48% against 61%). However, in general, a greater balance is perceived in relation to what was on the 6th edition guide. The term "hybrid" grows only a little bit in relation to previous edition, with (16% against 15% before).

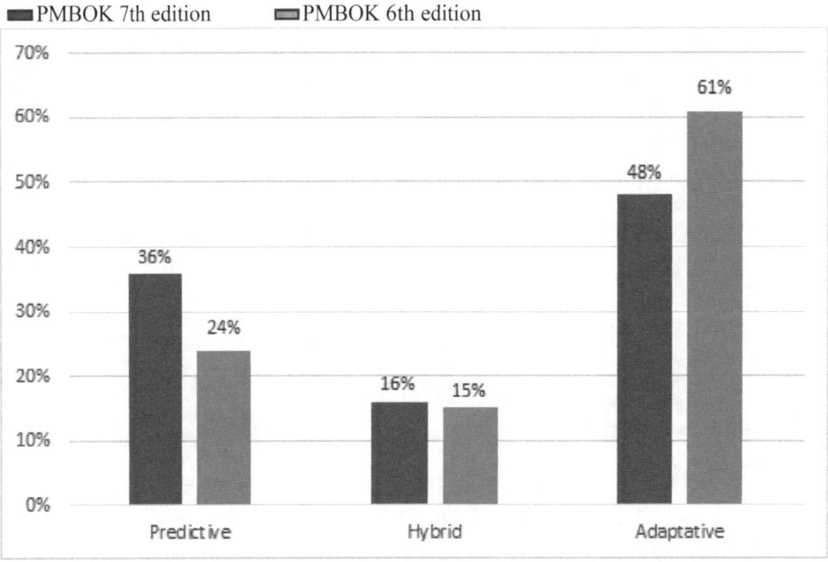

Figure 2. Management Approach Perspective. Source: from the author

5.2 Knowledge Areas Perspective

Although the new guide (7th edition) is no longer tied to the previous Knowledge Area structure, the terms are still cited many times. On latest version of the guide, the term "stakeholders" has (20%) citations among the ten (10) areas of knowledge, as shown in Figure 3, while it only appeared in (12%) on the 6th edition guide. On the new guide, "stakeholders" has become a domain and a management principle. The second term most cited for the knowledge area on the 7th edition guide is "risk", which was previously a separate chapter in the 6th edition guide and has now been replaced by a domain (uncertainty) and a principle (risk).

We can see that, in general, Knowledge Areas continue to be heavily cited in the 7th edition guide, despite their replacement in the chapter structure by management principles and performance domains.

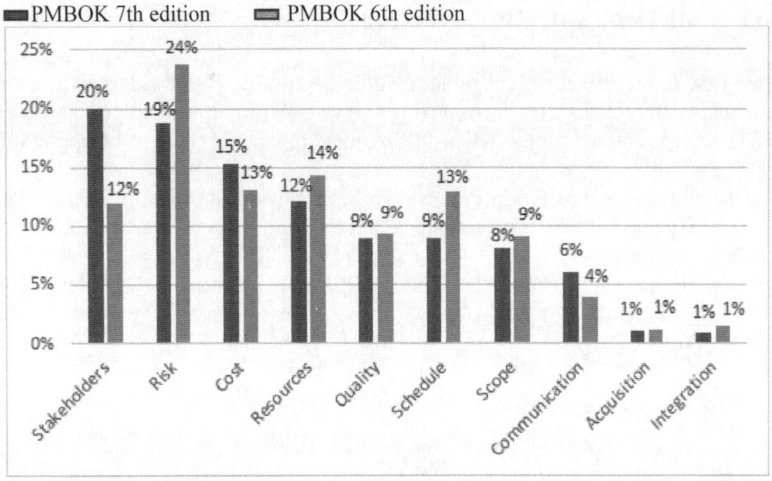

Figure 3. Knowledge Areas Perspective. Source: from the author

5.3 Process Group Perspective

Process groups are no longer part of the new guide (7th edition), but their terms continue to be mentioned with emphasis (Figure 4). The only process group from the 6th edition that appears as a domain is "Planning", which corresponds to (44%) of all citations in this perspective, followed by the term "Control" with (20%), "Initiation", with (16%), "Execution", with (11%), "Closing", with (5%) and "Monitoring and Control", with (4%).

On the 6th edition guide, the term "Planning" represented a process group that had 24 processes out of a total of 49 existing processes and is the 2nd one most cited in the guide, with (20%), the 1st one most cited was "Control", with (46%), and in the sequence, starting from 3rd place: "Execution", with (14%), "Monitoring and Control", with (9%), and "Closing", with (7%).

Due to the term "Control" appearing in the text, many times, outside the context of the process groups and, consequently, not associated with "Monitoring and Control", it was treated as an additional item. However, nothing prevents us from adding the two results into a single percentage when the interpretation so requires. On that way, we would have, for the PMBOK Guide 7th edition (24%) and for the PMBOK Guide 6th edition (55%) occurrences by the term "Monitoring and Control".

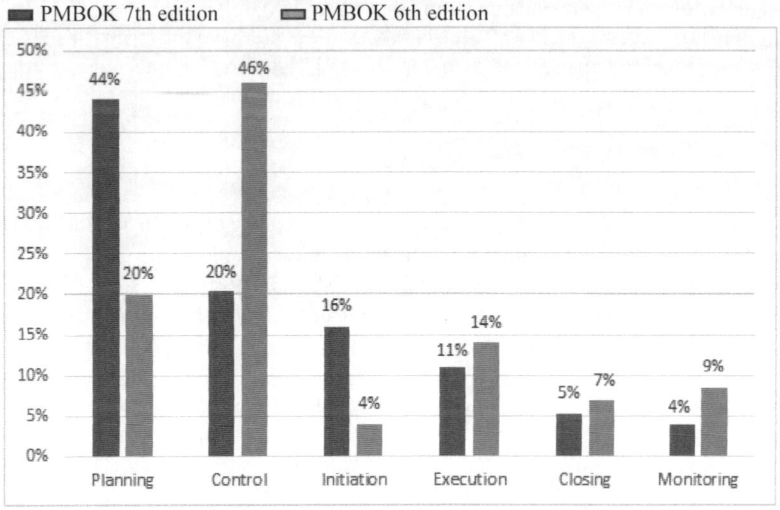

Figure 4. Process Groups Perspective. Source: from the author

5.4 Management Principles Perspective

These terms are new to the Project Management Guide 7th edition. PMI® adopted additional good practices that a project manager should work daily respecting twelve (12) principles that previously existed as important recommendations on the Agile Guide (PMI®, 2017-b) and revamped them to be applied throughout the type of project, that is, for any scope.

Figure 5 presents the result of the informetric analysis carried out from the perspective of Management Principles in the new guide (7th edition). It appears that the term "Team" was the most cited (31%), followed by "Value" (13%), "Stakeholders" (12%), "Changes" (12%), "Risk" (12 %), "Quality" (6%), "Leadership" (5%), "Complexity" (3%), "Resilience" (2%) and finally, "Stewardship" and "Systems Thinking", with (1%) each one.

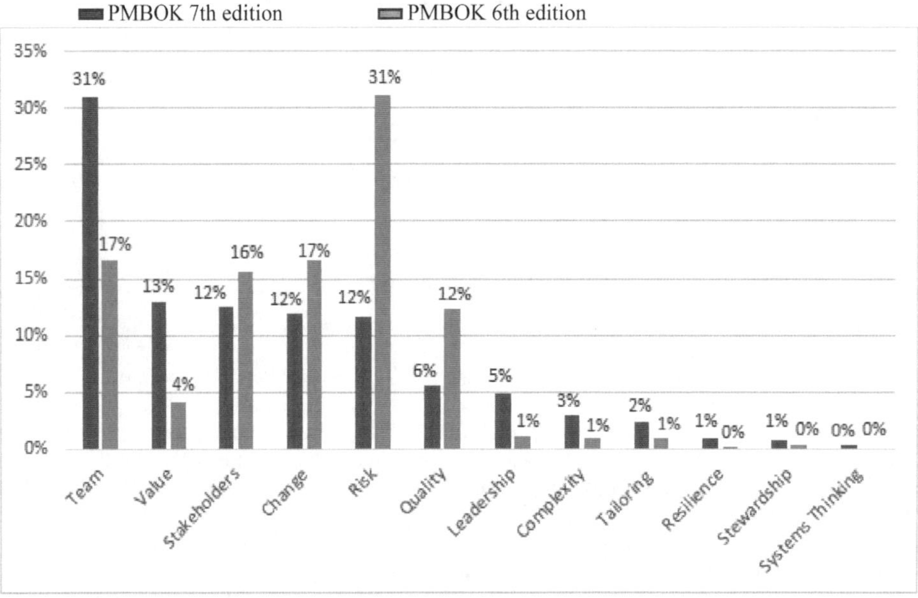

Figure 5. Management Principles Perspective. Source: from the author

Although, the 6th edition guide did not include a separate chapter on management principles, these terms already appeared, with "risk" being the most important one (31%), followed by "team" (17%), "change" (17%), "stakeholders" (16%), "quality" (12%), "value" (4%), and we still have the terms "leadership", "complexity", "adaptation", "resilience", "management ", "planning" and "systems thinking" adding up to 3% among all of them.

5.5 Performance Domains Perspective

This analysis showed that the new Guide (7th edition) emphasizes the importance of managing people to deliver value. In fact, the work to be done must be a responsibility of the people on the project team and provides value in deliveries, as preached by agile thinking since 2001 (PMI®, 2017-b).

Figure 6 demonstrates the terms, from the perspective of the eight (8) new domains ("Life Cycle"; "Team"; "Stakeholders"; "Planning"; "Uncertainty"; "Work"; "Measurement"; and "Delivery"). It appears that the most cited domains in the PMBOK® Guide-7th edition are, at first, "Team" (30%), followed by the domains "Delivery" (22%), "Work" (16%), "Stakeholders" (12%), "Planning" (7%), "Life Cycle" (6%), "Uncertainty" (5%) and "Measurement" (2%).

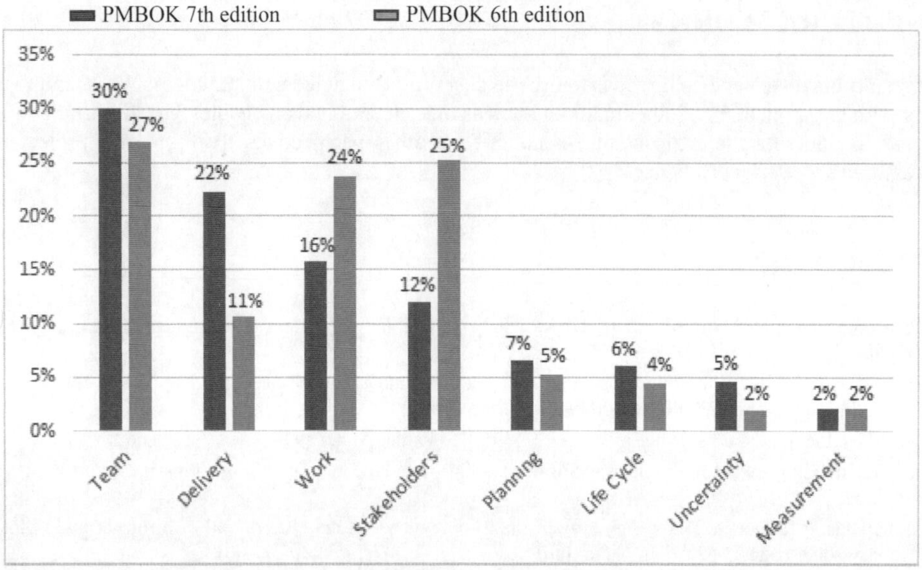

Figure 6. Performance Domains Perspective. Source: from the author

Although the guide in the 6th edition did not include a separate chapter for performance domains, these terms already appeared in its content, with the following degree of importance: "team" (27%), "stakeholders" (25%), "work" (24%), "delivery" (11%), "planning" (5%), "lifecycle" (4%), "uncertainty" (2%), and "measurement" (2%).

The reason for the term "Team" to be repeated more often in the new guide is because it is now one of the management principles and represents a performance domain, recommended as good practice for managing projects. Logically, the guide also reinforces the importance of managing projects across teams, whether in projects with a predictive or adaptive (agile or hybrid) scope.

6. FINAL CONSIDERATIONS

In this article, from the point of view of the informetric, the terms corresponding to the structure of the current and previous versions of the chapters of the PMI® project management best practices and standards guide - the PMBOK® guide were analyzed.

We could verify that the degree of importance given to the terms that formed the structure of the chapters of the guide to best practices in project management on its 6th edition continues to be present on the 7th edition, as well as that the terms that make up the new structure of the chapters in the 7th edition were already quite cited on the previous edition, the 6th one.

It was also possible to confirm that there is an emphasis, in this latest edition of the PMBOK®, on focusing on people management, as the most cited terms in the new version were "team" and "stakeholders".

An interesting curiosity that appeared with this research was that on the Management Approach Perspective, in the previous version, the term "adaptive" was already the most cited of the three one (the two others are predictive and hybrid), with (61%), and in the current version it appears only in (48%) of the cases.

For adaptive approaches, you can use the best practices available on the Agile Guide (PMI®, 2017-b), and on the "Choose your WoW"(PMI®, 2022), this one which helps project teams to choose and develop the better way of working, thus completing the knowledge about the three approaches used to practice project management with the 7th edition guide (PMI®, 2021).

It is important to note that at the end of 2022, PMI® issued a new process guide (PMI®, 2023), to address the use of the management model by process group, being more specific for the predictive lifecycle approaches, which reinforces the result of this study regarding the importance of processes in project management, despite the change made to the organization of chapters in the new best practices guide, now based on domains.

7. FUTURE WORKS

The results obtained serve to direct us to use the best project management practices. We intend to continue this study with the application of other methods such as those mentioned on chapter 3 of this article (methodology), as well as applying them to obtain evaluations on other perspectives that can help project management professionals to work even better.

REFERENCES

Agile Alliance. Agile Manifest. Utah, USA: 2001. Available in:__https://www.agilealliance.org/agile101/the-agile-manifesto/

Bender, E. M. Linguistic Fundamentals for Natural Language Processing. Springer: 2013. Available in: https://link.springer.com/book/10.1007/978-3-031-02150-3

Gil, A. C. Métodos e técnicas de pesquisa social. 5.ed. São Paulo: Atlas, 1999.

Godin, B. On the Origins of Bibliometrics. Springer: 2006. Avalilabe in: https://link.springer.com/article/10.1007/s11192-006-0086-0

Judit-Bar, Ilan. Informetrics at the beginning of the 21st century—A review. Journal of Informetrics, Volume 2, Issue 1, January 2008, Pages 1-52. Availble in: https://doi.org/10.1016/j.joi.2007.11.001

Inomata, D. O.; Manhães, M. C.; Fraga, B. D.; Rados, G. J. V. Mapeamento de conhecimento: Identificação de palavras através de coocorrência. RDBCI: Revista Digital de Biblioteconomia e Ciência da Informação, Campinas, SP, v. 13, n. 2, p. 279–297, 2015. doi: 10.20396/rdbci.v13i2.2121. Available in: https://periodicos.sbu.unicamp.br/ojs/index.php/rdbci/article/view/2121

PMI®. Project Management Institute. Process Groups: A Practice Guide. Pennsylvania, USA: PMI®, 2023.

PMI®. Project Management Institute. Choose your WoW: A Disciplined Agile Approach to Optimizing Your Way of Working – 6sc edition. Pennsylvania, USA: PMI®, 2022.

PMI®. Projetct Management Institute. The standard for project management and a guide to the project management body of knowledge (PMBOK® guide 7th edition). Pennsylvania, USA: PMI®, 2021.

PMI®. Projetct Management Institute. The standard for project management and a guide to the project management body of knowledge (PMBOK® guide 6th edition). Pennsylvania, USA: PMI®, 2017-a.

PMI®. Project Management Institute. Agile Practice Guide. Pennsylvania, USA: PMI®, 2017-b.

PMI®. Projetct Management Institute. The standard for project management and a guide to the project management body of knowledge (PMBOK® guide 3rd edition). Pennsylvania, USA: PMI®, 2004.

BUSINESS PROCESSES MANAGEMENT AND RESPONSIBLE USE OF BIG DATA

Galena Pisoni[1] and Bálint Molnár[2]
[1]*Université Cote d'Azur*
Polytech Nice Sophia, Campus ShopiaTech, 930 Route des Colles, 06410 Biot, France
[2]*Eötvös Loránd University (ELTE)*
Information Systems Department, Faculty of Informatics Pázmány Péter 1/C, 1117 Budapest, Hungary

ABSTRACT

Organizations today seek to improve and adapt their business processes because of the competitive economy. The use and application of Data Science (DS) and Artificial Intelligence (AI) for different business process aims is often discussed and put in place, yet it can have a negative impact if DS and AI are implemented in the wrong way. We discuss the use of DS and AI for the identification, verification, and improvement of business processes, and how to ensure responsible DS and AI use in enterprises for this aim. We propose an information system design for responsible and trustworthy business processes, and we envision that businesses will need strong and well-defined control points in their information systems for managing processes and creating associated audits to enforce their principles. We define questions and challenges companies need to reflect on and follow for an application of responsible DS and AI in the enterprise context.

KEYWORDS

Business Processes, Business Process Management (BPM), Responsible AI, Data Science, AI, Enterprise Architecture

1. INTRODUCTION

The fast evolution of business process management systems and architectures has brought a generation of a waste amount of data coming from business process execution (Weske, 2007). These data can be used to discover or validate knowledge regarding existing processes operators have or help improve processes and provide flexibility and possibility for human intervention. A business process is "a collection of tasks executed in a specific order to achieve the business goal" (Weske, 2007). This definition suggests that business process management systems track the execution of the process it supports and ensures that the process confirms to set of restrictions. The application of data science (DS), and artificial intelligence (AI), opens the possibility to knowledge workers to obtain further knowledge, previously not known, and provides additional flexibility without endangering the correct execution of the business processes itself.

The use of DS and AI is on rise in companies. Data science (DS) studies how to collect, structure, and transform data into information and knowledge, it is an umbrella term for statistical techniques, design techniques, and development methods, while AI is the implementation of a predictive model to foresee events, it has to do with predictive algorithm design, development, efficiency, and the deployment in products and services (Waller & Fawcett, 2013; Newman et al., 2016). In business contexts, DS has termed business intelligence and analytics (BI&A), while the application of AI is referred to as artificial intelligence and analytics (AI&A). Both BI&A and AI&A support the collection, management, analysis, and visualization of large amounts of data, which is of great importance for providing managers, especially in terms of their own operations and business processes, with recommendations and insights (de Medeiros et al., 2020).

The topic of the application of DS and AI to business process management is relevant because organizations that use their business operations data to drive their decisions through BI&A and AI&A can achieve better performance (Brynjolfsson et al., 2011; Müller et al., 2018). According to Newman et al. (2016), the ability to manage operations with DS and AI has become significant for organizations, therefore also the adoption of the BI&A and AI&A approaches for this aim.

Organizations have understood the power of data analytics for mining and enhancing business processes, however, there are great concerns about the use of data for this aim as well. However, the power inherent in DS and AI naturally poses certain threats, especially in terms of fairness, trust, and privacy (Eitel-Porter, 2021; Van Der Aalst, 2016). DS and AI projects could deliver erroneous or biased outcomes and thus breach regulation or cause damage to the company reputation. These outcomes can happen due to different reasons, like bias in the data, bias encoded in the algorithms, or irresponsible management of both, data, and algorithms (Martin, 2022). Data decisions may be unfair or non-transparent, and confidential data may be shared unintentionally or abused by third parties (van der Aalst et al., 2017). Inaccuracies can be produced in each step of the DS or AI analysis, that is if the data used to train the model reflects biases, the output is likely to incorporate these biases as well (Van Der Aalst, 2016). Therefore, detection and prevention of bias and discrimination is an important aspect when applying DS or AI, especially for companies, where their brand and compliance with regulations at stake.

In the context where business processes and business process management are supported by DS and AI, all business processes should be able to run as intended and preserve the ability to recover and retract from undesirable and inconsistent outcomes. Interactive dashboards and business intelligence interfaces, in relation to the execution and adaptation of business processes, and options on how to mitigate problems observe, together with the suggestion of countermeasures, should help the knowledge operator with options and information regarding the business process at hand and provide new insights not available before.

To be able to exploit to the best of the potential the use of DS and AI, the business process management system should be able to interact with agents in an optimized manner. Implementing big data-enhanced business processes in companies and organizations whose information systems had not been originally structured for structuring and processing of big data, or that do not have management structures that enable big data analysis and value creation through the generation of actionable insights, is a big challenge. Moving to data-driven business process management requires both, suited personnel to apply DS and AI in the first place, a change in the underlying architectures and systems to allow for suited collection and analysis of big data, and a change in mindset.

To be able to interact with humans in the best possible way is an important characteristic of a business process management system enhanced with DS and AI. There are numerous ways in which DS and AI can help in this respect, they can provide more and new insights about the execution context and should be able to suggest process-related goals and actions, based on observed situational information, and should be structured so that can work and function in synchronous or asynchronous input. In addition, ideally, they can adapt the mode of working based on the preferences of the business user, adapt the information provided to the type of user it interacts with, and the situation in which the interaction happens. Acceptance of such DS and AI-empowered business process will depend on if the users find the advice rational and justified for the situation; thus, users should be able to understand the provided information, and the system provides faithful explanations for the choices. DS and AI can only be effective if people trust the results, therefore should not be viewed as a black box, accountability and comprehensibility are essential for transparency and therefore trustworthiness of the outcome. (van der Aalst et al., 2017).

Responsible data science implementations must ensure the fulfillment of the following principles (van der Aalst et al., 2017)

– Fairness, that is outputs should avoid unfair conclusions even if they are true
– Accuracy, that is the outputs and results should be accurate, and not a guesswork
– Confidentiality, that is results should answer questions without revealing secrets
– Transparency, that is outputs should provide an explanation to the final user on how the decision was made, and that explanation is clear and makes sense

For use of AI, there's the AI ethics guideline for trustworthy AI by an EU Independent High-Level Expert Group on Artificial Intelligence, that highlights the need for AI systems to be human-centric. The new EU regulatory framework applies to products and services relying on AI. Ethics Guidelines for Trustworthy AI advocate for AI technology that is more human-centric and doesn't discriminate, therefore also responsible and trustworthy business processes based on big data should follow these guidelines and behave in compliance with them.

Improper implementations of AI and DS can bring systematic discrimination and invasions of privacy, therefore it's important to prevent non-transparent and inaccurate conclusions, and to avoid the negative side effects that data may have in any context (van der Aalst et al., 2017).

Given all the above, in this article we first hypothesize an information system design for responsible and trustworthy business processes, next we outline, still to answer challenges, research questions, and opportunities for research in the domain, and finally, we outline actors and stakeholders that should work together to answer the outstanding challenges and questions in this domain. We conclude the paper with a short discussion/reflection of outstanding questions and outline future directions.

2. BACKGROUND

In order to have a responsible and trustworthy application of DS and AI in a business processes context, there must be adequate tools, methods, and technologies to support such governance and decision-making based on big data (Chen et al., 2012). These elements, that is governance frameworks and technologies, should come together, so responsible DS and AI principles are applied at each stage of big data analysis of business operations context.

Given the new demands of companies to constantly innovate and to stay relevant, the research in the domain of information systems is united that IS are considered as 'never complete' and constantly need to be improved (Tilson et al., 2010; Tiwana et al., 2010). The development of governance of business processes, based on big data, requires that sociotechnical constructions are revisited, and new decision points, based on data and observations from outputs of the application of DS and AI methods are introduced. These new strategic decision control points, in return, introduce new stable socio-technical constructions. The new strategic decision points require re-development of the management platforms, and there's a process of flexibility/stability that follows until a new IS stable configuration is found (Figure 1).

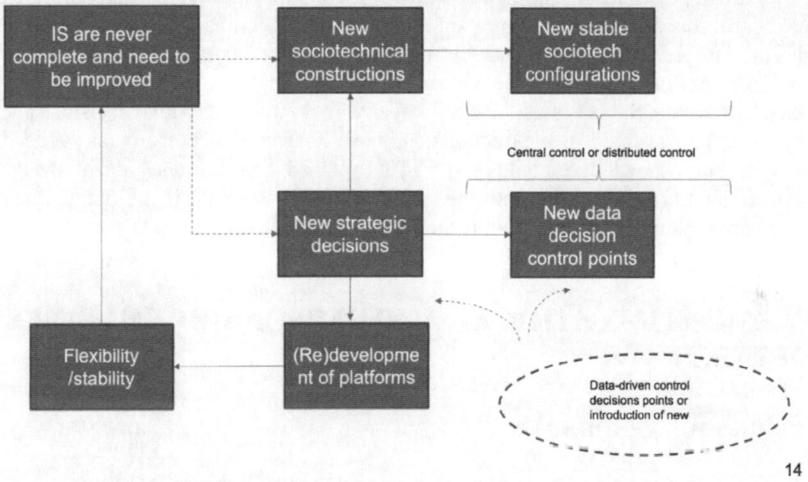

Figure 1. Process of governance of business processes management, with new sociotechnical constructions and decision points decided on big data and application of AI and DS, inspired by Tilson et al. (2010)

The new IS design to support such business process execution, requires that IS architecture is modular by design, decomposed, and follows simple design rules, the design, in turn, must have a good fit with IS use and governance for business operations, therefore, decision points and control mechanisms, are decided based on data, and application of DS and AI on operations data. This IS organization is influenced by the environment in which the company operates and the technological trajectory of the products and services of the adjacent companies and competitors, as well as their influence (Figure 2). The business issues request data warehouse or data lake design suited to the requirements, therefore they also drive competitors in a similar way in terms of IS design and search for optimal solutions for the domain at hand.

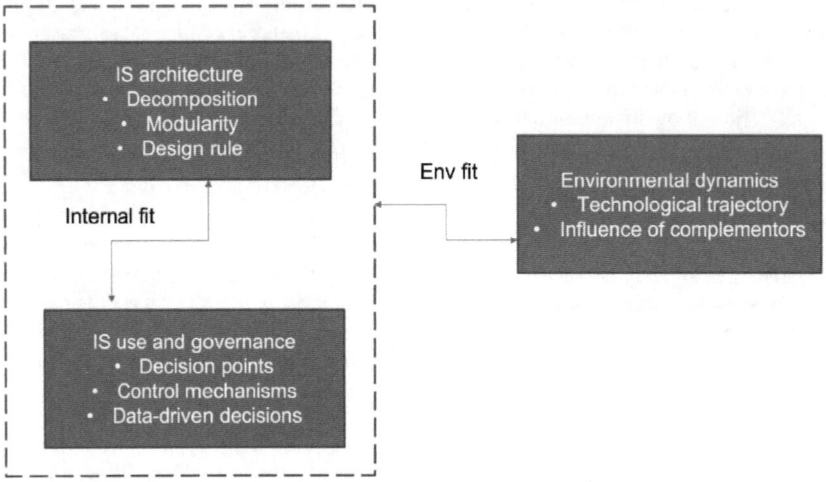

Figure 2. IS architecture is influenced internally by the use and governance of IS, and new decision points, based on data, while the whole IS organization and management is decided in the wider environmental context, in which the competitors and adjusts technologies affect the different selections internally of the company for its operations, inspired by Tiwana et al. (2010)

Ethical DS and AI governance in businesses foresee that first the company determines, based on existing guidelines, the ethical principles that apply to its own work and to which it will adhere. Preferably there should be an ethical board, that among other important members of the company, consists of ethicists, and approve the strategies then implemented in DS and AI implementations, especially for own company operations. As proposed in our framework, there must be a clear outlines governance structure, based on data collected and the application of AI and DS, there must be clarity over who is expected to take decisions about which aspects of the business operations, and possible tradeoffs and benefits from the company, as deduced from the AI and DS analysis. Next, such knowledge should be spread across the whole company and all the company members, and finally, there should be strong monitoring, preferably with metrics, if the outputs of both, data-driven approaches and governance do give ethical, responsible, and trustworthy results

3. IMPLEMENTING ETHICAL AND RESPONSIBLE BUSINESS PROCESSES

3.1 Guidelines for Companies

The problem as we outline in this paper lies in the intersection of human-centric AI and enterprise architectures and applications, with a focus on business process optimization for businesses. In the previous section, we outlined a governance model for IS for business process management, however, different questions and challenges need to be answered before such a governance model, enhanced with AI and DS, is put in place in organizations.

Explainable AI (XAI), for instance, promises to address the explainability problem, that is to enable users to understand the algorithm and parameters it used to make the decision. The aim of XAI is to provide the reasons for the outcome of the process of deciding a way to make it understandable for the final user. The research on XAI had mainly been performed in two directions: visualization of ML processes and explainable ML algorithms. These approaches so far have delivered limited results, due to the algorithms' limited capability to explain decisions in humanly understandable ways or rely on abstract visualization methods, which may further increase complexity for final users.

In an organization, there are different kinds of users and stakeholders, and different stakeholders may need different explanations. In addition, not everyone or every role needs or wants an explanation, it may be that the same explanation may be good for more than one role (Langer, M et al., 2021). Therefore, the first question that companies will need to answer in this respect is

1) Which stakeholders need an explanation? What kind of explanation each stakeholder/user needs?

Subsequently, there'll be the need to test the effectiveness of the explanations generated and how users understand the explanations. There's a need for participatory involvement of all and co-creation of meanings for different users, that is developers of DS and AI solutions and business experts, the need to also teach business users regarding explainability and how to "consume" explanations generated, risks involved, and common ways in which the explanations will be used (Chromik et al, 2021). After being provided an explanation, some participants may want or need even more information, on how one can do this efficiently the companies will need to understand of their own:

2) How can we test if the explanation is good for the needs of the organization? How can we provide more information for the roles/stakeholders that need such additional information? How can we achieve better alignment of the explanations with the needs of the different stakeholders in the company?

A known problem in DS is the phenomenon of "overfitting", or better looking for patterns that don't generalize outside of the given dataset, in addition, AI algorithms fail as well, and there are risks concerned with the actions stakeholders usually take or might need to take, so another question is

3) How risky AI or DS failures are for the company?

If users understand how DS and AI work, then they'll understand also preventively what kind of problems may arise, for companies. It may be easier to provide access to people with such knowledge that can later be explained, especially when the explanatory information is not good or is superficial, not useful; moreover, they are not available, as sometimes to make the results understandable, when the results are good, can be achieved after consultation of such people.

Therefore, the other two questions to consider for companies:

4) Do different stakeholders understand the explanations produced by AI or DS?

5) Is it possible to have DS and AI scientists available on spot to provide explanations to different stakeholders?

Sometimes explanations provided are not the desired one and may be inadequate, for deciding in the complex world of business. Sometimes the explanation can be of no-good quality, or too detailed, in different formats, and different kinds of contents, like diagrams, matrices, and logic trees (Wang et al, 2019). Previous research confirms that it's good to visualize data or make a reduction but clear analogies, especially in problem-solving domains, in highly detailed technical explanations are not favored often, although having cross-disciplinary skills would help the users to feel more secure in the results as they will be able to control the outputs and the data better in their own.

6) What should we do if the provided explanations are too technical?

In the use of DS and AI approaches and data in general it may be better to also know better the data origin, and the data itself and to see the –input-output demonstration, and therefore understand the biases

7) How will we provide more information about the data origin? In which format?

In a context like this, it is important also for all stakeholders to understand how the system can fail or mislead.

8) Can we identify a common way in which the system can fail? Can we provide such training to different stakeholders in the company?

Interactive ML is an approach to ML in which algorithms interact with agents (these agents can be humans too) and thus through these interactions they can optimize their behavior (Holzinger, 2016) for a problem like this, the use of interactive ML (iML) is a key as well. It may be the case that the traditional ML approaches might have limited success, in the case of events not available in the training dataset.

The next challenge for the company to solve would be which data should be used for developing such a system. There are privacy-and security-related consequences, as well as, as outlined above ethical issues that are relevant and important to be considered (Clavell & Peuvrelle, 2020). There is the observatory of algorithms with social impact studies that enlists different algorithms and provides information about their aim, therefore aiming to demystify opaque and unaccountable algorithms that have proved to be systematically biased against women and minority groups, this can be another valuable resource regarding selection of algorithms on which the system can be based.[1]

In addition, companies need to be compliant with regulations, therefore the system needs to comply with regulations too, especially guidelines coming from the EU regarding the development of human-centric AI systems (European Commission, 2019). There are also existing widgets to use for the development of a fair and not biased decision-making system (based on e.g., fairness IBM Toolbox and responsible AI widgets) that can make the development of AI solutions easier for companies.

The methods for the analysis of data should be mixed and encourage ethical and socially responsible behavior. Computational social science approaches and computational analytics methods based on machine learning and computational models to contribute to comprehensible AI, taking into account the business processes and business needs should be designed, to accelerate the transition to actionable, responsible, and bias-free insights from big data. There is a need of further research to evaluate the practices regarding knowledge management and data analysis, as well as the gathering, and usage of data in the generic business process management ecosystem of the company, to test the application of relevant existing tools, widgets, and DS and AI methods so to have good quality output.

3.2 What Kind of Team to Gather?

The presented challenges and questions for companies require knowledge and expertise from different domains, and form a team combining a diverse set of needs to answer them:

– Data custodians, data curators, and knowledge operators, that would prepare the data coming from different operations for analysis, especially from big data and data coming from different sources of the company

– Data scientists, that would use the generated data from business process execution to build robust machine learning models that are responsible, trustworthy, and explainable

– Business managers, that are familiar with the knowledge domain of the company, and existing business processes the company relies upon,

– Regulation authorities, to confirm that the explanations on how the decision was made, are in line with regulation if it is clear and makes sense

– Ethicists, and company external references regarding ethical criteria in the domain of the company.

4. DISCUSSION AND FUTURE DIRECTIONS

In this paper, we outlined governance mechanisms for business process management, based on big data, DS and AI, and a set of guidelines for companies, in the form of a checklist to ensure good implementation of DS and AI-enhanced business processes. In addition, we reflect on what kind of team to gather to be sure that there is ethical and responsible use of AI and DS for business process improvement.

There are many possible future directions and problems still to solve.

One of the issues in research like this is which decisions should be fully automated (based on data) and for which decisions human input shall be needed and why? And how can companies decide on this? An important step would be to understand and distinguish functions that should be carried out by DS or AI-empowered systems, and functions that should be performed entirely by humans, and study their order in each context, to understand how intelligent functions can best support human actions, and vice versa.

---

[1] https://eticasfoundation.org/oasi/register/

Another challenge is how to put together the same visualization insights generated from data and the process itself. Another recurring challenge is the relationship between data and processes. State-of-the-art approaches like UML still have different diagrams covering different aspects, that is, class models for data, activity diagrams for processes, yet there are no suited visualizations that combine data, business intelligence insights, and business process representations.

Petri nets fully integrate both but are difficult to use for complex designs of information systems. Further research in the domain is timely.

ACKNOWLEDGEMENT

The paper was supported by the “Application Domain-Specific Highly Reliable IT Solutions" project, implemented with the support provided by the National Research, Development and Innovation Fund of Hungary, financed under the Thematic Excellence Programme TKP2021-NVA-29 (National Challenges Subprogramme) funding scheme, and by the COST Action CA19130 - "Fintech and Artificial Intelligence in Finance Towards a transparent financial industry" (FinAI) https://www.cost.eu/actions/CA19130/.

REFERENCES

Brynjolfsson, E., Hitt, L. M. & Kim, H. H. (2011), ‘Strength in numbers: How does data-driven decision-making affect firm performance?’, Available at SSRN 1819486 .

Chen, H., Chiang, R. H. & Storey, V. C. (2012), ‘Business intelligence and analytics: From big data to big impact’, MIS quarterly pp. 1165–1188.

Chromik, M., Eiband, M., Buchner, F., Krüger, A., & Butz, A. (2021, April). I think i get your point, AI! the illusion of explanatory depth in explainable AI. In *26th International Conference on Intelligent User Interfaces* (pp. 307-317).

Clavell, G. G., & Peuvrelle, V. (2020). Ethical Issues in Big Data Analytics for Time Critical Mobility Forecasting. In Big Data Analytics for Time-Critical Mobility Forecasting

de Medeiros, M. M., Hoppen, N. & Maçada, A. C. G. (2020), ‘Data science for business: benefits, challenges and opportunities’, The Bottom Line .

Eitel-Porter, R. (2021), ‘Beyond the promise: implementing ethical ai’, AI and Ethics 1(1), 73–80.

European Commission (2019). High-level expert group on Artificial Intelligence, Ethics Guidelines for Trustworthy AI, European Commission

Holzinger, A. (2016). Interactive machine learning for health informatics: when do we need the human- in-the-loop?. Brain Informatics, 3(2), 119-131

Langer, M et al. (2021). What do we want from Explainable Artificial Intelligence (XAI)?–A stakeholder perspective on XAI and a conceptual model guiding interdisciplinary XAI research. *Artificial Intelligence*, 296, 103473

Martin, K. (2022), Algorithmic bias and corporate responsibility: How companies hide behind the false veil of the technological imperative, in ‘Ethics of data and analytics’, Auerbach Publications, pp. 36–50.

Müller, O., Fay, M. & Vom Brocke, J. (2018), ‘The effect of big data and analytics on firm performance: An econometric analysis considering industry characteristics’, Journal of Management Information Systems 35(2), 488–509.

Newman, R., Chang, V., Walters, R. J. & Wills, G. B. (2016), ‘Model and experimental development for business data science’, International Journal of Information Management 36(4), 607–617.

Tilson, D., Lyytinen, K. & Sørensen, C. (2010), ‘Research commentary—digital infrastructures: The missing is research agenda’, Information systems research 21(4), 748–759.

Tiwana, A., Konsynski, B. & Bush, A. A. (2010), ‘Research commen- tary—platform evolution: Coevolution of platform architecture, governance, and environmental dynamics’, Information systems research 21(4), 675–687.

Van Der Aalst, W. (2016), Process mining: data science in action, Vol. 2, Springer.

van der Aalst, W. M., Bichler, M. & Heinzl, A. (2017), ‘Responsible data science’. Waller, M. A. & Fawcett, S. E. (2013), ‘Data science, predictive analytics, and big data: a revolution that will transform supply chain design and management’.

Weske, M. (2007), Business process management architectures, Springer.

Wang, D., Yang, Q., Abdul, A., & Lim, B. Y. (2019, May). Designing theory-driven user-centric explainable AI. In *Proceedings of the 2019 CHI conference on human factors in computing systems* (pp. 1-15).

SHORT PAPERS

POTENTIAL OF GAMIFICATION FOR ENVIRONMENTAL MANAGEMENT TRAINING IN THE CONSTRUCTION INDUSTRY

Insyirah Abd Razak, Nafisah Abdul Rahiman and Norazam Othman
Department of Quantity Surveying, Faculty of Built Environment & Surveying
Universiti Teknologi Malaysia Johor Bahru. 81310 Johor Bahru Johor, Malaysia

ABSTRACT

Construction activities are a major source of environmental pollution. Environmental Management Systems (EMS) which aim to minimize adverse environmental effects and maximize environmental benefits, have gained attention recently. However, the human capital in EMS is insufficient to realize its full potential in preventing environmental issues. Environmental management training (EMT) is required to provide knowledge and skills regarding good practices in sustainability, a safe and hygienic work environment and reducing environmental risks resulting from construction activities. Gamification approaches for EMT have the potential to empower knowledge and skills effectively for construction players. This study's objectives are (i) to highlight challenges in EMT, (ii) to highlight effective measures in EMT, and (iii) to discuss the potential of gamification for effective EMT. Challenges in EMT include low environmental awareness, saturated training content, lack of hands-on approach, lack of visualization from training with real practice. Effective measures in EMT includes increases environmental awareness, increases motivation with rewards system, employee engagement, and strategy of designing effective training delivery. The potential of gamification can be seen through improving employees' motivation and attractive engagement, meanwhile serious game capacity to transfer skills and knowledge of environmental management innovatively and effectively. The limitation of the study is that it only explored the theoretical integration of EMT and gamification in the construction industry. Future research should focus on the actual application of gamification for EMT in the industry.

KEYWORDS

Environmental Management, Training, Construction Industry, Gamification, Serious Game

1. INTRODUCTION

Development is inevitable and one of the significant effects is pollution (Lau *et al.*, 2016). 67.5% of the ecosystem and 21% of the natural resources in Malaysia are affected by construction activities (Zolfagharian et al., 2012). Currently, environmental management system, a process management system that enables organizations to further reduce their environmental impact (Daud, Yusof and Mokhtar, 2019) is being promoted. Every organization should equip its workers with the skills and knowledge of environmental management (EM). Environmental management training (EMT) is crucial to provide knowledge and skills regarding good practices in sustainability, a safe work environment and minimize environmental risks resulting from construction activities. However, EMT is not well acknowledged in the construction industry. Lack of awareness for environmental factors are obvious (Ojo, Oladinrin and Obi, 2021) as construction companies tend to prioritize time and money over environmental concerns (Abdullah, Madros and Ahmad, 2001). Besides, lack of emphasis on EMT caused low recognition of EM in organizations (Ololade and Rametse, 2018). Despite the scarcity of skilled workers in EM for the construction industry, there are no articles discussed on relevant issues that identify challenges related to human resources (Campos *et al.*, 2016). Among significant human resource aspects is EMT which aims to prepare change agents to encourage the growth of EM in organizations (Jabbour *et al.*, 2010). This study focused issues on a shortage of skilled workers for EM in the construction industry, insufficient training content for construction environmental training, and the potential gamification for EMT in construction. Hence, the objectives of this study are (i) to highlight challenges in EMT, (ii) to highlight effective measures in EMT, and (iii) to discuss the potential of gamification for effective EMT. This paper is structured into an introduction, gamification rationale, challenges and effective measures of EMT, gamifications potentials, and a conclusion.

2. WHY GAMIFICATION AS A STRATEGY?

Gamification is defined as use of game elements in non-gaming contexts to enhance user engagement and experience (Deterding *et al.*, 2011) and promotes behavioral change (Mazur Stommen and Farley, 2016). Also, gamification refers to the mix of game elements' selection, application, implementation, and integration to enhance users' experiences and create engaging gameplay (Werbach, 2014). Common visible game elements are points, badges, leaderboards, performance graphs, meaningful stories, avatars and teammates. Besides, the needs of the players for psychological satisfaction is crucial during the design of gamification tools (Sailer *et al.*, 2017). Gamification can highlight objectives and their applicability, guide users along predetermined paths, provide rapid feedback, reward excellent behavior, and condense complex topics into simple tasks (Krath, Schürmann and von Korflesch, 2021). There are higher preferences for "just-in-time" training due to its ability to tailor programs to the specific and immediate needs of employers and deliver quick training (Gekara and Snell, 2018). This raises the possibility of linking just-in-time training and gamification for EMT in the construction industry, as proven in healthcare education (ONeill *et al.*, 2018).

3. CHALLENGES IN EMT

Factors that discourage construction workers from joining training program are a lack of training environments on site, lack of policies to hire trained workers as permanent employees, a lack of research and development in the training system and a lack of training infrastructure (Johari and Jha, 2019). Moreover, participants perceived neutrality on training contents, training environments, facilities and materials, the training schedule and presentation style and training effectiveness. This suggests that training activities do not meet trainees' needs and expectations. Statistically, training contents, training environments, facilities and materials, training schedules and presentation styles show a significant positive correlation with training effectiveness (Hajjar and Alkhanaizi, 2018). Also, the Construction Industry Development Board (CIDB, 2018) provided EMT for the construction industry however this course is currently inactive due to a lack of participation (CIDB, personal communication, September 25, 2022). In Malaysia, EMT provided are more relevant for industrial sectors compared to construction sector. Hence, standardization of EMT would be helpful, acting as a proper guideline to assist construction players in EM.

Many construction activities have immediate and direct negative effects on the environment (Yahaya and Abidin, 2020) as it happened gradually such as flood and landslide, different from health and safety risks whose consequences happened immediately, especially suffered by labors. Environmental harm is difficult to comprehend, but its detrimental effects are progressively developed. Significant gaps between the training provided and the abilities demanded by the construction industry are that most training is classroom-based, despite the industry needs more workers with practical experience, it is disconnected from real-world tasks and lacks practicality on the work site, it does not consider the various construction jobs performed by different classes of contractors, and most contractors attend training because it is required of them (Zahrizan *et al.*, 2013). EMT should be interactive, immersive, practical and provide participants with the skills they need to manage the environment safely and effectively. However, existing training delivery is lacking in these areas; it is difficult to learn from mistakes and simulate hazardous demonstrations in the real world.

4. EFFECTIVE MEASURES IN EMT

Successful training outcomes are significantly affected by training design and delivery which are challenged with training space, interaction and conduct in training design and provision with a market-based approach (Gekara and Snell, 2018). The practical implementation, organizational factors, motivational factors, human-related factors and behavioral factors are the major success factor for construction safety training (Tezel *et al.*, 2021). Comprehensive environmental training received by employees is needed for successful EMS development. Human resources factors are key elements in EMS practice, which includes top management support, environmental training, employee empowerment, teamwork and reward systems (Daily and Huang, 2001). Top management commitment, employee training and green programs are found to be statistically significant for perceived environmental performance (Lather and Shikha, 2015). Besides, there is a positive relationship between barrier factors; a lack of guidelines for the setting of objectives and the involvement of employees, suppliers and other stakeholders, and a lack of guidelines to achieve the continuous improvement of the standard, leading to the implementation of an EMS (Ismail *et al.*, 2015).

5. GAMIFICATION POTENTIALS IN EMT

Although the construction industry is largely dependent on technology, construction EMT has not yet evolved towards embedding technological elements especially gamification. Gamification is defined as "the process of making activities more game-like," which emphasis the significant gap between the elements of games and the whole experience of gamefulness (Werbach, 2014). Meanwhile, serious games aim to communicate a message for the purpose of training or to develop particular skills and behaviors that can be transferred to the real world (Mettler and Pinto, 2015). Capabilities of serious game can be seen in promoting lean construction training (Liu *et al.*, 2020), risk and hazard identification in the construction industry (Mohd *et al.*, 2019) and increases occupational safety knowledge (Kazar and Comu, 2021). This supports the idea that serious game-based training is effective to ensure safety knowledge retention over time. Besides, serious games are also noticeable in different job training industries such as flood safety training (Mokhtar, Ismail and Muda, 2019), enhance problem-solving skills (Uskov and Sekar, 2014), better knowledge interpretation and engagement (Li *et al.*, 2017). Thus, this provides a good opportunity to explore gamification potentials and improve current training delivery for construction EMT. Hence, this study proposes to integrate gamification and a serious game approach with construction environmental training.

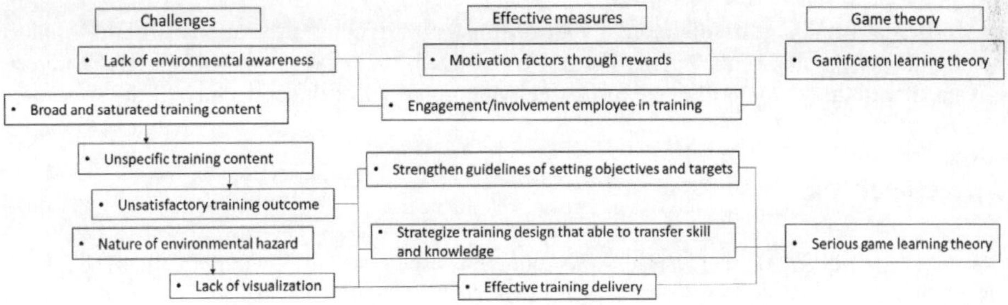

Figure 1. Theoretical framework of gamification and serious games for environmental management training

Figure 1 illustrates the theoretical framework which provides an initial view of gamification's potential to improve the efficacy of EMT. The link between EMT and gamification can be made meaningful by identifying challenges and its effective measures. From the gamification focal point, environmental behavior can be stimulated through improving motivation of workers. A rewards system in gamification has the potential to attract, engage and encourage workers towards positive environmental behavior. Trainees would become more environmentally conscious and motivated to understand the concept of EMS. Engagement through points, badges, and leaderboards would provide a competitive approach among trainees and challenge them to perform better. Trainees able to get involved in EMS can bring about changes in terms of workers feeling more responsible, environmentally aware and having a better image. Meanwhile, from the serious game dimension, knowledge and skills in EMS can be attractively transferred to trainees. Training objectives must be identified before strategizing the training design to meet those needs. Saturated EMS training content can be grouped into smaller subject matters and arranged with better engagement and visualization. Nevertheless, through the development of gamification and serious games for EMT, the effectiveness and outcomes can be discussed further.

6. CONCLUSION

This paper highlights the challenges in EMT, which are the lack of environmental awareness, the lack of participation in environmental training, the broad structure of training content, and the lack of visualization due to the indirect nature of environmental hazards. Furthermore, effective measures of EMT discussed are employees' motivation, employees' involvement and engagement, strengthening guidelines for setting objectives and strategic training design that is able to transfer skill and knowledge, and effective training delivery. From these challenges and effective measures, gamification and serious game strategy have seen their potential to assist in improvised EMT. Gamification concepts have the opportunity to increase trainees' motivation and engagement during training, which later also improves environmental performance. Meanwhile, the serious game concept has seen its potential by embedding the concept of purposeful knowledge and skill transfer in EM. However, it is also crucial to study the training objectives, which can later be designed into effective training delivery. Limitations of this study are that the topics of study are quite specific, which are EMT in construction projects, gamification, and serious games. The methodology of the study focused on synthesis from a literature review, and it is expected to provide a significant outcome from a combination quantitative and qualitative research approach. Although the proposed framework is merely an initial work, there is a need for more research on the application of gamification for EMT in construction projects. Also, the realization and adoption of gamification and serious games in EMT can be explored further.

ACKNOWLEDGEMENT

This work was funded and supported by the Ministry of Higher Education (MoHE) Malaysia under the Fundamental Research Grant Scheme (Vote No. FRGS/1/2021/SSI03/UTM/02/1) and Universiti Teknologi Malaysia. The authors would like to express their appreciation for the assistance of the sponsors.

REFERENCES

Abdullah, A.M., Madros, N.H. and Ahmad, A.S. (2001) 'Environmental Problems Confronting The Construction Industry in Producing Sustainable Developement', in *Conference Proceedings of the National Conference of Construction Industry, Skudai, Malaysia*.

Campos, L.M.S. *et al.* (2016) 'Environmental management systems in the construction industry: A review', *Environmental Engineering and Management Journal*, 15(2), pp. 453–460. doi:10.30638/eemj.2016.048.

CIDB (2018) *Professional course in environmental management*.

Daily, B.F. and Huang, S.C. (2001) 'Achieving sustainability through attention to human resource factors in environmental management', *International Journal of Operations and Production Management*, 21(12), pp. 1539–1552. doi:10.1108/01443570110410892.

Daud, S., Yusof, N. and Mokhtar, M. (2019) 'The Effectiveness of the Environmental Management System (EMS) Implementation in Green Supply Chain: A Case Study', in *FGIC 2nd Conference on Governance and Integrity 2019*, pp. 943–962. doi:10.18502/kss.v3i22.5105.

Deterding, S. *et al.* (2011) 'Gamificación . Utilizando elementos de diseño de juegos en contextos que no sean de juego', *CHI'11 extendido ...*, pp. 2425–2428. Available at: http://dl.acm.org/citation.cfm?id=1979575.

Gekara, V. and Snell, D. (2018) 'Designing and delivering skills transferability and employment mobility: the challenges of a market-driven vocational education and training system', *Journal of Vocational Education and Training*, 70(1), pp. 107–129. doi:10.1080/13636820.2017.1392996.

Hajjar, S.T. EL and Alkhanaizi, M.S. (2018) 'Exploring the Factors That Affect Employee Training Effectiveness : A Case Study in Bahrain', *SAGE Open*, pp. 1–12. doi:10.1177/2158244018783033.

Ismail, R. *et al.* (2015) 'The Implementation of Environmental Management in Malaysian Construction Project', *Australian Journal of Basic and Applied Sciences*, 7(11), pp. 222–231.

Jabbour, C.J.C. *et al.* (2010) 'Managing environmental training in organizations: Theoretical review and proposal of a model', *Management of Environmental Quality: An International Journal*, 21(6), pp. 830–844. doi:10.1108/14777831011077673.

Johari, S. and Jha, K.N. (2019) 'Challenges of attracting construction workers to skill development and training programmes', *Engineering, Construction and Architectural Management*, 27(2), pp. 321–340. doi:10.1108/ECAM-02-2019-0108.

Kazar, G. and Comu, S. (2021) 'Effectiveness of Serious Games for Safety Training: A Mixed Method Study', *Journal of Construction Engineering and Management*, 147(8). doi:10.1061/(ASCE)CO.1943-7862.0002119.

Krath, J., Schürmann, L. and von Korflesch, H.F.O. (2021) 'Revealing the theoretical basis of gamification: A systematic review and analysis of theory in research on gamification, serious games and game-based learning', *Computers in Human Behavior*, 125(January), p. 106963. doi:10.1016/j.chb.2021.106963.

Lather, A.S. and Shikha, G. (2015) 'Impact of Green Human Resource Factors on Environmental Performance in Manufacturing Companies : an Empirical Evidence Impact of Green Human Resource Factors on Environmental Performance in Manufacturing Companies ':, *International Journal of Engineering and Management Sciences*, 6(1), pp. 23–30.

Lau, J.L. *et al.* (2016) 'Understanding the environmental worldviews of Malaysian project managers', *Smart and Sustainable Built Environment*, 5(4), pp. 307–324. doi:10.1108/SASBE-06-2016-0012.

Li, K. *et al.* (2017) 'Measuring the Learning Effectiveness of Serious Gaming for Training of Complex Manufacturing Tasks', *Simulation and Gaming*, 48(6), pp. 770–790. doi:10.1177/1046878117739929.

Liu, C. *et al.* (2020) 'Accelerating the last planner system® (LPS) uptake using virtual reality and serious games: A sociotechnical conceptual framework', *IGLC 28 - 28th Annual Conference of the International Group for Lean Construction 2020*, (January 2021), pp. 481–492. doi:10.24928/2020/0058.

Mazur Stommen, S. and Farley, K. (2016) *Games for Grownups: The Role of Gamification in Climate Change and Sustainability, Indicia Consulting LLC.*

Mohd, N.I. *et al.* (2019) 'Exploring gamification approach in hazard identification training for Malaysian construction industry', *International Journal of Built Environment and Sustainability*, 6(1), pp. 51–57. doi:10.11113/ijbes.v6.n1.333.

Mokhtar, N., Ismail, A. and Muda, Z. (2019) 'Designing model of serious game for flood safety training', *International Journal of Advanced Computer Science and Applications*, 10(5), pp. 331–339. doi:10.14569/ijacsa.2019.0100541.

Ojo, L.D., Oladinrin, O.T. and Obi, L. (2021) 'Critical Barriers to Environmental Management System Implementation in the Nigerian Construction Industry', *Environmental Management*, 68(2), pp. 147–159. doi:10.1007/s00267-021-01473-y.

Ololade, O.O. and Rametse, P.P. (2018) 'Determining factors that enable managers to implement an environmental management system for sustainable construction: A case study in Johannesburg', *Business Strategy and the Environment*, 27(8), pp. 1720–1732. doi:10.1002/bse.2237.

ONeill, K. *et al.* (2018) 'Mobile technology, just-in-time learning and gamification: Innovative strategies for a CAUTI education program', *Online Journal of Nursing Informatics*, 22(2), pp. 1–11.

Sailer, M. *et al.* (2017) 'How gamification motivates: An experimental study of the effects of specific game design elements on psychological need satisfaction', *Computers in Human Behavior*, 69, pp. 371–380. doi:10.1016/j.chb.2016.12.033.

Tezel, A. *et al.* (2021) 'Critical success factors for safety training in the construction industry', *Buildings*, 11(4). doi:10.3390/buildings11040139.

Uskov, A. and Sekar, B. (2014) 'Serious games, gamification and game engines to support framework activities in engineering: Case studies, analysis, classifications and outcomes', in *IEEE International Conference on Electro Information Technology*. IEEE, pp. 618–623. doi:10.1109/EIT.2014.6871836.

Werbach, K. (2014) '(Re) Defining Gamification', *Springer Lecture Notes in Computer Science* [Preprint].

Yahaya, I. and Abidin, N.Z. (2020) 'The implementation of environmental practices by Malaysian contractors', *International Journal of Integrated Engineering*, 12(4), pp. 310–318.

Zahrizan, Z. *et al.* (2013) 'Exploring the barriers and driving factors inimplementing Building Information Modeling (BIM) in the Malaysian Construction Industry: A Preliminary Study', *The Journal of The Institution of Engineers, Malaysia*, 75(1), pp. 384–393.

Zolfagharian, S. *et al.* (2012) 'Environmental impacts assessment on construction sites', *Construction Research Congress 2012: Construction Challenges in a Flat World, Proceedings of the 2012 Construction Research Congress*, (March 2016), pp. 1750–1759. doi:10.1061/9780784412329.176.

ORGANISATION AND IMPLEMENTATION OF WELFARE TECHNOLOGY - AN INTERVIEW STUDY IN SWEDEN AND NORWAY

Ann Svensson[1], Camilla Gjellebæk[2] and Selma Kylén[1]

[1]*School of Business, Economics and IT, University West, P.O., 461 86 Trollhättan, Sweden*

[2]*Faculty of Health, Welfare and Organisation, Østfold University College, 1671 Fredrikstad, Norway*

ABSTRACT

This paper reports from an interview study on organisation and implementation of welfare technology in municipalities in a rural interregional area in Sweden and Norway. The aim of this paper is to analyse how municipalities organize their work with implementation of welfare technology. The results show that there are differences in organization, prioritization and decision-making between the municipalities. The bigger municipalities seem to have more resources to develop and structure test and implementation processes. The smaller municipalities seem to be more dependent on "fiery souls" managers' commitments in implementing welfare technology.

KEYWORDS

Welfare Technology, Rural Municipalities, Social Care, Healthcare, Implementation, Organization

1. INTRODUCTION

Municipalities are intended to accelerate digital transformation in care services, as this is expected to improve the quality and cost-effectiveness of care provision. The concept of welfare technology is used in the Scandinavian countries, and it covers all the technology used in health and care. In some contexts, Welfare technologies and e-health is sometimes equated with the concept welfare technology (Frennert & Baudin, 2021). Such technologies can be described as assistive technologies providing physical, social and cognitive assistance (Kouppamäki, 2021). In this paper, it refers to all kinds of techniques aimed to improve the quality of welfare services through increased security, activity, participation or independence for recipients of health and care services, as usually called user-related technologies. Such technologies consist of safety alarms, night monitoring, digital surveillance, sensor and movement detectors, assistive robots and exercise apps, and they are aiming to increase empowerment, safety, autonomy and independence among older or disabled people (Emilsson, et al., 2023). Also, process-related technologies are covered by the concept of welfare technology. These are intended to improve professional practice as well as to improve quality on welfare services by facilitating, improving and streamlining care and nursing from the staff's point of view. Such technologies could be planning tools, digital medication apps and so on. The concept of welfare technology also concerns learning of welfare technology (SOU 2020: 14; Svensson, et al., 2021). However, the implementation of digital technology meets challenges du to organisational resistance, insufficient infrastructure, as well as ethical and juridical issues. Implementation of welfare technology obviously requires knowledge of digitalization, and to organize and lead in implementation processes (Gjellebæk, et al., 2020; Nilsen, et al., 2016; Svensson, 2021b). New ways of working is needed in adopting and using welfare technology in care practice. This implies changes in professional roles and identities, and requires learning and competence development among health and social care professionals (Glomsås, et al., 2021; Svensson, et al., 2023). Moreover, learning can be supported by external actors, as academia (Grundén, et al., 2020; Svensson, 2022).

An initial study showed that the Norwegians and the Swedish rural municipalities had little experience regarding implementation and that the competence in welfare technology was relatively low in municipalities. A case study was then conducted to found out how rural municipalities in Norway and Sweden manage to implement welfare technology. Thus, the aim of this paper is to analyse how municipalities organize their work with implementation of welfare technology.

2. RESEARCH METHOD

A total of eight representatives from eight municipalities have participated in an interview study on which this paper is based. The study was conducted in the beginning of 2021. The included municipalities are based on the participating municipalities in an interregional project funded by Interreg Sweden-Norway, European Regional Development Fund. Representatives from health and social care from ten municipalities were asked to be interviewed, and eight of those representatives accepted. Four of the included municipalities are smaller and four of them are bigger. Seven of the municipalities are located in Fyrbodal, Sweden, and one is located in Viken, Norway, all close to the border between the countries. The representatives and municipalities have been anonymized and the municipalities are referred to as Municipality A to H in this paper. All the municipalities have, in one way or another been active in the collaborative and interregional project concerning organization, implementation and use of welfare technology. The interviewees were at the time of the interview in any way involved in the work with implementing welfare technology, and worked in roles as business developers, digitization strategists, department heads or social workers with a certain responsibility of welfare technology implementation. The interviews were conducted as semi-structured interviews via video link, and lasted between one and two hours each. Thematic analysis was used to analyse the collected data (Braun & Clarke, 2006). The data were analyzed based on six different themes; planning, decisions, information, competence development, and implementation, for smaller and larger municipalities respectively.

3. FINDINGS

The motives for implementation of welfare technologies are the need for a meaningful everyday life, increased participation and sense of independence for the people that need support. Municipalities want to increase individuals' opportunities for independence and participation and to improve public health and welfare. They also want to invest in using digitalization to prevent the challenges in elderly care that comes within the sparsely populated areas with large geographical distances. Welfare technology is considered to be an important solution to the challenges which comes with an aging population, as fewer staff in health and social care. The aim of the municipalities is to use welfare technology, enable for innovation and develop useful models for how the technologies can be used. An extra effort is added on skills development and work-integrated learning at the workplaces, on developing the organizations to be able to create common municipal arenas for knowledge exchange. More details of the organization of the welfare technology implementation in this rural and interregional area are presented in a book with the results from the project (Svensson & Gjellebæk, 2021).

3.1 Organizing for Implementation in Larger Municipalities

Municipality A works actively to integrate the welfare technology in the health and social care. The municipality has collaboration with other municipalities. In the overall strategy, descriptions of requirements are developed, and a mapping of needs are conducted. Professionals, patients and relatives are involved in focus groups where needs are discussed. The municipality has a strategy for prioritizing welfare technology, but this is not yet followed for each project, which leads to random prioritization between different projects. It is the municipal board that decides on the overall framework for funding and priorities, while the management for health and welfare decides on what should be included. Selected professionals and managers are trained in how the technology works and how it should be handled, and these in turn disseminate the knowledge on to colleagues. The training often takes place via clear written instructions and via instruction films about what the procedure with and around the technology looks like. After implementation, the projects are followed up regularly by the municipality's department for e-health and an ongoing dialogue takes place between those involved.

Within the care administration in Municipality B, they work with needs-driven development in the field of welfare technology. The municipality is primarily looking for the welfare technology that improves the conditions for both professionals in care and for patients who receive the care, but which also makes the municipality's operations more efficient. The municipality collaborates with other municipalities to gain inspiration and knowledge. User questionnaires, relative questionnaires and observations of users have been used as a basis for collecting the needs. An implementation strategy is made for each project, which includes a project plan and a communication plan. A standardized approach to decision-making around welfare technology does not currently exist, as the decision-making look different depending on the proposal and project. The municipality establishes an implementation strategy for each project, which includes a project plan and a communication plan. The communication plan specifies how professionals, patients and relatives are to be informed and trained. When testing welfare technology, pilot projects are often carried out. The needs for technology as a means of communication for both patients and professionals as well as an improved work environment has been confirmed, as has a need for more efficient health and social care.

Municipality C works to seek welfare technological solutions to challenges that arise in health and social care and to secure users' well-being and professionals' working environment. The welfare technology that the municipality chooses to introduce comes from inspiration from other municipalities. The municipality is also involved in a cross-regional project which aims to give patients a greater role in the choice of technology. The municipality engages in dialogue with patients, relatives and health and social care professionals to ascertain needs that could be covered with the support of welfare technology. The need for efficiency and the need to become a more attractive workplace for health and social care professionals are prioritized. Currently, there are no formal regulations on how decision-making should take place. Prior to the implementation of welfare technology, affected professionals are informed and trained. The municipality wants to test certain technologies on a smaller scale before full-scale implementation via so-called pilot projects. The municipality evaluates the results of pilot projects and compares cost versus benefit using surveys and in-depth interviews.

Municipality D works actively with welfare technology in healthcare through continuous implementation. The municipality monitors which products are available on the market by participating in seminars on the subject. Sometimes health and social care professionals come up with proposals for welfare technology. The need for welfare technology is based on patients or the work conducted by the professionals. The municipality then carries out a needs survey, which involves first collecting information through interviews with patients, professionals and possibly others who will take part. However, professionals and patients are not as involved in the choice of welfare technology as the municipality strives for. The social administration's management team is usually the decision-maker, but in the case of decisions on major financial issues, it is also brought up in the municipal council. A plan for training and dissemination of information is created when a decision on the implementation of welfare technology has been made. When testing welfare technology, the municipality uses pilot projects where a selected group of, for example, patients and professionals are involved.

3.2 Organizing for Implementation in Smaller Municipalities

Municipality E works actively to implement welfare technology that will benefit the patients and the professionals. The municipality works with a digitalization strategist and an e-council where the most prioritized needs are discussed. The needs inventory is made by each health and social care manager who organize workplace meetings where needs are discussed. The municipality does not yet have a strategy for a more comprehensive collection of needs. There is still no widespread user participation in the prioritization of welfare technology. Health and social care professionals are intended to be involved in the development and decision-making around welfare technology, but the municipality has not yet reached the goal. The municipality also cooperates with other municipalities. When deciding on welfare technology that may affect politics, the proposal is presented to the social welfare board, otherwise the social administration itself decides on introduction. When introducing welfare technology, a communication plan is created on how the information should be disseminated and plans are made for how training and meetings are to be set up. Web-based training courses are often launched that the professionals can participate in. When testing new technology, a project is first implemented on a small scale, in a limited geographical area in order to possibly broaden the introduction if everything works as expected.

Municipality F has implemented some welfare technology, however there is no strategy for how decision-making, prioritization and implementation should take place. It is up to each health and social care department to decide what they want to implement. No structured needs analysis takes place in the selection of welfare technology, but it is chosen based on a perception that it will be helpful. The municipality takes inspiration from other municipalities, and via various regional councils, and implements what is deemed to work well. The decision-making process looks different depending on which welfare technology is to be decided upon. For welfare technology that requires a lot of resources, the social administration highlights to the social committee which welfare technology the municipality wants, which in turn makes decisions about funding. Regarding welfare technology that does not cover large sums, the social administration itself makes decisions about implementation. When a decision on implementation has been made, selected professionals are trained in how the technology works, who in turn teach their colleagues. Workshops for staff on how the technology worked have also occurred during implementation. The municipality tests the technology on a smaller scale to examine the ease of use, before procurement starts.

Municipality G works with needs-driven development of welfare technology. The municipality sees advantages with the type of technology that makes the municipality's operations more efficient and improves the conditions for both professionals in health and social care and for patients who receive the care. To arrive at which welfare technology should be introduced in the municipality, the management teams of the care administration and the social administration, together with the municipality's digitalization strategist, map the needs of their operations. The municipality collaborates to a certain extent with other municipalities to find common solutions in terms of welfare technology. There are also various forums within the region. Prioritization of which welfare technology is to be implemented is based on the municipality's financial resources, time and that implementation is prioritized where the need is judged to be greatest. When making decisions, the management of the care administration jointly decides which project should be prioritized based on needs. Before implementation, professionals are informed about the technology and any training efforts are put in place. When testing new technology, a smaller pilot project is usually introduced. After the pilot project, an evaluation is carried out that leads to the decision whether the project should be expanded and benefit more patients, and in that case how such a wide introduction should be carried out.

Municipality H has not come as far in the development of welfare technology as they had hoped for, where the welfare technology is aimed at patients. However, there has been a small-scale implementation of user-related welfare technology projects. The municipality does not actively cooperate with other municipalities in the field of welfare technology, but takes inspiration from selected municipalities. The benefit and the long-term perspective of welfare technology implementation is central to the choice of welfare technology. There is a municipal council, consisting of activity managers, where welfare technology is discussed and where the activity managers can exchange knowledge about welfare technology with each other. In the case of decision-making about the implementation of welfare technology, the proposal is first raised from health and social care managers to the social administration, which makes the decision. For larger projects that involve larger resources, the matter is decided at the political level. By informing patients and professionals at an early stage, the municipality hopes to prevent possible resistance to welfare technology. In some cases, professionals have been trained in the welfare technology prior to the commissioning of the technology. There is a so-called "training center" where professionals can test technologies and receive training. In order to test the welfare technology, the municipality starts a pilot project in a smaller, controlled, small-scale test environment. A pilot project is continuously evaluated during the test period and a decision is then made about implementation on a full-scale level.

4. CONCLUSION

The results show that there are differences in organization, prioritization and decision-making between the municipalities. It can be assumed that the differences are in how resourceful the municipalities are is as well as how strong the commitment in question is in each municipality. It is obvious that some aspects cause resistance to implementation of welfare technology in municipal healthcare (Nilsen, et al., 2016). Management also face challenges in digitalization of healthcare services (Gjellebæk, et al., 2020). The bigger municipalities seem to have more resources to develop and structure test and implementation processes. The smaller municipalities seems to be more dependent on "fiery souls" commits to implement welfare technology.

It is clear from the results that all municipalities are working to broaden the implementation of welfare technology in their health and social care operations. However, it shows that the municipalities at the same time have different strategies and uses different amounts of resources in the development within this field. This research contributes to inspire the field of work of in the municipalities and to encourage them to exchange knowledge and experiences as well as to collaborate.

ACKNOWLEDGEMENT

This work was supported by the Interreg Sweden-Norway, European Regional Development Fund (ERDF) (grant numbers: 20201564 and 20202391), and by the Health Academy West.

REFERENCES

Braun, V., & Clarke, V. (2006). Using thematic analysis in psychology, Qualitative Research in Psychology, 3(2), 77-101.

Emilsson, M., Karlsson, C., & Svensson, A. (2023). Experiences of using surveillance cameras as a monitoring solution at nursing homes: The eldercare personnel's perspectives, BMC Health Services Research, 23(144), 1-13.

Frennert, S., & Baudin, K. (2021). The concept of welfare technology in Swedish municipal eldercare. Disability and Rehabilitation, Disability and rehabilitation, 43(9), 1220–1227.

Gjellebæk, C., Svensson, A., Fladeby, N., Bjørkquist, C., & Grundén, K. (2020). Management challenges for the future digitalization of healthcare services, Futures, 1(124), 102636.

Glomsås, HS., Knutsen, IR., Fossum, M., Halvorsen, K.. (2021). 'They just came with the medication dispenser'- a qualitative study of elderly service users' involvement and welfare technology in public home care services, BMC Health Services Research, 21(1), 245.

Grundén, K., Svensson, A., Forsman, B., Karlsson, C., & Obeid, A. (2020). Dialogue meetings as an arena for collaboration and reflection among researchers and practitioners in a pre-study of a welfare technology testbed, International Journal of Engineering Management and Economics, 14(8), 629-634.

Kuoppamäki, S. (2021). The application and deployment of welfare technology in Swedish municipal care: a qualitative study of procurement practices among municipal actors, BMC Health Services Research, 21(918), 1-12.

Nilsen, ER., Dugstad, J., Eide, H., Gullslett, MK., & Eide, T. (2016). Exploring resistance to implementation of welfare technology in municipal healthcare services–a longitudinal case study, BMC Health Services Research, 16(1), 1-4.

Samhan, B., & Joshi, KD. (2015). Resistance of Healthcare Information Technologies; Literature Review, Analysis, and Gaps, Proceedings of 48th Hawaii International Conference on System Sciences,. 2992–3001.

Svensson, A., Bergkvist, L., Bäccman, C. & Durst, S. (2021a). Challenges in implementing digital assistive technology in municipality healthcare, In Ekman, P., Keller, C., Dahlin, P. & Tell, F. (Eds.). Management and Information Technology in the Post-Digitalization Era, Routledge.

Svensson, A., & Gjellebæk, C. (red.) (2021). Organisering, implementering och användning av välfärdsteknologi. Resultat från eTeam-projektet, Högskolan Väst, Trollhättan.

Svensson, A., Grundén, K., & Larsson, L.G. (2021b). Studying resistance to changes and learning in social care organizations, In Proceedings of the15th annual International Technology, Education and Development Conference (INTED 2021), Valencia, Spain, March 8-10.

Svensson, A. (2022). Digital Ecosystem in Academia to Support Learning for Innovative Practices in Health Services, In Proceedings of European Distance and e-Learning Network (EDEN 2022), Series ISSN: 2707-2819, Tallinn, Estonia, June 20-22

Svensson, A., Aggestam, L., & Vallo Hult, H. (2023). Management and organization of change processes in digital transformation of healthcare: The role of workplace learning, in Proceedings of the 17th annual International Technology, Education and Development Conference (INTED 2023), Valencia, Spain, March 6-8.

DEEP LEARNING-BASED APPROACH FOR JAPANESE KEYPHRASE GENERATION

Padipat Sitkrongwong[1], Nakarin Sritrakool[1,2],
Phannakan Tengkiattrakul[1], Pongsakorn Jirachanchaisiri[1,2] and Atsuhiro Takasu[1,2]
[1]*National Institute of Informatics, Tokyo, Japan*
[2]*The Graduate University for Advanced Studies, Kanagawa, Japan*

ABSTRACT

Retrieving keywords or keyphrases from a text document is one of the essential features in many applications. For example, the dataset search systems may use those keyphrases to suggest more relevant data to users. However, obtaining the keyphrases from a Japanese text is challenging due to its unique sentence structure. Moreover, most existing methods derive an extraction approach incapable of producing new Japanese keyphrases for each document. Thus, we propose a method for generating Japanese keyphrases based on a deep learning-based text-to-text generative model. Our method can accurately generate the existing and the additional relevant keyphrases for each document text. A model architecture used in our method also helps produce the Japanese keyphrases that preserve their original meanings.

KEYWORDS

Japanese Keyphrase Generation, Dataset Search, T5

1. INTRODUCTION

Recently, open data has become an important resource for analyzing what happens in the real world. Since open data is provided by various organizations, ranging from national and local governments to citizens, search engines are essentially important for retrieving relevant data. Google launched Google Dataset Search (https://datasetsearch.research.google.com), and we are developing a search engine for open data in Japan (https://search.ckan.jp). Search by keywords is a primary approach to the dataset search, but it is not easy for users to choose effective keywords for this new type of information. This paper, therefore, aims to propose a method to generate keyphrases for enhancing the dataset search results.

There are two main approaches to obtain the list of keyphrases from a document text: extraction and generation. Keyphrase extraction (Le et al., 2013; Teng, 2021) aims to extract keyphrases that are previously mentioned in each document. In comparison, keyphrase generation (Meng et al., 2017; Shen et al., 2022) aims to generate a list of keyphrases that may or may not exist in the document text.

Most existing works proposed under those approaches failed to produce high-quality keyphrases when applied to Japanese text because the Japanese sentence structure differs from English. For example, in one sentence, the Japanese words or phrases might be written consecutively without explicit word boundary, which is different from English sentences, leading to a challenge in designing the tokenization methods that work well with Japanese text. Also, unlike English words, most Japanese words could be composed of more than one token. Separately extracting those tokens from one word might completely abandon its original meaning.

Acknowledged by these unique characteristics, some researchers proposed techniques for retrieving Japanese keywords and keyphrases (Le et al., 2013; Teng, 2021). For example, Le et al. proposed a chunk-based keyword extraction that treats Japanese keywords as chunks of text that yield each document's important contents (Le et al., 2013). However, these methods are based on the extraction approach that can extract only the mentioned keyphrases in a document. Therefore, the keyphrases for each document may not necessarily need to be matched with the phrases mentioned in a document. In many applications, the ability to generate new keywords or keyphrases for each document could be a potential advantage. For example, the dataset search system could provide more relevant search results based on the newly generated tags for each dataset.

To solve these challenges, we propose a deep learning-based approach for Japanese keyphrase generation. Instead of following the extraction approach, we derive a text-to-text generative model as our model architecture. Our main contributions are:

1. We propose a model architecture for Japanese keyphrase generation based on a deep learning-based text-to-text generation approach. This model can accurately generate keyphrases (tags) for each document (dataset description) and the additional relevant keyphrases that most keyphrase extraction methods cannot retrieve. Moreover, it can generate new keyphrases that have not existed in the keyphrase vocabulary.
2. The masking mechanism used in our derived model can mask the consecutive tokens, which helps produce the Japanese keyphrases that preserve their original meaning.

2. THE PROPOSED METHOD

2.1 Deep Learning-Based Text-to-Text Generation

We adopt a pre-trained model called T5 (Text-to-Text-Transfer-Transformer) (Raffel et al., 2020) for the Japanese keyphrase generation. T5 is an encoder-decoder model trained on a large corpus of text and metadata in multi-task learning, which makes it generalized for various natural language processing (NLP) tasks. Furthermore, it is designed based on a unified text-to-text generation framework, meaning its input and output are always in a string format.

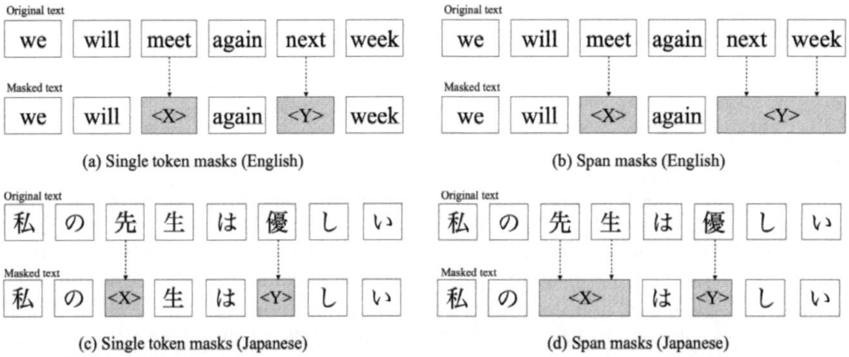

Figure 1. Applying two masking mechanisms to a text in two languages. (a) Single token masks with English text, (b) Span masks with English text, (c) Single token masks with Japanese text, and (d) Span masks with Japanese Text

Similar to Bidirectional Encoder Representations Transformers (BERT) (Devlin et al., 2019), T5 was trained with the masked language model objective, where some words of the input text are randomly masked. The representations of those mask words are then learned by leveraging the information derived from their left and right context words. The example of a masked text done by BERT is presented in Figure 1a, where the words "meet" and "next" in the original text are masked by the mask tokens <X> and <Y> before feeding into the model. However, there are two main differences between BERT and T5. Since BERT comprises only the encoder model, it aims to produce a dense input representation, which can be used mainly for text classification tasks. In contrast, T5 is an encoder-decoder model designed with the objective of text generation. The text-to-text generative nature of T5 makes it applicable to the NLP tasks that BERT cannot achieve, including machine translation or text summarization (Agarwal et al., 2020).

The masking mechanism is the other component that makes T5 different from BERT and suitable for this work. Normally, BERT randomly replaces a single-word token with a masked token, as shown in Figure 1a. This masking, however, can cause a problem when working with Japanese text where most words are composed of two or more tokens (which are obtained by applying Japanese word tokenizers such as SentencePiece (Kudo and Richardson, 2018)). If only one token from those words is masked, they might lose their original meaning. For example, Figure 1c illustrates the possible masking of BERT applied to a Japanese sentence 「私の先生

は優しい」 (My teacher is kind). In this sentence, a token「先」 from a word 「先生」 (teacher) is masked, whereas the token 「生」 remains unmasked. These two tokens, however, also have their individual meanings (「先」 means "previous" and 「生」 means "life"). Separately masking only one of them could produce a text representation far from its original meaning.

Fortunately, the masking problem can be alleviated by the masking mechanism of T5. In T5, a mask token can be used to mask more than one consecutive word token. We believe this masking scheme could work especially well for the Japanese keywords and keyphrases. Considering the same sentence but masks with T5 in Figure 1d, both tokens from the word 「先生」 are now masked together. We believe that T5's masking scheme could help preserve the original meaning of Japanese keywords, leading to a more meaningful representation and fidelity of the model.

2.2 Japanese Keyphrase Generation

In order to apply T5 to Japanese text, we use the version of T5 that was pre-trained with Japanese text corpora (https://huggingface.co/sonoisa/t5-base-japanese), such as Japanese Wikipedia and OSCAR.

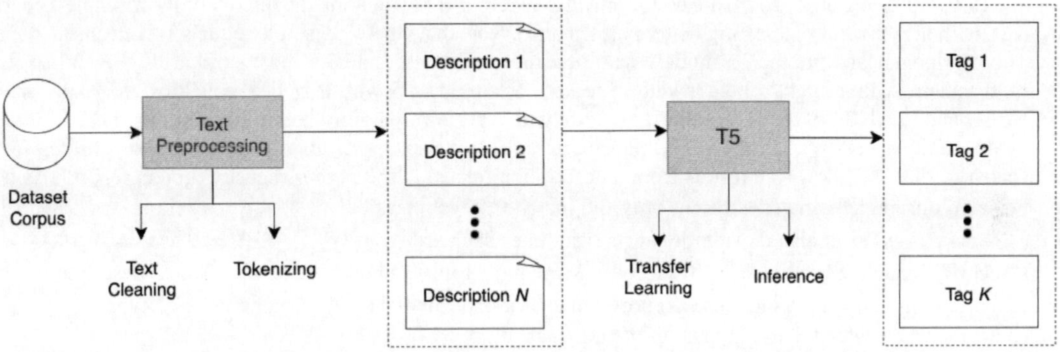

Figure 2. An overview of our Japanese keyphrase generation pipeline using T5

The pipeline of the method is in Figure 2. We first retrieve dataset metadata from the dataset corpus. We then extract only the description of each dataset (as a document) and its corresponding tags (as keyphrases) from the metadata. After that, the Japanese texts are normalized, such as full-width conversion and removing special characters, whereas English texts are converted into lowercase. Both descriptions and tags are then tokenized using SentencePiece (Kudo and Richardson, 2018). After obtaining a cleaned and tokenized dataset description and its corresponding tags, they are fed into T5 for the Japanese phrase generation task, which consists of two phases. In the transfer learning phase, we fine-tuned the pre-trained T5 by feeding the pairs of <description, tags> as input and output of the model. The main objective is to let T5 learn to generate the corresponding tags given a description as input. In the inference phase, we use the fine-tuned T5 to generate the list of tags by providing a dataset description as input. This model can generate the tag list for tagged and untagged descriptions and new tags that have never appeared before in the tag vocabulary.

3. EXPERIMENTS

3.1 Experiment Settings

The model is evaluated on the metadata obtained from our dataset search system (https://search.ckan.jp). From this metadata, a total of 27,682 dataset descriptions and 5,585 unique tags are extracted. After that, the descriptions are cleaned. Then, the input (descriptions) and labels (tags) are tokenized and truncated to 512 and 200 tokens at maximum. Next, the dataset is split into 80%, 10%, and 10% for training, validating, and testing. Finally, the dataset is used to fine-tune the T5 model (https://github.com/sonoisa/t5-japanese) with a learning rate of 1e-4, batch size of 16, training epoch of 10,000, and an early stop when the loss of validation set is not improved for 10 epochs. The other parameters are set to their default values used in T5.

3.2 Experimental Results

Table 1. Comparison of T5 with different repetition penalties on various measurements

Model	Repetition Penalty	Hit Rate	Coverage Ratio	BLEU (Unigram)	ROUGE (Unigram)
T5	1.0	0.8952	0.8940	0.8567	0.8733
T5	1.5	**0.8963**	**0.8959**	**0.8585**	**0.8744**
T5	3.0	0.8953	0.8932	0.8552	0.8732

Table 1 shows the performance comparison of T5 with different repetition penalties. The evaluation metrics include hit rate, coverage ratio, BLEU, and ROUGE. The hit rate and coverage ratio indicate how well the model can correctly identify and generate text, with higher values indicating better performance. The BLEU and ROUGE (Yang et al., 2018) are commonly used metrics for evaluating the quality of the machine-generated text, with higher values indicating better performance. Note that when the penalty equals 1, it means no penalty. The results indicate that the T5 models with penalties of 1.0, 1.5, and 3.0 have similar hit rate and coverage ratio values, with a slightly higher value for T5 1.5. Among T5 with different penalties, they have similar BLEU and ROUGE, except T5 with penalty 1.5, which performs slightly better than the others.

In addition to the accuracy performances, we also give examples of the generated keyphrases in two scenarios. Table 2 shows the results from a description related to the "cyber security project report". As it can be seen, our model can generate not only the matched keyphrases (「クラウド」: "cloud", 「セキュリティ」: "security") but also the additional relevant ones such as "security", 「セキュリティガイドライン」("security guideline") or「安全」("safety"). Moreover, Table 3 shows the results from a description related to the "energy / power-saving project report". In this case, the model can even generate the keyphrase 「節電」(power saving), which does not exist in the tag vocabulary.

Table 2. Example of generating additional keyphrases

Description	平成 26 年度サイバーセキュリティ経済基盤構築事業クラウドセキュリティ監査制度の見直し調 査報告 書 iso/iec 27001 及び 27002(2013 年版)に基づき、情報セキュリティ管理基準の改訂を検討し た資料、 及び、so/iec 27001 及び 27002(2013 年版)、クラウドセキュリティガイドライン、iso/iec 27017 の策 定動向に基づき、クラウド情報セキュリティ管理基準の改訂を検討した資料。(127 文字)		
Matched Keyphrases	クラウド, セキュリティ	**Additional Keyphrases**	security, セキュリティガイドライン, 企業_会社情報, 商取引, 商業, 安全, 工業, 法 律, 産業, 研究, 社会, 経済

Table 3. Example of generating a new (out of vocabulary) keyphrase

Description	平成 26 年度エネルギー使用合理化促進基盤整備事業(電力需要抑制に係る設備導入効果の実態分析調 査)調査報告書「平成 23 年度補正建築物節電改修支援事業」の補助金交付を受けた事 業者を対象とし て、事業完了後 1 年間の電力抑制実績及び目標値に対する実績値の傾向分析を 行った。		
Matched Keyphrase	エネルギー	**New Keyphrase**	節電

4. CONCLUSION

We proposed a model architecture for Japanese keyphrase generation based on a deep learning-based text-to-text generation approach. This model can generate the existing and additional relevant keyphrases for each document text and preserve their original meanings. For future works, we want to try other state-of-the-art encoder-decoder models to evaluate the performances of Japanese keyphrase generation tasks. Moreover, we want to design a way to evaluate the correctness of the newly generated keyphrases obtained by our proposed method to ensure that they are reliable when using them in the downstream tasks.

ACKNOWLEDGEMENT

This work was supported by the Cross-ministerial Strategic Innovation Promotion Program (SIP) Second Phase, "Big-Data and AI-Enabled Cyberspace Technologies" by New Energy and Industrial Technology Development Organization (NEDO).

REFERENCES

Agarwal O, Kale M, Ge H, et al. (12 2020) Machine Translation Aided Bilingual Data-to-Text Generation and Semantic Parsing. In: *Proceedings of the 3rd International Workshop on Natural Language Generation from the Semantic Web (WebNLG+)*, Dublin, Ireland (Virtual), 12 2020, pp. 125–130. Association for Computational Linguistics.

Devlin J, Chang M-W, Lee K, et al. (2019) BERT: Pre-training of Deep Bidirectional Transformers for Language Understanding. In: *Proceedings of the 2019 Conference of the North American Chapter of the Association for Computational Linguistics: Human Language Technologies, Volume 1 (Long and Short Papers)*, Minneapolis, Minnesota, June 2019, pp. 4171–4186. Association for Computational Linguistics.

Kudo T and Richardson J (2018) SentencePiece: A simple and language independent subword tokenizer and detokenizer for Neural Text Processing. In: *Proceedings of the 2018 Conference on Empirical Methods in Natural Language Processing: System Demonstrations*, Brussels, Belgium, November 2018, pp. 66–71. Association for Computational Linguistics.

Le TTN, Le Nguyen M and Shimazu A (2013) Unsupervised Keyword Extraction for Japanese Legal Documents. In: *JURIX*, 2013, pp. 97–106.

Meng R, Zhao S, Han S, et al. (2017) Deep Keyphrase Generation. In: *Proceedings of the 55th Annual Meeting of the Association for Computational Linguistics (Volume 1: Long Papers)*, Vancouver, Canada, July 2017, pp. 582–592. Association for Computational Linguistics.

Raffel C, Shazeer N, Roberts A, et al. (2020) Exploring the Limits of Transfer Learning with a Unified Text-to-Text Transformer. *Journal of machine learning research: JMLR* 21(1).

Shen X, Wang Y, Meng R, et al. (2022) Unsupervised Deep Keyphrase Generation. *Proceedings of the AAAI Conference on Artificial Intelligence* 36(10): 11303–11311.

Teng M (2021) Using the Ship-Gram Model for Japanese Keyword Extraction Based on News Reports. *Complexity* 2021. Hindawi.

Yang A, Liu K, Liu J, et al. (2018) Adaptations of ROUGE and BLEU to better evaluate machine reading comprehension task. In: *Proceedings of the Workshop on Machine Reading for Question Answering*, Stroudsburg, PA, USA, 2018. Association for Computational Linguistics.

LEVERAGING PYTHON IN INFORMATION SYSTEMS COURSES

Ray Kresman
Department of Computer Science, Bowling Green State University
Bowling Green, OH 43403, USA

ABSTRACT

Spreadsheets are ubiquitous and tools like Excel and Minitab have been the workhorse of IS courses for decades. While these tools continue to excel at what they do, IS students need to be cognizant of the evolving skillsets needed in today's workforce, specifically the business skillsets needed to handle data that varies in size (big and small), format (potentially different from tabular structures such as spreadsheets), and medium (web, social media, etc.). We propose the use of certain educational pedagogies to help prepare IS students for this transition and argue the need for introducing elementary Python concepts to undergraduate students in IS. Students leverage what they already know, and by connecting to intuitive coding concepts in Python, can stay engaged, handle repeated tasks and simple workflow automation, and be prepared for the emerging needs of the information industry.

KEYWORDS

IS, Educational Pedagogy, Spreadsheets, Python

1. INTRODUCTION

Spreadsheets are ubiquitous, and Excel has been the workhorse in information systems courses for decades. Excel with VBA supports native integration of MS applications, for example: Excel with Power BI provides analytics and visualization capabilities; and one can spawn an application (such as email) in response to Excel cell values meeting a threshold (Maabo, 2020). Integration with external APIs, however, is difficult and VBA syntax is not all that intuitive. Google Sheets is another tool, but it needs an internet connection.

Many IS programs we reviewed include, among other items, business-facing and project management courses to design real-world systems (that use computing tools such as Excel, VBA, and PowerBI), and a general education computing course that is at best loosely coupled with the major. Recognizing that introductory Python is becoming a valuable skillset for students who graduate in IS/business (Khudov, 2020; Nye, 2022), we propose a constructivist approach using certain educational pedagogies to better integrate this computing course; students use their previous knowledge to build on their foundation, leverage what they already know, and by connecting to intuitive coding concepts in Python, stay engaged, handle repeated tasks and simple workflow automation, and be prepared for the emerging needs of the information industry.

1.1 Motivation and Business Case

Recent research (Coffman, et al, 2023) based on a randomized comparative study of students' perception of visual vs textual language (python) in an introductory general education computing course open to all majors shows that students overwhelmingly perceive Python to be more valuable. Whether it is data collection from multiple sources or a computation across time periods or market segments, business users are confronted with repeated tasks and Python provides mechanisms for automating such workflows with a robust, reusable pipeline. The web, social media and other digital data repositories house enormous amount of data that far exceeds the capability of traditional spreadsheet processing programs such as Excel. While serious analysis of such datasets is left to experts, entry level employees with a college degree in IS or business may still be expected to (or at least be cognizant and willing to learn to) do simple collection and processing of large datasets, and Python provides such capabilities. Python can help complement their Excel skillsets, for example: a) use familiar GUI such as Excel as the front-end, and use back-end 3rd party Python tools to process the data; b) use openpyxl library to extract data from a database with Excel in the pipeline to do pre or post processing in Python; c) use native Pandas library to handle data (read, repair holes, cleanse duplicates, etc.) in a variety of formats including spreadsheets – Python can do this efficiently no matter what the data size is, a task that is particularly challenging for spreadsheet programs (Bosacki, n.d).

Students who graduate in IS with exposure to Python are in high demand and our proposal for better integration of the computing course into their major provides opportunities for reinforcement and helps them leverage what they already know. Even if these graduates don't write any code on the job, programming skillsets can help improve their participation in technical conversations (April, et. al, 2018) to gain credibility with their technical team members and to stay current with digital trends and technology developments. Additionally, the divide between IS, IT, and CS is narrowing, and college graduates are likely to encounter multidisciplinary teams as they enter the workforce; such teams help remove institutionalized silos and build team synergy, and the ability to work together with peers who have complementary skills and expertise is a critical asset for the future workforce.

Python is open source with a significantly large and continuously expanding ecosystem. Spreadsheet copy and paste operations can be tricky and formulas add an additional level of complexity, and intermediate results may be suppressed in such formulae though they can be more revealing to business analysts; consider using discount factor—information system students and even average consumers know inflation erodes value of money—to figure out whether a projected investment is profitable, i.e. net present value (NPV) is positive. As compared to XNPV of Excel, a benefit of coding (in Python, for example) is that can also see the present values of intermediate cashflows as opposed to only the final NPV (Moffatt, 2019; CFI Team, 2022).

2. EDUCATIONAL PEDAGOGY

2.1 Scaffolding

Our task as teachers is to help students build on their experiences and knowledge as they learn new skills; the help that we give can be relaxed as they progress in their learning. Scaffolding, a teaching pedagogy, creates the bridge between learning gaps and helps construct new knowledge (Harris, 2016). By breaking up a learning experience into manageable parts, we can give our students the assistance they need to learn each part. As instructors we must take it as a challenge to impress upon our IS undergraduates that coding is a creative endeavor that can produce a creatively generated work with relevance in the business world.

The power of jigsaw puzzles cannot be overstated. Students are already familiar with jigsaw puzzles and one approach to is to give them the code for a Python program but jumbled up, and their task is to put them together in the right sequence. Parsons problems (Borchert and Valia, 2022) are coding puzzles in which students drag-and drop code snippets to put them in the right order. The difficulty level can be varied; for example, one can do even simpler activities such as using a visual programming languages (Snap!, for example) where the blocks are visually rearranged to end up with the correct sequencing of the blocks. Conversely, one can increase the difficulty level by adding distractors. Research has shown that Parsons problems can help scaffold students' transition from learning in Snap! to Python (Shah, 2020).

2.2 Adaptive Programming

Sigmund Freud (Freud, 2012) laid the foundation for psychoanalysis and psycho-education when he noted that what was unconscious had to be made conscious to affect a change in symptomatic behavior. Adaptive programming attempts to let something be "known again," so it can be "known differently." This principle applies to any field including IS: reviewing past knowledge can lead to new, and beneficially updated understanding (Munshi, et al, 2022; Seltzer, 2019). This pedagogy can be applied to entry level classes for students in IS. Just as jigsaw puzzles help make the transition to Python, so can the spreadsheet itself. Students are exposed to spreadsheets as early as middle school so one approach is to start with doing the things in Excel and supplement it with a coding language such as Python (Shah, 2020); start with very simple examples (such an open an Excel file and print it) and progressively ramp up. Each such activity in Excel provides a bridge to learning the comparable way of doing the tasks in Python. Ramped up excel activity may also be as simple as figuring out the standard deviation of student scores or other interesting statistic.

One student may not be at the same level as another, and the instructor may like to adapt to their varied abilities. This can help bring a spark back into the classroom and help students discover 'spreadsheets again,' so spreadsheets can be 'known differently.' As instructors we may be pleasantly surprised at how tech savvy today's information systems students are and that they may be eager and ready to engage in this adaptive programming pedagogy; together, we help them rediscover through Python what they already know.

Both pedagogies have the same end goal: by intentionally associating coding into the (spreadsheet) context they are already familiar with, we can ensure that the new content does not negatively affect their extraneous cognitive load. The illustrative examples in the next section attempt to employ these pedagogies.

3. ILLUSTRATIVE EXAMPLES

Jupyter Notebook, an interactive web tool available for all platforms including Windows, provides a convenient visual environment to explore Python. IS students already know how to write VBA code to output "Hello World" (Figure 1(a)). Corresponding one-line Python app in the Jupyter environment, shown in Figure 1 (b), is rather intuitive. Suppose the "Hello World" string is instead to be written to cell [1,2] of an Excel file, Test.xlsx, using VBA. As seen in the VBA (column 1) of Figure 2 (adapted from Tom (AnalystCave), 2022), one must open the spreadsheet and invoke a few functions to write the string to that cell. Corresponding Python code (column 2) is much simpler and it is instructive to compare the two.

(a) VBA　　　　　　　　　　(b) Python

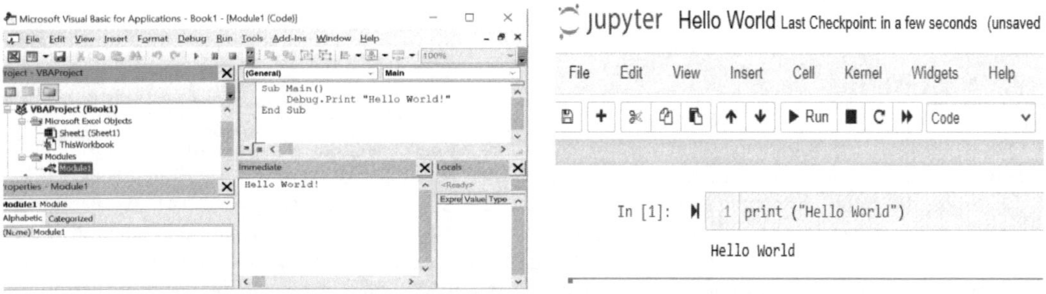

Figure 1. Output 'Hello World'

Sub Main() Dim app As Excel.Application Dim wb As Excel.Workbook Dim ws As Excel.Worksheet Dim fileName As String fileName = "C:\Test.xlsx" Set app = New Excel.Application Set wb = app.Workbooks.Add Set ws = wb.Sheets(1) ws.Cells (1, 2) = "Hello World" wb.SaveAs filename End Sub	import openpyxl as op wb = op.Workbook() ws = wb.active ws.cell (1,2).value = "Hello World" wb.save (r"C:\... \Test.xlsx") //replace cell [1,2] of Test

Figure 2. Write 'Hello World' to cell [1, 2] of an Excel file

As another example, let us recap some of the summary functions in spreadsheets that IS students experiment with like sum, mean, etc. One can compute these and more in Python; in fact, Python has a rich library, pandas, to manipulate tabular structure very efficiently and with minimal coding. An example of such a computation is shown in Figure 3. Line 2 of Figure 3 Python code reads an excel file, 'sales data.xlsx,' while the next line prints it (see the output in column 2 with five rows with 'Order No,' 'Date,' Qty,' and 'Amount.'). Line 5 prints various stats (note the use of 'describe' function) on the 'Qty' and 'Amount' fields, such as count, mean, standard deviation. A spreadsheet program on the other hand would need many clicks through the formula icon to generate similar statistics. Another computation quite relevant to MIS/IS students is the SQL construct to do aggregates based on groups. Excel users may be familiar with its pivot operation. Line 6 of Figure 3 Python code does the (sum) aggregation of 'Amount' by date and the output is shown to the far right of Figure 3. Of course, aggregation can involve multiple categories and the like. Again, what appeals to students is the ability to do some useful computation in Python with minimal coding that is also intuitive and simple to understand.

Recall that information systems students use VBA to do SQL and one can do the same thing with the Pandas library. Figure 4 shows the Python code that runs a SQL against an MS Access database to retrieve all tuples in the table, 'student.' Line 4 connects to the database and the next line runs the query.

Python code

```
1 import pandas as pd
2 myData = pd.read_excel('sales data.xlsx')
3 print(myData)
4 # print stats on Qty and Amount
5 print (myData [["Qty", "Amount"]].describe())
6 pd.pivot_table(data=myData,
7      index='Date',values=['Amount'],aggfunc='sum')
```

Output

```
   Order No        Date  Qty  Amount
0       101  2022-12-01    2     120
1       103  2022-12-03    4     160
2       104  2022-12-01    7     200
3       105  2022-11-01    3      90
4       456  2022-12-03    4      40
            Qty      Amount
count  5.000000    5.000000
mean   4.000000  122.000000
std    1.870829   61.806149
min    2.000000   40.000000
25%    3.000000   90.000000
50%    4.000000  120.000000
75%    4.000000  160.000000
max    7.000000  200.000000
```

	Amount
Date	
2022-11-01	90
2022-12-01	320
2022-12-03	200

Figure 3. Process an Excel file and print some statistics

Code

```
1 import pyodbc
2 import pandas as pd
3
4 myConn = pyodbc.connect('DSN=studentData;')
5 myQuery=pd.read_sql_query
6   ('''select * from student''',myConn)
7 myResult = pd.dataFrame(myQuery)
8 print (myResult)
```

Output

```
   ID  SSN       Name
0  22    1    John S.
1  23    2   David T.
2  24    5   Cindy W.
3  25    4  Megan L.
```

Figure 4. Run a SQL query against an MS Access database

Now let us turn our attention to the metric noted in Section 1 - discount factor and the net present value (NPV). As the saying goes, money now is better than money in future. Business savvy students need to know if an investment is profitable (such as loaning money to someone or starting a small business). Net present value (NPV), the net after adding inflow and subtracting outflows, can help students pick an investment that is better among competing investments (CFI Team. 2022); for example, is investing \$X now that returns \$Y after n years better than, say putting the money in the bank at a rate of interest, r. Without belaboring the point, suffice to say that one can answer such cashflow question rather easily and with minimal coding using Python libraries. For brevity, the Python code is not shown here.

This paper proposed a constructivist approach in the design of a Python-based introductory computing course for IS majors. Couple of instructional pedagogies were introduced to help students make the transition from spreadsheets to doing similar computations in Python. Our illustrative examples use a constructivist approach to perk up students' interest in Python by connecting the new concepts to what they already know as spreadsheet users. We believe this approach should help IS students rediscover what they already know so it is 'known differently,' and prepare them to contribute to multidisciplinary teams of the future workforce by working together with peers who have complementary skills and expertise.

ACKNOWLEDGEMENT

We are grateful for the support through BGSU's Faculty Allies grant and for the constructive comments on an earlier draft from anonymous reviewers.

REFERENCES

April Y. et al, 2018. Mismatch of Expectations: How Modern Learning Resources Fail Conversational Programmers. *Proceedings of the 2018 CHI Conference on Human Factors in Computing Systems* (Montreal QC, Canada) (CHI '18). ACM, New York, NY, USA, pp. 1–13.

Borchert, O. and Valia, G. 2022. ScaffoldSQL: Using Parson's Problems to Support Database Pedagogy. *Proceedings of the 55th Hawaii International Conference on System Sciences*. Hawaii, USA. pp. 1032 - 1041.

Bosacki, A. How is Python Used in Finance? — Python Applications in Finance. https://www.softkraft.co/how-is-Python-used-in-finance/

CFI Team. (2022, November 29). What is a Discount Factor? corporatefinanceinstitute.com/resources/financial-modeling /discount-factor/

Coffman, J. et al, 2023. Visual vs. Textual Programming Languages in CS0.5: Comparing Student Learning with and Student Perception of RAPTOR and Python. *Proceedings of the SIGCSE 2023 Technical Symposium*. Toronto, Canada. *to appear*.

Freud, S. (2012). A general introduction to psychoanalysis. Wordsworth Editions

Harris, K. (2016, February 12). Creating a Bridge to Learning with Scaffolding. https://teaching.nmc.edu/creating-a-bridge-to-learning-with-scaffolding/

Khudov, N. (2020, November 24). Why Python is Essential for Business Analysts. https://towardsdatascience.com/why-Python-is-essential-for-business-analysts-ed3d5a2b194c

Maabo, J. (2020, September 12). VBA vs Python: Key Differences Plus a Dose of History. https://software-solutions-online.com/vba-vs-Python/

Moffatt, M. (2019, April 10). What Is a Discount Factor? https://www.thoughtco.com/discount-factor-definition-1146077

Munshi, A. et al, 2022. Analyzing Adaptive Scaffolds that Help Students Develop Self-Regulated Learning Behaviors. doi:10.48550/ARXIV.2202.09698. *under review.*

Nye, W. (2022, December 2). Transitioning From Excel To Python: Essential Functions For SEO Data Analysis" https://www.searchenginejournal.com/transitioning-from-excel-to-Python-essential-functions-for-seo-data-analysis/472147/

Seltzer, L. (2019, May 8). You Can Only Learn What You Already Know. Psychology Today. Online. https://www.psychologytoday.com/us/blog/evolution-the-self/201905/you-can-only-learn-what-you-already-know

Shah, M. (2020). Exploring the Use of Parsons Problems for Learning a New Programming Language. *Technical Report* No. UCB/EECS-2020-88. 2020. https://www2.eecs.berkeley.edu/Pubs/TechRpts/2020/EECS-2020-88.pdf

Tom (AnalystCave). (2022, June 3). VBA to Python – 10 Simple Python vs VBA Examples. https://analystcave.com/vba-to-Python-10-examples-Python-vs-vba/

A RESEARCH DESIGN FOR CREATING A DIGITAL TRANSFORMATION MATURITY ASSESSMENT TOOL FOR DEVELOPMENT NGOS

Anand Sheombar
HU University of Applied Sciences Utrecht, The Netherlands

ABSTRACT

This paper explores a research approach for creating a digital transformation maturity (DTM) assessment tool specific to development NGOs. This paper focuses on the initial phase of the co-creation approach for such a tool with practitioners of these organisations. The process ensures relevance and adjustment to appropriate and understandable language for development practitioners. Rigour is ensured later through a detailed literature review on the concept of digital transformation of development NGOs as a specific group of non-profit organisations. We present the findings of the first phase of the research with the evaluation of five digital maturity assessment tools for non-profit organisations. This paper contributes to setting out design criteria for a quick & shorter digital transformation maturity assessment more focused on the context of development NGOs. This quick scan will help development NGOs decide on the next steps, like the choice for more detailed measurements. Secondly, we identify a possible shortcoming of current DTM tools that are not linked to the development paradigm and strategy of the NGOs. We conclude the evaluation by reflecting on limitations and the need to adjust DTM assessment tools to organisational development paradigms and goals of NGOs, suggesting the need for future research.

KEYWORDS

Digital Transformation, Digital Maturity, Development NGOs, Non-Profit Organisations, Digital Development

1. INTRODUCTION

International development NGOs operate in a fast-changing environment. The work of international development is changing in the face of the advent of various digital technologies leading to a digital transformation of the sector. Development NGOs try to make sense of these technologies on if and how to implement them in their development projects based on the organisational capabilities. This paper describes the approach we have taken to develop a practical and easy-to-use assessment tool for practitioners for the level of maturity of the development NGO's digital transformation. The research question addressed is how can we design an appropriate digital transformation maturity tool to assess (Dutch) development NGOs quickly? With this study, we contribute to the knowledge of digital transformation in the organisational context of development NGOs and on practical requirements for developing a quick scan for digital transformation maturity assessment. The paper first addresses the nature of development NGOs and a practical concept for digital transformation. Then it describes the research design process we take for co-creating an assessment tool on digital transformation maturity for Dutch development NGOs. The results of the first phase of that process are presented in the Results chapter, followed by a short conclusion and explanation of the next step of the ongoing research.

2. DEVELOPMENT NGOS AND DIGITAL TRANSFORMATION

Non-governmental organisations (NGOs) are active players in international development, both as providers of aid and services to underprivileged communities and policy advocates (Davies, 2018). NGOs have the following characteristics: *institutionalised organisation, separation from the government (non-state), non-profit, self-governing, and often have some degree of voluntary participation in their activities* (Brunner, 2019, Davies, 2019). Development NGOs are considered a subset of organisations belonging to the non-profit sector (Northern Bridge, 2019). They are recognised as important actors in the landscapes of international development, humanitarian action, human rights, the environment, and many other areas of public action (Salamon and Sokolowski, 2016).

The concept of Digital Transformation has many definitions. For this Digital Transformation Maturity tool development, we start with an existing one used by practitioners in the (non)-profit sector: *"Digital transformation is the process of determining and implementing policies, increasing staff capacity, and specific technology systems which allow organisations to deliver their services with greater impact for the individuals they serve, their own decision-making processes, and policy decision in their communities"* (Techsoup, 2022). In a follow-up paper, we will further explore and carefully define Digital Transformation for development NGOs. As stated in the Introduction, development NGOs want to know where they stand at their digital transformation level and what the next step means. This implies knowledge of the digital transformation maturity level. A maturity evaluation means the ability to (self-) assess an organisation's digital capabilities and identify the growth trajectory for further developing the capabilities (OECD, 2021).

In the Method chapter, this short paper presents the steps to design a DTM quick scan that assumes this starting definition and how insights from an academic literature review are later compared and synthesised to an updated definition of digital transformation *for development* suitable to development NGOs.

3. METHOD

The digital maturity assessment tool is developed with the Dutch development NGOs and their (overarching) representative association Partos. There are approximately one hundred Dutch development NGOs (Partos, 2012). Development NGOs try to make sense of the possibilities and issues digital technologies bring when adopted in international development projects and their organisational operations. Therefore there is a need for better situational awareness of where an organisation stands and what can be done next if the development NGO pursues to increase the capabilities in using digital technologies for their organisational goals (i.e. maturity). Maturity assessment tools are not uncommon in the development sector for evaluation of, for example, the monitoring and evaluation of development project performance.

We outline the entire research approach, from which this short paper covers the first phase. As an initial step, as shown in Figure 1, we have conducted desk research to identify Digital Transformation Maturity (DTM) assessment tools currently used by non-profit organisations across the globe. Our approach is to work from the practitioners' perspective and develop a tool that addresses both practical relevance and academic rigour. This aligns with applied research where practical solutions are sought for existing problems. Furthermore, starting from understandable and sometimes familiar tools for the development NGOs improved the approval of this applied research process ensured willingness to participate in co-creation and testing of the Digital Transformation Maturity (DTM) assessment tool by the involved practitioners of the development NGOs.

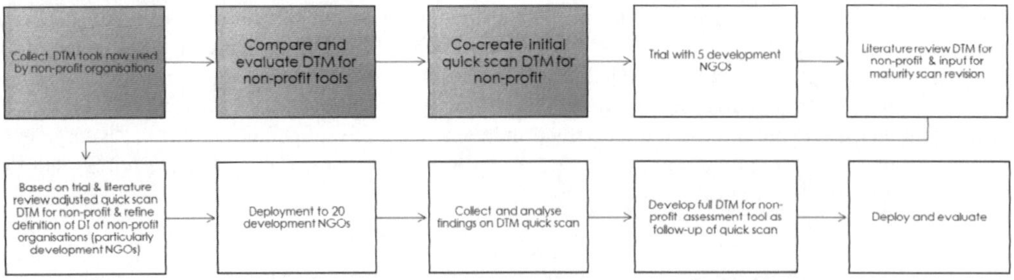

Figure 1. The full applied research approach for developing a Digital Transformation Maturity assessment for Development NGOs, from which this short paper only covers the initial phase depicted by the three grey boxes

The process approach has both elements of a design science approach where the three grey boxes discussed in this short paper cover the 'design cycle' (Hevner et al., 2008) as well as design thinking (Razzouk and Shute, 2012) in the way it approaches a 'wicked problem' of getting grips with digital transformation maturity (DTM) while designing and co-creating together with the intended users an appropriate prototype of a quick scan DTM tool for development NGOs in a short time. The trial and later field test with 20 development NGOs are related to the 'relevance cycle' of design science. In contrast, the rigour cycle is linked to the academic literature review, the resulting adjustment of the digital transformation maturity (DTM) tool, and, more precisely, the concept of Digital Transformation for development NGOs.

The scope of this paper is the three grey boxes. In this phase, the co-creation workshop sessions were preceded by time-intensive desk research and comparing and contrasting existing DTM tools in the non-profit sector. One of the tools to be evaluated was suggested by representatives of the Partos association of development NGOs., who wished to explore the possible use of Digital Principles for Development (further explained in the Results chapter). These representatives from the Partos association and the participants from the pilot group of development NGOs are all active in working groups on data for development and therefore were sufficiently knowledgeable and interested in measuring digital transformation maturity. From the onset, the common goal was clear: creating a short, easy-to-understand, quick scan in a format the development NGO practitioners are familiar with. Five co-creation sessions were used to get a common base on what is out there and what the development NGOs want to achieve with a quick scan instrument. After condensing the list of questions to approximately thirty to forty, more emphasis was put on merging questions that were asking topics close to each other and reformulating them so that they were more understandable to development practitioners instead of information and data specialists. The next chapter presents our findings.

4. RESULTS

In this chapter, we summarise the results of our desk research on Digital Transformation Maturity assessment tools used by non-profit organisations and what would be appropriate for a quick scan tool for development NGOs. We start with an overview of tools often used by non-profit organisations, as shown in Table 2.

4.1 Evaluation & Quick Scan Design Criteria

The desk research for Digital Transformation Maturity tools was conducted in English. Based on the characteristics of the Dutch development NGOs, we observed that specific tools used by Northern-based non-profit organisations could be included in our evaluation. The initial requirements we received from the association of development NGOs, Partos, were that the tool should be in English (most NGOs internally used English as their communication language one development projects), explore the usefulness of the Digital Principles instrument, assess the appropriateness for the development sector in cross-boundary and geographically remote activities, and use understandable language for the development practitioners. We identified the following design criteria for the quick scan for digital transformation maturity self-assessment:

1. The quick scan (in English) should not take more than 20-30 minutes. The surveys' experiences also provide a preferred length of the quick scan tool consisting of not more than 25-30 questions or statements to keep the time for filling in less than half an hour.
2. All digital transformation aspects are covered: process, people, technology, ánd digital leadership and organisational culture. The leadership-related questions from the IFRC model seem to be a helpful addition.
3. Questions should address a mix of operational, tactical and strategic levels; even a quick scan should address the digital transformational aspects on all these levels at the development NGO.
4. There should be a focus on the primary process of international development NGOs, thus the development projects in Global South countries, rather than the back-office and secondary processes of development NGO. The NGO Reference Model provides a common approach by defining standard business processes for the non-profit sector and allows them to plan for their digital future. This may result in additional questions regarding positioning Digitalisation or Digital Transformation efforts in the NGO's 'Primary activities' or 'Enabling activities' (Snow et al., 2016).

5. Include parts of the core tenets of the Digital Principles – the elaboration of the meaning of the nine principles- in the quick scan questions or their explanations (Principles, 2019). That means a more succinct explanation of the digital principles helps practitioners better understand the quick scan.

6. The language or phrasing of questions should be such that development practitioners can quickly grasp the meaning.

4.2 Comparison of Digital Transformation Maturity Tools

Starting from the suggested Digital Principles for Development self-assessment tool, these principles are as stated on the website (https://digitalprinciples.org/about/): "a set of living guidance intended to help practitioners succeed in applying digital technologies to development programs". Right now, there are nine principles: Principle 1: Design with the User; Principle 2: Understand the Ecosystem; Principle 3: Design for Scale; Principle 4: Build for Sustainability; Principle 5: Be Data Driven; Principle 6: Use Open Standards, Open Source, Open Data, and Open Innovation; Principle 7: Reuse and Improve; Principle 8: Address Privacy and Security; Principle 9: Be Collaborative. The principles are not considered compulsory measures but can be seen as recommendations supported by the experiences of practitioners in the development sector, nor do they have to be adopted simultaneously (Waugaman, 2016). Although these principles do not directly point toward digital transformation maturity assessment, this self-assessment tool can be modified to cater for that purpose. The tool is published under Creative Commons, which makes modifications possible. Such a modification needs to incorporate the strategic aims and vision of development NGOs (so it should be possible to 'personalise' the outcome goals when plotted on the nine principle themes, helping an organisation choose what to focus on. Furthermore, when we analysed the around 83 questions of the survey, the three-answer options for the questions are relatable to the maturity levels of digital maturity models, namely the beginning level 1 Initial: Processes poorly controlled and reactive; via level 3 Defined: Processes characterised for the organisation and is proactive; to level 5 Optimised/Transformed: Focus on process improvement. The tool, however, does not delve deep into the so-called organisational or strategic digital leadership capabilities needed to go from one level to a higher level.

The second tool we evaluated is the TechSoup Digital Assessment Tool (DAT). The tool website states that the DAT is designed to guide the organisation "along the path to digital resiliency". Interestingly the tool has a kind of introductory assessment consisting of only 20 questions. This may provide some clues on the state of matter for the organisation, but further investigation requires one to fill out an extensive survey that needs the knowledge of multiple professionals within the organisation. This is actually a realistic approach as not all required information is available to one person for this kind of self-assessment. The tool seems to be more focused on a digitalisation step-buy-step approach rather than a holistic assessment of digital transformation.

The NetHope Digital Non-profit Ability (DNA) Assessment is the third tool we evaluated. It states that it is an assessment of readiness for digital transformation. The survey covers Readiness, People, Process, Technology, and Data & Investment. The DNA tool fits well with these topics for a digital transformation maturity framework. It has four quadrants that describe possible states of digital transformation. The actual questions of the survey may put off respondents as there are too many repetitive questions -each question is repeated four times- focused on different organisational levels), and could be misinterpreted by development practitioners whose first language is not necessarily English.

The fourth tool is called IFRC Digital Maturity Framework. This is developed by the International Federation of the Red Cross Red Crescent (IFRC), specifically designed for use on a national level by the 192 Red Cross and Red Crescent National Societies (NSs). The framework is aligned with the IFRC Digital Transformation Strategy document published in 2021, which presents a roadmap for digital maturity improvement. The language of the five maturity levels has been adapted to the language and jargon used by national organisations. The survey questions cover all significant processes, leadership and an organisational culture assessment. The tool itself is not specifically development-goals oriented but valuable for non-profit organisations. It provided examples for formulating goals for a digital strategy.

Table 1. Overview of evaluation of Digital Transformation Maturity assessment tools used by non-profit organisations

Tool	**Digital Principles Self-Assessment**	**Techsoup Digital Assessment Tool (DAT)**	**NetHope Digital Nonprofit Ability (DNA) Assessment**	**IFRC Digital Maturity Framework**	**Toolkit 2.0 – Digitalisation in Development Cooperation**
Goal	Assessing awareness & use of the Digital Principles	the DAT is designed to guide your organization along the path to digital resiliency.	The Digital Nonprofit Ability (DNA) Assessment for readiness for digital transformation	The digital maturity framework aims to measure for continuous improvement of operations through the application of data analytics and digital technology	Evaluating Digitalisation in development projects.
Survey size	83 questions over 9 Principles domains	Introductory assessment is 20 questions, but many (100!) questions for specific categories. These can be delegated to colleagues.	Many (89) questions covering Readiness, People, Process, Technology, Data & Investment	50-60 questions/statements with 5-level range (beginner/basic to expert-future proof) for each.	Over 80 questions and checklist statements.
Pros	Easy to understand principles. benchmarking with a large group of NGOs worldwide. Useful when organizations want to go ahead with Digital Principles. Aligns with prior communications by Partos on these Principles.	Provides Digital Capability Score and a recommendations that can help improve organisational capabilities. Assesses along common maturity roadmap.	Fits well with topics of digital transformation maturity frameworks. DNA has four quadrants that describe possible states to digital transformation.	Covering all processes. Leadership & culture assessment	Digitalisation in development context.
Cons	The survey seems to focus on the level of engagement in implementing the Digital Principals. However, this can be modified toward digital transformation. Lacking a bit on organisational or strategic digital leadership capabilities needed.	It has a mechanist approach to DT, by stipulating tactical goals as a starting point, for change in technology, people's procedures of working etc. Results present steps to digitalisation (not transformation) and TechSoup services offered.	Too many repetitive questions (each question is 4x repeated) focused on different organisational levels; these may put off the respondents.	Not specific development-goals oriented, but useful for non-profits.	Focuses on digitalisation on the project level, not on maturity at an organisational level.
Remarks	Published under Creative Commons, so adaptions are allowed. Additional tools like Business Model Sustainability Toolkit	Next to the Principles, this model could be suitable for Partos members.	Has also (Data) Digital Skills Framework for the Nonprofit	Helps with formulation goals for a digital strategy	Toolkit developed by German Federal Ministry for Economic Cooperation and Development (BMZ)
Website	https://digitalprinciples.org	https://assessment.techsoup.org	https://nethope.org/toolkits/digital-skills/	https://www.510.global/the-digital-maturity-framework-establishing-a-collective-vocabulary-for-digital-transformation/	https://www.giz.de/expertise/downloads/Toolkit-2.0-Digitalisation-in-Development%20Cooperation.pdf

The fifth toolkit we discuss in this evaluation is developed by the German Federal Ministry for Economic Cooperation and Development (BMZ) and is called Toolkit 2.0 – Digitalisation in Development Cooperation. The toolkit focuses on evaluating digitalisation in development projects and, as such, is not primarily looking at the digital transformation maturity on an organisational level of the development NGO. It does use language related to digitalisation in a development context. The survey length is over 80 questions and contains some checklist statements. The first tool we discussed actually highlights the use of open-source technologies or project team digital literacy capabilities.

With the before mentioned criteria in mind, the five tools were evaluated and a quick scan pilot survey of approximately 25 questions has been developed. Based on this evaluation of the five digital transformation maturity assessment tools, we suggest constructing a quick scan based on the Digital Principles Self-Assessment tool, but drastically reduced and the principles directed to targets set for maturity level goals attuned to the specific development NGO. We added questions on digital leadership, inclusiveness, data bias and decolonisation of data and technologies, relevant for certain development paradigms that we found lacking in all evaluated tools. We are going to test this (prototype) quick scan for digital transformation maturity assessment with a small group of development NGOs and the Partos association. The results of this are going to be discussed in a follow-up paper.

5. CONCLUSION, LIMITATIONS, AND FUTURE RESEARCH

This paper has provided a possible design approach to the research question of how we can design an appropriate digital transformation maturity tool to assess (Dutch) development NGOs quickly. The step-by-step approach, as outlined in this paper, includes co-creation activities with the target uses (representatives of the development NGOs) and uses elements of design thinking and design science methods to design and develop a quick scan assessment tool on digital transformation maturity for development NGOs while combining relevance cycles and rigour cycles in the process. This ensures a balance between the needs of the practitioners at development NGOs for a quick scan on one side and rigour by the academic literature review and analysis to develop a precise concept of Digital Transformation for Development NGOs, which is somewhat different from a study on Digital Transformation for Development (DX4D aimed the end goals of development), e.g. Heeks et al. (2022). A possible limitation in a co-creation approach may be the subjectivity or choices made for selecting questions for a quick scan. We tried to mitigate this by remaining close to the nine principles and seeking to formulate questions similar to the original survey improving their readability to a larger audience of development practitioners. In that sense, the participants acted as proofreaders. The co-creation approach may introduce a bias in the tool, as the perspectives and opinions of the participants may influence the final product. Therefore, we encourage the authors to address this limitation. An observation from our evaluation of the digital transformation maturity (DTM) assessment tools reveals that these tools do not embed or guide toward a particular development paradigm that has been adopted by the development NGO. In our follow-up paper, we will address this and present how this can be related to, for example, certain digital principles of the Digital Principles Self-Assessment that may help to improve and 'personalise' the quick scan we develop for development NGOs. The evaluation of the digital transformation maturity tools has resulted in developing a quick scan mainly based on a selection of questions of the Digital Principles Self-Assessment, of course covering all principles but extended with areas such as digital leadership, where additional questions/statements are inspired by the others tools that we evaluated. In our follow-up paper, we will discuss the results of the remainder of the research process as outlined in Figure 1. The quick scan may be a valuable, practical contribution to development NGOs beyond the target group in The Netherlands.

FUNDING & ACKNOWLEDGEMENT

We want to thank the participating development NGOs and the Partos association for their cooperation. There are no conflicting interests to report. This work was supported by the Taskforce for Applied Research SIA, The Netherlands, under grant number HBOPD.2018.05.030.

REFERENCES

Brunner, B. R. 2019. *Public Relations Theory: Application and Understanding*, Wiley.

Davies, T. 2018. The historical development of NGOs. *Handbook of Research on NGOs.* Edward Elgar Publishing.

Davies, T. 2019. *Routledge Handbook of NGOs and International Relations*, Taylor & Francis.

Heeks, R., Ezeomah, B., Iazzolino, G., Krishnan, A., Pritchard, R. & Zhou, Q. 2022. *Development Transformation as the Goal for Digital Transformation* [Online]. Available: https://ict4dblog.wordpress.com/2022/12/13/development-transformation-as-the-goal-for-digital-transformation/ [Accessed 28 January 2023].

Hevner, A. R., March, S. T., Park, J. & Ram, S. 2008. Design science in information systems research. *Management Information Systems Quarterly,* 28, 6.

Northern Bridge. 2019. *What is the third sector and what does it do?* [Online]. Northern Bridge Doctoral Training Partnership. Available: http://toolkit.northernbridge.ac.uk/engagingwithpolicymakers/engagingwiththethirdsector/whatisthethirdsectorandwhatdoesitdo/ [Accessed 2019].

OECD 2021. Digital Transformation Maturity Model. *OECD Tax Administration Maturity Model Series.*

Partos. 2012. *About Partos* [Online]. Partos. Available: http://www.partos.nl/index.php?page=_9 [Accessed 19 February].

Principles. 2019. *The Principles* [Online]. Available: https://digitalprinciples.org/ [Accessed].

Razzouk, R. & Shute, V. 2012. What is design thinking and why is it important? *Review of educational research,* 82, 330-348.

Salamon, L. M. & Sokolowski, S. W. 2016. Beyond Non-profits: Re-conceptualising the Third Sector. *VOLUNTAS: International Journal of Voluntary and Non-profit Organizations,* 27, 1515-1545.

Snow, G., Smith, M. & Stecher, K. 2016. NGO Reference Model. *An enabler for digital transformation. Available online at https://www. ngoreferencemodel. org.*

Techsoup. 2022. *Using the TechSoup Digital Assessment Tool for Your Digital Planning* [Online]. Available: https://www.slideshare.net/TechSoupGlobal/using-the-techsoup-digital-assessment-tool-for-your-digital-planning-252242069?from_action=save [Accessed 27 January 2023].

Waugaman, A. 2016. From principle to practice: implementing the principles for digital development. *Proceedings of the Principles for Digital Development Working Group,* 4.

POSTER

EVALUATION OF LINGUISTIC AGGRESSION IN CYBERBULLYING AGAINST WOMEN ON SOCIAL MEDIA IN PUBLIC SECTOR UNIVERSITIES OF PAKISTAN

Syeda Irsa Batool and Mahmood Shah[1]
Newcastle Business School, Northumbria University, Newcastle, UK
[1]Dr

ABSTRACT

Internet has brought many changes in human life. This technology has an impact on every sphere of life. It has also had some negative effects on our lives, for instance, cyberbullying (CB). Cyberbullying started in late nineties on online forums. But it caught attention when the first case of suicide was reported in the mid-2000s. In Pakistan and other south Asian countries this phenomenon is growing rapidly. Young people, especially females, are becoming the target of cyberbullying. This research used systematic literature review to study the problem regarding the phenomenon of cyberbullying in relation with linguistic features and prevention strategies. From the detection to the prevention stages, a detailed analysis of existing literature provided an overview of the issue. The next phase of the study will focus on collecting primary data from females who faced the severe effects of CB.

KEYWORDS

Cyberbullying, Cybercrime, Preventions, Methods, Victims, University

1. LITERATURE REVIEW

Numerous studies have affirmed that social media is being used as a new platform by cyber criminals in practicing various kinds of cybercrimes, like phishing (Aggarwal et al., 2012), malware spreading (Yang & Tate, 2012), spamming (Yardi et al., 2010), and cyberbullying (Weir et al., 2011). Cheng et al., conducted a study designed by using a multi-model context on cyberbullying detection (Cheng et al., 2019). Peled (2019) studied the influence of cyberbullying on the academic, social and emotional development of undergraduate students (Peled, 2019). Numerous types of cyberbullying were explained by Watts et al. (2017) including online harassment, flaming, cyberstalking, masquerading, trickery and outing, exclusion and denigration. Similarly, López-Meneses et al. (2020) highlighted some socio-economic factors and socio-environmental factors connected with cyberbullying (López-Meneses et al., 2020). Furthermore, Hamuddin et al. (2020) proposed prevention techniques with regard to anti-cyberbullying that cover promotive, preventive, curative and rehabilitation approaches. Cross-cultural study between Pakistan and Sweden on females revealed that cyberbullying exists in both nations (Imran, 2014). Females in a country like Pakistan seldom report cases of cyberbullying (Magsi et al., 2017). A large number of people are involved in online bullying as revealed by studying two major cities of Pakistan (Musharraf & Anis-ul-Haque, 2018). Unknown men victimize women due to various psychological reasons (Rafi & Sarwar, 2019). Studies has reported that females in the universities are victimized more as compared to males (Bauman, 2013; Holfeld & Grabe, 2012; Kowalski et al., 2019; Mesch, 2009; Wang et al., 2019). Though, based on the evidence from the findings of systematic literature review, the data covers the detection, impacts on mental health, types, and factors of cyberbullying. A few studies also suggested prevention by using online software. Recent cross-cultural research (Carter, 2013; Livingstone et al., 2011; Mishna et al., 2012; Sittichai & Smith, 2015; Smith et al., 2018; Wright et al., 2018) showed that cyberspace is frequently the platform for bullying.

The language used in cyberbullying has many types, including the spread of gossip by phones, using WhatsApp for threating somebody, creating offensive or menacing remarks through social media, and insulting others on digital platforms (Faucher et al., 2014; Garaigordobil, 2015) has revealed that bullies can use language to condemn, negotiate, irritate, threat, bar, isolate, ridicule, humiliate, chase, expose individual details, or contain antagonistic, disrespectful or contemptuous comments, to harm or upset the sufferer.

However, existing literature is lacking in examining methods and prevention strategies for cyberbullying. This paper will be an attempt to uncover the issue by studying its current methods and practices. Rather than relying on a single aspect, this empirical study will address distinct dimensions involved in cyberbullying.

2. NEXT PHASE

Systematic review of the literature summarized above, provides an overview of the current state of cyberbullying research in Pakistan. By using pre-set inclusion criteria articles were selected to synthesize the existing literature. Three prominent databases were included to target the required literature. The databases included IEEE Xplore, Science Direct and Emerald Insight. Moreover, the search engine Google Scholar was also utilized. Following the next phase of this research, both qualitative and quantitative methods will be used. Data will be gathered by conducting 30 semi-structured interviews and a survey questionnaire from at least 1000 females studying at public sector universities in Pakistan. Thus, it will study the current methods and practices involved in cyberbullying to propose better prevention strategies.

Research methodology is a systematic way to resolve a research problem. In this paper, a mixed method approach will be adopted to analyze information. In qualitative analysis, semi-structured interviews will be used to collect data from female university students. The targeted age group ranges from 18-25 years. The reason for choosing university students is their increased exposure to cyberbullying. The convenience sampling technique will be used to approach the victims. Semi-structured interviews will give an in-depth analysis of the victims' ordeals which will provide a thorough insight of the problem. It will provide an insight of the language manipulation in the digital platforms used to bully people. The findings from the interview phase will be used to develop a survey questionnaire.

3. RESEARCH LIMITATION

The systematic literature review was confined to the last 10 years i.e., in between 2012-2022. To access focused literature, four prominent databases were incorporated: Emerald Insights and Business Source Premier, Google Scholar, IEEE, and Science Direct. Moreover, the sample will be restricted to the age group of 18-25 years. Furthermore, the sample will focus on female students only. This will reduce the chance to explore the responses of all genders.

4. ORIGINALITY

Synthesizing the existing literature at each phase of cyberbullying will make a distinctive contribution in conducting this research. It will bridge the gap by studying existing methods and preventions strategies.

5. PRACTICAL IMPLICATION

Negative effects can be prevented by taking action against both short-term and long-term outcomes. By analyzing the discourse related to this problem from a developing world, this would highlight a variety of aspects involved in cyberbullying and its preventions. The findings may be beneficial for youngsters in educating them about the harmful effects of cyberbullying. It may aid educational institutions in helping cyber victims.

REFRENCES

Aggarwal, A., Rajadesingan, A., & Kumaraguru, P. (2012). PhishAri: Automatic realtime phishing detection on twitter. 2012 eCrime Researchers Summit,

Bauman, S. (2013). Cyberbullying: What does research tell us? *Theory into practice*, *52*(4), 249-256.

Carter, M. A. (2013). Third party observers witnessing cyber bullying on social media sites. *Procedia-Social and Behavioral Sciences*, *84*, 1296-1309.

Cheng, L., Li, J., Silva, Y. N., Hall, D. L., & Liu, H. (2019). Xbully: Cyberbullying detection within a multi-modal context. Proceedings of the Twelfth ACM International Conference on Web Search and Data Mining,

Faucher, C., Jackson, M., & Cassidy, W. (2014). Cyberbullying among university students: Gendered experiences, impacts, and perspectives. *Education Research International*, *2014*.

Garaigordobil, M. (2015). Cyberbullying in adolescents and youth in the Basque Country: prevalence of cybervictims, cyberaggressors, and cyberobservers. *Journal of Youth Studies*, *18*(5), 569-582.

Hamuddin, B., Rahman, F., Pammu, A., Sanusi Baso, Y., & Derin, T. (2020). Cyberbullying among EFL students'blogging activities: motives and proposed solutions. *Teaching English with Technology*, *20*(2), 3-20.

Holfeld, B., & Grabe, M. (2012). Middle school students' perceptions of and responses to cyber bullying. *Journal of Educational Computing Research*, *46*(4), 395-413.

Imran, S. (2014). Students' perception of cyber bullying: A comparative analysis in Sweden and Pakistan. In.

Kowalski, R. M., Limber, S. P., & McCord, A. (2019). A developmental approach to cyberbullying: Prevalence and protective factors. *Aggression and Violent Behavior*, *45*, 20-32.

Livingstone, S., Haddon, L., Görzig, A., & Ólafsson, K. (2011). Risks and safety on the internet. *The perspective of European children. Full findings and policy implications from the EU Kids Online survey of*, *26*.

López-Meneses, E., Vázquez-Cano, E., González-Zamar, M.-D., & Abad-Segura, E. (2020). Socioeconomic effects in cyberbullying: Global research trends in the educational context. *International Journal of Environmental Research and Public Health*, *17*(12), 4369.

Magsi, H., Agha, N., & Magsi, I. (2017). Understanding Cyber Bullying in Pakistani Context: Causes and Effects on Young Female University Students in Sindh Province. *New Horizons (1992-4399)*, *11*(1).

Mesch, G. S. (2009). Parental mediation, online activities, and cyberbullying. *Cyberpsychology & behavior*, *12*(4), 387-393.

Mishna, F., Khoury-Kassabri, M., Gadalla, T., & Daciuk, J. (2012). Risk factors for involvement in cyber bullying: Victims, bullies and bully–victims. *Children and Youth Services Review*, *34*(1), 63-70.

Musharraf, S., & Anis-ul-Haque, M. (2018). Cyberbullying in different participant roles: exploring differences in psychopathology and well-being in university students. *Pakistan Journal of Medical Research*, *57*(1).

Peled, Y. (2019). Cyberbullying and its influence on academic, social, and emotional development of undergraduate students. *Heliyon*, *5*(3), e01393.

Rafi, M. S., & Sarwar, S. (2019). Language of Cyberbullying: Implications for Mental Health on Pakistani University Female Students: Reasons and Preventions. *Pakistan Journal of Professional Psychology: Research and Practice Vol*, *10*(1).

Sittichai, R., & Smith, P. K. (2015). Bullying in south-east Asian countries: A review. *Aggression and Violent Behavior*, *23*, 22-35.

Smith, P. K., Sundaram, S., Spears, B. A., Blaya, C., Schäfer, M., & Sandhu, D. (2018). 17 Editorial Reflections. *Bullying, Cyberbullying and Student Well-Being in Schools: Comparing European, Australian and Indian Perspectives*, 352.

Wang, M.-J., Yogeeswaran, K., Andrews, N. P., Hawi, D. R., & Sibley, C. G. (2019). How common is cyberbullying among adults? Exploring gender, ethnic, and age differences in the prevalence of cyberbullying. *Cyberpsychology, Behavior, and Social Networking*, *22*(11), 736-741.

Watts, L. K., Wagner, J., Velasquez, B., & Behrens, P. I. (2017). Cyberbullying in higher education: A literature review. *Computers in Human Behavior*, *69*, 268-274.

Weir, G. R., Toolan, F., & Smeed, D. (2011). The threats of social networking: Old wine in new bottles? *Information security technical report*, *16*(2), 38-43.

Wright, M. F., Wachs, S., & Harper, B. D. (2018). The moderation of empathy in the longitudinal association between witnessing cyberbullying, depression, and anxiety.

Yang, H., & Tate, M. (2012). A descriptive literature review and classification of cloud computing research. *Communications of the Association for Information Systems*, *31*(1), 2.

Yardi, S., Romero, D., & Schoenebeck, G. (2010). Detecting spam in a twitter network. *First monday*.

AUTHOR INDEX